The International Handbook of Stepfamilies

The International Handbook of Stepfamilies

Policy and Practice in Legal, Research, and Clinical Environments

Edited By

Jan Pryor

WILEY

John Wiley & Sons, Inc.

Library of Congress Cataloging-in-Publication Data:

The international handbook of stepfamilies: policy and practice in legal, research, and clinical environments/edited By Jan Pryor.
        p. cm.
    Includes index.
    ISBN 978-0-470-11458-2 (cloth)
    1. Stepfamilies. 2. Stepfamilies—Cross-cultural studies.   I. Pryor, Jan.
    HQ759.92.I68 2008
    306.874'7—dc22   2008001377

Printed in the United States of America

10 9 8 7 6 5 4 3 2 1

This book is dedicated to Simon, Emily, and Esther, and to the memory of Alexander.

Contents

Foreword

IN THE past, most stepfamilies were formed after the death of a parent. Today stepfamilies are more likely to be formed after a parental divorce or a nonmarital birth. Whatever the cause, stepfamilies are common because most people find it difficult to be single parents and long for a chance to find happiness with new partners. Stepfamilies represent new beginnings, opportunities to correct prior mistakes, and visions of a better future. Of course, the optimism of many parents is soon tempered by the everyday realities of stepfamily life—including children's more skeptical views of these new unions.

We have always known that stepfamilies are complicated. Children in stepfather households, for example, have two father figures rather than one. And if the biological father remarries, then children also have two mother figures. Moreover, each partner may bring children from a previous relationship into the household, resulting in an intricate—and often volatile—mixture of people with different histories, expectations, and working models of family life. Understanding how parents and children navigate the complexities of stepfamily life has been a major focus of much prior research. But the increasing trend of nonmarital cohabitation has made this family form even more interesting—and more difficult to study. Consider the following questions: How do unmarried stepparents differ from married stepparents? In what ways are their roles similar or different? Do unmarried stepparents invest as much time and money in their families as do married stepparents? Are children better off if their parents and new partners marry? Finally, do the answers to questions like these depend on the cultures, policy environments, and legal systems in which stepfamilies are formed?

Although much has been learned about stepfamilies during the past several decades, this information is scattered across journals and books from multiple disciplines. Demographers have focused on counting the number of stepfamilies and documenting trends in their formation. Sociologists have asked questions about how stepfamily life varies by social class and other structural variables. Family psychologists have examined the multiple sources of stress that often emerge in stepfamily relationships. Child psychologists have studied the implications of stepfamily life for children's development, adjustment, and well-being. Clinicians and counselors have focused on interventions to facilitate the adjustment of stepfamily members. And law scholars have grappled with the legal ambiguities that stepfamilies generate, such as stepparents' financial obligations to stepchildren and whether divorced stepparents should have visitation rights. Given this diversity of scholarship, a critical need exists for a single volume that pulls this information together to provide a resource for counselors, policy makers, and scholars working in diverse fields.

Jan Pryor has assembled an impressive collection of chapters on stepfamilies, the most comprehensive set of writings on stepfamilies currently available. The contributing authors include demographers, sociologists, family psychologists, clinicians, legal scholars, and communication researchers. All of these authors are among the top scholars in their fields. The chapters address a variety of topics, such as trends in the prevalence and incidence of stepfamilies, marital quality in stepfamilies, parent-child relationships in stepfamilies, children's views of stepfamilies, sibling relationships in stepfamilies, stepfamilies and the law, and interventions for stepfamilies.

Perhaps the most unique aspect of this volume is the fact that the contributors come from a variety of countries, including the United States, France, Japan, Belgium, New Zealand, England, Wales, Canada, and Australia. This international flavor is missing from previous works on this topic. It is fascinating to know how the experiences of stepfamilies differ around the world. Studies conducted in the United States have tended to dominate the research literature on this topic, but good work is being done in many countries, and it is critical for family scholars to be aware of these contributions.

In addition to compiling and summarizing what we currently know about stepfamilies, this volume will undoubtedly stimulate new theoretical and empirical work. As our world becomes smaller and our methods of communication become faster, much of this new work will have a comparative and international perspective. I can foresee the formation of research teams comprising scholars from multiple countries, working on the same problems but viewing them through the lenses of their own cultures and legal systems. This type of arrangement is rare today, but it may become a more common research paradigm in the next several decades.

In summary, this edited collection will be a useful resource for scholars, students, and practitioners for many years. I congratulate the editor and the contributors to this volume for helping to shift the study of stepfamilies to a higher level of sophistication.

PAUL R. AMATO
Distinguished Professor of Sociology and Demography
Pennsylvania State University

Preface

BOOKS ABOUT stepfamilies, and families generally, abound. Yet most would agree that we are still in the dark as far as understanding the complexities, challenges, and joys of the ever-increasing numbers of stepfamilies. And increasing it is: As the rates of separations and divorces continue to rise, so too do the hopes of adults as they repartner in the earnest desire that *this* relationship and new family will work.

Sadly, the statistics tell us that second and third relationships are even more vulnerable than first ones. So families and households face further transitions and turmoil as they set about reorganizing themselves. Yet, many stepfamilies—often those unheralded by commentators and researchers—settle into a family life in which everyone thrives.

One response to the challenging aspects of stepfamilies is to discourage their formation by making divorce harder to achieve. David Popenoe has suggested that societies should be endeavoring to "halt the growth of stepfamilies" (Popenoe, 1994), and others have described them as incomplete institutions with few societal scripts available for guidance. There is no doubt that to try to understand stepfamilies is to aim at a moving and constantly changing target. However, it is true more generally that many families are now "incomplete institutions" as the traditional nuclear household is increasingly joined by other family structures such as cohabiting families, families headed by same-sex parents, and other combinations of adults and children. An alternative response to those who would discourage stepfamilies, and one taken by this book, is to acknowledge the reality that is family life in this century, which includes large numbers of stepfamily households.

Why, then, another book on this topic? It is my hope that this book is different from the others. First, it brings an international perspective on the subject; we have authors from Japan, France, Belgium, Australia, New Zealand, England, Canada, and the United States, and one U.S.-based chapter focuses on Mexican American stepfathers. This perspective highlights the similarities faced by stepfamilies worldwide, as well as differences brought about by the culture in which they live.

Second, it brings together scholars from a wide range of disciplines, many well known and respected for their work, others young and innovative in their approaches. Included are sociologists, demographers, legal scholars, psychologists, and clinicians.

Third, the aim of the book is to record what we know and, importantly, to identify what we have yet to understand; further, it includes suggestions to further our knowledge about stepfamilies and to use that knowledge to the benefit of those stepfamilies yet to be formed.

In short, it is an exciting compendium of current knowledge combined with pointers to further our understanding of this burgeoning, complicated, and often thriving family form.

REFERENCE

Popenoe, D. (1994). The evolution of marriage and the problem of stepfamilies: a biosocial perspective. In A. Booth & J. Dunn (Eds.), *Stepfamilies: Who benefits? Who does not?* Hillsdale, NH: Erlbaum.

Contributors

Tamara D. Afifi, PhD
Department of Communication
University of California
Santa Barbara, California

Graham Allan, PhD
Department of Sociology
Keele University
Staffs, United Kingdom

Bill Atkin, BA, LLM
Department of Law
Victoria University of Wellington
Wellington, New Zealand

Melinda E. Baham
Department of Psychology
Arizona State University
Tempe, Arizona

Sanford L. Braver, PhD
Department of Psychology
Arizona State University
Tempe, Arizona

Claire Cartwright, PhD
Department of Psychology
University of Auckland, Tamaki
Auckland, New Zealand

Stephen Claxton-Oldfield, PhD
Department of Psychology
Mount Allison University
New Brunswick, Canada

Marilyn Coleman, PhD
Sinclair School of Nursing and
Department of Human
Development and Family Studies
University of Missouri
Columbia, Missouri

Scott Coltrane, PhD
College of Humanities, Arts and
  Social Sciences
University of California
Riverside, California

Graham Crow, PhD
Division of Sociology and Social
  Policy
University of Southampton
Southampton, United Kingdom

Britt Dehertogh
Research Center for Longitudinal
  and Life Course Studies, Faculty
  of Political and Social Sciences
University of Antwerp
Antwerp, Belgium

William V. Fabricius, PhD
Department of Psychology
Arizona State University
Tempe, Arizona

Lawrence Ganong, PhD
Sinclair School of Nursing and
  Department of Human
  Development and Family Studies

University of Missouri
Columbia, Missouri

Erika Gutierrez, MA
Department of Sociology
University of California
Riverside, California

W. Kim Halford, PhD
Director, Griffith Institute of Health
Dean (Research), Faculty of Health
Griffith University
Gold Coast, Australia

Gordon T. Harold, PhD
School of Psychology
Cardiff University
Cardiff, United Kingdom

Sheila Hawker, PhD
C & S Academic Services
Dorset, United Kingdom

Tyler Jamison, MS
Sinclair School of Nursing and
  Department of Human
  Development and Family Studies
University of Missouri
Columbia, Missouri

Sarah E. C. Malia, JD, MS
Knoxville, Tennessee

Howard J. Markman, PhD
Professor of Psychology, University
  of Denver
Director, Center for Marital and
  Family Studies
Denver, Colorado

Jean-François Mignot
Observatoire Sociologique du
  Changement
Laboratoire de Sociologie
  Quantitative
Paris, France

Dimitri Mortelmans, PhD
Research Center for Longitudinal
  and Life Course Studies, Faculty
  of Political and Social Sciences
University of Antwerp
Antwerp, Belgium

Jan M. Nicholson, PhD
Murdoch Children's Research
  Institute
Royal Children's Hospital
Melbourne, Australia

Shinji Nozawa, MS
Department of Sociology
Meiji Gakuin University
Tokyo, Japan

Patricia L. Papernow, EdD
Private Practice
Hudson, Massachusetts

Ross D. Parke, PhD
Department of Psychology
University of California
Riverside, California

Kay Pasley, PhD
Department of Family and Child
  Sciences
Florida State University
Tallahassee, Florida

Maddy Phillips, PhD
Queensland Center for Mental
  Health Learning
Park Center for Mental Health
Queensland, Australia

Jan Pryor, PhD
Roy McKenzie Center for the Study
  of Families
Victoria University of Wellington
Wellington, New Zealand

Jeremy Robertson, PhD
Roy McKenzie Center for the Study
of Families
Victoria University of Wellington
Wellington, New Zealand

Matthew R. Sanders, PhD
School of Psychology
University of Queensland
Brisbane, Australia

Katherine H. Shelton, PhD
School of Psychology
Cardiff University
Cardiff, United Kingdom

Marjorie Smith, PhD
Institute of Education
University of London
London, United Kingdom

Laurent Snoeckx, MA
Department of Political and Social
Sciences
Research Center for Longitudinal
and Life Course Studies
University of Antwerp
Antwerp, Belgium

Jay Teachman, PhD
Department of Sociology
Western Washington University
Bellingham, Washington

Lucky Tedrow, PhD
Department of Sociology
Western Washington University
Bellingham, Washington

Jessica Troilo
Sinclair School of Nursing and
Department of Human
Development and Family Studies
University of Missouri
Columbia, Missouri

Brad van Eeden-Moorefield, PhD
Department of Human
Environmental Studies
Central Michigan University
Mount Pleasant, Michigan

Sasha L. Walters, MS
School of Psychology
Cardiff University
Cardiff, United Kingdom

Amy A. Weimer, PhD
Department of Psychology and
Anthropology
University of Texas–Pan American
Edinburg, Texas

Sarah W. Whitton, PhD
Center for Anxiety and Related
Disorders
Boston University
Boston, Massachussetts

Introduction

IT IS easy to be pessimistic about stepfamilies. Their very origins are steeped in notions of death: The word "step" derives from the Old English word *steop*, which in turn is related to *astieped*, meaning "bereaved." Words such as "stepbairn" and "stepchild" were used in the past as synonyms for orphan. Today, as chapters in this book attest, stepfamilies are still beset by stigma and stereotyping and by seemingly endless chronicles of their difficulties. Are stepfamilies today more or less challenged than those formed in the past mainly as a result of death? It is probably impossible to know. In the past, the death of a parent called for repartnering, particularly, as was often the case, if a mother died in childbirth leaving other children to be reared.

Stepfamilies today are more likely to be formed as a result of divorce, and they are both more pervasive and more highly visible than in the past. One difference between stepfamilies now and 200 years ago may be stability. Today, if stepfamily households are unstable it is because, in the main, the couple relationship fails and the decision is made to part. In the past, a stepfamily formed because of the death of a mother in childbirth may have been more stable at least partly because far less was demanded of marriage in terms of satisfaction, and divorce was both less feasible and less acceptable than it is today.

One symptom of the lingering stigma attached to stepfamilies is the repeated finding that stepfamilies do not want to be considered different from "normal" families and resist the stepfamily label (Ganong & Coleman, 2004). Another symptom is the prevalance of negative views and attitudes toward stepfamilies that abound, even in those who live in them. A compelling symptom of the wider reluctance to acknowledge stepfamilies as "real" families is the fact that countries such as Japan have had to invent a word based on the English word. In Sweden, too, common terms for stepparents are "plastic dad" and "plastic mom," conveying an attitude of impermanence or superficiality. In this volume, some of the authors who live outside the United Kingdom and the United States are the first in their countries to undertake research that focuses on stepfamilies, reflecting the lack of interest in this family form in some countries and the greater willingness of the United Kingdom, the United States, and parts of Europe to acknowledge its pervasiveness.

The reality is that living in stepfamilies is an aspect of the lives of increasing numbers of adults and children worldwide. Stepfamilies are remarkably persistent and resilient as a family form, if numbers mean anything. And they are increasingly under scrutiny as their presence is more visible and, some would argue, increasingly troublesome. This is reflected in the increased attention to stepfamilies from clinicians, family scholars, and the law.

This volume represents recent work from an international group of researchers, clinicians, and legal scholars. It is divided, broadly, into four sections: the contexts in which stepfamilies form and establish themselves, dynamics within stepfamily households, influences beyond the household, and clinical and legal issues for stepfamilies.

In Section I, Jay Teachman and Lucky Tedrow establish a demographic framework by describing the prevalence and incidence of stepfamilies and the changing processes through which they are formed. Although their chapter is based predominantly on U.S. data, it is a fair reflection of trends in other Western countries. The perceptions and stereotypes of stepfamilies are then explored by Stephen Claxton-Oldfield in Chapter 2, where he describes research over the past few decades that suggests that stereotypes, if not disappearing, may be weakening over time.

Two chapters then address issues for stepfamilies in countries outside the United States and the United Kingdom. In Chapter 3, Jean-François Mignot describes demographic and historical aspects of stepfamilies in France and reports data from a recent study there. He interprets the state of stepfamilies in France and elsewhere using an evolutionary psychology framework to explain the negative aspects of stepfamily life. In Chapter 4, Shinji Nozawa presents the findings of the first Japanese study of stepfamilies, putting these into the context of Japan's recent history of family cultures and family change. Finally in this section, Scott Coltrane and his colleagues explore differences and similarities between stepfathers in Mexican and Euro-American families. Taken together, these chapters give a context for stepfamilies that emphasizes ubiquity, diversity, and the importance of the cultural milieu in which stepfamilies live.

A great deal of scholarly effort has gone into understanding dynamics *within* stepfamily households, and some of these are addressed in Section II. The perspectives of stepfathers have received attention only relatively recently, and in Chapter 6 Jeremy Robertson discusses findings from an English study in which stepfathers talked about their roles. Of particular interest are his findings that stepfathers prefer not to be called stepfathers and that most of them welcome—or at least do not discourage—contact between nonresident parents and their children. In Chapter 7 Marjorie Smith, using data from the same U.K. study as Robertson, explores the place of mothers in stepfamily households, noting the pivotal role they play between partners and children in holding the family together.

Sibling relationships in stepfamilies have similarly received comparatively little attention. In Chapter 8 Melinda Baham and her colleagues develop a conceptual model of sibling relationships and present data that support their framework. They widen the common focus on dyads to consider sibling relationships and their associations with other relationships in stepfamilies and with child well-being.

The child's relationship with *resident* biological parents is another area that has received relatively scant attention from scholars. In Chapter 9 Claire Cartwright discusses three New Zealand studies that have investigated the impact of parental repartnering on the parent-child relationship and is able to illuminate factors that help and hinder it. Her work is an excellent example of how qualitative studies can uncover aspects of family dynamics that are not easily apparent in survey data.

In Chapter 10, Brad van Eeden-Moorefield and Kay Pasley examine the trajectory of marital stability and quality in four family groups: married couples with only biological children, stepfather-only families, stepmother-only families, and complex (stepfather-stepmother) families. Katherine Shelton and colleagues in Chapter 11 report on a study in Wales in which paths of influence from interparental conflict to child well-being both overlap and differ in families and stepfamilies. Their study is probably the first to apply parental conflict models to the study of stepfamilies.

In Chapter 12, Laurent Snoeckx and colleagues consider the division of labor between partners in newly formed stepfamily households. They describe these household dynamics in the context of the welfare regimes in which they are nested. Finally in this section, Tamara Afifi takes a whole-family approach to the understanding of stepfamily dynamics by focusing on stepfamilies as social units and reviewing recent research on communication in stepfamilies in Chapter 13.

In Section III, dynamics and influences beyond the stepfamily household itself are addressed. First, in Chapter 14, Graham Allan and his colleagues consider the question of how stepfamily members think about relationships with family members outside the household, the "family kin" network. He concludes that kinship operates rather differently for stepfamilies from the way it is used in first families. In Chapter 15 I focus on the relationship between children and nonresident parents and the overlaps between children's relationships with resident and nonresident parents of the same sex. This issue has become increasingly salient as nonresident parents become more involved with their children after divorce and when resident parents repartner.

Marilyn Coleman and her colleagues in Chapter 16 address the differences in the experiences of stepmothers depending on whether or not they live with children. She considers the role of conceptualizations and evaluations of stepmothers and the factors contributing to these, and she moves beyond earlier studies of stepmothers that have tended to treat them as a homogeneous group to consider the different experiences of resident and nonresident stepmothers.

Another aspect of stepfamily life that is attracting recent attention is the pattern of intergenerational relationships that are created when stepfamilies form. In Chapter 17 Lawrence Ganong addresses these complicated relationships, pointing out the different ways a person can become a step-grandparent and the particularly vague expectations of the relationships between stepchildren and their step-grandparents. The concept of incomplete institutionalization is particularly relevant to these relationships, as elders struggle to determine roles for themselves in stepfamilies.

Section IV focuses on clinical and legal issues for stepfamilies. Patricia Papernow emphasizes the importance for clinicians of recognizing that models based on first families will not work for stepfamilies; she describes "stepfamily architecture" and its implications for successful clinical work with stepfamilies. In Chapter 19, Sarah Whitton and colleagues review the literature and the interventions addressing couple relationships in stepfamilies. They note the importance of well-designed evaluations of programs that aim to help couples to function optimally. Jan Nicholson and her colleagues in Chapter 20 report on findings of two intervention studies carried out in Australia that focused on children's functioning in stepfamilies.

The law has moved slowly in many countries to intervene legally in the lives of stepfamilies. Stepparents and stepchildren have been described as legal strangers, and where legitimization of their relationship has been put in place it varies in terms of its power and of its implications for other relationships the child has. In Chapter 21, Bill Atkin identifies some of the key issues and questions faced by legal systems in regulating stepfamily life. He uses the New Zealand example to illustrate the complexities and difficulties involved in this venture. Sarah Malia in Chapter 22 provides a comprehensive description and critique of the law as it applies to stepfamilies in the United States.

In the final chapter, I identify some of the key questions, challenges, and trends that emerge from the chapters in this book. There is a promising transition that is apparent: from a focus on stepfamilies as units and assemblages of relationships to a consideration of the wider social, political, legal, and cultural contexts in which they function. I look to the near future in terms of how research with stepfamilies might advance.

No book can cover all topics, and I am aware of two major omissions. First, same-sex stepfamilies are not addressed, despite the fact that they are an increasingly prevalent group in which dynamics both overlap and differ from those in heterosexual families (see van Eeden-Moorefield, Henley, and Pasley, 2005, for a discussion on this topic). Second, there is no chapter that addresses African American stepfamilies, again a group that deserves more attention than they receive.

Terminology in regard to stepfamilies is difficult and ambiguous. Some authors here have addressed issues of definition, and others have not. Despite the many objections to the term "stepfamily," most writers, including myself, come back to it because it is widely understood and other terms can be vague or misleading or just silly (see Ganong & Coleman, 2004, for a discussion of terminology). Similarly, terms for the family structure against which stepfamilies are most often compared include nuclear, intact, biological, and first families. None of these is particularly accurate; even the word "biological" excludes families formed by adoption, and many stepfamilies would consider themselves to be intact. Again, authors have used varying terms in this book.

REFERENCES

Ganong, L., & Coleman, M. (2004). *Stepfamily relationships: Development, dynamics, and interventions*. New York: Kluwer Academic/Plenum Press.

van Eeden-Moorefield, B., Henley, K., & Pasley, K. (2005). Identity enactment and verification in gay and lesbian stepfamilies. In V. Bengston, A. C. Acock, K. R. Allen, P. Dilworth-Anderson, & D. M. Klein (Eds.), *Sourcebook of family theory and research* (pp. 230–233). Thousand Oaks, CA: Sage.

Acknowledgments

I WANT to thank the authors of the individual chapters for their skill and good humor as the book was brought together, and for their timeliness (in the main!) in getting chapters finished. Editing has been a far less arduous task than I had imagined thanks to you.

I want to acknowledge the forbearance and understanding of family and friends as this book was being written; in particular, my family—Simon, Emily, Esther, Roger, and Maggie—and fictive kin Duncan, Rhonda, Julian, Suzanne, Ian, Marilyn, and Mark.

Thank you to Patricia Rossi of John Wiley & Sons, who has been constantly supportive, encouraging, and helpful.

INTERNATIONAL, DEMOGRAPHIC, AND CULTURAL CONTEXTS

CHAPTER 1

The Demography of Stepfamilies in the United States

JAY TEACHMAN
LUCKY TEDROW

HOUSEHOLD STRUCTURE in the United States has evolved over time. For example, between 1970 and 2000, the proportion of married couple households with children declined from 40% of all households to 24% of all households (U.S. Bureau of the Census, 2001a). Over the same period, the percentage of other types of family households (those not including two married parents) increased from 10% to 16%. These changes in household structure were generated by changes in basic demographic processes that create different types of households (e.g., marriage, divorce, out-of-wedlock childbearing, cohabitation). One important consequence of these changes in household structure and demographic processes has been their effect on the living arrangements of children. A particularly important change has been the steep increase in the proportion of households that include stepchildren and the increasing likelihood that a child will spend at least part of his or her formative years in a stepfamily.

In this chapter we explore the prevalence of stepfamilies and stepchildren, as well as the incidence of important events that generate households containing stepparents and stepchildren. We begin by noting the changing definition of stepfamilies and the methodological complications associated with measuring stepfamilies. These methodological difficulties are one reason for the surprising lack of accurate demographic information about stepfamilies. Second, we examine the existing data about stepfamilies. Third, we turn our attention to the demographic processes that create stepfamilies, noting changes over time and what subsequent changes may imply for stepfamilies in the future. Although our attention is focused on the United

States, we present some comparative data from other Western industrialized nations that have experienced many of the same demographic changes.

MEASURING STEPFAMILIES

Although at first glance it may seem an easy task, defining what constitutes a stepfamily can be complicated. This difficulty mirrors debates about what constitutes a family (Benokraitis, 1999; Dilworth-Anderson, 1992). Do cohabiting couples constitute a family? What about gay and lesbian couples? Should blood, marriage, and other legal connections be used to define families to the exclusion of intimate relationships (Scanzoni, Polonko, Teachman, & Thompson, 1989)? Do family members need to share a common household? What about the role fictive kin play in defining families (Dilworth-Anderson, 1992)? Many of these same questions apply when attempting to define what constitutes a stepfamily. The issues involved are often not demographic. Rather, they revolve around issues of culture, socialization, and individual preference. These debates can be politicized as various groups seek to have their status legitimated by various organizations and government agencies.

Because the issue is so complex, to simplify the chore demographers generally rely on a household definition that is based on coresidence. In the U.S. Census, a "household includes all the people who occupy a housing unit as their usual place of residence" (U.S. Bureau of the Census, 2006). A family is defined as a type of household in which "two or more people . . . reside together and . . . are related by birth, marriage, or adoption." A stepfamily is a particular type of household and is defined as a "married couple family in which there is at least one stepchild of the householder present. If the child has been adopted by the householder, that child is classified as an adopted child and the family is not classified as a stepfamily, unless another nonadopted stepchild is present."[1] One weakness of this definition of a stepfamily is that it ignores linkages and interactions that occur across households (Levin & Trost, 2000). For example, suppose that John and Martha marry and have a child, Samuel. Then John and Martha divorce. Within 5 years of their divorce, John and Martha both remarry spouses with no prior children. Samuel resides with Martha and her new husband but spends two nights per week and every other weekend with John and his

---

[1] The terms "stepchildren" and "stepfamilies" also fail to fully capture the relationships in "blended families." For example, there are many more children living in blended families than there are stepchildren (e.g., because a remarried couple with stepchildren may also have their own biological children). Thus, children who are the biological offspring of both parents may have one or more half-brothers or half-sisters living in the household. The 1996 Survey of Income and Program Participation counted 11,798,000 children living in blended families, of which only 4,902,000 were stepchildren.

new wife. Demographers would generally count Martha's new household as a stepfamily. John's new household would not be counted as a stepfamily even though Samuel spends a portion of his time with John and John interacts regularly with Martha and her new husband concerning Samuel's upbringing.

The demographic definition is simple because it follows the Western tradition of thinking of families as being contained in a single household (Cherlin & Furstenberg, 1994). It is also tidy because households form easy units for counting individuals and their presumed relationships. Yet this definition misses some of the interaction associated with stepfamily relationships. Unfortunately, however, there is no way to measure stepfamily relationships across households that can be easily incorporated into large-scale survey efforts (e.g., the Current Population Survey) or a census that demographers rely on for gathering data on households. Thus, our demographic accounting of stepfamilies is necessarily based on a household definition.

The demographic definition of stepfamilies has other difficulties related to data collection, definition, and comparability. In part, these difficulties stem from changes over time in the types of events that create new stepfamilies. Historically, stepfamilies were created by two sets of paired processes: the death of one married parent followed by remarriage of the surviving parent, and later, divorce of married parents followed by remarriage of one or both parents. Thus, following the dissolution of a marriage, almost all stepfamilies were created by remarriage, with at least one of the married partners acting in the role of stepparent (both partners could be stepparents if both brought biological children to the marriage). Indeed, some of the earlier reviews on the subject of stepchildren and stepparents were at least partially written as reviews of the remarriage literature (Coleman & Ganong, 1990; Coleman, Ganong, & Fine, 2000; Glick, 1989).

Recent trends in two phenomena have changed the way stepfamilies are formed and thus how people think about them. One substantial change has been out-of-wedlock childbearing (National Center for Health Statistics, 2005; Wu & Wolf, 2001). Increased rates of nonmarital fertility have created a pool of parents entering the marriage market who have not been previously married. Thus, an increasing number of first marriages involve stepchildren and do not involve processes of remarriage.[2] Using data from the National Survey of Families and Households, Bumpass, Raley, and Sweet (1995) estimate that about one-quarter of mothers and nearly one-third of

---

[2] Of course, a nontrivial fraction of marriages with a nonmarital birth includes both biological parents. In addition, a nontrivial fraction of nonmarital births occurs to women (and men) who were previously married. Thus, although their next marriage will be a remarriage, divorce was not directly involved in the formation of the stepfamily.

children enter a stepfamily relationship via nonmarital childbearing rather than divorce. Although these families would be captured by the standard demographic definition of stepfamilies, census data do not distinguish them from stepfamilies created by remarriage. To the extent that the differences in how stepfamilies are formed are important for the way they function, this limitation is important to consider.

A second phenomenon, nonmarital cohabitation, is also related to how stepfamilies are formed and has consequences for the way they are counted. Substantial increases in cohabitation have meant that more and more children are living with one biological parent and the parent's partner without the umbrella of marriage (Bumpass & Lu, 2000; Bumpass & Raley, 1995; Bumpass et al., 1995). If cohabitation is counted as a family type, about two-thirds of both mothers and children enter a stepfamily relationship via cohabitation (Bumpass et al., 1995). These households would not be included in counts of *families* compiled by the U.S. Census Bureau, although they would be included in counts of *households*.

A third concern when examining data on stepfamilies and stepchildren relates to simple data collection procedures. For example, as indicated in the next section, the U.S. Census collects information about stepfamilies and stepchildren by asking for the relationship between each child in the household and the householder (most commonly the adult who completes the census form). Thus, a biological child of the householder would not be reported as a stepchild even if the householder's spouse was not the child's biological parent. These are all concerns that must be taken into account when comparing data collected across time, organizations, and geographic regions. Differences in the prevalence of stepchildren and stepfamilies can be substantial, but care must be taken to discount the possibility that differences are not due to variations in definition or how data are collected. In presenting data about the United States, we take care to point out cases in which comparisons should be made with caution.

THE U.S. CENSUS

With these concerns in mind, precisely how does the U.S. Census Bureau measure stepfamilies? Figure 1.1 shows the question that was used to ascertain household structure and composition in the 2000 decennial census. As indicated earlier, at the core of the census definition is a household, that is, individuals who share living quarters. Each household is represented by a householder (formerly a head of household). The householder is the reference person to whom the relationship of all other members of the household is determined. This is basically the structure that has been used in the decennial census since 1880. What has changed over time is the set of codes that have been used to determine the relationship between each person in

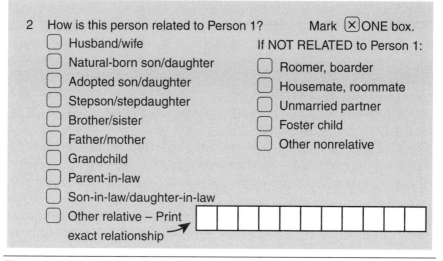

Figure 1.1 Reproduction of the Question on Relationship to Householder from Census 2000.
Source: "Census 2000 Questionnaire," by U.S. Bureau of the Census, 2000, Washington, DC: U.S. Government Printing Office.

the household and the householder. For our purposes, the most significant change occurred in 1990, when new codes were added for unmarried partners, stepchildren, and grandchildren. Reflecting continued change in the living arrangements of Americans, codes were added in 2000 for foster child, adopted child, parent-in-law, and child-in-law.

Although the changes made in 1990 and 2000 better reflected the changing living arrangements of Americans, allowing for the first time the identification of stepchildren and stepfamilies, U.S. Census data are constrained when it comes to counting these entities. For example, stepchildren are missed in couple households (married or unmarried) if the child being enumerated is the biological child of the householder but not of the householder's partner. For example, if in the hypothetical family considered earlier, Martha and her biological child, Samuel, form a new family via Martha's remarriage and Martha is listed as the householder, the family will not be counted as a stepfamily and Samuel will not be counted as a stepchild. This categorization would occur because Samuel is the biological child of the householder, Martha. The census would not ascertain the relationship between Samuel and his mother's partner.

This issue could be resolved if the U.S. Census Bureau changed the reporting requirements so that the relationship of every household member to every other household member was ascertained. This is not an insignificant data collection challenge but is already being accomplished in other countries, for example, in Great Britain (as of 2001) and Australia.

Another group of stepchildren is missed when, in unmarried house-holds, the partner listed as the householder fails to list nonbiological children living with him or her as stepchildren. Again, suppose that Martha and her son, Samuel, form a new household, but in this instance Martha cohabits rather than marries. If Martha's partner is listed as the householder, he may choose not to list Samuel as a stepchild even though Samuel is not his biological child and lives in the household. In this case, he could list Samuel as an "other nonrelative." This problem is tied to emerging social definitions of what constitutes a stepchild (Marsiglio, 2004). The U.S. Census allows respondents to use their own interpretation of the meaning of the coding categories presented. As premarital cohabitation becomes more widespread and accepted as a context for child rearing, we anticipate that more cohabiting households will report stepchildren. This possibility also means that trends over time in the proportion of children living with a parent and cohabiting partner must be interpreted with caution. In particular, increases in the prevalence of stepchildren could, at least in part, be due to the increased willingness of partners to list nonbiological children living with them as stepchildren.

SURVEY DATA

Several surveys have been used to generate estimates of stepchildren and stepfamilies in the United States, including the Current Population Survey (Glick, 1989), the National Study of Families and Households (Bumpass et al., 1995), and the Survey of Income and Program Participation (U.S. Bureau of the Census, 2001b). In Canada, estimates of stepfamilies have been derived from the National Longitudinal Survey of Children and Youth (Marcil-Gratton, 1998), in Great Britain from the British Household Panel Study (Ermisch & Francesconi, 2000), and for much of Europe the European Fertility and Family Surveys (Thomson, 2004, see also www.demographic-research.org.).

Due to its large size (about 37,000 households), and the fact that it counted the relationship of each person to every other person in the household, the 1996 Survey of Income and Program Participation (SIPP) is particularly important to consider. Indeed, we can use information from SIPP to provide some estimate of the degree to which the census may undercount stepchildren because of its limitations, including counting only the relationship of each household member to the householder.

The 1996 SIPP indicated that 4,902,000 children under age 18 were living with at least one stepparent, or about 7% of all children. This figure compares to 3,292,000 children under age 18 living with a stepparent enumerated in the 2000 census, or about 5% of all children. Thus, the census appears to capture only about two-thirds of all stepchildren. Yet, the census remains our primary source of demographic information about stepfamilies and stepchildren due to its large size and national coverage. Although the census undercounts stepchildren and stepfamilies, it remains useful when making comparisons across censuses (i.e., for trend data) and among groups within a census under the assumption that the undercount is likely to be relatively constant across different censuses and across groups within a census. In other words, even though the census may be underestimating the absolute numbers, we are likely to obtain reasonable estimates of differences across various groups in the prevalence of stepchildren and stepfamilies.[3] With these points in mind, we now turn to some basic results painting a portrait of stepfamilies and stepchildren in the United States.

PREVALENCE OF STEPFAMILIES AND STEPCHILDREN

Shown in Table 1.1 is the number and percentage of married-couple and cohabiting-couple households *with children* that contain a stepchild. Approximately 9% of married-couple households with children contain stepchildren (recall that U.S. Census figures likely understate the number of households containing stepchildren). Among cohabiting-couple households, 11.5% contain a stepchild. This latter figure is likely more of an underestimate than that for married couples, given the fact that cohabiting householders may not voluntarily list their partner's biological child as their stepchild. Despite concerns about their numerical accuracy, these figures indicate that cohabiting-couple households are more likely to contain a stepchild than married-couple households.

It is also important to recall that these estimates are cross-sectional. At a single point in time, only a relatively small fraction of family households with children contain stepchildren. In part, it is this snapshot characteristic of the data that yields what some observers may think is a relatively low level of prevalence. It is important to note, however, that these numbers do not reflect the proportion of parents and children who will ever experience life in a stepfamily because individuals move into and out of various family statuses over time. Lifetime prevalence is much higher than cross-sectional prevalence. As evidence, Bumpass et al. (1995) estimate that about 33% of all mothers and 25% of all children will spend at least part of their lifetime in a stepfamily. These figures increase to nearly 40% of all mothers and 30%

---

[3] The fact that the census undercounts children by about two-thirds does not mean that it undercounts households or families with stepchildren by two-thirds. This inequality holds because households with stepchildren often have more than one stepchild present. Thus, if one were to adjust upward by one-third the number of households with stepchildren, the result would likely be an overestimate.

Table 1.1
Family Households with Children by Marital Status of Parents and
Relationship of Children, 2000

Household Composition	Married Couples		Cohabiting Couples	
	Number	Percent	Number	Percent
With children	30,686,991	100.0	2,280,537	100.0
With stepchildren	2,694,014	8.8	261,631	11.5

Source: "Examining American Household Composition: 1990 and 2000," by U.S. Bureau of the Census, 2005, *Census 2000 Special Reports: CENSR-24*, Washington, DC: U.S. Government Printing Office.

of children when the definition of a stepfamily is expanded beyond that of married-couple families to include cohabiting couples.

In Table 1.2 we take a (short) historical approach and contrast the prevalence of stepfamily households as a fraction of *all* family households, including those without children (in Table 1.1 we presented stepfamily households as a fraction of family households *with children*) between 1990 and 2000 using census data. As was the case in Table 1.1, we present data separately for married couples and cohabiting couples. In 1990, about 57% of all married-couple households had children. By 2000 this figure had shrunk slightly to about 56%. The decline in the percentage of married-couple households with children was not due to a decline in the number of stepfamilies, which actually increased. Despite this increase, the fraction of married-couple households that contained stepchildren actually dropped slightly (from 5.0% to 4.9%), due to the fact that the number of married-couple families without children increased even more rapidly.

Among cohabiting couples, the proportion of households with biological children increased from about 38% to about 42%. Unlike the case for married-couple households, the fraction of households that contained stepchildren increased substantially, from 2.9% to 4.8%. Although part of this increase may be the result of increased willingness on the part of cohabiting individuals to report a partner's biological child as their stepchild, it most likely reflects real growth in the proportion of cohabiting relationships with children, many of whom contain children who are not the biological offspring of one of the partners (Bumpass et al., 1995). Thus, individuals with children are increasingly more likely to form new families through cohabitation.

Table 1.2 also suggests that over the 1990–2000 decade, the increase in stepchildren was much more common in cohabiting relationships than in marriages. About 84,000 new stepfamilies were reported among married couples, compared to about 165,000 new stepfamilies among cohabiting couples. Again, however, caution must be used when making this comparison given the fact that definitional changes may have been more important in generating the increase in stepchildren among cohabiters.

Table 1.2

Family Households by Marital Status of Parents, Presence of Children, and Relationship of Children, 1990 and 2000

Household Composition	Married Couples				Cohabiting Couples			
	1990	Percent	2000	Percent	1990	Percent	2000	Percent
All households	51,718,214	100.0	54,493,232	100.0	3,309,716	100.0	5,475,768	100.0
Households with biological children	29,643,541	57.3	30,686,991	56.3	1,245,960	37.7	2,280,537	41.7
Households with stepchildren	2,610,044	5.0	2,694,014	4.9	97,266	2.9	261,631	4.8

Source: "Examining American Household Composition: 1990 and 2000," by U.S. Bureau of the Census, 2005, *Census 2000 Special Reports: CENSR-24,* Washington, DC: U.S. Government Printing Office.

11

Table 1.3

Households by Type in 1990 and 2000 Ranked according to 2000 Prevalence

Type of Household	1990	Percent	2000	Percent	Percent Change 1990–2000
All households	91,993,582	100.0	105,480,101	100.0	14.7
Living alone (1)	22,421,114	24.4	27,230,075	25.8	21.4
Householder plus:					
Spouse and biological child (2)	25,013,513	27.2	24,591,606	23.3	–1.7
Spouse (3)	20,172,988	21.9	22,382,944	21.2	11.0
Biological child (4)	7,504,178	8.2	9,110,735	8.6	21.4
Unmarried partner (5)	1,647,208	1.8	2,682,247	2.5	62.8
Housemate (6)	2,020,598	2.2	2,332,386	2.2	15.4
Unmarried partner and biological child (7)	859,192	0.9	1,620,891	1.5	88.7
Spouse, biological child, and stepchild (8)	1,137,426	1.2	1,236,813	1.2	8.7
Spouse and stepchild (9)	1,195,656	1.3	1,105,151	1.0	–7.6
Biological child and grandchild (10)	683,994	0.7	832,606	0.8	21.7
Other stepchild arrangements:					
Unmarried partner, biological child, and stepchild (39)	42,186	0.04	112,407	0.1	140.1
Unmarried partner and stepchild (42)	35,627	0.04	102,541	0.1	187.8

Note: Value in parentheses indicates prevalence rank in 2000.
Source: "Examining American Household Composition: 1990 and 2000," by U.S. Bureau of the Census, 2005, *Census 2000 Special Reports: CENSR-24*, Washington, DC: U.S. Government Printing Office.

Table 1.3 shows a somewhat different perspective on households: the ranking of different household types in 1990 and 2000. The results indicate considerable change in the way Americans sorted themselves into households. Between 1990 and 2000, living alone supplanted living with a spouse and a biological child as the most common household type, with 25.8% of all households in 2000 consisting of a single individual. About 23% of American households consisted of a married couple plus their biological children. The third most common type of living arrangement in 2000 was living with a spouse without children (about 21%).

If we want to find households with stepchildren, we need to look down the list to the category "householder plus spouse, biological child, and stepchild," ranked eighth in prevalence. Although this household type represented only 1.2% of all households, it expanded rapidly over the 1990–2000 decade (by nearly 9%).[4] Ranked ninth in prevalence was the category "householder plus spouse and stepchild," which decreased by about 8% over the decade and represented 1% of all households. Note that the total of these two household types does not equal the number of households with stepchildren reported in Table 1.2 because there are numerous other living arrangements involving married couples and stepchildren that are not shown (e.g., householder plus spouse, stepchild, and other relative). Indeed, the U.S. Census recorded nearly 25,000 different types of household living arrangements given the coding scheme they used in 2000.

These figures again indicate the relatively low prevalence of American families with stepchildren in cross-section (although the total number of families implicated is not insignificant). It is also important to note, however, that one of the most rapidly growing family types among those indicated involve stepchildren. Between 1990 and 2000, using the figures shown in Table 1.3, unmarried couples with stepchildren more than doubled (recall that these increases may be related to differences across time in a householder's propensity to report a partner's biological children as his or her stepchildren). Indeed, using the top 45 household types reported in 2000, there were roughly 146,000 new households with stepchildren created over the decade, and nearly 95% of these households involved cohabiting partners. Clearly, changes in the preferred living arrangements of adults in the U.S. population (with particular emphasis on cohabitation) are having a significant impact on the nature and experience of stepfamilies.

In Table 1.4 we switch perspectives from that of households to that of children. Because households can have more than one stepchild, the experiences of children are not necessarily identical to the experiences of

---

[4] The percentages shown in Table 1.3 are much lower than those shown in Tables 1.1 and 1.2 because Table 1.3 includes nonfamily households in the base.

Table 1.4

Children by Type of Relationship to Householder and Age, 2000

Relationship of Child	All Children		Children <18		Children 18 and Older	
	Number	Percent	Number	Percent	Number	Percent
Total	83,714,107	100.0	64,651,959	100.0	19,062,148	100.0
Adopted	2,058,915	2.5	1,586,004	2.5	472,911	2.5
Stepchildren	4,384,581	5.2	3,292,301	5.1	1,092,280	5.7

Source: "Adopted Children and Stepchildren: 2000," by U.S. Bureau of the Census, 2003, *Census 2000 Special Reports: CENSR-6RV*, Washington, DC: U.S. Government Printing Office.

households. As shown in Table 1.4, about 5% of all children in 2000 were reported as stepchildren, compared to 2.5% of children reported as adopted children. There were about 4.3 million children reported as stepchildren of householders, about 3.3 million of which were younger than 18. Table 1.4 shows clearly that many stepchildren are older; about 25% of all stepchildren are over 18 (compared to about 23% of biological children). The abundance of older stepchildren has likely resulted from the fact that many stepfamilies have traditionally resulted from remarriages that contain older children.

It is important to recognize, however, that data restricted to stepchildren will underestimate the exposure of all children to stepfamilies because many biological children live in blended families. That is, many children who are not themselves stepchildren have stepsiblings or halfsiblings living with them who are the biological children of their parents. For example, in our hypothetical family, if Martha and her new husband have a child together, this child will not be a stepchild, although he or she will live in a blended family because Samuel will be his or her halfbrother.[5] Whereas only about 5% of children in the United States are stepchildren, 16.5% of children live in blended families (including stepchildren and biological children).[6] Black children are particularly likely to be living in a blended family (20.4%).

---

[5] The situation can become even more complex. For example, suppose that John and his new wife also have a child together. Samuel will now have two half-siblings living in different households. He may continue to spend two nights per week and every other weekend with John and his new wife and their biological child.

[6] Caution must be used when comparing the 5% figure to the 16.5% figure because they come from different data sources. The former figure is based on the U.S. Census and is likely biased downward because only the relationship of the child to the householder is reported. The latter figure is based on data taken from the SIPP. In the SIPP, children's relationships to both parents in the household are reported. In addition, the SIPP data count cohabiting couples as families, contrary to the census data. Thus, the difference between the two figures is exaggerated by differences in how data are collected and reported.

Table 1.5

Characteristics of Adopted, Step, and Biological Children, 2000

Characteristic of Child	Adopted Children		Stepchildren		Biological Children	
	Number	Percent	Number	Percent	Number	Percent
Total	1,586,004	100.0	3,292,301	100.0	59,773,654	100.0
Age						
Under 1 year	41,795	2.6	12,384	0.4	3,148,542	0.4
1 year	55,857	3.5	21,266	0.6	3,173,342	0.6
2 years	63,250	4.0	36,000	1.1	3,167,328	1.1
3 years	71,211	4.5	57,986	1.8	3,227,496	1.8
4 years	74,717	4.7	86,298	2.6	3,316,803	2.6
5 years	82,466	5.2	114,444	3.5	3,368,921	3.5
6 years	85,298	5.4	142,935	4.3	3,400,350	4.3
7 years	92,634	5.8	174,308	5.3	3,464,985	5.3
8 years	100,144	6.3	205,419	6.2	3,506,676	6.2
9 years	106,403	6.7	231,797	7.0	3,581,011	7.0
10 years	106,626	6.7	254,456	7.7	3,555,349	7.7
11 years	107,221	6.8	262,207	8.0	3,426,166	8.0
12 years	106,116	6.7	272,989	8.3	3,374,253	8.3
13 years	105,336	6.6	281,502	8.6	3,321,218	8.6
14 years	105,184	6.6	292,639	8.9	3,341,000	8.9
15 years	98,249	6.2	289,992	8.8	3,218,126	8.8
16 years	93,859	5.9	281,016	8.5	3,118,713	8.5
17 years	89,638	5.7	274,663	8.3	3,063,375	8.3
Race and Hispanic Origin						
White alone	1,017,666	64.2	2,482,249	75.4	42,358,683	75.4
Black or African American alone	254,161	16.0	402,821	12.2	7,911,317	12.2
American Indian and Alaska Native alone	25,681	1.6	39,822	1.2	597,780	1.2
Asian alone	116,909	7.4	38,905	1.2	2,069,271	1.2

(continued)

Table 1.5 *(Continued)*

Characteristic of Child	Adopted Children		Stepchildren		Biological Children	
	Number	Percent	Number	Percent	Number	Percent
Native Hawaiian and other Pacific Islander alone	4,184	0.3	4,272	0.1	88,019	0.1
Some other race alone	89,894	5.7	205,221	6.2	4,373,885	6.2
Two or more races	77,509	4.9	119,011	3.6	2,374,699	3.6
Hispanic or Latino (of any race)	215,909	13.6	479,101	14.6	9,720,023	14.6
White alone, not Hispanic or Latino	918,044	57.9	2,261,667	68.7	37,957,788	68.7
Nativity and English Ability						
Native	1,386,868	87.4	3,159,566	96.0	57,461,010	96.0
Foreign born	199,136	12.6	132,735	4.0	2,312,644	4.0
Foreign born aged 5 to 17	147,073	100.0	127,771	100.0	2,076,420	100.0
Speaks non-English language at home[1]	45,372	30.8	107,271	84.0	1,836,079	84.0
Speaks English very well	25,138	17.1	57,474	45.0	999,482	45.0
Disability Status[1]						
Aged 5 to 17	1,279,174	100.0	3,078,367	100.0	43,740,143	100.0
At least one disability	150,451	11.8	213,663	6.9	2,279,024	6.9
Sensory disability	18,930	1.5	34,488	1.1	404,988	1.1
Physical disability	19,595	1.5	21,814	0.7	360,976	0.7
Mental disability[2]	132,700	10.4	174,842	5.7	1,768,187	5.7
Self-care disability	20,706	1.6	30,471	1.0	417,677	1.0
Multiple disabilities[3]	27,498	2.1	33,863	1.1	463,179	1.1

Source: "Adopted Children and Stepchildren: 2000," by U.S. Bureau of the Census, 2003, *Census 2000 Special Reports: CENSR-6RV,* Washington, DC: U.S. Government Printing Office.

We change directions now to examine some of the characteristics of step-children in the United States by comparing them to adopted children and biological children. Tables 1.5 and 1.6 indicate selected characteristics of the households in which adopted, step, and biological children lived in 2000. The figures in this table indicate that stepfamilies are not a random subset of all households, or even of family households.

For example, stepchildren are somewhat more likely to be older than adopted children and biological children. Stepchildren are also more likely to be white and of non-Hispanic origin. Compared to adopted children, stepchildren (and biological children) are much less likely to be foreign born and are less likely to speak a non-English language. Similarly, stepchildren and biological children are less likely than adopted children to report having a disability. In addition, adopted and stepchildren are more likely than biological children to live in a household headed by someone who self-identifies as White. Adopted children and stepchildren are also much more likely to be of a different race than the householder with whom they live (the difference being particularly striking for adopted children).

Although nonmarried households with stepchildren are experiencing the most rapid growth, stepchildren are still much more likely than either adopted children or biological children to live in a married-couple house-hold. Stepchildren are also more likely to live in a cohabiting-couple house-hold where the male partner is the householder. This makes sense given the fact that most children remain with their mother after either divorce or a nonmarital birth (Goldscheider & Sassler, 2006). Stepchildren are greatly underrepresented among households headed by single women, even though over 30,000 women are raising children who are not biologically re-lated to them and whom they report as their stepchildren. It is interesting to note that single men are more likely than single women to be raising a step-child (50,000 versus 30,000).

In terms of household income, adopted children tend to live in house-holds with the most financial resources. Compared to biological children, stepchildren also tend to live in slightly better-off households, largely be-cause they are more likely to live in married-couple households (although they are less likely than other children to live in households with incomes above $100,000). As might be expected given differences in household in-come, adopted children live in households where the householder pos-sesses more education. Stepchildren tend to live in households with the least education, a finding consistent with research using survey data (Gold-scheider & Sassler, 2006). Finally, adopted children are much more likely than either stepchildren or biological children to live with parents who own their home.

Table 1.6

Characteristics of Households with Adopted, Step, and Biological Children, 2000

	Adopted Children		Stepchildren		Biological Children	
	Number	Percent	Number	Percent	Number	Percent
Total	1,586,004	100.0	3,292,301	100.0	59,773,654	100.0
Race:						
White	1,198,959	75.6	2,536,082	77.0	43,017,780	72.0
Black	231,459	14.6	415,460	12.6	7,980,985	13.4
Other	155,586	9.8	340,759	10.4	8,774,889	14.6
Child of different race than householder	271,454	17.1	356,441	10.8	4,010,538	6.7
Living arrangement of householder:						
Married couple	1,237,784	78.0	2,904,701	88.2	44,121,622	73.8
Male householder, partner present	28,641	1.8	264,404	8.0	1,335,277	2.2
Male householder, no partner	50,057	3.2	50,424	1.5	1,731,501	2.9
Female householder, partner present	29,052	1.8	42,487	1.3	1,703,394	2.8
Female householder, no partner	240,470	15.2	30,285	0.9	10,881,860	18.2
Household income:						
None	14,829	0.9	14,825	0.5	662,300	1.1
$1–$9,999	71,340	4.5	77,572	2.4	3,624,677	6.1

$10,000–$14,999	51,469	3.2	87,492	2.7	2,768,130	4.6
$15,000–$24,999	128,769	8.1	290,371	8.8	6,366,324	10.7
$25,000–$34,999	155,711	9.8	417,565	12.7	6,935,222	11.6
$35,000–$49,999	253,548	16.0	690,279	21.0	10,062,178	16.8
$50,000–$74,999	376,080	23.7	904,601	27.5	13,412,763	22.4
$75,000–$99,999	224,247	14.1	426,277	12.9	7,254,553	12.1
$100,000–$149,000	183,138	11.5	261,558	7.9	5,350,650	9.0
$150,000–$199,999	65,281	3.5	62,852	1.9	1,537,731	2.6
$200,000 or more	70,592	4.5	58,909	1.8	1,799,126	3.0
Median family income	$56,138	—	$50,900	—	$48,200	—
Educational attainment:						
Less than high school	226,646	14.3	568,065	17.3	10,741,542	18.0
High school graduate	359,142	22.6	1,132,925	34.3	15,808,215	26.4
Some college	470,571	29.7	1,074,775	32.6	17,769,199	29.7
Bachelor's degree	288,435	18.2	354,485	10.8	9,630,917	16.1
Graduate or professional degree	241,210	15.2	162,051	4.9	5,823,781	9.7
Owns home	1,233,692	77.8	2,200,742	66.8	39,950,491	66.8

Source: "Adopted Children and Stepchildren: 2000," by U.S. Bureau of the Census, 2003, Census 2000 Special Reports: CENSR-6RV, Washington, DC: U.S. Government Printing Office.

PROCESSES LEADING TO THE FORMATION OF STEPFAMILIES

What are the demographic processes that lead to the creation of stepfamilies, and how have they changed over time? As indicated earlier, before the dramatic rise in divorce rates during the second half of the twentieth century, death followed by remarriage used to be the primary means by which stepfamilies were formed. Following declines in mortality, an increased risk of divorce (followed by remarriage) became the agent of growth in the number of stepchildren and stepfamilies. Figure 1.2 represents changes that have occurred in divorce, marriage, and remarriage over much of the past century.[7]

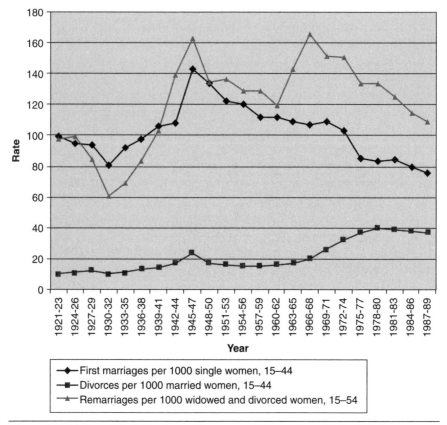

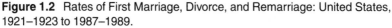

Figure 1.2 Rates of First Marriage, Divorce, and Remarriage: United States, 1921–1923 to 1987–1989.

Source: Marriage, Divorce, and Remarriage in the 1990s, by U.S. Bureau of the Census, 1992, Washington, DC: U.S. Government Printing Office.

---

[7] The data in Figure 1.2 are truncated at 1989 because of changes in the way vital statistics are collected in the United States. Specifically, in 1996 the National Center for Health Statistics suspended collection of detailed data on marriage and divorce from states, and no comprehensive analysis of these data has been published since 1989.

Figure 1.2 illustrates the surge in divorce rates that occurred from the early 1960s until about 1980. Since about 1980, divorce rates in the United States have not increased and have even declined slightly. Initially, when divorce rates began to climb, so did rates of remarriage, creating an increasing pool of couples likely to form a stepfamily. Starting in about 1970, however, rates of remarriage began to decline, well before rates of divorce declined. Thus, the number of children who have become stepchildren through remarriage has been an increasingly smaller proportion of children exposed to the probability of living in a stepfamily. This change is reflected in the rapid growth of single parents living with their children (see Table 1.3, showing that the growth in single-parent households was 21% over the 1990–2000 decade). In turn, the growth in single-parent families has fueled the growth in cohabiting couples with stepchildren.

Also shown in Figure 1.2 is America's retreat from marriage. Rates of first marriage have been dropping since 1970. The decline in marriage has meant that women are spending a greater proportion of their lifetime single. This pattern in turn increases the risk of nonmarital childbirth. Indeed, as Figure 1.3 indicates, the percentage of births among unmarried women

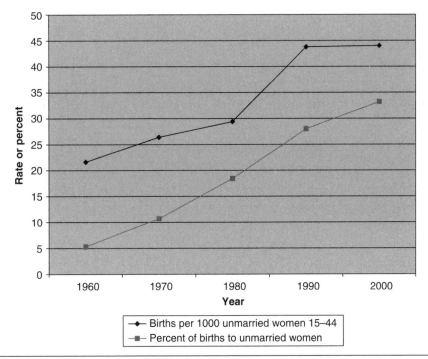

Figure 1.3 Births per 1,000 Unmarried Women Ages 15 to 44 and Percent of Births to Unmarried Women.
Source: Statistical Abstract of the United States: 2004–2005, by U.S. Bureau of the Census, 2004, Washington, DC: U.S. Government Printing Office.

has increased dramatically since 1960, from about 5% to about 33%. Figure 1.3 also shows that the birth rate of unmarried women has increased over the same period. Thus, not only have women retreated from marriage, increasing their risk of having a nonmarital birth, but the rate at which they have such births has increased. The result is that substantially more unmarried women with children are likely to form stepfamilies through either marriage or cohabitation.

The importance of cohabitation is shown in Figure 1.4; the number of unmarried-couple (cohabiting) households has increased substantially over the past 40 years, while the number of married-couple households has remained relatively constant. By 2000, there were about 5 million unmarried-couple households, representing 17% of all couple households in the United States. Combined with rapid increases in nonmarital childbirth, these figures indicate a sharp increase in the fraction of unmarried couples with stepchildren (as indicated in Table 1.3).

Consistent with these figures, Bumpass and Lu (2000) report that 40% of all children will spend some time in a cohabiting family before reaching age 16. They also report that 20% of all children born to married parents will

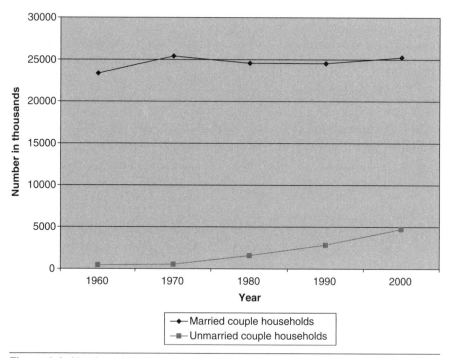

Figure 1.4 Number of Married and Unmarried Couples: United States 1960–2000.

Sources: For married-couple households, www.census.gov/population/socdemo/ hh-fam/fm1.pdf; for unmarried-couple households, www.census.gov/population/ socdemo/hh-fam/uc1.xls.

experience a cohabiting family by age 16 because of parental divorce; for children born to single mothers, the figure is 75%. Clearly, cohabitation has become an important source of family relationships to which biological children and stepchildren are exposed.

These changes indicate that the routes by which adults and children find themselves living in stepfamilies have changed over time. Divorce followed by remarriage is no longer the demographic process most often leading to a stepfamily. Bumpass et al. (1995) estimate that 27% of women enter a stepfamily via a nonmarital birth, and 65% via cohabitation. The figures for children are 32% and 64%, respectively. Thus, a substantial majority of stepfamilies are now being created by cohabitation, not marriage. Nonmarital childbirth has become another emerging and important demographic source underlying the formation of stepfamilies. Indeed, among Blacks, nearly two-thirds of children enter a stepfamily as a result of nonmarital childbirth.

SOME INTERNATIONAL COMPARISONS

We now turn our attention to some international comparisons to place the figures for the United States in a larger social and cultural context. We focus on selected European nations: France, Sweden, and the United Kingdom. These are all countries with well-developed postindustrial economies that have finished the demographic transition and have, according to some authors, entered the second demographic transition (Van de Kaa, 1987), characterized by low fertility, delayed marriage, historically high rates of divorce, and a disassociation of childbearing from marriage.

Figures 1.5 and 1.6 present crude marriage and divorce rates for these countries and the United States for the period 1980 to 2001.[8] Figure 1.5 shows a decline in marriage rates for all countries. The decline is particularly sharp for the United States and the United Kingdom, where rates of marriage have historically been higher. In Sweden, the rate of marriage is only about half that observed in the United States. Sweden has observed very little change between 1980 and 2001 in its already low rate of marriage. Despite recent declines, the United States remains the country with substantially higher marriage rates.

Figure 1.6 shows small increases in the divorce rate for France, stability in Sweden, and declines for the United Kingdom and the United States. The divorce rate is particularly high in the United States, even after declines over the past 2 decades. The rate of divorce in the United States is more than twice the rate in France. Figures 1.5 and 1.6 show that marital

---

[8] Note that the values shown in Figures 1.5 and 1.6 for marriages and divorces are not refined rates. That is, whereas these values represent marriages and divorces per 1,000 population, the values in Figure 1.1 for marriage represent marriages per 1,000 single women, and the values for divorce represent divorces per 1,000 married women.

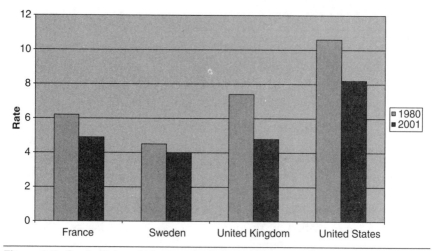

Figure 1.5 Crude Rates of Marriage for Selected European Countries and the United States, 1980 and 2001.

Source: The Clearinghouse on International Developments in Child, Youth, and Family Policies at Columbia University. See www.childpolicyintl.org.

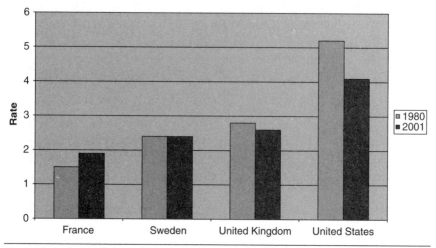

Figure 1.6 Crude Rates of Divorce for Selected European Countries and the United States, 1980 and 2001.

Source: The Clearinghouse on International Developments in Child, Youth, and Family Policies at Columbia University. See www.childpolicyintl.org.

transitions (both marriage and divorce) in the United States are much more common than they are in Europe. This pattern suggests that stepfamilies should be more common in the United States than in the European countries being considered.

Figure 1.7 illustrates the percentage of births that occur to unmarried mothers in each of the countries being considered. The first thing to notice

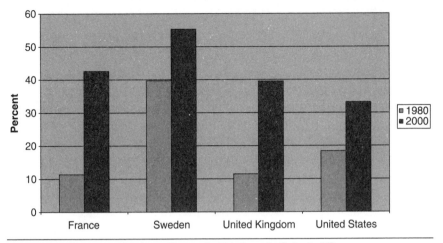

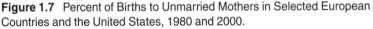

Figure 1.7 Percent of Births to Unmarried Mothers in Selected European Countries and the United States, 1980 and 2000.
Source: The Clearinghouse on International Developments in Child, Youth, and Family Policies at Columbia University. See www.childpolicyintl.org.

is the rapid increase in out-of-wedlock childbearing that has occurred in each country, continuing the disassociation of childbearing from marriage, associated with countries in the second stage of the demographic transition. At least 33% of all births now occur to unmarried mothers. In Sweden, this figure is now well above 50%. The high level of nonmarital childbearing in most of these countries indicates the potential for the creation of stepchildren and stepfamilies.

Figure 1.8 provides some indication of the prevalence of cohabitation by noting the percentage of women who cohabit before marriage. These data were gathered from various national surveys and refer to the early to mid-1990s. Two age groups are considered: women ages 25 to 29 and women ages 35 to 39. In every country, with the exception of Sweden, where premarital cohabitation has been almost universal for some time, the percentage of women ages 25 to 29 cohabiting prior to marriage is substantially greater than the proportion of women ages 35 to 39 cohabiting before marriage. This pattern indicates considerable growth in cohabitation over a short period of time. In all countries at least 60% of women can now expect to cohabit before they marry. Just as trends in out-of-wedlock childbearing suggest an increased prevalence of stepchildren and stepfamilies, so do the increasingly high rates of premarital cohabitation.

We illustrate the implications of differences in these basic demographic processes for the creation of stepfamilies in Figure 1.9, which shows the percentage of all families (including cohabiting-couple families) that are stepfamilies circa 2000 (the value for the United States is adjusted upward from about 9% to 13% to account for the undercount of stepchildren that occurs

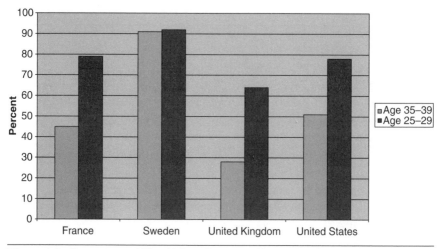

Figure 1.8 Percentage of First Unions Begun as Nonmarital Cohabitation in Selected European Countries and the United States by Age of Women.
Source: Cohabitation and Divorce across Nations (CASE paper No. 65) by K. Kiernan, 2003, London: Centre for Analysis of Social Exclusion, London School of Economics.

in the use of census data). Figure 1.9 shows that stepfamilies are most common in the United States, followed by the United Kingdom, Sweden, and France. That stepchildren are most prevalent in the United States is not surprising given its much higher rates of marriage and divorce.

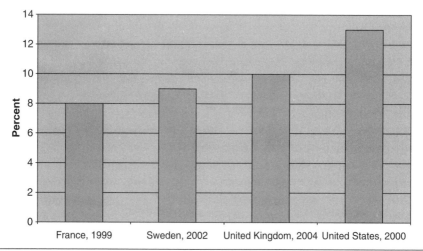

Figure 1.9 Percent of All Families That Are Stepfamilies.
Sources: For the United States, www.census.gov/prod/2001pubs/p20–537.pdf; for the United Kingdom, www.statistics.gov.uk/CCI/nugget.asp?ID=1164; for Sweden, www.scb.se/statistik/BE/LE0102/2002A01/LE0102_2002A01_BR_02_BE51S-T0307ENG.pdf; for France, www.insee.fr/fr/ffc/docs_ffc/lrsoc033.pdf.

This relatively simple conclusion belies more complex processes that may be operating, however. For example, more detailed data indicate the same ranking of countries with respect to the percentage of married-couple families that are stepfamilies (United States at 13%, United Kingdom at 8%, and Sweden at 7.8%). Yet, when cohabiting-couple families are included, the United States and the United Kingdom switch places. Indeed, the percentage of cohabiting-couple families in the United Kingdom is exceptionally high (38%) when compared to percentages in the United States (17%) and Sweden (11.7%). The reason for the much higher percentage in the United Kingdom is not immediately clear. Several factors may be at play, including differential timing of cohabitation (e.g., more cohabitations may occur after marriage, when children are more likely to be present) or a greater likelihood of forming cohabitating unions following an out-of-wedlock birth. Only more detailed analyses can provide the answer, but the question suggests the intricate patterns of stepfamily formation in countries where demographic processes have undergone substantial change.

CONCLUSION

In this chapter we have provided an overview of the demography of stepfamilies, with an emphasis on the United States. We began by considering the difficulties associated with measuring stepfamilies. Although the term is commonly used in the literature, it is not a simple exercise to define what constitutes a stepfamily. To simplify matters, and because we had to rely on census data, we presented a standard demographic definition of a stepfamily as a family household in which there is at least one stepchild of the householder present. As we noted, this definition misses important linkages that occur across different households. At the turn of the twentieth century, stepfamilies constituted about 13% of all families in the United States.

We also devoted attention to the demographic processes that generate stepfamilies, noting that there have been substantial changes over time in these processes, including increased rates of out-of-wedlock childbearing, marital disruption, and nonmarital cohabitation. These changes have led to substantial changes in the nature of stepfamilies. For example, between 1990 and 2000 the fraction of stepfamilies involving married parents remained virtually constant, whereas the fraction of families involving unmarried parents more than doubled.

We provided limited international comparisons, focusing on France, Sweden, and the United Kingdom. The prevalence of stepchildren is higher in the United States than in these European countries, most likely due to the much higher rate of divorce. However, changes in family structure in Western Europe associated with trends in marriage, divorce, and nonmarital cohabitation suggest that the prevalence of stepchildren will continue to grow.

More and more children will be spending at least a portion of their childhood in blended families. One can only speculate on the implications this will have for family structure and functions in the next generation. Will it be as Bengtson (2001) suggests, that relationships involving three or more generations will become increasingly important? If "multigenerational bonds are becoming more important than nuclear family ties for well-being and support over the course of [children's] lives" (p. 14), how will stepchildren fare compared to biological children in this scenario? Will the future for stepchildren be as dismal as portrayed in most fairy tales? Or is the alternative fairy tale provided by Bernstein (1999) more likely, where the stepchild returns home to live happily ever after, just like everyone else?

REFERENCES

Bengtson, V. (2001). Beyond the nuclear family: The increasing importance of multigenerational bonds. *Journal of Marriage and the Family, 63*, 1–16.

Benokraitis, N. (1999). *Marriages and families: Changes, choices, and constraints.* Upper Saddle River, NJ: Prentice-Hall.

Bernstein, A. (1999). Reconstructing the Brothers Grimm: New tales for stepfamily life. *Family Process, 38*, 415–429.

Bumpass, L., & Lu, H. H. (2000). Trends in cohabitation and implications for children's family contexts in the United States. *Population Studies, 54*, 29–41.

Bumpass, L., & Raley, R. K. (1995). Redefining single-parent families: Cohabitation and changing family reality. *Demography, 32*, 97–109.

Bumpass, L., Raley, R. K., & Sweet, J. (1995). The changing character of stepfamilies: Implications of cohabitation and nonmarital childbearing. *Demography, 32*, 425–436.

Cherlin, A., & Furstenberg, F. (1994). Stepfamilies in the United States: Reconsideration. *Annual Review of Sociology, 20*, 359–381.

Coleman, M., & Ganong, L. (1990). Remarriage and stepfamily research in the 1980s: Increased interest in an old family form. *Journal of Marriage and the Family, 52*, 925–940.

Coleman, M., Ganong, L., & Fine, M. (2000). Reinvestigating remarriage: Another decade of progress. *Journal of Marriage and the Family, 62*, 1288–1307.

Dilworth-Anderson, P. (1992). The cultural emergence, meaning and future of Black extended kin networks. *Generations, 17*, 29–36.

Ermisch, J., & Francesconi, M. (2000). The increasing complexity of family relationships: Lifetime experience of lone motherhood and stepfamilies in Great Britain. *European Journal of Population, 16*, 235–249.

Glick, P. (1989). Remarried families, stepfamilies, and stepchildren: A brief demographic profile. *Family Relations, 38*, 24–27.

Goldscheider, F., & Sassler, S. (2006). Creating stepfamilies: Integrating children into the study of union formation. *Journal of Marriage and the Family, 68*, 275–291.

Kiernan, K. (2003). *Cohabitation and divorce across nations* (CASE paper No. 65). London: Centre for Analysis of Social Exclusion, London School of Economics.

Levin, I., & Trost, J. (2000). Step family as dyads—Direct and indirect relationships. *Journal of Comparative Family Studies, 31*, 137–153.

Marcil-Gratton, N. (1998). *Growing up with Mom and Dad? The intricate family life courses of Canadian children* (Catalogue No. 89–566-XIE). Ottawa: Statistics Canada.

Marsiglio, W. (2004). When stepfathers claim stepchildren: A conceptual analysis. *Journal of Marriage and the Family, 66*, 22–39.

National Center for Health Statistics. (2005). *Births: Final data for 2003* (National Vital Statistics Reports Vol. 54, No. 2). Washington, DC: U.S. Government Printing Office.

Scanzoni, J., Polonko, K., Teachman, J., & Thompson, L. (1989). *The sexual bond: Rethinking the family and close relationships*. Newbury Park, CA: Sage.

Thomson, E. (2004). Step-families and childbearing desires in Europe. *Demographic Research, 3*, 117–134.

U.S. Bureau of the Census. (1992). *Marriage, divorce, and remarriage in the 1990s*. Washington, DC: U.S. Government Printing Office.

U.S. Bureau of the Census. (2000). *Census 2000 Questionnaire*. Washington, DC: U.S. Government Printing Office.

U.S. Bureau of the Census. (2001a). *America's families and living arrangements*. Washington, DC: U.S. Government Printing Office.

U.S. Bureau of the Census. (2001b). *Living arrangements of children* (Current Population Reports, Series P70–74). Washington, DC: U.S. Government Printing Office.

U.S. Bureau of the Census. (2003). *Adopted children and stepchildren: 2000* (Census 2000 Special Reports: CENSR-6RV). Washington, DC: U.S. Government Printing Office.

U.S. Bureau of the Census. (2004). *Statistical abstract of the United States: 2004–2005*. Washington, DC: U.S. Government Printing Office.

U.S. Bureau of the Census. (2005). *Examining American household composition: 1990 and 2000* (Census 2000 Special Reports: CENSR-24). Washington, DC: U.S. Government Printing Office.

U.S. Bureau of the Census. (2006). *American fact finder*. Retrieved February 21, 2006, from http://factfinder.census.gov/home/en/epss/glossary_s.html.

Van de Kaa, D. (1987). Europe's second demographic transition. *Population Bulletin, 42*(1).

Wu, L., & Wolf, B. (2001). *Out of wedlock: Causes and consequences of nonmarital fertility*. New York: Russell Sage Foundation.

CHAPTER 2

Stereotypes of Stepfamilies and Stepfamily Members

STEPHEN CLAXTON-OLDFIELD

STEPPARENTS AND stepchildren have been subject to negative stereotypes for a very long time. Whenever people hear the word "stepmother," for example, images of a wicked, evil, cruel, ugly, and jealous woman almost immediately come to mind (Coleman & Ganong, 1987a; Ganong & Coleman, 1995, 1997; Salwen, 1990); being sexually harassing and physically abusive is readily associated with stepfathers (L. R. Bryan, Coleman, Ganong, & Bryan, 1986; Claxton-Oldfield, 2000); and the word "stepchild" usually brings to mind a youngster who is unwanted, unloved, neglected, or mistreated (Coleman & Ganong, 1987a).

Schneider (2005, p. 24) defines stereotypes as "qualities perceived to be associated with particular groups or categories of people." An argument can be made that stereotypes are useful because they help us to reduce the enormous amount of information about people that we have to deal with. Simply lumping together all members of the same group is much easier (and much quicker) than having to get to know each new member of the group we meet as an individual (Sampson, 1999): "Oh, you're one of them. I already know a lot about you."

Although stereotypes can be positive, negative, neutral, or mixed, most people tend to be more aware of the negative stereotypes that exist about various groups (Nelson, 2002). When a group of people, such as stepmothers, are seen as having many negative characteristics (e.g., wicked, evil, cruel), they may become the object of prejudice. For example, a young girl says that she does not like stepmothers because she has read or heard about them in fairy tales, and she thinks they are mean and ugly. That same girl expects her friend's stepmother to be horrible and, for this reason, does not want to visit her friend's house. This is an example of how stereotypes and prejudices can serve to increase the distance that people put between themselves and members of a disliked group. Overcoming her anxiety about meeting her friend's stepmother, the young girl eventually goes to her friend's home. Inside, she notices a mop and bucket by the back door and assumes that the stepmother makes her friend sweep and scrub the floors because that is what "wicked stepmothers" do. This demonstrates how stereotypes can sometimes lead people to see what they expect to see; if Cinderella's stepmother did not make her scrub the floors, then the young girl probably would not have noticed the mop and bucket at her friend's house. The young girl's stereotyped beliefs may influence how she behaves when she actually meets her friend's stepmother (e.g., she may be unfriendly and cool toward her). These behaviors may, in turn, elicit behaviors from the stepmother that are consistent with the young girl's expectations that stepmothers are not very nice (the stepmother may not make much of an effort to get to know her stepdaughter's aloof new friend). This illustrates how stereotypes can become self-fulfilling prophecies, producing the very behaviors that fit the stereotype (Snyder & Swann, 1978).

The focus of this chapter is on reviewing the empirical evidence for the existence of stereotypes about stepfamily members and stepfamily units. In addition, questions regarding the origins and implications of these stereotypes are examined. Finally, the limitations of past research are discussed and suggestions for future research are offered.

WHERE DO STEP STEREOTYPES COME FROM?

Stereotypes about stepparents, stepchildren, and stepfamilies can be found in all types of media, from movies and television to fairy tales and adult literature (Claxton-Oldfield, 2000). At a very young age, children are exposed to stepmothers in popular fairy tales about Hansel and Gretel, Snow White, and Cinderella. There can be little doubt that children learn stereotypes about stepmothers from reading or hearing these tales (Smith, 1953). Consider, for example, the tale of the little boy called Hansel and his sister Gretel, who live with their father (a poor woodcutter) and his second wife. Worried about not having enough food for herself to eat, Hansel and Gretel's mean and unloving stepmother persuades her husband to abandon his children in the forest. Unable to find their way home again, Hansel and Gretel will surely perish, leaving two fewer mouths for the stepmother to feed. In another well-loved tale, which also involves a failed attempt to murder a stepchild, Snow White's vain and wicked stepmother tries to kill her with a poison-laced apple. And what about poor Cinderella? Her evil stepmother gave her torn and ragged old clothes to wear and the most disgusting household chores to do and, of course, would not let her go to the ball. It is no wonder that young children are often fearful and anxious about acquiring a stepmother. Long before a stepmother even arrives on the scene, children have already learned that stepmothers are almost always bad. As Ganong and Coleman (1997, p. 102) put it, "It is not too far fetched, considering how stepfamily life is often portrayed, for stepchildren to assume that they will be abused and unloved." Ahrons (as cited in Doheny, 1998, p. F16) "recalls a 10-year-old boy she saw in therapy, concerned about his father's upcoming remarriage. 'I don't want a stepmother!' he told her. His concern, she later found out, was related to a movie he had seen whose cast included a wicked stepmother."

Although stepfathers do not feature prominently in children's fairy tales, there are plenty of abusive stepfathers in adult literature (Claxton-Oldfield, 2000). In Dickens's (1849–1850) *David Copperfield*, for example, we meet David's stepfather, the domineering Mr. Murdstone: "'David,' he said, making his lips thin by pressing them together, 'if I have an obstinate horse or dog to deal with, what do you think I do? . . . I beat him. . . . I make him wince and smart.'" In Nabokov's (1955) *Lolita*, we meet Humbert Humbert, who has a sexual love affair with his 12-year-old stepdaughter, Dolores, affectionately called Lolita: "'Lolita, light of my life, fire of my loins. My sin. My soul."

Abusive stepfathers can also be found in movies. Nabokov's *Lolita*, for example, has been made into a movie twice, in 1962 and 1997. Using an Internet movie database, Claxton-Oldfield and Butler (1998) examined movie plot summaries that specifically mentioned a stepfather character. The majority of the summaries (58%) portrayed stepfathers in a negative way (as physically abusive or sexually harassing, as scheming, bad, and evil, or as unwanted). For example, in the movies *The Stepfather* (1987) and its sequel, *The Stepfather II: Make Room for Daddy* (1989), a psychopathic stepfather marries widows with children and then gruesomely murders them when they fail to live up to his idealized image of the perfect family. Stepmothers are usually portrayed in movies as murderous, mean-spirited, money-grubbing, unwanted, or very strange (Claxton-Oldfield & Butler, 1998; Ganong & Coleman, 1997). In a more recent study, Leon and Angst (2005) found that stepfamilies in movies were typically portrayed in either a negative or mixed way. Stepparents also tend to be portrayed in predominantly negative ways in newspaper stories (Christian, 2005; Claxton-Oldfield, 2000). For example, the headline "Stepfather Jailed for Sex with Adolescent Stepdaughter" may lead people to believe that it is not unusual for stepfathers to lust after their stepdaughters. It is possible that sensational newspaper headlines and shocking story lines in fictional books and movies may lead people to believe that abusive stepfathers are commonplace, thanks to the availability heuristic (Tversky & Kahneman, 1973).

In addition to the negative stereotypes of stepparents found in fairy tales, books, movies, and newspaper stories, others have argued that negative attitudes toward stepfamilies derive from "the image of the contemporary stepfamily that is often the aftermath of divorce" (Johnson, 1980, p. 304). As Ganong and Coleman (2004, p. 30) point out, stepfamilies are often seen as "the consequences of failed marriages and broken homes." Although divorce and remarriage are more acceptable today than in the past, Ganong and Coleman believe that "there is still an undercurrent of moral outrage directed toward individuals who divorce" (p. 30), many of whom remarry and form stepfamilies.

With divorce and remarriage a common occurrence these days, the shame around divorce and the stigma surrounding stepfamilies is likely much less robust than it used to be. However, this has not stopped some stepfamilies from using labels without the step prefix to describe their family status (e.g., remarried, blended, merged, reconstituted, recoupled, combined). Some stepfamilies go to the extreme of denying their step status to be seen by others as a "normal" (biological) family and to avoid the negative step stereotypes (Coleman & Ganong, 1987a; Dainton, 1993). The kinds of characteristics Ganong and Coleman's (2004) students generated to describe stepfamilies (e.g., conflicts, anger, confusion, dysfunctional, wicked, complex, rocky/shaky, lots of arguing) and the problem-focused approach in many magazine articles and self-help books about stepfamilies (Coleman & Ganong, 1987b; Coleman, Ganong, & Gingrich, 1985; Pasley & Ihinger-Tallman, 1985) would seem to suggest that stepfamilies are not as healthy as biological families.

EMPIRICAL STUDIES OF STEPFAMILY STEREOTYPES

Since the early 1980s, a number of studies have been conducted to examine what people think about stepparents and stepchildren. Typically, three main research methods have been used: ratings of family position labels (Claxton-Oldfield & Voyer, 2001; Fine, 1986; Fluitt & Paradise, 1991; Ganong & Coleman, 1983), ratings of adults and children identified as (step)parents and (step)children in brief, neutral written descriptions (L. R. Bryan et al., 1986; S. H. Bryan, Ganong, Coleman, & Bryan, 1985), and ratings of written descriptions in which the individuals identified as (step)parents and (step)children are actually depicted interacting with one another (Claxton-Oldfield, 1992; Dukes, 1989).

FAMILY POSITION LABELS

In 1983, Ganong and Coleman published the first study examining American college students' perceptions of stepmothers and stepfathers. Using a semantic differential scale consisting of nine pairs of bipolar adjectives (e.g., good-bad, affectionate-hateful, kind-cruel, loving-unloving), half of the students were asked to rate the family position labels "grandmother," "brother," "nephew," "cousin," "mother," and "stepfather." The other half rated the first four labels along with the labels "father" and "stepmother." Each pair was responded to on a 7-point scale, with a higher score indicating a more positive perception of the family position. The labels were presented at random on separate pages, and students were instructed to respond to each label "in general," that is, "not to a specific person they might know in that family position" (p. 920). A comparison of the responses to mothers and stepmothers revealed that mothers were rated more positively than stepmothers on seven of the nine scales, and fathers were rated more positively than stepfathers on eight of the nine scales. Based on these findings, Ganong and Coleman concluded, "The stereotype of stepmothers and stepfathers as being hateful, cruel, and unloving still seems to be in operation" (p. 921).

Fine (1986) and Fluitt and Paradise (1991) also found evidence of stereotyped perceptions of the family position labels "stepmother" and "stepfather" among college students. These researchers employed the same nine bipolar adjective pairs used by Ganong and Coleman (1983). The results of both studies were consistent with the earlier findings: Mothers were perceived more positively than stepmothers, and fathers were perceived more positively than stepfathers. Both Fine and Fluitt and Paradise added the variable "student's current family structure" (biological, single-parent, stepparent) to the analyses. In Fine's study, a comparison of the responses to stepmothers and stepfathers revealed that students from all three family backgrounds had less positive perceptions of stepmothers than they did of stepfathers, including those students who were stepchildren themselves, while Fluitt and Paradise found no differences between students' perceptions of stepmothers and stepfathers. Fine also found that students from single-parent and stepparent homes had less stereotyped perceptions of stepmothers compared to students from biological family homes. These results were

interpreted as supporting the notion that increased exposure to stepfamilies (many of those in single-parent homes also related to stepmothers living with noncustodial fathers) attenuates negative stereotypes of stepmothers through increasing sensitivity, familiarity, and appreciation of the challenges facing remarried mothers. (Fine, 1986, p. 537)

Claxton-Oldfield and Voyer (2001) investigated university students' perceptions of stepchildren and children from biological families using four family position labels (stepsister, stepbrother, sister, and brother)—these labels had not been included in any of the previous studies—and Ganong and Coleman's (1983) nine pairs of bipolar adjectives. The results revealed that sisters were perceived more positively than stepsisters, and brothers were perceived more positively than stepbrothers. There was no difference in the students' overall ratings for stepsister and stepbrother. The results of this study appear to indicate that the labels "stepsister" and "stepbrother" elicit more negative (or less positive) reactions than do the labels "sister" and "brother."

Clearly, step labels have the power to activate stereotypes (i.e., bring stereotyped content to mind). Over half a century ago, Bernard (1956, p. 14) argued that step labels should be avoided whenever possible because "they are, in effect, smear words." If step labels did not influence how people view stepfamilies, then stepfamily members would have no reason to hide or deny their stepfamily status (Visher & Visher, 1979). One way of overcoming the powerful effects of labels is to avoid using them, as when a stepson publicly refers to his stepfather as his dad or a stepmother introduces her husband's child from a previous relationship as her own son or daughter. After all, if I do not tell you "I am Lisa's stepfather," how would you know? Your stereotype of stepfathers would not be activated and, because stepfathers do not look different in any way from biological fathers, you would probably assume that I am Lisa's father and evaluate me accordingly.

Instead of trying to conceal their step status, some stepparents have come up with new terms for their roles (e.g., "Lydia's coparent," "Amy's other father"; Coleman & Ganong, 1987a; Maddox, 1975), indicating their awareness that step labels may evoke negative stereotypes. However, this strategy is likely to yield only short-term results; over time, these new terms are likely to acquire the negatively tinged connotations of step terms (Ganong, Coleman, & Kennedy, 1990). As Maddox (1975, p. 202) put it, "If the connotation is unpleasant, the reason should be faced, not glossed over with a change of label."

BRIEF NEUTRAL WRITTEN VIGNETTES

A second method of studying family structure stereotypes involves presenting participants with brief, neutral written descriptions (or vignettes) of adults and children in families with married, remarried, widowed, divorced, or never-married parents (L. R. Bryan et al., 1986; S. H. Bryan et al., 1985). For example, the vignettes used by L. R. Bryan et al. were variations of the following:

> *Ann (Alan) Davis is 41, married (divorced, remarried, widowed, never married) and lives in suburban Chicago with her (his) husband (wife) [if divorced, widowed or never married, "her (his) husband (wife) and" was omitted] and her (his) 17-year-old daughter (son, stepdaughter, stepson) Linda (Larry). Ann (Alan) has a master's degree*

from the University of Illinois and works as a writer. Linda (Larry) is a senior in high school. (Coleman & Ganong, 1987a, p. 26)

After reading the vignette, the participants (undergraduate students) were asked to rate the adult and the adolescent using the First Impressions Questionnaire (FIQ). The FIQ consists of 40 pairs of bipolar adjectives loading on six factors: Social Evaluation, Potency, Satisfaction/Security, Personal Character, Activity, and Stability. The results revealed that stepparents and stepchildren were perceived less positively than parents and children from biological families on all six factors of the FIQ. Stepparents were viewed more negatively than widowed parents but similarly to divorced and never-married parents, and children in stepfamilies were seen less positively than children from all other family structures on five of the six factors.

In a previous study, using vignettes similar to those in the L. R. Bryan et al. (1986) study, S. H. Bryan et al. (1985) asked mental health counselors (employed professionals) and graduate and undergraduate students enrolled in counseling and social work courses to give their "first impressions" of a father, stepfather, mother, or stepmother and his or her (step)son or (step)daughter, depending on the parent-child combination. The participants' ratings were made on the First Impressions Semantic Differential (FISD), consisting of 25 pairs of bipolar adjectives loading on four factors: Evaluative, Potency, Activity, and Adjustment/Well-Being. S. H. Bryan et al. found that stepparents were viewed as less potent and less well-adjusted compared to biological parents. The results also revealed that perceptions of stepfathers and fathers were more negative than perceptions of stepmothers and mothers on the Potency and Adjustment/Well-Being factors. This finding is inconsistent with the results of Fine's (1986) study using family position labels, in which stepmothers were evaluated more negatively than stepfathers. In the S. H. Bryan et al. study, stepchildren were evaluated less positively and rated as less potent, less active, and less well-adjusted than their biological counterparts. Additional analyses revealed that the amount of professional experience the participants had influenced their perceptions of persons from biological and stepfamilies. Experienced counselors (i.e., those with at least 2 years of work experience) did not view stepfamily and biological family members differently. Inexperienced counselors, however, viewed stepparents less positively on the Evaluative factor and as less potent and less well-adjusted than biological parents; they also viewed stepchildren less positively than biological children on the Evaluative and Adjustment/Well-Being factors.

Ganong, Coleman, and Kennedy (1990) investigated the effects of not using step labels to indicate one's stepparent status. In this study, the target adult in a brief written vignette was identified as either a parent, a stepparent, or someone with whom his (or her) partner's children lived (to avoid using the step label). After reading the paragraph, the participants (undergraduate students) rated the target person using the FIQ (L. R. Bryan et al., 1986). The results revealed that students rated persons identified as stepparents less positively on the Evaluative factor of the FIQ than persons identified as parents and persons who were not labeled as stepparents. These findings suggest that

> stepmothers and stepfathers who refer to themselves with alternative labels, such as "mother" and "father," or who avoid using any label for their stepparenting role, may indeed be reducing the negative attitudes of others by their avoidance of negatively connotated terms. (Ganong, Coleman, & Kennedy, 1990, p. 460)

However, as Visher and Visher (1988, as cited in Ganong, Coleman, & Kennedy, 1990, p. 462) note, "This kind of denial is probably detrimental to one's sense of self and may hinder stepfamily adjustment."

The results of studies using family position labels and brief, neutral written vignettes suggest that stepparents and stepchildren are generally viewed more negatively (or less positively) than parents and children from biological families. A major criticism of these studies, however, concerns the largely static way in which the comparisons between stepfamily members and biological family members have been made. For example, the information presented about the target person being evaluated in these studies—family position label or name, age, place of residence, and occupation (e.g., writer or senior in high school)—is, at best, neutral (Ganong, Coleman, & Mapes, 1990) and is not particularly useful in terms of making evaluative judgments about the person in question. For example, how can I possibly say whether "Alan who lives in suburban Chicago with his wife and his 17-year-old stepdaughter" is a good person or a bad person, a loving person or an unloving person, a kind person or a cruel person? Based on the limited information that I have just read, I do not know anything about what Alan is like as a person or as a stepfather. If the only "information" that comes to mind when I think about Alan is a stereotype of stepfathers, then I can either use that as a basis for evaluating Alan or I can rate him in the middle of each bipolar scale to indicate that, in the absence of any individuating information about him, I cannot really say that either trait (good-bad, loving-unloving, etc.) applies to him.

As noted earlier, the vignettes used in the L. R. Bryan et al. (1985) and S. H. Bryan et al. (1986) studies contain no information about the actual behavior of the parent or stepparent being evaluated. That is, they do not describe the (step)parent interacting with his or her (step)child. It makes sense that how well or how poorly someone carries out his or her (step)parental role is more important than the name of the person's role (e.g., stepfather,

father). Surely, a badly behaving biological father would be viewed more negatively than a stepfather interacting positively with his stepchild. However, in the absence of any individuating information (e.g., actual [step]parental behavior), raters can base their evaluations only on labels, and when people respond only to labels, negative stereotypes are more likely to be apparent (Schneider, 2005).

WRITTEN VIGNETTES DESCRIBING (STEP)PARENTAL BEHAVIOR

The first researcher to introduce actual parenting behavior into the situation in which the (step)parent is being evaluated was Dukes (1989). In this study, undergraduate students were presented with three brief written vignettes, each describing a (step)parent interacting either effectively or ineffectively with a child (e.g., turning off the TV to listen attentively to a child who is obviously excited about something or telling a child who is obviously excited about something to be quiet until the TV show is over). After reading each vignette, the students were asked to make a single rating of the (step)parent's effectiveness in the situation, using a 7-point scale. The results revealed no differences in the students' ratings of the stepparent's or biological parent's behavior over the three vignettes. In other words, "what parents did in the situation overwhelmed any differences that were due to whether the adult in the vignette is a stepparent or a natural parent or whether the child is a natural child or a stepchild" (p. 69).

Claxton-Oldfield (1992, Study 1) found that British college students rated stepfathers as being less affectionate, fair, kind, loving, and likeable than biological fathers when they were depicted (in written vignettes) punishing a misbehaving (step)child (i.e., spanking a 5-year-old [step]child on the leg because he or she was having a "temper tantrum" while out shopping with his or her [step]father). In addition, the stepfather's disciplinary behavior was rated as less justified and excusable. However, when stepfathers and biological fathers were depicted behaving affectionately toward a (step)-child in Study 2 (i.e., being playful with and hugging and kissing a 5-year-old [step]child), there were few differences in how students rated them.

The results of the Dukes (1989) and Claxton-Oldfield (1992, Study 2) studies suggest that individuating information is more important than stereotypes in forming impressions of stepparents. In other words, the power of step labels to provoke stereotypes can be overcome by providing information about actual stepparental behaviors, so long as these behaviors are viewed as acceptable and appropriate. For example, spanking a child may be viewed as an acceptable behavior for biological fathers (who are perceived as having a legitimate authority to punish their own children) but not acceptable or appropriate for a stepfather, who lacks a blood relationship with the child. In Claxton-Oldfield's Study 1, it is also possible that the "abusive stepfather" stereotype may have influenced the students' ratings of the stepfather's disciplinary behavior. Once a stereotype is activated, there is a tendency for people to seek out information that confirms their stereotyped beliefs and expectations (Johnston & Macrae, 1994). For the target person identified as a stepfather, the information about him spanking his stepson or stepdaughter on the leg and marching him or her out of the store may have served to confirm the "abusive stepfather" stereotype, whereas the stereotype-inconsistent information in Claxton-Oldfield's Study 2 (i.e., a stepfather being playful with and affectionate toward his stepchild) did not. Another possible explanation for Claxton-Oldfield's findings is that people may have more than one stereotype of stepfathers (Claxton-Oldfield, O'Neill, Thomson, & Gallant, 2005).

PERCEPTIONS OF STEPFAMILY UNITS

There has been less research looking at people's stereotypes of stepfamilies as a family unit. In one such study, Bryant, Coleman, and Ganong (1988) compared undergraduate students' perceptions of Black and White biological families and stepfamilies. A brief neutral written vignette was used to describe the Smiths' family structure (stepfamily, biological family) and race (Black, White). After reading the description, students evaluated the family unit using the FIQ (L. R. Bryan et al., 1986). The results revealed that Black students generally perceived the vignette families more positively than did White students and that students (irrespective of race) viewed stepfamilies less positively than biological families. Contrary to the researchers' expectations that the Black stepfamily would be rated less positively than all other family structures, the White stepfamily was consistently rated less positively than the Black stepfamily and the Black and White biological families. Several possible explanations were offered for these findings, including the idea "that White and Black families are evaluated by different standards" (Bryant et al., 1988, p. 8).

Ganong, Coleman, and Kennedy (1990) assessed the effects of using different labels to denote stepfamily status. Undergraduate students read about the Walkers, described as either a family, a stepfamily, a blended family, a remarried family, a reconstituted family, or a nuclear family living in a large midwestern American city. Responses to the different family targets were made using the FIQ (L. R. Bryan et al., 1986). Somewhat surprisingly, no differences were found in how students rated families with different labels, suggesting that the step prefix may have negative connotations only when it is used to describe a person (e.g., stepmother, stepfather) but not an entire stepfamily unit.

More recently, Claxton-Oldfield and O'Neil (2007) explored undergraduate students' perceptions of stepfamilies headed by gay and lesbian couples. According to the 2001 Canadian Census, 15% of female same-sex couples and 3% of male same-sex couples had children living with them (Statistics Canada, 2001). In the United States, the 1990 census found that 22% of households headed by lesbian couples and 5% of households headed by gay male couples had children living with them (Black, Gates, Sanders, & Taylor, 2000). In Claxton-Oldfield and O'Neil's study, undergraduate students read a brief vignette describing one of four family units (gay stepfamily, lesbian stepfamily, heterosexual stepfamily, or biological family). The vignettes used were a variation of the basic vignette used by Bryant et al. (1988). The gay and lesbian stepfamily versions read as follows:

> Joan (John) Davis lives in suburban Toronto with her (his) partner Mary (Mike) Smith. Living with Joan (John) and Mary (Mike) are Mary's (Mike's) children from a previous marriage (Alan, aged 14, and Susan, aged 10). Joan (John) and Mary (Mike), who are lesbians (gay), both teach high school social studies. (Claxton-Oldfield & O'Neil, 2007, p. 4)

After reading the vignette, students were asked to rate their impressions of the family unit using the FIQ (L. R. Bryan et al., 1986). The results revealed a significant difference between the biological family and all three stepfamily units on the Activity factor of the FIQ, with gay, lesbian, and heterosexual stepfamilies perceived as being more active than biological families. This finding may reflect the participants' belief that life in a first-marriage family is more steady, reliable, or predictable, whereas life in a stepfamily is more changeable and unpredictable (e.g., stepchildren frequently go back and forth between two households). The only other difference involving the biological family was that it was rated as being more stable than the heterosexual stepfamily. Overall, there were few differences in how students viewed the different family units, and there was no evidence of a "double negative" stereotype for gay and lesbian stepfamilies.

Although Bryant et al. (1988) found that stepfamilies as a whole are seen less positively than biological families, Claxton-Oldfield and O'Neil (2007) found few differences in people's perceptions of biological families and homosexual or heterosexual stepfamilies. Similarly, the study assessing the effects of using alternative labels to describe stepfamilies found that all family units were evaluated the same (Ganong, Coleman, & Kennedy, 1990). As Bryant et al. (1988, p. 453) suggest, "It may be that 'step' labels are meaningful only when applied to individuals." For example, when we think about Cinderella, we tend to remember the mistreated stepchild, the wicked stepmother, and the ugly stepsisters. We tend not to think about the fact that Cinderella lives in a stepfamily household.

MULTIPLE STEREOTYPES OF STEPPARENTS

Clearly, when it comes to making judgments or evaluations about step-parents, individuating information is important (e.g., Dukes, 1989). For example, when actual (step)parental behaviors were included in Claxton-Oldfield's (1992) vignettes, the students rated a stepfather depicted spanking a child less positively than an identically behaving biological father (Study 1), whereas there were hardly any differences in the students' ratings of a father or a stepfather depicted being playful with and affectionate toward his (step)child (Study 2). These findings suggest that people may have a number of different stereotypes of stepfathers (e.g., the abusive stepfather, the loving stepfather).

Research on stereotypes of the elderly suggests that people have more than one stereotype of older persons (e.g., Brewer, Dull, & Lui, 1981; Hummert, Garstka, Shaner, & Strahm, 1994; Schmidt & Boland, 1986). For example, Brewer et al. found that when asked to sort photographs of older adults into groups, participants put them into different subcategories (or subtypes), such as respected elder statesman, sweet grandmother, and inactive senior citizen. Other researchers have found that people have different stereotypes for subtypes of women (e.g., housewife, career woman, women's libber; Eckes, 1994) and African Americans (e.g., athletes, businessmen, ghetto dwellers; Devine & Baker, 1991).

In the first of three separate studies, Claxton-Oldfield et al. (2005) asked undergraduate students to list all of the things they typically think about, hear about, or read about stepfathers, using single words or short phrases. After combining semantically similar traits, the list of over 500 was reduced to a set of 77 traits, of which 45 were negative and 32 were positive. In Study 2, undergraduate students were asked to sort the 77 traits into one or more groups, each group consisting of traits that could be found together in the same stepfather. Hierarchical cluster analysis resulted in nine negative and six positive trait clusters, suggesting that students have several different stereotypes for subtypes of stepfathers (e.g., the decent stepfather, the supportive stepfather, the unloving stepfather, the exploiting stepfather). Encouragingly, the positive stereotypes were seen as being more typical of stepfathers than the negative stereotypes (Study 3).

It seems likely that how people perceive stepfathers will depend on which stereotype is activated. For example, if I have just read a vignette describing a stepfather playing with and behaving affectionately toward a stepchild, then the "decent stepfather" stereotype (i.e., a stepfather who is nice, loving, warm, and caring) may come to mind and I will evaluate him favorably. On the other hand, if I've just read a vignette describing a stepfather spanking a stepchild and marching him or her out of a store (even though the stepfather's behavior may have been justified), then the "unloving stepfather" stereotype may be activated and influence how I evaluate this particular stepfather—not favorably.

One of the problems with subtypes is that any negative stereotypes people may hold about a particular group do not necessarily change simply because they encounter a single stereotype-inconsistent group member (Weber & Crocker, 1983). For example, if my general view of stepfathers is that they are bad, but I happen to encounter a warm, kind, and loving stepfather, I may place him in an exception-to-the-rule category of "decent stepfathers" while maintaining my original belief that most stepfathers are a nasty piece of work.

IMPLICATIONS OF STEPPARENT STEREOTYPES

Clearly, stereotypes can influence our interpretations of others' behavior in one direction or another. This is especially true when the information at hand is ambiguous (Darley & Gross, 1983). For example, one stereotype of stepfathers is that they are abusive, sexually and physically (L. R. Bryan et al., 1986; Claxton-Oldfield, 2000), an image perpetuated in movies (Claxton-Oldfield & Butler, 1998), newspaper stories, and adult literature (Claxton-Oldfield, 2000). In a 2002 study, Claxton-Oldfield, Goodyear, Parsons, and Claxton-Oldfield investigated whether ambiguous evidence of child abuse would lead people to be more suspicious of a stepfather's behavior than of a identically behaving biological father. In Study 1, undergraduate students read a brief vignette describing an adolescent girl talking to a high school counselor about how her (step)father likes to tickle her unexpectedly (e.g., when she's doing the dishes or talking on the phone) and how this bothers her. The students were instructed to imagine themselves as the high school counselor and to indicate the likelihood that they would be suspicious of the (step)father's behavior, using a 7-point scale. They were also asked to provide a written explanation for their answer. The results revealed that students were more suspicious of the stepfather's behavior than they were of the same behavior from the girl's biological father. In explaining their judgments, more than half of the students (64%) felt that the stepfather's behavior was inappropriate, disrespectful, unwanted, or possibly abusive. The most common explanation for the same behavior by the biological father was that he was just being playful.

In Claxton-Oldfield et al.'s (2002) Study 2, a hospital examination for a soccer injury (twisted ankle) revealed bruises on a young boy's back and arms. In background information, the young boy was identified as living with his mother and father or his mother and stepfather. Responding as imagined doctors, students indicated the extent to which they were suspicious about the boy's bruises, using a 7-point scale. The results revealed no differences between the stepfather and father conditions. It is possible that the stereotype of stepfathers as sexually harassing may have been operating in Study 1. As one student put it, "My first inclination is to be concerned that the stepfather's behavior is suspicious just because it sounds like a typical scenario." When information about an individual's behavior is ambiguous, the activation of a stereotype may lead people to interpret the behavior in a way that makes it fit the stereotype (Sagar & Schofield, 1980). For example, if the stereotype of stepfathers as sexually harassing is widely believed, then even weak or inconclusive evidence of abuse may be enough to arouse people's suspicions about a stepfather's behavior. In Study 2, however, the stereotype of the "physically abusive stepfather" did not seem to be activated; most students in the stepfather and father conditions thought that the boy's bruises probably came from playing soccer. Perhaps the stereotype of the "sexually harassing stepfather" is stronger than the stereotype of stepfathers as physically abusive. It is also possible that the students were aware of the "physically abusive stepfather" stereotype but chose not to use it. As one student in Study 2 wrote, "Though there is no direct evidence to who or what caused the bruises on John, it is suspicious that he does have these markings on him. It is presumptuous to implicate the stepfather. This would be a negative stereotype."

Do people think that child abuse occurs more often in stepfather families than it does in biological families? Claxton-Oldfield and Whitt (2003) asked 186 undergraduate students to indicate whether they thought that girls who live with stepfathers are at greater, about the same, or lower risk for sexual abuse compared to girls who live with their biological father. They were also asked whether they thought that boys who live with stepfathers are at greater, about the same, or lower risk of physical abuse than boys who live with their biological father. In addition, students were asked to explain how they arrived at their decisions. Interestingly, fewer than half of the students believed that children living with stepfathers were at greater risk of sexual or physical abuse (45.4% and 34.1%, respectively). The reasons given for believing that girls who live with stepfathers are at greater risk of sexual abuse included the lack of a biological relationship, the absence of the incest taboo, media portrayals of stepfathers as sexual abusers, and the lack of bonding. The nonbiological relationship and the greater likelihood of conflict in stepfather families contributed to the belief that boys are at greater risk of physical abuse if they live with a stepfather. More than half of the students believed that the risks of sexual or physical abuse were the same for children living in stepfather and biological father families (i.e., it happens in both kinds of families) and that it depends more on the personality of the abuser than the nature of the relationship. Many of the students in this study were aware of the negative stereotypes of stepfathers (e.g., "The media often tends to portray stepfathers as being the most common sexual abusers of young girls"). What is encouraging, however, is that a number of them made a conscious decision not to use these stereotypes when making their judgments about stepfathers (e.g., "While a popular belief [that stepdaughters are at more risk of sexual abuse by stepfathers], I believe it is a stereotype").

If inexperienced social workers and counseling psychologists view stepparents and stepchildren differently from parents and children in biological families (S. H. Bryan et al., 1985), how might knowledge of a person's family structure influence other helping professionals' (e.g., nurses, teachers) perceptions of stepfamily members? Blaine, Coleman, and Ganong (1985; as cited in Coleman & Ganong, 1987a) examined nursing students' perceptions of a 5-year-old child whose bedwetting was caused by either psychological problems or physical problems. The child's family structure was presented as stepfamily (stepmother and father, stepfather and mother) or biological family, or no family information was presented. The researchers' expectation that children from stepfamilies would be evaluated less positively than children from the biological or no family information conditions was only weakly supported; children from both stepfamily conditions were rated less positively on the Evaluative scale of the FISD (S. H. Bryan et al., 1985), but no differences were found in how the child was perceived on the other scales.

Guttman and Broudo (1989) examined teachers' perceptions of an 11-year-old fifth-grade boy described as living with both biological parents, with his divorced mother, with his mother and stepfather, or with both biological parents who do not get along (conflicted family). After reading a brief vignette describing the boy's personal and background characteristics and family type, female teachers in Israel were asked to rate the boy's scholastic performance (e.g., receives good grades, receives poor grades), social behavior (e.g., socially active in class, socially passive in class), and emotional functioning (e.g., happy, sad). The results showed that teachers evaluated the social and emotional functioning of the child from the biological family as significantly better than that of the children from the divorced, stepfather, and conflicted families; no differences were found between the child from the divorced and the stepfather families, both of whom were evaluated as functioning better socially and emotionally than the child from the conflicted family. No differences in academic functioning were found between the child from the biological family and the child from the divorced or stepfather families. "These findings would appear to reflect the belief of teachers that although having an intact family is best for children, they are better off living with divorced [or remarried] parents than in a conflicted family" (p. 325).

Ganong, Coleman, and Jones (1990) and Claxton-Oldfield and Kavanagh (1999) also investigated the effects of family structure information on people's impressions of a (step)child in a school setting. In the Ganong,

Coleman, and Jones (1990) study, college students planning to be teachers read a brief paragraph describing an adolescent male meeting with his high school counselor. Three different family structures (biological, single-parent, or stepfather family) were inserted into the paragraph, and the boy's recent behavior was described as good (trying to pull his grades up), bad (skipping classes), or neutral. The results showed that family structure information had no effect on the college students' predictions about the boy's behavior at school or at home, and no differences were found in their impressions of him on the FIQ (L. R. Bryan et al., 1986). However, in an open-ended question ("If you were his high school counselor, what thoughts would you have about his situation?"), the students were more likely to give negatively tinged responses when the boy lived in a stepfamily rather than in a biological or single-parent family.

In Claxton-Oldfield and Kavanagh's (1999) study, undergraduate students were asked to view an 8-year-old child's report card. The report card indicated that the child was of average intelligence. The child's family structure was identified in the following instructions: "The child whose report card you are about to see is named Jane (John). She (he) is 8 years old and lives in Halifax with her (his) mother and father (stepfather). Jane (John) is in grade three" (p. 149).

After viewing the child's report card, the students were asked to rate their impressions of the child's scholastic performance, social behavior, and emotional functioning, using a shortened (12-item) version of Guttman and Broudo's (1989) questionnaire. The students were also asked to rate the child's predicted behavior in school (e.g., "How likely is he [she] to break school rules and regulations?"; "How likely [it is that] he [she] is popular with his [her] friends at school?"), using a 7-point scale (1 = "very likely" to 7 = "very unlikely"). The results revealed that male (but not female) students perceived stepchildren as functioning worse socially and emotionally compared to children from biological families. One possible explanation for this finding is that males are more willing than females to judge a child based on limited information. As in Guttman and Broudo's study, scholastic performance was not affected by family structure information, nor was the child's predicted behavior in school.

LIMITATIONS OF PAST RESEARCH AND DIRECTIONS FOR FUTURE RESEARCH

The empirical studies reviewed in this chapter are not without their limitations. For example, most of the studies were conducted with college or university students as participants. The opinions of these young, educated, open-minded people may not reflect those of the general population, thereby posing a threat to the external validity of these studies (Gravetter &

Forzano, 2006). Participant age may be an overlooked variable; for example, it is possible that middle-aged and older participants hold more traditional views of the family (i.e., as a unit consisting of a mother, father, and two or three children) and may be less accepting of nontraditional families, including stepfamilies, compared to younger participants. Another limitation is that most of the studies described in this chapter were conducted in North America, although some were conducted in other countries, for example, England (Claxton-Oldfield, 1992) and Israel (Guttman & Broudo, 1989).

Furthermore, in those studies in which stepfamily members were perceived more negatively than biological family members, it should be noted that, as Coleman and Ganong (1987a, p. 36) pointed out, the participants' "responses seldom were negative in an absolute sense. Mean scores for stepfamily positions on the various semantic differential items tended to be near the midpoint, with mean scores for comparison stimuli falling toward the positive side of the scales." In other words, responses to stepmothers, stepfathers, and stepchildren tended to be more neutral than negative, yet less positive (or more negative) than responses to biological mothers, fathers, and children.

Another problem with using semantic differential scales to compare people's views regarding stepparents and biological parents on various dimensions (e.g., evaluation, potency, personal character) has to do with what exactly is being measured. In other words, we do not know whether participants are responding to the target persons in these studies (e.g., stepmother) using their knowledge of the cultural stereotype of stepmothers or their own personal (idiosyncratic) beliefs about stepmothers (Braithwaite, Gibson, & Holman, 1986; Devine, 1989). For example, although most people are aware of the "wicked stepmother" stereotype and know where it comes from (fairy tales and movies), they may not personally accept, endorse, and apply this stereotype. In Claxton-Oldfield et al.'s (2002) and Claxton-Oldfield and Whitt's (2003) studies, a number of participants indicated that they were aware of the "abusive stepfather" stereotype but did not use it. Future studies need to determine whether it is people's personal beliefs about stepparents, stepchildren, and stepfamilies that are being assessed and not just cultural stereotypes, which they may or may not believe to be true.

More research is needed to determine the content of people's step stereotypes. For example, it would be interesting to conduct a study comparing people's perceptions of stepmothers and stepfathers using both the semantic differential method (e.g., Ganong & Coleman, 1983) and the free-response method, in which participants simply list the characteristics and traits that come to mind when they think about stepmothers or stepfathers. Surely, a person's instant (or gut-level) reaction to stepmothers is more meaningful than his or her rating the family position label "stepmother" on a series of bipolar adjectives scales provided by the researcher.

Another suggestion for future research is to learn more about young children's stereotypes of stepparents and stepfamilies. One way of investigating children's feelings about step relationships is to use a storytelling task. For example, children could be shown a picture of a happy-looking (step)family or an unhappy-looking (step)family and then asked to tell a story about what they think might have just happened in the picture, how the child feels about the (step)parent, how the (step)parent feels about the child, what is going to happen next, and so on. This would be a gentle way of exploring young children's views about step relationships, while at the same time giving their imaginations free rein.

Future research could also focus on people's perceptions of adoptive stepparents. For example, is a stepparent who adopts his or her stepchild(ren) viewed more positively than one who does not, or is stepparent adoption viewed as a desperate attempt by stepparents to re-create a biological family (i.e., to make the stepparent feel like a "real" parent)? What about people's perceptions of step-grandparents: Do people think that step-grandparents treat their step-grandchildren differently compared to how biological grandparents treat their grandchildren? Studies using other research methods (e.g., videotaped interactions between a [step]child and [step]parent or a [step]child and teacher) should be conducted to better understand people's perceptions of stepparents. Another question that has not been investigated has to do with how knowledge of a person's step status influences others' behavior toward him or her. A person's preconceptions about stepmothers or stepfathers may lead him or her to act in ways that elicit the kinds of behaviors that confirm stereotyped expectations, creating a self-fulfilling prophecy. This could be studied by arranging for participants to interact with someone identified as being a (step)father or (step)mother and recording what they do or say, the length of the interaction, the interpersonal distance maintained between them, and so on. It would also be interesting to know whether step stereotypes influence interactions within stepfamilies, especially between young children and new stepparents.

Different types of self-report measures could be developed to assess people's stereotypes about stepparents. For example, a questionnaire item that asks "Would you let your adolescent daughter have a sleepover at a friend's house if you knew that her friend's mother was remarried?" addresses a more subtle form of prejudice against stepfathers than simply asking someone if stepfathers in general are good or bad. Claxton-Oldfield et al.'s (2005) study provides evidence for the existence of multiple stereotypes of stepfathers (some positive, others negative), suggesting that people may react to stepfathers in more than one way. More research is needed to discover which situations activate certain stereotypes. Based on the previous research (e.g., Claxton-Oldfield, 1992, Study 2; Dukes, 1989), it would appear that stepparents who are depicted behaving reasonably (i.e., within the typical range of stepparenting behavior) are an effective counter to negative stereotypes.

Being a stepparent or stepchild is different from being a member of various other groups (e.g., racial, gender) in that group membership is not necessarily permanent. It would be interesting to see how people's attitudes toward stepfamilies change as their own family circumstances change. For example, as a young child growing up in a biological family, I may have a negative view of stepparents and stepfamilies based on what I have read, heard, or seen about them. Then, after my parents get divorced and my mother remarries, I find myself living in a stepfamily with a stepfather. If my stepfather makes my mother happy, helps out with the family, cares about me, and acts as another father figure, my attitude toward him will likely be positive, and this may generalize to other stepfathers and stepfamilies, especially if I see my stepfather as being typical of stepfathers in general. On the other hand, if my stepfather bosses me around, tries to replace my biological father, and does not care about me, my negative view of stepfathers and stepfamilies will be reinforced. (See Claxton-Oldfield, Garber, & Gillcrist, 2006, for a discussion of the advantages and disadvantages to having a stepfather.) Fortunately, there is nothing about becoming a stepparent that inevitably brings out the worst in people. In fact, most stepparents try very hard to be good stepmothers and stepfathers.

CONCLUSION

In 2001, there were over half a million stepfamilies in Canada, compared with 430,500 in 1995; this represents a 17% increase in the number of stepfamilies over a 6-year period (Statistics Canada, 2002). About half of these stepfamilies consist of married couples; the other half are composed of common-law or cohabiting couples (Statistics Canada, 2002). The majority of Canadian stepfamilies—approximately three-quarters—are stepfather families (Juby, 2003–2004). As the number of stepfamilies in Canada continues to grow, it is likely that negative stereotypes about stepfamily members will eventually disappear.

Now that stepfamilies have become a prominent part of our society, the media has an important role to play in presenting the message that step relationships can be satisfying. As Ganong and Coleman (1997, p. 102) note, "A more balanced emphasis by the media on the positive and negative aspects of stepfamilies would be helpful in setting expectations and attitudes." Books focusing on the good things about living in a stepfamily, such as Boyd's (1990) *The Not So-Wicked Stepmother* and Steel's (1990) *Martha's New Daddy*, can help stepchildren understand what it is like to have a stepparent. Over the years, a number of American television shows have presented positive models of stepfamilies (e.g., *Eight Is Enough, Step by*

Step, Something So Right), albeit mostly in situation comedies (i.e., geared for laughs) rather than realistic portrayals of everyday stepfamily life. Some Hollywood movies have presented positive models for stepparents: *Stepmom* (1998) starred Julia Roberts as a stepmother trying to please her stepchildren, and *Man of the House* (1995) starred Chevy Chase as a stepfather trying to build a positive relationship with his soon-to-be stepson. "Things are changing, say some filmmakers, who contend that as they become stepparents themselves, their productions are reflecting more realism and less sensationalism and negativity" (Doheny, 1998, p. F16). It seems reasonable that positive media portrayals of stepfamily life will go a long way toward reducing negative stereotypes of stepfamily members.

Another sign that stepfamilies are more accepted is the availability of greeting cards for stepfathers, stepmothers, stepsons, and stepdaughters. I recently came across a Father's Day card for a "loving and concerned stepfather." Although I was not overwhelmed by the selection of cards for various step relationships, things are changing as society becomes more sensitized to stepfamilies. Twenty years ago, Coleman and Ganong (1987a, p. 34) noted that "the relative absence of greeting cards for stepmothers, stepfathers, and stepchildren is another example of the symbolic avoidance of stepfamilies." Step terms are no longer "smear words," as Bernard (1956) regarded them over a half century ago.

Stepfamilies are all around us. Today, nearly everyone knows at least one person who is a stepparent or a stepchild. Within stepfamilies, personal relationships with well-intentioned and well-meaning stepmothers and stepfathers will also help to break down negative stereotypes, especially if a genuine friendship develops between stepchildren and their stepparents. Furthermore, according to the extended contact hypothesis (e.g., Wright, Aron, McLaughlin-Volpe, & Ropp, 1997), observing one's friends interacting positively (i.e., getting along) with their stepparents and stepchildren may serve as a basis for modifying the remnants of any negative stereotypes of stepfamily members. In other words, today's stepparents and stepchildren can act as peer socializers by talking to their friends about their positive experiences in their own stepfamilies. The more this kind of counterstereotypic information gets spread across more and more stepparents and stepchildren, the less likely it is that people will regard happy stepfamilies as being exceptions to the rule, and the more likely it is that these positive views will generalize to stepparents, stepchildren, and stepfamilies in general.

REFERENCES

Bernard, J. (1956). *Remarriage: A study of marriage.* New York: Russel & Russel.

Black, D., Gates, G., Sanders, S., & Taylor, L. (2000). Demographics of the gay and lesbian population in the United States: Evidence from available systematic data sources. *Demography, 37*(2), 139–154.

Boyd, L. (1990). *The not-so-wicked stepmother*. London: Puffin Books.

Braithwaite, V., Gibson, D., & Holman, J. (1986). Age stereotyping: Are we oversimplifying the phenomenon? *International Journal of Aging and Human Development, 22*(4), 315–325.

Brewer, M. B., Dull, V., & Lui, L. (1981). Perceptions of the elderly: Stereotypes as prototypes. *Journal of Personality and Social Psychology, 41*(4), 656–670.

Bryan, L. R., Coleman, M., Ganong, L. H., & Bryan, S. H. (1986). Person perception: Family structure as a cue for stereotyping. *Journal of Marriage and the Family, 48*(1), 169–174.

Bryan, S. H., Ganong, L. H., Coleman, M., & Bryan, L. R. (1985). Counselors' perceptions of stepparents and stepchildren. *Journal of Counseling Psychology, 32*(2), 279–282.

Bryant, Z. L., Coleman, M., & Ganong, L. H. (1988). Race and family structure stereotyping: Perceptions of Black and White nuclear families and stepfamilies. *Journal of Black Psychology, 15*(1), 1–16.

Christian, A. (2005). Contesting the myth of the "wicked stepmother": Narrative analysis of an online stepfamily support group. *Western Journal of Communication, 69*(1), 27–47.

Claxton-Oldfield, S. (1992). Perceptions of stepfathers: Disciplinary and affectionate behavior. *Journal of Family Issues, 13*(3), 378–389.

Claxton-Oldfield, S. (2000). Deconstructing the myth of the wicked stepparent. *Marriage and Family Review, 30*(1/2), 51–58.

Claxton-Oldfield, S., & Butler, B. (1998). Portrayal of stepparents in movie plot summaries. *Psychological Reports, 82*, 879–882.

Claxton-Oldfield, S., Garber, T., & Gillcrist, K. (2006). Young adults' perceptions of their relationships with their stepfathers and biological fathers. *Journal of Divorce and Remarriage, 45*(1/2), 51–61.

Claxton-Oldfield, S., Goodyear, C., Parsons, T., & Claxton-Oldfield, J. (2002). Some possible implications of negative stepfather stereotypes. *Journal of Divorce and Remarriage, 36*(3/4), 77–88.

Claxton-Oldfield, S., & Kavanagh, P. (1999). The effect of stepfamily status on impressions of children's report card information. *Journal of Divorce and Remarriage, 32*(1/2), 145–153.

Claxton-Oldfield, S., & O'Neil, S. (2007). Perceptions of gay and lesbian stepfamilies. *Journal of Divorce and Remarriage, 46*(3/4), 1–8.

Claxton-Oldfield, S., O'Neill, S., Thomson, C., & Gallant, B. (2005). Multiple stereotypes of stepfathers. *Journal of Divorce and Remarriage, 44*(1/2), 165–176.

Claxton-Oldfield, S., & Voyer, S. (2001). Young adults' perceptions of stepchildren. *Journal of Divorce and Remarriage, 35*(1/2), 107–114.

Claxton-Oldfield, S., & Whitt, L. (2003). Child abuse in stepfather families: Do people think it occurs more often than it does in biological father families? *Journal of Divorce and Remarriage, 40*(1/2), 17–33.

Coleman, M., & Ganong, L. H. (1987a). The cultural stereotyping of stepfamilies. In K. Pasley & M. Ihinger-Tallman (Eds.), *Remarriage and stepparenting: Current research and theory* (pp. 19–41). New York: Guilford Press.

Coleman, M., & Ganong, L. H. (1987b). An evaluation of the stepfamily self-help literature for children and adolescents. *Family Relations, 36*(1), 61–65.

Coleman, M., Ganong, L., & Gingrich, R. (1985). Stepfamily strengths: A review of the popular literature. *Family Relations, 34*(4), 583–589.

Dainton, M. (1993). The myths and misconceptions of the stepmother identity: Descriptions and prescriptions for identity management. *Family Relations, 42*(1), 93–98.

Darley, J. M., & Gross, P. H. (1983). A hypothesis-confirming bias in labelling effects. *Journal of Personality and Social Psychology, 44*(1), 20–33.

Devine, P. G. (1989). Stereotypes and prejudice: Their automatic and controlled components. *Journal of Personality and Social Psychology, 56*(1), 5–18.

Devine, P. G., & Baker, S. M. (1991). Measurement of racial stereotypes subtyping. *Personality and Social Psychology Bulletin, 17*(1), 44–50.

Dickens, C. (1849–1850). *David Copperfield*. London: Bradbury & Evans.

Doheny, K. (1998, December 31). Steps toward change: Audiences applaud projects like "Stepmom" for countering stereotypes. *Los Angeles Times*, p. F16.

Dukes, R. L. (1989). The Cinderella myth: Negative evaluations of stepparents. *Sociology and Sociological Research, 73*(2), 67–72.

Eckes, T. (1994). Explorations in gender cognition: Content and structure of female and male subtypes. *Social Cognition, 12*(1), 37–60.

Fine, M. A. (1986). Perceptions of stepparents: Variation in stereotypes as a function of current family structure. *Journal of Marriage and the Family, 48*(3), 537–543.

Fluitt, M. S., & Paradise, L. V. (1991). The relationship of current family structures to young adults' perceptions of stepparents. *Journal of Divorce and Remarriage, 15* (3/4), 159–174.

Ganong, L. H., & Coleman, M. (1983). Stepparent: A pejorative term? *Psychological Reports, 52*, 919–922.

Ganong, L. H., & Coleman, M. (1995). The content of mother stereotypes. *Sex Roles, 32*(7/8), 495–512.

Ganong, L. H., & Coleman, M. (1997). How society views stepfamilies. *Marriage and Family Review, 26*(1/2), 85–106.

Ganong, L. H., & Coleman, M. (2004). *Stepfamily relationships: Development, dynamics, and interventions.* New York: Kluwer Academic/Plenum Press.

Ganong, L. H., Coleman, M., & Jones, G. (1990). Effects of behaviour and family structure on perceptions. *Journal of Educational Psychology, 82*(4), 820–825.

Ganong, L. H., Coleman, M., & Kennedy, G. (1990). The effects of using alternate labels in denoting stepparent or stepfamily status. *Journal of Social Behavior and Personality, 5*(5), 453–463.

Ganong, L. H., Coleman, M., & Mapes, D. (1990). A meta-analytic review of family structure stereotypes. *Journal of Marriage and the Family, 52*, 287–297.

Gravetter, F. J., & Forzano, L. B. (2006). *Research methods for the behavioural sciences* (2nd ed.). Scarborough, Canada: Nelson/Thomson Learning.

Guttman, J., & Broudo, M. (1989). The effect of children's family type on teachers' stereotypes. *Journal of Divorce, 12*, 315–328.

Hummert, M. L., Garstka, T. A., Shaner, J. L., & Strahm, S. (1994). Stereotypes of the elderly held by young, middle-aged, and elderly adults. *Journal of Gerontology: Psychological Sciences, 49*(5), 240–249.

Johnson, D. (1980). Working with stepfamilies: Principles of practice. *Social Work, 25*, 304–308.

Johnston, L., & Macrae, C. N. (1994). Changing social stereotypes: The case of the information seeker. *European Journal of Social Psychology, 24*(5), 581–592.

Juby, H. (2003–2004, Winter). Yours, mine, and ours: New boundaries for the modern stepfamily. *Transition, 33*(4), 3–6.

Leon, K., & Angst, E. (2005). Portrayals of stepfamilies in film: Using media images in remarriage education. *Family Relations, 54*(1), 3–23.

Maddox, B. (1975). *Step-parenting: How to live with other people's children.* London: Unwin Paperbacks.

Nabokov, V. (1955). *Lolita.* Paris: Olympia.

Nelson, T. D. (2002). *The psychology of prejudice.* Boston: Allyn & Bacon.

Pasley, K., & Ihinger-Tallman, M. (1985). Portraits of stepfamily life in popular fiction: 1940–1980. *Family Relations, 34*(4), 527–534.

Sagar, H. A., & Schofield, J. W. (1980). Racial and behavioural cues in Black and White children's perceptions of ambiguously aggressive acts. *Journal of Personality and Social Psychology, 39*(4), 590–598.

Salwen, L. V. (1990). The myth of the wicked stepmother. *Women and Therapy, 10* (1/2), 117–125.

Sampson, E. E. (1999). *Dealing with differences: An introduction to the social psychology of prejudice.* Orlando, FL: Harcourt.

Schmidt, D. F., & Boland, S. M. (1986). Structure of perceptions of older adults: Evidence for multiple stereotypes. *Psychology and Aging, 1*(3), 255–260.

Schneider, D. J. (2005). *The psychology of stereotyping.* New York: Guilford Press.

Smith, W. C. (1953). *The stepchild.* Chicago: University of Chicago Press.

Snyder, M., & Swann, W. (1978). Behavioural confirmation in social interaction: From social perception to social reality. *Journal of Experimental Social Psychology, 14*(2), 148–162.

Statistics Canada. (2001). *The proportion of "traditional" families continues to decline.* Retrieved August 15, 2007, from www12.statscan.ca/english/census01/products/analytic/companion/fam/canada.cfm.

Statistics Canada. (2002, July). *Changing conjugal life in Canada.* Catalogue No. 89–576-XIE.

Steel, D. (1990). *Martha's new daddy.* New York: Delacorte Press.

Tversky, A., & Kahneman, D. (1973). Availability: A heuristic for judging frequency and probability. *Cognitive Psychology, 5*(2), 207–232.

Visher, E., & Visher, J. (1979). *Stepfamilies: A guide to working with stepparents and stepchildren.* New York: Brunner/Mazel.

Weber, R., & Crocker, J. (1983). Cognitive processes in the revision of stereotypic beliefs. *Journal of Personality and Social Psychology, 45*(5), 961–977.

Wright, S. C., Aron, A., McLaughlin-Volpe, T., & Ropp, S. A. (1997). The extended contact effect: Knowledge of cross-group friendships and prejudice. *Journal of Personality and Social Psychology, 73*(1), 73–90.

CHAPTER 3

Stepfamilies in France Since the 1990s: An Interdisciplinary Overview

JEAN-FRANÇOIS MIGNOT

SOCIAL SCIENCE research focusing on stepfamilies in France did not develop until the early 1990s. This phenomenon is emphasized by the fact that the phrase for "stepfamily" in French—*famille recomposée*, that is, recomposed family—was not coined until the late 1980s. Although adequate statistical and ethnographic data about stepfamilies have been lacking for a long time and social scientists' interest in these families has not increased as rapidly as their number, research conducted since the 1990s offers some findings concerning their prevalence and functioning. Therefore, this contribution aims to give a synthetic overview of the information currently available in this newly developed field of interest.

Although stepfamilies are sometimes defined as a kind of family, that is, as a type of kinship unit, they are best seen as a kind of household, that is, as a type of *residential unit*. In this chapter, stepfamilies are defined as a kind of household in which a (usually heterosexual, married or unmarried) couple lives with at least one child who is the (biological or adopted) child of only one of the members of this couple; the other member of this couple is the child's stepparent. Therefore, when I refer to "stepfamilies," it should be understood that this term refers to stepfamily households.

I would like to thank Jan Pryor and Amanda Fenn for helping me write the English version of this chapter, and Xavier Bebin for drawing my attention to Martin Daly and Margo Wilson's noteworthy articles.

A stepfamily is formed through the repartnering or remarriage of a parent who is either separated or divorced from, or widowed by, a former partner or spouse. Once a stepfamily is formed, the new couple can have children, who are then called the half-brothers and half-sisters of the children born from former unions. If both members of the new couple had children from former unions, then these children, who are biologically unrelated, are called stepbrothers and stepsisters. Consequently, children can live with either *one* of their parents (if they are children their parents had before forming the stepfamily) or with *both* of them (if they are children born since the stepfamily was formed); a child can also live either with or without half-siblings (depending on whether the coresiding parent had another child inside the stepfamily) and stepsiblings (depending on whether the coresiding parent's new partner or spouse also had children before forming the stepfamily).

Defining stepfamilies in this manner—as a kind of household, rather than as a kind of family—implies that a parent who repartnered or remarried after separation or divorce, but who does not have custody of the child(ren) he or she had from a former union, is *not* part of the stepfamily. This is a somewhat arbitrary definition; however, for clarity's sake, this chapter follows it. Beginning with a historical overview of the study of stepfamilies in France, this review of the existing literature focuses on stepfamilies in France since the 1990s, and more specifically on the demography (incidence, prevalence, and composition) of these families, the ethnographic accounts of the relationships between their members (children, parents, stepparents, and siblings), their ties with the law, and their functioning as explained by evolutionary psychology.

HISTORICAL BACKGROUND ON STEPFAMILIES IN FRANCE

In French, the word *marâtre* has a double meaning: "stepmother" and "cruel mother." *Parâtre* means both "stepfather" and, to some extent, "cruel father." Indeed, in France as in many other countries, stepfamilies have long been regarded, at best, with suspicion and, at worst, with horror. This section illustrates this fact and tries to explain why this perception has existed for a long time.

Until the twentieth century, those who formed stepfamilies were almost exclusively widows or widowers who had children from a first marriage and remarried. However, these remarriages had several fierce enemies. The first of these emerged during the twelfth century, when the Church decreed that marriage was indissoluble, which meant that widows and widowers should ideally never remarry. However, because many people were finding it hard to forgo sex and the benefits from the sexual division of labor (between household and market sectors), the Church tolerated remarriage as a somewhat necessary evil: necessary because remarriage was considered much more acceptable than nonmarital sex, but still evil because it was a clear indication of man's weakness in his struggle against the temptations of bodily pleasure (Cadolle, 1998; Fulchiron, 1993). In this context, widows remarrying relatively young husbands (and, to a lesser extent, widowers marrying younger wives) were commonly suspected of doing so for indecent, sex-related reasons. Second, remarriages, especially those involving an older husband and a younger wife, were strongly frowned upon by young males who thought that these marriages were depriving them of potential wives: These remarried men were taking two wives, sometimes leaving the young males without any women to marry. In rural communities, this is one of the reasons why remarriages often faced *charivaris*, that is, young men making a scene on the couple's wedding day to express their deep disapproval of such unions.

However, remarriages were not the only reason why stepfamilies gained a bad reputation. More specifically, they were frowned upon because they were remarriages that included children from a former marriage. The problem here was twofold. First, because raising stepchildren or marrying an older spouse was seen as inherently undesirable, the reason the stepparent had chosen to marry a widow or widower, instead of a childless spouse, *had* to be shameful. Typically, young women marrying older widowers and young men marrying older widows were suspected of doing so only for financial reasons. The second part of the problem was due to the fact that the remarriage of the parent threatened the transmission of family heritage to his or her children from a former union (Cadolle, 1998; Fulchiron, 1993). The concern was that the new spouse would try to rob the stepchildren of their inheritance either for his or her own advantage or for that of the children he or she would have in the marriage. Indeed, according to popular belief, this possibility was all the more credible because the stepparent was already suspected of having married for financial reasons. In cases in which a man married a widow instead of a more attractive, younger wife, the widow was even suspected of being forced to promise to give him her children's inheritance as compensation for the marriage (Fulchiron, 1993). More generally, common sense suggested that nothing would restrain greedy stepparents—and especially wicked stepmothers—from maltreating or, at best, neglecting their stepchildren.

Therefore, traditional suspicion of stepfamilies was not utterly arbitrary; people generally had some "good reasons" (Boudon, 2003) to be distrustful of those forming stepfamilies. A detailed study has shown that traditional fictional literature, not limited to the stories of Cinderella and Snow White, widely spread these suspicions (Cadolle, 1998). In these tales, although a stepfather is sometimes depicted as a precious help to a needy widow with children, he is more often depicted as a usurper; when he does not simply kill the child's father to rob him of his power position or wealth (sometimes with the mother's consent, if she was his lover), he unscrupulously robs the children of their inheritance, and often the male child's right to the throne. This model is the well-known *abusive stepfather* figure; however, this recurring character is not quite as horrific or encountered as frequently as that of the *wicked stepmother*. Indeed, this literature usually portrays a stepmother as a degenerate person, a malicious woman, a mother who is eaten up with jealousy and therefore treats her stepchildren cruelly. It is not only her lack of maternal instinct toward her stepchildren, but also—and maybe more important—her greedy and exclusivist temper that supposedly make her act in this way. More precisely, she is said to have several reasons to be jealous. On the one hand, if she loves her husband, she is jealous of her stepchildren because their existence implies that she cannot monopolize her husband's love and consideration; she is also jealous of her husband's former spouse, and the stepchildren become a constant reminder of the intolerable fact that before the formation of the stepfamily there was another woman that her husband loved. On the other hand, if she married for financial motives, she must be jealous of her stepchildren because they use money that would otherwise be given to her and her children, and they will continue to do so until the split of the inheritance. In other words, the core reason why the stepmother hates her stepchildren and why her children also hate their half-siblings is that they force her and her children to share the same man's love and money. It is no surprise, then, that she turns out to be unfair, favoring her own children when distributing the household's burdens, such as chores, and goods, such as food and clothes and, of course, motherly love. The stepmother is perceived as being particularly jealous of her stepdaughter, whom she sees not only as a rival in the competition to gain the man's favors, but also as a future rival for her own daughters when they enter the marriage market; this is why she stubbornly tries to inflict material deprivations and symbolic humiliations on her.

In those times, and well into the eighteenth and even the nineteenth century, relatively high mortality risks created numerous young widows and widowers, thus paving the way for remarriage and the formation of stepfamilies. However, as France was experiencing its demographic transition from high to lower mortality, stepfamilies became less common. Moreover, as France was experiencing socioeconomic modernization and a move from "ascribed" to "achieved" status, inheritance issues became less central, which consequently made the relationships within stepfamilies healthier. Therefore, from the nineteenth century on, stepfamilies became less problematic than in the past and people's opinions about these families began to change. Consequently, when stepfamilies became more common again following the rise in divorce and separation in the 1970s (Villeneuve-Gokalp, 1993), their reputation, although not quite enviable, was not as negative as it had been for centuries. The following sections show that, while the demography of stepfamilies has changed dramatically since the 1970s, the functioning of stepfamilies, although becoming easier than before, retained some of its core elements.

THE DEMOGRAPHY OF STEPFAMILIES, 1990–1999

Demography relies on relevant statistical data. Currently, French data on stepfamilies remain scarce because censuses are inadequate for the study of these families and there are few surveys that focus on them (Leridon, 1993). Thus, to learn more about stepfamilies, demographers rely on the French Family Surveys (Enquête Famille, 1990, and Enquête Étude de l'Histoire Familiale, 1999). The advantage of these surveys is that they are reliable and easy to compare; however, they do not permit researchers to study stepfamilies before the 1990s, which is why this section does not dwell at length on that period.

Following the increase of the number of stepfamilies in the 1970s and the 20% rise in this number in the 1980s (Desplanques, 1993), the number of children living in stepfamilies increased rapidly. In 1985 (Villeneuve-Gokalp, 1993), 980,000 children were living in stepfamilies: 680,000 were living with a parent and a stepparent (usually, their mother and stepfather), and 300,000 were living with their two parents and half-siblings. Of course, the central difference from the period before the 1960s was not only one of prevalence, but also one of composition (Villeneuve-Gokalp, 1993): In 1985, as many as 80% of the 800,000 children who were living or had ever lived with a stepparent were or had been part of a stepfamily due to the divorce or separation of their parents, whereas only 6% of them entered a stepfamily due to widowhood (the remaining 14% were born into a one-parent family). In the early 1990s, stepfamilies had already become much more common than in previous decades, and they were also most often caused by remarriage or re-partnership after divorce or separation rather than after widowhood. The following data, discussing the precise prevalence and composition of stepfamilies in France in the 1990s, come from two pairs of texts: one on stepfamilies in 1990 (Desplanques, 1993, 1994) and one on stepfamilies in 1999 (Barre, 2003, 2005). The survey focuses first on stepfamilies in relation to all families and then on children living in stepfamilies in relation to all children.

Stepfamilies in the 1990s

The percentage of stepfamilies among all households is described first. As Figure 3.1 shows, in 1999 stepfamilies composed 8% of all families with at least one child under the age of 25. By comparison, "traditional" families— in which both parents live together—made up 73.4% of all families, and single-parent families made up 18.6% of the total.

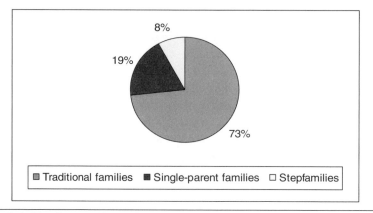

Figure 3.1 The Composition of Families by Family Type—France's Family Survey, 1999. *Note:* Field = Families with at least one child under 25.
Source: "1,6 Million d'Enfants Vivent dans une Famille Recomposée," by C. Barre, 2003, *INSEE Première, 901,* pp. 1–4.

Second, as shown in Figure 3.2, between 1990 and 1999 the number of stepfamilies increased from 646,000 to 708,000. This 9.6% increase over 9 years raised the percentage of stepfamilies from 7.1% to 8%. In the same time, the percentage of single-parent families increased from 15.3% to 18.6%, and that of traditional families decreased from 77.6% to 73.4%.

The form of stepfamily that increased the most in the 1990s was that in which there were not only children from a former union but also children from the present union. The percentage of these stepfamilies rose by 13.1%

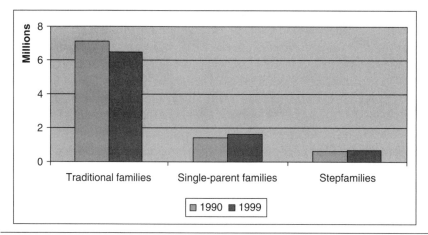

Figure 3.2 The Evolution of the Number of Families by Family Type—France's Family Surveys, 1990–1999. *Note:* Field = Families with at least one child under 25.
Source: "1,6 Million d'Enfants Vivent dans une Famille Recomposée," by C. Barre, 2003, *INSEE Première, 901,* pp. 1–4.

(from 336,000 to 380,000), while the number of stepfamilies in which there were no children from the present union rose by only 5.8% (from 310,000 to 328,000). One effect of this phenomenon is that in the 1990s the proportion of stepfamilies with at least one child from the present union rose from 52% to 54%.

Another persistent characteristic of stepfamilies is their relatively underprivileged social background. Indeed, women who form stepfamilies tend to have below-average education levels (Desplanques, 1994) and are disproportionately low-income earners (Barre, 2003). Although more educated women tend to be divorced more often, less educated women are more often widowed or single mothers and, more important, tend to remarry or repartner more often after divorce or separation (doubtless because they have more to gain financially by repartnering or remarrying) and to have at least one child from their first union (Desplanques, 1993, 1994).

Now that the French landscape concerning stepfamilies in relation to all families has been clarified, I will continue by focusing on children living in stepfamilies in relation to all children.

CHILDREN LIVING IN STEPFAMILIES IN THE 1990s

As Figure 3.3 shows, in 1999 children living in stepfamilies made up 8.7% of all children under the age of 25. By comparison, 65.7% of children were living in traditional families, 15% of them were living in single-parent families, and 10.6% were not living in any household, but in a boarding school or foster center.

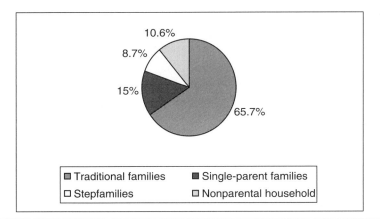

Figure 3.3 The Distribution of Children by Family Type—France's Family Survey, 1999. *Note:* Field = People under 25.

Source: "1,6 Million d'Enfants Vivent dans une Famille Recomposée," by C. Barre, 2003, *INSEE Première, 901*, pp. 1–4.

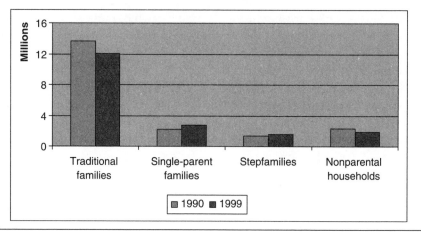

Figure 3.4 The Evolution of the Number of Children by Family Type—France's Family Surveys, 1990–1999. *Note:* Field = People under 25.
Source: "1,6 Million d'Enfants Vivent dans une Famille Recomposée," by C. Barre, 2003, *INSEE Première, 901,* pp. 1–4.

As shown in Figure 3.4, between 1990 and 1999 the number of children under 25 living in stepfamilies increased from 1,429,000 to 1,583,000. This 10.8% increase raised the percentage of children living in stepfamilies from 7.3% to 8.7%. At the same time, the percentage of children living in single-parent families increased from 11.4% to 15%, while that of children living in traditional families decreased from 69.3% to 65.7% and that of children not living in any household decreased from 12% to 10.6%.

As Figure 3.5 shows, in 1999 children living in stepfamilies were distributed into three roughly equal groups (Toulemon, 2004): One third of them

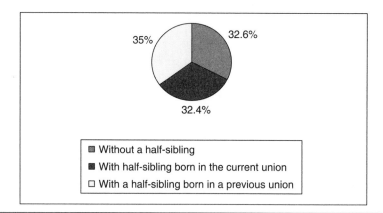

Figure 3.5 The Distribution of Children Living in Stepfamilies by Number of Half-siblings Born in Each Union—France's Family Survey, 1999. *Note:* Field = People under 25.
Source: "1,6 Million d'Enfants Vivent dans une Famille Recomposée," by C. Barre, 2003, *INSEE Première, 901,* pp. 1–4.

(32.6%), who were born in a former union, lived with a parent and a step-parent and had no half-sibling born in the new union; another third (32.4%), also born in a former union and living with a parent and a stepparent, had at least one half-sibling born in the present union; and the last third (35%) of children living in stepfamilies, who were born in the new union and lived with both of their parents, had at least one half-sibling born from a former union. Between 1990 and 1999, the number of children without any half-siblings rose by 33.4%, from 386,000 to 515,000, while the number of children who had half-siblings remained stable.

Breaking down these results by the children's ages, it is evident that in 1999 the proportion of children living with a stepparent was very low before 5 and, to some extent, 10 years old, but relatively high at higher ages (Barre, 2005). This pattern results from the fact that by the time a parent has sepa-rated or divorced and found a new partner, the children have grown up.

THE FERTILITY OF STEPFAMILIES

Stepfamilies tend to be relatively large families. In 1999, as in 1990, the fact that stepfamilies often contained children from two or three different unions made them overrepresented among large families. For instance, in 1990, stepfamilies composed 6% of families with only one child, but 15% of families with four children (Desplanques, 1994). It has been shown that underprivileged stepfamilies in France tend to have more children in the present union than do more privileged stepfamilies (Desplanques, 1993). But the most interesting results concerning the fertility behavior of stepfa-milies come from a study involving not only France but also three other European countries: West Germany, Austria, and Finland (Thomson, 2004). This study found that in these countries stepfamilies' propensity to give birth to a first shared child was higher than would be expected given the number of children the couple already had from former unions, which sug-gests the unique role that a first shared child plays in solidifying the newly composed couple's commitment. This explanation is given more credibility by the fact that in stepfamilies with two or more children, couples tend to *want* one more child much more often if they do not yet have a shared child. Moreover, the study found that stepfamily couples' birth rate may also be higher than expected for a second shared child, which may show the impor-tance of having a second shared child to become the first one's full sibling. This phenomenon could also be interpreted as an additional indication that, at least in the parents' eyes, a full sibling is better for a child than a half-sibling. (This study also found that stepfamily couples' birth rate was not higher if one of the partners was not a parent before the stepfamily formed, which could contradict the idea that adults who mate with a partner who is already a parent attach any value to parental status.)

In general, stepfamilies and children living in stepfamilies, whose numbers rose by around 10% in the 1990s, reached a prevalence among families and among children of nearly 10% in the late 1990s. Whereas until the nineteenth century, and to some extent until the mid-twentieth century, stepfamilies were typically composed of at least one widowed, remarried parent, by the 1990s they most often included a divorced or separated parent who may or may not have remarried or married after having spent some time as a single parent. The fact that divorce, rather than widowhood, became the root of the formation of stepfamilies modifies stepfamilies' functioning substantially because, as will become clear in the next section, it implies that the stepparent may no longer replace the nonresident parent.

ETHNOGRAPHIC ACCOUNTS OF THE RELATIONSHIPS BETWEEN STEPFAMILY MEMBERS IN THE 1990S

French researchers often claim that the study of stepfamilies should include a study of both household and kinship networks, which go hand in hand (Meulders-Klein & Théry, 1993, 1995; Théry, 2001). Indeed, not only is a stepfamily household often closely connected to the nonresident parent's household (and sometimes to the nonresident parents' households), but a stepfamily household itself includes various two-person kinship relationships. The main dyads I discuss in this section are child-mother, child-father, child-stepparent, child–half-siblings, and child-stepsiblings. Due to the absence of any quantitative research on the relationships between stepfamily members in France, this section draws mainly on interviews conducted by Cadolle (1998) in the mid-1990s with 60 stepfamily members. However, before reviewing this rich collection of data, I examine how stepparents are described in youth literature published in the 1990s, looking specifically at whether the abusive stepfather or wicked stepmother figures were still prominent.

Studying the content of this literature written for French youth seems to be a feasible method of detecting the degree of the social acceptability of stepfamilies (Cadolle, 1998). These books generally claim that stepfamilies are "true families" that one should prefer to single-parent families, if only because it is better for children to live with two parents than with only one. Most of these books claim that another advantage that stepfamilies have over single-parent families is that they may produce siblings (half-siblings and also stepsiblings), which should be seen as an opportunity to share more love. However, these children's books do not deny that accepting a stepparent can be difficult. For instance, some of them recount the conflicts emerging between a child and his or her stepparent, especially at the start of cohabitation. Despite the hardships recounted, the central message of this genre is one of relaxation and encouragement: One must not overdramatize the situation and should even try to make the best of it. For children, the worst thing to do is to hold on to the dream that their parents will reconcile. In stark contrast with older tales, this literature claims that stepparents improve after one gets to know them; neither the stepfather nor the stepmother is usually seen as greedy or cruel, neither of them is trying to replace the nonresident parent (except if he or she is dead or has never lived with the child), and both of them can be understanding and have positive effects on the child. A stepfather can have educational functions, although of a more discreet nature than a father's. A stepmother can also play an educational and emotional role; this forms a juxtaposition with the traditional view of the wicked stepmother. Therefore, although recently published children's books admit that accepting a stepparent can be difficult for a child, they tend to give a positive, sometimes even humorous view of stepfamilies. This is also true of the majority of articles and TV reports in the popular media, as well as of personal development books published since the 1990s, which usually try to free stepfamilies of their anxieties (Cadolle, 1998).

However, even if this recent view of stepfamilies is likely to have had an impact on people's beliefs, it tells us little about the actual relationships among stepfamily members. When questioned about their stepfamily lives, adults often claim that it has become better and better and is now going fairly well. However, children living in stepfamilies often express bitterness when questioned about their parents' separation or divorce. To understand the nature of the relationships among stepfamily members, it is necessary to go into more detail, starting by analyzing the relationships between children and their parents, followed by the crucial relationship between children and stepparents, and finally the relationships between the different types of siblings in the stepfamily (Cadolle, 1998). As to the relationships between adults in stepfamilies, and their relationships with their former partners or spouses, these are addressed in passing.

CHILDREN AND BIOLOGICAL PARENTS

Children do not generally blame their parents for making the decision to separate or for becoming repartnered or remarried. However, following a separation or divorce they often miss their father, since custody of the children is almost always given to the mother, and generally children do not see their father as often as before the breakup. For instance, in 1985, only 25% of children who resided with their mother saw their father at least every 2 weeks, and more than 50% of children saw their father less than once a month (30% of them never saw their father; Villeneuve-Gokalp, 1993). Laws that established the sharing of parental rights after divorce were passed in 1993 and 2002, but they do not seem to have had much effect on the frequency of contact between children and their (nonresident) father (Théry, 2001). As a result, the idea that "one may divorce one's spouse but not one's children" remains largely an unenforced ideal for men.

This frequent estrangement between children and fathers is sometimes revealed or exacerbated by the fact that the children have a bedroom of their own at the mother's (and stepfather's) home but not at the father's home; therefore, these children are likely to feel less at home in their father's home, especially when the father lives with a new partner or wife and their children. It should be noted, though, that children who live with a stepfather do not see their father less often than children living in single-mother families, except when their mother and stepfather have children. Despite these trends, the key factor influencing the frequency and intensity of the relationships between a child and his or her father after separation or divorce seems to be the quality of the father's relationship with the mother, which depends on whether or not they ended their relationship on good terms. If the divorce was amicable, the nonresident father usually sees his child quite frequently; however, if a bitter breakup fostered hatred between the former spouses, then the father usually sees his child rarely, if ever.

Moreover, tension between the parents is likely to create distressing loyalty conflicts for the child. Given that breakups tend to be more acrimonious in underprivileged families, children from low socioeconomic families tend to see their father less often than children from higher socioeconomic backgrounds (Le Gall & Martin, 1993). In addition, tension often arises in poorer families due to the father's missing child support payments, which in turn causes children to suffer more from their parents' conflicts.

Whether or not children see their father is often an important determinant of the type of relationship they will have with their stepfather (Cadolle, 1998). If a child has strong relationships with both parents, he or she will very probably have a relatively distant relationship with the stepparent, because the former takes precedence over the latter in the child's emotional life. Consequently, children from lower socioeconomic backgrounds, who see their father less often after divorce than children from less poor backgrounds, are more likely to have a close relationship with their stepfather, who then becomes a sort of substitute to the absent biological father (Théry, 2001). Thus it is hard to escape the conclusion that the relationship between a child and another member of the kinship network surrounding a stepfamily—be it the father, his new partner or wife, the stepfather, half-siblings or stepsiblings—is heavily dependent on the mother's relationship with that person (Cadolle, 1998). Only the relationship between a child and his or her full siblings seems as strong as that between a mother and her child. The difficulties following the parental divorce and perhaps the formation of the stepfamily as well seem to strengthen the intensity of the bond between full siblings (Cadolle, 1998). Let us remember, though, that these results, some of which are contrary to those obtained in the United States and the United Kingdom, are mainly based on a single (although high-quality) qualitative study and should therefore be taken with caution.

<small>CHILDREN AND STEPPARENTS</small>

It is not easy to build a satisfying relationship between children and stepparents. In times when the formation of stepfamilies resulted from widowhood, the role of the stepparent in the new family was clear: That person had to replace the deceased parent in authority and loving functions. Thus, until the 1970s, it was expected that stepparents would take on the role of a surrogate parent. However, now that stepfamilies are most often formed as a result of divorce, the nonresident parent is usually still alive, making it less straightforward for the stepparent to replace him or her. In this new configuration, a stepparent's replacement of a biological parent might feel to both the child and the parent like an encroachment on the parent's rights and a violation of the child's interests; family experts and child psychologists also agree that this can be a consequence (Théry & Dhavernas, 1993). Thus, taking this possibility into consideration, it is important to determine what rights and duties might exist between a stepparent and a stepchild.

The role of stepparent has become quite unclear, if not empty, as indicated by the fact that there is no customary, legal, or socially widespread name by which stepchildren call their stepparent (Théry, 2001). Usually, stepchildren and stepparents agree on the fact that the former should not call the latter "Daddy" ("Papa") or "Mommy" ("Maman"), but there is no consensus on what terminology should be used: their first name only, or "Daddy" (or "Mommy") followed by their first name, or "false daddy" (or "mommy"), or still others (Hurstel & Carre, 1993). Stepchildren can also refer to their stepparents as "my stepparent," "my parent's partner," or "my second father/mother." Stepparents often describe their role as being difficult to define; it is "neither that of a parent nor that of a friend" (Théry & Dhavernas, 1993, p. 160). From both perspectives, then, this role is not well defined. However, it seems fair to say that the relationship between a stepparent and a stepchild can best be understood as a relationship that consists of some components of parenthood and some components of friendship; which of these dominates the relationship varies from one stepfamily to the other.

As a parent figure within the family, a stepparent exercises authority over the stepchildren, raises them, and takes care of them. However, most stepparents do not want to replace the child's nonresident parent; they avoid becoming the child's primary provider of material resources and emotional gratifications, they have less of an authority role, and when they do exercise authority it is often with reserve (for instance, by giving advice rather than orders), and they do not interfere in the parent's decisions about the child's future. As a coresident who is not a parent, a stepparent can resemble an older friend the child can rely on more than a parent; in some cases, stepparents develop very convivial relationships with their stepchildren. This is perhaps particularly true between stepmothers and stepdaughters, although some stepmothers who are not much older than their stepdaughters want to avoid becoming their stepdaughters' best friend. In either case, a stepparent is usually not a substitute for the parent—or is far from a perfect one—in terms of the child's education and emotional life (Cadolle, 1998).

"Cautious nonparticipation" is a widespread attitude among stepparents regarding their stepchildren's upbringing (Cadolle, 1998). This proves to be a useful strategy for stepparents because it exempts them from dedicating too much time and energy to their stepchildren. The nonresident parent may also prefer this attitude because the threat to the parental role is reduced. Moreover, if the new couple breaks up, the bond between the stepparent and the stepchild is likely to be severed. It is for this reason that several French sociologists have called relationships between children and stepparents a bond based on "revocable mutual choice" (Théry, 2001) rather than duty or spontaneous affection beginning with the start of cohabitation.

Relationships between a stepparent and a stepchild are also prone to hostility as a consequence of mutual jealousy. In this case, each one accuses or at least suspects the other of trying to monopolize the time, attention, affection, and sometimes money of the stepchild's parent. Thus, a stepparent and a stepchild can be seen as competitors for these scarce resources, which inevitably results in some tensions. For the most part, interviews conducted in the 1990s support this view of stepfamilies. Studies have found that the tensions between the stepparent and the stepchild usually start upon cohabitation; this coresidence proves to be especially difficult if the stepparent moves into the stepchild's house (Le Gall & Martin, 1993). In this case, several conflicts crystallize around the organization of the household and the distribution of space within it. The child may try to take advantage of the fact that he or she lived in the house first (Le Gall, 2005).

According to stepparents, a significant number of stepchildren are simply hard to deal with because they are lying, insolent, untidy, and careless; these faults are often attributed to the nonresident parent of the child (Cadolle, 1998). It is not surprising, then, that the presence of stepchildren increases the risk of separation or divorce (Mignot, 2005). Nevertheless, several family characteristics can improve the relationship between the stepparent and the stepchild (Cadolle, 1998). If the stepchild was relatively young—typically, under 7 years old—at the start of cohabitation with the stepparent, the stepchild tends to see his or her stepparent less as an intruder in the family, thus making their relationship more satisfying. If the new couple has a child—that is, gives the stepchild a half-sibling—the stepchild and the stepparent tend to be closer. Even the stepparent's intention to have a child—that is, the plan to give the stepchild a half-sibling—seems sufficient to bring the stepchild and the stepparent closer. Indeed, stepparents are more prone to look after and to share meaningful moments with a stepchild if they hope that this stepchild will soon become their child's older half-sibling. In a situation where a stepmother has already had children before forming the stepfamily and is unlikely to have more children, she is less likely to create a meaningful relationship with her stepchildren.

According to many stepchildren, their stepparents are unworthy of being the partner or spouse of their parents (Cadolle, 1998). Quite a lot of stepchildren even admit to despising their stepparents; however, they usually do not tell their parents to what extent they detest their stepparents. Nevertheless, many children easily tolerate the presence of stepparents, especially if they do not play a large disciplinary role. Other stepchildren even admire their stepparents, or at least consider them older friends or confidants to whom they can go for support, help, and advice. Stepchildren who have a positive image of their stepparents often like them for having helped their parents to put an end to a period of grief and loneliness, especially when a stepfather makes a mother happy again. It is also more common for girls to like their stepparents; girls say more often that they would like to continue to see their stepparent even if the couple were to divorce. Overall, it seems that the quality of the relationships between children and their stepparents tends to improve over time, an effect of the duration of contact between them, although it may also deteriorate when the child becomes a teenager, an effect of the age of the stepchild.

In current times men are stepparents much more often than women (Toulemon, 2005). In 1998 12.7% of men were raising stepchildren, whereas only 4.5% of women were doing so. This difference between men and women has been increasing over time; whereas women were not raising a higher (average yearly) number of stepchildren in 1998 than in 1975, men were raising 3 times more stepchildren in 1998 than in 1975. Now, in addition to frequent tensions between stepparents and stepchildren, some problems emerge more often when the stepparent is female. As a rule, it seems harder for a woman to be a stepparent. Due to the traditional division of labor, which exists more often in stepfamilies than in traditional two-parent families, there is an inherent contradiction in what is expected of a stepmother, whereas this is not the case among stepfathers (Cadolle, 1998; Théry & Dhavernas, 1993). Indeed, a stepmother's role of raising her stepchildren is likely to be less gratifying than a stepfather's role of pursuing his career.

If the stepmother takes good care of her stepchildren, she may easily be accused of being too caring, thus severing the bond between her stepchildren and their mother. But if the stepchildren are not satisfied with their stepmother, which may be likely if they wish to be treated as they were by their mother or if they resent her for favoring her own children, she may easily be accused of being a careless mother. In other words, a stepmother has a much more uncomfortable position than a stepfather, which may be one of the reasons why stepmothers often refuse to take care of their stepchildren, demanding that their father assume his paternal responsibilities.

It also seems easier to be a stepfather than a stepmother due to the fact that stepchildren view their stepfather more positively than their stepmother (Cadolle, 1998). Stepchildren sometimes depict their stepfather as generous, but they most often depict their stepmother as self-interested and stingy and claim that she insists on their financial independence earlier than they would want. Interestingly, stepmothers often claim that their stepchildren are extravagant. Therefore, the basic financial conflict between a stepmother and her stepchildren, which has been the topic of many fairy tales and which has undoubtedly posed problems for past generations, is still very much alive, as if it were a defining characteristic of many stepmother families.

A very specific problem arises for stepfathers who have a stepdaughter: the temptation of incest. Although romantic or sexual relationships between a stepfather and a stepdaughter do not constitute incest in the usual sense of the term because a stepfather and a stepdaughter have no kin relationship, they do constitute a certain kind of incest in the eyes of many people and in the eyes of the law. Article 161 of the French Civil Code outlaws marriage between a stepchild and a stepparent if the stepparent was married to the stepchild's parent, rather than just cohabiting with him or her; however, since 1938 it has been possible to request special permission to marry, but only if the stepparent was widowed rather than divorced from the stepchild's parent (Théry, 2001). This policy was probably put into place because these kinds of relationships can be viewed as indirect incest. This kind of incest, which was exemplified by the relationship between Woody Allen and Sun Yi, the adopted daughter of his former partner Mia Farrow, is a concern often expressed in the media. Stepfamilies also seem to take this concern seriously because they often take action to avert it: Many stepfathers avoid close physical contact with their stepdaughters when they reach adolescence (Cadolle, 1998).

SIBLING RELATIONSHIPS IN STEPFAMILIES

In comparison to the relationship between the stepparent and the stepchild, the relationship between half-siblings or stepsiblings is a relatively easy one

(Cadolle, 1998). Children most often perceive their half-siblings and stepsiblings as very closely related kin and refer to them as brothers and sisters. In effect, the majority of children view their half-siblings as full siblings, even if they do not see those half-siblings frequently (typically because they are their father's children) or dislike the half-sibling's other parent (typically the mother). Children do not generally consider themselves as close to their stepsiblings as to their half-siblings because they have generally not lived together—at least for a significant amount of time—and have much lower quality relationships with them. A consequence of this distance is the possible creation of strong sexual attraction between stepsiblings, whereas this is rarely the case between half-siblings.

LEAVING HOME IN STEPFAMILY HOUSEHOLDS

All relevant empirical studies have found that in France children raised in stepfamilies leave their parental household earlier than children raised in one-parent or traditional two-parent families. Children raised in stepfamilies leave their parental households 1.5 to 2 years earlier than children raised in traditional two-parent families when their academic and economic situations are comparable (Villeneuve-Gokalp, 2005). This phenomenon is evident among both girls and boys who were raised in any kind of stepfamily—formed after widowhood, divorce, or separation—and has existed since at least the 1990s (Barre, 2003; Desplanques, 1993; Villeneuve-Gokalp, 2005). The most plausible explanation for this phenomenon is that an unsatisfying relationship with the stepparent gives stepchildren an incentive to leave early. Stepchildren residing in their father's home actually leave even earlier than those residing in their mother's home (Villeneuve-Gokalp, 2005). This may be explained by the fact that it is harder to live with a stepmother than with a stepfather. Stepchildren also leave home earlier if they do not have any half-siblings, which may be explained by the fact that the presence of half-siblings makes the stepfamilies more satisfying for stepchildren because it makes them closer to their stepparents and it gives them new brothers and sisters with whom they usually get along well (Desplanques, 1993).

STEPFAMILIES AND THE LAW

This section discusses a specific legal issue related to stepfamilies: the existence and nature of the legal ties between the stepparent and the stepchild. Legislation in European countries concerning the rights and duties of the stepparent in relation to his or her stepchildren tend to be either all or nothing. Either the stepparent and the stepchild share no legal ties, in which case the stepparent has no rights or responsibilities toward the child, or there is a legal filiation link between them, in which case the stepparent has the same rights and responsibilities as a parent (Sosson, 1993). If there is no legal link between the stepparent and the stepchild, then the child's legal status, which was decided after separation or divorce, remains the same: Parental rights, child's residence, and alimony are not modified by the presence of a stepparent. In this case, the stepparent is a third party who has practically no rights and no duties toward the child (although in some countries—but not France—the stepparent gains parental status if both parents are incapable of raising or feeding the child). If, on the contrary, there *is* a legal filiation link between the stepparent and the stepchild (through either adoption or "accommodating" legal recognition of the child, both of which are usually possible only if the child has only one legal, living parent), then the child's legal status is based entirely on this fictional filiation link and no longer on the initial biological link with the unavailable parent. In this case, the stepparent is a legal parent with all the rights and duties parents have.

The French law is an example of this all-or-nothing conception of parenthood that is applied to stepparents: They have no rights or duties toward their stepchildren unless they deliberately create a filiation link with them (Sosson, 1993). In any case, stepparents and stepchildren in France do not have any legal link that is specific to their relationship (Théry, 2001). Some political debate has been going on since the late 1990s and seems quite close to reaching a consensus concerning the creation of a flexible legal status for stepparents; however, because the subject continues to be debated and no law has been passed as of June 2007, this section does not dwell at length on that topic.

The formation of a (married or unmarried) stepfamily has no legal effect in itself; therefore no legal link is created between the stepparent and the stepchild (Bourgault-Coudevylle & Delecourt, 1993; Fulchiron, 1993; Théry, 2001). In other words, after separation or divorce, the two biological parents have the same parental rights and shared authority, and grandparents keep their right to have personal relationships with their stepchildren. Thus these legal relationships remain unchanged after the formation of the stepfamily. Stepparents, whether married or not, have no legal duty to provide for their stepchildren, and if the stepchildren are minors the stepparents are not responsible for any legal problem their stepchildren may cause. Reciprocally, stepchildren have no duty toward their stepparents even if they participated actively in their education, and stepchildren do not automatically inherit their stepparents' wealth. The only way that a stepparent can legally become the adult who is responsible for a stepchild as well as for receiving family allowances and other welfare payments is if the biological parents cannot care for the child; however, even in that case, the stepparent is not responsible because of being the child's stepparent, but rather because of having offered to take in the child. From a strictly financial viewpoint, if a person remarries after divorce, French law also powerfully protects the interests of the children born with the first spouse from their stepparent, half-siblings, and stepsiblings with the tax penalties that stepparents face when leaving their stepchildren a legacy.

Although no automatic legal ties (and related rights and duties) are created between stepparents and stepchildren, they can be created under certain circumstances. French law actually offers stepfamilies two ways of making the relationship between a stepparent and a stepchild legal (Brunet, 1993). The first way of legalizing a step relationship is for a stepfather—but not a stepmother—to establish a (true or false) paternal filiation through blood (Brunet, 1993). There are several different procedures for this purpose, which depend on the marital status of the stepfamily, the marital status of the child's parents at birth, and whether or not the father acknowledged the child at birth. If the stepfamily couple is not married, the stepchild's parents were not married when he or she was born, and the stepchild has no paternal filiation, the stepfather may acknowledge or become the father by *possession d'état* (whether or not he really is the biological father). In all other cases—if the stepfamily couple is married, or is not married but the stepchild's parents were married at the time of birth, or if the stepfamily couple is not married and the stepchild's parents were not married at the time of birth but the stepchild has a paternal filiation—the stepfather needs to contest his stepchild's paternity in order to replace it with his own paternal filiation.

The second way of legalizing a step relationship is for a stepmother or a stepfather to establish a parental filiation through adoption (Brunet, 1993). There are two types of adoption in France. "Plenary adoption" of children severs all the ties they had with their family of origin; "simple adoption" (which is similar to America's "open adoption") maintains most of these ties. In simple adoption, the adoptive parents have a duty to provide for their stepchildren (this then becomes a reciprocal duty later in life). However, nonresident parents maintain their parental rights and have a duty to provide for their children if the stepparents cannot fulfill that duty; they may also have visitation rights to maintain the relationship with their children. In plenary adoption, the adoptive parents share with the biological parents all the parental rights and duties: They both have parental rights, manage the children's wealth, and take care of them.

There are two different procedures to adopt children, depending on the marital status of stepfamilies. First, if the stepfamily couple is married, the stepparent can choose to adopt the stepchild using either procedure—plenary or simple. Stepfamilies often prefer simple adoption because it creates an adoptive parenthood without erasing the previous one. However, if a stepparent prefers plenary adoption, the stepchild can be adopted as long as the child is under 15 years old; since 1993 a stepparent has been able to adopt a stepchild through plenary adoption only if the child has no filiation with the biological parent's former partner. Second, if the stepfamily couple is not married, the stepparent cannot adopt the stepchild through plenary adoption but can do so through simple adoption. A serious drawback, however, is that the simple adoption of a child by a stepparent does not enable the child's resident parent to keep parental rights.

Considering these new legal filiation links, the question then becomes: What happens if the stepfamily couple decides to separate or divorce? Whereas paternal filiation through blood is very vulnerable, parental filiation through adoption is almost completely invulnerable (Brunet, 1993). The stepfather himself may contest his own paternal filiation through blood, and if the paternal filiation was false, it can be contested by the mother (after her separation from him), by the biological father, by the child, or by any member of the child's family. By contrast, neither the stepparent nor anyone else may contest the stepfather's parental filiation through adoption, unless it is a simple adoption that the stepparent has "serious motives" to end.

THE EVOLUTIONARY PSYCHOLOGY OF STEPFAMILIES WORLDWIDE

This chapter has examined—in both historical and present-day contexts—the relationships among stepfamily members in France and has found that in general these relationships are less meaningful and gratifying than those of traditional two-parent families. This is largely due to the coresidence of a stepparent and a stepchild with potentially conflicting interests, since the majority of stepchildren admit that they prefer biological parents to stepparents and the majority of stepparents admit that they prefer biological children to stepchildren (Cadolle, 1998). I have also explored why French—and, for that matter, European—law protects the relationship between the parent and child over that of the stepparent and stepchild: This protection promotes the child's interest because a biological parent is assumed to be more committed than a stepparent concerning child care. Therefore, it appears that, according not only to rumor and assumption but also to the long-held view of stepfamilies, stepfamily members themselves, and lawmakers, a biological parent is likely to make a better parent than a stepparent. This widespread idea, which is largely held not only in France but also in every other society on which reliable data exist (Daly & Wilson, 1996), should not be taken for granted, but rather should be explained. This is precisely what evolutionary psychology, the theoretical synthesis between the modern theory of evolution and contemporary psychology, permits us to do.

The central assumption of evolutionary psychology is that the human psyche, like every element of every reproducing organism, has evolved by selection. Thus, present humans are endowed with a psyche whose characteristics, after appearing through random genetic variation in very remote generations of hominids, were selected across generations through processes of differential survival (natural selection) and differential reproduction (sexual selection). In other words, present-day humans have their specific mind-sets because these originally enabled the first individuals with these mind-sets to have more children than those who did not have them. Therefore, this mind-set was transmitted via genetics more often than others, and consequently it was only those individuals possessing this mind-set who finally attained genetic posterity.

Evolutionary psychology, formerly called sociobiology, has a heretical reputation among social scientists, probably due mostly to nonscientific reasons, such as the fear that social scientists will be replaced by biologists in the study of human behavior or the fear that biologists' explanations of human behavior will justify the domination of one sex over the other or of one race over others. In fact, the objections that have been raised against the intellectual foundations of evolutionary psychology (in comparison to the objections raised against certain auxiliary assumptions or models used by certain evolutionary psychologists) do not withstand scrutiny. This section summarizes the teachings of evolutionary psychology on stepfamilies, without trying to justify the use of evolutionary psychology itself. It does so despite the absence of any French research in that field, or of any research focused specifically on French data.

The main insight that evolutionary psychology brings to the subject of stepfamilies is simple: Evolution has selected in humans a tendency to "discriminative parental solicitude" (Daly & Wilson, 1996, p. 17), that is, to invest more material and emotional resources in one's own children than in someone else's children. Indeed, individuals investing more resources in other people's children than in producing and rearing their biological children would have lower fertility and/or higher child mortality, which implies that they would have fewer biological children surviving to fecund ages. Consequently, they would transmit fewer of their genes to subsequent generations, and they would transmit fewer of the genes predisposing them to caring more for another's offspring, thus making it impossible for the genes predisposing to care more for another's offspring to spread across generations. By contrast, individuals investing more resources in their own children than in other people's children passed on more of their genes to subsequent generations, so that it is *their* parental psychology, including a preference for own children rather than for stepchildren or any other children, that proliferated across generations.

This theory is supported by the fact that individuals are more likely to protect their biological children than their stepchildren from violence. Internationally, parents are more likely to neglect, exploit, and assault their stepchildren than their genetic children (Daly & Wilson, 1996, 2001). Most strikingly, stepparents are considerably more likely than biological parents to abuse and/or kill their stepchildren; it has been found that living with a married or unmarried stepparent is the single most powerful predictor of severe child abuse. The fundamental reason for this propensity for abuse probably stems from the evolutionary development of mankind in which a stepchild's welfare was not as valuable to the adult's genetic posterity as a biological child's. Therefore, the psychological mechanisms of parental feeling (including a willingness to sacrifice for the child's welfare) were selected only in relationships with biological children, not in relationships with stepchildren. These mechanisms of parental feeling thus tend to be lessened when one assumes a parental role with a stepchild rather than a biological child.

Some additional remarks may be useful to dispel several misunderstandings that were generated by this evolutionary psychology explanation of the relatively high incidence of child abuse among stepfamilies. Although it seems difficult to deny that adults have a much higher propensity to mistreat their stepchildren than their biological children, it is also undeniable that only a tiny fraction of stepparents mistreat their stepchildren. It should be noted, though, that this fact is far from incompatible with—and may even be derived from—the evolutionary psychology approach to stepfamilies. The reason evolution seems *not* to have selected a very sharp hostility against stepchildren (but only less powerful violence inhibitors for them) may be because if stepparents harm their stepchildren, they may lose the opportunity to breed with the child's parent and thus create their own genetic legacy, which would have prevented (genes predisposing to) antagonism against stepchildren from spreading across human generations. Some researchers have also questioned the existence of discriminative parental solicitude because certain parents who are genetically unrelated to their children—adoptive parents and males who do not know that the children they raise are actually not their biological children—have not been shown to mistreat their children more frequently than biological parents. However, adults can adopt children only after having been screened by government agencies and after going through a process that is costly in time and energy (and often money), so that it is no wonder that adoptive parents, being highly selected, do not abuse their children more often than biological parents. It may not be so surprising either—although it has never been established empirically—that males who raise their wife and another man's children without knowing that they are not their biological father do not abuse those children more often than biological fathers, because only the knowledge or at least the unconscious suspicion that these children are not their own would deactivate the various psychological mechanisms of parental feeling.

It should also be noted that certain explanations of the relatively high incidence of child abuse among stepfamilies, which are sometimes viewed as competing with the explanation offered by evolutionary psychology, should actually be seen as derived from it. For instance, the explanation according to which it is the stepmother's relatively low level of contact with the child during his or her early years that prevents her from building up a protective attitude or from internalizing the incest taboo—which in turns explains stepmothers' higher propensity for abuse—is best seen as one version of the evolutionary psychology explanation. In fact, in the evolutionary history of mankind, females who tended to have stronger parental feelings toward children with whom they lived from infancy on, compared to females who had no such tendency, were able to invest more of their emotional and material resources in biological (rather than genetically unrelated) children because living with the child when he or she was very young increased the chances of being the child's biological mother. This enabled those females to transmit more of their genes to subsequent generations and, notably, more of the genes predisposing them to prefer children with whom they first had contact at early ages. This is presumably why, today, females tend to have more parental feeling (and a lower propensity for ill treatment) with children they saw as babies than with children they met at relatively advanced ages.

Therefore, it seems reasonable to consider the evolutionary psychology explanation of the relatively high incidence of child abuse among stepfamilies, at least until contrary evidence is found. More exactly, evolutionary psychology helps explain the *widespread* character of the relatively high incidence of child abuse among stepfamilies, although it may be of no use in explaining the cross-cultural variations in this relatively high incidence. According to Daly and Wilson (1998; Daly, Wilson, & Wiseman, 1997), there are two significant consequences of discriminative parental solicitude. First, in a stepfamily, the presence of a stepchild is a risk factor for conflict between the parent and the stepparent and for possibly lethal violence against the wife. The presence of the stepchild creates conflicts about the allocation of the family's resources: The child's genetic parent wants to give him or her more than what his or her (genetically unrelated) stepparent would want. Second, given that discriminative parental solicitude makes it relatively difficult to live in a stepfamily, widows and widowers may prefer to remarry a relative of their former spouse rather than a genetically distant individual (Daly & Wilson, 1996). This would allow their children to be brought up by someone who also has some genetic interest in their upbringing and therefore will have less disagreement with them about the allocation of family resources to their genetic children. This may be an (admittedly partial) explanation for the practice of levirate (a widow marrying her dead spouse's brother) and sororate (a widower marrying his dead spouse's sister) in certain human societies.

FUTURE DIRECTIONS FOR RESEARCH: OUTCOMES OF CHILDREN OF STEPFAMILIES

This overview of the research on stepfamilies in France since the 1990s has used history, demography, ethnography and sociology, law, and evolutionary psychology to shed light on diverse phenomena affecting stepfamilies and their possible explanations. Further studies in each of these disciplines are still necessary to confirm, modify, or even disprove present knowledge. This process requires that more and better statistical data become available on stepfamilies in both France and other countries. In addition to this improvement, other disciplines simply need to *start* studying stepfamilies in France.

One of the main questions that still needs to be addressed is if there are any consequences from the formation of stepfamilies on children's psychological adjustment and school performance. After a child has lost a parent, does the formation of a stepfamily help or harm the child? It both increases the child's living standard (relative to a one-parent family) and creates tensions with a stepparent, but the overall effect on the child's well-being remains unknown. Studies dating back to the late nineteenth century claim that children from stepfamilies were disproportionately delinquents, drug addicts, and suicide victims, but these studies were far from rigorous enough to enable us to ascertain these facts, let alone to draw any causal connection between stepfamily formation and child behavior (Lefaucheur, 1993). Researchers should also more specifically examine whether or not the therapeutic practices aimed at preventing or treating maladjusted children are effective. Again, this is a subject on which French research is significantly lacking.

REFERENCES

Barre, C. (2003). 1,6 million d'enfants vivent dans une famille recomposée. *INSEE Première, 901*, 1–4.

Barre, C. (2005). 1,6 million d'enfants vivent dans une famille recomposée. In C. Lefèvre & A. Filhon (Eds.), *Histoires de famille, histoires familiales* (pp. 273–281). Paris: Ined.

Boudon, R. (2003). *Raison, bonnes raisons: La rationalité—Notion indispensable et insaisissable?* Paris: PUF.

Bourgault-Coudevylle, D., & Delecourt, F. (1993). Les familles recomposées: Aspects personnels, aspects alimentaires. In M.-T. Meulders-Klein & I. Théry (Eds.), *Les recompositions familiales aujourd'hui* (pp. 257–279). Paris: Nathan.

Brunet, L. (1993). Heurs et malheurs de la famille recomposée en droit français. In M.-T. Meulders-Klein & I. Théry (Eds.), *Les recompositions familiales aujourd'hui* (pp. 229–255). Paris: Nathan.

Cadolle, S. (1998). *La relation beau-parent bel-enfant dans les familles recomposées: Des représentations communes aux trajectoires identitaires.* Paris: Institut d'Etudes Politiques de Paris.

Daly, M., & Wilson, M. (1996). Evolutionary psychology and marital conflict: The relevance of stepchildren. In D. M. Buss & N. Malamuth (Eds.), *Sex, power, conflict: Feminist and evolutionary perspectives* (pp. 9–28). New York: Oxford University Press.

Daly, M., & Wilson, M. (1998). Lethal and nonlethal violence against wives and the evolutionary psychology of male sexual proprietariness. In R. E. Dobash & R. P. Dobash (Eds.), *Rethinking violence against women* (pp. 199–230). Thousand Oaks, CA: Sage.

Daly, M., & Wilson, M. (2001). An assessment of some proposed exceptions to the phenomenon of nepotistic discrimination against stepchildren. *Annales Zoologici Fennici, 38,* 287–296.

Daly, M., Wilson, M., & Wiseman, K. A. (1997). Women with children sired by previous partners incur excess risk of uxoricide. *Homicide Studies, 1*(1), 61–71.

Desplanques, G. (1993). Les familles recomposées en 1990. In M.-T. Meulders-Klein & I. Théry (Eds.), *Les recompositions familiales aujourd'hui* (pp. 81–96). Paris: Nathan.

Desplanques, G. (1994). Les familles "recomposées" en 1990. *Population et Sociétés, 286,* 1–4.

Fulchiron, H. (1993). La transmission des biens dans les familles recomposées: Entre trop de droit et pas de droits. In M.-T. Meulders-Klein & I. Théry (Eds.), *Les recompositions familiales aujourd'hui* (pp. 281–298). Paris: Nathan.

Hurstel, F., & Carre, C. (1993). Processus psychologiques et parentés plurielles. In M.-T. Meulders-Klein & I. Théry (Eds.), *Les recompositions familiales aujourd'hui* (pp. 191–214). Paris: Nathan.

Institut National de la Statistique et des Études Économiques. (1990). Enquête Famille.

Institut National de la Statistique et des Études Économiques. (1999). Enquête Étude de l'Histoire Familiale.

Lefaucheur, N. (1993). Sur la scène de l'anormalité familiale. In M.-T. Meulders-Klein & I. Théry (Eds.), *Les recompositions familiales aujourd'hui* (pp. 123–136). Paris: Nathan.

LeGall, D. (2005). La conception de l'habiter à l'épreuve de la cohabitation familiale. *Espaces et Sociétés, 120–121*(1/2), 45–60.

LeGall, D., & Martin, C. (1993). Transitions familiales, logiques de recomposition et modes de régulation conjugale. In M.-T. Meulders-Klein & I. Théry (Eds.), *Les recompositions familiales aujourd'hui* (pp. 137–158). Paris: Nathan.

Leridon, H. (1993). Recomposer les familles dans les sources statistiques. In M.-T. Meulders-Klein & I. Théry (Eds.), *Les recompositions familiales aujourd'hui* (pp. 51–66). Paris: Nathan.

Meulders-Klein, M.-T., & Théry, I. (Eds.). (1993). *Les recompositions familiales aujourd' hui.* Paris: Nathan.

Meulders-Klein, M.-T., & Théry, I. (Eds.) (1995). *Quels repères pour les familles recomposées? Une approche pluridisciplinaire internationale.* Paris: LGDJ, Droit et Société.

Mignot, J.-F. (2005). La rupture d'union dans la France contemporaine: Vers une explication unifiée. Available from http://halshs.archives-ouvertes.fr/halshs-00009489/en/.

Sosson, J. (1993). Le statut juridique des familles recomposées en Europe: Quelques aspects de droit comparé. In M.-T. Meulders-Klein & I. Théry (Eds.), *Les recompositions familiales aujourd'hui* (pp. 299–312). Paris: Nathan.

Théry, I. (Ed.). (2001). *Recomposer une famille, des rôles et des sentiments*. Paris: Textuel.

Théry, I., & Dhavernas, M.-J. (1993). La parenté aux frontières de l'amitié: Statut et rôle du beau-parent dans les familles recomposées. In M.-T. Meulders-Klein & I. Théry, (Eds.), *Les recompositions familiales aujourd'hui* (pp. 159–187). Paris: Nathan.

Thomson, E. (2004). Step-families and childbearing desires in Europe. *Demographic Research, Special Collection, 3*, article 5.

Toulemon, L. (2004). Qu'est-ce qu'une famille nombreuse? Définitions à partir d'indicateurs démographiques variés. *Informations Sociales, 115*, 18–33.

Toulemon, L. (2005). Enfants et beaux-enfants des hommes et des femmes. In C. Lefèvre & A. Filhon (Eds.), *Histoires de famille, histoires familiales* (pp. 59–77). Paris: Ined.

Villeneuve-Gokalp, C. (1993). De la famille d'origine à la famille recomposée. In M.-T. Meulders-Klein & I. Théry (Eds.), *Les recompositions familiales aujourd'hui* (pp. 67–79). Paris: Nathan.

Villeneuve-Gokalp, C. (2005). Conséquences des ruptures familiales sur le départ des enfants. In C. Lefèvre & A. Filhon (Eds.), *Histoires de famille, histoires familiales* (pp. 235–249). Paris: Ined.

CHAPTER 4

The Social Context of Emerging Stepfamilies in Japan: Stress and Support for Parents and Stepparents

SHINJI NOZAWA

UNTIL VERY recently stepfamilies in Japan have caught little attention socially and academically, an omission which is reflected in the fact that there has not been a Japanese counterpart to the English word "stepfamily." Members of Japanese stepfamilies have been a socially invisible minority with neither name nor social identity. According to Andrew Cherlin (1978), they were an "incomplete institution" in the sense that there was an absence of institutionally based social support (Engel, 2004; Nozawa, 2006).

However, the rising numbers of divorces and remarriages coupled with the rise in Internet use, particularly in the past decade, have resulted in stepfamilies holding a more socially visible position. A new Japanese word, *suteppufamiri,* adopted from the English word "stepfamily," has been

This chapter is based on the findings from our joint research project on Japanese stepfamilies, which was supported by grants from the Ministry of Health, Labor, and Welfare (2002–2003) and from the Japan Securities Scholarship Foundation (2004–2005). I thank Akiko Nagai, Mari Kikuchi, Shigeki Matsuda, and Naoko Ibaraki for their collaboration in the project. Although a preliminary collaborative analysis, which includes similar findings, appeared in Nozawa, Nagai, Kikuchi, & Matsuda (2006) in Japanese, I am solely responsible for the reanalysis in this chapter. An earlier version of this chapter was presented at the panel "New Family Ways: Partnership and Parenting among Divorcees, Single Mothers, and Stepfamilies in Japan" at the Association for Asian Studies' annual meeting in Boston on March 22, 2007. I thank Masako Ishii-Kuntz, the discussant of the panel, for her useful comment. My thanks also go to Kay Pasley and Jan Pryor for their helpful comments and editorial help on earlier versions of the manuscript.

spread mainly through mass media appearances of members of the Step-family Association of Japan (SAJ), a support group established in 2001 to provide a variety of self-help activities for stepfamilies both online and off-line (Nozawa, Ibaraki, Hayano, & Stepfamily Association of Japan, 2006). As stepfamily households are becoming socially more visible, stepfamilies are gradually gaining a social identity. This may be one of the indications that "the postwar family system in Japan" has reached a turning point (Ochiai, 1997).

The modernization or Westernization of Japanese society from the late nineteenth century until the end of World War II was a long-term social process of institutionalization and stabilization of Japanese marriages. The number and rate of divorces decreased drastically after 1898, when the first modern civil law in Japan began, and continued to decrease gradually thereafter until World War II (see Figure 4.1), and remarriages followed a similarly decreasing trend (Iwai, 2000).

In this period, under the prewar civil law, Japanese families were ideal-ized and institutionalized as a stem-family system, or a kind of extended family household (*ie*), in which the norm was that more than two genera-tions lived together in a patrilineal tradition. It was also a long-term social process whereby divorces and remarriages were increasingly characterized as deviant behaviors.

After World War II, the new democratic constitution was established and the new individualistic civil law was enacted under the strong influence of the United States. The trend of stabilization of marriage, however,

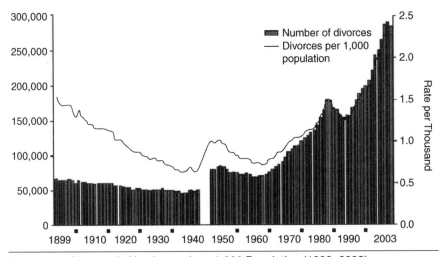

Figure 4.1 Divorces in Number and per 1,000 Population (1899–2003).

Source: Jinko no doko nihon to sekai: Jinkotokei shiryoshu 2005 [Demographic Trends in Japan and World 2005], by the National Institute of Population and Social Security Research 2005, Tokyo: Health and Welfare Statistics.

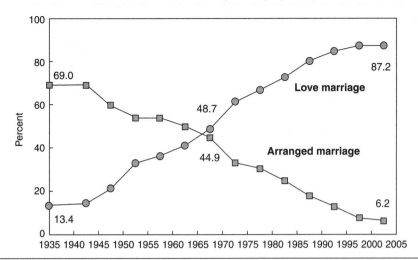

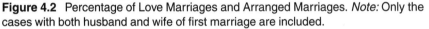

Figure 4.2 Percentage of Love Marriages and Arranged Marriages. *Note:* Only the cases with both husband and wife of first marriage are included.

Source: Wagakuni fufu no kekkon katei to shusshoryoku: Dai 13 kai shussho doko kihon chosa [Marriage process and fertility of Japanese married couples: Report on the thirteenth Japanese national fertility survey in 2005, volume I], by the National Institute of Population and Social Security Research, 2007, Tokyo: National Institute of Population and Social Security Research.

continued until the 1960s (Japan's high economic growth period), when "love marriages" outnumbered the older style arranged marriages (see Figure 4.2). With the emergence of Japan's new middle class in this period, a new family model, based on love marriages between *salary man* husbands and housewives, became widely accepted by the general population as a new standard (Blood, 1967; Ochiai, 1997; Vogel, 1963). The mainly (sub)urban nuclear families following this model embraced rigid gender-role segregation and a strong emphasis on the importance of wives' mothering role (Imamura, 1987; Vogel, 1963). This postwar family system seems to have been effective in providing younger generations with another set of social norms about family life, to the extent that the divorce and remarriage rates remained relatively low until the 1970s (Iwai, 2000; Ochiai, 1997).

However, there have been changes in this regard since then. The number and rate of divorces in Japan have greatly increased, particularly in the 1990s (see Figure 4.1). The cumulative probability of marital dissolution within 20 years of marriage in Japan is estimated to be 30%, which means that the risk of divorce for new marriages in Japan now matches the highest level in Europe (similar to that of Germany, slightly higher than that of Sweden, and substantially higher than that of France), even though it is still considerably lower than the risk in the United States (Raymo, Iwasawa, & Bumpass, 2004). The increase in divorces parallels the change in social norms. Japanese people became considerably more tolerant about divorce in general as well as divorce involving minor children during the 1980s (Iwai, 2000). In fact, roughly 60% of all the annual divorces in recent years occur among couples with minor children.

The remarriage rate has also gone up steadily (see Figure 4.3). In 2005, 25% of new marriages were remarriages for at least one of the spouses. Although there are no precise statistics on Japanese stepfamilies, these data suggest that the number of stepfamily households has also been increasing substantially. Although the standard nuclear family model is far from losing its dominant position, all these changes in people's attitudes and behaviors regarding divorce and remarriage as well as stepparenting indicate that the Japanese postwar family system as social norm is in transition (Ochiai, 1997).

It should be noted that the prewar extended family tradition was not totally abandoned during the era of the postwar family system, but was modified as a more flexibly practiced pattern of intergenerational coresidence and interdependence in cases of family emergencies and transitions. In sum, the still prevalent postwar standard family model and the coexisting older extended family tradition provide the sociocultural context within which Japanese stepfamily members form their family relations.

In this chapter, I present findings from the first exploratory study of stepfamilies in Japan, which incorporates a survey and in-depth interviews (Nozawa, Nagai, Kikuchi, & Matsuda, 2006). For the findings described, I analyzed data from our interviews of 60 stepparents and biological parents

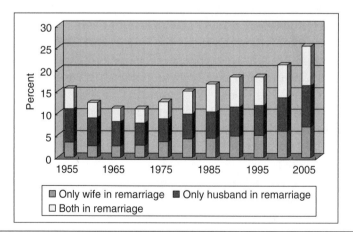

Figure 4.3 Percentage of Remarriages in Total Number of New Marriages (1955–2005).
Source: Heisei 17 nen jinko doktai tokei [The vital statistics of Japan 2005, volume I], by the Statistics and Information Department, Minister's Secretariat, Ministry of Health, Labour, and Welfare, 2005, Tokyo: Health and Welfare Statistics Association.

in stepfamilies to explore the social mechanisms and processes involved in stepfamily formation in Japan. Special attention was paid to the difficulties associated with stepmothering. Following Jacobson (1990), the intention was to focus on stressful and supportive outcomes from various network structures in the cultural context of changing Japanese families.

THE JAPANESE STUDY

Semi-structured interviews were conducted with 60 relatively young step-parents and biological parents between October 2001 and November 2005. The average age was 37.8 for 43 female participants (in two cases, age was unknown) and 39.9 for 11 male participants, with ranges of 24 to 51 and 34 to 49, respectively. The interviews lasted 2 hours on average. We recruited interview participants from the respondents to our survey, from the SAJ's self-help activities, and through snowball sampling via previous interview participants. Of the interviewees, 44 (73.3%) had also responded to our survey (26.5% of the 166 survey respondents). The interview questions include (a) family profiles and background information (life histories), (b) experiences in (step)parenting, (c) relationships with partners, (d) supportive networks, (e) use of the Internet for getting information and emotional support, and (f) participation in self-help groups such as the SAJ.

Of the 60 interviewees, 22 individuals were married couples and were interviewed separately (all 11 male interviewees were members of the couple participants). The mean length of their present marriage for the 45 female married participants was 4 years and 8 months, ranging from 6 months to 16 years (we included those in the 11 married couples and another 34 married individuals, and we excluded four legally unmarried ones in these figures). The interviewees lived in various types of stepfamily households, but they overrepresented resident (first-married) stepmother households with only the father's children in residence (Type E in Table 4.1), and they underrepresent other types of stepfamily households (see Table 4.1).

In the following sections, the findings from this study are described. In particular, sources of stress for stepfamilies, such as pressures for early (re)-marriage, gendered role expectations, and complex networks of old and new family ties, are at the center of the discussion. Participation in self-help activities of online and offline support groups for stepfamilies are depicted as an important source of social support for step- and biological parents.

Romantic Love against All Odds: The Push toward Marriage

In contrast to the general trend of prolonged courtship before first marriage in Japan, many stepfamily members reported a relatively short courtship, usually less than 1 year and in some cases just a few months. Typically

Table 4.1

Stepfamily Household Types Based on Where Children Live

Household Types by Children from Prior Union	Interviewed Wives (Cases with Mutual Child in Each Type)		Interviewed Husbands (Cases with Mutual Child in Each Type)		Existence of Resident (Nonresident) Stepparent
	Number	Percentage	Number	Percentage	
A: Both have child(ren) from prior unions, and all of the children live in their household.	11 (4)	22.4 (36.4)	3 (0)	27.3 (0.0)	Stepmother and Stepfather
B: Both have child(ren) from prior unions, but husband's children live elsewhere.	6 (1)	12.2 (16.7)	2 (1)	18.2 (50.0)	Stepfather (Stepmother)
C: Both have child(ren) from prior unions, but wife's children live elsewhere.	1 (0)	2.0 (0.0)	0 (0)	0.0 (0.0)	Stepmother (Stepfather)
D: Only wife has child(ren) from prior union.	8 (5)	16.3 (62.5)	2 (2)	18.2 (100.0)	Stepfather
E: Only husband has child(ren) from prior union.	23 (12)	46.9 (52.1)	4 (2)	36.4 (50.0)	Stepmother [first married except 2]
Total	49 (22)	100.0 (44.9)	11 (5)	100.0 (45.5)	

couples came to know each other in various social contexts, such as workplaces, a favorite bar or pub, introductions by common friends, and church affiliations (a kind of arranged matching or *omiai*), as well as social networking web sites for divorcees (*batsu-ichi*) and/or single parents. Yet, wherever they reported having met and falling in love, most of them started to consider marriage almost immediately. For example, a first-married stepmother who had lived with her husband and his 20-year-old son for 6 years remembered her initial "intuitive" feeling before marriage:

> *This was going be a deep relationship, what should I say, a spiritually deep relationship or something totally reliable which would lead to marriage, I thought.*

The existence of child(ren) on either or both sides of the couple was a common factor prompting their decision to marry quickly rather than to delay. Unlike people without children, single parents faced the problem of managing time for dating away from their children. Dating also involved some feelings of guilt by both adults, especially when the children were young. One way of solving this dilemma was to plan dates with the children included. Once the children were involved in this way, the quality of the relationship turned toward having a serious sense of responsibility for the children. For example, another first-married stepmother, who had lived with her husband and his 12-year-old daughter for nearly 6 years, recalled her feelings about dating her present husband and his (then preschool-age) daughter at an amusement park and similar places before marriage:

> *I believed that she [my stepdaughter] would expect me to be her mother. As we went on dating over and over again in that way, it occurred to me that I should not behave too irresponsibly. If she should expect me to become her mother, and if I should disappoint her, it would surely make her feel sad. So, I felt I should make a quick decision if I go for it [marriage] or not.*

Similarly, a stepfather in his second marriage with no biological child from his previous relationship explained that the age of his present wife's child, who was about to enter elementary school, was the main factor encouraging him to get married at that time:

> *I just wanted to let him [my stepson] start his school life here rather than make him change schools later [because of our marriage], which pushed me [toward marriage]. If he had already reached school age, I wouldn't have rushed into marriage.*

Some parents and stepparents also believed that the younger the children were, the easier it would be to build their step relationships. Thus, in general, the children's involvement likely prompted their decision to marry sooner rather than to delay.

A related factor affecting couples' decision to marry was the negative re-action toward their ongoing relationship from significant people in their lives, such as parents and close friends. In particular, parents whose adult child was marrying into a resident stepparent situation tended to object to the marriage, hoping to avoid their child's (especially daughter's) antici-pated struggles as a stepparent. The other parents were more willing to ac-cept their child's future partner as a "new mother" or "new father" of their grandchild(ren). Unlike courtship in first marriage, remarrying couples found themselves in a defensive position in relation to negative reactions from the very beginning of their relationship. It is probable that many cou-ples in this situation dissolved the courtship prior to marrying. We suspect that our interviewees were the survivors of such conflict, marrying against all odds and giving up trying to persuade their parents. Many seemed to have rushed into marriage, intending to disprove the negative predictions of those around them.

Interestingly, these factors did not lead the couples to serious considera-tion or examination of the prospective difficulties in their future stepfamily, except in a few cases. Most of our interviewees said that they or their part-ner (usually the biological parent) were so optimistic that they believed there would be no problems. For instance, the stepmother previously quoted said that she had been "confident, but recklessly confident, so to speak, or overly confident, in retrospect, without knowing any specific pro-cess" about becoming the stepmother of an elementary school boy when she got married 6 years before. Many stepmothers' optimistic anticipations were based on a variety of reasoning, such as being a lover of children, hav-ing a career as a teacher and thus being more skilled with handling chil-dren, finding future stepchildren "docile," and having a good experience parenting their own biological children.

On the other hand, many of the biological parents expected, at least implicitly, that their emotionally and economically stressful single-parent life would be back to normal once both a father and a mother were in the home, doing their own job as "an ordinary family" (see Arnaut, Fromme, Stall, & Felker, 2000, for similar "myths and expecta-tions about normative families" among biological parents in American stepfamilies). Some of the stepparents and biological parents reported that they realized after marriage that they had not paid enough attention to the feelings of their (step)children, partly because they were busy dealing with other, opposing parties. Whatever the reasons, and despite the intensity of their romantic love, it was typical among the stepfamily couples in our study that they did not spend much time before marriage developing their relationships, much less developing their step relationships.

Among the many kinds of unexpected difficulties that parents and stepparents face in their new family life after remarriage, most central are developing stepparent-stepchild relationships and performing stepparent roles (see Felker, Fromme, Arnaut, & Stoll, 2002; Ganong & Coleman, 2004; Pasley & Ihinger-Tallman, 1982; Visher & Visher, 1991, for American stepfamilies). Being a stepmother is noted as particularly stressful in Western literature (Christian, 2005; Fine & Schwebel, 1992; Levin, 1997; Nielsen, 1999; Whitsett & Land, 1992). An analysis of our survey data from 88 female respondents who were stepmothers and/or biological mothers in Japanese stepfamilies also suggests that being a stepmother is more stressful than being a biological mother in a stepfamily (Nozawa, in press; see also Nozawa, Nagai, et al., 2006). Although they had good intentions in regard to mothering before marriage, stepmothers in our study began to notice soon after they started living with their stepchildren that being a "new mother" was not an easy task.

A typical stepmother in our study faced two conflicting feelings: not being accepted as a mother by her stepchildren and even by herself and, at the same time, being expected to be the stepchildren's good mother by her husband and other close kin, such as his parents, and again by herself. While everybody in her social circle, including herself, believed that a stepmother can be a good mother almost instantly as long as she sincerely tries, in reality the stepmother-stepchild relationships lacked intimacy and shared experiences. In such a situation, trying even harder to be a mother led to friction with stepchildren—usually one particular stepchild among others (similar reports are noted by Felker et al., 2002, on American stepparents). She is most likely to find herself being trapped in a growing psychological gap between her idealized affectionate mother role identity and her actual negative interactions with her stepchild. She is apt to blame either herself or her stepchild, or both in many cases, for the gap. Some stepmothers in our study expressed their frustrations by saying that they sometimes felt like a "housekeeper" or "live-in maid" rather than a mother.

In the case of stepmothers who live with both their stepchildren and biological children, these kinds of frustrations tended to be intermingled with the feelings of guilt about the gap between their attachment to their biological children and their attachment, or lack thereof, to stepchildren. A mother living for 1.5 years with her own preschool children and her husband's preschool child as well as their newborn baby expressed her initial feeling about stepmothering:

> *First of all, I wanted to regard my husband's child as a real child of mine. . . . Anyway, I wanted to have the same consciousness [of my stepson as I had of my biological*

children], or I wanted to let him [my stepson] emotionally depend [amae] on me just like my children do, and wanted to scold him just like my children. I just wanted to feel the same way.

Perhaps he [my husband] wants me and his child to get along well with each other anyway. He wants me to be able to see his child as my child.

Both she and her husband shared the role expectation that she should and could be a "real" mother, yet he could hardly share her feelings, as he explained:

In sum, our problem is all about her [my wife's] feelings. She wouldn't change her feeling that she doesn't like my son and that's all. . . . She says to me, "I can't viscerally accept [your son], and maybe our marriage can't go on with such a feeling, because it causes pain for you and your child." She says, "I can't change it [my feeling] and I wish I could have resolved it." . . . I can't understand why she feels so much pain. I wish I could.

At least in the early stage of stepfamily life, many stepmothers and their husbands experienced this kind of miscommunication. Biological fathers, who assume that stepmothering is not too difficult or different from mothering and are away from home during the day, when most of the step interactions occur, fail to understand or even notice their wife's struggle in becoming a mother. Another first-married stepmother of an elementary school boy and biological mother of a preschool mutual daughter in the present marriage described the gap she faced early in her marriage:

The biggest gap I found between us was about what he [my husband] said just a week after we got married. He said, "I feel as if I had been living with you for years now. I see you are here and I come home to you every day, and you cook our meals and take care of my child, so I feel as if we had been doing this for years." But I couldn't feel that way at all. Rather, I was feeling "How come I got mixed up in this confusion every day?" So when I heard him saying so, I thought to myself, "Oh my! If things keep going in this way, I will end up with more and more pain." I could never feel the way he did, which made me realize keenly how overly optimistic we, both of us, had been.

Some couples in our study attempted to breach the gap in understanding by talking with each other about stepparenting. Many stepmothers, however, reported difficulties in confiding to their husband their psychological conflict and agony over not being a good mother. Because the husbands had strong expectations and assumptions about the wives' ability to be a good mother, some wives kept trying hard to fulfill these expectations until the last moment, when the friction and stress peaked. A remarried stepmother, having lived for 4 years with two stepchildren and two biological children (all of them in an elementary school), recalled her husband's reaction when she confided to him about her struggles with and loathing for one of his children:

> *I couldn't talk about it to my husband for a long time, because I thought he might get offended if I speak ill of his child. Just after one year passed, I talked to my husband about it. Because he often told me that he wanted to be more intimate with me and that we could tell each other anything, I thought I should talk about it, too. But he reacted saying, "You are wrong. You must be out of your mind." Since then, I could not talk with him about it. . . . I was totally at a loss. I may be wrong for feeling this way, but anybody [in my shoes] may feel the same way. So I went to see a psychiatrist.*

A father who had lived for 3 years with his remarried wife and her two elementary school children as well as his two teenage children described a similar marital conflict in his family as a "proxy war," for he felt he had been fighting on behalf of his children:

> *Her [my wife's] direct criticism comes out about the second child, one of my children, and it comes out gushing. I start with the notion that I would like to consider both my wife's position and my child's position objectively and calmly and to mediate between the two so they can get along with each other. But after all, I unexpectedly realize that I have come to act as my child's spokesperson in the course of our argument. . . . I know she is my wife, but that fact disappears somewhere in the middle of this "proxy war" [dairi-senso] between her and me acting as my son's spokesperson. That's the way things go.*

As the conflict gets more serious, sides are taken and a vicious spiral is created in the household; the harder a stepmother attempts to be her step-child's mother, the more intense the friction between them and between her and her husband. It is ironic that both spouses' efforts to reconstitute a standard family bring more psychological difficulties with them.

Stepfathers experienced more or less parallel role strains in their steppar-enting. Some of them reported similar feelings of frustration and confusion in developing close relations with stepchildren and in disciplining them, particularly if they expected to behave and to be treated as a father. Some stepfathers also reported feeling alienated in the face of preestablished close mother-child relationships. Stepfathers who lived with their own biological children were aware of the need to deal with their different feelings about their biological and stepchildren.

Overall, however, stepfathers expressed less discomfort about their step-parent role identities than stepmothers did. This may be because of the more vague social norms regarding the father role, allowing stepfathers to be flexible in terms of their parenting. In fact, they are far less likely to be in a primary parenting role than are stepmothers. For example, a stepfather who used to be a teacher explained his position in his stepfamily with two stepdaughters (elementary school girls) after 1 year of living together:

Stepfather: There are a lot [of difficulties in being a stepfather]. I grew up in a family of four, my parents and my younger brother and me, and among us, a single authoritative word from my father decided everything. But in my present family, things don't go that way, so I have to change my thinking, which irritates me. Among the daughters [my stepdaughters] and the mother [my wife], a single authoritative word from the mother is it. . . .

Interviewer: What do you think you are to your stepchildren?

Stepfather: I am not a father. I may be a teacher. I was not with them from the beginning, and I am not sure how they feel; I think it [the teacher image] will be on my mind to a smaller extent in the future. . . . My attitude is more like a researcher in that I devote myself solely to observing them, not actually educating them. . . .

Interviewer: So you are not actively pursuing any father image?

Stepfather: No. Perhaps this is a rather passive approach, but I think it's a better way to look ahead. . . . I would feel more comfortable if I brought my character to the fore, insisting on my own single authoritative word. However, if I persist in doing this, I run a risk. I feel that the risk is either one of two extreme results: things going all right or things going totally wrong [with my stepdaughters]. I want to avoid the latter. I would rather take a passive but less risky approach.

For both stepmothers and stepfathers, it held equally true that pursuing the "ordinary" or standard family model too rigidly and attempting too hard to be a new parent caused a great deal of tension and conflict in the stepfamily relations (similar emotional difficulties among American stepparents are documented in Felker et al., 2002). Yet, in general, Japanese stepfathers felt more at ease than did stepmothers in being slow to assume a parenting role and managing to create their own style of stepparenting. Perhaps this is also the case in many Western societies, where the idealization of motherhood and the gendered family role identities are relatively strong (Levin, 1997; Nielsen, 1999).

STRESS AND SUPPORT IN NETWORK STRUCTURE: FRICTION
AMONG OLD AND NEW TIES

It is argued that being a stepmother is more stressful than being a stepfather because stepmothers are liable to compete with biological mothers in parenting (Nielsen, 1999). This is also the case with Japanese stepmothers, and in addition there were many cases in our study where stepmothers were involved in more complicated competition with multiple quasi-parents, such as stepchildren's grandparents.

One common coping strategy of biological parents when they were single parents before remarriage was to seek help from their parents (or their deceased former spouse's parents, in a few cases) in parenting their children. If available, most divorced or bereaved single parents lived with or in proximity to their parents (and other kin, such as their siblings) at least for some period so their children could be taken care of while they were working. Coresidence with parents may be a relatively unusual coping strategy for Western counterparts. For example, it is estimated that the proportion of 35- to 39-year-old divorced women coresiding with parents is 25% in Japan but only 2% in the United States (Raymo et al., 2004). It can be a favorable choice, however, for Japanese single parents and their parents to coreside and coparent, given the more or less viable Japanese tradition of an extended (stem) family system and its recent shift toward more bilateral rather than rigidly patrilineal kinship orientations (Ochiai, 1997).

After experiencing this living arrangement with grandparents as coparents, the transition to a new stepfamily household is likely to increase "family boundary ambiguity" among the adult and child members more than would occur among their North American White middle-class counterparts (Pasley, 1987; Stewart, 2005). The extended family network, partly based on the Japanese stem-family tradition, can function as a safety net in case of emergencies, such as parenting after divorce. Yet, it can also be a source of friction between a stepmother as a new mother under the nuclear family model and the grandparents as former coparents under the extended family model. For example, the stepmother quoted previously about her dating with her present husband along with his preschool daughter before marriage had lived with her husband's parents early in their marriage, as she had just started parenting her stepdaughter. She explained her frustration at the time:

> [My stepdaughter's] grandma was a very mature and understanding person, and she said to me, "Now you are here, so I follow your way of disciplining." So basically I thought I would do things in my own way, following my husband's encouragement. But even if I told her [my stepchild] to do it my way, she unconsciously continued to follow the way she had been told by her grandma. . . . That she didn't change her behavior made me frustrated a bit, as I was apt to feel that grandma's words had priority over my words. . . . Now I think she didn't mean such a thing, but somehow I was inclined to think that way at that time.

Another stepmother, who had lived in a stepmother-stepfather household for 3 years, experienced a similar feeling when she found that her teenage stepson had had meals at her husband's deceased former wife's parents' house, which used to be near them. This stepson sometimes refused to eat what she had cooked. Some stepmothers who took a new mother role tended to define it as their responsibility to rediscipline their stepchildren who had been "spoiled" by too-permissive grandparents. In such a situation, the role strain in stepmothering came from the preexisting family networks in which a stepmother was newly embedded as well as from the relationships with her stepchild and new spouse.

The psychological stress of stepmothers becomes more serious if they are isolated in their personal networks. Many stepmothers reported that they had no one to talk with about their struggles as stepmothers when their family relationships were difficult. They assumed that people who had never been stepmothers could not understand their psychological pain. They were also aware of the social stereotype of "wicked stepmothers" and the risk of being blamed for not being a good mother (Christian, 2005; Ganong & Coleman, 1997). In addition, because most stepmothers had married over their parents' and friends' objections, they were unwilling to let these intimates know of their troubled stepfamily life. Thus, stepmothers reported experiencing the pile-up of psychological stress at the same time that they become increasingly isolated from their former networks.

Some stepfathers with no biological children also reported being isolated from their disapproving parents. Yet, these stepfathers and their wives (biological mothers with no stepchildren) were less likely to be in competition with their stepchildren's grandparents. We found no tendency among biological mothers with no stepchildren to isolate themselves from their preexisting networks, unless they moved a great distance because of their remarriage. On the other hand, biological fathers (with or without their stepchildren in the household) expressed their feelings of being torn between their wife (stepmother) and their parents. A typical coping behavior was to keep their distance from both the parents and other old network members by moving to a new house. In sum, the relative seriousness of stress deriving from stepmother-stepchild relationships is more or less related to how embedded or isolated the stepmother is in her old and new network structures.

EMERGING AMBIGUITY ABOUT VISITATION

Another possible old family tie in most stepfamilies is the relationship between a (step)child and his or her nonresident biological parent. Under the present Japanese judicial system, there is no legal way for a divorced couple to have joint custody, and in an increasing number of cases (approximately 80%), custody is awarded to the mother (Engel, 2004; Nozawa, 2006). Until recently it was customary that the relationships between nonresident biological parents (usually fathers) and their children were diminished after the parents' divorce, and even more so if either or both remarried. Thus, visitation between nonresident parents and children in practice occurs among fewer Japanese stepfamilies than among their counterparts in many Western countries. It follows logically that Japanese stepfamilies may be less affected by family boundary ambiguity around visitation arrangements.

With the rise of social awareness in Japan concerning the importance of fathering, it is probable that an increasing number of stepfamilies practice some kind of visitation between children and nonresident parents (Nozawa, 2006). Some biological mothers in our study said that they had mixed feelings about relationships being maintained between their children and their former husband. A mother living with her daughter and two stepsons as well as her remarried husband of 1 year told us of her worrying about her daughter's visiting her biological father:

> Now he [my former husband] is an unrelated person to me, but he is still my daughter's father. He wasn't a bad father, so my daughter seems to remember him once in a while and think, "How pitiful my dad is!" So I was very worried about the visitation. Each time she returns home after seeing her father, she remembers the good days of her past and gets depressed. Then she gives her [step]-father at home the cold treatment. . . . She seems to think, "If my mom didn't marry him, she would have returned to my dad." I agree with the stepfamily book [Haruna & Takahashi, 1991, the Japanese edition of Visher & Visher, 1991] saying that children will keep dreaming of going back to their original family. . . . In the beginning, my husband said we'd better not have my daughter see her father [any more], so I had him read the stepfamily book so he could understand alternative ideas. Because the idea in the book was that the visitation as practiced in the United States benefits children, I persuaded him to agree to it, but he doesn't like me to see him [my former husband] when my daughter visits.

It is evident that arranging this kind of visitation and coping with the stress concerning family boundary ambiguity are emerging issues for step-families in Japan. If the practice of visitation between nonresidential parents and children becomes more common in Japan in the near future, many parents and stepparents in stepfamilies will face a new challenge of inter-household stress management.

PARTICIPATION IN SUPPORT GROUPS

Finally, the importance of participation in support groups, whether online or offline, emerged as a key theme. As we recruited the participants partly through publication (Haruna & Takahashi, 1991), web sites, events, and activities of the SAJ, many of the interviewees had at least some experience of exchanging social support off- and/or online. Some of them, in fact, are staff members of such support groups. As is shown in recent American studies (Christian, 2005; Flexman, Berke, & Settles, 1999), participation in online and offline support groups for family members under similarly stressful situations, such as being stepmothers, provides them with an opportunity to share their feelings with others who have had similar experiences. Among other interviewees who participated in a stepfamily-related support group, stepmothers in particular emphasized that they were emancipated from feelings of isolation and alienation and that they came to have a positive view of their own identity as stepmothers. For example, the stepmother who described her experiences of premarital dating with her husband and his daughter as well as her difficulty in stepmothering under the influence of grandma participated in face-to-face session activities, "feeling like clutching even at straws." She described what she felt at the sessions:

> I was very much relieved. I'm not sure if I've seen the light [of a solution] yet, but for sure I found so many hints there. Then I thought to myself, "I can keep going a little farther." In addition, I was not wrong in doing all these all along. I learned that everybody [in my shoes] experienced the same path. It's a common pathway. Now I understand I was not alone in having this experience, and my experience was not because I did anything wrong. I got some confidence, and I got motivated to keep going.

Her husband (a biological father), who participated in one of the sessions with her, explained the shift in his viewpoint:

> Father: By reading it [the bulletin board on the web site of the support group], I can tell you for sure that a man often assumes, when he remarries along with his own child, that it's only natural that the stepmother takes care of his child. . . . But first of all, unless you can change that very idea, I don't think you can make things work well. . . . A man is apt to feel that now his wife is a [new] mother, so it would be normal that she does [take care of his child]. That was my case, too.
> Interviewer: By experience, you learned it didn't work?
> Father: Yes, and I found many people in SAJ have similar opinions.
> Interviewer: You changed your view there?
> Father: That's right. It's very good to get an objective view. If you are confined in your own family, all you can see is your own family.

Another stepmother, who had remarried only 4 months before to live with her new husband and his two teenage children along with her own two teenage children, made a related comment on the merit of their couple participation in a similar session where adult stepfamily members had shared their family experiences with other participants:

> [In the session] he [my husband] can hear the other [step]mothers directly say they can't feel any attachment to their stepchildren, or they can't feel the same way toward their stepchildren as toward their own children. He can understand it better that way. Even if I repeat it many times, he would be inclined to see it as my own case, just an individual case. But [in the session] he can see that's not true, because it's also the case with everybody else. And as my husband is the only one [stepfather] that I can see in my daily life, I would wonder if other stepfathers are really like him or not. But I can see [other step-] fathers [in the session] and find there are a variety of people. So we can generalize about all the participants' views, and we can understand our own family's

case in comparison to others', saying, "We are doing all right on this matter, but over-looked that one," or "We can do it better."

It was a liberating event for many of our interviewees to meet other step-parents and biological parents in more or less similar stepfamily situations. By exchanging views and sharing experiences, they found a way into the open air after a long struggle in a closed place. Some of them mentioned how exciting it was for them just to learn a new word, *suteppufamiri* (step-family) to describe their family experiences, which symbolized how strong their feeling of being alone was. Participation in support groups is not nec-essarily a perfect solution for every stepfamily or for every problem. Yet it provided them with an opportunity to shift their view of their own family relations from a closed, idiosyncratic view to an open, comparative view. Through this shift, they could redefine their own or their partner's role identities as a stepmother, a stepfather, or a biological parent in a stepfam-ily. At the same time, they reexamined their unspoken strong assumptions about the standard family model. Their newly developed networks of non-kin ties with similar people in similar family experiences can serve as an avenue to the collective construction or reinvention of more flexible alterna-tive family models, particularly in the case of a couple's joint participation.

CONCLUSION

The analysis of our interview data suggests two major findings regarding the reasons for stepmothers' highly stressful experiences in Japanese stepfa-milies. First, the limited availability of alternatives to the standard family model, which assumes gender-role segregation with an emphasis on wom-en's mothering role, fosters the social expectation for stepmothers to take on a new mother role as soon as they attempt to restructure the dynamics of their preexisting families (Ganong & Coleman, 1997). The inflexible expect-ation regarding the mother role leads stepmothers (and most probably their stepchildren) to experience psychological stress to the point where success-ful coping is almost impossible.

In this context, it can be argued that Cherlin's (1978) classic argument about remarriage as "an incomplete institution" seems to hold better in Japan than in the United States. In the present Japanese society, available supportive resources, including books on stepfamilies and family support professionals trained to help stepfamilies, are still scarce (Ibaraki, 2006). Even the concept of stepfamily itself is not yet fully recognized. In Japan, the standard family model has been more completely built into the social norms regarding most social institutions, such as the educational system. This institutional incompleteness of stepfamilies might be an additional so-cial condition making stepparenting more difficult in Japan, particularly for stepmothers. Interestingly, the lack of guidelines for stepparenting is conditioned by the rigidity of guidelines for gender-role relations in society at large.

Second, the family and nonfamily network structures surrounding Japanese remarried couples are closely related to the stressful nature of their stepfamily life. The relatively interdependent nature of the extended family network in Japan can produce stress and can prompt couples to rush into remarriage. It can also promote stepmothers' competition with former mothering figures and, ironically, isolation from their old personal network. Although the intergenerational interdependence among extended family members is a relatively remarkable cause of family boundary ambiguity early in a marriage, the relationships between children and their nonresident parents is a minor source of ambiguity for Japanese stepfamilies, because visitation is not common. In other words, the family stress caused by the *vertical* family boundary ambiguity may be higher, and the *horizontal* family boundary ambiguity may be lower in Japan than in many Western societies. Emerging support groups for stepfamilies, largely based on the Internet, serve as a new opportunity for stepfamily members to share stressful and successful experiences with each other and to collectively create more flexible alternatives to the standard family model.

Although the discussion in this chapter has centered on stressful aspects of stepfamilies having relatively complex relations under the difficult social conditions, it should be noted that there were positive aspects of stepfamily experiences. In particular, some remarried wives in biological mother–stepfather families expressed their satisfaction with their remarriage as they had a better coparenting partner compared to their troubled previous marriage and following single parenthood. There was also an exceptionally successful case in our study in which a first-married young stepmother took a more careful and long-term approach to build a more trusting stepmother-stepchild relationship, taking more than 4 years before marriage and taking a "big sister" role instead of a mother role even after marriage (Nozawa, Nagai, et al., 2006; see also Church, 1999, and Weaver & Coleman, 2005, for a variation in stepmother roles in North America). Furthermore, our interviewees were not a representative sample. Stepfamilies in relatively stressful situations were likely to be overrepresented, as many of them had originally been recruited through publications, web sites, and events and activities of the SAJ, while more positive aspects of stepfamily life might be underrepresented in our study.

In addition, our analysis of mainly one-time interview data might have missed the full stories of stepfamily dynamics, focusing too much on family conflict in the early stages of the stepfamily formation. In our study, however, some veteran stepmothers who had come into strong antagonism with one of their stepchildren in his or her adolescence told us stories about how the quality of the stepmother-stepchild relationship had changed over time into a more supportive and enjoyable one as the stepchild entered his or her adulthood, usually after spending some time living apart from the stepfamily. These cases suggest that the development of stepfamily relationships is indeed a long-term process, as Papernow (1984 and this volume) shows (see also Baxter, Braithwaite, & Nicholson, 1999).

Needless to say, explorations into more diverse aspects and issues of Japanese stepfamilies are yet to come. Obviously, studies with a longitudinal design and on children's and stepchildren's viewpoints, as well as more representative data collections (see, e.g., Ahrons, 2004), are on the list of what we lack and need. Having these, we will be able to explain more fully the variations and processes of relational dynamics among stepfamilies in Japan. We have just taken the first step forward.

REFERENCES

Ahrons, C. (2004). *We're still family: What grown children have to say about their parents' divorce.* New York: HarperCollins.

Arnaut, G. L. Y., Fromme, D. K., Stall, B. M., & Felker, J. A. (2000). A qualitative analysis of stepfamilies: The biological parent. *Journal of Divorce and Remarriage, 33*(3/4), 111–128.

Baxter, L. A., Braithwaite, D. O., & Nicholson, J. (1999). Turning points in the development of blended family relationships. *Journal of Social and Personal Relationships, 16*(3), 291–313.

Blood, R. O., Jr. (1967). *Love match and arranged marriage: A Tokyo-Detroit comparison.* New York: Free Press.

Cherlin, A. (1978). Remarriage as an incomplete institution. *American Journal of Sociology, 84*(3), 634–650.

Christian, A. (2005). Contesting the myth of the "wicked stepmother": Narrative analysis of an online stepfamily support group. *Western Journal of Communication, 69*(1), 27–47.

Church, E. (1999). Who are the people in your family? Stepmothers' diverse notion of kinship. *Journal of Divorce and Remarriage, 31*(1/2), 83–105.

Engel, M. (2004). Stepfamilies worldwide: A comparative review of legal approaches in selected countries. In R. Brown & L. W. Morgan (Eds.), *2005 family law update* (pp. 219–287). Rockville, MD: Aspen Press.

Felker, J. A., Fromme, D. K., Arnaut, G. L., & Stoll, B. M. (2002). A qualitative analysis of stepfamilies: The stepparent. *Journal of Divorce and Remarriage, 38*(1/2), 125–142.

Fine, M. A., & Schwebel, A. I. (1992). Stepparent stress: A cognitive perspective. *Journal of Divorce and Remarriage, 17*(1/2), 1–15.

Flexman, R., Berke, D. L., & Settles, B. H. (1999). Negotiating families: The interface between family and support groups. *Marriage and Family Review, 28*(3/4), 173–190.

Ganong, L. H., & Coleman, M. (1997). How society views stepfamilies. *Marriage and Family Review, 26*(1/2), 85–106.

Ganong, L. H., & Coleman, M. (2004). *Stepfamily relationships: Development, dynamics, and interventions.* New York: Kluwer Academic/Plenum Press.

Haruna, H. (Ed.), Takahashi, T. (Trans.). (2001). *Suteppufamiri: Shiawasena saikon kazoku ni narutameni.* Tokyo: Wave Shuppan.

Ibaraki, N. (2006). Suteppufamiri eno shien no genjo [Professional support services for stepfamilies in Japan]. In S. Nozawa, N. Ibaraki, T. Hayano, & Stepfamily Association of Japan (Eds.), *Q&A suteppufamiri no kisochishiki* [An introduction to stepfamilies] (pp. 113–125). Tokyo: Akashi Shoten.

Imamura, A. E. (1987). *Urban Japanese housewives: At home and in the community.* Honolulu: University of Hawaii Press.

Iwai, N. (2000). Divorce in Japan: Historical changes and current issues. In R. R. Miller & S. L. Browning (Eds.), *With this ring: Divorce, intimacy, and cohabitation from a multicultural perspective* (pp. 53–77). Stamford, CT: JAI Press.

Jacobson, D. (1990). Stress and support in stepfamily formation: The cultural context of social support. In B. R. Sarason, I. G. Sarason, & G. R. Pierce (Eds.), *Social support: An interactional view* (pp. 199–218). New York: Wiley.

Levin, I. (1997). The stepparent role from a gender perspective. *Marriage and Family Review, 26*(1/2), 177–190.

National Institute of Population and Social Security Research. (2005). *Jinko no doko nihon to sekai: Jinkotokei shiryoshu 2005* [Demographic Trends in Japan and World 2005]. Tokyo: Health and Welfare Statistics.

National Institute of Population and Social Security Research. (2007). *Wagakuni fufu no kekkon katei to shusshoryoku: Dai 13 kai shussho doko kihon chosa* [Marriage process and fertility of Japanese married couples: Report on the thirteenth Japanese national fertility survey in 2005. Volume I]. Tokyo: National Institute of Population and Social Security Research.

Nielsen, L. (1999). Stepmothers: Why so much stress? A review of the research. *Journal of Divorce and Remarriage, 30,* 115–148.

Nozawa, S. (2006). Suteppufamiri wo meguru shakaijokyo [Stepfamilies in contemporary Japan: An overview]. In S. Nozawa, N. Ibaraki, T. Hayano, & Stepfamily Association of Japan (Eds.), *Q&A suteppufamiri no kisochishiki* [An introduction to stepfamilies] (pp. 17–38). Tokyo: Akashi Shoten.

Nozawa, S. (in press). Intahnetto wa kazoku ni nani wo motarasunoka? [What does the Internet bring about for families? Role strains and support networks among stepfamilies]. In K. Miyata & S. Nozawa (Eds.), *Onrainkasuru nichijoh-seikatsu: Sapohto wa doh kawarunoka?* [Everyday life online: Any difference in social support exchange?]. Tokyo: Bunkashobo/Hakubunsha.

Nozawa, S., Ibaraki, N., Hayano, T., & Stepfamily Association of Japan (Eds.). (2006). *Q&A suteppufamiri no kisochishiki* [An introduction to stepfamilies]. Tokyo: Akashi Shoten.

Nozawa, S., Nagai, A., Kikuchi, M., & Matsuda, S. (2006). Suteppufamiri no kazoku katei to kankei keisei [Family formation and relational dynamics among Japanese stepfamilies]. In S. Nozawa, N. Ibaraki, T. Hayano, & Stepfamily Association of Japan (Eds.), *Q&A suteppufamiri no kisochishiki* [An introduction to stepfamilies] (pp. 55–111). Tokyo: Akashi Shoten.

Ochiai, E. (1997). *The Japanese family system in transition: A sociological analysis of family change in postwar Japan*. Tokyo: LCTB International Library Foundation.

Papernow, P. L. (1984). The stepfamily cycle: An experiential model of stepfamily development. *Family Relations, 33*, 355–363.

Pasley, K. (1987). Family boundary ambiguity: Perceptions of adult stepfamily members. In K. Pasley & M. Ihinger-Tallman (Eds.), *Remarriage and stepparenting: Current research and theory* (pp. 206–224). New York: Guilford Press.

Pasley, K., & Ihinger-Tallman, M. (1982). Stress in remarried families. *Family Perspective, 16*(4), 181–190.

Raymo, J. M., Iwasawa, M., & Bumpass, L. (2004). Marital dissolution in Japan: Recent trends and patterns. *Demographic Research, 11*(14), 395–419.

Statistics and Information Department, Minister's Secretariat, Ministry of Health, Labour, and Welfare. (2005). *Heisei 17 nen jinko doktai tokei* [The vital statistics of Japan 2005. Volume I]. Tokyo: Health and Welfare Statistics Association.

Stewart, S. (2005). Boundary ambiguity in stepfamilies. *Journal of Family Issues, 26*(7), 1002–1029.

Visher, E. B., & Visher, J. S. (1991). *How to win as a stepfamily* (2nd ed.). New York: Brunner/Mazel.

Vogel, E. (1963). *Japan's new middle class: The salary man and his family in a Tokyo suburb*. Berkeley: University of California Press.

Weaver, S. E., & Coleman, M. (2005). A mothering but not a mother role: A grounded theory study of the nonresidential stepmother role. *Journal of Social and Personal Relationships, 22*(4), 477–497.

Whitsett, D., & Land, H. (1992). Role strain, coping, and marital satisfaction of stepparents. *Families in Society: Journal of Contemporary Human Services, 73*(2), 79–92.

CHAPTER 5

Stepfathers in Cultural Context: Mexican American Families in the United States

SCOTT COLTRANE, ERIKA GUTIERREZ,
and ROSS D. PARKE

FAMILIES ARE undergoing a period of gradual change, with new family forms emerging in the United States and elsewhere. One of the major shifts has been the rise in stepparent families. High rates of divorce and nonmarital birth mean that about half of all children in the United States will spend time not living with a biological parent (typically the father). And because most divorced people remarry, about a third of all U.S. children will live with a stepparent—usually a stepfather—before reaching adulthood (Amato & Sobolewski, 2004; Bumpass, Raley, & Sweet, 1995). Researchers note that these trends undermine children's links to one parent while simultaneously expanding the universe of potential kin in the form of stepparents, stepsiblings, and step-grandparents (Logan & Spitze, 1996). Although we are beginning to understand more about reconstituted families, we cannot yet predict the long-term consequences of exchanging one very close tie for

Support for this project was provided by grants from NIMH: MH 64828, "Effects and Meaning of Fathers for Adolescents: UCR Site" (Scott Coltrane, principal investigator), and "Effects and Meaning of Fathers for Adolescents: ASU Site" (Sanford Braver, principal investigator). We thank the UC Riverside Center for Family Studies and the ASU Prevention Intervention Research Center for technical and material support. We especially thank Shoon Lio, Kate Luther, and Marie Miller for valuable research assistance and express our profound gratitude to the many families who participated in the study.

a wider network of ties (Bumpass, 1990; Furstenberg & Cherlin, 1991). In this chapter, we argue that one key to understanding this trade-off for future families is to focus on the cultural contexts that shape marriage and divorce patterns as well as the causes and consequences of different forms of stepfathering.

We draw on our studies of Mexican American families living in the southwestern United States to illustrate how culture and ethnicity shape patterns of marriage, remarriage, and stepfathering. Latinos (or Hispanics) are now the largest and fastest-growing ethnic group in the United States and are projected to constitute one-fourth of the U.S. population by 2050 (U.S. Census Bureau, 2003). Research on divorce, remarriage, and stepparenting among Mexican Americans is still rare, but we use our recent work to illustrate some benefits of considering cultural context in studies of reconstituted families.

One of the most distinctive historical features of Mexican American family life is reliance on extended networks of kinfolk for emotional and material support. Not only is household size comparatively larger for Mexican American families throughout the Southwest, but the family also consists of an extended network of relatives living outside the household. *La familia* includes grandparents, aunts, uncles, cousins, married brothers and sisters, and their children. A unique *compadrazgo* system also links godparents and children in a system of mutual exchange and support. *Padrinos,* or godfathers, and *madrinos,* or godmothers, are nonbiologically related individuals who become members of the extended family and participate in the major ceremonies of the children's lives. Godparents act as *compadres,* or coparents, disciplining children, offering companionship to parents and children, providing emotional support, and offering financial aid (Coltrane & Collins, 2001; Griswold del Castillo, 1984).

Many of these traditions continue today, and scholars often rely on the concept of *familism* to describe both traditional and contemporary Mexican American families (Rumbaut & Portes, 2001). Familism refers to a constellation of values that give overriding importance to the family and the needs of the collective as opposed to individual and personal needs (Bean, Curtis, & Marcum, 1977). Embeddedness in close-knit extended kin networks and valuing family solidarity over individuality or personal achievement is a Mexican cultural pattern handed down through the generations, but research also suggests that reliance on actual and fictive kin (nonrelatives defined as family members) is similarly common among lower-class African Americans and some non-Hispanic Whites in the United States (Stack, 1974; Zavella, 1987). To understand how and why marriage patterns and kin networks vary, and to better model and assist families in coping with the challenges of remarriage, it is important to assess cultural differences as well as similarities.

FOCUSING ON THE STEPFATHER

More family research now includes fathers, but stepfathers are still relatively understudied in the research on father involvement (Marsiglio, 2004a, 2004b; Marsiglio, Day, & Lamb, 2000). There are some notable exceptions, however, that include analysis or mention of stepfathers in their books on fatherhood (Marsiglio, 1995, 2004a; McKee & O'Brien, 1982; Parke, 1981, 1996). This raises the following questions: Where do stepfathers fit in? and Are they really different from biological fathers?

Although almost a third of American youth will acquire stepfathers (Cherlin & Furstenberg, 1994; Coleman, Ganong, & Fine, 2000; Hetherington & Stanley-Hagan, 2002), there is little research that examines systematically how stepfathers influence their children, especially during the turbulent adolescent years. We do know that the effects of stepfathers on children are highly variable (Hetherington & Clingempeel, 1992), in part depending on the intrusiveness of the stepfather and the speed with which he tries to establish both his authority and close ties to the stepchildren (Hetherington, Bridges, & Insabella, 1998). Some research suggests that following remarriage, adolescent stepchildren are likely to attribute motives to stepfathers that create emotional distance and discourage warm feelings (Coleman et al., 2000; Fine, Voydanoff, & Donnelly, 1993; Love & Murdock, 2004; Russell & Searcy, 1997). Above all, the research literature demonstrates that children in stepfather families are at risk for a variety of reasons, including the loss of their birth father (Amato & Keith, 1991; Biblarz & Gottainer, 2000; Hetherington & Clingempeel, 1992; Ross & Mirowsky, 1999). Recent data reveal that children in stepfather families are at double the normal risk for mental health disorders (Biblarz & Raferty, 1999; Bray, 1999; Buehler & Pasley, 2000; Kim, Hetherington, & Reiss, 1999; Nicholson, Fergusson, & Horwood, 1999; Phares, 1997). Moreover, these children score lower in academic achievement and in the quality of peer relationships (Amato & Sobolewski, 2004). However, culture and ethnicity also play a role: Children in African American families are better off in a married stepfamily than in a single-mother household, as indexed by lower rates of school dropout and less early sexual activity and fewer teenage pregnancies (McLanahan & Sandefur, 1994; Moore & Chase-Lansdale, 2001).

But what does this literature tell us about the unique effects of the stepfather? White and Gilbreth (2001) summarize the empirical literature as generally concluding that stepfathers have little or no effect on child outcomes, but this conclusion is typically drawn based on comparisons of a simple family structure variable (e.g., stepfather families versus single-mother families; see McLanahan & Sandefur, 1994). Researchers often describe stepfathers as disengaged (Hetherington, 1988), and a significant minority of stepfathers and stepchildren do not even think of each other as family (Furstenberg, 1987). White and Gilbreth (2001, p. 156) note that

> *regardless of the good intentions with which they entered the stepparenting role, many stepfathers experience sufficient rebuffs from the children and sometimes from their spouse that they eventually withdraw to the role of chauffeur, bankroller, and handyman, eschewing any attempts at authoritative parenting.*

From the moment a man becomes a stepfather, he holds a nebulous role, as his responsibilities are vague and ill defined (Marsiglio, 2004a, 2004b). Many men become formal stepfathers by marrying a single mother; others develop an informal fatherhood role, often but not necessarily living with the child and the child's mother. Debates over when a man actually becomes a stepfather suggest that stepfathering remains a complicated matter with fuzzy boundaries (Stewart, 2005). Failure to control for a range of social and contextual variables such as social class and culture has been a problem in remarriage research, and few studies have attempted to measure the meanings people assign to their stepfamily experiences or examined how these meanings change over time, despite the promise that such studies hold for increasing our understanding of stepfamilies (Coleman et al., 2000). Symbolic meanings as well as behavior patterns associated with stepfamilies are especially likely to be influenced by cultural context.

FACTORS CONTRIBUTING TO STEPFATHER INVOLVEMENT

The literature on stepfather involvement is based primarily on research involving White non-Hispanic stepfathers; however, identified factors that are linked to involvement may not only be important for fathers of other cultural/ethnic backgrounds, but may operate in different ways in various cultural/ethnic groups. Important factors include the stepfather's relationship with his partner, whether the stepfather has children of his own, whether the biological father of the stepchildren is still alive, and the age and gender of the stepchildren.

The stepfather's relationship with his partner is a crucial determinant of the amount and quality of involvement with his stepchildren. Fine and Kurdek (1995) found that the marital relationship has a stronger impact on the parent-child relationship in stepfamilies than in first marriages, suggesting that the boundary between the marital and stepparent-stepchild dyads is more permeable than that between the marital and parent-child dyads. Fathers are more involved with coresident children (whether biological or stepchildren) if they have a positive relationship with the mother (Belsky,

Youngblade, & Rovine, 1991; Carlson & McLanahan, 2004; Gottman, 1998). In unmarried couples, a conflicted spousal relationship discourages positive father involvement, whereas a positive spousal relationship promotes healthy father-child interaction (Coley & Chase-Lansdale, 1999; Danziger & Radin, 1990; Seltzer, 1991).

A significant factor related to the level of involvement of a stepfather is whether he has children of his own (Coleman et al., 2000). Burgoyne and Clark (1982) found that stepfathers with biological children are relieved to have new partners to help them, despite having acquired new stepchildren. Marsiglio (1991) found that fathers coresiding with both biological children and stepchildren were more likely to engage in play activities with all children as opposed to fathers living only with their stepchildren. However, in complex stepfamilies, stepfathers devote more time and direct more affection to their own children (Hetherington, 2006; Hetherington & Stanley-Hagen, 2002).

Another factor to consider is whether the biological father of the stepchildren is still alive and has an active role in his children's lives. The literature that addresses the relationships children have with their stepfathers and nonresident fathers is addressed elsewhere in this book (Pryor, Chapter 15). The age and gender of the stepchildren are also important to consider in relation to stepfather involvement, and Robertson (this volume) discusses this research. There is usually an easier transition into the family and acceptance of a stepfather if his stepchildren are younger rather than older. Adolescents, in particular, have a hard time accepting a stepfather into the family (Hetherington, 2006). Typically it is easier for a stepfather to become involved with a stepson than with a stepdaughter, since girls seem to have a more difficult time interacting with and accepting a stepfather (Buchanan, Maccoby, & Dornbusch, 1996; Vuchinich, Hetherington, Vuchinich, & Clingempeel, 1991).

In general, the research literature suggests that the more a stepfather is involved with his stepchildren, the fewer behavioral problems the child has and the better the child does in school (Manning & Lamb, 2003; White & Gilbreth, 2001). Although the type and level of stepfather involvement may differ, a stepchild typically responds well to a stepfather who seeks to be involved with his stepchild (Galatzer-Levy, 2001; Hetherington & Jodl, 1994). Nevertheless, three in-depth longitudinal studies of stepfamilies found that relationships between stepfathers and stepchildren generally became more negative over time (Bray & Kelly, 1999; Hetherington, 1993; Hetherington & Clingempeel, 1992). In addition, compared to fathers in continuously married families, stepfathers devote less time and attention to their (step)children (Amato, 1987; Hofferth, Pleck, Stueve, Bianchi, & Sayer, 2002; Pleck, 1997). Theoretical explanations for unique stepparent influences on stepchildren suggest that levels of stress, extent of parent involvement, and parenting styles all contribute to a higher incidence of mental health disorders and behavior problems in children in stepfamilies (Coleman et al., 2000; Fisher, Leve, O'Leary, & Leve, 2003).

MEXICAN AMERICAN FAMILIES AS A CASE STUDY IN CULTURAL CONTEXT

Although there has been a noticeable increase in research on fathers in the past few years (Cabrera, Tamis-LeMonda, Bradley, Hofferth, & Lamb, 2000; Marsiglio et al., 2000), various limitations of this research remain, including a failure to examine how the impacts of fathering behaviors vary according to family type (step versus nonstep), and with little attention given to cultural differences and commonalities in fathering. Many researchers and advocacy groups have called for fatherhood research that includes samples of subgroups in the population with unique characteristics or special needs, such as ethnic minority fathers and stepfathers. We know little about how fatherhood is modified by ethnic background and marital status and what impact different forms of fathering have on children's development and well-being in different groups. King (2006) notes that some studies find that African American fathers have more contact with their nonresident children than White or non-Black fathers (King, 1994; Seltzer, 1991), but others find no differences (Seltzer & Bianchi, 1988). One study found that African American adolescents reported being closer to their nonresident father than Whites did (King, Harris, & Heard, 2004). The few studies that assess possible differences between racial/ethnic groups in stepfather-stepchild relations report mixed findings (Hofferth & Anderson, 2003; King, 2006; Marsiglio, 1995). In her review of the literature, Valerie King (2006, p. 912) writes, "Little is known about nonresident father-child relationships or stepfather-stepchild relationships in immigrant families," though she notes that migration among U.S. Latinos often negatively affects nonresident father contact (see Landale & Oropesa, 2001). In her study using a national sample, King also found no differences in U.S. adolescents' closeness to stepfathers or nonresident fathers by race/ethnicity or immigrant status.

Among the groups most at risk for economic stress, adolescent problems, and school dropout are Latinos, who, as noted, are projected to compose one-quarter of the U.S. population by the year 2050. Two-thirds of U.S. Latinos are Mexican Americans, a population disproportionately composed of two-parent, working-poor families with unique needs and cultural resources. Compared to families that are of White European (Anglo) descent, Mexican American families have low social mobility and experience relatively little change in family income across generations (Chapa & Valencia, 1993). Latinos, especially Mexican Americans, tend to be employed in agriculture, construction, manufacturing, and service and occupy jobs with low pay, limited benefits, few opportunities for advancement, and periodic instability (Duncan, Hotz, & Trejo, 2006; Reimers, 2006). Although Latinos have higher rates of marriage and employment than other minority groups, because of their parents' low wages over a third of Latino children under the age of 18 live in poverty, a rate that is over 3 times higher than that of non-Latinos in the United States (Proctor & Dalaker, 2002).

Latino fathering has received little attention from family scholars, although several studies have appeared in the past decade that focus on Latino men's participation in family life (Cabrera & Garcia Coll, 2004; Coltrane, Parke, & Adams, 2004; Formoso, Gonzalez, Barrera, & Dumka, 2007; Mirandé, 1997) and other studies have compared Latino men's parenting to men in other racial/ethnic groups (Hofferth, 2003; Toth & Xu, 1999). Mexican American families are worthy of study because of their prevalence and poverty, but also because of their high regard for marriage and traditional emphasis on familism (Bean et al., 1977; Buriel & DeMent, 1997; Keefe & Padilla, 1987; Oropesa, 1996). Mexican Americans have higher birth rates and higher levels of kin coresidence than other ethnic groups, with exceptionally low rates of divorce compared to other groups of similar socioeconomic status. Although researchers have recently turned their attention toward Latino families, we still know little about diversity among them, nor how Mexican American fathers in particular might contribute to their family or influence their children's development (Coltrane & Valdez, 1993; Gonzales, Knight, Morgan-Lopez, Saenz, & Sirolli, 2001).

Some argue that Mexican American fathers remain more traditional (authoritarian, rigid, and patriarchal) than European American fathers, while others suggest that Mexican American families and fathers are becoming more egalitarian (Zavella, 1987; Zinn & Wells, 2000). Most research finds that Mexican American parents who are not born in the United States and who are less linguistically and socially acculturated endorse the traditional role of the man as the head of the household and primary economic provider, though other studies find that Mexican American (and African American) respondents, compared with European American respondents, have more positive attitudes toward wives working, probably because of financial necessity (Kane, 1992; McLoyd, Cauce, Takeuchi, & Wilson, 2000; Taylor, Tucker, & Mitchell-Kernan, 1999).

Divorce and nonmarital birth rates have been increasing in Latino families, just as they have in other racial/ethnic groups in the United States. Although there is a growing literature on intact Latino families, Latino stepfamilies are rarely assessed via organized research projects. In this chapter's focus on Latino stepfamilies, we investigate the role of the stepfather in Mexican American stepfamilies, his relationship to his partner/spouse and stepchildren, and his involvement within the family structure.

As noted, a core value in many Latino families is familism, or having a cohesive bond and an emphasis on cooperation, as well as keeping to traditional gender ideals (Cauce & Rodriguez, 2002; Cotera, 1976; Hondagneu-Sotelo & Avila, 1997; Mirandé, 1997; Tafolla, 1985). Stepfamilies encounter a particular dilemma in the face of familism because separation or divorce would have had to occur in order for a stepfamily to be created, that is, unless the partner is widowed. A certain degree of stigma may arise for Latino families, especially the blended types, from the perception that they are not unified or cooperative, which violates the value of familism. Therefore, some Latino families may be reluctant to readily specify that they are a stepfamily or to discuss the origins of their current family structure. Similarly, stigma may also arise from divorce given that many Latinos in the United States are Catholics. Divorce among Catholics is complicated by the fact that the Catholic Church requires an annulment if either party to a failed marriage wants to be remarried in the Church. In general, the influence of religion over divorce has been declining in the past several decades, and though divorce rates for Catholics remain below those of Protestants, and for Latinos below those of Anglos, they have all followed a similar historical trajectory (Coltrane & Collins, 2001; Sander, 1993). Patterns of remarriage are somewhat different, with two-thirds of White women but only about half of Black and Latino women remarrying (Teachman, 2000).

How commonplace are Latino stepfamilies? Although it is difficult to estimate specific marriage and divorce rates with current demographic data, the consensus among population scholars is that stepfamily formation among Latinos is rising at a slightly lower rate than that of non-Hispanic Whites but is increasing as the Latino population increases (Bramlett & Mosher, 2002; DaVanzo & Rahman, 1993; Stewart, 2007). What are the implications of having more Latino stepfamilies? Specifically, how are Latino stepfathers interacting with their partner and their partner's children? Does the involvement of a Latino stepfather differ from that of a biological father? If so, how and why? These are a few of the questions our research is attempting to answer. We hope to provide a much needed focus on a group that is rarely discussed in family literature.

THE LATINO FAMILY AND STEPFAMILY

Our particular study focused on both Mexican American and European (Anglo) American intact families and stepfamilies. One of the major differences we noted in comparing Latino stepfamilies to Anglo stepfamilies was the need to consider the effects of immigration, particularly the generation of arrival of the Latino parent or parents (although there are some Latino families that have been in the United States for more generations than some Anglo-Americans). In our sample, half of the Latino parents we interviewed were born in Mexico and hence can be classified as first-generation immigrants. The United States has seen an increase in Latino immigration since 1965 (Acuña, 2000; Gutierrez, 1995; Rumbaut & Portes, 2001).

From the outset of our study, we were concerned about how the generational status of the Latino stepparents might impact family structure, parental behaviors and expectations, and child development. We were particularly interested in Latino stepfather families and the potential stresses associated with being a relatively recent immigrant. The analysis of adjustment among Latino stepfathers is practically nonexistent in family scholarship. Half of the Latino stepfathers we sampled reported that they were born in Mexico, and the other half were born in the United States.

Characteristics of Mexican American Stepfamilies

In our study, we looked specifically at Mexican American couples in which both parents were of Mexican descent. We made this sampling decision to control for the confounding effects of mixed ethnicity marriages. Although ethnically mixed families are increasingly common, we opted for a sampling design that would yield consistent ideal types. We sampled intact families and stepfamilies in which the biological mother was remarried or cohabiting with a male partner and had a child in the seventh grade from a previous relationship. In the course of recruiting our stepfamily sample from the public schools, we ended up with over 60% of families with stepfathers who had also been married previously. Although we sampled and interviewed Anglo stepfamilies as well, in this discussion we focus on the characteristics of our Mexican American stepfamily sample, occasionally making comparisons to Anglo-American stepfamilies to show contrasts between the two groups.

Despite simple stereotypes about the composition of Latino families in the American Southwest, the reformed families we interviewed represented a range of complex forms. To qualify for participation in the study, the men had to be living in the home for a minimum of 1 year and be "acting in a father role." Over half of the stepfathers had moved in with the mother and stepchild by the time the child was 6 years old. The focal stepchild was 12 or 13 years old at the time of the first interview. Over 75% of the Mexican American stepfamilies we interviewed contained multiple siblings who shared the same parents (typically the mother and the nonresident biological father). Just under 50% contained stepsiblings, and almost 25% contained other adult relatives. When compared to Anglo stepfamilies, the Mexican American stepfamilies had significantly more coresident siblings and adult relatives. Fewer than 10% of the families counted grandparents among household residents, but over 16% included other adult relatives in the household (aunts, uncles, cousins, etc.). The reasons for joint residence were often financial, as the mean income for families in our sample was under $50,000 in a region known for high housing costs and a standard of living exceeding most suburban American locales. Almost half of the Mexican American stepfathers (45%) had children from a previous relationship, whereas less than a third of the Anglo American stepfathers did. Those Mexican American stepfathers who had children from a previous relationship tended to see them regularly, with over half (51%) having contact with their nonresident children once a week or more, and half having their nonresident children over to their (stepfamily) houses to visit. Two-thirds of the Mexican American stepfathers with nonresident children paid child support to the mother of those children.

SPOUSAL RELATIONS

A large majority of the Mexican American stepfathers in the study (58%) were not married to the mother. In contrast, 75% of the Anglo stepfathers were married to the mother. Seventy-five percent of the Mexican American stepfathers reported that they were Catholic, with another 20% reporting that they were non-Catholic Christians (e.g., Protestant). Nevertheless, 27% reported that they had not attended church in the past year, and 32% reported that they had attended church six or fewer times in the past year. The Mexican American stepfamilies (and their intact-family counterparts) tended to espouse traditional gender ideals in which women are seen as the primary family caregivers who should defer to their husband. For example, 56% of the stepfathers agreed that a wife should always support her husband's decisions, even if she did not agree with him. Nevertheless, due primarily to economic insecurity, over 60% of the Mexican American mothers in our stepfamilies held paying jobs. These contradictory economic and ideological pressures set up tensions in these families that were not easily resolved.

BIRTH FATHER RELATIONS

Mexican American adolescent children reported more distant or strained relations with their birth father than did Anglo children. About 20% of the Mexican American families reported that the target adolescent had no contact with a nonresident biological father; 7% had a father who had died; and another 12% did not know whether their father was still living. Almost two-thirds (64%) lived with their mother and had no overnight visits with their biological father; 25% lived with their mother but had some overnight visits with their biological father; and 11% had frequent overnights with their biological father or lived with both mother and father equally. Although only 4% of adolescents reported that they lived with their mother and father equally, 29% voiced a preference for this arrangement when asked.

Only 22% of the Mexican American stepchildren were described by their stepfather as getting along well with their birth father, with a similar proportion (20%) described as having relations with a birth dad that were "just okay." Two-thirds (68%) of the Mexican American adolescents reported that their birth father and their stepfather never had contact with each other, and an additional 19% reported that their birth father and their stepfather rarely had contact with each other. Over a third (37%) of the mothers had no contact with the birth father, and over a quarter (29%) were reported to not get along well with him. Very few of the mothers (7.6%) were described as getting along well with the birth father. The pattern that emerges from our data suggests that Mexican American stepfamilies are composed of adolescent children who are more alienated from their birth father than are their Anglo counterparts.

STEPFATHER RELATIONS

What sorts of relationships do these adolescents have with their stepfather? Our data show that these relationships tend to be very positive. Two-thirds of the adolescents (65%) strongly agreed and 21% agreed with the statement "My dad really cares about me." Similarly, 86% of Mexican American adolescents strongly agreed or agreed that they "really mattered" to their stepdad. Eighty-six percent of adolescents reported that they did fun things with their stepdad, with over 60% saying that this occurred often. Contrary to stereotypes of distant or authoritarian Latino stepfathers, 58% of the Mexican American adolescents we interviewed indicated that their stepfather hugged them, patted them on the back, or otherwise showed them physical affection. Almost half of the Mexican American adolescents (48%) reported that their stepfather often told them that he loved them, with an even larger proportion (59%) indicating that their stepfather often did things that showed that he loved them. Similarly, well over half of Mexican American adolescents (59%) reported that their stepfather remembered things that were important to them, and about half (49%) reported that their stepfather "took their side."

Mexican American stepfathers, in turn, tended to report that they had good relationships with their stepchildren: 95% reported that their relationships were "good," "very good," or "the best." Over a third of stepfathers (37%) reported that they got along "extremely well" with their stepchildren, and another half (51%) reported that they got along "pretty well." Almost two-thirds (63%) of Mexican American stepdads reported that they played a sport or other outdoor activity with a stepchild "often" or "very often," and 44% indicated that they "often" or "very often" went shopping with their children. Against the narrow stereotype of Latino fathering, 44% of Mexican

American stepfathers also indicated that they "often" or "very often" cooked or prepared a meal with their stepchild.

Mexican American stepfathers reported being very involved with their stepchildren, and most embraced the fathering role wholeheartedly. Three-fourths of Mexican American stepfathers rejected the idea that a stepfather does not have the full responsibility of being a parent, and 70% agreed that having a stepchild was just as satisfying for a stepfather as having his "own" children. Fewer than a third (29%) agreed that it was harder for a stepfather to love his stepchildren than it was for him to love his "own" children, and 62% agreed that it was just as easy for a stepfather to discipline his stepchild as his "own" children. Nevertheless, 55% agreed that raising stepchildren was hard for a stepfather because they were used to different rules. In addition, 51% of stepfathers reported that it was hard for a stepfather to get his relatives to treat his stepchild the same as his "own" children.

STEPFATHER PARENTING PRACTICES

Mexican American stepfathers were actively engaged in monitoring their stepchildren's behavior. Over half (52%) reported that they knew "everything" about where the child went and what he or she did after school, and 35% reported that they knew "most things" about where the child went and what he or she did after school. Well over half (59%) of stepfathers indicated that they knew when their stepchildren had exams or papers due at school. In line with the Mexican American tradition of instilling respect, 87% of adolescents reported that their stepfather was doing well at teaching them right from wrong and instructing them to be respectful. The vast majority of adolescents also reported that their stepfather was doing a good job of helping them to feel safe (83%) and at teaching them to be responsible (87%). Adolescents also recognized their stepfather's role in the family system: 88% said that their stepdad was doing well at being a good husband or partner to their mother. Similarly, 84% said that their stepdad was doing well at respecting their mother's parenting decisions. As a marker of the acceptance of stepfathers as authority figures, a full 30% of Mexican American adolescents indicated that they called their stepfather "Dad." Calling the stepfather "Dad" was not related to whether he was married to the mother, but was associated with having lived with the child a longer time, as well as the child having less contact with the nonresident biological father.

BARRIERS AND CHALLENGES

Stepfathers in this sample faced some special challenges. About half (49%) of the stepfathers spoke predominantly Spanish, as indicated in their choice to be interviewed in Spanish. But the sample is not one composed mostly of recent immigrants. Half of the sample fathers were born in Mexico, but over half of these men (56%) migrated to the United States before 1990. New immigrants face special challenges, but here we are describing a group of fathers with fairly long-term and stable residence in the United States, but still with a cultural heritage linked to Mexico. The Mexican American men ranged in age from 24 to 53 at the time of the interview, with a median age of 34. Over a third (35%) had a ninth-grade education or less; 20% attended some high school; 26% graduated from high school; just 19% attended some college; and fewer than 4% had earned at least a BA degree. As noted earlier, family incomes were relatively low by local standards, and the men were employed in occupations with low skill levels, high job turnover, limited benefits, and few opportunities for career advancement.

In part because of language barriers, the Mexican American stepfathers were relatively uninvolved in their stepchild's school, even though over 90% said they felt welcome at the school. Almost three-quarters (72%) reported that it was hard for parents who spoke only Spanish to communicate with teachers and other school staff, and 38% agreed that the school had different goals for their children than they did. Eighty-eight percent of stepfathers belonged to no organizations at their stepchild's school, and 44% had no interaction with their stepchild's teachers. This does not mean that the stepfathers were uninvolved in their stepchild's education: 41% reported that they talked to their stepchild about school on a daily basis, and another 29% reported that they talked to their stepchild about school on a weekly basis. Nevertheless, very few helped their children with homework on a daily (4%) or weekly (13%) basis, and over half said they rarely or never helped their children with homework, a school project, or to prepare for a test. Clearly, language barriers and the limited education of Mexican-born stepfathers limited opportunities for fulfilling the traditional father roles of educating their offspring, and few were able to build bridges to upward social mobility. The class position of the fathers limited their abilities to augment their children's out-of-school education in traditional enrichment activities, with only 32.6% reporting having ever taken the stepchild to a museum, a zoo, an aquarium, a concert, a play, or a lecture.

COMPARISON TO EUROPEAN AMERICAN STEPFATHERS

Compared to Anglo stepfamilies, as noted earlier, Mexican American stepchildren appear to have worse relations with their birth father. In addition, according to adolescent reports, Mexican American stepfathers do less parental monitoring than their Anglo counterparts but have closer marital interactions. According to Mexican American stepfathers, they do more activities with their stepchildren than do Anglo American stepfathers. On the whole, however, mean levels of father involvement and parenting in Mexican American stepfamilies look remarkably similar to mean levels of father involvement and parenting in European American stepfamilies (even though the European American stepparents are much more likely to be married to each other). Of the 21 comparisons of parenting practices between Mexican Americans and Anglo-Americans that we analyzed, only the three just noted were statistically significant. In general, we can say that patterns of parenting in these two groups are much more similar than they are different. In terms of level of stepfather involvement, amount of interaction with stepchild, quality of relationship with stepchild, and parenting style, Mexican American stepfathers and European American stepfathers looked very similar. For example, there were no significant differences across the groups in the level of acceptance or warmth, in the amount of rejection, or in the frequency of discipline by stepfathers (as assessed by children, mothers, and fathers).

PREDICTORS OF FATHER INVOLVEMENT

What leads to more involved stepfathering in Mexican American families? In part, this depends on which aspects of father involvement one considers. In general, we found that stronger husband-wife bonds and more cooperation between parents were associated with higher levels of father involvement. For example, fathers were more involved in monitoring their adolescent stepchildren if they rated high in cooperative parenting, were older, and were married. For other aspects of father involvement in parenting, however, we found that being married was surprisingly *un*related to embracing the father role. For example, Mexican American fathers and children interacted more frequently if husbands and wives spent more time interacting in shared activities (regardless of whether they were married or unmarried, acculturated or recently immigrated, rich or poor, living in small or large households). According to the evaluations of child, mother, and father, stepfathers were more involved in disciplining their stepchild if that child was a boy. Mothers and adolescents report that stepfathers show more love and nurturing to children when they are involved in more loving and nurturing relationships with their wife and partner and when they enjoy high levels of cooperative parenting. Mexican American stepfathers tend to have closer emotional and loving relationships with their stepchildren when they have cooperative parenting relationships with their female partner and when they are more accepting of ideals suggesting that men and women are equal and should have similar roles in the family. Similarly, when the romantic relationship between the mother and father is stronger and when their parenting practices are more cooperative, the father and child are likely to report that they have a better (step)father-child relationship.

We analyzed predictors of stepfather involvement in Mexican American families using multivariate models that included such demographic variables as generational status, parents' age, number of siblings, gender of child, number of extended family in the home, number of hours employed, household income, and mother's share of earnings. With very few exceptions, these factors did not predict higher or lower levels of stepfather involvement. One exception that mirrors the larger literature is that stepfathers were significantly more likely to discipline stepsons than stepdaughters. Another exception is that older fathers and those whose wife worked more hours tended to participate more actively in monitoring their stepchild. Also, there was a tendency ($p = .06$) for Mexican-born stepfathers to participate in more child monitoring than their U.S.-born Latino counterparts. Only for parental monitoring did married stepfathers have higher levels of involvement than unmarried stepfathers. In addition, we included measures specific to stepfamilies, including the age of the child when the stepfather began living in the household and whether the stepfather had children under 18 from a previous relationship who did not live in the household. These did not reach statistical significance, though there was a tendency ($p = .06$) for fathers who had children from a former relationship to do more monitoring of their stepchildren.

Finally, patterns of family work allocation appear to follow somewhat different causal pathways than the affective relationship or parenting practices. Contrary to faith-based marriage and fatherhood promotion claims in the United States, religiosity was negatively associated with fathers' share of responsibility for supervising stepchildren in multivariate models; those who were the most religious shared the least amount of direct child oversight with their wife. Those fathers who were employed fewer hours were also somewhat more likely ($p = .09$) to take on more of the child supervision. The level of stepfathers' involvement in performing housework appears to respond to practical concerns. Mexican American stepfather families in which wives earn a greater share of the household income (like their Anglo counterparts) are the most likely to have husbands who do a greater proportionate share of the housework, even when controlling for gender attitudes. Thus, when we consider time spent in child and home maintenance issues, it is likely that practical and monetary concerns are more important than gender and cultural beliefs about who should do what around the house or with the children. Even in these Mexican American families, previously characterized as being governed by traditional patriarchal divisions of household labor, we can see that family-level decisions about parenting and housework are more influenced by near-term economic influences than by gender or family ideals supposedly fixed by cultural ideals.

CHILD OUTCOMES

What child adjustment outcomes are associated with higher levels of fathering in these Mexican American stepfamilies? Findings from our preliminary analyses are quite similar to findings from previous research into these questions using nonminority samples or intact families. For example, Mexican American children's behavior problems were significantly related to the father's level of love and acceptance of the stepchild in the expected direction. Internalizing problems and externalizing problems (as rated by both mother and teacher) were higher in stepfamilies with low levels of stepfather-stepchild interaction. Similarly, rejecting patterns of parenting from the stepfather were associated with more internalizing and externalizing in stepchildren. Conversely, adolescent externalizing, internalizing, and depression were lower in families in which stepfathers showed more warmth and acceptance of stepchildren. More consistent discipline from stepfathers was also associated with less internalizing and externalizing (mother and teacher reports) and less depression (adolescent report), as well as more positive adolescent behaviors (mother report). Finally, overall relationship quality between stepfather and adolescent was associated with fewer internalizing and externalizing behaviors exhibited by the adolescent (mother and teacher reports) and more positive adolescent behaviors (mother report). According to these early findings, the effects of positive parenting appear to be remarkably similar across both family type (step and intact) and ethnicity (Anglo and Mexican American).

CONCLUSION

Our review of the literature on Mexican American stepfathers in the United States suggests that they face many special challenges, but that their involvement with stepchildren is important for several reasons. In many cases, and especially in ethnic minority populations like the Mexican American families we are studying, a stepfather can provide financial, practical, and emotional support to mothers and children. Although there are many forms of stepparenting, most are beneficial for children, and most depend on a well-functioning relationship with the children's mother.

One of the most surprising findings concerning predictors of stepfathering in Mexican American families is the relative similarity between Mexican Americans and European Americans. Similar factors associated with the husband-wife relationship and practical aspects of jobs and family life predict greater involvement of stepfathers in their children's lives. Also surprising, most of the differences we observed either within or across groups were not due to variables commonly used in previous studies. Contrary to some previous work (on other ethnic groups), being married to the mother was unrelated to being involved with the stepchildren. Similarly, income, generational status, household size, and length of relationship to the child generally did not significantly influence the pattern of father involvement.

Our findings about the effects of involved stepfathering on the mental health and overall well-being of Mexican American children are consistent. When the stepfathers were more involved, their stepchildren did much better; they were less likely to be depressed, to act out, and to internalize, and they were more likely to exhibit positive behaviors. Although the small size of our sample and the exploratory nature of our data analysis render our conclusions tentative, they are noteworthy because we know so little about this group. Hopefully more research will be conducted on stepfather families in other ethnic groups, varied social classes, and diverse regional locations in the United States. By comparing findings about these groups to those in other regions of the world we might better understand how cultural context plays a role in shaping family functioning and child adjustment. Only then will we be in a position to judge whether stepfathering patterns and processes should be considered cross-culturally relevant.

REFERENCES

Acuña, R. (2000). *Occupied America: A history of Chicanos* (4th ed.). San Francisco: Longman.

Amato, P. R. (1987). Family processes in one-parent, stepparent, and intact families: The child's point of view. *Journal of Marriage and the Family, 49,* 327–337.

Amato, P. R., & Keith, B. (1991). Parental divorce and the well-being of children: A meta-analysis. *Psychological Bulletin, 110*(1), 26–46.

Amato, P. R., & Sobolewski, J. M. (2004). The effects of divorce on fathers and children: Nonresidential fathers and stepfathers. In M. E. Lamb (Ed.), *The role of the father in child development* (4th ed., pp. 341–367). Hoboken, NJ: Wiley.

Bean, F. D., Curtis, R. L., & Marcum, J. P. (1977). Familism and marital satisfaction among Mexican Americans: The effects of family size, wife's labor force participation, and conjugal power. *Journal of Marriage and the Family, 39*(4), 759–767.

Belsky, J., Youngblade, L., & Rovine, M. (1991). Patterns of marital change and parent-child interaction. *Journal of Marriage and the Family, 52,* 487–498.

Biblarz, T. J., & Gottainer, G. (2000). Family structure and children's success: A comparison of widowed and divorced single-mother families. *Journal of Marriage and the Family, 62,* 533–548.

Biblarz, T. J., & Raferty, A. E. (1999). Family structure, educational attainment, and socioeconomic success: Rethinking the "pathology of matriarchy." *American Journal of Sociology, 105*(2), 321–365.

Bramlett, M. D., & Mosher, W. D. (2002). *Cohabitation, marriage, divorce, and remarriage in the United States.* Retrieved from www.cdc.gov/nchs/data/series/sr_23_022.pdf.

Bray, J. (1999). From marriage to remarriage and beyond: Findings from the Developmental Issues in Step-families research project. In E. M. Hetherington (Ed.),

Coping with divorce, single parenting, and remarriage: A risk and resiliency perspective (pp. 253–271). Mahwah, NJ: Erlbaum.

Bray, J., & Kelly, J. (1999). *Stepfamilies: Love, marriage, and parenting in the first decade.* New York: Broadway Books.

Buchanan, C. M., Maccoby, E. E., & Dornbusch, S. M. (1996). *Adolescents after divorce.* Cambridge, MA: Harvard University Press.

Buehler, C., & Pasley, K. (2000). Family boundary ambiguity, marital status, and child adjustment. *Journal of Early Adolescence, 20*(3), 281–308.

Bumpass, L. L. (1990). What's happening to the family? Intersection of demographic and institutional change. *Demography, 27,* 484–498.

Bumpass, L. L., Raley, R. K., & Sweet, J. A. (1995). The changing character of stepfamilies: Implications of cohabitation and nonmarital childbearing. *Demography, 32,* 425–436.

Burgoyne, J., & Clark, D. (1982). From father to step-father. In L. McKee & M. O'Brien (Eds.), *The father figure* (pp. 196–207). London: Tavistock.

Buriel, R., & DeMent, T. (1997). Immigration and sociocultural changes in Mexican, Chinese, and Vietnamese American families. In A. Booth, A. C. Crouter, & N. Landale (Eds.), *Immigration and the family: Research and policy on U.S. immigrants* (pp. 165–200). Mahwah, NJ: Erlbaum.

Cabrera, N., & Garcia Coll, C. (2004). Latino fathers: Uncharted territory in need of much exploration. In M. E. Lamb (Ed.), *The role of the father in child development* (pp. 98–120). Hoboken, NJ: Wiley.

Cabrera, N., Tamis-LeMonda, C. S., Bradley, R., Hofferth, S. L., & Lamb, K. A. (2000). Fatherhood in the 21st century. *Child Development, 71,* 127–136.

Carlson, M. J., & McLanahan, S. S. (2004). Early father involvement in fragile families. In R. D. Day & M. E. Lamb (Eds.), *Conceptualizing and measuring father involvement* (pp. 241–271). Mahwah, NJ: Erlbaum.

Cauce, A. M., & Rodriguez, M. D. (2002). Latino families myths and realities. In J. Contreras, K. A. Kerns, & A. M. Neal-Barnett (Eds.), *Latino children and families in the United States* (pp. 3–26). Westport, CT: Praeger.

Chapa, J., & Valencia, R. R. (1993). Latino population growth, demographic characteristics, and educational stagnation: An examination of recent trends. *Hispanic Journal of Behavioral Sciences, 15,* 165–187.

Cherlin, A., & Furstenberg, F. (1994). Stepfamilies in the United States: A reconsideration. *Annual Review of Sociology, 20,* 359–381.

Coleman, M., Ganong, L. H., & Fine, M. (2000). Reinvestigating remarriage: Another decade of progress. *Journal of Marriage and the Family, 62,* 1288–1307.

Coley, R. L., & Chase-Lansdale, P. L. (1999). Stability and change in paternal involvement among urban African American fathers. *Journal of Family Psychology, 13,* 1–20.

Coltrane, S., & Collins, R. (2001). *Sociology of marriage and the family: Gender, love, and property* (5th ed.). Belmont, CA: Wadsworth.

Coltrane, S., Parke, R. D., & Adams, M. (2004). Complexity of father involvement in low income Mexican American families. *Family Relations, 53,* 179–189.

Coltrane, S., & Valdez, E. O. (1993). Reluctant compliance: Work-family role allocation in dual-earner Chicano families. In J. C. Hood (Ed.), *Men, work, and family* (pp. 151–175). Newbury Park, CA: Sage.

Cotera, M. P. (1976). *Diosa y hembra: The history and heritage of Chicanas in the U.S.* Austin, TX: Information Systems Development.

Danziger, S., & Radin, N. (1990). Absent does not equal uninvolved: Predictors of fathering in teen mother families. *Journal of Marriage and the Family, 52,* 636–642.

DaVanzo, J., & Rahman, M. O. (1993). American families: Trends and correlates. *Population Index, 59*(3), 350–386.

Duncan, B., Hotz, V. J., & Trejo, S. J. (2006). Hispanics in the U.S. labor market. In M. Tienda & F. Mitchell (Eds.), *Hispanics and the future of America* (pp. 228–290). Washington, DC: National Academies Press.

Fine, M. A., & Kurdek, L. A. (1995). Relationship between marital quality and (step)-parent-child relationship quality for parents and stepparents in stepfamilies. *Journal of Family Psychology, 9,* 216–223.

Fine, M. A., Voydanoff, P., & Donnelly, B. W. (1993). Relations between parental control and warmth and child well-being in stepfamilies. *Journal of Family Psychology, 7*(2), 222–232.

Fisher, P. A., Leve, L. D., O'Leary, C. C., & Leve, C. (2003). Parental monitoring of children's behavior: Variation across stepmother, stepfather, and two-parent biological families. *Family Relations, 52*(1), 45–52.

Formoso, D., Gonzales, N. A., Barrera, M., & Dumka, L. E. (2007). Interparental relations, maternal employment, and fathering in Mexican American families. *Journal of Marriage and Family, 69,* 26–39.

Furstenberg, F. F. (1987). The new extended family: The experience of parents and children after remarriage. In K. Pasley & M. Ihinger-Tallman (Eds.), *Remarriage and stepparenting: Current research and theory* (pp. 42–61). New York: Guilford Press.

Furstenberg, F. F., & Cherlin, A. (1991). *Divided families: What happens to children when parents part?* Cambridge, MA: Harvard University Press.

Galatzer-Levy, R. M. (2001). Stepfathers: Clinical explorations. In S. H. Cath & M. Shopper (Eds.), *Stepparenting: Creating and recreating families in America today* (pp. 127–142). Hillsdale, NJ: Analytic Press.

Gonzales, N. A., Knight, G. P., Morgan-Lopez, A., Saenz, D. S., & Sirolli, A. (2001). Acculturation, enculturation and the mental health of Latino youths: An integration and critique of the literature. In J. Contreras, K. A. Kerns, & A. M. Neal-Barnett (Eds.), *Latino children and families in the United States* (pp. 45–74). Westport, CT: Praeger.

Gottman, J. M. (1998). Toward a process model of men in marriages and families. In A. Booth & A. C. Crouter (Eds.), *Men in families: When do they get involved? What difference does it make?* (pp. 149–192). Mahwah, NJ: Erlbaum.

Griswold del Castillo, R. (1984). *La familia: Chicano families in the urban southwest, 1848 to the present.* Notre Dame, IN: University of Notre Dame Press.

Gutierrez, D. G. (1995). *Walls and mirrors: Mexican Americans, Mexican immigrants, and the politics of ethnicity.* Berkeley: University of California Press.

Hetherington, E. M. (1988). Parents, children, and siblings: Six years after divorce. In R. A. Hinde & J. Sevenson-Hinde (Eds.), *Relationships within families: Mutual influences* (pp. 311–331). Oxford: Clarendon Press.

Hetherington, E. M. (1993). An overview of the Virginia Longitudinal Study of Divorce and Remarriage with a focus on early adolescence. *Journal of Family Psychology, 7,* 39–96.

Hetherington, E. M. (2006). The influence of conflict, marital problem solving and parenting on children's adjustment in nondivorced, divorced, and remarried families. In A. Clarke-Stewart & J. Dunn (Eds.), *Families count: Effects on child and adolescent development* (pp. 203–237). New York: Cambridge University Press.

Hetherington, E. M., Bridges, M., & Insabella, G. M. (1998). What matters? What does not? Five perspectives on the association between marital transitions and children's adjustment. *American Psychologist, 53,* 167–184.

Hetherington, E. M., & Clingempeel, W. G. (Eds.). (1992). *Coping with marital transitions: A family systems perspective.* Chicago: University of Chicago Press for the Society for Research in Child Development.

Hetherington, E. M., & Jodl, K. M. (1994). Stepfamilies as settings for child development. In A. Booth & J. Dunn (Eds.), *Stepfamilies: Who benefits? Who does not?* (pp. 55–79). Hillsdale, NJ: Erlbaum.

Hetherington, E. M., & Stanley-Hagan, M. M. (2002). Parenting in divorced and remarried families. In M. H. Bornstein (Ed.), *Handbook of parenting: Vol. 3. Being and becoming a parent* (pp. 287–315). Mahwah, NJ: Erlbaum.

Hofferth, S. L. (2003). Race/ethnic differences in father involvement in two-parent families: Culture, context, or economy. *Journal of Family Issues, 24,* 185–216.

Hofferth, S. L., & Anderson, K. G. (2003). Are all dads equal? Biology versus marriage as a basis for paternal investment. *Journal of Marriage and the Family, 65,* 213–232.

Hofferth, S. L., Pleck, J., Stueve, J. L., Bianchi, S., & Sayer, L. (2002). The demography of fathers: What fathers do. In C. S. Tamis-LeMonda & N. Cabrera (Eds.), *Handbook of father involvement* (pp. 63–90). Mahwah, NJ: Erlbaum.

Hondagneu-Sotelo, P., & Avila, E. (1997). "I'm here, but I'm there": The meanings of Latina transnational motherhood. *Gender and Society, 11,* 548–571.

Kane, E. W. (1992). Race, gender, and attitudes toward gender stratification. *Social Psychology Quarterly, 55,* 311–320.

Keefe, S. E., & Padilla, A. M. (1987). *Chicano ethnicity.* Albuquerque: University of New Mexico Press.

Kim, J. E., Hetherington, E. M., & Reiss, D. (1999). Associations among family relationships, antisocial peers, and adolescents' externalizing behaviors: Gender and family type differences. *Child Development, 70,* 1209–1230.

King, V. (1994). Nonresident father involvement and child well-being: Can dads make a difference? *Journal of Family Issues, 15,* 78–96.

King, V. (2006). The antecedents and consequences of adolescents' relationships with stepfathers and nonresident fathers. *Journal of Marriage and the Family, 68,* 910–928.

King, V., Harris, K. M., & Heard, H. E. (2004). Racial and ethnic diversity in nonresident father involvement. *Journal of Marriage and the Family, 66*(1), 1–21.

Landale, N. S., & Oropesa, R. S. (2001). Father involvement in the lives of mainland Puerto Rican children: Contributions of nonresident, cohabiting and married fathers. *Social Forces, 79,* 945–968.

Logan, J. R., & Spitze, G. (1996). *Family ties: Enduring relations between parents and their grown children.* Philadelphia: Temple University Press.

Love, K. M., & Murdock, T. B. (2004). Attachment to parents and psychological well-being: An examination of young adult college students in intact families and stepfamilies. *Journal of Family Psychology, 18*(4), 600–608.

Manning, W. D., & Lamb, K. A. (2003). Adolescent well-being in cohabiting, married, and single-parent families. *Journal of Marriage and the Family, 65,* 876–893.

Marsiglio, W. (1991). Paternal engagement activities with minor children. *Journal of Marriage and the Family, 53,* 973–986.

Marsiglio, W. (1995). Stepfathers with minor children living at home: Parenting perceptions and relationship quality. In W. Marsiglio (Ed.), *Fatherhood: Contemporary theory, research, and social policy* (pp. 211–229). Thousand Oaks, CA: Sage.

Marsiglio, W. (2004a). *Stepdads: Stories of love, hope, and repair.* Lanham, MD: Rowman & Littlefield.

Marsiglio, W. (2004b). When stepfathers claim stepchildren: A conceptual analysis. *Journal of Marriage and the Family, 66,* 22–39.

Marsiglio, W., Day, R. D., & Lamb, M. E. (2000). Exploring fatherhood diversity: Implications for conceptualizing father involvement. *Marriage and Family Review, 29*(4), 269–293.

McKee, L., & O'Brien, M. (Eds.). (1982). *The father figure.* London: Tavistock.

McLanahan, S. S., & Sandefur, G. D. (1994). *Growing up with a single parent.* Cambridge, MA: Harvard University Press.

McLoyd, V. C., Cauce, A. M., Takeuchi, D., & Wilson, L. (2000). Marital processes and parental socialization in families of color: A decade review of research. *Journal of Marriage and the Family, 62,* 1070–1093.

Mirandé, A. (1997). *Hombres y machos.* Boulder, CO: Westview Press.

Moore, M. R., & Chase-Lansdale, P. L. (2001). Sexual intercourse and pregnancy among African American adolescent girls in high poverty neighborhoods: The role of family and perceived community involvement. *Journal of Marriage and the Family, 63,* 1146–1157.

Nicholson, J. M., Fergusson, D. M., & Horwood, L. J. (1999). Effects on later adjustment of living in a stepfamily during childhood and adolescence. *Journal of Child Psychology and Psychiatry and Allied Disciplines, 40*(3), 405–416.

Oropesa, R. S. (1996). Normative beliefs about marriage and cohabitation: A comparison on non-Latino Whites, Mexican Americans, and Puerto Ricans. *Journal of Marriage and the Family, 58,* 49–62.

Parke, R. D. (1981). *Fathers.* Cambridge, MA: Harvard University Press.

Parke, R. D. (1996). *Fatherhood.* Cambridge, MA: Harvard University Press.

Phares, V. (1997). Psychological adjustment, maladjustment, and father-child relationships. In M. E. Lamb (Ed.), *The role of the father in child development* (pp. 261–283). New York: Wiley.

Pleck, J. H. (1997). Paternal involvement: Levels, sources, and consequences. In M. E. Lamb (Ed.), *The role of the father in child development* (pp. 67–103). New York: Wiley.

Proctor, B., & Dalaker, J. (2002). *Current population reports: Poverty in the United States, 2001.* Washington, DC: U.S. Census Bureau.

Reimers, C. (2006). Economic well-being. In M. Tienda & F. Mitchell (Eds.), *Hispanics and the future of America* (pp. 291–361). Washington, DC: National Academies Press.

Ross, C. E., & Mirowsky, J. (1999). Parental divorce, life-course disruption, and adult depression. *Journal of Marriage and the Family, 61,* 1034–1045.

Rumbaut, R. G., & Portes, A. (2001). *Ethnicities: Children of immigrants in America.* Berkeley: University of California Press.

Russell, A., & Searcy, E. (1997). The contribution of affective reactions and relationship qualities to adolescents' reported responses to parents. *Journal of Social and Personal Relationships, 14*(4), 539–548.

Sander, W. (1993). Catholicism and marriage in the United States. *Demography, 30*(3), 373–384.

Seltzer, J. A. (1991). Relationships between fathers and children who live apart: The father's role after separation. *Journal of Marriage and the Family, 53,* 79–101.

Seltzer, J. A., & Bianchi, S. M. (1988). Children's contact with absent parents. *Journal of Marriage and the Family, 50,* 663–677.

Stack, C. B. (1974). *All our kin: Strategies for survival in a Black community.* New York: Harper & Row.

Stewart, S. D. (2005). Boundary ambiguity in stepfamilies. *Journal of Family Issues, 26,* 1002–1029.

Stewart, S. D. (2007). *Brave new stepfamilies: Diverse paths toward stepfamily living.* Thousand Oaks, CA: Sage.

Tafolla, C. (1985). *To split a human: Mitos, machos y la mujer Chicana.* San Antonio, TX: Mexican American Cultural Center.

Taylor, P. L., Tucker, M. B., & Mitchell-Kernan, C. (1999). Ethnic variations in perceptions of men's provider role. *Psychology of Women Quarterly, 23,* 741–761.

Teachman, J. D. (2000). Diversity of family structure: Economic and social influences. In D. Demo, K. Allen, & M. Fine (Eds.), *Handbook of family diversity* (pp. 32–58). New York: Oxford University Press.

Toth, J. F., & Xu, X. (1999). Ethnic and cultural diversity in father's involvement: A racial/ethnic comparison of African American, Hispanic, and White fathers. *Youth and Society, 31,* 76–99.

U.S. Census Bureau. (2003). *Current population reports: The Hispanic population in the United States: March 2002.* Washington, DC: U.S. Government Printing Office.

Vuchinich, S., Hetherington, E. M., Vuchinich, R., & Clingempeel, W. G. (1991). Parent-child interaction and gender differences in early adolescents' adaptation to stepfamilies. *Developmental Psychology, 27,* 618–626.

White, L., & Gilbreth, J. G. (2001). When children have two fathers: Effects of relationships with stepfathers and noncustodial fathers on adolescent outcomes. *Journal of Marriage and the Family, 63,* 155–167.

Zavella, P. (1987). *Women's work and Chicano families: Cannery workers of the Santa Clara valley.* Ithaca, NY: Cornell University Press.

Zinn, M. B., & Wells, B. (2000). Diversity within Latino families: New lessons for family social science. In D. H. Demo, K. R. Allen, & M. A. Fine (Eds.), *Handbook of family diversity* (pp. 252–273). New York: Oxford University Press.

DYNAMICS WITHIN STEPFAMILY HOUSEHOLDS

CHAPTER 6

Stepfathers in Families

JEREMY ROBERTSON

INCREASES IN rates of cohabitation, birth outside marriage, separation and divorce, and repartnering have focused the attention of researchers on the impact of these family transitions on children's well-being. It has been estimated that about a third of all U.S. children will live with a stepparent before reaching adulthood (Amato & Sobolewski, 2004; Bumpass, Raley, & Sweet, 1995) and that 30% of mothers in Great Britain will live in a stepfamily before their 45th birthday (Ermisch & Francesconi, 1996). As most children remain with their mother after parental separation, the typical experience for children is to have a stepfather residing in their household. In comparison, stepmothers are less likely to have resident stepchildren and tend to exercise their stepparenting role to visiting stepchildren (Bumpass et al., 1995; Haskey, 1994).

There is evidence of a range of negative outcomes for children living in stepfamilies compared to those living with both biological parents. For example, stepchildren tend to have more health and behavior problems; adolescents in stepfamilies tend to leave home and school earlier, engage in sexual activity earlier, and have a greater likelihood of being involved in criminal activity (Amato & Keith, 1991; Coleman, Ganong, & Fine, 2000). Research also indicates that stepchildren are at a greater risk of both physical and sexual abuse (Giles-Sims, 1997; Sariola & Uutela, 1996). With regard to stepfamily functioning, Bray and Hetherington (1993, p. 5) summarized the results of past research: "Stepfamilies are described as less cohesive, more problematic, and more stressful than first marriages. . . . Stepparent-child and sibling relationships are characterized as more negative and distant and less warm and involved."

It has been proposed that many of these negative outcomes arise not only from the effects of parental separation, but also from the disruptive effect of a stepfather entering the household (Coleman et al., 2000). Differences between stepfathers and biological fathers in levels of involvement, warmth, supervision, aspirations, and parenting practices (Coleman et al., 2000; Hofferth & Anderson, 2003) have been suggested as possible explanations for these outcomes. Other possible factors include those often associated with stepfamily formation, such as the impact of changes in residence, changes in schools, disruption of extra-household relationships (e.g., friends and extended family), differences in employment patterns, and changes in economic circumstances.

We can estimate the chances of a mother and child living in a stepfamily, but we have rather less information on the chances of a man living in a stepfamily at some time in his adult life (Juby & LeBourdais, 1998). Relatively little is therefore known about the relationship histories of those men who become stepfathers and how these influence their approach to stepparenting. While we now have a sizable body of research on children's adjustment in stepfamilies, there is relatively little research that explores stepfathers' adjustment and their experiences and perceptions of stepfamily life (Bray & Kelly, 1999; Burgoyne & Clarke, 1984; Marsiglio, 1992, 2004; Marsiglio & Hinojosa, 2007).

It is likely that forming a relationship with a new partner who has children raises a number of challenges for both stepfathers and other family members. While developing a close relationship with his new partner, a stepfather must also form a relationship with her children. Because the new partner and her children have developed their own routines, a stepfather must also work to either integrate into these routines or negotiate new ones. Issues such as degree of parenting involvement, involvement in control and discipline, standards of behavior for children, allocation of household tasks, and management of money are but some of the issues stepfathers must negotiate. In addition, there are often extra-household relationships to be considered, for example, contact with his nonresident children, contact between stepchildren and their nonresident parent, contact with the nonresident parent's extended family (usually paternal grandparents), and relationships with ex-partners.

Earlier studies of stepfamilies often relied on clinical reports (or samples), which resulted in small heterogeneous samples containing a high proportion of stepfamilies with relationship problems (Dawson, 1991; Santrock, Sitterle, & Warshak, 1988). Other samples were recruited from stepfamily associations (Fine & Kurdek, 1994). Although they help to identify many of the issues just noted, there are potential problems with the bias in these samples. Participating in therapy and joining a stepfamily association are both more likely in families that are experiencing difficulties (Coleman et al., 2000). In addition, these are often families who have taken on a stepfamily identity. This raises the question of the extent to which these stepfather adjustment issues are problematic for community samples of stepfather stepfamilies. It could be the case that in more representative samples most stepfathers and stepfamilies have been able to negotiate these issues without negative effects on family functioning.

This chapter briefly reviews research on stepfathers' adjustment, relationships, engagement in parenting, and perceptions of their role. Following this review, results from a U.K. study of stepfamilies is presented (see also Chapter 7), focusing on stepfathers' reports of their experiences. Using a representative community sample, the study describes the diversity of stepfathers' backgrounds, their experiences of aspects of stepfamily life, and their perceptions of their role within a stepfamily. These results give an indication of how stepfathers themselves see their place within the stepfamily. It also provides some indication of how common some of these experiences and perceptions are in a nonclinical sample.

DEFINING STEPFAMILIES AND STEPFATHERS

Trying to provide a simple definition of a stepfamily is difficult because of the great diversity and potential complexity of family relationships in stepfamilies. At core is the idea that a couple has formed a relationship in which one or both of the partners have children from a previous relationship. However, such a relationship can exist in a number of variations, depending on such factors as the gender of the stepparent, who has children (his, hers, and theirs), the relationship history of either partner (e.g., previously married, never partnered, cohabiting or romantically attached but not living together), and where the children reside (e.g., full time, shared, or visiting). These variations in stepfamily type may have a significant influence on stepfamily functioning. For example, it has been found that relationships in stepmother stepfamilies are generally more problematic and that complex stepfamilies do less well than simple stepfamilies (e.g., J. Dunn, Davies, O'Connor, & Sturgess, 2000).

Previous stepfamily research has also tended to focus on married stepfamilies (e.g., Fine, Ganong, & Coleman, 1997; Fine & Kurdek, 1995; Hetherington, 1993; Kurdek & Fine, 1991; Santrock et al., 1988). However, there is increasing recognition that cohabiting stepfamilies now make up a significant proportion of stepfamilies (Cherlin & Furstenberg, 1994; J. Dunn, Deater-Deckard, Pickering, O'Connor, & Golding, 1998; Ferri & Smith, 1998; MacDonald & DeMaris, 1996). Although half of cohabiting stepfamilies are thought to proceed to marriage (Bumpass et al., 1995), there may be important differences in family functioning between married and cohabiting stepfamilies. With increasing recognition of stepfamily diversity, it is important to include these cohabiting stepfamilies in future research.

RESEARCH ON STEPFATHERS

This section briefly reviews research on stepfathers' adjustment and perceptions of stepfamily life. I concentrate on research that has explored stepfathers' perceptions of their roles and relationships within the stepfamily, rather than studies that have relied on mothers' or children's reports.

Stepfather Well-Being

Findings with regard to stepfather well-being in stepfamilies are mixed (Coleman et al., 2000). Although there are studies that suggest there are differences in rates of psychological ill health between fathers and stepfathers (e.g., Hetherington & Clingempeel, 1992), others have found no difference in reported well-being (Lansford, Ceballo, Abbey, & Stewart, 2001).

However, a number of recent studies done in the United Kingdom have identified a higher incidence of depressive symptomatology in stepfathers. Ferri and Smith (1998) found that stepfathers were twice as likely to score high on a measure of vulnerability to depression compared to fathers in first families (12% versus 5%). In another U.K. study, Deater-Deckard, Pickering, Dunn, and Golding (1998) found that stepfathers who had recently experienced the birth of a child had a rate of depression just over twice that for a comparable group of fathers in first families. This increased rate of depression appeared to be mediated by their partner's level of depressive symptoms, the stepfather's educational level, the number of life events experienced, the extent of social support and social network, and the level of aggression in the relationship.

It has been suggested that heightened levels of depression may be associated with less involvement in parenting by stepfathers (Blair & Hardesty, 1994), may reflect selection factors (Coleman et al., 2000), or may be a reflection of stepfamily stresses, possibly as a result of conflict arising from high levels of stepfather parenting (Ferri & Smith, 1998). It is possible that a number of these processes are at work, with preexisting mental health problems leading to less parental involvement and measures of current distress reflecting stepfamily conflict over parenting by highly involved stepfathers.

Stepfather Relationships with Partners

The quality of stepfathers' relationships with both their partner (i.e., the marital[1] relationship) and her children have been central to most of the

---

[1] In this chapter I use the phrase "marital relationship" to refer to both married and cohabiting couples.

research on stepfamilies. These relationships are seen as pivotal in explaining stepfamily adjustment and stepchild well-being and are explored in greater depth in other chapters in this volume.

With regard to the stepfather-partner relationship, the research findings on the quality of the marital relationship in stepfamilies are mixed (Coleman et al., 2000). Early research indicated that those who were remarried were likely to report lower marital satisfaction, although the practical effect was small (Vemer, Coleman, Ganong, & Cooper, 1989). Research also found a greater probability of divorce for those who remarried (Booth & Edwards, 1992). However, not all those who remarry have children, and there is a large group of stepfamilies in which the partners are not married (Cherlin & Furstenberg, 1994). Caution must be taken in applying to stepfamilies the results of research that has compared remarried to first-married couples. More recent research comparing reports of stepfathers to fathers in first families found no difference in relationship quality, satisfaction with the relationship, or disagreements with a partner (Lansford et al., 2001).

Some studies suggest a difference in the nature of the marital relationship for stepfamilies compared to first families. Bray and Hetherington (1993, p. 5) concluded, from their respective research studies, that remarried couples view their relationship as "more open in communication with a greater willingness to confront conflict, more pragmatic and less romantic, and more egalitarian with respect to child rearing and housekeeping roles." This greater openness does not necessarily lead to greater conflict or disagreement. For example, Acock and Demo (1994) found that remarried mothers in stepfamilies actually reported fewer arguments over household tasks, money, time spent together, their sexual relationship, and in-laws. MacDonald and DeMaris (1995) also report that remarriage did not result in an increase in the frequency of open disagreements between spouses compared to couples in first marriages. In fact, if both partners were remarried, disagreements were fewer than if only one partner had been previously married. MacDonald and DeMaris concluded, "Contrary to our expectations, our findings suggest that remarriage and stepchildren are not necessarily associated with more frequent marital conflict, and in some cases are associated with less frequent conflict" (p. 387).

In contrast to these findings, recent research from a U.K. sample has reported higher levels of disagreement in stepfamilies. Ferri and Smith (1998) reported that stepfathers were not as happy with their relationship with their partner and with "life so far" compared to fathers in first families. They also reported more disagreement over child care and household tasks compared to those in first families.

Bray and Berger's (1993) longitudinal study provides important information on the changing nature of the association between the marital relationship and parenting. They found that stepfamilies who had been re-married for 6 months had happier relationships when stepfathers were not expected to assume a parental role or form close relationships with step-children (see also Hetherington, Cox, & Cox, 1982). However, 2.5 years after remarriage, marital adjustment was more satisfactory when stepfathers had formed closer relationships with stepchildren. Surprisingly, after 5 years of remarriage, stepparent roles were again no longer associated with marital adjustment. In part, these results may reflect the aging of the stepchildren, with children in adolescence requiring less active parenting and mothers needing different forms of parenting support from stepfathers.

Differences in findings with regard to the marital relationship may reflect what is being measured (e.g., satisfaction, communication, disagreements), who is reporting (e.g., mother or stepfather), how it is measured (e.g., self-report or observation), and who is being compared (e.g., remarried versus first married, stepfather versus father).

Stepfather Relationships with Stepchildren

The stepfather-stepchild relationship has received considerable attention from researchers. Findings generally indicate that most relationships are positive, although on average they are rated lower than relationships between fathers and their children (Hofferth et al., 2007; Pryor, this volume). The quality of the stepfather-stepchild relationship potentially depends on a number of factors, including the age of the child, the child's gender, how old the child was when the stepfamily formed, contact with the nonresident father, stepfamily complexity (e.g., presence of other children in the household), and the stepfather's and partner's relationship history and mental health (Dunn et al., 2000). Relationships have also been shown to change over time and generally become more problematic as children reach adolescence (Bray & Kelly, 1999; Hetherington, 1993; Hetherington & Clingempeel, 1992).

Hetherington and Stanley-Hagan (2000, p. 187) conclude that it is better for stepfathers to start with a "warm, supportive friendship" with their step-children and "to engage in control and discipline only through their support of mothers' parenting efforts." Initially stepfathers are similar to fathers in terms of their positivity toward their stepchildren but engage in less monitoring and control of the stepchildren (Bray & Kelly, 1999; Hetherington & Clingempeel, 1992). The subsequent development of stepfathers' parenting depends on the age, and possibly the gender, of the stepchildren. For younger stepchildren the relationship tends to improve for boys, whilst that with girls continues to be problematic. Boys may benefit from stepfathers increasing their involvement in monitoring and control, in contrast to the situation with older stepchildren, where levels of monitoring and control remain low and are likely to be resented.

There is also evidence that stepchildren play an active role in shaping their stepfather's behavior and his relationship with them. Using longitudinal data, Hetherington (1993; Hetherington & Clingempeel, 1992; O'Connor, Hetherington, & Clingempeel, 1997) found that stepchildren's externalizing and negative behavior led to later increases in negative behavior in stepfathers. On the other hand, stepfathers' behavior was less effective in leading to subsequent changes in stepchildren's behavior (Hetherington & Clingempeel, 1992).

More frequent contact with their nonresident father results in children feeling closer to him (Peterson & Zill, 1986), but does not appear to affect the quality of their relationship with their stepfather (Dunn, Cheng, O'Connor, & Bridges, 2003; White & Gilbreth, 2001). However, there has been little research to date on the effect of this contact on stepfathers' involvement in parenting activities. At the very least, frequent contact between the stepchild and his or her nonresident father reduces the time available for stepfather-stepchild interactions. Contact may also lead stepfathers to feel less inclined to take on an active parenting role. Fathers may also resent stepfathers' parenting efforts and make it difficult for stepfathers to take on a parenting role. On the other hand, Hetherington, Cox, and Cox (1982) found that half the nonresident fathers in their study approved of their ex-wife's new partner, which suggests that there may be some support from nonresident fathers for stepfathers' parenting involvement. It may be important to consider the nature of the parenting activities, with disciplinary activities more likely to meet with nonresident fathers' opposition.

Stepfather Parental Engagement

There has been an increasing body of research on stepfathers' participation in household and parenting activities. This research suggests that compared to fathers in first families, stepfathers are less involved in activities with their stepchildren, on average, than fathers are with their children (Cooksey & Fondell, 1996; Hofferth et al., 2007; Lansford et al., 2001). With regard to general household activities (e.g., cooking, household maintenance), the findings suggest that stepfathers are just as involved as fathers (Acock & Demo, 1994; Ferri & Smith, 1998) and possibly more so. In their study, Ishi-Kuntz and Coltrane (1992, p. 229) concluded that although not reaching statistical significance, "on average, all types of remarried households tend to share more housework than their first-married counterparts." As in first families, however, mothers still do most of the housework (Coltrane, 1996; Demo & Acock, 1993; Sullivan, 1997).

Comparing means can be misleading, as there is considerable variation in stepfathers' engagement (e.g., Ferri & Smith, 1998) and a substantial proportion of stepfathers participate fully in parenting and household activities. For example, Ahrons and Wallisch (1987) found that about one quarter of the stepfathers in their sample were considered to be "very" involved in stepparenting, while just under one fifth had a "very low" level of involvement. Hetherington, Cox, and Cox (1982) also report that stepfathers in their study tended either to be disengaged from parenting or "they were extremely actively involved." This greater variability may be the result of a number of factors unique to the stepfathering context, including stepfathers' own family and relationship history (Cooksey & Fondell, 1996), their partner's relationship history (Sullivan, 1997), previous experience as a parent (Hetherington & Stanley-Hagan, 2000), time trade-offs with visiting biological children, stepchildren's contact with their nonresident parent, the development of the current relationship, and the stepfathers' and their partner's perceptions of the stepfather role (Marsiglio, 1992). As with parenting by biological fathers (Pleck, 1997), levels of parenting involvement by stepfathers is likely to be multiply determined.

What is largely unknown is the ways roles are negotiated and how they vary with the development of the stepfamily. For example, there has been some discussion in the literature on "gatekeeping" by mothers (Allen & Hawkins, 1999), including mothers in stepfamilies (Marsiglio, 2004). Mothers may limit stepfathers' engagement with the stepchildren, particularly with regard to discipline. On the other hand, mothers may also encourage and direct stepfathers' parenting. The process of negotiating roles may be explicit (e.g., family meetings to discuss issues) or involve implicit understandings reached between partners with minimal discussion. Some stepfamilies may discuss issues prior to cohabitation, whereas others may discuss issues only when, or if, difficulties arise.

Stepfather Roles

The perceptions of stepfamily members have been an area of interest to stepfamily researchers, particularly as these may be associated with relationship quality and stepfamily functioning. A number of studies have sought to examine the perceptions of stepfamily members concerning the role of the stepfather (Fine, Coleman, & Ganong, 1998; Fine et al., 1997; Kurdek & Fine, 1991; Marsiglio, 1992, 2004). As in first families, perceptions of roles within families may differ among stepfamily members, and these differing perceptions may lead to problems with stepfamily adjustment, although there is perhaps greater room for differing role perceptions given the lack of clear social norms or expectations for stepfamilies (Cherlin, 1978). This lack of behavioral norms can lead to difficulties with stepfamily adjustment, including problems in arranging and negotiating child care and household tasks. In addition, "family space" often has to include other households, for example, that of nonresident children or of absent parents. Without guidelines for dealing with this added complexity, stepfamilies are susceptible to conflict across households (MacDonald & DeMaris, 1995).

Research has found that the behaviors expected of stepparents are less clear than those for parents (role clarity; Fine et al., 1998). It is generally agreed, however, that stepparents are not expected to do everything that parents do (Coleman & Ganong, 1997; Fine, 1995). Bray, Berger, and Boethel (1994) report that parents and stepparents in the same family generally agree on stepfamily roles and on child-rearing arrangements. In fact, in their study there was more consensus on these roles than there was between first-marriage spouses. Adult stepfamily members felt it was more acceptable for stepparents to assume a parental role than did parents in first-marriage families (when asked about stepparent roles). Stepfathers are expected to be supportive of mothers and friendly toward stepchildren but not to act as the stepchild's primary disciplinarian (Fine et al., 1998).

Stepfathers have also been found to vary in their agreement with statements regarding stepparenting roles and behaviors (Fine & Kurdek, 1995; Marsiglio, 1992). For example, Marsiglio found that 52% of stepfathers disagreed with the notion that it is harder to love stepchildren than your own children, and 33% reported that it was at least somewhat true that they were more like a friend than a parent to their stepchildren. In this study stepfathers were most likely to report "fatherlike" perceptions when they (a) had both step- and biological children resident in the household, (b) became a stepfather to younger children, and (c) were happy with their marital or cohabiting partner. Stepfathers with more fatherlike perceptions of their role also reported having a better relationship with their stepchild. Given the cross-sectional nature of the data, it is not clear whether these fatherlike perceptions preceded the development of the relationship with the stepchild or were the result of a close relationship.

The clarity of the stepparent role for stepfathers has been found to be related to aspects of stepfathers' satisfaction with stepfamily life. Kurdek and Fine (1991) report that stepfathers' cognitions, especially their reports of role ambiguity, were related to their satisfaction with their relationship with their stepchildren. A study by Fine et al. (1997) found that positive stepfather outcomes were related to (a) stepfathers' perceptions that they frequently engaged in parenting behaviors and that they should engage in these behaviors; (b) small discrepancies between the way they actually behaved and their standards of how they should behave as a stepfather, particularly with respect to the warmth dimension of parenting; and (c) role clarity.

A further issue with regard to stepfathers is the difficulty of having to balance different roles. Role strain may exist when a stepfather is required to fulfill a number of different, and potentially conflicting, roles (Hetherington & Stanley-Hagan, 2000). A common difficulty for stepfathers, especially those in "complex" stepfamilies, concerns the challenge of fulfilling the role of parent to their own children and of "parent figure" to their stepchildren (Hetherington & Stanley-Hagan, 2000).

Research has also focused on the possible effects of negative public perceptions and attitudes toward stepfathers (Ganong & Coleman, 1997). Stepfamily life and stepparenting are the subject of a number of commonly held myths, the "wicked" stepmother and the abusing stepfather being the classic examples (Ganong & Coleman, 1997). However, there is relatively little research on the prevalence of these myths and stereotypes or on stepfathers' direct experience of negative treatment, or on their effect on stepfamilies and stepfathers themselves. For example, it is not known if the stereotype of the stepfather as a possible abuser impacts stepfathers' propensity to engage in intimate parenting behaviors (e.g., bathing or dressing stepchildren) or to express affection to their stepchildren.

THE U.K. NEW STEPFAMILIES STUDY

The data presented here come from an English study of a community sample of newly formed stepfamilies (Smith, Robertson, Dixon, Quigley, & Whitehead, 2001).[2] This study focused on recently formed stepfamilies because this is generally a time when family roles and routines are being negotiated (Bray & Berger, 1993; Hetherington, 1993). Focusing on established stepfamilies, those that have been together for many years, is likely to bias samples toward stepfamilies that function well, as poorly functioning stepfamilies tend to select themselves out of such samples.

The study gave a short questionnaire to parents of schoolchildren to identify children living in stepfamilies. The questionnaire asked about changes children had experienced in the past 4 years, including changes in household and parent figures. Of the 101 schools in London approached to take part in the study, 78% agreed to participate. All children between 7 and 11 years of age in the school were given a questionnaire to

[2] The U.K. New Stepfamilies Study was funded by the U.K. Department of Health, whose support is gratefully acknowledged. Any views expressed in this chapter, however, are those of the author and not necessarily those of the Department of Health.

take home to their parent or guardian. Of the 16,453 questionnaires sent out, 60% were returned. Most children were living with both parents (70%); a further 21% lived with one parent (mostly a mother). Seven percent of the children were currently living in a stepfamily (either cohabiting or married), mostly with a stepfather, and a few children (0.7%) lived with other parental figures (e.g., foster parents or grandparents). These figures are similar to those found in an analysis of U.K. national population data (Haskey, 1994).

The study focused on recently formed stepfamilies (couples who had been together between 1 and 4 years) with at least one resident stepchild between 7 and 11 years of age. All families who, based on the screening questionnaire, appeared to meet these criteria and who had indicated an interest in hearing about the study (83% of stepfather families) were contacted by the researchers. Visits were made to explain the research. The biological parent was interviewed in just over 60% of those stepfamilies contacted and found to be eligible (the refusal rate was somewhat lower than 40% as some stepfamilies were not contacted or an interview could not be arranged before the end of the study). This chapter reports on the 111 stepfamilies in which the stepfather and mother were interviewed separately (Smith reports on the findings from the larger sample of interviews with mothers in Chapter 7).

Semi-structured, interviewer-led interviews were conducted with the mothers, stepfathers, and children. These followed the format described by Graham and Rutter (1968), with different sorts of questions and probes used to elicit information on actual events or behavior, compared to those used to elicit feelings or attitudes. The interview was precoded; in addition, actual responses or quotes from interviewees were recorded where these were apposite or where unexpected or unusual views were expressed. Categories used to code interview material were derived from previous interview measures (e.g., the Maudsley marital rating [Quinton, Rutter, & Rowlands, 1976] and symptom score [Smith & Jenkins, 1991]), from a review of the relevant stepfamily literature, and from pilot interviews.

Interviews with mothers and stepfathers were similar, covering family demographics, quality of relationships (e.g., couple, mother-child, and stepfather-stepchild), family functioning, current relationship history, previous relationships, contact with nonresident parents, visiting by nonresident children, stepchild behavior, parenting activities, stepfather health, and perceptions of roles. To avoid social desirability biases, reference to stepfamilies and relationships was kept to a minimum and terms used by interviewers to identify stepfamily members were those used by interviewees.

Table 6.1

Characteristics of Stepfathers in U.K. New Stepfamilies Study

Characteristics	Percentage
Age	35.9 (*SD* 7.5) range 19 to 57 years
Ethnicity (percent non-White/European)	14
Educational qualifications:	
None	17
CSE	14
O level	29
A level and above	40
Marital status:	
Cohabiting	62
Married	38
Number of stepchildren:	
1	20
2	49
3 plus	31
New children of this relationship	33
Stepfather has previous children	41 (34% nonresident, 7% some resident)

FINDINGS

Family Structure

There was considerable diversity in the stepfamilies interviewed. Table 6.1 presents basic demographic information on the stepfathers and stepfamilies. Focusing first on resident children, 60% of stepfamilies had only stepchildren resident in the household; 33% also included a new child of the current relationship, as well as the stepchildren; and in 7% of stepfamilies at least one of the stepfather's children from a previous relationship was also resident. Forty-one percent of stepfathers had children from a previous relationship, with most of these children being resident in their mother's household. Comparison with findings of a U.K. cohort study (Ferri & Smith, 1998) indicated that the current sample contained more cohabiting couples and fewer new children of the relationship, although there were similar proportions of stepfathers with previous children. These differences may principally be due to the restriction on length of relationship in the current study, compared to Ferri and Smith's lack of such restriction.

Previous Relationships and Children

Stepfathers entered the stepfamily having experienced a variety of previous cohabiting relationships (of 3 months or more). Although 32% had never previously cohabited or married and 38% had only one previous cohabitation or marriage, almost 33% of the men had had more than one period of cohabitation or marriage (and some had had 10 or more). Previous cohabitation was as common as previous marriage, with 34% of men having been previously married. Of those with previous relationships, a small number (12% of the total) had in fact been living in a stepfamily, and it is interesting to speculate how this previous experience influences their subsequent behavior.

Although 45 fathers had children from a previous relationship, this did not necessarily mean that they had lived with these children or been actively involved in their parenting. Eight fathers had lived with their children for less than 1 year, and some reported minimal involvement as a parent during this time. On the other hand, 15 fathers had lived with their children for at least 10 years and had typically been very involved in their upbringing.

Mothers reported that approximately half the children had previous experience of living in a stepfamily (cohabitation for at least three months). That is, for many of the children this was not their first experience of a stepparent, and this previous (unsuccessful) experience is likely to color their response to their new stepfather.

Relationship Development and Building

There was also diversity in the ways partners developed their relationship, including the extent to which they included the children in the courtship. Almost a third (31%) of the men knew their new partner and her children in a different role, for example, as a work colleague, family friend, or neighbor. In these cases the children often knew them, although in a nonparental role, which sometimes assisted the relationship but at times also required considerable adjustment in roles. Most couples (83%) began cohabiting within a year of beginning a relationship. Some began cohabiting soon after meeting, leaving little time to get to know the children, and in a few cases the children first met their new stepfather when he moved into their home. Most men (63%), however, reported spending time with the children prior to cohabiting in order to build a relationship, and over 75% felt they knew the child well prior to cohabitation. On the whole it was mothers who managed this process, introducing the stepfather to her children and arranging outings to encourage shared activities. This time was often seen as a period of trial parenting by mothers.

Stepfathers were asked about preparation for cohabitation and whether there had been any discussion of parenting issues and roles with their partner prior to their living together. With only a quarter of the stepfathers reporting discussing any parenting issue prior to cohabitation, there appeared to be relatively little planning for the allocation of child care responsibilities.

Where there was discussion this usually occurred after cohabitation. For example, only a fifth of the stepfathers recalled discussing issues to do with discipline and control before cohabitation, and almost half had discussed these issues subsequent to living together. It is likely that discipline and control issues became more salient once couples cohabited, as stepfathers were increasingly exposed to the full range of their stepchildren's behavior. Setting boundaries and controlling aspects of this behavior is a normal part of parenting and becomes more of an issue for couples when they are resident in the same household.

Least often discussed, at any time in the relationship, was the issue of physical contact between the stepfather and the stepchild. It is possible that this was due to the age range of the sample (7 to 11 years). The issue of physical contact may become more important as the stepchildren, especially stepdaughters, reach puberty. Discussions with some stepfathers suggested that they perceived physical contact to be a more salient issue with their older stepdaughters rather than with the stepchild who was the focus of the study.

Those who discussed issues prior to cohabitation and who had gotten to know the stepchildren were more involved in current parenting activities. This association between current parenting and activities with stepchildren prior to cohabitation may illustrate MacDonald and DeMaris's (1995) comment that dating activities may serve to prepare potential spouses for the stepparenting role.

Current Stepfather Involvement

Mothers were seen as the main caretaker by almost three quarters of the stepfathers, with almost a quarter reporting shared care of children. In a few (4%) of the stepfamilies, stepfathers were reported as being the main caretakers, usually because they were at home full time with the children while their partner worked. Despite the primary role of mothers in child care, 75% of the stepfathers reported being fully involved in parenting their stepchildren, while the remainder reported some limited involvement (22%) and a few (2%) were uninvolved, leaving parenting to the mother. These reports were confirmed by measures of the frequency with which stepfathers engaged in a variety of housework and child care activities.

Although stepfathers generally reported regularly being involved in a range of child care and housework activities, mothers were consistently more engaged in these activities, as they are in first families. Comparative data on fathers from an earlier study indicated that, according to mothers, although there was a similar level of involvement by fathers and stepfathers on housework activities, stepfathers were significantly less involved in activities with the children (Smith et al., 2001). In terms of specific activities, stepfathers were most often involved in "general" household activities and fun (e.g., play) activities, but less often involved in more "intimate" (see also Marsiglio, 1991) or one-to-one activities, such as helping the stepchildren with their homework or reading to them.

Multivariate analysis suggests that different factors influenced stepfathers' involvement in different types of activity (e.g., housework such as cooking and cleaning versus child care activities such as help with homework, dressing children; Robertson, 2004). The results suggest that general household activities may be influenced more by work patterns, whereas child care activities, such as time spent playing with the child, may be more a function of a particular child's characteristics (e.g., externalizing behavior). This may be particularly so in stepfamilies, where the child care tasks involve a decision to interact with stepchildren, while many housework tasks would need to be undertaken whether stepchildren were resident or not.

As noted, the monitoring, control, and disciplining of stepchildren can be particularly problematic in stepfamilies. Most stepfathers in the study (59%) reported leaving control and disciplining of stepchildren to the mother, although 36% reported being as involved as mothers in disciplining children. In only 15% of stepfamilies did the stepfather report that he was mainly responsible for discipline (10% of mothers reported this). Stepfathers rarely used physical forms of discipline (7% reported spanking), instead using verbal control, withdrawal of privileges, or time-out.

Views on Parenting Involvement

Most mothers (82%) reported that stepfathers' level of parenting involvement was "about right," although 15% would have preferred stepfathers to be more involved. Only three mothers wanted their partner to be less involved. In line with previous research, mothers reported better relationships with their partner when they were more satisfied with the help and support they got from him and when he was more involved in household and parenting activities. Mothers' reports of being more satisfied with help and support with child care were positively associated with stepfathers' higher actual levels of involvement in child care, and both were associated with greater relationship satisfaction for mothers. These results confirm previous findings indicating that mothers want stepfathers to be involved and are more satisfied with their partner when he engages in child care and housework activities (Ahrons & Wallisch, 1987).

Stepfathers were asked if there were any parenting activities they would not engage in with their stepchildren. Although 43% could not identify any activity they would avoid, 26% reported limiting their involvement in some areas of parenting. The remainder (31%) reported definitely avoiding some parenting activities or being uninvolved in most.

Mothers reported less limiting or avoidance of parenting by stepfathers than stepfathers themselves reported (e.g., 17% of mothers said stepfathers definitely avoided some areas of parenting). Over a quarter (27%) of stepfathers reported that they would not bathe stepchildren, and an additional 13% reported limited involvement, for example, helping the mother but not bathing the children on their own. Although only three stepfathers (3%) said they did not engage in displays of affection toward their stepchildren, rather more (21%) put limits on the ways they showed affection to their stepchildren. Stepfathers might kiss a child goodnight in the presence of his or her mother but were cautious about physical contact (e.g., hugs) at other times.

Although there is clear evidence here that some stepfathers consciously limit their parenting, it is important to determine the reasons for limiting these parenting behaviors. The majority of stepfathers who limited their parenting activities (81%) did so because of their stepfather (or nonbiological parent) status. However, some said that the age and gender of the child were important considerations and that they might, for example, also limit their parenting of their own older female child.

Stepfathers who mentioned more limits to their involvement in parenting were less likely to be involved in actual activities with stepchildren and housework activities. It may seem rather obvious to say that those who limit or avoid certain activities are likely to be less involved in child care activities, yet the significance of this finding is that it was the stepfathers themselves who were limiting their involvement. Furthermore, the reason most often given for this was the fact that they were the child's stepfather (or not the child's biological father). Thus it was their perception of what was appropriate parenting behavior for a nonbiological parent that led to their avoidance of certain activities and hence less involvement in parenting activities.

Those stepfathers who limited their parenting involvement were asked directly who had decided on these limits. In the majority of cases (72%), stepfathers reported making the decision themselves, without consultation with the child's mother. Just over 10% reported that there was an implicit agreement with the mother, often after general discussions regarding parenting roles. Almost as many had made these agreements explicit, discussing and agreeing between them that the stepfather would not engage in certain parenting behaviors (e.g., bathing the children). In few cases (7%) were mothers seen to have made a summary decision. These results contrast with mothers' reports, where fewer (46%) reported stepfathers made the decision to limit parenting and more (37%) reported that limitations were the result of implicit agreement. However, mothers agreed that they were responsible for limiting stepfather involvement in relatively few cases (10% said they made the decision).

Stepchildren's Contact with Nonresident Fathers

As reviewed earlier, there has been some discussion of potential competition between children's relationships with their nonresident father and with their stepfather. In the current sample, a third of the children had not had contact with their nonresident father in the past year. Some of these children had not had contact with their father for many years, and he did not feature in their life. However, for almost half the children (44%) contact occurred at least monthly. Stepfathers were asked about their stepchild's contact with their nonresident father and the potential impact this contact had on the stepchild and stepfamily relationships (asked of those with stepchild–nonresident parent contact in the past year). Over a third (39%) noted that contact had a negative effect on the child's behavior, but most reported no changes (36%) in stepchild behavior, or thought that the stepchild seemed happier and better behaved after contact (25%). Just under a third (29%) felt that contact was detrimental to their relationship with their stepchild, but again most (58%) felt it had no impact or was actually beneficial (13%).

Stepfathers' main concern regarding contact was the impact on their stepchild of the nonresident father's perceived lack of interest (38%) in the stepchild or his unreliability (32%). Stepfathers often recounted occasions when stepchildren had been let down by their nonresident parent. Less frequently cited concerns were the impact of different household rules (17%) and children being spoiled by their nonresident parent (19%), especially if the stepfamily was under financial pressure. Finally, relatively few were concerned that the nonresident father was making denigrating comments to the stepchild about the stepfather (8%) or mother (4%).

In terms of the impact of contact on their ability to parent their stepchildren, most stepfathers (68%) felt contact had no effect or was actually beneficial (3%; e.g., the nonresident father supported the stepfather's parenting). Almost a third, however, felt that contact had limited their ability to act as a parent, for example by limiting their perceived authority, reducing time spent with the stepchildren, making them less confident in showing affection, and reminding them that they did not have the same status as the child's father. These results indicate that although stepchildren's contact with nonresident parents sometimes has negative effects, stepfathers' main concerns with contact related to its impact on the stepchild, particularly where children were upset after being let down by their nonresident parent. In response to these concerns stepfathers sometimes talked to the child or the child's mother, and in a few cases stepfathers had spoken directly to the nonresident father.

For those stepfathers whose stepchildren did not have contact, most thought that contact should occur (68%) between the stepchildren and their nonresident father. The third of stepfathers who felt that there should continue to be no contact cited past sexual or physical abuse as the main reason for this view. These results suggest that stepfathers are supportive of contact between stepchildren and their nonresident father, even though it can occasionally have negative impacts on the stepchild and family relationships and functioning.

Stepfathers' Contact with Nonresident Children

Fewer than half the stepfathers had nonresident children, and although 21% had not had contact in the past year, half of those with previous children had them visiting at least every 2 weeks. For those with contact, half the stepfathers reported problems arising from visits from their children. Most often cited was the relationship between visiting children and resident stepchildren, including the visiting child's jealousy of the time the stepchild had with his or her father. Some stepfathers noted their or their partner's strained relationship with the visiting children, partly created by the need to divide their time between activities with children and problems enforcing household rules (for similar U.K. findings, see Bradshaw, Stimson, Skinner, & Williams, 1999). For some, practical difficulties also existed, for example a lack of beds and the need to move toys and clothes between households.

Stepfamily Identity and Labels

Past research indicates that many families do not identify with the term "stepfamily," preferring instead to see themselves as a "normal" family (Burgoyne & Clark, 1984; Ganong & Coleman, 1997). This may particularly be the case with stepfamilies that have been together for many years. It is also possible that stepfamilies that have been together for a relatively short period of time, or who are in a cohabiting relationship, are less likely to identify as a stepfamily. Stepfathers were asked if they regarded themselves as a stepfather to their stepchildren. Just over half (51%) reported that they were definitely not the child's stepfather. A further quarter (27%) gave qualified agreement to being a stepfather, and the remainder (22%) definitely thought of themselves as a stepfather. Those who gave qualified support to being a stepfather generally said that the degree of identification depended on the circumstances. In public they might see themselves as the child's father, whereas when with others who know of the family relationships they might identify as a stepfather.

These results are reflected in stepfathers' reports of the extent to which they identified themselves as a stepfather in public. Half (51%) reported that they never or rarely made clear their stepfather status in relation to their stepchildren. Just over a third reported occasionally identifying as a stepfather, usually when they were forced to reveal their stepfather status (e.g., to doctors). The remainder (15%) reported that they usually made clear their stepfather status. In these latter cases, it was often clear that there may not be a biological relationship between stepfather and stepchild, for example when they were close in age to their older stepchildren or where there was a clear ethnic difference.

When asked why they did not consider themselves as a stepfather, most (55%) said they considered themselves to be a normal father living in a normal family; others considered the term stepfather to be stigmatizing (17%); still others simply did not consider themselves to be a stepfamily (13%), usually because the parents were not married. These findings are similar to those of Ahrons and Wallisch (1987), who found that, when asked if they saw themselves as stepparents to their partner's children, only 40% of stepfathers saw themselves as a stepparent. In both the present study and Ahrons and Wallisch's study, more stepfathers actually saw themselves as parents rather than stepparents.

Identification with a stepfather or father role also appeared to reflect the degree to which stepfathers were committed to a family relationship, as against a relationship with their partner alone. Thus stepfathers would report that they saw their relationship with their partner as one also necessarily involving the stepchildren. For these stepfathers this commitment to a family is likely to have been associated with the development of a parental identity as a stepfather or father. A small group of stepfathers, however, considered the main relationship to be with their new partner, with the stepchildren separate from this relationship. These stepchildren were regarded as the responsibility of the partner, with little expectation of parenting involvement on the part of the stepfather. In this latter case, it is unlikely that these men would regard themselves as having a parental role as either a stepfather or a father to their stepchildren.

In part this identification as a "normal" family reflects the lack of clear public markers for stepfamily status (with the exceptions described earlier) and a perceived negative public perception of stepfamilies. Stepfathers were asked what they thought public perceptions were of stepfamilies. Over half (55%) cited predominantly negative public perceptions of stepfamilies (e.g., as being abusive or dysfunctional); just over a third (35%) felt that there were both negative and positive perceptions of stepfamilies; the remainder (10%) reported only positive aspects (e.g., stepfathers supporting a partner and her children). Despite the view that the public perception of stepfamilies was largely negative, very few stepfathers (18%) reported being treated differently by the public because they were a stepfather, although, as noted earlier, their stepfather status was seldom obvious.

It is also likely that this self-identification is a function of the stepfather's background and the family context. It may be relatively easy for a young man with no children who enters a cohabiting relationship with a partner who has a relatively young child to develop a self-identity as a father. Certainly research suggests that relationships with stepfathers are better when stepchildren are younger at stepfamily formation (Bray & Kelly, 1999; J. Dunn et al., 2000; Hetherington & Jodl, 1994). Fine (1995) suggests that roles are less ambiguous for younger children than older because of differences in developmental needs. This may be particularly so if the stepchild has no contact with his or her biological father (and may not even know who he is; Bray & Kelly, 1999). In fact, in this case the stepchild may take a lead in establishing a fatherlike relationship, for example by referring to him as Dad, both in public and in the household. Some stepchildren in the study appeared to be very much missing a reliable father figure and to welcome the presence of a male who gave them positive attention and love. The influence of children on fathering has been underresearched and may be particularly important in stepfamilies.

Finally, those interviewed were asked to comment on what they thought was the general difference between a father and a stepfather, as distinct from their experiences reported earlier. Almost half (46%) mentioned a difference in the ability of stepfathers to discipline stepchildren, and almost as many thought that the child-father bond was stronger than that with a stepfather. Nearly a third (31%) mentioned that stepfathers were less likely to show their love and affection to their stepchildren, and 21% felt that fathers' greater responsibility for children was an important difference. Relatively few (6%) felt that an important distinction was the greater satisfaction fathers derived from parenting compared to stepfathers.

CONCLUSION

This chapter has reviewed research involving stepfathers and presented some related results from a study of newly formed stepfamilies. This study recruited a community sample of stepfather stepfamilies living in London. The sample included both cohabiting and married couples who had been living together for between 1 and 4 years and had at least one resident stepchild between 7 and 11 years of age. Given these restrictions on the sample, caution needs to be taken in generalizing these results to other stepfather samples.

These findings further underline the potential difficulties faced by couples, and their children, in forming a well-adjusted and satisfying stepfamily unit. Stepfathers entered the stepfamily with diverse relationship and parenting histories that influenced how they approached family life. The partners and stepchildren also had diverse family experiences prior to stepfamily formation (e.g., experiences of family violence or previously living in a stepfamily). Future research needs to consider how stepfathers' and partners' histories relate to current stepfamily functioning and to examine how the past experiences of children influence their response to a new parent figure.

The current research indicated that some couples work to consciously develop stepfamily relationships prior to cohabitation, and this helped stepfathers to get to know their stepchildren and so better prepare them for living together. It was surprising, however, how little discussion of stepfather roles and parenting occurred prior to cohabitation, with many couples working out issues as they arose once they were living together. It is possible that if the trial parenting is successful and relationships and routines are formed, there is no reason for couples to discuss these issues. However, where difficulties arise, for example due to differing expectations, it may be necessary to explicitly negotiate roles and routines.

Once they were living in the new family, stepfathers engaged in a range of parenting activities, with only a minority having little involvement in parenting their stepchildren. Mothers appear to want stepfathers to be involved in parenting their children and encourage engagement in a variety of ways (e.g., by suggestion or direction or by arranging parenting opportunities). Despite discussion in the literature of possible gatekeeping by mothers in stepfamilies, stepfathers (and mothers) reported relatively little explicit limiting by mothers of stepfathers' parenting. Rather, it was stepfathers themselves who drew back from fully engaging in some parenting activities, mainly because they were not the biological parent of the child. In particular, they were relatively reluctant to bathe and dress the children on their own and saw mothers as having the main role in disciplining the children. This finding is consistent with the high levels of awareness by stepfathers of the negative stereotypes of stepparents, which might explain their concerns about physical contact with the stepchildren.

Stepfathers also cited these negative stereotypes as a reason for avoiding identifying as a stepfather. In line with previous research, most stepfathers did not identify with this label, preferring to be seen as a father or friend to their stepchildren. Partly this also reflected the desire of stepfamilies to be seen as a "normal" family, and in some cases it was because at an early stage of the relationship a family identity had not yet formed. It was also evident that stepfathers sometimes moved between identifying as a stepfather and identifying as a father, depending on the particular context.

The possible impact of stepchildren's contact with their father on stepfathers' willingness to parent has also been mentioned in the literature. In the current study, two thirds of stepfathers reported that contact had little impact on their ability to parent their stepchildren; for a third, though, contact seemed to result in a number of difficulties for stepchildren and stepfamily relationships. Where stepfathers had concerns about contact, these were mainly about fathers' disinterest and unreliability and how this upset and unsettled the children. Few stepfathers, however, were against stepchildren's contact with their father. Those stepfathers with their own children also reported that having their children visit created tensions within the stepfamily, particularly when they had to manage the demands of their own children and their stepchildren.

These results show the challenges faced by many, but by no means all, stepfathers. But it is also important to focus on the rewards of stepfamily life for stepfathers. What came through from many of the interviews was the great joy stepfathers obtained from family life and their relationship with their stepchildren. One professional, high-achieving stepfather with an 11-year-old stepdaughter stated that she was quite reserved toward him initially. He then described the elation he felt when she had recently held his hand while crossing a busy road. This simple nonverbal acknowledgment of his role as an adult "protector" meant a great deal to him.

There is much yet to be learned about stepfathers' experiences of stepfamily life. Qualitative studies, such as Marsiglio's (2004) recent study, provide insights into how stepfathers develop different parenting roles and relationships within the stepfamily, how these change over time, and the degree to which they may vary with context. These studies can then be used to develop measures for larger scale quantitative studies that can evaluate the impact of factors such as the development and negotiation of parenting roles on stepfamily functioning. Above all, there is a need to focus not only on what is best for stepchildren in stepfamilies, but also what is best for all stepfamily members, including stepfathers.

REFERENCES

Acock, A. C., & Demo, D. H. (1994). *Family diversity and well-being*. London: Sage.

Ahrons, C. R., & Wallisch, L. (1987). Parenting in the binuclear family: Relationships between biological and stepparents. In K. Pasley & M. Ihinger-Tallman (Eds.), *Remarriage and stepparenting: Current research and theory* (pp. 225–256). New York: Guilford Press.

Allen, S. M., & Hawkins, A. J. (1999). Maternal gatekeeping: Mothers' beliefs and behaviors that inhibit greater father involvement in family work. *Journal of Marriage and the Family, 61*, 199–212.

Amato, P. R., & Keith, N. (1991). Parental divorce and the well-being of children: A meta analysis. *Psychological Bulletin, 110*, 26–46.

Amato, P. R., & Sobolewski, J. M. (2004). The effects of divorce on fathers and children: Nonresidential fathers and stepfathers. In M. E. Lamb (Ed.), *The role of the father in child development* (4th ed., pp. 341–367). Hoboken, NJ: Wiley.

Blair, S. L., & Hardesty, C. (1994). Paternal involvement and the well-being of mothers and fathers of young children. *Journal of Men's Studies, 3*(1), 49–68.

Booth, A., & Edwards, J. N. (1992). Starting over: Why remarriages are more unstable. *Journal of Family Issues, 13*(2), 179–194.

Bradshaw, J., Stimson, C., Skinner, C., & Williams, J. (1999). *Absent fathers*. London: Routledge.

Bray, J. H., & Berger, S. H. (1993). Developmental issues in stepfamilies research project: Family relationships and parent-child interactions. *Journal of Family Psychology, 7,* 76–90.

Bray, J. H., Berger, S. H., & Boethel, C. L. (1994). Role integration and marital adjustment in stepfather families. In K. Pasley & M. Ihinger-Tallman (Eds.), *Stepparenting: Issues in theory, research, and practice* (pp. 15–32). Westport, CT: Greenwood Press.

Bray, J. H., & Hetherington, E. M. (1993). Families in transition: Introduction and overview. *Journal of Family Issues, 7*(1), 3–8.

Bray, J. H., & Kelly, J. (1999). *Stepfamilies*. New York: Broadway Books.

Bumpass, L. L., Raley, R. K., & Sweet, J. A. (1995). The changing character of stepfamilies: Implications of cohabitation and nonmarital childbearing. *Demography, 32*(3), 425–436.

Burgoyne, J., & Clark, D. (1984). *Making a go of it: A study of stepfamilies in Sheffield*. London: Routledge & Kegan Paul.

Cherlin, A. J. (1978). Remarriage as an incomplete institution. *American Journal of Sociology, 84,* 634–650.

Cherlin, A. J., & Furstenberg, F. F. (1994). Stepfamilies in the United States: A reconsideration. *Annual Review of Sociology, 20,* 359–381.

Coleman, M., & Ganong, L. H. (1997). Stepfamilies from the stepfamily's perspective. *Marriage and Family Review, 26*(1/2), 107–121.

Coleman, M., Ganong, L., & Fine, M. (2000). Reinvestigating remarriage: Another decade of progress. *Journal of Marriage and the Family, 62,* 1288–1307.

Coltrane, S. (1996). *Family man: Fatherhood, housework, and gender equity*. Oxford: Oxford University Press.

Cooksey, E. C., & Fondell, M. M. (1996). Spending time with his kids: Effects of family-structure on fathers' and children's lives. *Journal of Marriage and the Family, 58*(3), 693–707.

Dawson, D. A. (1991). Family structure and children's health and well-being: Data from the 1988 National Health Interview Survey on Child Health. *Journal of Marriage and the Family, 53,* 573–584.

Deater-Deckard, K., Pickering, K., Dunn, J. F., & Golding, J. (1998). Family structure and depressive symptoms in men preceding and following the birth of a child. *American Journal of Psychiatry, 155*(6), 818–823.

Demo, D. H., & Acock, A. C. (1993). Family diversity and the division of domestic labor: How much have things really changed? *Family Relations, 42*(3), 323–331.

Dunn, J., Cheng, H., O'Connor, T., & Bridges, L. (2003). Children's relationships with their non-resident fathers: Influences, outcomes and implications. *Journal of Child Psychology and Psychiatry, 45,* 553–566.

Dunn, J., Davies, L. C., O'Connor, T. G., & Sturgess, W. (2000). Parents' and partners' life course and family experiences: Links with parent-child relationships in different family settings. *Journal of Child Psychiatry and Psychology, 8,* 955–968.

Dunn, J., Deater-Deckard, K., Pickering, K., O'Connor, T., & Golding, J. (1998). Children's adjustment and prosocial behaviour in step-, single-parent, and non-stepfamily settings: Findings from a community study. *Journal of Child Psychology and Psychiatry and Allied Disciplines, 39*(8), 1083–1095.

Ermisch, J., & Francesconi, M. (1996). *The increasing complexity of family relationships: Lifetime experience of single motherhood and stepfamilies in Great Britain.* Wivenhoe Park, Colchester, England: University of Essex.

Ferri, E., & Smith, K. (1998). *Step-parenting in the 1990s.* London: Family Policy Studies Centre.

Fine, M. A. (1995). The clarity and content of the stepparent role: A review of the literature. *Journal of Divorce and Remarriage, 24*, 19–34.

Fine, M. A., Coleman, M., & Ganong, L. H. (1998). Consistency in perceptions of the step-parent role among step-parents, parents and step-children. *Journal of Social and Personal Relationships, 15*(6), 810–828.

Fine, M. A., Ganong, L. H., & Coleman, M. (1997). The relation between role constructions and adjustment among stepfathers. *Journal of Family Issues, 18*(5), 503–525.

Fine, M. A., & Kurdek, L. A. (1994). A multidimensional cognitive-development model of stepfamily adjustment. In K. Pasley & M. Ihinger-Tallman (Eds.), *Stepparenting: Issues in theory, research, and practice* (pp. 15–32). Westport, CT: Greenwood.

Fine, M. A., & Kurdek, L. A. (1995). Relation between marital quality and (step)parent child relationship quality for parents and stepparents in stepfamilies. *Journal of Family Psychology, 9*(2), 216–223.

Ganong, L., & Coleman, M. (1997). How society views stepfamilies. *Marriage and Family Review, 26*(1/2), 85–106.

Giles-Sims, J. (1997). Current knowledge about child abuse in stepfamilies. *Marriage and Family Review, 26*(3/4), 215–230.

Graham, P., & Rutter, M. (1968). The reliability and validity of the psychiatric assessment of the child: Pt. II. Interview with the parent. *British Journal of Psychiatry, 114*(510), 581–592.

Haskey, J. (1994). Stepfamilies and stepchildren in Great Britain. *Population Trends, 76*, 17–28.

Hetherington, E. M. (1993). An overview of the Virginia Longitudinal Study of Divorce and Remarriage with a focus on early adolescence. *Journal of Family Psychology, 7*, 39–56.

Hetherington, E. M., & Clingempeel, W. G. (1992). Coping with marital transitions: A family systems perspective. *Monographs of the Society for Research in Child Development, 57*(2/3, Serial No. 227).

Hetherington, E. M., Cox, M., & Cox, R. (1982). Effects of divorce on parents and children. In M. E. Lamb (Ed.), *Nontraditional families: Parenting and child development* (pp. 233–288). Hillsdale, NJ: Erlbaum.

Hetherington, E. M., & Jodl, K. (1994). Stepfamilies as settings for development. In A. Booth & J. Dunn (Eds.), *Stepfamilies: Who benefits? Who does not?* (pp. 55–80). Cambridge, MA: Harvard University Press.

Hetherington, E. M., & Stanley-Hagan, M. (2000). Diversity among stepfamilies. In D. Demo, K. Allen, & M. Fine (Eds.), *Handbook of family diversity* (pp. 173–196). Oxford: Oxford University Press.

Hofferth, S. L., & Anderson, K. G. (2003). Are all dads equal? Biology versus marriage as a basis for paternal investment. *Journal of Marriage and the Family, 65*(1), 213–232.

Hofferth, S. L., Cabrera, N., Carlson, M., Coley, R. L., Day, R., & Schindler, H. (2007). Resident father involvement and social fathering. In S. Hofferth & L. M. Casper (Eds.), *Handbook of measurement issues in family research* (pp. 335–374). Mahwah, NJ: Erlbaum.

Ishi-Kuntz, M., & Coltrane, S. (1992). Remarriage, stepparenting and household labor. *Journal of Family Issues, 13*, 215–233.

Juby, H., & LeBourdais, C. (1998). The changing context of fatherhood in Canada: A life course analysis. *Population Studies: A Journal of Demography, 52*(2), 163–175.

Kurdek, L. A., & Fine, M. A. (1991). Cognitive correlates of satisfaction for mothers and stepfathers in stepfather families. *Journal of Marriage and the Family, 53*, 565–572.

Lansford, J. E., Ceballo, R., Abbey, A., & Stewart, A. J. (2001). Does family structure matter? A comparison of adoptive, two-parent biological, single-mother, stepfather, and stepmother households. *Journal of Marriage and the Family, 63*, 840–851.

MacDonald, W., & DeMaris, A. (1995). Remarriage, stepchildren, and marital conflict: Challenges to the incomplete institutionalisation hypothesis. *Journal of Marriage and the Family, 57*, 387–398.

MacDonald, W., & DeMaris, A. (1996). Parenting stepchildren and biological children: The effects of stepparents' gender and new biological children. *Journal of Family Issues, 17*(1), 5–25.

Marsiglio, W. (1991). Paternal engagement activities with minor children. *Journal of Marriage and the Family, 53*, 973–986.

Marsiglio, W. (1992). Stepfathers with minor children living at home: Parenting perceptions and relationship quality. *Journal of Family Issues, 13*(2), 195–214.

Marsiglio, W. (2004). When stepfathers claim stepchildren: A conceptual analysis. *Journal of Marriage and the Family, 66*, 22–39.

Marsiglio, W., & Hinojosa, R. (2007). Managing the multifather family: Stepfathers as father allies. *Journal of Marriage and the Family, 69*, 845–862.

O'Connor, T. G., Hetherington, E. M., & Clingempeel, W. G. (1997). Systems and bidirectional influences in families. *Journal of Social and Personal Relationships, 14*(4), 491–504.

Peterson, J. L., & Zill, N. (1986). Marital disruption, parent-child relationships, and behavior problems in children. *Journal of Marriage and the Family, 48*, 295–307.

Pleck, J. H. (1997). Paternal involvement: Levels, sources, and consequences. In M. E. Lamb (Ed.), *The role of the father in child development* (3rd ed., pp. 66–103). New York: Wiley.

Quinton, D., Rutter, M., & Rowlands, O. (1976). An evaluation of an interview assessment of marriage. *Psychological Medicine, 6*, 577–586.

Robertson, J. P. (2004). *Factors associated with stepfathers' parenting of stepchildren.* Unpublished doctoral dissertation, University of London, Institute of Education.

Santrock, J. W., Sitterle, K. A., & Warshak, C. L. (1988). Parent-child relationships in stepfather families. In P. Bronstein & P. A. Cowan (Eds.), *Fatherhood today* (pp. 144–165). New York: Wiley.

Sariola, H., & Uutela, A. (1996). The prevalence and context of incest abuse in Finland. *Child Abuse and Neglect*, *20*(9), 843–850.

Smith, M. A., & Jenkins, J. M. (1991). The effects of marital disharmony on prepubertal children. *Journal of Abnormal Child Psychology*, *19*(6), 625–645.

Smith, M. A., Robertson, J., Dixon, J., Quigley, M., & Whitehead, E. (2001). *A study of stepchildren and step-parenting: Final report to the Department of Health*. London: Thomas Coram Research Unit.

Sullivan, O. (1997). The division of housework among "remarried" couples. *Journal of Family Issues*, *18*(2), 205–223.

Vemer, E., Coleman, M., Ganong, L. H., & Cooper, H. (1989). Marital satisfaction in remarriage: A meta-analysis. *Journal of Marriage and the Family*, *51*(3), 713–725.

White, L., & Gilbreth, J. G. (2001). When children have two fathers: Effects of relationships with stepfathers and noncustodial fathers on adolescent outcomes. *Journal of Marriage and the Family*, *63*(1), 155–167.

CHAPTER 7

Resident Mothers in Stepfamilies

MARJORIE SMITH

THE LARGE majority of stepfamily households that are children's primary residences are stepfather families—that is, families with a mother and her children and a stepfather. In the United Kingdom, the most recent figures from the General Household Survey (Fido, Gibbins, Hurt, Matthews, & Thomas, 2006) show that 86% of stepfamily households are stepfather households, defined as "a couple with child(ren) from the woman's previous marriage/cohabitation"; 11% are stepmother households (a couple with children from the man's previous marriage/cohabitation); and 3% comprise a couple with children from both partners' previous marriage/cohabitation. Figures from the United States, based on the National Survey of Families and Households, are directly comparable, with 90% of children in stepfamilies living with their mothers and stepfathers (Thomson, Mosley, Hanson, & McLanahan, 2001). Although the prevalence of stepfamilies varies between different countries (Prskawetz, Vikat, Philipov, & Engelhardt, 2003), it seems probable that the balance of stepfather to stepmother stepfamilies is fairly

In line with recent changes in demographic usage (Bumpass et al., 1995; Prskawetz et al., 2003), in this chapter, the term "stepfamily" is used to mean both marriages and cohabiting relationships involving the child or children of only one partner.

The U.K. New Stepfamilies Study was funded by the U.K. Department of Health, whose support is gratefully acknowledged. Any views expressed in this chapter, however, are those of the author and not necessarily those of the Department of Health.

In addition to the author, the research team for the U.K. New Stepfamilies Study comprised Jo Dixon, Margaret Quigley, Emma Whitehead, and Jeremy Robertson, who between them carried out most of the interviews with mothers in stepfamilies with great skill and sensitivity, and whose help and insights made a major contribution to the study.

I am particularly grateful to the mothers in stepfamilies (and their children and partners) who consented to be interviewed and tell us about their lives and their histories. The study would not have been possible without their participation and willing assistance.

constant, with about 90% of stepfamilies comprising a resident mother, her children, and a stepfather.

The preponderance of stepfather households simply reflects the fact that after parental separation or divorce, a child is far more likely to have their primary residence with their mother rather than their father. It follows that because many of these children will spend some time with their fathers, often including staying with them, the majority of "part-time stepfamily" households are stepmother households. These households, which often operate as stepfamilies on weekends and during the school holidays, comprise a father and his new partner.

This chapter, however, is about mothers now in stepfamily households that are their children's primary homes. By definition, in all of these households there will be children who are not the biological children of the stepfather, but in some households there will also be a child or children who are the biological children of the stepfather and have been born since the start of their new relationship. About half of the mothers in stepfamilies go on to have children with their new partner (Prskawetz et al., 2003; Stewart, 2005; Thomson, 2004).

As Coleman, Ganong, and Fine (2000) conclude in their reassessment of the state of stepfamily research, dynamic factors and change over time are "critical and constant" in the life course of stepfamilies. For most mothers currently in stepfamilies, it represents one stage in a series of events and changes that has included a partnership with the birth of a child or children, a separation or divorce, a period as a lone parent, and then a repartnering or remarriage. There may also be several iterations to this, with additional separations, periods as a lone parent, and repartnerings.

In the United States, it has been estimated that about 40% of mothers will spend some time as part of a stepfamily before they are age 45 (Bumpass, Raley, & Sweet, 1995), and comparable figures for the United Kingdom have been estimated to be nearly a third of mothers (Ermisch & Francesconi, 2000). But as Ermisch and Francesconi identify, these figures have to be viewed in the context of other family changes:

> 40% of mothers will spend some time as a lone parent. The duration of lone parenthood is often short, one half remaining lone mothers for 4.6 years or less. About three-fourths of these lone mothers will form a stepfamily, with 80% of these stepfamilies being started by cohabitation and 85% following the dissolution of a union. Stepfamilies are not very stable: one quarter dissolve within a year. (p. 235)

Each of these stages may involve changes in residence, changes in financial circumstances, and changes in levels of stress. Each of the changes in status from partnered to lone to repartnered parent are, to some extent, markers for a series of other changes that are associated and are likely to follow.

When a woman with children decides to repartner, in addition to the structural changes that are likely to occur, the situation will create stresses in all the existing relationships (White, 1994) and necessitate the development or nurturance of new relationships. The mother becoming part of a new stepfamily faces the challenging task of developing a cohabiting relationship with her new partner, while simultaneously maintaining and continuing her relationship with her child or children and continuing to parent them; at the same time, she needs to nurture a relationship between her children and the new adult member of the household. In addition, since repartnering often follows quite soon after separation, for most women there is also a changed relationship with an ex-partner to create and maintain in order to enable the children's continuing contact and relationships with their nonresident father. Mothers must do this in the presence of their relationship with their new partner, and often their ex-partner's new partner.

Of course, the particular circumstances for women in these situations will vary widely. Some will have had relatively long-standing and good practical relationships with their new partners before they decide to cohabit, and similarly, some children will already know their new stepfathers well and have developed good relationships with them before they become part of the household. For other women there may be less preparation or forethought to the decision to cohabit, with the consequence that the relationship with their new partner will still be in its early stages, and their children are likely to have had little if any contact with their new stepfather and may feel negative or resentful of his presence. This latter situation applies for many women in stepfamilies; Montgomery, Anderson, Hetherington, and Clingempeel (1992) found that for most divorced women with children embarking on a new relationship, the decision to cohabit usually occurs fairly early on in the relationship. In the new stepfamilies studied by Smith and colleagues (described by Robertson, this volume), mothers were asked how long and how well their children had known the stepfather before he became part of the household. Although more than a quarter of children had known the stepfather for more than 3 years, over half had known him for less than a year, and of these nearly 20% either did not know the stepfather at all or had known him for less than 3 months. Overall, 36% of the children were described by their mothers as not knowing the stepfather well, and 8% of these as not knowing him at all, before cohabitation.

As the central and linking figure, the role of the mother is key to the functioning and success of the stepfamily. Yet the pivotal role of the resident mother in the stepfamily is often ignored in research on stepfamilies, where the focus has tended to be on stepparents, and particularly stepfathers, and on contact and relationships between children and the nonresident parent. There has been a great deal of focus on outcomes for children in stepfamilies, without the apparent acknowledgment or recognition of the importance of the mother in relation to this, in terms of her continuing parenting of, and relationship with, the child. As Coleman et al. (2000) point out, there are surprisingly few studies of mothers in stepfamilies, and we know more about nonresidential fathers than we do about mothers in stepfamily households.

This chapter examines what is known about mothers now in stepfamilies, in terms of their histories, their past and current mental health, and their role within the stepfamilies. Discussion is based on what is known from the clinical literature and, to a greater extent, from the published research findings in this area, but I also draw largely on a study of new stepfamilies, the U.K. Study of New Stepfamilies (described more fully in Chapter 6). This study was a cross-sectional investigation of a community sample of stepfamilies that had been in existence for at least 1 year and not more than 4 years. The families were identified by means of a screening questionnaire delivered via schools in three local education authority areas in and around London, to the parents or guardians of all children between 7 and 11 years old. The questionnaire focused on changes that the children had experienced in the previous 3 to 4 years and did not specifically mention stepfamilies or the purpose of the study. Overall, nearly 10,000 completed questionnaires were returned by parents, giving a response rate of 60%. An investigation in one school revealed no differences in family type or the number of changes children had experienced between those who did and did not return the questionnaire, so it was concluded that the identified stepfamilies, representing 8.7% of the responses, were a representative sample.

About half of the 840 identified stepfamilies had been in existence for more than 3 or 4 years and were therefore ineligible to take part in the study, but not all of the 368 identified new stepfamilies participated; some had not agreed on the questionnaire to further contact (15%), and others declined further involvement when contacted (15%) or could not be contacted or involved in the research for various reasons. A small number (5%) turned out to be ineligible when contacted, usually because the stepfamily had been in existence for longer than 4 years. In the end, 184 new stepfamilies—50% of those identified—participated in the research, and of these, 177 (96%) were, or had been until recently, stepfather families, with a resident mother and stepfather (families were included in the research if the stepparent was no longer in the household but had been for at least a year within the previous 3 years).

Interviews were conducted in the family home with 151 mothers currently in stepfamilies and 26 mothers who had been in stepfamilies until recently. All the mothers had at least one child between 7 and 11 years old living with them, but some had more than one. Mothers were asked about up to two children in this age range, providing information on a total of 225 children, 193 of them currently in stepfamily households and 32 who had been until recently. The interviews were semi-structured and interviewer-led and obtained a mixture of qualitative and quantitative information. They covered a wide range of topics, which included information on the mother's history in terms of her previous relationships, child rearing, and periods as a lone parent; the history of the current relationship; and detailed information on stepfamily functioning and parenting and the quality of relationships within the household. In addition, information was obtained on the mother's past and current mental health and well-being. As well as mothers, interviews were conducted with up to two children between 7 and 11 years old in each stepfamily (a total of 149 children currently in stepfather families, plus 23 children from past stepfather families), and where they agreed to it, with stepfathers (data from these interviews are described in Chapter 6, this volume).

The majority of mothers interviewed were White British (80%), with 8% of African Caribbean descent, 5% of South Asian origin, and 7% of other descent. Overall, 90% of the interviewed mothers were born in Britain. Nearly two thirds of the mothers currently in stepfamilies were cohabiting in their stepfamily relationships, rather than married: 93 (62%) were cohabiting, and 58 (38%) were married to their new partners.

To compare the parenting and functioning of mothers in stepfamilies with that of non-stepfamilies and, in particular, with two-parent families, other sources of data relating to community samples of families were used for comparative purposes. The data used were obtained from a randomly selected community sample of nearly 200 families with children ages 7 *or* 11 years, also drawn from London and the Southeast of England (Nobes & Smith, 2002). The families had been involved in an earlier study investigating parental control strategies and physical punishment in the home, and directly comparable data were available on a number of variables, including those relating to the mother-child relationship, activities within the family, the quality of the marital relationship, and maternal mental health. Most of the comparative analyses have utilized data from the mothers in the 192 two-parent families in the sample, but for some analyses, comparisons have been made with data from the 45 lone-mother families.

HISTORIES OF MOTHERS NOW IN STEPFAMILIES

It is clear that stepfamily formation is not a random process, and that there are some selection effects that operate to make it more likely that some women will have complex family relationships, including becoming part of a stepfamily household.

In an analysis of the Christchurch cohort data from New Zealand, Nicholson, Fergusson, and Horwood () investigated the effects on children at the age of 18 of living in a stepfamily for the first time when they were between 6 and 16 years old. They noted that several of the factors that differentiated stepfamilies and needed to be taken into account in understanding outcomes for children were factors that predated the existence of the stepfamily. For instance, mothers in stepfamilies tended to have been younger when they had their first child: 31% were under the age of 20 years, compared with 14% of the mothers not in stepfamilies; they were more likely to have a history of depression, and they were more likely to smoke. Other factors, such as having experienced a separation, having been a single parent, and having experienced high levels of life events and conflict, were more directly attributable to a parental separation or divorce, which preceded the stepfamily formation. Because early childbearing and early marriage are both associated with increased risk of divorce (Baldwin, 1993; Bumpass, Martin, & Sweet, 1991; Furstenberg, 1990) these appear to be key variables in terms of subsequent selection into a stepfamily.

There is also evidence of intergenerational risks in becoming part of a stepfamily, with those who grew up as part of a stepfamily more likely to be part of a stepfamily as an adult. This risk is based on evidence of the intergenerational transmission of divorce (Amato, 1996) and the fact that most divorced people remarry (Ermisch & Francesconi, 2000; Furstenberg & Cherlin, 1991). The effect is perhaps exacerbated by the finding that girls brought up in stepfamilies are more likely than those not brought up as part of a stepfamily to leave home and form relationships earlier (Aquilino, 1991; White & Booth, 1985) and that children of divorced or remarried parents are more likely to have children in their teens (Cherlin, Kiernan, & Chase-Lansdale, 1995; Kiernan, 1992), thus re-creating the risk of early partnering and early child rearing.

In line with the data on early parenthood, the average age at which mothers in the U.K. New Stepfamilies sample had their first child was 22.9 years $(SD = 4.9)$, which was considerably below the U.K. national mean age for first births at about the time the children were born, which was 26.8 years (Armitage & Babb, 1996). Over a quarter of the sample (27.4%) had been teenage mothers.

MENTAL HEALTH HISTORIES OF MOTHERS IN STEPFAMILIES

Nicholson et al. (1999) also found that women now in stepfamilies were more likely to have histories of depression: 31% of the cohort mothers in stepfamilies had a history of depression compared with 17% of mothers not in stepfamilies. Poorer mental health histories of mothers in stepfamilies have also been noted by others (e.g., Demo & Acock, 1996; O'Connor, Hawkins, Dunn, Thorpe, & Golding, 1998) and include higher rates of alcoholism, Antisocial Personality Disorder, and Social Phobia, as well as depression (Foley et al., 2004).

In the U.K. New Stepfamilies Study, based on comprehensive and detailed interview assessments of maternal mental state, backed up with standardized measures of affective disorder (Malaise Inventory; Rodgers, Pickles, Power, Collishaw, & Maughan, 1999), most aspects of mothers' mental health were markedly worse in mothers now in stepfamilies than in mothers in the comparison two-parent sample; this related particularly to past mental health histories. Nearly half the mothers currently in stepfamilies ($N = 151$) had a history of depression in the previous 5 years (47.6%), compared to 19% of mothers in two-parent families. Mothers in stepfamilies were more than 4 times more likely to have been moderately or severely depressed (29.1% versus 7% in two-parent families).

As well as histories of poorer mental health, current mental health was also worse in mothers in stepfamilies. Rates of depression in the previous year were twice those of mothers in two-parent families, with 32.5% of mothers in stepfamilies being depressed to some degree and nearly 20% having received treatment for depression, compared to fewer than 10% of mothers in two-parent families. Reflecting this, thoughts of suicide or suicide attempts were much more commonly reported by mothers in stepfamilies. None of the mothers in the comparison sample reported that they had made a suicide attempt in the previous year, but 14 mothers in stepfamilies had done so, and 8 times as many mothers in stepfamilies reported having had thoughts of suicide (25% versus 3%). There were also significantly higher rates of both situational and nonsituational anxiety in mothers now in stepfamilies; 30% of mothers in stepfamilies were judged to have symptoms of an anxiety state, and 17% to a moderate or severe degree, compared to 12% of mothers in two-parent families, of whom fewer than 4% had moderate or severe symptoms.

It is not clear how much these very significantly raised rates of past depression are a cause or consequence of earlier relationship breakdown. In this connection it was notable that rates of depression and suicidal ideation were even higher in the small group of mothers ($N = 26$) who had been in stepfamilies until recently; 18 had been depressed in the previous 5 years, 10 of them with symptoms of moderate or severe depression, and 12 of them had received treatment for depression. Eight of the 26 mothers reported symptoms of depression in the past year; more than half of this small group of mothers (14) had had suicidal thoughts in the previous year; and, according to their own reports, four had made suicide attempts.

Relationship breakdown is known to be associated with increased risk of depression (Aseltine & Kessler, 1993; Bifulco & Moran, 1998; Kessler, Walters, & Forthofer, 1998), as is earlier or continuing interpartner conflict, noted by Nicholson et al. (1999) as more common in histories of women now in stepfamilies (Amato & Keith, 1991). But other factors more prevalent in the histories of women now in stepfamilies are also associated with increased risk of depression. For example, previous lone-parent status, or indeed of multiple changes in status, and the associated stresses (O'Connor et al., 1998) are also associated with increased risk of depression.

Looked at another way, it is clear that current stepfamily status is, to some extent, a marker for other factors in women's history and circumstances, since the strength of the association between depression and stepfamily status reduces when other factors are controlled (O'Connor et al., 1998).

Over a third of mothers in the U.K. New Stepfamilies Study (34%) had experienced physical violence in their previous relationships. These mothers had significantly higher scores on the Malaise Inventory than those who had not experienced physical violence, and they were also more likely to have had a history of depression, to have been hospitalized for psychiatric symptoms at some time, to have made a suicide attempt, and to have experienced a moderate or severe depression or anxiety state in the previous year.

MOTHER-CHILD RELATIONSHIPS IN STEPFAMILIES

It has been suggested by clinicians that relationships between mothers and children are likely to suffer with the formation of a stepfamily, as children have to share their mother's attention with the stepfather, and they may lose the close and confiding relationships that often exist in lone-parent families (Ganong & Coleman, 1994). It is also suggested that resentment of the stepfather's presence or behavior may impact on children's behavior and create difficulties in the mother-child relationship following a repartnering. Empirical evidence, on the other hand, suggests that children, particularly boys, tend to have poorer mother-child relationships after parental divorce (Booth & Amato, 1994; Hetherington, 1993; Zill, Morrison, & Coiro, 1993), with the implication that these improve following repartnering (Thomson et al., 2001).

There are, however, few longitudinal studies that have investigated the impact of stepfamily formation on mother-child relationships. Such data as there are (e.g., Hetherington & Clingempeel, 1992; Hetherington & Jodl, 1994) have tended to focus more on changes in parenting behaviors, with any consequent changes in the relationship implied rather than assessed. These data are suggestive of a disruption in parenting, and therefore a negative impact on relationships between mothers and children, in the early stages of stepfamily formation. This is in line with family stress hypotheses that suggest that transitions, such as parental separation or the formation of a new stepfamily, negatively impact relationships. Hetherington and

Clingempeel, for example, found that remarriage was initially associated with higher levels of mother-child conflict, but over time mother-child relationships in stepfamilies did not differ from those in the comparison nondivorced families.

Based on cross-sectional data, others have reported that, compared to postdivorce mother-child relationships, remarriage was associated with an improvement in the mother-child relationship (Peterson & Zill, 1986), at least from the children's point of view (Thomson et al., 2001), which suggests that the length of time between a separation and a repartnering is relevant.

Bray and Berger (1993) conducted a cross-sectional investigation of three groups of White middle-class stepfamilies, all with children ages 6 to 8 years at stepfamily formation, at different points after remarriage, and compared them with a group of families with two biological parents and children of comparable ages. Mother-child relationships were assessed by means of coded observation of six 10-minute videotaped interactions. Relationships in the stepfamilies that had only been together for 6 months demonstrated more negativity and less positivity than those in the non-stepfamilies. Mother-child relationships in stepfamilies that had been in existence for 2.5 years were comparable to those in the families with two biological parents with children of comparable ages. But in the longest established stepfamilies, remarried for 5 years and with adolescent children, there were fewer positive interactions between mothers and children than in the comparison group of two-parent families. These results were attributed to the lower levels of family cohesion and poorer communication (i.e., more disengagement) observed in stepfamilies. Within stepfamilies, more negative interactions between mothers and children were predicted by negative couple interactions and stepfathers' lower levels of marital satisfaction.

Based on parent report questionnaire and interview measures of the mother-child relationship, and using data from the families in the Avon Longitudinal Study of Parents and Children cohort study, O'Connor, Dunn, Jenkins, and Rasbash (2006) compared the quality of resident mother-child relationships in stepfamilies and two-parent families. They found that, compared to two-parent families, there was no difference in the quality of mother-child relationships in terms of either conflict or warmth and positivity in simple stepfamilies. Differences in complex stepfamilies, and the greater variability in the quality of mother-child relationships with different children, were accounted for by differences in relatedness and the fact that some of the mothers in complex stepfamilies were also stepmothers.

In a study based on secondary analysis of survey data, Thomson et al. (2001) found no differences, from mothers' reports, between mothers and their children in stepfamilies, two-parent families, and lone-mother families on the global measure of the mother-child relationship, warmth between mother and child, or the frequency of enjoyable times with their child.

These findings are broadly consistent with the findings from the U.K. New Stepfamilies Study, despite that fact that the stepfamilies studied were in their early stages. Assessments of the quality of mother-child relationships were based on detailed data obtained during the interviews with mothers and with children. For mothers, this included information on positive recognition of the child, warmth, enjoyment of company, criticism, irritability, hostility, loss of control, confiding, shared interests, and shared activities. From these, two composite measures of the mother-child relationship, positivity and negativity, were created. In addition, a measure of the overall quality of the mother-child relationship, based on high positivity and low negativity, was made in one of five categories: very good, good, mixed/ambivalent, poor, or very poor.

Based on mothers' accounts of the relationship, the large majority described very good ($N = 101, 50.2\%$) or good ($N = 59, 29.4\%$) relationships with their children. The overall quality of the mother-child relationship was not associated with the age or gender of the child, although there was an association between child gender and being described as having a very good relationship with the parent: More girls than boys in stepfamilies were described as having very good relationships with their mothers (53.5% of girls versus 46.5% of boys). Fourteen children—seven boys and seven girls, all but two in current stepfamilies—were described as having poor ($N = 9, 4.5\%$) or very poor ($N = 5, 2.5\%$) relationships with their mothers.

The quality of the mother-child relationship was not associated with stepfamily type (i.e., whether it was a current stepfather family or a mother from a stepfamily that had now broken up; or whether it was a simple stepfamily, a "simple plus" stepfamily, or a complex stepfamily), or with the marital status of the stepfamily.

Comparing the data from the U.K. New Stepfamilies Study with exactly comparable information on the quality of the mother-child relationship from the comparison sample, there were no significant differences in the overall quality of mother-child relationships between children in current stepfamilies and children in two-parent families (Figure 7.1). As might be anticipated from this, there were no differences in the measures of positivity or negativity between mothers in stepfamilies and mothers in two-parent families, and no differences in the majority of the individual variables that made up the composite measures, with two exceptions. Mothers in stepfamilies were more positive than mothers in two-parent families in describing their children, and the pattern of irritability with the child was different in stepfamilies, with more reports at both extremes (of frequent and infrequent irritability) than in two-parent families. There were no differences between the two groups in warmth toward the child, enjoyment of

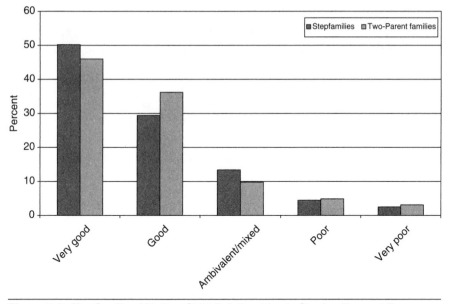

Figure 7.1 The Quality of Mother-Child Relationships in Stepfamilies and Two-Parent Families.

the child's company, criticism of the child, confiding by the child, or the child's reluctance to confide.

Children's reports of their relationships with their mothers were similar: Over 75% of the children in the U.K. New Stepfamilies Study described enjoying their mother's company, and 60% were very warm in their descriptions of their mother. Nearly 66% said that they confided in their mother, and only 11 children (6.4%) said that they did not confide at all. More than half ($N = 102, 57.6\%$) described high levels of physical contact with their mother—although there was a tendency for older children and boys to report less physical contact than younger children and girls. The large majority of children were neither critical of their mothers (15% were moderately critical and only one child was highly critical) nor displayed hostility toward them (2%). Sometimes criticism of the mother was in relation to the stepparent. One girl, when asked what she would change about her mother or how she would like her to be different, said, "I'd like her to break up with Dad [stepfather]. He's horrible." Others were critical about changes that had taken place in the wake of the stepfamily. A boy said, "I'd like to have a cuddle [with his mother] but I don't get a chance now because of the baby."

From these descriptions about different aspects of the relationships and other information obtained in the interviews with the children, interviewers made a global rating of the quality of the relationship. Most children described relationships with their mothers that were very good ($N = 84, 47.2\%$) or good ($N = 71, 39.9\%$). Only four children (2.2%) were judged to have poor relationships with their mothers, and none of the relationships was rated very poor.

MOTHERING IN STEPFAMILIES

Several studies have reported that there are more negative life stresses for stepfamilies, particularly in the early stages (Bray, 1988; Hetherington, 1993). This creates challenges for all stepfamily members, but particularly so for the mother, who is the pivotal figure in the stepfamily. Described as "the glue that holds stepfamilies together" (Ganong & Coleman, 2004, p. 109), mothers in stepfamilies have a major role in parenting their children, at the same time that they play a number of roles in relation to the stepfather and others, such as the nonresident father. Weaver & Coleman (unpublished manuscript, as cited in Ganong & Coleman, 2004) found that mothers acted as the protectors of their children by acting as gatekeepers, defenders, mediators, and interpreters. Several other researchers have identified the role of mothers in stepfamilies as gatekeepers for their children, not only to the stepfather, but in relation to contact with the nonresident father. Gatekeeping by mothers within the stepfamily household is likely to be a feature of the early stages of a stepfamily, but may continue at a lesser level in longer established stepfamilies. It can work both ways: to protect the children from the stepfather, and to protect an unaccustomed stepfather from the realities of parenting and child rearing. There was evidence of both of these in the U.K. New Stepfamilies Study, although in general there was rather little evidence of mothers having prepared their new partners for the role of stepfather to their children. For some mothers, however, discussion of what the stepfather was facing was clearly essential. One mother said:

> I had to be sure he knew what he was taking on. I don't think he knew. He had to know that she [the child] came first. He was surprised at the constraints—that he couldn't go out drinking every weekend; that she takes up a lot of time—her behavior and the mess she makes. I don't think he'd got a clue.

Some mothers had discussed issues relating to the stepfathers' general role in the household and toward children before cohabitation, but it was clear that in some instances this was initiated by the prospective stepfather, in anticipation of his role and behavior with the children, and that in these cases the mother was acting as a mediator rather than a gatekeeper between her new partner and her children. Mothers were asked whether there had been any discussion with their new partner either before or after the stepfather became part of the household or subsequently, on his general behavior and role toward the children, his role in the household, his role and behavior in relation to child care, and specifically in relation to discipline and control and to physical contact with the children. About a third of the mothers had discussed some aspects of the stepfathers' behavior toward their children with them before they cohabited; for example, 35% had specifically discussed aspects of discipline and control, and 34% had discussed his general behavior with the children or in the household (32%) or in relation to child care (29%). Mothers who had discussed one of these aspects of behavior tended to have discussed others as well. The topic least likely to be discussed before cohabitation was how the stepfather was going to behave in relation to physical contact, or the lack of it, with the children; only 15% of mothers said they had done this. For many stepfamilies these conversations did not occur until the stepfather was living in the household, when discussion presumably was triggered by the stepfather's behavior with the child. The topic that was most likely to have been discussed, either before or after cohabitation, was the stepfather's behavior and role in relation to discipline and control of the child, which 74% of mothers said had been discussed at some point. But 49% of the mothers reported that they had never discussed household roles, 46% had never discussed issues relating to child care, and 74% had never discussed the stepfather's behavior in relation to physical contact with the child. In 19% of stepfamilies ($N = 33$) there had never been any discussion of any of these aspects of the stepfather's role or behavior in the household.

PARENTING BY MOTHERS IN STEPFAMILIES

Apart from the additional roles of gatekeeper (and defender), is there any evidence that parenting changes when mothers and their children become part of a stepfamily (usually after being lone parents), or that parenting by mothers in stepfamilies differs from parenting in two-parent families? Thomson and colleagues (2001) discuss a number of reasons why parenting might change with repartnering after a period as a lone parent. These include an improved financial situation leading to lower stress, sharing of household and child-rearing tasks, and the presence of social support for the mother, all of which might be anticipated to result in improvements in parenting. At the same time these researchers acknowledge that there may be other factors that have negative influences on mothering, such as household changes (in residence, routines, etc.), which cause stress; disruptions to mother-child relationships and to the child's behavior as a result of the presence of a new stepfather; and competition for attention.

In the Virginia Longitudinal Study of Divorce and Remarriage, Hetherington and Clingempeel (1992) found that, particularly in the early years of the stepfamily, mothers in stepfamilies exhibited lower levels of monitoring and control of their adolescent children than mothers in two-parent families and were less involved with their children. There were, however, no differences in family functioning or parenting by mothers in longer established stepfamilies, as long as they were simple stepfamilies (Hetherington, 1999). These findings, from a small-scale intensive study, are not consistent with those of Bray and Berger (1993), also based on a small-scale study, or those of Thomson, McLanahan, and Curtin (1992), based on cross-sectional secondary analysis of large-scale survey data. Bray and Berger reported that mothers in stepfamilies tend to parent in a more authoritarian way and are likely to be stricter with their children. Thomson et al. also reported that, compared to mothers in two- or lone-parent families, mothers in stepfamilies supervised their children more closely and had stricter rules for their children. They interpret this as demonstrating that, compared to the lone-parent situation that normally precedes it, a stepfamily and a new partner free the mother to spend more time parenting.

In a subsequent analysis based on secondary analysis of data from the U.S. National Survey of Families and Households (NSFH), mothering before and after divorce was compared, including the impact of remarriage (Hanson, McLanahan, & Thomson, 1998). Based on reports of how often they engaged in four different sorts of activities (leisure activities away from home, working on a project or playing together, having private talks, helping with reading or homework), divorced mothers were involved in more activities with their children than mothers in two-parent families, and this pattern continued after remarriage; that is, mothers did not revert to their previous partnered pattern of mothering. This was not the case in relation to supervision. In a further analysis, utilizing two waves of the NSFH data, Thomson and colleagues (2001) did not replicate their earlier findings, as supervision by mothers in the relatively new stepfamilies was found to be less than in stable lone-parent households. They concluded that family disruption as a result of repartnering also disrupted supervision by mothers.

Activities with the Index Child

In the U.K. New Stepfamilies Study, mothers were asked about their involvement with the index child (the child in the household between 7 and 11 years old, or if there was more than one, a randomly selected child in this age group) in six specific activities in the previous week: watching television, reading or listening to the child read, helping with homework, playing games or computer games, playing outside games or sports, and doing household chores together. For each activity, mothers were questioned about whether they had engaged in this activity with the index child in the previous week; if they had, they were asked to provide further information and details of the activities. For example, if the mother reported that she had watched television with the child the previous day, she would be asked what they had watched together and so on for each instance. The aim of this detailed questioning was to assess accurately the actual frequency of activities with the child rather than the hypothetical frequency; it was often the case that mothers who felt they often helped with homework or frequently read to their child had not actually done so in the previous week. This detailed information was then coded in one of four categories: daily or more often, three to six times in the past week, one or two times in the past week, and not in the past week.

The most frequently shared activities were watching television together (which 17% of mothers and children in stepfamilies did daily, and only 12% had not done at all in the previous week) and helping with school homework (which only 2% had done every day, but over 20% had done on three or more occasions and 33% had done once or twice). The least frequent shared activities were outside games and sports (fewer than 30% had done so at all in the previous week, and for most of these it had been on only one or two occasions).

Comparing these data with those from the comparable sample of mothers in two-parent families, on the whole there was remarkable concordance. There were no differences in the frequency or pattern of activities in relation to reading to the child, helping with school homework, playing games with the child, or involvement in outside games and sports. There were, however, differences in relation to patterns of television watching and marked differences in the frequency of helping with household chores. Mothers in stepfamilies were less likely to watch television with the index child on a daily basis but were more likely to have watched some television with the child in the previous week, and mothers in stepfamilies were less likely to have involved the index child in housework within the previous week. Only 2% of children in stepfamily households had helped their mother with household chores every day in the previous week, compared with 8% of those in two-parent households, and 64% of those in stepfamily households had not done so at all in the previous week, compared with 42% of those in two-parent households.

It seems probable that the differences in involvement in housework in stepfamilies are a residual effect of lone-parent status, since comparison with data from a small group of 44 lone mothers (from the comparison sample) revealed that they were also less likely to involve their children in housework than were mothers in two-parent families, and that lone mothers did not differ significantly from mothers in stepfamilies in the pattern of involvement. Of the mothers in lone-parent households, 59% had not involved their children in any housework in the previous week, compared with 42% of children in two-parent households and 64% in stepfamilies.

Although this finding may largely explain the immediate origin of this difference in stepfamilies, it is not clear why children in lone-mother households should be less likely than children in two-parent families to help their mothers with household activities, such as cooking, washing up, and cleaning.

Differences in the patterns of television watching between mothers in stepfamilies and in two-parent families are also hard to explain. They were not accounted for by the fact that more stepfamilies had babies or young children, as the differences persisted when this factor was controlled for. They were, moreover, only partly explained by the number of children who were regularly away or out of the household on the weekend, for example visiting their nonresident fathers.

PUNISHMENT AND CONTROL

For children, growing up in a stepfamily was said to be a risk factor for abusive punishment and maltreatment (Giles-Sims & Finkelhor, 1984) and for harsh or punitive parenting (Hashima & Amato, 1994). The studies that gave rise to these conclusions were conducted some time ago, when the prevalence of stepfamilies was much lower than now; they often had small and nonrepresentative samples, and in many of them there was poor information on the perpetrator of the violence or harsh parenting. For example, in their analyses of the U.S. NSFH, Hashima and Amato (1994) conclude that children in stepfamilies are at increased risk of punitive parental behavior based on parents' self reports that they yelled at or slapped their young children "very often," but parents were not distinguished from stepparents in the analyses, so it is not possible to know whether this finding relates to mothers in stepfamilies, or to stepfathers, or both. More recent studies, and studies that have looked more specifically at the identity of the parent, have tended to conclude that stepfathers are no more likely than fathers to be severely violent to their stepchildren (Gelles & Harrop, 1991), and indeed that after a period of settlement and adjustment, parental control and punishment of children in established stepfamilies does not differ significantly from that of children in two-parent families. However, both Bray (1988) and Hetherington (1993) reported differences in mothers' behavior in the early stages of stepfamily formation, although these disappeared over time. Based on small-scale but intensive data, Bray found that mothers in stepfamilies reported less effective discipline practices in the early days after stepfamily formation. Hetherington, also using small-scale but detailed data, reported higher levels of conflict between mothers and their children in the initial stages of the stepfamily, in conjunction with lower levels of control, but noted that after a few years maternal punitiveness did not differ from parenting in two-parent families.

This is broadly in line with what Thomson and colleagues (2001) concluded from secondary analyses of two waves of the NSFH data. Thomson et al. looked at the impact of remarriage or cohabitation after a period as a lone parent on mothers' supervision and punitiveness. They found that, compared to lone parents, mothers in stepfamilies supervised their children less closely (which was in contrast to findings from their earlier cross-sectional analysis; Thomson et al., 1992), but that they were also less likely to use harsh discipline (based on limited questions about how often children were yelled at, spanked, or hit).

In terms of timing, these data should be broadly consistent with the cross-sectional data from the U.K. New Stepfamilies Study, since the stepfamilies studied were in their relatively early stages, but in this case the comparisons are with mothers in two-parent families. As discussed earlier, in the U.K. study, the issue of punishment and control appeared to be the aspect of parenting that had most often been discussed between mothers and stepfathers. According to mothers, it had been discussed in detail in more than half the current stepfamilies, and in a further quarter it had not been discussed, but there was clear evidence of gatekeeping by the mothers, with limits set for the stepfather or acceptable practice specified. Mothers in only 17 families (11%) said that they had never discussed the issue of punishment or control with the stepfather.

In both stepfamilies and non-stepfamilies the mother usually described herself as the main disciplinarian. In 13 stepfamilies (8.4%) the mother was the only punisher, as the stepfather either did not or was not allowed to discipline the children. One mother said, "They're my children, so he [stepfather] tells me what has happened. I deal with it." Another mother described why she had stopped the stepfather from disciplining the child: "I suggested not to discipline at first as [stepchild] was seeking approval [from the stepfather]. Only when [stepchild] became comfortable could [stepfather] discipline."

Most mothers in stepfamilies had spanked the index child at some time, although 29 (16.2%) said that they had never done so, and 68 (37.8%) said that they had not done so in the past year. Compared with mothers in two-parent families from the comparison sample, the prevalence and frequency of spanking was very different in current stepfamilies (Figure 7.2). Mothers in stepfamilies were significantly less likely to have ever spanked the child or to have hit the child in the previous year. Where they reported that they had (46.0% compared with 71.6% of mothers in two-parent families), they also reported spanking less frequently. This was a marked difference. While several possible explanations could be hypothesized, for example, mothers wishing to model nonpunitive styles of control to the stepfathers or lower rates of physical punishment being a residue of the lone-parent status (Nobes & Smith, 2002), two important caveats must be attached to these

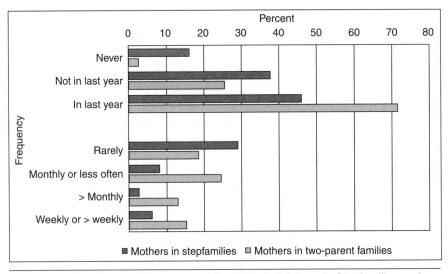

Figure 7.2 Spanking and Frequency of Spanking by Mothers in Stepfamilies and Mothers in Two-Parent Families (%).

findings. The first is that the comparison data were obtained as part of a study in which the main focus was on parental control and punishment of children, and this will have acted to maximize reporting of these behaviors, in comparison to the U.K. New Stepfamilies Study, in which the data were obtained as a much smaller and less significant part of an interview covering a wide range of parental behaviors and a variety of other topics. A second reason for caution relates to the fact that the comparison data were obtained some 3 to 6 years earlier than the stepfamily data, and the apparently lower level of physical punishment may reflect a general temporal trend of decreasing use of physical punishment by parents in the United Kingdom, and not anything specific to membership of a stepfamily. The fact that, according to mothers' historical recall, the differences predate stepfamily formation lends some support to this possibility. In the absence of contemporaneous comparison data it is not possible to know how much of the disparity might be due to either or both these causes. In support of the validity of the findings it is worth noting that they are broadly consistent with the findings of less, or less effective, control by mothers (Bray, 1988; Hetherington, 1993) and less use of harsh punishment (Thomson et al., 2001) in the early years of the stepfamily.

The clearest evidence of mothers' roles as gatekeepers and defenders within the stepfamily was in relation to discipline and physical punishment. In response to questions about whether they approved of the stepfather spanking (or otherwise physically punishing) their child, nearly half the mothers in stepfamilies ($N = 60, 47.2\%$) said they would have concerns or definite anxieties about this. In this group, 48 of the stepfathers had never spanked the index child, but 12 had, six of them within the previous year. Nearly a quarter of mothers ($N = 30, 23.6\%$) said they disapproved of anyone hitting their child, and only three stepfathers in this group had ever hit the child, none of them in the past year. More than a quarter of mothers ($N = 36, 28.3\%$) gave either full or qualified approval to the idea of their partner physically disciplining their child. This did not necessarily mean that the stepfather had done so, although he was more likely to.

CONCLUSION

As the prevalence of stepfamilies as a family form has increased, so has research on stepfamilies: Coleman et al. (2000) point out that the number of research papers on stepfamilies in the previous decade exceeds that of the preceding 90 years. At the same time, stepfamily research has become more sophisticated in terms of its hypotheses, design, and methodology. Despite this, the state of knowledge about stepfamily dynamics and how "ordinary" stepfamilies function has not advanced very significantly in recent years. It is not clear, for example, as remarriage and repartnering become a more common experience for women and the stepfamily experience less atypical, whether the past evidence on stepfamily functioning is still valid, or whether there is any indication that stepfamily dynamics have changed with the changes in prevalence. This is partly a consequence of the methodological difficulties of obtaining stepfamily samples, with the result that the studies that are undertaken tend either to be investigations of stepfamilies as a subgroup within large-scale studies, such as national cohorts, or small-scale intensive studies. The former, where stepfamilies are not the specific focus of the study, are good at identifying associations between variables but poor at providing detailed and rich explanatory information, necessary for understanding family functioning. Small-scale studies, which can potentially provide this, often involve nonrepresentative volunteer samples and lack statistical power. The lack of advancement in our understanding is also a result of the tendency to focus on the step or atypical aspects of the stepfamily, by focusing on stepfathers, nonresident fathers, or outcomes for children. Resident mothers, who after all were mothers before the stepfamily and remain mothers in the stepfamily, and their role in the functioning and well-being of the stepfamily have largely been ignored.

The U.K. New Stepfamilies Study has gone some way to redressing this situation. It involved a broadly representative population of new stepfamilies identified by means of a community screening exercise, and it obtained detailed interview information from a sample of over 150 mothers currently in stepfamilies, as well as children and stepfathers. The major limitation of the study is that it was cross-sectional, looking at stepfamilies and their functioning at a moment in time. As discussed earlier, stepfamilies, and particularly the new stepfamilies studied, are families in transition. For the mothers currently in stepfamilies it represents one stage in a series of events that preceded the stepfamily and, for most women, started in their families of origin.

This chapter has taken a somewhat blinkered view of mothers now in stepfamilies in focusing on their accounts of their histories, and particularly their mental health histories, their relationships with their children, and their parenting in the stepfamily.

Excluded from this view has been any discussion of the quality of mothers' relationships with their current partners, the stepfathers of their children, and with their ex-partners, the nonresident fathers of their children. Nor have the implications for children, in terms of child outcomes, been described. These are relevant, as in order to understand family functioning, the pattern of relationships in the whole family should be studied (Hetherington et al., 1999). Within stepfamilies, however, there is evidence that there are positive associations between the quality of mother-child relationships and children's relationships with their fathers and stepfathers, as well as those between stepfathers and nonresident fathers (Smith, 2004). This could plausibly be interpreted as suggesting that where there is a good and strong relationship between the mother and child or children in a stepfamily, other relationships within the stepfamily network are also likely to be good. Dunn and colleagues (Dunn, Davies, O'Connor, & Sturgess, 2000) also found positive correlations between mother-child relationships and stepfather-child relationships, but noted that both relationships were also associated with each adult's early life course experiences in terms of early parenthood and the number of previous relationships. This reinforces the view that the role of mother is pivotal in determining the functioning and well-being of the stepfamily, but at the same time that the factors that to a large extent determine this predate the stepfamily. It also indicates that the well-being of the mother is an important influence on the well-being and dynamics of the stepfamily.

The U.K. New Stepfamilies Study provided clear evidence of the potential vulnerability of mothers now in stepfamilies, in terms of their past mental health histories. Importantly, though, there was no evidence of the disruptions in the mother-child relationships reported by others (Bray & Berger, 1993; Hetherington, 1993) in the early years after stepfamily formation, despite the fact that the stepfamilies studied were in the early years of their relationships. Also in contrast with the findings of others (Hansen et al., 1998; Hetherington & Clingempeel, 1992), there was no evidence that mothers disengaged from parenting after stepfamily formation or were more involved parents, since there was remarkable similarity to mothers in two-parent families in terms of their activities with their children.

At the same time, there was evidence of an additional layer of parenting activities being performed by many mothers in stepfamilies, in the form of gatekeeping and defending, but also acting as broker, mediator, and facilitator. There was evidence of mothers tutoring stepfathers in the parenting role and how they should behave toward the children, defending their children from the stepfather, particularly in relation to the issue of punishment and control; there was also evidence (not described in this chapter) of many mothers performing these roles in relation to the nonresident father as well, and often between the stepfather and the nonresident father.

Mothers are the cause of the stepfamily to the extent that they have entered into a relationship with a new partner, and the children come, as described by Hetherington (1999), as an "adjunct" to this relationship. The cost is that at least in the relatively early stages of the stepfamily, mothers must perform a multiplicity of roles—in fact, acting as the linchpin or central pivot in the stepfamily. As such, their role is key to the dynamics and success of the stepfamily. At the same time, factors that select women into stepfamilies, in particular their early partnering and child rearing, failed relationships, and, to a greater extent, poor mental health histories, suggest that women in stepfamilies are a potentially vulnerable population. This has clear implications for their future support needs, although there were no indications of disruptions to parenting or to relationships with their children in the mothers involved in the U.K. New Stepfamilies Study who were in the honeymoon stage of the stepfamily. The fact that stepfamilies are to a large extent an invisible population poses real challenges for support services, but it should be remembered that, despite the complexity of their situations and processes, the large majority of stepfamilies do function well, and that this is, in large part, attributable to the resident mothers.

REFERENCES

Amato, P. R. (1996). Explaining the intergenerational transmission of divorce. *Journal of Marriage and the Family, 58*, 628–640.

Amato, P. R., & Keith, B. (1991). Parental divorce and the well-being of children: A meta-analysis. *Psychological Bulletin, 110*, 26–46.

Aquilino, W. S. (1991). Family structure and home leaving: A further specification of the relationship. *Journal of Marriage and the Family, 53*, 999–1010.

Armitage, B., & Babb, P. (1996). Population review: (4) Trends in fertility. *Population Trends, 84*, 1–13.

Aseltine, R. H., & Kessler, R. C. (1993). Marital disruption and depression in a community sample. *Journal of Health and Social Behavior, 34*, 237–251.

Baldwin, W. (1993). The consequences of early childbearing: A perspective. *Journal of Research on Adolescence, 3*, 349–353.

Bifulco, A., & Moran, P. (1998). *Wednesday's child: Research into women's experience of neglect and abuse in childhood and adult depression.* London: Routledge.

Booth, A., & Amato, P. (1994). Parental marital quality, divorce, and relations with parents. *Journal of Marriage and the Family, 53*, 21–34.

Bray, J. H. (1988). Children's development during early remarriage. In E. M. Hetherington & J. D. Arasteh (Eds.), *Impact of divorce, single parenting, and stepparenting on children* (pp. 279–298). Hillsdale, NJ: Erlbaum.

Bray, J. H., & Berger, S. H. (1993). Developmental issues in Stepfamilies Research Project: Family relationships and parent-child interactions. *Journal of Family Psychology, 7*, 76–90.

Bumpass, L. L., Martin, T. C., & Sweet, J. A. (1991). The impact of family background and early marital factors on family disruption. *Journal of Family Issues, 12*, 22–42.

Bumpass, L. L., Raley, R. K., & Sweet, J. A. (1995). The changing character of stepfamilies: Implications of cohabitation and nonmarital childbearing. *Demography, 32*, 425–436.

Cherlin, A. J., Kiernan, K. E., & Chase-Lansdale, P. L. (1995). Parental divorce in childhood and demographic outcomes in young adulthood. *Demography, 32*, 299–318.

Coleman, M., Ganong, L., & Fine, M. (2000). Reinvestigating remarriage: Another decade of progress. *Journal of Marriage and the Family, 62*, 1288–1307.

Demo, D. H., & Acock, A. C. (1996). Singlehood, marriage, and remarriage: The effects of family structure and family relationships on mothers' well-being. *Journal of Family Issues, 17*, 388–407.

Dunn, J., Davies, L. C., O'Connor, T. G., & Sturgess, W. (2000). Parents' and partners' life course and family experiences: Links with parent-child relationships in different family settings. *Journal of Child Psychology and Psychiatry, 41*, 955–968.

Ermisch, J., & Francesconi, M. (2000). The increasing complexity of family relationships: Lifetime experience of lone motherhood and stepfamilies in Great Britain. *European Journal of Population, 16*, 235–249.

Fido, M., Gibbins, R., Hurt, C., Matthews, D., & Thomas, T. (2006). *General Household Survey 2005*. Newport, England: Office for National Statistics.

Foley, D. L., Pickles, A., Rutter, M., Gardner, C. O., Maes, H. H., Silberg, J. L., et al. (2004). Risks for conduct disorder symptoms associated with parental alcoholism in stepfather families versus intact families from a community sample. *Journal of Child Psychology and Psychiatry, 45*, 687–696.

Furstenberg, F. F. (1990). Divorce and the American family. *Annual Review of Sociology, 16*, 379–403.

Furstenberg, F. F., & Cherlin, A. J. (1991). *Divided families: What happens to children when parents part*. Cambridge, MA: Harvard University Press.

Ganong, L. H., & Coleman, M. (1994). *Remarried family relationships*. Thousand Oaks, CA: Sage.

Ganong, L. H., & Coleman, M. (2004). *Stepfamily relationships: Development, dynamics and interventions*. New York: Kluwer Academic/Plenum Press.

Gelles, R. J., & Harrop, J. W. (1991). The risk of abusive violence among children with nongenetic caretakers. *Family Relations, 40*, 78–83.

Giles-Sims, J., & Finkelhor, D. (1984). Child abuse in stepfamilies. *Family Relations, 33*, 407–414.

Hanson, T. L., McLanahan, S. S., & Thomson, E. (1998). Windows on divorce: Before and after. *Social Science Research, 27*, 329–349.

Hashima, P. Y., & Amato, P. R. (1994). Poverty, social support, and parental behavior. *Child Development, 65,* 394–403.

Hetherington, E. M. (1993). An overview of the Virginia Longitudinal Study of Divorce and Remarriage with a focus on early adolescence. *Journal of Family Psychology, 7,* 39–56.

Hetherington, E. M. (1999). Family functioning in nonstepfamilies and different kinds of stepfamilies: An integration. *Monographs of the Society for Research in Child Development, 64*(4), 184–191.

Hetherington, E. M., & Clingempeel, W. G. (Eds.). (1992). Coping with marital transitions: A family systems perspective. *Monographs of the Society for Research in Child Development, 57*(2/3).

Hetherington, E. M., Henderson, S. H., Reiss, D., Anderson, E. R., O'Connor, T., Jodl, K. M., et al. (1999). Family functioning and adolescent adjustment of siblings in nondivorced families and diverse types of stepfamilies. *Monographs of the Society for Research in Child Development, 64*(4, Serial No. 259).

Hetherington, E. M., & Jodl, K. M. (1994). Stepfamilies as settings for child development. In A. Booth & J. Dunn (Eds.), *Stepfamilies: Who benefits? Who does not?* (pp. 55–79). Hillsdale, NJ: Erlbaum.

Kessler, R. C., Walters, E. E., & Forthofer, M. S. (1998). The social consequences of psychiatric disorders: Pt. III. Probability of marital stability. *American Journal of Psychiatry, 155,* 1092–1096.

Kiernan, K. E. (1992). The impact of family disruption in childhood on transitions made in young adult life. *Population Studies, 46,* 213–234.

Montgomery, M. M., Anderson, E. R., Hetherington, E. M., & Clingempeel, W. G. (1992). Patterns of courtship for remarriage: Implications for child adjustment and parent-child relationships. *Journal of Marriage and the Family, 54,* 686–698.

Nicholson, J. M., Fergusson, D. M., & Horwood, L. J. (1999). Effects on later adjustment of living in a stepfamily during childhood and adolescence. *Journal of Child Psychology and Psychiatry, 40,* 405–416.

Nobes, G., & Smith, M. (2002). Family structure and the physical punishment of children. *Journal of Family Issues, 23,* 349–373.

O'Connor, T. G., Dunn, J., Jenkins, J. M., & Rasbash, J. (2006). Predictors of between-family and within-family variation in parent-child relationships. *Journal of Child Psychology and Psychiatry, 47,* 498–510.

O'Connor, T. G., Hawkins, N., Dunn, J., Thorpe, K. J., & Golding, J. (1998). Family type and maternal depression in pregnancy: Factors mediating risk in a community sample. *Journal of Marriage and the Family, 60,* 757–770.

Peterson, J. L., & Zill, N. (1986). Marital disruption, parent-child relationships, and behaviour problems in children. *Journal of Marriage and the Family, 48,* 295–307.

Prskawetz, A., Vikat, A., Philipov, D., & Engelhardt, H. (2003). Pathways to stepfamily formation in Europe: Results from the FFS. *Demographic Research, 8,* 107–149. Available from www.demographic-research.org/volumes/vol8/5.

Rodgers, B., Pickles, A., Power, C., Collishaw, S., & Maughan, B. (1999). Validity of the Malaise Inventory in general population samples. *Social Psychiatry and Psychiatric Epidemiology, 34,* 333–341.

Smith, M. (2004). Relationships of children in stepfamilies with their non-resident fathers. *Family Matters, 67,* 28–35.

Stewart, S. D. (2005). How the birth of a child affects involvement with stepchildren. *Journal of Marriage and the Family, 67*, 461–473.

Thomson, E. (2004). Step-families and childbearing desires in Europe [Special collection]. *Demographic Research, 3*(5). Available from www.demographic-research.org.

Thomson, E., McLanahan, S. S., & Curtin, R. B. (1992). Family structure and parental socialization. *Journal of Marriage and the Family, 54*, 368–378.

Thomson, E., Mosley, J., Hanson, T. L., & McLanahan, S. S. (2001). Remarriage, cohabitation, and changes in mothering behavior. *Journal of Marriage and the Family, 63*, 370–380.

White, L. K. (1994). Growing up with single parents and stepparents: Long term effects on family solidarity. *Journal of Marriage and the Family, 56*, 935–948.

White, L. K., & Booth, A. (1985). The quality and stability of remarriages: The role of stepchildren. *American Sociological Review, 50*, 689–698.

Zill, N., Morrison, D. R., & Coiro, M. J. (1993). Long term effects of parental divorce on parent-child relationships, adjustments and achievements in early adulthood. *Journal of Family Psychology, 7*, 91–103.

CHAPTER 8

Sibling Relationships in Blended Families

MELINDA E. BAHAM, AMY A. WEIMER,
SANFORD L. BRAVER, and WILLIAM V. FABRICIUS

A LARGE NUMBER of children will experience the separation, divorce, and remarriage of their parents during their childhood. Approximately half of all first marriages will end in divorce, and the majority of adults will remarry (e.g., Bray & Berger, 1993; Hetherington & Jodl, 1994). Additionally, it is estimated that 40% of parents currently in first marriages will remarry before their youngest child reaches adulthood (Glick, 1989). Thus, it becomes increasingly important to investigate the social, emotional, cognitive, and behavioral impact that living in a stepfamily has on children and adolescents. Although recent research has focused on changes in the parent-child relationship and in parenting practices within the new family and how those changes are related to child outcomes, relatively little research has examined how the changing family formation impacts sibling relationships.

Sibling relationships are potentially important determinants of psychological outcomes, yet they are relatively understudied, and researchers have not articulated a clear theoretical approach. Thus, the goal of this chapter is to synthesize the existing research on siblings in blended families into a single, comprehensive conceptual model that can both summarize current knowledge and guide further research. This model, in turn, should and does relate to and extend theoretical approaches to siblings in *intact* families. In addition, we present some new preliminary data that examine links between the quality of sibling relationships, parent-child relations, and child well-being among blended families.

However, before these goals can be achieved, we must first clearly define our terminology.

DEFINING VARIOUS SIBLING AND FAMILY TYPES

We distinguish three types of siblings: full siblings, stepsiblings, and half-siblings. A full sibling is a sibling of the target child who has the same biological parents as the target child. A stepsibling is a sibling of the target child who is not biologically related to the child and has entered the family system via the child's stepparent. A half-sibling is a sibling of the target child who shares one biological parent with the child, but the sibling's other biological parent is not biologically related to the child (Reiss et al., 1994; Rende, Slomkowski, Lloyd-Richardson, & Niaura, 2005). The half-sibling can be a result of the union between the target child's biological parent and the target child's stepparent, or could be the result of the target child's biological parent's union with a prior partner. For children with more than one sibling, there may be more than one type of sibling. For example, a child may have both a full sibling and a stepsibling.

Step- and half-siblings arise in the context of blended families, which can include various combinations of stepparents and single parents. In a simple stepparent family (either stepfather or stepmother family) one parent is the biological parent of the target child, and the other parent is not the biological parent. A complex stepfamily is one in which both parents are stepparents to different children in the family (a *Brady Bunch* family). We call this a stepmother and stepfather family. A complex stepfamily may also include a half-sibling: a child that is the result of a genetic union between both parents in the family and would be a half-sibling to a child of the mother's or a child of the father's.

THEORIES OF SIBLING AND FAMILY RELATIONSHIPS

The existing literature on sibling relationships within blended families does not provide an adequate theoretical perspective that both explains the known relationships and suggests areas of future research. Developing and proposing such a model is a major goal of this chapter. However, ideally, this model should relate to and extend existing theoretical insights into processes and dynamics that are similar. In fact, several important theories of sibling relationships in *intact* families have been proposed, and these will likely serve as productive frameworks as we seek to summarize processes involved in the development of sibling relationships in blended families. The theoretical views that follow represent the primary theoretical approaches from the literature.

Sibling deidentification is the experience of being dissimilar from one's sibling (Neaves & Crouch, 1990; Schachter, 1982). Sibling deidentification is a way of appropriately dealing with feelings of sibling rivalry, to the extent that children are able to indirectly promote their superiority over their sibling by differentiating themselves from their sibling (Schachter, 1982). Thus, deidentification might be construed as an active process through which children become increasingly dissimilar to their siblings as they develop (e.g., McHale, Updegraff, Helms-Erikson, & Crouter, 2001). In terms of sibling relationships in blended families, deidentification theory might suggest a process for the ways stepsiblings in particular disassociate themselves from each other in order to establish their own identity. This could be particularly true for young adolescents who are actively undergoing identity formation.

SOCIAL LEARNING THEORY

Social learning theory emphasizes that behavior is learned through imitation, modeling, and reinforcement. For example, siblings are much more likely to get along if their parents get along (Dunn, 1993). Likewise, parental conflict-resolution techniques predict siblings' negative behaviors toward each other (Reese-Weber, 2000). In particular, children whose parents are violent toward each other and children and who are victims of parental abuse have significantly higher levels of sibling violence (Straus, Gelles, & Steinmetz, 1980).

Siblings are also models for each other. In particular, older siblings might be especially important models for younger siblings because of their position of authority (Buhrmester & Furman, 1990). They can help younger siblings become more competent at many tasks. For example, children who have older siblings as tutors fare better in school (Koester & Johnson, 1984); in turn, older siblings benefit from the tutoring experience (Paulhus & Shaffer, 1981).

Similar to social learning theory, the social-interactional perspective also suggests ways that siblings influence each other's behaviors (Patterson, Dishion, & Bank, 1984). This perspective views deviant behavior (delinquency, antisocial behavior, aggression) as a product of operant conditioning, in which children and parents train each other to act in a coercive manner, which produces a pattern of coercive behavioral interactions that increases in intensity over time. This approach also suggests that siblings train each other to act in a coercive manner. For example, after one sibling acts in a coercive manner, the other sibling is very likely to *reciprocate* that behavior.

The principles of social learning theory likely apply similarly among siblings in blended families. That is, children model the behavioral patterns of parents and full, step-, and half-siblings with whom they have frequent contact. That siblings influence one another, can create a similar environment for one another, and that there is a bidirectional nature to the child's relationships and that this impacts the future functioning of the family as a whole are key aspects of the theory that can inform sibling relationships in blended families.

Family Systems Theory

Family systems theory (Bowen, 1971, 1972) examines the family in terms of various subsystems, each of which can impact other subsystems and the overall family system (S. Minuchin, 1974). For example, a family may have a sibling subsystem, a marital subsystem, and a parent-child subsystem. Family systems theory proposes that a triangular relationship (a relationship involving three individuals) is a more stable unit than a two-person relationship. Individuals and relationships are consistently interacting and mutually influencing one another, as opposed to a unidirectional influence of one person or relationship to another. Another core concept is that both stability and change in families are expected over time (P. Minuchin, 1985, 1988). Families will engage in typical reaction patterns to one another, and these reaction patterns are relatively stable over time. However, these patterns may change as new challenges for the family emerge to which the family must adapt.

Family systems theory has been used both by sibling relationships researchers and stepfamily researchers. Sibling relationship researchers use family systems theory as a way of explaining how changes in the sibling relationship may influence other aspects of family life, and how the parent-child relationship and the marital relationship might influence the quality of the sibling relationship. Stepfamily researchers have used family systems theory to explain the ways in which the forming of a new family system through remarriage may have influences on other aspects of the family (Bray & Berger, 1993; Hetherington, 1991). For example, two biologically unrelated children who are living together because of the marriage between their parents have a new, stepsibling relationship, and changes in that sibling relationship, or simply focusing on that relationship, can impact the relationship between one of the children and his or her biological parent. Thus, the stepsibling subsystem is affecting the parent-child subsystem.

Nonshared Environment

Researchers have noticed that siblings residing in the same household have very different experiences, due in part to the different environments they choose (e.g., peers, activities), and in part because similar events (e.g., a divorce) might impact siblings in very different ways. These environmental factors that are different between siblings growing up in the same household are referred to as the *nonshared environment* (Plomin & Daniels, 1987; Turkheimer & Waldron, 2000). Explaining the various factors that influence the nonshared environment has become a goal of many researchers.

Stepsiblings in particular have a history of experiencing a nonshared environment because they grow up in two different households. Those households have dissolved and been reformed into the new family in which the stepsiblings reside. Given the different histories of the stepsiblings, they, perhaps more than full siblings, are likely to have different influences on their development. They are likely to have the opportunity to have different peer groups and to engage in different activities. Additionally, even full siblings may have reacted differently to their parents' divorce and remarriage, and therefore a different environment is created for each child, due to his or her reaction to the family changes. Thus, when examining sibling relationships in blended families, it is important to consider the different influences on each child that may influence the relationship.

EVOLUTIONARY THEORY

Evolutionary theorists (Barkow, Cosmides, & Tooby, 1992; Irons, 1979) contend that both psychological processes and behavioral mechanisms evident in humans today have evolved because they were adaptive for our ancestors. This view of development has been applied to understanding family relationships in stepfamilies and thus has many implications for the dynamics of sibling interactions within them. For example, Popenoe (1994) claims that stepfathers take less active roles in parenting than custodial fathers because they are not as invested in the survival of unrelated children. Applying Popenoe's reasoning, perhaps children from blended families have less invested stepparents (in particular stepfathers) who are more likely to treat siblings differently. This could foster sibling rivalry, given that differential treatment from parents has been found to affect sibling relationships. In particular, relationships tend to be less conflictual when parents do not favor one child over the other, but rather respond warmly and sensitively to all of their children (Boyle, Jenkins, & Georgiades, 2004; Brody, 1998; McHale et al., 2001).

FURMAN AND BUHRMESTER'S THEORY OF THE QUALITY OF SIBLING RELATIONSHIPS

Through open-ended and questionnaire surveys, Furman and Buhrmester's (1985) work on sibling relationships established four factors, or macro aspects, of sibling relationships: warmth, relative power, conflict, and rivalry. Warmth and conflict were unrelated to each other, suggesting two distinct dimensions, and were both uncorrelated with relative power, whereas conflict and rivalry had a moderate (.35) positive correlation. This highlights the necessity of considering positive and negative aspects of sibling relationships as separate dimensions. Additionally, 15 specific features, or micro aspects, of sibling relationships were observed, including intimacy, companionship, nurturance, and affection (all aspects of the warmth factor), dominance (an aspect of relative power), quarreling, antagonism, and competition (aspects of conflict), and parental partiality (an aspect of rivalry).

In addition to specifying particular aspects of the quality of sibling relationships, Furman and Buhrmester (1985) suggested a model that describes the hypothesized influences on the quality of the sibling relationships (see Figure 8.1).

This model describes such family constellation variables as family size, birth order, and age discrepancies as having a direct impact on both the parent-child relationships and the sibling relationship (relative age refers to whether the child is the older or younger sibling). Furthermore, the connection between the parent-child relationship and the sibling relationship, which is characterized by the four relationship factors, is bidirectional in nature, allowing the parent-child relationships to impact the sibling relationship and the sibling relationship to impact the parent-child relationships. Finally, characteristics of the children themselves, such as their personalities, directly influence the quality of the sibling relationship and the parent-child relationships.

Research (Buhrmester, 1992; Furman & Buhrmester, 1985) indicates that sibling relationships provide an important opportunity to experience intimacy (disclosure), affection, and companionship; these relationships vary by gender and change with development. For example, same-sex sibling

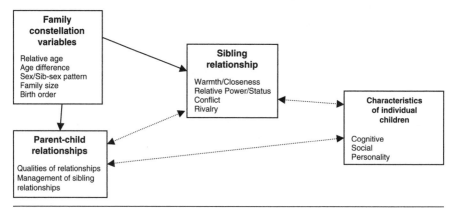

Figure 8.1 Furman and Buhrmester's (1985) Model of the Influences of Sibling Relationship Quality.

Source: "Children's Perceptions of the Qualities of Sibling Relationships," by W. Furman and D. Buhrmester, 1985, *Child Development, 56,* pp. 448–461.

pairs report higher levels of companionship, affection, and intimacy. Regarding age, older siblings have more status and power in the relationship than do younger siblings. Children report higher levels of intimacy with older siblings as opposed to younger siblings, with whom they report more frequent conflict. Siblings close in age report higher levels of conflict than siblings who are far apart in age (Buhrmester, 1992; Furman & Buhrmester, 1985). Yet, as children enter adolescence, sibling relationships become more balanced, such that older siblings lose the power they had over their younger siblings, nurture their younger siblings less, dominate their younger siblings less, whereas younger siblings nurture and dominate their older siblings more as the children develop (Buhrmester, 1992). Moreover, as siblings age, their relationships become less emotionally charged; levels of all major dimensions of sibling relationship (warmth, conflict, rivalry, and power) diminish, and this decrease is postulated to be due in part to the diminished frequency of interaction as children mature. However, although reported levels of warmth decrease with age, this is mostly due to decreased levels of companionship, whereas levels of affection remain fairly strong (Buhrmester, 1992). These findings underscore the importance of considering age and gender, the relative match in age and gender between siblings, and how relationships change over time when investigating the quality of sibling relationships.

Many of these same ideas can be applied to the development of step- and half-sibling relationships. The impact of family constellation variables, such as age and gender similarities, the influence of parent-child relationships, and the impact of the characteristics of the two children in the dyad, will certainly play a role in the development of sibling relationships in blended families. In particular, the consideration of parent-child relationships will need to be expanded to include stepparent-stepchild relationships and the relationship each child has with his or her nonresidential parent. Finally, Furman and Buhrmester (1985) suggest a useful way of examining the quality of sibling relationships in terms of warmth, conflict, rivalry, and relative power that will help guide our understanding of sibling relationships in blended families.

DUNN'S INDIVIDUAL DIFFERENCES IN SIBLING RELATIONSHIPS

Dunn's (1993) work has focused on the individual differences in various sibling relationships rather than their commonality, especially in young siblings. Dunn recalls the work of several researchers that indicate clearly distinct positive (e.g., a sense of attachment, connected conversations, self-disclosure, humor, and shared experiences of fantasy or pretend play) and negative (e.g., rivalry and conflict) dimensions of sibling relationships. Sibling pairs can be high on both dimensions, low on both dimensions, or high on one dimension and low on the other dimension. Remarkable individual differences are noted in the amount of conflict between young siblings, with some sibling pairs having relatively little conflict, and others experiencing high levels of conflict.

Dunn (1993) highlights the significance of each child's individual temperament and the temperament match (or mismatch) between the two siblings on the quality of the sibling relationship. Children with difficult or active temperaments, or temperaments in which they are unable to easily adapt to changes in the environment, often have a more conflictual sibling relationship. Siblings who differ greatly in their temperament styles will also experience a less harmonious sibling relationship. Dunn also acknowledges the role that family constellation variables, such as gender, the age difference between children, and birth position, may have on the developing sibling relationship. Moreover, Dunn recognizes the influences other relationships, including the parent-child, parent-sibling, and marital relationships, may have on individual differences in sibling relationships.

The focus that Dunn (1993) places on individual differences in sibling relationships is applicable to the sibling relationships in blended families literature. Step-, half-, and full sibling relationships in blended families are very likely to differ from pair to pair, and thus it is critical to examine the reasons for these differences, specifically the mechanisms that might lead one pair of siblings to have a high-quality relationship and another pair to have a relationship marked by conflict.

BRODY'S HEURISTIC MODEL

Brody (1998) summarized and amalgamated the literature on the quality of sibling relationships (full siblings from intact families) and created a heuristic model that synthesized the research to date and guided future research. Brody focused on the influence of child temperament, marital processes, parental depression, parent-child relationships, parental differential treatment, and parental conflict-management strategies on sibling relationship quality (see Figure 8.2).

Several contributions of child temperament and marital relationship quality to sibling relationship quality were observed. Brody (1998) reviewed work that suggests children's temperaments are related to the quality of the sibling relationship, such that older siblings' difficult temperament (characterized by high activity levels and emotional intensity) related to less positivity in the sibling relationship, and younger siblings' difficult temperament related to more negativity in the sibling relationship (Brody, Stoneman, & McCoy, 1994). The most harmonious sibling relationships were observed between siblings who both had low activity levels; siblings who both had high activity levels had the most conflictual relationships (Stoneman & Brody, 1993).

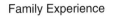

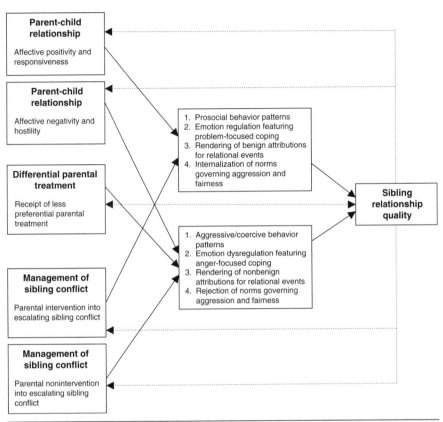

Figure 8.2 Brody's (1998) Model of the Mediators Between Family Processes and Sibling Relationship Quality.

Source: "Sibling Relationship Quality: Its Causes and Consequences," by G. H. Brody, 1998, *Annual Review of Psychology, 49,* pp. 1–24.

Additionally, Brody (1998) summarizes research findings regarding stress in the marital relationship, which suggest that children respond to their parents' stress by experiencing negative emotions such as distress and anger, and these negative emotions are often directed toward others, especially siblings. Similarly, parental depression is often related with poorer quality parenting and children's experiences of negative emotions, which then may impact the sibling relationship.

Brody (1998) also highlighted the effect of family process variables, such as parent-child relationships, differential parental treatment, and management of sibling conflict, on the quality of the sibling relationship. Moreover, these family processes are thought to influence sibling relationship quality through the mediators of children's behavior patterns (prosocial or aggressive), the child's ability to regulate his or her emotions, the attributions the child uses to explain various behavioral events, and the norms relating to appropriate interaction between siblings. These mediators exert their influences in a variety of ways. Through mechanisms such as social learning, children learn how to engage in relationships via their interactions with their parents and apply that knowledge to their interactions with their siblings. Also, by observing their parents ameliorating conflict in the sibling relationship, children learn how to interact with their siblings in a more positive manner. Furthermore, children who are able to control negative emotions that arise from their observation of differential treatment or interactions with their parents are less likely to act aggressively towards their sibling than children who cannot manage their emotions. Finally, the reasons children give to explain experiences in their relationships with their parents, and the way in which children accept or discard the rules regarding appropriate behavioral interactions with their siblings, influences the quality of their relationships with their siblings.

The great advantage of this model is that it provides hypotheses regarding the specific processes that are involved in mediating the link between family variables and qualities of the sibling relationship. Other models of sibling relationship have not concentrated nearly as much on the processes through which particular variables, such as parent-child relationships, impact sibling relationship quality. This focus can be equally applied to sibling relationships in blended families. In addition to describing the various circumstances and relationships that might influence step-, half-, and full sibling relationship quality, we should also explore the mechanisms that produce these influences.

Summary

Several key aspects of these various theories of sibling relationships deserve further consideration and application to the realm of sibling relationships in blended families. There are six critical points regarding the theoretical perspectives that must be highlighted. First, the conceptualization of the quality of the sibling relationship along the broad dimensions of conflict and warmth/closeness provides a framework for examining these types of relationships and can be easily applied to sibling relationships in blended families. Second, most of the theoretical approaches considered the substantial impact that the parent-child relationship can have on the sibling relationship, and this should also apply to sibling relationships in blended families. Third, family systems theory suggests the importance that other family relationships, such as the marital relationship and each child's relationships with other siblings, may have on the sibling relationship. Fourth, a few theories introduce characteristics of the child and of the sibling dyad, such as temperament, age, gender, and the match between the siblings on these characteristics, that are thought to be related to the quality of the sibling relationship and to interact with other important variables, such as the parent-child relationship, and thus change the impact that those variables have on the sibling relationship quality. Fifth, sibling relationships may have significant consequences and outcomes, such as the influence of the relationship on the formation of the child's identity. Sixth, Brody's (1998) theory in particular focuses on the processes that might mediate the relationship between family experiences (such as the parent-child relationship and differential treatment) and sibling relationship quality. These processes may be involved in explaining the mechanisms through which sibling relationships in blended families are developed and maintained.

RESEARCH FINDINGS REGARDING SIBLING RELATIONSHIPS IN BLENDED FAMILIES

Having summarized and reviewed the major theoretical approaches underlying sibling relationships in intact families, we proceed next to a review of research findings regarding sibling (including full, half-, and stepsibling) relationships in blended families. Recall that it is our eventual goal to fashion and organize these findings into a conceptual model that both summarizes existing results and guides future research.

Stepsiblings and full siblings in blended families are distinct from full siblings in intact families because they have experienced the loss of a former family system and have gained a new family system. Additionally, siblings in blended families must adjust to their new family members, including potentially new step- and half-siblings. These are among the dynamics that make blended families unique, but note that the older child in intact families must adjust to the idea of a new baby. As can be seen from the earlier discussion, while there are noteworthy differences between sibling relationships in blended families and sibling relationships in intact ones, there are clear similarities as well. Thus, it is useful to keep in mind the theoretical perspectives of the general (intact) sibling research literature as we review the findings on sibling research in blended families. In light of this, we choose to organize the review of the empirical research on blended family sibling relationships in a manner similar to the models of sibling relationships proposed by Furman and Buhrmester (1985) and Brody (1998). Thus, we first discuss parent-child relationships and other family variables, then child and dyad characteristics as they impact sibling relationships, then research directly on the quality of the sibling relationship, and finally how the sibling relationship relates to psychosocial outcomes.

Parent-Child Relationships and Other Family Variables

Research has documented that both mothers and fathers report feeling closer to and having more positive relationships with their own (biological) children than with their stepchildren and that they monitor their biological children more than their stepchildren. Mothers experience more conflict with their biological children than with their stepchildren (Henderson & Taylor, 1999; Mekos, Hetherington, & Reiss, 1996). In fact, when parents had both biological and stepchildren, they reported feeling closer to their biological children than parents who had only biological children (Ganong & Coleman, 1993). O'Connor, Dunn, Jenkins, and Rasbash (2006) also found that stepfamilies' differential parenting as compared to intact families was related to age differences and sex differences between the siblings.

Several other family variables might plausibly impact the quality of the sibling relationship in blended families. These variables include the sometimes lower availability of resources (both financial and emotional), lifestyle changes associated with the formation of the stepfamily, the relationships the child has with other siblings, and the quality of the marital relationship. In large part, although these factors reasonably may influence the quality of the sibling relationship, and the quality of the stepsibling relationship in particular, researchers have yet to include these factors in their studies.

It would also appear important to consider how long the child has been in the new family, and, especially in the case of stepsiblings, how long the children have been living together as siblings. However, despite the suggestion that families take 2 to 3 years to adjust to a divorce (e.g., Hetherington, 1989) and another 2 to 4 years to adjust to a new stepfamily after the remarriage (Bray & Berger, 1993), few researchers have considered this factor in their studies.

Child and Sibling Dyad Characteristics

Child characteristics, such as age, gender, and temperament, as well as dyad characteristics, such as the difference in ages, the gender match or mismatch, and the fit of temperaments, also impact the quality of the sibling relationship. Anderson (1999) investigated the connections between the age of the siblings (combining full, half-, and stepsiblings) and aspects of the sibling relationships. Older adolescents had relationships characterized by less negativity (including rivalry, aggression, and avoidance) and more empathy (but not companionship) than did younger adolescents. Additionally, the greater the difference in ages between the two siblings (which ranged from 0 to 5 years difference), the more aggression and avoidance characterized the relationship and the less companionship was observed in the relationship. Mekos et al. (1996) found that the age difference between siblings was unrelated to differential treatment by parents, but sibling age differences were related to differences in problem behavior: The larger the age difference, the more noticeable were the differences in problem behaviors between siblings.

Regarding the impact of gender on the sibling relationship, Anderson (1999), who limited participants to same-sex sibling pairs, found that girl pairs had more observed positivity in their sibling interactions than did boy pairs, regardless of whether they were full, half-, or stepsiblings. Additionally, girls had higher levels of empathy in their relationships than did boys. There were no significant differences between boys and girls in the amount of companionship exhibited in the sibling relationship. However, Ganong and Coleman (1993) found that cross-sex pairs of stepsiblings taught each other less than any other type of sibling pair (cross-sex half- or full sibling pairs and same-sex step-, half-, or full sibling pairs).

QUALITY OF SIBLING RELATIONSHIPS IN BLENDED FAMILIES

At the heart of research on sibling relationships in blended families is the quality of the relationship itself, which is typically measured in terms of positivity, which often includes warmth and affection, and negativity, which includes conflict and rivalry. With respect to negativity, the results are rather consistent across studies: Stepsiblings have the least and full siblings the most. Anderson (1999) found that stepsiblings exhibited significantly less negativity in their relationships than half- and full siblings, even after controlling for the age of the siblings and the age difference. Furthermore, stepsiblings engaged in the lowest levels of rivalry, aggression, and avoidance. Deater-Deckard, Dunn, and Lussier (2002) also found that stepsiblings (youngest child and middle child) had significantly less negativity in their relationships than did half-siblings or full siblings (who did not differ from each other), even after controlling for the child's age and gender, the gender composition of the dyad (same or opposite sex), and family income. Jenkins, Dunn, O'Connor, Rasbash, and Behnke (2005) also found that half-siblings have significantly lower levels of negativity over time when compared to full siblings, and relationships were less negative the older the oldest child. However, full siblings do not significantly differ from stepsiblings in the amount of change in negativity over time, nor do differential treatment and age difference predict change in negativity. Furthermore, there was a moderate amount of similarity in dyad negativity between dyads within the same family, which suggests that family processes may be involved in the development and maintenance of sibling negativity. Finally, Ganong and Coleman (1993) also found that stepsiblings fought less and that only approximately a third of parents reported typical sibling rivalry between stepsiblings.

The findings are a bit more mixed with respect to positivity. Anderson (1999) found that stepsiblings had more positive interactions than did half-siblings, but Deater-Deckard et al. (2002) found no significant differences in positivity in the sibling relationships for all three sibling pairs (youngest-middle, youngest-oldest, and middle-oldest). Ganong and Coleman's (1993) stepsiblings taught each other less and helped each other less than did full siblings, and stepsiblings played with each other less, helped each other less, and taught each other less than did half-siblings. Together, these findings suggest that stepsibling relationships may be less polarized than the relationships of full siblings, given that stepsiblings appear consistently to engage less frequently in negative behaviors than do full siblings, although the findings are mixed with respect to positivity. On the whole, the majority (78%) of parents felt that their children had good or excellent relationships with their stepsiblings.

Psychosocial Outcomes

A major feature of existing work involves how sibling relationships affect psychosocial outcomes, which include identity formation, socialization, and internalizing and externalizing behavior problems. Anderson (1999) measured adolescent adjustment by a variety of factors, including externalizing behavior problems and social responsibility (characterized by how well they get along with others; how dependable, honest, understanding, obedient, and modest they are; and how closely they comply with adult norms and values). Findings indicate that for all sibling types combined, both negativity and positivity in the sibling relationship were predictive of externalizing problems, whereas only positivity was significantly related to social responsibility. There was a stronger relationship between positivity and externalizing problems for boy sibling pairs compared to girl sibling pairs, regardless of sibling type. Furthermore, a weaker relationship was noted between negativity and social responsibility for both younger and older stepsiblings compared to other sibling types (Anderson, 1999).

Longitudinally, results indicated that positivity in the sibling relationship was related to externalizing behavior problems several years later. Additionally, greater positivity in the sibling relationship was related to higher levels of social responsibility several years later, and those levels of social responsibility predicted future positivity in the sibling relationship (this indicates a bidirectional flow of influence between positivity and social responsibility). This connection held for all sibling types, suggesting that even for stepsiblings, greater positivity in the stepsibling relationship has important positive outcomes for each individual. However, Anderson (1999) found less similarity in externalizing behavior problems between stepsiblings than between full and half-siblings, indicating that full and half-siblings are more similar in the amounts of externalizing behavior problems they exhibit than are stepsiblings.

Furthermore, Deater-Deckard et al. (2002) found that positivity in the youngest-middle child sibling relationship was significantly related to fewer externalizing problems for the younger child, and negativity in this relationship was related to more externalizing problems for the middle child. Negativity in the youngest-oldest child sibling relationship was associated with higher levels of internalizing behavior problems for the oldest child and higher levels of externalizing problems for the youngest child. Finally, negativity in the middle-oldest child sibling relationship indicated more externalizing behavior problems for the oldest child. These significant relationships did not differ as a function of sibling type, which suggests that stepsibling relationships impact child outcomes in a way similar to full sibling relationships.

SUMMARY

Research involving the quality of sibling relationships in blended families and related constructs has revealed several significant findings. First, mothers and fathers have different qualities of relationships with their biological children compared to their stepchildren. Typically these differences are such that the parent–biological child relationships are both more positive and more negative than relationships with stepchildren. Parents also vary in their parenting styles toward their biological and stepchildren, having the tendency to monitor their biological children more than their stepchildren. Second, associations with age are such that older children typically have less negativity and more positivity in their relationships, and the larger the age difference, the more negativity and the less companionship. Third, girl sibling pairs engaged in more empathy but exhibited similar levels of companionship compared to boy sibling pairs, regardless of sibling type. However, other research indicated that cross-sex stepsibling pairs engaged in less teaching in their relationship than did same-sex stepsibling pairs.

Fourth, in general, stepsiblings had lower levels of negativity and similar levels of positivity in their relationships compared to full sibling relationships, although some research indicates that stepsiblings engaged in less teaching than full siblings, and other research suggests that stepsiblings are both less negative and less positive in their relationships than full siblings. This discrepancy might in part depend on whether global (e.g., positive or negative) or specific (e.g., companionship, empathy, teaching, rivalry, conflict, aggression) dimensions of the relationship are being considered. Dunn (1993) suggests that researchers move beyond global demarcations and toward more specific aspects of relationship quality, in part to help clarify

precisely how different relationships are associated. The stepsibling literature should make note of this suggestion, as it is likely that conflicting findings will continue to occur unless researchers become more specific in the
particular aspects that relate to their investigations. Finally, the associations
between sibling relationships and internalizing and externalizing behavior
problems appear similar for step- and full siblings, such that positivity
and negativity are predictive of internalizing and externalizing outcomes.
This indicates that some of the same mechanisms might be involved in
the relation between full and stepsibling relationship quality and psychological outcomes. However, this finding also highlights the importance of
studying stepsibling relationships, given that they also impact psychological functioning.

A MODEL OF THE QUALITY OF SIBLING RELATIONSHIPS IN BLENDED FAMILIES

After discussing the theoretical models pertaining to full sibling relationships in intact families, and after reviewing the research conducted to date
regarding sibling relationships in blended families, it is necessary to examine what we can abstract from those theories and empirical studies and the
links that can be made between the theoretical perspectives and the empirical research. A way of summarizing the current knowledge, as well as providing hypotheses to guide future research, is needed. Without such a
synthesis, the relationships between the theoretical perspectives and the
empirical research would be difficult to decipher, and the mechanisms involved in sibling relationships in blended families might be overlooked.
To address these issues, we propose a model of sibling relationships, based
on the findings of the literature and extending from current theorizing on
siblings in intact families, as a way of synthesizing, organizing, and discussing the findings as well as suggesting avenues for further research (see
Figure 8.3).

The model highlights five main categories of constructs. In the middle is
the quality of the sibling relationship. This relationship is posited to be influenced by three categories of factors (parent-child relationships, other
family relationships, and child and sibling dyad characteristics) and, in
turn, to predict the child's psychosocial outcomes. It should be noted that
the linkages between the various aspects of the model should not be viewed
as paths per se, but simply as possible connections between predictors and
outcomes of stepsibling relationships. Thus, although no direct relationships are marked between psychosocial outcomes and parent-child relationships, family variables, and child and sibling dyad characteristics, this does
not imply that the direct relationships do not exist. These direct relationships do exist, but given that the focus of the chapter is the quality of sibling

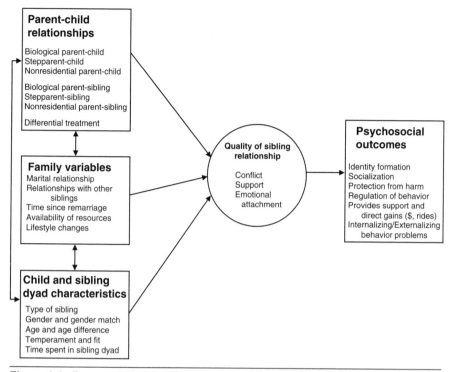

Figure 8.3 Proposed Model of the Quality of Sibling Relationships in Blended Families.

relationships and not psychosocial outcomes, these paths are not modeled to aid in clarity of the diagram. Next, we elaborate on each category of constructs in the model.

PARENT-CHILD RELATIONSHIPS

The majority of theoretical perspectives discussed thus far highlight the importance of parent-child relationships and the potential impact that parent-child relationships may have on sibling relationships. Specifically, a major tenet of family systems theory is the idea that changes in one relationship, such as the parent-child relationship, affect other subsystems of the family, such as the sibling relationship. Similarly, Dunn's (1993) theory of individual differences in sibling relationships discusses the role of parent-child relationships in the development of the sibling relationship. Additionally, Furman and Buhrmester's (1985) sibling relationship quality theory and Brody's (1998) heuristic model both underscore the critical significance the parent-child relationship can have on the sibling relationship, and the parent-child relationship is a key factor in the development of sibling relationship quality in both models. Brody's model draws attention to parental differential treatment and the impact this can have on the sibling relationship. These theoretical approaches clearly stress the vital role that parent-child relationships play in the quality of the sibling relationship, but these approaches also note the ways in which the sibling relationship can impact the parent-child relationships. As such, the parent-child relationship and the sibling relationship can be considered to mutually influence one another.

Furthermore, research with siblings in blended families has indicated that parents tend to have more emotionally intense relationships with their biological children than with their stepchildren, such that parent–biological child relationships are marked by more positivity and more conflict, as well as more monitoring of the child's behaviors and greater feelings of closeness to the biological child compared to the stepchild. Additional research indicates that differential monitoring by parents and differential negativity by fathers were related to differences in problem behaviors between siblings; the children who were monitored less and who experienced more negativity exhibited more antisocial behaviors.

Thus, it is clear that we must include in our model the various parent-child relationships that children in stepfamilies have, as well as potential differential treatment of children by the parents. Children in stepfamilies have relationships with their *residential biological parent*, their *stepparent*, and their *nonresidential biological parent*, all of which need to be considered for both the child and his or her sibling. In light of the theoretical and empirical research, these parent-child relationships, and the interaction of these relationships with child characteristics (e.g., gender, age) are expected to impact the quality of the sibling relationship. In addition, the quality of the parent-child relationships could relate to the quality of the marital relationship and to various psychosocial outcomes.

FAMILY VARIABLES

Both family systems theory and Dunn's (1993) individual differences theory suggest that the quality of the *marital relationship* is associated with the quality of the sibling relationship. Although sibling research in blended families has not examined these linkages, investigations of full siblings in intact families generally suggest that a high-quality marital relationship is linked to high-quality parent-child relationships, whereas a difficult marital relationship is connected with poor parent-child relationships (Dunn, 1993). Family systems theory also asserts that other family subsystems, including the *relationships the siblings have with other siblings* in the household, may be related to the quality of the sibling relationship. One study (White & Riedmann, 1992) did indeed find that having other siblings reduced the amount of contact with a stepsibling, which suggests that these potential relationships should not be overlooked.

Moreover, research has indicated that a period of adjustment, lasting several years, is typical following a remarriage. Considering that siblings in blended families by nature most likely have experienced the remarriage of one of their parents, and knowing that a period of acclimation to the new family is quite common, it is crucial to include *time since remarriage* as an aspect of the model. And although not specifically outlined by theoretical models, it is reasonable to assume that other factors associated with the remarriage, such as the *availability of resources* (both emotional and physical) and the impact of the new family formation on *lifestyle changes* (changes in schools, friends, geographical locations, family roles, etc.), might have an influence on the stepfamily as a whole (Ganong & Coleman, 2004), and hence might impact the sibling relationship. Additionally, the model allows for potential interactions between these family variables, the parent-child relationships, and characteristics of the child and the sibling dyad.

CHILD AND SIBLING DYAD CHARACTERISTICS

Of course, the *type of sibling* must be considered, for differences are often found depending on whether full siblings, half-siblings, or stepsiblings are examined. The theoretical perspectives of Brody (1998), Dunn (1993), and Furman and Buhrmester (1985) each emphasize some aspect of child or sibling dyad characteristic that may relate to the quality of the sibling relationship. Furman and Buhrmester consider how the *gender* and *gender match* of the siblings, as well as the *ages* and *age difference* of the siblings, impact the sibling relationship and the parent-child relationships. Research with siblings in blended families supports including these variables, given that older adolescents typically have less hostile relationships, and the greater the age difference between the siblings, the more hierarchical the relationships become and the greater the differences between children in observed problem behaviors. Likewise, relationship quality has been found to depend in part on the gender of the children, such that girl sibling pairs had higher levels of positivity than did boy sibling pairs.

Brody (1998) and Dunn (1993) both discuss *temperament* and the match or *fit of the temperament* styles of the two siblings as important aspects related to sibling relationships, whereas Furman and Buhrmester (1985) include personality, a psychological concept closely related to temperament. Children with difficult temperaments, or with temperament styles that do not fit their sibling's temperament well, are unlikely to have a harmonious sibling relationship. Although not explicitly mentioned in the theories of sibling relationships or examined in the empirical work on siblings in blended families, research with full siblings (Updegraff, McHale, Whiteman, Thayer, & Delgado, 2005) has included *time spent with siblings* in shared activities as another aspect of sibling life that deserves further consideration. These characteristics are expected to relate to the family variables and the parent-child relationships variables, as well as to the quality of the sibling relationship. Moreover, there are expected to be interactions of child age, gender, and temperament with the family variables and parent-child relationships, such that the nature of the relationship between parent-child relations and the children, and the association between the parent-child relationship and the quality of sibling relationship, might be altered depending on each child's age, gender, and temperament and the amount of similarity between the children.

Quality of the Sibling Relationship

Three theories in particular focused on explicit dimensions of the quality of sibling relationships. Dunn (1993), Brody (1998), and Furman and Buhrmester (1985) focused on positive and negative features of sibling relationships. Positive qualities most often include warmth, closeness, support, and emotional attachment, whereas negative qualities include conflict, dominance, and rivalry. Numerous findings have involved the variables that may help foster the development of these dimensions of sibling relationships and consequences or outcomes of these dimensions. For example, research has found that stepsibling relationships are less negative than full sibling relationships, and that stepsiblings engage in similar or lower levels of positivity than full siblings. Accordingly, the model describes the quality of the sibling relationship as being portrayed by the dimensions of *conflict* (negativity), *support*, and *emotional attachment* (both aspects of positivity). As previously mentioned, the quality of sibling relationships is expected to be influenced by parent-child relationships, family variables, and child and sibling dyad characteristics, and to have a mutual impact on those factors. Further, the quality of sibling relationships is thought to be associated with various psychosocial outcomes.

Psychosocial Outcomes

One of the potential results of having a relationship with a sibling is the role that relationship may play in aiding a child in the process of *identity formation* (Ganong & Coleman, 2004; Bank & Kahn, 1997). Deidentification and nonshared environment theories in particular address this role directly. Deidentification models suggest that children actively distinguish themselves from their siblings, and thus their identity is formed in relation to another person. For example, a child might distinguish herself as being good at math, which her brother is not. Thus, a portion of her sense of self, that which is derived from her mathematical ability, is developed through a direct comparison of her abilities to her brother's. Nonshared environment theory suggests that differences in sibling behaviors and identities are due in part to the different influences (peers, differential interpretation of and reaction to common events) they experience while growing up. Research has indicated that differences in sibling relationship quality were related to externalizing behavior problems and thus highlights the need to include these types of outcomes in the model of sibling relationships in blended families. Therefore, the model contains several psychosocial outcomes suggested by prior research (Ganong & Coleman, 2004; Bank & Kahn, 1997; Anderson, 1999; Deater-Deckard et al., 2002), including the extent to which the sibling aids in identity formation, *socialization, protection* (e.g., from marital and familial conflict and from conflict with other adolescents), and *regulation of behavior; provides support and direct gains* (rides, money, etc.); and displays the child's *internalizing* and *externalizing behavior problems.* All of these outcomes are thought to be related to the quality of the sibling relationship, but many are also related to the parent-child relationships and the family, child, and sibling dyad characteristics (these connections are not displayed in the model).

POTENTIAL MODERATORS, PROCESSES, AND MECHANISMS

Given the dearth of research on the quality of sibling relationships in blended families, it seems premature to specify the exact mechanisms through which the previously described variables impact these relationships. However, failing to suggest any mechanisms would be a disservice to the future of research in this area. Consequently, we mention a few potential processes as a guide for generating additional moderators and mediators. This list is not meant to be comprehensive, and due to the exploratory nature of these conjectures, these processes are not displayed in the model.

First, recall that Brody's (1998) heuristic model described several mediators through which family processes influenced the quality of sibling relationships. These mediators included prosocial or hostile patterns of behavior, the ability to regulate emotion, attributions of behavioral events, and the acceptance or refusal of norms regarding aggression and fairness. Certainly all of these mediators are potential mechanisms through which various aspects of family life may impact sibling relationships in blended families. More specifically, differential treatment may be more likely in stepfamilies, because the stepparent treats his or her biological child differently from the stepchild. Thus, children who can regulate the negative emotions that result from this preferential treatment are less likely to have hostile interactions with their siblings (the object of the preferred treatment) than children who are unable to control their emotions. Additionally, the behavior patterns learned from observing parent-child interactions and the internalization of beliefs about appropriate behaviors are likely to mediate the effects of family processes, such as parent-child and marital relationships on the quality of sibling relationships.

Furthermore, the attributions children make about various behavioral events are likely to impact the sibling relationship. The reasons children give for their parents' behavior could be a process through which negative parent-child relationships lead to negative sibling relationships. If, for example, a child sees his stepfather give his stepsister a hug, and that child explains the hug by saying that the stepfather cares more about his biological daughter than he cares about his stepson, the child may experience negative emotions toward his stepsister and thus have more negative interactions with her. Research conducted with children in intact and stepfamilies has found that a stronger relationship occurred between children's attributions of their father's behavior and the children's perception of being important to their father when the children were from a stepfamily, reporting about a stepfather, than when the children were from an intact family and were reporting about their biological father (Saenz et al., 2007). Thus, attributions may have particular importance in stepfamilies, perhaps because the children have only a few years' worth of experiences with their stepfather to draw upon, or because children don't have the expectation that their stepfather will automatically care about them, as may be the case with biological relationships. Additional research indicates that attributions regarding the fairness of parental differential treatment had implications for the full sibling relationship (Kowal & Kramer, 1997). Overall, if children described the parental differential treatment as fair, they reported more positivity in their sibling relationship. Certain types of attributions, specifically those involving the sibling's needs that were different from the child's, were associated with more warmth in the sibling relationship than were other types of attributions (e.g., those involving personal traits of the children or those involving a differential family relationship). Thus the various types of attributions children make for their parents' behaviors might help explain the mechanism through which parental differential treatment impacts the sibling relationship.

Finally, the child's beliefs, attitudes, and values about family and who is considered family will also likely impact the sibling relationship, most specifically the stepsibling relationship. In particular, what the child thinks constitutes a family (e.g., biological relatedness, living together, shared interests) and whether the child views stepsiblings in general as a part of a family could have important implications for both the quality of the relationship the child has with his or her stepsibling and the influence the stepsibling relationship has on various outcomes. If the child doesn't consider his or her stepsibling family, then the quality of the relationship may have little impact on the child's identity formation or externalizing behaviors. If, however, the child views stepsiblings as part of the family, then the quality of the relationship may have an impact on different psychosocial outcomes. Additionally, whether the child views his or her stepsiblings as family may impact the degree to which the child feels compelled to get to know his or her siblings and interact with them. Furthermore, children from cultures in which families are highly regarded and family values esteemed may feel a stronger connection to their stepsiblings and may be more invested in developing relationships with them. In general, researchers suggest that society lacks social norms regarding stepfamilies and stepsiblings, and thus individuals are unsure of how to categorize these step kin (Ihinger-Tallman, 1987; Rosenberg & Hajal, 1985). However, it is possible that specific cultures, perhaps those that already place a strong influence on the importance of family, may not differentiate between biological family relations and stepfamily relations, and thus stepfamily relationships may follow more traditional family roles.

These possible mechanisms are just a starting point for researchers in the field. It is hoped that these mechanisms, along with other processes inspired by those here, will be thoroughly investigated and the ways in which parent-child relationships, the marital relationship, and child characteristics influence the sibling relationship will be elucidated.

SUMMARY

This model is a consolidation of the theories of sibling relationships and an organization of the research thus far on sibling relationships in blended families that should serve as a catalyst for future research, both in helping generate ideas that warrant additional investigation and in delineating potential processes involved in the sibling relationships. We would expect this model to change and be revised according to further research in the field of sibling relationships in blended families.

PRELIMINARY DATA PROBING THE MODEL

A study we are involved in provides an opportunity to make a preliminary examination into the ways some of these variables might be related.

PARTICIPANTS AND PROCEDURES

All participants were part of a 5-year longitudinal study (Parents and Youth Study; PAYS) that investigated the role of fathers in adolescent development. Specifically, the project was designed to examine the contribution of the father-child relationship and fathering behaviors to adolescent outcomes and the social construction of the "meaning" of fathers. In addition, the study focused on sampling adolescents who might be deemed at risk, which included Mexican American adolescents as well as adolescents from stepfamilies. Adolescents (in the 7th grade at the time of recruitment and initial participation) and their mothers and fathers (or stepfathers) participated in the study. To be considered eligible to participate in the study, all members of the family needed to be of the same ethnic group, and children in stepfamilies needed to have lived with the "stepfather" for at least one year prior to participation, although the child's biological mother and stepfather could be cohabitating rather than married.

Adolescents were recruited from various schools in the Phoenix, Arizona, and San Bernardino/Riverside, California areas. Recruitment was aimed at obtaining participation from approximately 100 families in each of the four populations of interest: European American (EA) intact, EA step, Mexican American (MA) intact, and MA step families. Specific details on recruitment procedures for the two sites will be discussed next.

RECRUITMENT: ARIZONA SITE

Ten schools, whose enrollment was at least 30% MA, were recruited in the Phoenix area. Of these, eight schools agreed to further involvement with the project. In these eight schools, all adolescents in the 7th grade completed information cards aimed at determining their eligibility to participate in the study. A school recruiter reviewed the information and sorted the information cards into eligible and ineligible categories. Of the 5,415 children who completed the survey, 2,459 met basic study ethnic and family type criteria (e.g., EA intact family). Randomly selected families who met eligibility requirements were contacted by the recruiter and invited to participate; those who expressed interest were asked to contact the project staff and were subsequently mailed an information packet describing the study in more detail. Packets were sent to 640 families, and of those, 499 families were subsequently contacted by the project staff. After being contacted by the project staff, 124 (24.8%) were found to be ineligible and 133 (26.6%) refused to participate. Of the 242 families (48.5%) that agreed to participate, 2 could not be contacted again, 14 became ineligible, and 25 subsequently refused to participate; thus, a total of 201 participants were interviewed from the ASU site.

RECRUITMENT: CALIFORNIA SITE

Two school districts, whose enrollment was at least 30% MA, were selected by project staff to participate. Twelve of the 14 schools in these two districts agreed to participate. Based on the names of the children and their parents, project staff selected families they believed may have fit one of the four desired categories. Recruitment methods then differed by district. For one district (containing six schools), a school recruiter made phone calls to families and if they were eligible and interested in the study, their contact information was forwarded to the UCR staff who then contacted the family. In the other school district (containing another six schools), the project staff mailed families information packets about the project, and interested families contacted the project staff and were briefly interviewed to determine eligibility based on ethnicity, family type, and participation availability by the three family members (child, mother, father). Of the 540 families interested in participating, 66 (12%) could not be reached again, 165 (35%) were found to be ineligible, and 61 (13%) were not interviewed because project staff had already filled that category. Of the remaining 248 families, 56 (23%) refused participation and 192 (77%) agreed to participate.

SAMPLE

Participants consisted of 393 adolescents (205 girls, 188 boys) in the 7th grade, of which only the 175 who came from families with a stepfather are included in the current analyses. Adolescents ranged in age from 11 to 14 years old ($M = 12.94$ years, $SD = 0.54$) and were 49.36% Mexican American. Adolescents in stepfamilies had lived an average of 6 years with their stepfathers, with a range from 1 to 14 years. The adolescent, his/her mother, and residential father were interviewed separately in their homes in the language of their choice (English, Spanish). The median income of the families was $55,000, and each family was compensated $120 for participation. Informed consent and assent were obtained before administering the survey.

Adolescents in the study were asked to list any siblings they had who lived with them at least 50% of the time. Ninety-four adolescents had at least one full sibling living with them who met the specified criteria (sibling $M = 12.60$ years old, $SD = 3.22$, range 3 to 18 yrs; average age difference = 2.7 yrs), 86 had at least one half-sibling (sibling $M = 7.75$ years old, $SD = 4.87$, range 1 to 18 yrs; average age difference = 6.2 yrs), and 34 had at least one stepsibling (sibling $M = 11.82$ years old, $SD = 4.02$, range 3 to 18 yrs; average age difference = 3.2 yrs). In the instance that an adolescent had more than one sibling in a particular category, the adolescent was asked to think about the sibling closest to him or her in age. Only Wave 1 (7th-grade) findings are presented here.

RESULTS

The top (unshaded) part of Table 8.1 illustrates the correlations between selected variables in the three constructs on the left of the model and adolescents' relationships with their full, half-, and stepsiblings, respectively, in the middle. In partial support of three of the variables in the parent-child relationship construct, the more adolescents felt they mattered to their stepfather, the better

Table 8.1

Correlations with Sibling Relationship Quality from PAYS Dataset

	Full Sibling Relationship		Half-Sibling Relationship		Stepsibling Relationship	
	r	n	r	n	r	n
Mattering to mother	.10	94	-.03	86	.03	34
Mattering to stepfather	.21*	94	.27*	86	.12	34
Mattering to non-residential father	.11	77	-.14	64	.09	29
Relationship with mother	.30**	94	.28**	86	.13	34
Relationship with stepfather	.11	94	.24*	86	.09	34
Relationship with non-residential father	.07	79	-.16	66	.06	31
Mother's preferential treatment of full sibling	-.13	94	-.40*	32	-.08	19
Stepfather's preferential treatment of full sibling	-.12	94	-.39*	32	.00	19
Mother's preferential treatment of half-sibling	-.38*	32	-.26*	86	-.22	14
Stepfather's preferential treatment of half-sibling	-.46**	32	-.17	86	-.34	14
Mother's preferential treatment of stepsibling	-.18	19	-.63*	14	-.21	34
Stepfather's preferential treatment of stepsibling	-.13	19	-.47	14	-.30	34
Time lived with stepfather	-.10	94	-.24*	86	-.01	34
Child gender	.10	94	-.11	86	-.01	34
Gender match between child and full sibling	-.09	93	-.08	32	-.08	19
Gender match between child and half-sibling	-.14	32	-.01	86	-.60*	14
Gender match between child and stepsibling	-.52*	19	-.41	14	-.26	34
Child age	-.20*	94	.00	86	.02	34
Age difference between child and full sibling	-.05	94	.10	32	-.04	19
Age difference between child and half-sibling	.20	31	.27*	85	.20	14
Age difference between child and stepsibling	-.30	19	-.44	14	.09	33
Adolescent's internalizing behavior problems	-.24*	94	-.10	86	-.19	34
Adolescent's externalizing behavior problems	-.24*	94	-.08	86	-.11	34
Adolescent's positive behaviors	.33**	94	.24*	86	.24	34

*$p < .05$.

**$p < .01$.

200

relationship they had with not only their full but also their half-siblings. Mattering to the mother or to the biological father did not similarly relate. Also, the better the overall relationship between adolescents and their mother, the better the relationship between adolescents and their full sibling and half-sibling; only the latter correlated with the child-stepfather relationship. Several quite high correlations were found with the differential treatment variable; in virtually every case, the more adolescents perceived differential treatment by a parent, the worse became their sibling relationships.

Of the variables in the family variables construct, we investigated only the time since the child began living with the stepfather. Contrary to prediction, the greater this length of time, the poorer was the child's relationship with his or her half-sibling. Of those in the child and sibling characteristics constructs, we found no significant correlations with the child's gender nor the gender match with the respective sibling. However, we did find that older adolescents rated their full-sibling relationships less positively, and the greater the age difference between half-siblings, the significantly better relationship they experienced.

The shaded portion of Table 8.1 consists of selected correlations involving the quality of the sibling relationship and internalizing and externalizing problems and positive behaviors. The correlations represent the connections between the quality of the sibling relationship and several psychosocial outcomes suggested in the model. Several of these correlations reach significance, and all are in the expected direction. More specifically, the quality of the full-sibling relationship is significantly related to the adolescent's internalizing behavior problems (depression and anxiety), externalizing behavior problems (acting out, delinquency), and positive behaviors. The better quality relationship an adolescent has with his or her sibling, the fewer internalizing and externalizing problems he or she experiences. Conversely, the higher quality sibling relationship, the more positive behaviors exhibited by the adolescent. Thus, the quality of full-sibling relationships in blended families is importantly related to several behavioral outcomes. Moreover, the quality of the half-sibling relationship is correlated with adolescent positive behaviors, such that the better the adolescent and his or her half-sibling get along, the more the adolescent engages in positive behaviors. Although none of the adolescent outcome measures significantly related to the adolescent's relationship with his or her stepsibling, the correlations are in the predicted directions, such that better quality relationships are associated with fewer internalizing and externalizing problems and more positive behaviors. The sample size for these correlations is small, and it may be that once more stepsibling relationships are examined, the connections between the quality of the stepsibling relationship and adolescent outcomes will become clearer and reach significance.

These findings, although preliminary in nature, generally support the model and highlight the importance of investigating sibling relationships within blended families. Sibling relationships appear to have an effect on various outcomes, including internalizing and externalizing behavior problems, as well as on positive behaviors. Additionally, various family characteristics and parent-child relationship measures are related, mostly as specified by the model, to the quality of the sibling relationship, suggesting that these contextual factors may impact important connections between siblings. It should be noted that with such a small sample size for stepsiblings, there is most likely inadequate power to fully detect effects among the variables. Thus, more research is needed that specifically examines these types of sibling relationships.

CONCLUSION AND FUTURE DIRECTIONS

Despite the paucity of research in the field of sibling relationships in blended families, there are some important aspects to highlight. First, theories from the stepfamily and sibling literatures appear to largely apply to sibling relationships in blended families, most notably the focus on how various changes in the family (marital relationship, parent-child relationship) can impact the sibling relationship. Additionally, family systems theory suggests that the quality of sibling relationships can impact various aspects of the family, including the marital relationship and the parent-child relationship. Because the various family subsystems are interdependent, changes in one can impact another. Also, an important implication of Brody's (1998) model for sibling research in blended families is that future endeavors should move beyond simply describing aspects of sibling relationships and should start working on explaining the mechanisms through which these sibling relationships impact psychosocial outcomes. Moreover, it is important to look both at child characteristics (age, temperament, gender) and dyad characteristics (relative age difference, gender match or mismatch, temperament fit, time spent in dyad) when examining the impact on sibling relationships.

Second, empirical research, though scarce, seems to indicate that stepsibling relationships differ in important ways from those of full and half-siblings. Most researchers who have examined this issue find that stepsibling relationships are characterized by less negativity but similar amounts of positivity when compared to full and half-sibling relationships. It is unknown what impact these differences might have on children's behavioral and social outcomes, and it is also unknown precisely which mechanisms produce these changes. Although it is apparent that stepsibling relationships have important implications for children's outcomes, specifically externalizing and internalizing behavior problems, the extent to which these implications differ depending on other factors is still unclear. Moreover, because the qualities of stepsibling relationships predict behavioral outcomes for adolescents, the processes through which these effects occur should be investigated further.

Third, regarding future research, several guidelines need to be established for reporting information in published studies of sibling relationships in blended families. In research with blended families, it is often unclear if the sibling relationship mentioned is one of full biological siblings, half-siblings, stepsiblings, or some combination of the three. Thus, it is difficult to describe specifically what is occurring in each of these sibling relationships and the ways in which stepsibling relationships may be similar to, and may differ from, relationships with half- and full siblings. Therefore, researchers, especially in cases in which the participants are from a variety of family backgrounds, need to be specific as to which types of siblings were examined. Furthermore, researchers should report not only the average ages of the siblings but also the difference in ages between siblings as well as the gender constellation of the dyad. Additionally, researchers should mention the length of time since the parental remarriage and in particular the length of time that the stepsiblings and half-siblings have lived together. Although current research has typically restricted step- and half-sibling relationships to those siblings who live together at least 50% of the time, future research should report if this criterion was upheld, or if some other definition was used. These are just a few guidelines that would help researchers organize the literature on siblings in blended families, but future research should provide a more complete set of guidelines as the field expands. On a related note, future research should start to focus on more specific features of sibling relationships, such as companionship, nurturance, teaching, avoidance, and conflict, in addition to investigating global aspects of relationship quality. This may lead to clearer connections being drawn as to precisely how stepsibling and full sibling relationship qualities might differ and could help suggest avenues for potential interventions focused on these particular targets. Finally, longitudinal designs will contribute to the ability to understand causal pathways.

Fourth, the conceptual model we present is suggested as a promising way of both organizing what is known and inspiring future research. Many of the connections in the model were supported either by past research or in the preliminary research we reported. However, other relationships in the model have not been thoroughly examined, and several have not been examined at all. For example, one such question is proposed by the paths between parent-child relationships, sibling relationships, and psychosocial outcomes. It is of interest to know if positive sibling relationships in part buffer the deleterious effects of negative parent-child relationships on psychosocial outcomes. Additionally, in what ways do sibling relationships impact parent-child relationships? In what ways does the quality of sibling relationships impact the various social, emotional, cognitive, and behavioral outcomes? For example, what role might the sibling relationship play in the development and maintenance of deviant behaviors? Which aspects of the sibling relationship are related to academic success? These questions are a small subset of those suggested by the model, and researchers are encouraged to use the model as inspiration for future investigation.

Finally, researchers have just begun to study sibling relationships in blended families, and as investigation in this area increases, important discoveries will be made about the interplay among the various family systems and both the factors that impact the type of sibling relationship that develops and the implications that relationship has for future success. Researchers should start considering the processes and mechanisms that underlie the paths suggested in the model. Researchers are encouraged to continue the investigation into the complexities of families and familial relationships and to enlighten the community as to the impact that sibling relationships in blended families can have on psychological functioning and well-being.

REFERENCES

Anderson, E. R. (1999). Sibling, half sibling, and stepsibling relationships in remarried families. In E. M. Hetherington, S. H. Henderson, & D. Reiss (Eds.), Adolescent siblings in stepfamilies: Family functioning and adolescent adjustment. *Monographs of the Society for Research in Child Development, 64*(4, Serial No. 259), 101–126.

Bank, S. P., & Kahn, M. D. (1997). *The sibling bond.* New York: Basic Books.

Barkow, J. H., Cosmides, L., & Tooby, J. (1992). *The adapted mind: Evolutionary psychology and the generation of culture.* New York: Oxford University Press.

Bowen, M. (1971). Family therapy and family group therapy. In H. Kaplan & B. Sadock (Eds.), *Comprehensive group psychotherapy* (pp. 384–421). Baltimore: Williams & Wilkins.

Bowen, M. (1972). Family therapy and family group therapy. In H. Kaplan & B. Sadock (Eds.), *Group treatment of mental illness* (pp. 145–181). New York: Aronson.

Boyle, M. H., Jenkins, J. M., & Georgiades, K. (2004). Differential-maternal parenting behavior: Estimating within- and between-family effects on children. *Child Development, 75*(5), 1457–1476.

Bray, J. H., & Berger, S. H. (1993). Developmental issues in Stepfamilies Research Project: Family relationships and parent-child interactions. *Journal of Family Psychology, 7,* 76–90.

Brody, G. H. (1998). Sibling relationship quality: Its causes and consequences. *Annual Review of Psychology, 49,* 1–24.

Brody, G. H., Stoneman, Z., & McCoy, J. K. (1994). Forecasting sibling relationships in early adolescence from child temperaments and family processes in middle childhood. *Child Development, 65,* 771–784.

Buhrmester, D. (1992). The developmental courses of sibling and peer relationships. In F. Boer & J. Dunn (Eds.), *Children's sibling relationships: Developmental and clinical issues* (pp. 19–40). Hillsdale, NJ: Erlbaum.

Buhrmester, D., & Furman, W. (1990). Perceptions of sibling relationships during middle childhood and adolescence. *Child Development, 61,* 1387–1398.

Deater-Deckard, K., Dunn, J., & Lussier, G. (2002). Sibling relationships and social-emotional adjustment in different family contexts. *Social Development, 11,* 571–590.

Dunn, J. (1993). *Young children's close relationships: Beyond attachment.* Newbury Park, CA: Sage.

Furman, W., & Buhrmester, D. (1985). Children's perceptions of the qualities of sibling relationships. *Child Development, 56,* 448–461.

Ganong, L. H., & Coleman, M. (1993). An exploratory study of stepsibling subsystems. *Journal of Divorce and Remarriage, 19,* 125–141.

Ganong, L. H., & Coleman, M. (2004). *Stepfamily relationships: Development, dynamics, and intervention.* New York: Kluwer Academic/Plenum.

Glick, P. C. (1989). Remarried families, stepfamilies, and stepchildren: A brief demographic profile. *Family Relations, 38,* 24–27.

Henderson, S. H., & Taylor, L. C. (1999). Parent-adolescent relationships in nonstep-, simple step-, and complex stepfamilies. In E. M. Hetherington, S. H. Henderson, & D. Reiss (Eds.), Adolescent siblings in stepfamilies: Family functioning and adolescent adjustment. *Monographs of the Society for Research in Child Development, 64*(4, Serial No. 259), 79–100.

Hetherington, E. M. (1989). Coping with family transitions: Winners, losers, and survivors. *Child Development, 60,* 1–14.

Hetherington, E. M. (1991). Families, lies, and videotapes. *Journal of Research on Adolescence, 1,* 323–348.

Hetherington, E. M., & Jodl, K. M. (1994). Stepfamilies as settings for child development. In A. Booth & J. Dunn (Eds.), *Stepfamilies: Who benefits? Who does not?* (pp. 55–79). Hillsdale, NJ: Erlbaum.

Ihinger-Tallman, M. (1987). Sibling and stepsibling bonding in stepfamilies. In K. Pasley & M. Ihinger-Tallman (Eds.), *Remarriage and stepparenting: Current research and theory* (pp. 94–140). New York: Guilford Press.

Irons, W. G. (1979). Natural selection, adaptation, and human social behavior. In N. Chagnon & W. Irons (Eds.), *Evolutionary biology and human social behavior* (pp. 4–39). North Scituate, MA: Duxbury Press.

Jenkins, J. M., Dunn, J., O'Connor, T. G., Rasbash, J., & Behnke, P. (2005). Change in maternal perception of sibling negativity: Within- and between-family influences. *Journal of Family Psychology, 19,* 533–541.

Koester, L. S., & Johnson, J. E. (1984). Children's instructional strategies: A comparison of sibling and peer tutoring. *Acta Paedoligica, 1*(1), 23–32.

Kowal, A., & Kramer, L. (1997). Children's understanding of parental differential treatment. *Child Development, 68,* 113–126.

McHale, S. M., Updegraff, K. A., Helms-Erikson, H., & Crouter, A. C. (2001). Sibling influences on gender development in middle childhood and early adolescence: A longitudinal study. *Developmental Psychology, 37,* 115–125.

Mekos, D., Hetherington, E. M., & Reiss, D. (1996). Sibling differences in problem behavior and parental treatment in nondivorced and remarried families. *Child Development, 67*, 2148–2165.

Minuchin, P. (1985). Families and individual development: Provocations from the field of family therapy. *Child Development, 56*, 289–302.

Minuchin, P. (1988). Relationships within the family: A systems perspective on development. In R. A. Hinde & J. Stevenson-Hinde (Eds.), *Relationships within families: Mutual influences* (pp. 7–26). Oxford: Clarendon.

Minuchin, S. (1974). *Families and family therapy*. Cambridge, MA: Harvard University Press.

Neaves, R. D., & Crouch, J. G. (1990). Deidentification in two-child families. *Journal of Adolescent Research, 5*, 370–386.

O'Connor, T. G., Dunn, J., Jenkins, J. M., & Rasbash, J. (2006). Predictors of between-family and within-family variation in parent-child relationships. *Journal of Child Psychology and Psychiatry, 47*, 498–510.

Patterson, G. R., Dishion, T. J., & Bank, L. (1984). Family interaction: A process model of deviancy training. *Aggressive Behavior, 10*, 253–267.

Paulhus, D., & Shaffer, D. R. (1981). Sex differences in the impact of number of older and number of younger siblings on scholastic aptitude. *Social Psychology Quarterly, 44*(4), 363–368.

Plomin, R., & Daniels, D. (1987). Why are children in the same family so different from one another? *Behavioral and Brain Sciences, 10*, 1–16.

Popenoe, D. (1994). The evolution of marriage and the problem of stepfamilies: A biosocial perspective. In A. Booth & J. Dunn (Eds.), *Stepfamilies: Who benefits? Who does not?* (pp. 3–27). Hillsdale, NJ: Erlbaum.

Reese-Weber, M. (2000). Middle and late adolescents' conflict resolution skills and siblings: Associations with interparental and parent-adolescent conflict resolution. *Journal of Youth and Adolescence, 29*(6), 697–711.

Reiss, D., Plomin, R., Hetherington, E. M., Howe, G., Rovine, M., Tryon, A., et al. (1994). The separate worlds of teenage siblings: An introduction to the study of the nonshared environment and adolescent development. In E. M. Hetherington, D. Reiss, & R. Plomin (Eds.), *Separate social worlds of siblings: The impact of nonshared environment on development* (pp. 63–109). Hillsdale, NJ: Erlbaum.

Rende, R., Slomkowski, C., Lloyd-Richardson, E., & Niaura, R. (2005). Sibling effects on substance use in adolescence: Social contagion and genetic relatedness. *Journal of Family Psychology, 19*, 611–618.

Rosenberg, E. B., & Hajal, F. (1985). Stepsibling relationships in remarried families. *Social Casework: Journal of Contemporary Social Work, 66*, 287–292.

Saenz, D. S., Baham, M. E., Braver, S. L., Cookston, J., Fabricius, W. V., & Parke, R. (2007). *Father behaviors and perceived mattering in adolescents: The role of attributions.* Manuscript submitted for publication.

Schachter, F. F. (1982). Sibling deidentification and split-parent identification: A family tetrad. In M. E. Lamb & B. Sutton-Smith (Eds.), *Sibling relationships: Their nature and significance across the lifespan* (pp. 123–151). Hillsdale, NJ: Erlbaum.

Stoneman, Z., & Brody, G. H. (1993). Sibling temperaments, conflict, warmth, and role asymmetry. *Child Development, 64*, 1786–1800.

Straus, M. A., Gelles, R. J., & Steinmetz, S. K. (1980). *Behind closed doors: Violence in the American family*. New York: Anchor Press.

Turkheimer, E., & Waldron, M. (2000). Nonshared environment: A theoretical, methodological, and quantitative review. *Psychological Bulletin, 126,* 78–108.

Updegraff, K. A., McHale, S. M., Whiteman, S. D., Thayer, S. M., & Delgado, M. Y. (2005). Adolescent sibling relationships in Mexican American families: Exploring the role of familism. *Journal of Family Psychology, 19,* 512–522.

White, L. K., & Riedmann, A. (1992). When the Brady Bunch grows up: Step/half- and full sibling relationships in adulthood. *Journal of Marriage and the Family, 63,* 197–208.

CHAPTER 9

Resident Parent-Child Relationships in Stepfamilies

CLAIRE CARTWRIGHT

IT IS well established that relationships between parents and children are central to the well-being of children; as a result, family research often focuses on these relationships. However, stepfamily researchers have given scant attention to this biological relationship. Researchers may have assumed that relationships between parents from previous unions and their children are well established and resilient and turned their attention toward the new relationships in the stepfamily, especially the stepparent-stepchild relationship. Stepfamily clinicians have also attended less to this relationship than to others, and in early clinical literature often conceptualized the couple's relationship as the key or central relationship to stepfamily development. Hence, the parent-child relationship is somewhat underrepresented in both clinical and research literature. Much of what we know about parent-child relationships comes from longitudinal studies that have examined all of the different relationships within the stepfamily household.

In this chapter, I examine the research and clinical literature that provides insight into the effects that remarriage and stepfamily living have on relationships between parents and their children from previous unions. As has been widely discussed, stepfamilies are a complex family form, and researchers and clinicians conclude that adults living in stepfamilies must find ways of adapting to the challenges of learning to live in this different type of family. Yet many parents enter stepfamily life with unrealistic expectations of what is ahead of them in terms of relationship processes and stepfamily trajectories. As will be seen from the following analysis of the research literature, parent-child relationships come under considerable stress following repartnering or remarriage, especially in the first 2 years and again as children reach adolescence. As with other areas of divorce-related research, the outcomes are variable. Some parents and children fare well and maintain close relationships; others struggle and experience a weakening of bonds. Prior to examining the research literature, however, it is worth looking back on the historical position of the parent-child relationship within the early clinical and research literature.

HISTORICAL CLINICAL AND RESEARCH PERSPECTIVES ON PARENT-CHILD RELATIONSHIPS IN STEPFAMILIES

Stepfamily clinicians have been influential within the field of stepfamily studies. Clinicians began to write about their clinically (and sometimes personally) derived understanding of stepfamily living before the first major wave of empirical research began in the 1980s (e.g., Messinger, Walker, & Freeman, 1978; Mowatt, 1972; E. B. Visher & Visher, 1979; Whiteside, 1982). Clinicians recognized that stepfamilies were a new area of professional practice and that there was a lack of knowledge about how they functioned. Hence, the clinical literature dominated thinking about stepfamilies in the late 1970s and early 1980s (Ganong & Coleman, 1994).

The ideas put forward about stepfamily relationships and processes by clinicians in the early years have been given considerable support by results from empirical research. These have included the emphasis on the complexity of stepfamilies, the unrealistic expectations of stepfamily couples, the number of years it takes for a stepfamily to form, and the challenges associated with the stepparent role and discipline. However, an examination of the early clinical literature demonstrates a tendency among clinicians to conceptualize the couple's relationship as central to stepfamily development. Many clinical writers commented on the importance of maintaining the parent-child relationship and the potential "losses" for children when parents remarry. However, they often failed to address the importance of the parent-child subsystem within the stepfamily system and its role in stepfamily integration and adjustment. This was evident in two early and influential papers that conceptualized the process of stepfamily development (Mills, 1984; Whiteside, 1982). Mills (1984, p. 367), for example, stated that the stepfamily couple can be "the architect of the stepfamily system, to assume conscious executive control of the family." He talked about drawing a boundary around "the parental unit to cut across the preexisting biological parent-child bonds" (p. 367). Whiteside (1982) argued that the important tasks of early remarriage were to establish a "firm marital coalition," to develop step-parenting relationships, to maintain "strong ties" with the parent outside the home, and to develop positive alliances among step- and half-siblings. Neither of these authors discussed the maintenance of the parent-child relationship as essential to stepfamily development. Similarly, E. B. Visher and Visher (1993) did not include the maintenance of parent-child relationships as one of their defined "tasks" of stepfamily development.

Sometimes clinicians stated that the couple's relationship was the key or primary relationship. E. B. Visher and Visher (1996, p. 25), the most influential clinicians (Ganong & Coleman, 1994), talked about the couple as the "primary long-term relationship" in the stepfamily. Webber (1994, p. 10) in her Australian publication, described the couple's relationship in any family as "the most crucial relationship" for family integration but states that the couple's relationship is "even more important" in stepfamilies.

Martin and Martin (1992, p. 137) stated:

> *Clinicians must often focus their efforts on helping a newly married couple assist young children in the family. In-laws and older children obviously also have an impact on the development of a remarriage. It is important that boundaries be developed quickly. . . . One cornerstone is that couples must repeatedly emphasize to those around them the importance and primacy of the marital relationship. Through this action, couples make the statement that if others try to put them in the position of choosing between family members and their spouses, they will align with their spouses.*

Hence, as Papernow commented in 1993, the stepfamily literature was "full of exhortations for stepcouples to become a strong team" (p. 13).

It may be that clinicians attended to what they perceived as the most urgent difficulties. Perhaps the couple's relationship was emphasized because of the higher rates of dissolution of remarriages and a desire to assist couples to maintain strong relationships in order to avoid a further family disruption. Alternatively, it may be that some clinicians hesitated to emphasize the parent-child relationship in order to counteract the tendency toward dysfunctional alliances between parents and children in stepfamilies (Bray & Berger, 1993; Hetherington & Kelly, 2002). These alliances result in distress for stepparents, who feel like "outsiders," and in marital difficulties (Papernow, 1993; J. Visher & Visher, 1988).

Accompanying this early clinical emphasis on the centrality of the couple's relationship was a lack of research focus on parent-child relationships. While clinicians demonstrated a tendency toward prioritizing the couple's relationship, researchers focused more intensively on stepparents and children. A number of researchers have drawn attention to this lack of focus on parent-child relationships (e.g., Cartwright, 2005; Ganong & Coleman, 1994, 2004; Solomon, 1995).

The interest in and concern about the impact of the stepparent role was heightened by an early study that examined the relative importance of the marital relationship versus the step relationship in predicting family happiness in middle-class European stepfather households (Crosbie-Burnett, 1984).

The key variables measured in this study were family happiness, marital happiness, and aspects of the relationships between the stepparents and stepchildren. The results indicated that the stepparent-stepchild relationship was more highly associated with family happiness than was the marital relationship. These findings challenged the clinical emphasis on the couple's relationship. As Crosbie-Burnett (1984, pp. 462–463) stated:

> *If we assume a bond between natural parent and child and some type of positive attraction between the adult partners, then the relationships in the stepfamily that lack* raison d'etre *are those between stepparent and stepchild. . . . These results suggest that proactive attention should be given to the steprelationship if* all *members of the household are to be happy in the new family. In stepfamilies, it is not enough to nurture the conjugal relationships and assume that the others will "fall into place."*

It is understandable that researchers have focused on the less understood stepparent role; it is nevertheless surprising that the parent-child relationship, so closely associated with child well-being, has been relatively neglected. It may be that researchers have taken relationships between parents and children for granted and viewed them as resilient and of less urgent concern than the stepparent-stepchild relationship. This lack of research focus has continued, leaving a gap in our understanding of how parents and children relate to each other in stepfamily contexts (Ganong & Coleman, 2004) and the potential systemic importance of this biological relationship within the stepfamily system (Cartwright & Seymour, 2002).

OUTCOMES FOR PARENT-CHILD RELATIONSHIPS IN STEPFAMILIES

This section examines the outcomes for parent-child relationships in stepfamilies across the transition to stepfamily living, through childhood and adolescence and into adulthood. Because the great majority of mothers have custody of children, most stepfamily research has focused on stepfather families and less is known about relationships between residential fathers and children. A number of early studies provided some evidence that remarriage could impact the closeness between parents and children in stepfamilies (Parish & Dostal, 1980; Parish & Kappes, 1980). However, the most useful insights into the nature of relationships in stepfamilies have come from a number of longitudinal studies that have investigated stepfamilies and collected data relevant to parent-child relationships. Hetherington and associates have conducted three longitudinal studies that investigated stepfamily functioning, individual adjustment, and adaptation to remarriage and life in a stepfamily (Hetherington & Jodl, 1994). These include the Virginia Longitudinal Study of Divorce and Remarriage (VLSDR; Hetherington, 1987, 1993, 1999); the Hetherington and

Clingempeel (1992) study of Divorce and Remarriage; and, the National Study of Nonshared Environment (Hetherington, Henderson, & Reiss, 1999; Hetherington & Jodl, 1994).

Hetherington (1989) in the VLSDR found that mothers and daughters in divorced families expressed considerable satisfaction with each other 6 years after divorce, when the children were around 10 years of age. In contrast, when mothers remarried, mother-child relationships 6 years after parental divorce were conflicted and daughters were observed to be demanding, hostile, coercive, and less warm toward mothers compared to girls in both the single-parent and nondivorced groups. They appeared to adjust somewhat and behavior improved over time, but at 2 years after remarriage the girls were still more antagonistic and disruptive with parents than girls in the other two family types. On the other hand, relationships between mothers and sons in the single-parent group were characterized by cycles of coercive behavior and conflict (Hetherington, 1989). This pattern changed when mothers remarried. While mothers and stepfathers initially viewed the son's behavior as extremely difficult, over time this improved and, after 2 years, boys in stepfamilies were not showing different levels of aggressive, noncompliant behavior in the home or school compared to boys in nondivorced families.

Similarly, Bray and associates (Bray, 1999; Bray & Berger, 1993; Bray & Kelly, 1998) in the Developmental Issues in Stepfamily Project found that relationships between parents and children (and stepparents and stepchildren) were often fraught in the early stages of stepfamily living. Mothers at 6 months following remarriage, compared to those in nondivorced families, reported high personal levels of stress (3 times higher than nondivorced mothers) and were experiencing increased parenting difficulties with their children, whom they rated as having more behavioral problems compared to those in the nondivorced group. Mothers were observed to be less attuned to the needs of their children during this period, and some children appeared to compete with the new stepparent over the parent's time and energy and to experience a sense of parental abandonment (Bray & Kelly, 1998).

Hetherington and Clingempeel (1992) also found that parent-child relationships were disrupted during the early stages of stepfamily living. Interactions between preadolescent children and mothers in stepfamilies were more conflicted than those in nondivorced families, and mothers in stepfamilies demonstrated increased negativity and decreased positivity toward their children from previous unions. However, these researchers found that parenting by mothers had mostly recovered after 2 years and there was little difference between mothers in stepfamilies and those from nondivorced families (Hetherington & Clingempeel, 1992).

Bray (1999) and Hetherington (1999) both found that problems between parents and children increased again, relative to those in the nondivorced group, as children entered adolescence; they hypothesized that stepfamily adolescents were experiencing a "sleeper effect" from their parents' divorce. This, they proposed, was interacting with the normal struggles of adolescents to individuate and develop autonomy, resulting in increased difficulties for adolescents and parents. Perhaps because of the conflict and difficulties in relationships with parents and stepparents, around 33% of adolescent boys and 25% of adolescent girls in divorced and remarried families, compared to around 10% in nondivorced families, disengaged from their families and spent little time at home (Hetherington & Jodl, 1994). Other researchers have also found that adolescents in stepfamilies leave home at an earlier age than those in first-marriage families (Mitchell, Wister, & Burch, 1989) and single-parent families (Mitchell et al., 1989; Quilino, 1991; White & Booth, 1985), although gender differences have been found, with girls in stepfamilies having a significantly higher rate of early home-leaving than boys (Quilino, 1991). Analyzing data from the British National Child Development Study, Kiernan (1992) found that adolescents in stepfamilies were more likely than those in single-parent and nondivorced families to leave school and home earlier and to cite conflict as a reason for doing so. She proposed that conflict-ridden family relationships may act as a "push factor" in the leaving-home process.

The disruption to parent-child relationships in stepfamilies can also manifest itself in early adulthood. White (1992) examined data from the American National Survey of Families and Households to investigate the impact of parental divorce and remarriage on parental support for adult children. Examining three dimensions of support—social, instrumental, and financial—she found a significant and substantial support deficit from parents to young adult children when comparing divorced parents and remarried parents to parents in nondivorced families. Although there were gender interactions, support deficits were generally significant for both mothers and fathers. The deficit in financial support could be accounted for by decreased income of separated parents. However, she concluded that, in general, the effects from ever-divorced parents appeared to be due largely to lower parent-child solidarity rather than to decreased parental resources. This lack of support was also found to be reciprocal, as young adults from stepfamilies reported giving less to their parents, receiving less from them, and perceiving less support from them compared to young adults from nondivorced families (White, 1994).

These results strongly suggest that remarriage does not constitute a neutral event for children. Parent-child relationships are put under considerable stress following remarriage, and parents and children face challenges that are not experienced by parents in first-marriage and single-parent families. As with other areas of research into postdivorce families, parent-child relationships are at risk following remarriage, especially in the first 2 years and again during adolescence. This can result in less closeness and support between parents and offspring in early adulthood. Children's responses vary with age and gender, but even younger children who appear to have adjusted to their parent's remarriage can experience increased difficulties as they move into adolescence. Girls, and particularly pre- and early adolescent girls, appear to feel particularly threatened by the presence of the partner.

On the other hand, as has been discussed by a number of researchers (e.g., Amato, 2000; Coleman, Ganong, & Fine, 2000), although statistically significant differences exist in outcomes for children in first-marriage families compared to those in single-parent and stepfamilies, the effect sizes are relatively small. Also, stepfamilies are not a homogeneous group, and some stepfamilies learn to adjust and function well (Anderson & White, 1986; Bray, 1992; Kurdek, 1994; Ochiltree, 1990). Perhaps what is most remarkable about postdivorce families, as Hetherington (2003) points out, is the great variation in outcomes for adults and children. Similarly, many parents and children maintain close bonds. Some parents, stepparents, and children find ways of relating to each other that are adaptive and supportive, and established stepfamilies often provide good environments for child and adolescent development (Buchanan, Maccoby, & Dornbusch, 1996; Hetherington et al., 1999). Parent-child relationships have also been found to be more positive and less negative in nonclinical stepfamilies, and children are warmer, communicate more effectively and more assertively, and exhibit more positive moods toward both mothers and stepfathers (Anderson & White, 1986; Bray, 1992).

It is therefore important for researchers and clinicians to develop further understanding of how stepfamily characteristics and processes impact this biological relationship and the parenting practices that are associated with both child well-being and adjustment difficulties. In the next section, I examine the characteristics of stepfamilies and stepfamily processes that have implications for residential parent-child relationships. I have limited this discussion to residential stepfamily household issues. The areas of stepfamily life to be discussed are the extended period of adjustment that follows remarriage; the impact of the presence of the new parental partner in the household and the associated loss of time and attention for children; parental and child well-being; the impact of the stepparent role; loyalty issues between parents, partners, and children; and coalitions in stepfamilies. As will be seen, several of these areas interrelate.

THE IMPACT OF STEPFAMILY PROCESSES AND RELATIONSHIPS

My colleagues and I have conducted a number of qualitative studies that investigated parent-child relationships in stepfamilies and the parenting practices that impact, either positively or negatively, this relationship.

These studies have been previously published and are briefly outlined here. The first three studies focused participants' attention on parent-child relationships and parenting practices that were experienced as supportive or difficult by children. Participants were recruited through advertising. The fourth study used a questionnaire that began with a stepfamily vignette and asked university students from a range of family types for their views about parenting and children's expectations in the early stages after remarriage.

1. Therapist Study: Interviews with 9 therapists experienced in working with stepfamilies (Cartwright, 2003b).
2. Young Adult Study: Group interviews with 28 young adults who had lived in stepfamilies for an average of approximately 10 years (Cartwright & Seymour, 2002).
3. Multiple Case Study: Individual and follow-up interviews with 7 mother-child pairs (pre- to early adolescents, 4 girls and 3 boys) living in a stepfamily household and recruited through advertising (Cartwright, 2003a, 2005).
4. Vignette Study: A questionnaire study using a stepfamily vignette completed by 65 late adolescent/young adult participants from a range of family backgrounds. Participants were asked about their views and children's expectations of parenting following remarriage (Moore & Cartwright, 2005).

The results from these studies are integrated into the following sections as they are relevant to the discussion, and quotes and excerpts from interviews are used to illustrate some of the stepfamily processes.

THE EARLY STAGES OF STEPFAMILY DEVELOPMENT

Couples frequently enter into stepfamily living believing that they and their children will adjust easily to the new family situation (Bray & Kelly, 1998) and have unrealistic expectations of "instant love" between stepparents and children (Hetherington & Kelly, 2002; J. Visher & Visher, 1988). However, the transition to remarriage involves a reorganization of family roles, rules, and step relationships (Hetherington, 1999), and "instant love" is uncommon (J. Visher & Visher, 1988). According to Hetherington, it takes longer for children to adjust to living in a stepfamily than it does for them to adjust to living in a single-parent family. Estimates of the time needed to adjust to stepfamily living and to integrate into a functional family unit range from between 2 or 3 years to 7 years (Cherlin & Furstenberg, 1994; Hetherington & Jodl, 1994; Ihinger-Tallman & Pasley, 1997). Because more than a quarter of remarriages end in the first 5 years (Hetherington, Bridges,

& Insabella, 1998), some stepfamilies never experience the process of stabilization. Hence, parents and children in stepfamilies experience two extended periods of potential disruption to their relationships associated with the transitions of divorce and remarriage. Second and third remarriages are likely to impact even more on outcomes for parent-child relationships (Kurdek, 1994). On the other hand, as discussed previously, when remarried partners stay together and the stepfamily is stabilized, parenting in both stepmother and stepfather families is similar to first-marriage families, as are adolescent outcomes (Hetherington et al., 1999).

The Entrance of the Parental Partner into the Lives of Parent and Child

Children often experience difficulty accepting and adjusting to the parent's repartnering or remarriage and the presence of a stepparent in their lives. Clinicians point out that this can be eased somewhat if children are given time to adjust to their parents' divorce and to get to know a stepparent before remarriage (J. Visher & Visher, 1988). Some parents, however, begin to cohabit with a new partner early on in a relationship, and some children are likely to react against this. This was relevant for a number of young adults and children who took part in the Young Adult Study and Multiple Case Study (Cartwright, 2005). As one young woman said:

> He moved in quite soon in the relationship which my brother and I quite resented just because you know it was our house. . . . [Later] I think it's probably worse in my relationship with my Mum because I don't really respect the decisions that she's made with her life and also her relationships. (Female, aged 19 years)

Some of the young adults and children also experienced a lack of communication from their parents in regard to repartnering or remarriage (Cartwright & Seymour, 2002). They recalled feeling confused, hurt, or betrayed when parents did not communicate with them about decisions that would impact their lives.

> When my Mum got remarried, I didn't know she was going to, that she was engaged . . . like somebody else told me and I just couldn't believe it. Just because it happened when I was 9 years old. (Female, aged 20 years)

Once the parent repartners, in both cohabiting and remarried stepfather families, some children receive less attention and support from their mothers (Thomson, Thomas, & McLanahan, 1994), a shift in parenting that the researchers attributed to the competition of the new relationship for time and attention.

Stepfamily clinicians often talk about the losses that children sustain through divorce and remarriage (Cartwright, 2003b; Emery, 1999; Rodwell, 2002; J. Visher & Visher, 1988). The potential loss of time and attention was a strong theme that emerged across all of the qualitative studies mentioned previously. Some of the therapists viewed this loss of attention as almost inevitable (Cartwright, 2003b). Several young women in the Young Adult Study, without any prompting, talked about experiencing a loss of time and attention as children (Cartwright & Seymour, 2002). This was then interpreted as a loss of importance in the mother's life.

> *They're like in the middle of forming this new relationship. With your parents, they'd already formed that before you came along. And so when you came along it was something new for them to focus their attention on. But because your parent and stepparent are getting to know each other, you don't become nearly as, well in your own eyes, as important. . . . I definitely felt a bit isolated especially going from a household with one parent to two. There's a lot less attention from anyone really. (Female, aged 20 years)*

Pre- to early adolescent girls appear to find their parents' new relationship particularly difficult (Hetherington & Stanley-Hagan, 1995). Girls of this age have often developed a warm and supportive relationship with single mothers, and remarriage can lead to a loss of status and role within the family. Hence, the simple existence of the couple's relationship and an associated loss of time and attention can provoke distress, anger, or rebellion in some children. Even stepfathers who are kind, supportive, and noninterfering can be rejected in the early stages (Hetherington & Jodl, 1994), and it seems likely that children will harbor negative feelings toward a parent who has, from their perspective, brought an unwanted competitor into their lives.

As well as a loss of time and attention, the time available to parents and children can become more conflicted, as the following illustrates. Gemma, aged 12 years, who has previously been close to her mother, is asked about her relationship with her mother now that she has repartnered:

GEMMA: When he's not around then fine but if we start talking about him I get on really badly with Mum. I argue with her all the time about it. But if we're just talking about normal things, fine.
INTERVIEWER: What part or percentage of the time do you think you and Mum get on well? Half? Most of the time?
GEMMA: Um, about a quarter of the time.
INTERVIEWER: What [was] it like before John came?
GEMMA: I don't know. Three quarters or most of the time. Eighty percent.

However, with time, children can adjust. When the transition is managed carefully and well, with consideration for the children, the adaptation is likely to be easier and relationships with parents maintained. As one young woman said:

My Mum dated my Stepdad for 3 years. They got married and it was like one of my stepbrothers is likely [sic.] one of my brothers. We'd been on vacations together and so it wasn't a huge change to move in [,] which I think was good. It made it a lot easier. (Age 19)

PARENTAL AND CHILD WELL-BEING

Remarried mothers experience economic advantages compared to mothers in single-parent families (Hughes, 2000). Psychological health and well-being improve markedly when divorced adults form a satisfying and intimate relationship or remarry (Funder & Harrison, 1993; Hetherington & Kelly, 2002). However, remarriage is associated with an increase in both positive and negative events for parents (Hetherington & Kelly, 2002). Remarried mothers have reported being 3 times as stressed as mothers in non-divorced families (Bray & Kelly, 1998), and, although the well-being of parents improves after remarriage, there is still an increased rate of depression among mothers after 2 years, compared to those in first-marriage families (Hetherington & Jodl, 1994).

In an investigation of stepfamilies in the longitudinal British Child Development Study, the majority of biological and stepparents appeared contented with their lives, although a sizable minority were not (Ferri & Smith, 1998). The proportion that was vulnerable to depression and anxiety and the proportion expressing negative feelings were higher than in first marriages. Around 75% of mothers and stepfathers were satisfied with their lives compared to around 90% of first-marriage adults, although the researchers commented on the "striking optimism" of stepcouples in regard to their expectations of satisfaction in 10 years time, suggesting that most saw the difficulties and challenges as temporary and surmountable.

Individual and family factors present in the lives of stepfamily members prior to remarriage are likely to account for some of the differences between parents in first marriages and stepfamilies (e.g., Nicholson, Fergusson, & Horwood, 1999). However, some of the increased levels of depression and anxiety can be attributed to the stresses associated with the remarriage transition and stepfamily living, which in turn negatively impact parenting.

How well residential parents fare will also be influenced by children's psychological and emotional well-being and responses to stepfamily life. Children who are experiencing adjustment difficulties prior to remarriage may respond more negatively toward the new family situation. For example, children in a clinical sample of stepfamilies with "child-focused" problems responded with less reciprocity to stepfathers than children in nonclinical families, even though the two groups of stepfathers did not differ on the amount of authority-related or befriending behavior initiated by stepparents (Brown, Green, & Druckman, 1990). On the other hand,

Hetherington and Kelly (2002) concluded that some children appear to have a temperament that allows to them to cope well with the transitions of divorce and remarriage and to relate easily to parents and stepparents across these transitions. Finally, it is important to note that it has been observed that children in stepfamilies have more influence than children in first-marriage families (Bray & Kelly, 1998). Hetherington and Clingempeel (1992), for example, in their 26-month study found that adolescents in stepfamilies in the first 2 years were more effective in altering the behavior of parents and stepparents than stepparents and parents were in altering the behavior of adolescents.

THE STEPPARENT ROLE

The attitude of the new stepparent and the approach taken toward stepchildren also affects how children respond. Research findings indicate that a functional stepparent role is different from a parenting role. Researchers and clinicians agree that a stepfather's early adoption of a disciplinary role, even an authoritative one, tends to trigger resistance in children and is associated with adjustment difficulties and negative child outcomes (Bray, 1999; Hetherington & Jodl, 1994; Papernow, 2006; J. Visher & Visher, 1988), although there is some evidence that adolescents may respond well when both parent and stepparent adopt an authoritative parenting style (Hetherington & Jodl, 1994; Nicholson, Phillips, Peterson, & Battistutta, 2000). On the other hand, adolescents in one study rated the role of friend as more appropriate for stepparents compared to parents and stepparents, who more frequently believe that a parenting role is appropriate (Fine, Coleman, & Ganong, 1999). Hence, a parenting role for a stepparent, especially in terms of discipline, may be associated with child and family adjustment difficulties, at least in the early stages of stepfamily formation. This is in contrast to nondivorced families and perhaps also in contrast to established stepfamilies (Hetherington, 1999).

The stepparent role emerged as important also in the first three qualitative studies (Cartwright, 2005). The young adults and children in the studies expressed a strong preference for parental, and not stepparental, control. Therapists also perceived that stepparents' adoption of a parenting role was problematic for children and adolescents (Cartwright, 2003b). The following extract is a conversation between three of the young adult participants in a group interview, demonstrating their thoughts about the importance of parents maintaining discipline:

> *I think it's important to reinforce that you're not getting a new parent. . . . I'm getting married to a new man and he is your stepfather. But he is not your father. I think that really needs to be reinforced to children. (Male, aged 20 years)*

I think that when you've got older children and they get into adolescence, it's really hard for them to know whether to take that new person as a parent figure, or like their mother's spouse, cause there's still the process of discipline. Once you're in adolescence, the new person should be the mother's partner and your original parent should really discipline you. (Female, aged 20 years)

Yeah I think basically I agree with you completely. I think your parents, you expect they have a right to tell you what to do. . . . Basically your stepparents are just— they're there. And if they do [discipline the children], it's sort of unnatural and it becomes an intrusion. (Male, aged 19 years)

Children also appeared to find it difficult if they perceived that a parent was supporting a stepparent in taking on a disciplinary role, at least an authoritarian one. The next quote is from a young man reflecting back on his stepfamily situation:

I think one of the things my Dad did wrong was, I think he sat back quite a lot with Ann [stepmother] coming in and doing the disciplining of us and my little brother. He'd just sort of sit there, and not want to look at what she was doing, and say: No that's wrong. You're not supposed to do that to a kid. And he'd just sit there because he didn't want more conflict because it would just go on and on. (Age 19)

On the other hand, stepparents who are supportive of both partners and children, who take time to build relationships with children and to earn their respect, can enhance the lives of children and parents (Bray & Kelly, 1998; E. B. Visher & Visher, 1993). In a recent New Zealand qualitative study of young adults' narrative accounts of relationships with stepfathers, 5 of the 25 young adult participants told narratives of continual positive regard (Kinniburgh-White, 2007, p. 89). In this group, relationships with stepfathers began well and continued to grow and deepen across the childhood and adolescent years. The stepfathers were seen as warm, supportive, and/ or generous. Similarly, Hetherington and Kelly (2002) concluded that the choice of a supportive partner was closely associated with positive outcomes for children and for the stepfamily.

PARENT-CHILD COALITIONS IN STEPFAMILIES

Unlike first-marriage families, parent-child relationships in stepfamilies are well established before the entrance of the new partner to the household (Ganong & Coleman, 1994), and some parents and children have developed very close relationships during the single-parent period. It is not surprising, then, that coalitions are common in stepfamilies and that these are frequently along biological lines, especially between parents and children (Bray & Kelly, 1998; Hetherington & Jodl, 1994). Many of these coalitions are dysfunctional and exclude the stepparent.

However, there is evidence that some form of coalition or alliance between a parent and child may be adaptive in remarried families. Anderson and White (1986) examined relationship patterns in 63 family and stepfamily triads. The families were categorized as functional or dysfunctional according to scores on an adjustment scale and involvement (or not) in treatment for family or child dysfunction. The researchers found that functional stepfamilies were similar to functional first-marriage families in that both exhibited good marital adjustment, strong positive bonds between biological parent and child, a lack of reported desire to exclude family members, and an ability to make mutually acceptable family decisions. However, functional stepfamilies exhibited a tendency toward stronger biological parent-child coalitions than both functional and dysfunctional first-marriage families. Dysfunctional stepfamilies also had stronger parent-child coalitions, but these were accompanied by a negative stepparent-stepchild relationship and a tendency to exclude stepfamily members. These results suggest that the commonly observed coalition or alliance between parent and child in the stepfamily may, in some forms, be adaptive, as long as it is not associated with a negative relationship with the stepparent and active attempts to exclude him or her.

LOYALTY ISSUES FOR PARENTS

Closely related to issues involved in parent-child coalitions and the stepparent role discussed earlier are issues of loyalty. Divided loyalties are common in stepfamilies (Bray & Kelly, 1998; J. Visher & Visher, 1988). Children can feel torn between divorced parents and between the parent and stepparent of the same gender, and parents frequently feel torn between partners and children whose relationships are conflicted.

When children and stepparents are engaged in conflict, the parent experiences divided loyalties. Parents can respond in a number of different ways. They can stay out of the conflict, take protective or supportive action in regard to the child, support the partner, or attempt to be supportive toward both. Weaver and Coleman (in Ganong & Coleman, 2004), in a grounded theory study of the roles women enact as mothers in stepfamilies, found that mothers' loyalty generally lay with children when conflict arose between children and stepfathers and that mothers engage in protective behavior in four different ways. They can act as a "gatekeeper" and control the stepfather's access to the children; adopt a position of "defender" to protect children from perceived threats to safety or well-being; act as a "mediator" between the partner and children when conflict arises; and act as an "interpreter" to assist partners to understand their children.

Engaging in these protective behaviors is likely to be tiring and stressful for mothers. Some of the mothers in the Multiple Case Study (Cartwright,

2003b) talked about the distress and confusion they experienced when a partner and child were in conflict, although they did not always take their children's sides. The mother in the following quote is describing how she responds to conflict between her 14-year-old son and her partner:

> It either goes two ways for me. Either I'll think about it and I'll take Dave's [partner] side really and I'll think that was a really provocative [thing for son] to say. . . . So I'll be grumpy at him. . . . Or else I'll take Damien's [son] side and say: Oh don't worry about it! . . . [Later] I don't know who to support these days. I can't see where the solution is. . . . [Later] I think my relationship with my son gets compromised by moving between two camps.

There is also evidence that children expect mothers to protect them and to take their side during conflict with stepparents. One young boy said he prefers his mother to intervene when his stepfather is "mad" at him and feels closer to her as a result:

INTERVIEWER: What does your Mum do if Bob is feeling mad?

JOSH: Well, if it's sort of like real bad, he just keeps going on for no sort of reasons . . . and it's just like I'm feeling really really hurt and stuff, sometimes she'll come to my defense.

INTERVIEWER: If you're feeling hurt?

JOSH: Yeah.

INTERVIEWER: How do you feel when Mum does that, when she comes to your defense?

JOSH: I feel quite happy with her, like I feel close to her, yeah.

INTERVIEWER: How do you think you'd feel if you Mum never did that, if Mum always just stayed out of it?

JOSH: I'd feel really hurt and I wouldn't like Bob.

Similarly, when the participants in the Questionnaire Study were asked "What do you think the mother ought to do if one of the children is upset and arguing with the stepfather?" almost 70% said the mother ought to intervene in some way (Moore & Cartwright, 2005). They suggested a number of ways of intervening that fell into two main categories: mediating between the stepparent and child and being supportive and understanding toward the position of both. A smaller group (7 out of 65) thought that the mother ought to take sides with the child. The remaining 30% believed that the mother should try to stay out of the conflict and allow the stepparent and child to work it out between them. No participants said that the mother ought to take sides with or support the stepfather only.

Hence, it seems likely that mothers who do behave protectively toward children may be responding, at least in part, to children's expectations. As

Browning (1994) points out, however, if parents often feel driven to defend a child, over time the parent can begin to feel disenchanted with the child and more emotionally removed from him or her. Similarly, a child's rebellion or lack of acceptance of a stepparent can impact how a parent feels toward a child, as illustrated next.

I've found it very painful. I still do. . . . But what I've been aware of in the last week is how angry she is. I feel that she's very angry with me. . . . And funnily enough when she has then wanted a cuddle out of me I've felt really angry because I haven't wanted to give it to . . . this is a time that is difficult for me because I do feel angry when she's nasty to John, when she's quite mean. So a lot of the time we've been very angry at each other. (Mother of 12-year-old girl)

The stresses associated with parenting children in stepfamilies may impact how parents feel toward children from previous unions. Hobart (1987) interviewed 232 stepfamily couples in Canada and found that both mothers and fathers reported having more positive relationships and gaining more satisfaction with their mutual children than with their nonshared children. Hobart concluded that mutual children had a "first class" position in the stepfamily compared to stepchildren.

Results from the qualitative studies also suggest that some children and adolescents in stepfamilies perceived a shift in the parent's loyalty away from them and toward the new partner. This perceived shift was associated with feelings of hurt and betrayal. A shift in loyalty was experienced in regard to how conflict was managed by a parent. Participants recalled feeling betrayed if a parent consistently "took the side" of a stepparent who was in conflict with them.

One of the worst things is thinking that your stepparent is somehow kind of turning your own parent against you! In some ways like they're siding together against you. And it sort of, it's just that whole betrayal thing again. It's just, it feels wrong. At times, I felt that I wasn't being stuck up for, and I'd even start to side with my stepbrothers against him. (Male, aged 22 years)

In some instances, parental loyalty was seen as shifting away from the child and toward the "new family" formed with mutual children. Some also perceived that they were given less support, either financial or emotional, relative to others in the stepfamily.

Basically, the money goes to the family that they have in their head and it's real obvious that you are always a part of it. It's just convenient for them to just take off with the kids [mutual children] and go the Rainbow's End [a theme park] and then: "Oh, sorry. We forgot to tell you." That kind of thing. . . . And my mum always takes his side, you know. She's with him. (Female, aged 18 years)

Finally, it is important to consider the impact of expectations regarding primacy of relationships in stepfamilies. As discussed earlier, some clinicians conceptualized the couple's relationship as the primary relationship in the stepfamily. However, some young adult participants stated that children ought to have a primary position in their parents' lives:

> I think parents have just got to put their kids first. No matter what! Otherwise, there's no point in having kids. (Female, aged 18 years)
>
> I would try to make it clear to the child or children that they're still number one and no relationship is going to get in the way of that. (Female, aged 19 years)

To investigate expectations around primacy of relationships, participants in the Questionnaire Study were asked the following question: "In your opinion, should the mother give priority to anyone in the family (out of her husband and her children) and if so, why?" (Moore & Cartwright, 2005). Only two participants said that the mother ought to give priority to the husband. The remainder of the participants was equally divided between those who said that she ought to give priority to the children and those who said she ought to give priority to both. These findings contradict clinical wisdom that emphasizes the primacy of the couple's relationship.

Parent-child relationships are placed under stress by a parent's repartnering or remarriage. Children have difficulty accepting a new parental partner, and the period of adjustment to stepfamily living can take many years. Children, especially those who have adjustment difficulties prior to remarriage, and pre- to early adolescent girls, may experience more extreme difficulties. As a result, children can stretch parents' abilities to provide nurturance and discipline. Mothers' difficulties are exacerbated by the increased stress that they experience during this time, which further impacts their ability to parent authoritatively.

Clinicians have often seen stepparents as having an outsider position in the stepfamily system, yet some children appear to experience an outsider position to the new couple's relationship. Some experience a loss of time and attention. Others perceive that the parent's loyalty to them is diminished and has gone toward the stepparent and perhaps mutual children born to the new marriage. These difficulties are exacerbated when stepparents and stepchildren have conflicted relationships and parents are placed in a position of divided loyalty. Mothers may have a tendency to support children. However, some children in the qualitative studies perceived that their mother was supporting their stepparent during conflict and felt betrayed by this. Hence, the type of role adopted by the stepparent may significantly impact parent-child relationships. Children rebel against stepparents who attempt to discipline them or who engage with them in conflictual interchanges. A stepparent who seeks to build a relationship with children, who recognizes the prior relationship of parent and child, and who supports the parent in his or her role is likely—over time—to attract less negative attention from the child and place less stress on parents and children. Similarly, given the findings about adaptive parent-child coalitions in stepfamilies and children's needs for ongoing time, attention, and parental commitment, stepparents who are able to accept children's need for a primary relationship with parents may trigger less resistance and rivalry in children.

FUTURE DIRECTIONS: RESEARCH AND CLINICAL PRACTICE

This section looks briefly at future directions in research and practice with stepfamilies based on the clinical and research literature examined in this chapter.

CLINICAL PERSPECTIVES

Early clinical writers often emphasized the central importance of the couple's relationship. However, a shift may have occurred in recent years, with clinicians placing more emphasis on the development of all the key relationships in stepfamilies, including the parent-child relationship. Papernow (1995), for example, points out that stepfamilies are most likely to remain "primarily divided" in the early stages, in line with established family relationships, with nurturance and agreement of rules occurring most easily within these established relationships. Because of the "middle ground" that exists in the parent-child relationship in the early stages, but that is not established for newer relationships, "blending" is less effective than "compartmentalizing" (Papernow, 1993, 2006). Papernow suggests that different subsystems, including the parent-child, stepparent-stepchild, and couple, will all need time together to bond. She also argues that "active" families who move too fast to create a new family unit often deny children enough access to the biological parent and require too much change in too short a time (Papernow, 1995). These families, she says, do not attend enough to the child's need for connection and continuity in their relationship with the parent.

Rodwell (2002), a New Zealand clinician, deals with the issue of primacy in her recent publication by encouraging parents to consider how they can simultaneously be both "best partner" and "best parent": "Within a repartnered family the birth parent is required to maintain at least two primary relationships: the continuing one with his or her own children and the new one with the partner" (p. 58).

Clinical approaches, such as those of Papernow (1993, 1995, 2006) and Rodwell (2002), appear to fit better with the needs and expectations of children, as demonstrated here, compared to approaches that guide parents to consider the partner relationship as the primary relationship.

The results discussed in this chapter suggest that parents are in need of guidance about ways to relate to their children in stepfamily situations to ensure that they maintain strong positive parent-child relationships, thereby enhancing the possibility of positive child outcomes and also satisfaction in parenting. It seems essential that models of stepfamily development emphasize the importance of the parent-child relationship, as well as the couple's relationship and the stepparent-stepchild relationship. The results discussed in this chapter suggest that clinicians working with stepfamilies cannot assume that parents understand that they need to spend time with children and maintain their parenting roles after remarriage.

RESEARCH DIRECTIONS

The ongoing lack of research attention to the parent-child relationship is problematic given the lack of institutionalization of stepfamilies in society (Cherlin, 1978; Grizzle, 1999). This means that researchers and clinicians do not have sufficient understanding of how parents relate to children in this different type of family. On the other hand, parents and stepparents are in need of alternative models to guide them, especially when their parenting skills are often severely tested by children who are distressed about the family changes they have experienced. It seems important, then, that the parent-child relationship is not taken for granted and that stepfamily relationship research begins to establish a more intensive focus on this dyad.

In particular, it would be useful to understand more about the challenges that parents face in the transition to repartnering or remarriage; how they inform children of their decision to repartner or remarry; how they assist children with the transition into a stepfamily household; and the parenting practices that are most strongly associated with child well-being across these transitions. It is also important to investigate the challenges that parents face in maintaining parenting roles with children and parenting practices that support children to adapt to the new family situation or are associated with adjustment difficulties. Because children's lack of acceptance of and rebellion against the stepfamily situation underlie many of the difficulties facing parents and stepparents, it also is desirable to understand more about the views and experiences of children. Understanding the meaning of different stepfamily processes and events for children would provide insight into the parenting and communication processes that are associated with adaptation of children. Longitudinal studies that investigate parent-child relationships, across family transitions and through stepfamily living, will provide us with increased understanding of the diverse trajectories of these relationships; the impact of age and gender of children at remarriage; and the influence of individual and contextual factors that interact with parenting processes to influence outcomes for parents and children.

REFERENCES

Amato, P. (2000). The consequences of divorce for adults and children. *Journal of Marriage and the Family, 62,* 1269–1287.

Anderson, J. Z., & White, G. (1986). An empirical investigation of interaction and relationship patterns in functional and dysfunctional nuclear families and stepfamilies. *Family Process, 25,* 407–422.

Bray, J. (1992). Family relationships and children's adjustment in clinical and nonclinical stepfather families. *Journal of Family Psychology, 6,* 60–68.

Bray, J. (1999). From marriage to remarriage and beyond: Findings from the Developmental Issues in Stepfamilies Research Project. In E. M. Hetherington (Ed.), *Coping with divorce, single parenting, and remarriage: A risk and resiliency perspective* (pp. 253–273). Hillsdale, NJ: Erlbaum.

Bray, J., & Berger, S. (1993). Developmental Issues in Stepfamilies Research Project: Family relationships and parent-child interactions. *Journal of Family Psychology, 7,* 76–90.

Bray, J., & Kelly, J. (1998). *Stepfamilies: Love, marriage, and parenting in the first decade.* New York: Broadway Books.

Brown, A., Green, R., & Druckman, J. (1990). A comparison of stepfamilies with and without child-focused problems. *American Journal of Orthopsychiatry, 60,* 556–566.

Browning, S. (1994). Treating stepfamilies: Alternatives to traditional family therapy. In K. Pasley & M. Ihinger-Tallman (Eds.), *Stepparenting: Issues in theory, research and practice* (pp. 175–199). Westport, CT: Praeger.

Buchanan, C. M., Maccoby, E. E., & Dornbusch, S. M. (1996). *Adolescents after divorce.* Cambridge, MA: Harvard University Press.

Cartwright, C. (2003a). *Parent-child relationships in families of remarriage: What hurts? What helps?* Unpublished doctoral dissertation, University of Auckland, New Zealand.

Cartwright, C. (2003b). Therapists' perceptions of bioparent-child relationships in stepfamilies: What hurts? What helps? *Journal of Divorce and Remarriage, 38,* 147–166.

Cartwright, C. (2005). Stepfamily living and parent-child relationships: An exploratory investigation. *Journal of Family Studies, 11,* 265–283.

Cartwright, C., & Seymour, F. (2002). Young adults' perceptions of parents' responses in stepfamilies: What hurts? What helps? *Journal of Divorce and Remarriage, 37,* 123–141.

Cherlin, A. J. (1978). Remarriage as an incomplete institution. *American Journal of Sociology, 84,* 634–650.

Cherlin, A. J., & Furstenberg, F. F. (1994). Stepfamilies in the United States: A reconsideration. *Annual Review of Sociology, 20*, 359–381.

Coleman, M., Ganong, L., & Fine, M. (2000). Reinvestigating remarriage: Another decade of progress. *Journal of Marriage and the Family, 62*, 1288–1307.

Crosbie-Burnett, M. (1984). The centrality of the step relationship: A challenge to family theory and practice. *Family Relations, 33*, 459–463.

Emery, R. (1999). *Marriage, divorce and children's adjustment*. Thousand Oaks, CA: Sage.

Ferri, E., & Smith, K. (1998). *Step-parenting in the 1990s*. York, North Yorkshire, England: Joseph Rowntree Foundation.

Fine, M. A., Coleman, M., & Ganong, L. H. (1999). A social constructionist multi-method approach to understanding the stepparent role. In E. M. Hetherington (Ed.), *Coping with divorce, single parenting and remarriage* (pp. 273–294). Mahwah, NJ: Erlbaum.

Funder, K., & Harrison, M. (1993). Drawing a longbow on marriage and divorce. In K. Funder, M. Harrison, & R. Weston (Eds.), *Settling down: Pathways of parents after divorce* (pp. 13–32). Melbourne: Australian Institute of Family Studies.

Ganong, L. H., & Coleman, M. (1994). *Remarried family relations*. Thousand Oaks, CA: Sage.

Ganong, L. H., & Coleman, M. (2004). *Stepfamily relationships: Development, dynamics, and interventions*. New York: Kluwer Academic/Plenum Press.

Grizzle, G. L. (1999). Institutionalization and family unity: An exploratory study of Cherlin's (1978) views. *Journal of Divorce and Remarriage, 30*, 125–141.

Hetherington, E. M. (1987). Family relations six years after divorce. In K. Pasley & M. Ihinger-Tallman (Eds.), *Remarriage and stepparenting: Current research and theory* (pp. 185–205). New York: Guilford Press.

Hetherington, E. M. (1989). Coping with family transitions: Winners, losers, and survivors. *Child Development*, 1–14.

Hetherington, E. M. (1993). An overview of the Virginia Longitudinal Study of Divorce and Remarriage with a focus on early adolescence. *Journal of Family Psychology, 7*, 39–56.

Hetherington, E. M. (Ed.). (1999). *Coping with divorce, single parenting, and remarriage: A risk and resiliency perspective*. Mahwah, NJ: Erlbaum.

Hetherington, E. M. (2003). Social support and the adjustment of children in divorced and remarried families. *Childhood, 11*, 217–236.

Hetherington, E. M., Bridges, M., & Insabella, G. M. (1998). What matters? What does not? Five perspectives on the association between marital transitions and children's adjustment. *American Psychologist, 53*, 167–184.

Hetherington, E. M., & Clingempeel, W. G. (1992). Coping with marital transitions. *Monographs of the Society for Research in Child Development, 57*, 1–14.

Hetherington, E. M., Henderson, S. H., & Reiss, D. (Eds.). (1999). Adolescent siblings in stepfamilies: Family functioning and adolescent adjustment. *Monographs of the Society for Research in Child Development, 64*(4, Serial No. 259).

Hetherington, E. M., & Jodl, K. M. (1994). Stepfamilies as settings for child development. In A. Booth & J. Dunn (Eds.), *Stepfamilies: Who benefits? Who does not?* (pp. 55–80). Hillsdale, NJ: Erlbaum.

Hetherington, E. M., & Kelly, J. (2002). *For better or for worse: Divorce reconsidered.* New York: Norton.

Hetherington, E. M., & Stanley-Hagan, M. M. (1995). Parenting in divorced and re-married families. In M. H. Bornstein (Ed.), *Handbook of parenting* (Vol. 3, pp. 233–254). Mahwah, NJ: Erlbaum.

Hobart, C. (1987). Parent-child relations in remarried families. *Journal of Family Issues, 8,* 259–277.

Hughes, J. (2000). Repartnering after divorce. *Family Matters, 55,* 16–21.

Ihinger-Tallman, M., & Pasley, K. (1997). Stepfamilies in 1984 and today—A scholarly perspective. *Marriage and Family Review, 26,* 19–40.

Kiernan, E. K. (1992). The impact of family disruption in childhood on transitions made in young adult life. *Population Studies, 46,* 213–234.

Kinniburgh-White, R. (2007). *A qualitative study of the experiences of young adult step-children: Developing a relationship with a stepfather.* Unpublished doctoral dissertation, University of Auckland, New Zealand.

Kurdek, L. (1994). Remarriages and stepfamilies are not inherently problematic. In A. Booth & J. Dunn (Eds.), *Stepfamilies: Who benefits? Who does not?* (pp. 37–44). Hillsdale, NJ: Erlbaum.

Martin, D., & Martin, M. (1992). *Stepfamilies in therapy: Understanding systems, assessment, and intervention.* San Francisco: Jossey-Bass.

Messinger, L., Walker, K., & Freeman, S. (1978). Preparation for remarriage following divorce: The use of group techniques. *American Journal of Orthopsychiatry, 48,* 263–272.

Mills, D. M. (1984). A model for stepfamily development. *Family Relations, 33,* 365–372.

Mitchell, B. A., Wister, A. V., & Burch, T. K. (1989). The family environment and leaving the parental home. *Journal of Marriage and the Family, 51,* 605–613.

Moore, S., & Cartwright, C. (2005). Adolescents' and young adults' expectations of parental responsibilities in stepfamilies. *Journal of Divorce and Remarriage, 43,* 109–128.

Mowatt, M. H. (1972). Group psychotherapy for stepfathers and their wives. *Psychotherapy, Theory, Research and Practice, 9,* 328–331.

Nicholson, J., Fergusson, D., & Horwood, L. (1999). Effects on later adjustment of living in a stepfamily during childhood and adolescence. *Journal of Child Psychology and Psychiatry, 40,* 405–416.

Nicholson, J., Phillips, M. E., Peterson, C. C., & Battistutta, D. (2000). Relationship between the parenting styles of biological parents and stepparents and the adjustment of young adult stepchildren. *Journal of Divorce and Remarriage, 36,* 57–76.

Ochiltree, G. (1990). *Children in stepfamilies.* Sydney, Australia: Prentice-Hall.

Papernow, P. (1993). *Becoming a stepfamily: Patterns of development in remarried families.* San Francisco: Jossey-Bass.

Papernow, P. (1995). What's going on here? Separating (and weaving together) step and clinical issues in remarried families. In D. K. Huntley (Ed.), *Understanding stepfamilies: Implications for assessment and treatment* (pp. 3–24). Alexandria, VA: American Counseling Association.

Papernow, P. (2006, May/June). "Blended family" relationships: Helping people who live in stepfamilies. *Family Therapy Magazine,* 34–42.

Parish, T., & Dostal, J. (1980). Evaluations of self and parent figures by children from intact, divorced and reconstituted families. *Journal of Youth and Adolescence, 9*, 347–351.

Parish, T., & Kappes, B. (1980). Impact of father loss on the family. *Social Behavior and Personality: An International Journal, 8*, 107–112.

Quilino, W. S. (1991). Family structure and home-leaving: A further specification of the relationship. *Journal of Marriage and the Family, 53*, 999–1010.

Rodwell, J. (2002). *Repartnered families: Creating new ways of living together beyond the nuclear family*. Auckland, New Zealand: Penguin.

Solomon, C. R. (1995). The importance of mother-child relations in studying stepfamilies. *Journal of Divorce and Remarriage, 24*, 89–98.

Thomson, E., Thomas, L., & McLanahan, S. S. (1994). Family structure and child wellbeing: Economic resources versus parental behaviors. *Social Forces, 73*, 221–242.

Visher, E. B., & Visher, J. (1979). *Stepfamilies: A guide to working with stepparents and stepchildren*. New York: Brunner/Mazel.

Visher, E. B., & Visher, J. (1993). Remarriage families and stepparenting. In F. Walsh (Ed.), *Normal family processes* (pp. 235–253). New York: Guilford Press.

Visher, E. B., & Visher, J. (1996). *Therapy with stepfamilies* (Vol. 6). New York: Brunner/Mazel.

Visher, J., & Visher, E. (1988). *Old loyalties, new ties: Therapeutic strategies with stepfamilies*. New York: Brunner/Mazel.

Webber, R. (1994). *Living in a stepfamily*. Melbourne: Australian Council for Education Research Limited.

White, L. (1992). The effect of parental divorce and remarriage on parental support for adult children. *Journal of Family Issues, 13*, 234–250.

White, L. (1994). Stepfamilies over the life course: Social support. In A. Booth & J. Dunn (Eds.), *Stepfamilies: Who benefits? Who does not?* (pp. 109–137). Hillsdale, NJ: Erlbaum.

White, L., & Booth, A. (1985). The quality and stability of remarriages: The role of stepchildren. *American Sociological Review, 50*, 689–698.

Whiteside, M. F. (1982). Remarriage: A family developmental process. *Journal of Marital and Family Therapy, 4*, 61–70.

CHAPTER 10

A Longitudinal Examination of Marital Processes Leading to Instability in Remarriages and Stepfamilies

BRAD VAN EEDEN-MOOREFIELD
KAY PASLEY

STUDIES OF marital dynamics, quality, and stability have long been the focus of research on families, including stepfamilies (e.g., Bradbury, Fincham, & Beach, 2000; Coleman, Ganong, & Fine, 2000). Typically, findings on stepfamilies compare couples in first marriages with those in remarriages on indicators of both marital processes and marital outcomes. In general, reviews of these studies suggest mixed findings. Some findings show that poorer marital quality is more common in remarriages than in first marriages, whereas other studies find the opposite (e.g., Coleman et al., 2000). Results consistently show that of those involved in a first divorce approximately 85% will remarry (Kreider & Fields, 2002), and about 50% to 60% of couples who remarry will redivorce, suggesting a slightly higher probability of divorce among remarrieds compared to first-marrieds. However, since 1990 few studies have examined the causes of such instability in remarriage, which is of concern considering the recent national movement to strengthen marriages (see http://center.americanvalues.org/?p=7/). Additionally, it appears that the current decade has witnessed a renewed interest primarily in the effects of remarriage on children (e.g., Braithwaite & Baxter, 2006) and in interactions between former spouses (e.g., Fischer, de Graaf, & Kalmijn, 2005). Clearly, efforts to address couple dynamics and relationship processes predictive of redivorce are warranted (Ganong & Coleman, 2004) because of the need to identify potential points at which marital intervention might be successful.

Our purpose here is twofold. Using data from Waves 1–3 of the National Survey of Families and Households (NSFH; 1987–1988, 1992–1994, 2001–2002), we first examined the effects of certain marital processes (marital conflict, perceived fairness, and marital quality) on marital instability to identify the patterns of change over time. The literature suggests that structural complexity is a primary source of reduced marital quality and stability for those who remarry, because children from a prior marriage and former spouses potentially complicate family life (Ganong & Coleman, 2004). Thus, we also examined the moderating role of structural complexity by comparing the patterns of change in marital processes and stability among two groups: individuals in remarriages (those with no children in the current marriage or only biological children from the current marriage) and stepfamilies (those with at least one child from a prior marriage). In examining the changes in marital process and outcomes among different family structures, we begin to answer a key question about the influence of structural complexity that to date is primarily speculative.

OUR CONCEPTUAL MODEL

We posit a conceptual model claiming that early marital conflict, perceptions of fairness, and marital quality affect these same indicators of marital processes later and ultimately result in varying levels of marital instability, including divorce. Specifically, we argue that higher levels of disagreement regarding various aspects of family life (marital conflict), perceptions of unfairness in handling various matters (fairness), and being less satisfied with life and unhappy with one's marriage (marital quality) predict greater marital instability over time.

Although evidence suggests that relationship processes such as communication and other couple interactions are comparable in first marriages and remarriages, we agree with Adler-Baeder and Higginbotham (2004) that research has oversimplified these comparisons and neglected the true complexity inherent in stepfamily life. Moreover, research concerning marital conflict in remarriages and stepfamilies is scant (Coleman, Fine, Ganong, Downs, & Pauk, 2001). There is consistent evidence that marital conflict and its resolution is related to both future marital quality and divorce among first marriages (e.g., Gottman & Notarius, 2000; Kurdek, 1995; Matthews, Conger, & Wickrama, 1996). What is established even more clearly is that compared to first marriages, those in stepfamilies have more potential for conflict (Bray, 1999; Coleman et al., 2000). Specifically, interactions with former spouses, concern over finances, stepparenting, and child custody arrangements are unique sources of conflict (Coleman et al., 2000) and are related to marital outcomes. In fact, Bodenmann, Pihet, and Kayser (2006) found that dyadic interactions related to communication patterns predicted future changes in marital quality, similar to the findings of Beaudry, Boisvert, Simard, Parent, and Blais (2004). Taken together, we expected marital conflict to affect future marital quality, such that marital quality is reduced over time.

As marital conflict increases and future marital quality decreases, we expected that marital stability would decrease as thoughts of divorce begin to surface and permeate the relationship. Stated another way, it is logical to conclude that when marital conflict is high and marital quality is low, couples begin to contemplate divorce and report that their remarriage is in trouble. In fact, Yeh, Lorenz, Conger, and Elder (2006) studied 283 married couples longitudinally and found that decreased sexual and marital satisfaction (two indicators of marital quality) were related to decreased marital stability, although marital satisfaction mediated the relationship between sexual satisfaction and marital stability. Stewart (2005) found that as happiness decreased, thoughts of redivorce increased, leading to eventual separation, as is also suggested in our model. Earlier studies also support our assertion that decreased marital quality is related to marital instability (e.g., Aguirre & Kirwan, 1986; Kurdek, 1991; White & Booth, 1985) and that divorce is increasingly likely.

As stated earlier, there is little available research on redivorce (Ganong & Coleman, 2004). However, a recent study (Gager & Sanchez, 2003) examined the risk of divorce among those in first marriages using Waves 1 and 2 of the NSFH. These researchers found that instability at Wave 1 predicted divorce at Wave 2. There is no reason to believe that similar outcomes would not occur among remarriages and stepfamilies.

Because issues arise when stepchildren are present that are unique to stepfamily life, we expected that remarriage and stepfamily complexity would moderate the links between marital processes and marital instability in our model (Ganong & Coleman 2004). Clearly, those with no children or only common children will not experience many of the difficulties associated with attempting to parent another person's children, handling the complexity of different and competing developmental needs (e.g., new marriage competes with parenting school-age children), and coping with former spouses and multiple extended families, as suggested early by Pasley and Ihinger-Tallman (1982) and supported by other scholars later (e.g., Visher & Visher, 1998; Visher, Visher, & Pasley, 2003). Given that adolescent adjustment is reflective of couple adjustment (Ganong & Coleman, 2004), stepfamily complexity was included as a moderator.

SAMPLE AND DESIGN

We used data from Waves 1, 2, and 3 of the NSFH, a national longitudinal probability sample study conducted in 1987–1988, 1992–1994, and

2001–2003 where minority populations, early marrieds, and remarrieds were oversampled (Sweet & Bumpass, 2002). The original sample included a cross-section of 9,367 households ($N = 13,007$ individuals), of whom 10,007 respondents were reinterviewed at Wave 2, and those with an eligible focal child as well as those over age 45 were reinterviewed again at Wave 3 ($N = 4,600$). We refer the reader to the primary reference for additional sample- and design-related information (Sweet & Bumpass, 2002).

The sample used here was delimited to those who were (a) continuously in the same remarriage and/or stepfamily at Waves 1 and 2, but not necessarily at Wave 3 ($N = 455$), and (b) in their first remarriage. The average length of remarriage at Wave 1 was 8.33 years ($SD = 8.38$), suggesting a maritally stable group. Our sample included 197 (43.3%) men and 258 (56.7%) women (primary respondents and not matched couples) with an average age of 41.87 years ($SD = 9.9$). Of the 455 respondents, 335 (73.6%) were White, 98 (21.5%) were Black, 17 (3.7%) were Hispanic, 4 (.9%) were Native American, and 1 did not report race. A slight majority reported that they had not cohabited prior to their remarriage (233; 51.5%). At Wave 1, 238 (52.3%) held high school or GED degrees or less, 170 (37.4%) were attending college or held associate's or bachelor's degrees, and the remaining 47 (10.4%) were enrolled in a postgraduate program or held graduate degrees. Also at Wave 1, the mean total couple income was $55,663.26 ($SD = 11,524.94$), whereas the median income was $38,500. Geographic location in the United States included 88 (19.3%) in the Northwest, 125 (27.5%) in the North Central, 150 (33.0%) in the South, and 92 (20.2%) in the West. At Wave 3, 94 (20.70%) respondents reported being divorced.

MEASUREMENT

Descriptive statistics and reliabilities for all measures included in our conceptual model are found in Table 10.1.

Marital Quality

Marital quality consisted of nine items that asked about the degree of happiness from a series of questions assessed at both Waves 1 and 2. The items were scored on a 7-point Likert-type scale ranging from *very unhappy* to *very happy*. Responses were summed, with higher scores indicative of higher marital quality (sample item: happiness with the amount of time spent with your spouse). Overall, this sample was generally happy with their marriage at Wave 1 ($M = 53.45, SD = 12.58$) and slightly less happy 5 years later ($M = 48.62, SD = 10.88$). We note that the distribution of responses shifted from leptokurtic and negatively skewed at Wave 1 to an approximate normal distribution at Wave 2 (see Table 10.1).

Table 10.1

Descriptive Statistics, Reliabilities, and Correlations for Manifest Variables

Manifest Variable	1	2	3	4	5	6	7
Wave 1 Marital quality	—						
Wave 1 Fairness	.20*	—					
Wave 1 Marital conflict	−.30*	−.07	—				
Wave 2 Marital quality	.34*	.23*	−.30*	—			
Wave 2 Fairness	.16*	.31*	−.13*	.38*	—		
Wave 2 Marital conflict	−.19*	−.01	.43*	−.53*	−.46*	—	
Wave 3 Instability	−.25*	−.10*	.15*	−.60*	−.23*	.34*	—
Mean	53.45	8.98	10.83	48.62	8.80	11.60	2.49
SD	12.58	1.22	4.22	10.88	1.29	4.61	2.34
Actual Range	9–63	4–15	6–33	10–63	4–15	6–36	1–6
Alpha	.90	.60	.75	.90	.55	.76	—
Kurtosis	2.85	6.40	2.92	.54	4.59	2.39	2.39
Skewness	−1.70	−.26	1.36	−.88	−.54	1.26	1.68

*$p = < .05$.

Fairness

Fairness also was measured at both Waves 1 and 2 and is a composite measure of the summed responses to four questions asking about the level of perceived fairness. These items were scored on a 5-point Likert-type scale with responses ranging from *very unfair for the respondent* to *very unfair for the spouse*. The middle anchor is *fair to both* (sample item: fairness of household chores). The mean was 8.98 for Wave 1 ($SD = 1.22$) and 8.80 for Wave 2 ($SD = 1.29$) and had a sizable leptokurtic distribution (see Table 10.1). Clearly, this sample perceived their marriage as fair overall, with a slight bias toward being unfair for the respondent.

Marital Conflict

Marital conflict was measured at both Waves 1 and 2. It is a composite measure containing six items scored on a 6-point Likert-type scale and asking about the frequency of disagreement, with responses ranging from *never* to *almost every day*. Responses were summed, with higher scores reflective of more frequent marital conflict (sample item: amount of disagreement related to household tasks). As seen in Table 10.1, overall this sample did not report a high frequency of conflict in 1987–1988 or 1992–1994, with means of 10.83 ($SD = 4.22$) and 11.60 ($SD = 4.61$), respectively, as well as the slightly leptokurtic distribution of responses.

Marital Instability

Because instability was measured dichotomously at Wave 1, which differed from its measurement at Waves 2 and 3, the Wave 1 score was excluded from the model. Marital instability was measured at Wave 2 by asking respondents about the extent to which they believed that they eventually would divorce or separate from their current spouse; this item was measured on a 5-point Likert-type scale ranging from *very low* to *very high*. At Wave 3 the respondents were asked this question again. Additionally, respondents were asked to report whether they had divorced their current spouse. Responses were recorded as *yes* or *no*. Responses from these two questions were combined for the instability measure at Wave 3; if the respondent reported having divorced at Wave 3, he or she received an instability score of 6, otherwise they received their reported score for the first question only. Thus, the final variable ranged from *very low probability* of divorce to *actually did divorce*. The mean score at Wave 3 was 2.49 ($SD =$ 2.34), indicating a somewhat moderate level of stability, which also is supported by the positively skewed leptokurtic distribution (see Table 10.1).

Family Complexity

Family complexity was expected to moderate the hypothesized model and was measured using a combination of several variables related to the presence and relation of children to the respondents and their current spouse. This resulted in the identification of two groups: remarriages ($n = 292$; i.e., remarrieds with no children or only joint biological children) and stepfamilies ($n = 163$; i.e., stepfather-only families [only she has children from a prior marriage], stepmother-only families [only he has children from a prior marriage], stepmother-stepfather families [both have children from prior marriages], and those with both common and stepchildren). Only two groups were created as it was expected that remarriages that included no children or only common biological children face fewer family formation obstacles compared with those in which one or more children are stepchildren. For example, among stepfamilies, issues related to visitation and custody are common sources of added stress that easily spill over into the couple's relationship (Ganong & Coleman, 2004).

RESULTS

Preliminary Analyses

Correlations between the variables and descriptive statistics also appear in Table 10.1. Note that the alphas were acceptable across scale variables (.75 to .90) except for both of those indicating fairness (.60, .55). As expected, univariate and multivariate assumptions of normality were not met in these cases. Specifically, several kurtosis and skewness scores departed from 0, demonstrating higher than acceptable levels. However, this is not surprising given that Fletcher, Simpson, and Thomas (2000) suggested that when people self-report on their own relationships they rate them more positively than they actually are and more positively than observers rate them. Further, there were some missing data, which we assumed to be randomly missing. Full-information maximum likelihood estimation with imputation was used to fit the covariance structure to the data within AMOS 5.0 (Arbuckle, 2003) to handle estimation problems with nonnormal and missing data (Raykov, 2005).

Correlations were as expected, except that fairness was not correlated significantly with marital conflict at Wave 1, but was at Wave 2. Because Wave 1 marital conflict and marital quality were correlated, when we tested the model this was added so only the independent contributions of these exogenous variables were tested on Wave 2 and Wave 3 endogenous variables. Additionally, disturbance terms at Wave 2 were allowed to correlate. This is justified given that common extraneous variables likely exist among marital conflict, marital quality, and fairness (Kline, 1998).

First, a full cross-lagged model (Burkholder & Harlow, 2003) was tested, followed by a multigroup analysis to test for moderation. Suggestions by Baron and Kenny (1986) for tests of moderation (i.e., multigroup analyses) were followed. The importance of using a cross-lagged model is that it allows for an approximation of causal influences by accounting for cross-time construct stability, such that variance due to other variables and beyond the same construct assessed at multiple time points can be explained (Burkholder & Harlow, 2003). To simplify the models so they would produce estimates and control for the influence of Wave 2 instability on Wave 3 instability concurrently, Wave 3 marital instability was regressed on Wave 2 instability, and the residual scores were used in AMOS to test the conceptual model (Fletcher, Selgrade, & Germano, 2006). Specifically, for a model to fit the data and produce estimates, there must be more known values (e.g., variances and covariances of the constructs) than unknowns (i.e., parameters to be estimated such as paths). In our model, there were 21 known values (or 7 constructs $[7 - 1]/2 = 21$). Thus, we had to limit the estimation of parameters to 20. Further, the number of paths to be estimated is high for cross-lagged models. This number was further increased because we allowed marital conflict and martial quality to be correlated, such that only independent effects and the correlated disturbance terms were estimated. As such, we needed to reduce the number of "unknowns" to be able to test the model and have confidence in the result. One way to do this was to simplify the model using the method outlined above.

Full Sample Model

Results of the full sample model suggest that it is a plausible solution ($\chi^2[4] = 6.69, p = .15, \text{RMSEA} = .04, \text{NFI} = .99; \text{CFI} = .99$) with moderate stability coefficients (see Table 10.2 and Figure 10.1). Specifically, the model suggests that higher levels of early marital conflict decrease later marital

Table 10.2

Unstandardized and Standardized Parameter Estimates, Critical Ratios, and Significant Levels for the Full Sample Model (Standard Errors in Parentheses)

Parameter Estimate	Full Sample Model ($N = 455$)		
	Unstandardized (SE)	Standardized	Critical Ratio
W1MCON → W2MCON	.44 (.06)	.41	7.87*
W1MCON → W2MQUAL	−.58 (.13)	−.23	−4.40*
W1MCON → W2FAIR	−.03 (.02)	−.09	−1.77
W1MQUAL → W2MCON	−.28 (.17)	−.08	−1.65
W1MQUAL → W2MQUAL	1.75 (.39)	.23	4.49*
W1MQUAL → W2FAIR	.05 (.05)	.06	1.14
W1FAIR → W2MCON	.05 (.18)	.01	.80
W1FAIR → W2MQUAL	1.12 (.42)	.13	2.65*
W1FAIR → W2FAIR	.31 (.05)	.29	6.12*
W2MCON → W3INSTAB	.10 (.01)	.05	.93
W2MQUAL → W3INSTAB	−.05 (.01)	−.54	−10.48*
W2FAIR → W3INSTAB	−.03 (.03)	−.04	−.94

Notes: FAIR = Fairness; INSTAB = Marital instability; MCON = Marital conflict; MQUAL = Marital quality; W refers to Wave 1, 2, or 3.

*$p < .01$.

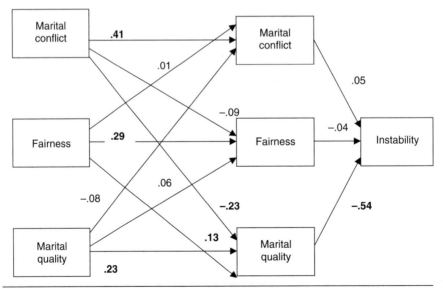

Time 1   Time 2

Time 3

Figure 10.1 Full Sample Path Model of Marital Processes Leading to Marital Instability (Standardized Solution). *Notes:* Significant paths in bold. $N = 455$; χ^2 [8] = 6.69; $p = .15$; CFI = .99; NFI = .99; RMSEA = .04.

Table 10.3

Unstandardized and Standardized Parameter Estimates and Critical Ratios for the Remarriage and Stepfamily Models (Standard Errors in Parentheses)

Parameter Estimate	Remarriage Model (N = 292)			Stepfamily Model (N = 163)		
	Unstandardized	Standardized	Critical Ratio	Unstandardized	Standardized	Critical Ratio
W1MCON → W2MCON	.55 (.07)	.49	7.64*	.27 (.09)	.27	3.12*
W1MCON → W2MQUAL	−.67 (.18)	−.26	−3.71*	−.46 (.20)	−.19	−2.36*
W1MCON → W2FAIR	−.04 (.02)	−.12	−1.79	−.02 (.03)	−.06	−.77
W1MQUAL → W2MCON	−.34 (.21)	−.10	−1.65	−.13 (.28)	−.04	−.47
W1MQUAL → W2MQUAL	1.70 (.50)	.22	3.40*	1.89 (.64)	.24	2.97*
W1MQUAL → W2FAIR	.07 (.05)	.08	1.35	.02 (.09)	.02	.22
W1FAIR → W2MCON	−.09 (.25)	−.02	−.35	.13 (.26)	.04	.50
W1FAIR → W2MQUAL	.77 (.61)	.08	1.28	1.31 (.59)	.18	2.24*
W1FAIR → W2FAIR	.41 (.06)	.37	6.46*	.21 (.08)	.21	2.66*
W2MCON → W3INSTAB	.01 (.02)	.05	.73	.01 (.02)	.05	.79
W2MQUAL → W3INSTAB	−.05 (.01)	−.49	−6.36*	−.06 (.01)	−.61	−8.71*
W2FAIR → W3INSTAB	−.02 (.05)	−.03	−.47	−.04 (.05)	−.05	−.81

*$p < .05$.

Note: W refers to Wave 1, 2, or 3; FAIR = Fairness; INSTAB = Marital instability; MCON = Marital conflict; MQUAL = Marital quality.

239

quality. Conversely, higher levels of perceived fairness early on increase later marital quality. Importantly, higher levels of marital quality increase later stability of the marriage. It is noteworthy that 34% of the variance in marital instability at Wave 3 was accounted for by the conceptualized process model.

EVIDENCE OF MODERATION

As stated earlier, it is important to consider how marital processes might differ between those in remarriages and those in stepfamilies, given the added pressures associated with the presence of stepchildren and stepparenting (e.g., distribution of family resources, handling parenting decisions; Ganong & Coleman, 2004). Thus, family complexity was examined as a moderator (see Table 10.3 and Figure 10.2). The comparison of the two groups in the moderated model fits the data quite well (χ^2 [8] = 8.37, p = .40, RMSEA = .01, NFI = .99, CFI = .99), and based on the χ^2 and RMSEA appears to have improved fit over the full model. However, both models did fit the data.

The moderated model is largely similar to the full model except for two key differences. First, the strength of the paths differed by family

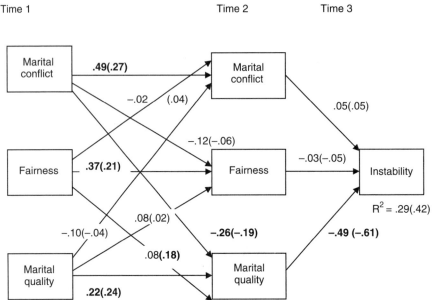

Figure 10.2 Remarriage and Stepfamily Path Model of Marital Processes Leading to Marital Instability (Standardized Solution). *Notes:* Significant paths in bold and estimates for the stepfamily model are in parentheses. Moderated Model: χ^2 [8] = 8.37; p = .40; CFI = .99; NFI = .99; RMSEA = .01.

complexity, and all significant and nonsignificant paths found in the full model were replicated in both groups here except for the path from early fairness to later marital quality. This path was significant only for those in stepfamilies. Further, there was a stronger path from marital conflict to marital quality for those in remarriages compared to those in stepfamilies. Although the strength of the path from marital quality to instability was strong for both groups, it was stronger for stepfamilies. Again, this likely is due to the role of earlier reported fairness among stepfamilies. Second, more variance in instability was accounted for by the various processes assessed among stepfamilies (.42) than remarrieds (.29). Clearly, the moderated model is somewhat superior to the full model, but there remains much unexplained variance.

DISCUSSION

Unlike in the 1990s, which saw a good deal of research on couple dynamics among the remarried (Coleman et al., 2000), more contemporary research often has neglected couple dynamics and relational outcomes. Instead, we have seen increases in the examination of child outcomes in stepfamilies (e.g., Braithwaite & Baxter, 2006) and of the interactions between former spouses (e.g., Fischer et al., 2005). Similar to work in the 1990s, much of the contemporary research on remarried couples has been qualitative, with few design enhancements (e.g., Michaels, 2006). However, there is evidence that the quality of quantitative research has improved, especially in the application of more longitudinal (e.g., Stewart, 2005) and daily diary designs (e.g., DeLongis, Capreol, Holtzman, O'Brien, & Campbell, 2004) methods. We addressed both of these issues by testing a conceptual model of couple dynamics that led to marital instability and using quantitative longitudinal data from Waves 1 through 3 of the NSFH. Our findings suggest support for our conceptual model.

Our finding that earlier marital conflict affected later marital quality is consistent with previous findings (e.g., Beaudry et al., 2004; Bodenmann et al., 2006). We also found that marital quality was related to marital instability, which is consistent both with earlier (e.g., White & Booth, 1985) and more contemporary (e.g., Stewart, 2005) findings. In fact, this path in our model was quite strong (−.54) and accounted for a significant amount of variance in the full model (.34). As suggested earlier by others (e.g., Gottman, 1993), it may well be that early marital conflict erodes marital quality over time and that such erosion encourages spouses to consider divorce as an option and for some to ultimately divorce. Importantly, the link between marital quality and later marital instability is much stronger for stepfamilies than for remarried couples (−.61 and −.49, respectively), and martial quality explains more variance in instability (.42 and .29, respectively). This is not surprising given the earlier literature suggesting that in stepfamilies the nature of the stepparent-stepchild relationship strongly undermines the quality of the marriage, placing it at risk. This would not be expected in remarriages with no children or those with only biological children, because they more closely resemble first-marriage biological families.

It also may be that the link between marital conflict and marital quality represents a key place in which prevention efforts could focus, before erosion of marital stability occurs—a link that consistently has held among studies of first marriages (Gager & Sanchez, 2003). We now extend that finding to remarriages and stepfamilies.

Further, our findings showed that early perceptions of fairness affect later marital quality, especially in stepfamilies. Thus, for stepfamilies both marital conflict and perceptions of fairness influence marital quality and ultimately affect later marital stability. In fact, our model suggests that earlier marital conflict is a risk factor in both remarriages and stepfamilies. However, earlier fairness may act as a protective factor to buffer against the erosion of marital quality, especially in stepfamilies, such that the stability of the union is maintained. Because marital conflict and fairness are marital phenomena that can be altered more easily than other phenomena, our results suggest that preventive efforts directed at these marital processes might be key to helping those in remarriages and stepfamilies strengthen their union. Importantly, fairness may be a primary area of prevention work for stepfamilies compared to remarriages, whereas our results suggest that marital conflict may be a primary area of prevention work for remarriages compared with stepfamilies.

Our study contributes to our understanding of how family structural complexity affects marital stability through certain marital processes. It is logical to assume that the more complex a family is (remarried versus stepfamily), the more potential there is for developmental difficulty. We draw attention to the differences between the models, suggesting that marital processes are important to marital stability in remarriages and stepfamilies over time; yet, these processes vary depending on the family structure.

IMPLICATIONS

As outlined throughout our discussion, the results of this study emphasized areas in which preventive efforts could be focused to assist in maintaining or enhancing marital stability among those in remarriages and those in stepfamilies. Specifically, the frequency of marital conflict has an especially deleterious effect, eroding marital quality and leading to increased marital instability over time. However, perceptions of fairness also play a key role in this erosive process, particularly for men and women in stepfamilies. Although we suggest that conflict management and identifying areas and behaviors associated with the perception of unfairness are prime places for preventive efforts in remarital education (for additional recommendations see Adler-Baeder & Higginbotham, 2004), as practitioners we realize that often these couples and families do not present for services until after problems arise. Even more common, stepfamilies present after such problems reach a critical level (Papernow, 1984). As such, clinical intervention efforts also may be warranted.

The literature addressing clinical intervention with stepfamilies is scant and typically applies a family systems perspective to focus primarily on the relationship between stepparent-stepchild roles and the associated conflict. In this literature scholars also discuss successful stepfamily development, but the focus remains on stepparent-stepchild relationships (e.g., Pasley, Dollahite, & Ihinger-Tallman, 1993). Although the stepparent-stepchild relationship is important, we must consider how problems within the marital dyad affect the marital and (step)parental relationships. We agree with Pasley and associates that many remarrieds and stepfamilies present by asking for assistance with infusing love and cohesiveness back into their marriage. Addressing these marital quality issues directly would do little more than put a Band-Aid on a wound that needs stitches. Instead, the results from this longitudinal analysis suggest that marital conflict is an important risk factor in both remarriages and stepfamilies in eroding marital quality over time. Thus, assessing marital conflict and communication skills early on and developing strategies to resolve conflict and communicate effectively may be most helpful for these families. In fact, a recent study by Beaudry et al. (2004) found that compared with the other unique challenges faced by members of stepfamilies, the nature of their general communication skills was more predictive of marital quality. In another study, Golish (2003) found that general communication skills (e.g., problem solving, using everyday talk) and stepfamily-specific communication skills (e.g., communication of positive images of former spouse) differentiated "strong" stepfamilies from those experiencing problems. Thus, findings from the related empirical research suggests that practitioners should focus on enhancing general communication skills as a beginning point in the initial assessment and intervention phases of working with a couple or family. We anticipate that remarried couples would be more receptive to such work because couples in general can benefit from being more effective communicators. Further, the early recommendation by Pasley and associates that early intervention efforts should focus on the dyad rather than the entire family system continues to have merit. An important key may be to adopt a more behavioral approach in working with remarried couples that teaches them basic communication and conflict resolution skills.

We also recognize that many problems, especially those experienced by stepfamilies, are related to child rearing and interactions with former spouses. When this is the case, it is not logical to have the children present during the initial sessions or psychoeducational process. Relatedly, the fact that perceptions of fairness were particularly important for those in stepfamilies compared to those in remarriages (recall that remarrieds had no children or only biological children) is important for intervention around these two issues. Once couples have garnered a good set of general communication and conflict resolution skills using behavioral techniques, the next step in marital therapy is to address some of the unique issues that arise in stepfamilies, such as stepparent-stepchild conflict, relationship with former spouse, and financial concerns (e.g., pooling of money, child support income or lack thereof).

An appropriate clinical approach to use at this step with stepfamilies is cognitive-behavioral therapy (CBT). The aim of CBT is to connect thoughts and behaviors such that emotions, in this instance marital quality, are positively influenced (Markman, Stanley, Jenkins, Petrella, & Wadsworth, 2006). One focus of CBT is to help clients learn new ways of reacting. It is common for members of stepfamilies to expect the new family to mirror their expectations of a first family, which is neither possible nor desirable. Thus, they might interact with family members in ways that are not appropriate in stepfamilies, as in the case of a new stepparent attempting to discipline a stepchild. Taking a CBT approach might be particularly useful in illuminating the meaning behaviors engender for individual family members and facilitate greater mutual understanding, something that could be done with the aid of a technique such as family sculpting. Once the meaning is known, insight grows, which can be validated or challenged if maladaptive, thereby promoting positive change and enhancing marital quality.

In sum, our results suggest that a two-step approach to marital and family therapy as an intervention is warranted and may prove most helpful in early and brief intervention efforts. First, therapists should adopt a behavioral approach to enhance general communication and conflict resolution skills. This could include participation in psychoeducational programs that are evidence-based, such as those designed as part of Prevention and Relationship Enhancement Program (PREP, Inc.; Markman, Stanley, & Blumberg, 1994). Second, therapists can build on behavioral approaches by using CBT to address unique issues, particularly those found among stepfamilies. We offer these suggestions being ever cognizant of the need for future research to address the efficacy of such an approach and other potentially effective approaches for use with remarrieds and stepfamilies.

As a concluding thought we wish to speculate about what our findings on changes in marital stability among those in remarriages and stepfamilies mean for the future of these families and discuss additional implications. Although research suggests that divorce rates (Kreider & Fields, 2002) and the potential for conflict (Coleman et al., 2001) are higher among remarriages, there is no evidence to suggest any significant increases in marital instability (divorce) in the immediate future among these groups. It also is important to note that any future increases might be attributed to those in first marriages rather than remarriages because of the increase in cohabitation prior to marriage and findings that show increased divorce among those with prior cohabitation experience (Bramlett & Mosher, 2002). In fact, we may begin to see small decreases in marital instability among remarrieds and stepfamilies, as individuals try out relationships in cohabiting between marriages and potentially reduce the chances of poor choices in a remarriage. Clearly, the rates of cohabitation, marriage, divorce, and remarriage are strongly linked. If people are cohabiting, there are fewer marriages to terminate; those that elect to marry may do so with more forethought.

Further, we base this speculation of a decrease in marital instability in remarriages on several other findings from the literature. First, those in re-marriages are spending both more time between divorce and remarriage and between remarriage and redivorce, which itself suggests increased stability rather than instability (Kreider & Fields, 2002). We also believe that the time between divorce and remarriage potentially allows individuals more opportunities to grieve the loss of their first marriage and settle into more amicable patterns of interaction with their former spouse, thereby reducing the amount of prior marital baggage that can affect marital stability in subsequent marriages. This is not to say that patterns of interaction are guaranteed to be positive, but it is logical to expect that, with more time, there will be more opportunities for healing. Second, the movement to strengthen marriages may increase public knowledge about preventive efforts available to assist all families, and the emergence of marital education programs specifically designed for remarriage and stepfamilies is encouraging (Adler-Baeder & Higginbotham, 2004). We believe that as these efforts become more widespread and as more families elect to participate in them, (re)marriages may become more stable and of higher quality.

An additional major challenge to increasing stability in remarriages and stepfamilies lies within the realm of family law and related family policy. Newer stepfamily research (e.g., Stewart, 2005) has begun to focus on the concept of boundary ambiguity, suggesting that its presence negatively influences marital stability. Other research has found that clear boundaries (i.e., knowing who is in and who is out of the family) (Boss, 2007; Carroll, Olson, & Buckmiller, 2007; Stewart, 2005) and assistance from professionals help stepfamilies succeed (Michaels, 2006). However, Mason, Harrison-Jay, Svare, and Wolfinger (2002) and Gately, Pike, and Murphy (2006) found that stepfamilies seek ways to gain social recognition through acquiring rights for their families that first-marriage families have. Because current law and social policy are not equipped to provide such recognition, boundary ambiguity persists, and thus the associated problems exist. In this instance, families themselves are telling professionals what they need to be more successful, and many in the legal arena simply are not listening, in spite of research that is consistent with what families are saying. Thus, we must make a concerted effort to create family laws and social policies consistent with today's myriad family forms that acknowledge the roles and responsibilities of all involved. Although there have been suggestions offered by U.S. scholars (e.g., Mason, Fine, & Carnochan, 2001) and models provided in other countries (e.g., United Kingdom), little has been done to adopt such suggestions or models. By making a concerted effort to address the diversity of family forms, many areas of contention (e.g., legal rights of stepparents) can become clearer, lessening the potential negative effects from some of the unique sources of conflict in remarriages and stepfamilies.

Last, we must not forget those who elect to cohabit and form nonlegal stepfamilies, as they represent a unique group who are at risk for relationship instability and about which little is known. Often these couples include a young mother of color with at least one young child from a prior union. She develops a relationship with a man who is not the father of her children but who also comes to the relationship with limited resources (e.g., education and financial). Their youth and their limited experience parenting children effectively in a context of few resources place them at the greatest risk for experiencing challenges that undermine the stability of their relationship. Thus, we must focus future research, practice, and policy efforts in a way that allows for the recognition and development of strategies for the myriad forms of remarriages and stepfamilies.

REFERENCES

Adler-Baeder, F., & Higginbotham, B. (2004). Implications of remarriage and stepfamily formation for marriage education. *Family Relations, 53*, 448–458.

Aguirre, B., & Kirwan, P. (1986). Marriage order and the quality and stability of marital relationships: A test of Lewis and Spanier's theory. *Journal of Comparative Family Studies, 17*, 247–276.

Arbuckle, J. (2003). *Amos 5.0 update to the Amos users guide.* Chicago: Small Waters.

Baron, R., & Kenny, D. (1986). The moderator-mediator variable distinction in social psychological research: Conceptual, strategic, and statistical considerations. *Journal of Personality and Social Psychology, 51*, 1173–1182.

Beaudry, M., Boisvert, J. M., Simard, M., Parent, C., & Blais, M. C. (2004). Communication: A key component to meeting the challenges of stepfamilies. *Journal of Divorce and Remarriage, 42*(1/2), 85–104.

Bodenmann, G., Pihet, S., & Kayser, K. (2006). The relationship between dyadic and marital quality: A 2-year longitudinal study. *Journal of Family Psychology, 20*, 485–493.

Boss, P. (2007). Ambiguous loss theory: Challenges for scholars and practitioners. *Family Relations, 56*, 105–111.

Bradbury, T., Fincham, F., & Beach, S. (2000). Research on the nature and determinants of marital satisfaction: A decade in review. *Journal of Marriage and the Family, 62*, 964–980.

Braithwaite, D., & Baxter, L. A. (2006). "You're my parent but you're not": Dialectical tensions in stepchildren's perceptions about communicating with the nonresidential parent. *Journal of Applied Communication Research, 34*, 30–48.

Bramlett, M. D., & Mosher, W. D. (2002). *Cohabitation, marriage, divorce, and remarriage in the United States* (DHH Publication No. PHS 2002-1998). Hyattsville, MD: Department of Health and Human Services, National Center for Health Statistics.

Bray, J. (1999). From marriage to remarriage and beyond: Developmental issues in Stepfamilies Research Project. In E. M. Hetherington (Ed.), *Coping with divorce, single-parenthood and remarriage: A risk and resiliency perspective* (pp. 253–271). Mahwah, NJ: Erlbaum.

Burkholder, G., & Harlow, L. (2003). An illustration of a longitudinal cross-lagged design for larger structural equation models. *Structural Equation Modeling, 10*, 465–486.

Carroll, J., Olson, C., & Buckmiller, N. (2007). Family boundary ambiguity: A 30-year review of theory, research, and measurement. *Family Relations, 56*, 210–230.

Coleman, M., Fine, M., Ganong, L., Downs, K., & Pauk, N. (2001). When you're not the Brady Bunch: Identifying perceived conflicts and resolution strategies in stepfamilies. *Personal Relationships, 8*, 55–73.

Coleman, M., Ganong, L., & Fine, M. (2000). Reinvestigating remarriage: Another decade of progress. *Journal of Marriage and the Family, 62*, 1288–1307.

DeLongis, A., Capreol, M., Holtzman, S., O'Brien, T., & Campbell, J. (2004). Social support and social strain among husbands and wives: A multilevel analysis. *Journal of Family Psychology, 18*, 470–479.

Fischer, T. F. C., de Graaf, P. M., & Kalmijn, M. (2005). Friendly and antagonistic contact between former spouses after divorce. *Journal of Family Issues, 26*, 1131–1163.

Fletcher, G., Simpson, J., & Thomas, G. (2000). The measurement of perceived relationship quality components: A confirmatory factor analytic study. *Personality and Social Psychology Bulletin, 26*, 340–354.

Fletcher, T. D., Selgrade, K. A., & Germano, L. M. (2006, May). *On the use of partial covariances in structural equation modeling.* Paper presented at the 21st annual conference of the Society for Industrial and Organizational Psychology, Dallas, TX.

Gager, C., & Sanchez, L. (2003). Two as one? Couples' perceptions of time spent together, marital quality, and the risk of divorce. *Journal of Family Issues, 24*, 21–50.

Ganong, L., & Coleman, M. (2004). *Stepfamily relationships: Development, dynamics, and intervention.* New York: Kluwer Academic/Plenum Press.

Gately, N. J., Pike, L. T., & Murphy, P. T. (2006). An exploration of the impact of the family court process on "invisible" stepparents. *Journal of Divorce and Remarriage, 44*(3/4), 31–52.

Golish, T. (2003). Stepfamily communication strengths: Understanding the ties that bind. *Human Communication Research, 29*, 41–80.

Gottman, J. M. (1993). A theory of marital dissolution and stability. *Journal of Family Psychology, 7,* 57–75.

Gottman, J., & Notarius, C. (2000). Decade review: Observing marital interaction. *Journal of Marriage and the Family, 62,* 927–947.

Kline, R. (1998). *Principles and practice of structural equation modeling.* New York: Guilford Press.

Kreider, R., & Fields, J. (2002). *Current population reports: Number, timing, and duration of marriage and divorce, 1996* (Series P70–80). Washington, DC: U.S. Government Printing Office.

Kurdek, L. (1991). Marital stability and changes in marital quality in newlywed couples: A text of the contextual model. *Journal of Social and Personal Relationships, 8,* 27–48.

Kurdek, L. A. (1995). Predicting change in marital satisfaction from husbands' and wives' conflict resolution styles. *Journal of Marriage and the Family, 57,* 153–164.

Markman, H. J., Stanley, S. M., & Blemberg, S. L. (1994). *Fighting for your marriage: Positive steps for preventing divorce and preserving lasting love.* San Francisco: Jossey-Bass.

Markman, H. J., Stanley, S. M., Jenkins, N. H., Petrella, J. N., & Wadsworth, M. E. (2006). Preventive education: Distinctives and directions [Special issue: *Cognitive-Behavioral Assessment and Treatment of Couples*]. *Journal of Cognitive Psychotherapy, 20,* 411–433.

Mason, M., Fine, M. A., & Carnochan, S. (2001). Family law in the new millennium: For whose family? *Journal of Family Issues, 22,* 859–881.

Mason, M., Harrison-Jay, S., Svare, G., & Wolfinger, N. (2002). Stepparents: De facto parents or legal strangers? *Journal of Family Issues, 23,* 507–522.

Matthews, L., Conger, R., & Wickrama, K. (1996). Work-family conflict and marital quality: Mediating processes. *Social Psychology Quarterly, 59,* 62–79.

Michaels, M. L. (2006). Factors that contribute to stepfamily success: A qualitative analysis. *Journal of Divorce and Remarriage, 44*(3/4), 53–66.

Papernow, P. (1984). The stepfamily cycle: An experimental model of stepfamily development. *Family Relations, 33,* 355–363.

Pasley, K., Dollahite, D., & Ihinger-Tallman, M. (1993). Bridging the gap: Clinical applications of research findings on the spouse and stepparent roles in remarriage. *Family Relations, 42,* 315–322.

Pasley, K., & Ihinger-Tallman, M. (1982). Stress in remarried families. *Family Perspective, 16,* 181–190.

Raykov, T. (2005). Analysis of longitudinal studies with missing data using covariance structure modeling with full-information maximum likelihood. *Structural Equation Modeling, 12,* 493–505.

Stewart, S. D. (2005). Boundary ambiguity in stepfamilies. *Journal of Family Issues, 26,* 1002–1029.

Sweet, J., & Bumpass, L. (2002). *The National Survey of Families and Households—Waves 1, 2, and 3: Data description and documentation.* Center for Demography and Ecology, University of Wisconsin-Madison. Available from www.ssc.wisc.edu/nsfh/home.htm.

Visher, E. B., & Visher, J. S. (1998). Stepparents: The forgotten family members. *Family and Conciliation Courts Review, 36,* 444–451.

Visher, E. B., Visher, J. S., & Pasley, K. (2003). Remarriage families and stepparenting. In F. Walsh (Ed.), *Normal family processes: Growing diversity and complexity* (3rd ed., pp. 153–175). New York: Guilford Press.

White, L., & Booth, A. (1985). The quality and stability of remarriages: The role of stepchildren. *American Sociological Review, 50,* 689–698.

Yeh, H. C., Lorenz, F. O., Conger, R., & Elder, G. (2006). Relationships among sexual satisfaction, marital quality, and marital instability at midlife. *Journal of Family Psychology, 20,* 339–343.

CHAPTER 11

Children's Appraisals of Relationships in Stepfamilies and First Families: Comparative Links with Externalizing and Internalizing Behaviors

KATHERINE H. SHELTON, SASHA L. WALTERS,
and GORDON T. HAROLD

IN A major review of international research findings examining the outcomes of children who have experienced parental separation and divorce, it was estimated that 35% of children born in the 1980s in the United States will enter a stepfamily before the age of 18 and that in the United Kingdom 20% of children will become part of a married or cohabiting stepfamily by the age of 16 (Pryor & Rodgers, 2001). Similar figures exist for New Zealand and Australia (Pryor & Rodgers, 2001). Most compellingly in terms of the rate of family change in the United Kingdom and associated implications for children is the statistic that in 1999, stepfamilies constituted 6% of all families in Britain where the head was 60 years or over, yet by 2010 it is estimated that more families will go through separation and restructuring than will stay together (Parentlineplus, 2005). This projection underscores the pace of family change in the United Kingdom, echoed in other Western

We would like to thank the families and schools who participated in the Welsh Family Study for their time and cooperation with this project. Appreciation is also extended to Janet Whitley for her assistance with aspects of data collection and preparation. The development of this chapter was supported by a grant awarded to Gordon Harold from the Economic and Social Research Council (R000222569).

countries, and highlights the importance of identifying what it is about children's experiences of family transitions that explains differences in their psychological adaptation.

This chapter explores the role of interparental conflict as a factor in accounting for variation in children's internalizing symptoms and externalizing problems across first family and stepfamily contexts. In particular, the respective role of children's attributions for parents' marital arguments versus their experiences of hostile neglecting parenting are considered as mechanisms underlying links between interparental conflict and children's symptoms of psychological distress.

FAMILY FACTORS AND CHILDREN'S PSYCHOLOGICAL DEVELOPMENT

The role of the family as a context for understanding differences in children's normal and abnormal psychological development has a long and established history. Children raised in households exposed to acute or chronic economic strain (Conger, Ge, Elder, Lorenz, & Simons, 1994), heightened levels of parental psychopathology (Downey & Coyne, 1990), interparental conflict and violence (Grych & Fincham, 1990; Rivett, Howarth, & Harold, 2006), negative parent-child relations (Erel & Burman, 1995), or parental separation, divorce, and remarriage (Hetherington, Bridges, & Insabella, 1998) have been shown to experience a variety of negative psychological outcomes, including increased anxiety, depression, aggression, hostility, and antisocial behavior. Research in this area, however, has progressed from establishing simple bivariate associations between measures of family experience and children's psychological adaptation to identifying the social, emotional, and cognitive architecture underlying links between family stress and child development (see Cummings & Davies, 2002). In considering the impact of parental separation and divorce on children, for example, it is now recognized that children's adaptation to marital transition may be determined more by the level of conflict that occurs between parents before, during, and after the breakup of the marital relationship than the actual breakup itself (Emery, 1982; Harold & Murch, 2005). Indeed, with regard to the indices of family functioning mentioned (e.g., economic stress, parent depression, negative parenting), conflict occurring between parents has been recognized as a factor common to all in accounting for adverse effects on children (Conger et al., 1994; Downey & Coyne, 1990; Harold & Conger, 1997). Recent experimental (see Cummings & Davies, 2002) and longitudinal (e.g., Harold, Shelton, Goeke-Morey, & Cummings, 2004) studies have highlighted the role of interparental conflict as a possible causative agent in accounting for the effects of family stress on children's psychological adaptation.

Research relating to the effects of interparental conflict on children has tended to concentrate efforts in two primary domains: first-family[1] households and households where children have experienced parental separation and divorce (see Amato, 2001; Cummings & Davies, 2002). An additional context where the effects of conflict between cohabiting adults has relevance to understanding differences in children's psychological development relates to those households in which parents have remarried (see Hetherington et al., 1998). Although a large volume of research exists describing the psychological outcomes for children who experience parental remarriage (Pryor & Rodgers, 2001), there is a paucity of research that investigates the processes through which adverse effects may be explained (for exceptions, see Hetherington, Henderson, & Reiss, 1999; O'Connor, Hetherington, & Reiss, 1998). Little research compares recognized processes relating to the child's own perspective of the interparental and parent-child relationships and psychological adaptation across family types (stepparent versus first families). The present chapter advances research in this area by considering the respective role of children's experiences of negative parenting and their attributions of threat and self-blame emanating from adult conflicts in accounting for variation in their internalizing symptoms and externalizing problems. To accommodate this primary conceptual objective, we briefly review research relating to the effects of parental separation, divorce, and remarriage, with particular emphasis on process-oriented research that considers children's adaptation to couple conflict across stepparent and first-family households.

FAMILY TRANSITION AND CHILDREN'S PSYCHOLOGICAL ADJUSTMENT: A BRIEF REVIEW

A large volume of international research now exists linking the type of family a child lives in to his or her emotional and behavioral well-being. Research conducted over the past 50 years suggests that children who experience parental separation and divorce, compared to children who live in continuously married households, consistently perform less well on measures of academic achievement, general conduct, psychological adjustment, and social relations (Amato & Keith, 1991; Pryor & Rodgers, 2001). The impact of separation and divorce on children, however, may be determined more by the level of conflict that exists between parents before, during, and after the breakdown of the parental relationship than the actual breakdown itself (Emery, 1982; Harold & Murch, 2005). Moreover, for many

---

[1] In this chapter the term "first families" is used to refer to families in which the adults are the biological or adoptive parents of the children. Other chapters use other terms, such as "nuclear" or "intact," to refer to the same kind of household.

children, divorce or separation of their parents is not the only major family change they will experience; many will also experience parental remarriage.

DIVORCE AND CHILDREN'S PSYCHOLOGICAL ADAPTATION

Amato and Keith (1991) conducted a seminal review of studies in the 1950s through the 1980s that compared children residing with divorced and continuously married parents. These authors concluded that children with divorced parents scored lower on a variety of measures of well-being, including measures of academic achievement, general conduct, psychological adjustment, self-concept, social relations, and the quality of relationships with their mother and father. In addition, it was noted that variation in children's adaptation to divorce could be explained by a number of factors associated with the separation rather than the divorce itself. Most children returned to levels of predivorce functioning within 2 years; those who did not experienced various problems, such as relationship difficulties with the custodial parent (usually the mother), being unsettled by changing neighborhoods, a worsening of their family's finances, further instability in custodial arrangements following parental separation, and continuing exposure to high levels of interparental conflict (e.g., Hetherington, 1989; Hetherington et al., 1998).

Across all studies reviewed, exposure to interparental conflict appears to act as a common denominator in differentiating those children who adjusted "normally" from those who did not. Amato (2001) highlights two noteworthy findings from more recent research. First, children who are exposed to chronic and unresolved predivorce conflict between parents appear to be better off in the long run when the marriage ends than if parents stay together. Second, when parents engage in relatively low-level predivorce conflict, children appear to be worse off following divorce.

These findings help to underscore the central role that conflict between parents plays in determining the effects of separation and divorce on children. Indeed, research conducted over the past 20 years focusing specifically on the effects of interparental conflict on children living in continuously married homes has important implications for understanding how children are affected by exposure to the adversarial conditions typically associated with separation and divorce (Emery, 1982; Grych, 2005; Harold & Murch, 2005).

INTERPARENTAL CONFLICT AND CHILDREN'S PSYCHOLOGICAL DEVELOPMENT

Interparental conflict is increasingly recognized as a significant influence on children's long-term psychological health and well-being. Children of all ages who are exposed to frequent, intense, and poorly resolved interparental conflict are at heightened risk for a variety of negative outcomes, including increased anxiety and depression (Davies, Harold, Goeke-Morey, &

Cummings, 2002; Harold & Conger, 1997), aggression and hostility (Dadds, Atkinson, Turner, Blums, & Lendich, 1999; Harold, Fincham, Osborne, & Conger, 1997), low social competence (Paley, Conger, & Harold, 2000), and academic underachievement (Harold, Aitken, & Shelton, 2007; Long, Forehand, Fauber, & Brody, 1987).

From as far back as the 1930s it has been recognized that discord between parents has a potentially debilitating effect on children (Towle, 1931). More recent theoretical models suggest that the effects of interparental conflict on children are determined through (a) disruptions in the parent-child relationship and (b) the negative emotions, cognitions, and representations of family relationships engendered in children who are exposed to hostile exchanges between their parents. Each of these perspectives will be reviewed in order to locate the theoretical relevance of the analyses proposed in the present study.

The Importance of the Parent-Child Relationship

Serot and Teevan (1961) proposed that one of the basic tenets of developmental psychology is that a child's early family environment, especially the pervading parental attitude or emotional tone of the parent-child relationship, is a fundamental factor in determining children's long-term emotional and behavioral development. Research conducted across attachment and parenting traditions in the decades that followed strongly supports this hypothesis (Waters & Cummings, 2000). However, research has also demonstrated that the emotional tone of the parent-child relationship is itself influenced by the emotional tone of the interparental relationship, offering an indirect mechanism through which interparental conflict adversely affects children's well-being (Cox, Paley, & Harter, 2001; Erel & Burman, 1995; Goldberg & Easterbrooks, 1984; Kaczynski, Lindahl, Malik, & Laurenceau, 2006).

A number of researchers suggest that parents embroiled in a hostile and distressed marital relationship are typically also more hostile and aggressive toward their children and less sensitive and emotionally responsive to their needs. The effects of interparental conflict on children are deemed to occur indirectly through a "spillover" of emotion from the couple relationship to the parent-child relationship. In support of this view, there is a robust association between emotion expressed in the marital relationship and emotion expressed in the parent-child relationship (Erel & Burman, 1995). However, if conflict between parents affected children only via disruptions in the parent-child relationship, children would be affected by such disruption irrespective of whether or not they actually witnessed conflict between their parents. Research evidence suggests that this is not the case (Emery, Fincham, & Cummings, 1992). As Serot and Teevan (1961) argued, the essential relationship between children's well-being and their relationship with their parents is that which exists between the children's perception of the parent-child relationship and their adjustment, rather than aspects of the parent-child relationship deemed important by adult reporters (parents or observers). This theme has been developed in recent decades following Emery's (1982) seminal review of the literature highlighting the role of children's perceptions of interparental conflict and has led researchers to consider a second set of hypotheses aimed at explaining the effects of interparental conflict on children.

THE IMPORTANCE OF THE CHILD'S PERSPECTIVE

Research conducted over the past 2 decades has shown that overt interparental conflict to which children are exposed has a greater impact on child distress than covert conflict to which children are not exposed (see Cummings & Davies, 2002). This finding has led researchers to consider a second set of hypotheses that focus on the underlying cognitive and emotional processes engendered in children who live in households marked by hostile interparental relations. Three primary theoretical perspectives have emerged that focus on the role of the child's own perspective when explaining the effects of interparental conflict on children's psychological well-being. Grych and Fincham (1990), in their cognitive-contextual framework, propose that the attributions children assign to their parents' marital arguments account for effects on well-being. Davies and Cummings (1994) emphasize the importance of attachment processes and highlight the role of children's emotional security as a factor in accounting for variation in well-being. Harold and Conger (1997) offer a familywide model and propose that the attributions children assign to conflict occurring in the marital relationship orient their expectations and representations of conflict in the parent-child relationship, which in turn affects their long-term psychological adaptation.

A Cognitive-Contextual Framework

Grych and Fincham (1990), in their cognitive-contextual framework, propose that children's responses to interparental conflict occur through their mental (cognitive) processing of the conflict. According to this perspective, the impact of conflict on children depends both on how it is expressed and how children interpret its meaning and potential implications for their well-being. These authors suggest that there are two stages of cognitive processing underlying the link between children's exposure to conflict and their interpretation of its meaning. The first of these, primary processing, is a stage in which the child first becomes aware that conflict is occurring and experiences an initial level of arousal. They suggest that specific characteristics of the conflict episode, such as its frequency, intensity, and resolution potential, as well as contextual factors such as the quality of the parent-child relationship(s), child temperament, gender, and history of exposure to conflict, influence this initial stage of appraisal. This primary stage of processing may then lead to a more elaborate secondary stage, during which the child attempts to understand why the conflict is occurring and what he or she should do in response. Secondary processing involves making sense of the cause of the event, ascribing responsibility and blame, as well as calculating how best to cope with the conflict (Grych & Fincham, 1990). Children who view conflict as threatening or who feel unable to cope effectively experience more anxiety and helplessness. Children who blame themselves for parental disagreements or feel responsible for not helping to end them experience guilt, shame, and sadness. If conflict is frequent, intense, and poorly resolved, these appraisals are believed to increase children's risk of emotional and behavioral problems (Grych & Fincham, 1990; Grych, Fincham, Jouriles, & McDonald, 2000).

Many of the hypotheses drawn from the cognitive-contextual framework have been supported empirically (e.g., Grych, Raynor, & Fosco, 2004; Kerig, 1998). In a recent longitudinal study, Grych, Harold, and Miles (2003) showed that children's attributions of threat and self-blame accounted for (or mediated) the relationship between marital conflict and children's internalizing symptoms (depression, anxiety) and their externalizing problems (aggression, hostility). Girls' feelings of self-blame and responsibility exacerbated their symptoms of depression and anxiety (internalizing) more so than for boys, and boys' perceived threat exacerbated their aggressive, hostile, and antisocial (externalizing) behaviors more so than for girls (Grych et al., 2003). These findings have important implications for understanding children's responses to conflict between parents and, importantly, why boys and girls may be differentially at risk in the context of a distressed marital relationship.

An Emotional Security Hypothesis

Davies and Cummings (1994) offer a complementary perspective suggesting that a child's sense of "emotional security" is threatened in the context of interparental conflict. Extending from the principles of attachment theory (Bowlby, 1969), these authors propose that the effects of destructive and badly managed conflict between parents are determined through disruptions to three conceptually related areas of children's emotional functioning. First, feelings of "emotional reactivity" may be affected such that children feel angry, sad, or scared in the context of conflict. Second, their "representations of family relationships" may be affected such that conflict between parents affects children's expectations that conflict will occur elsewhere in the family system (e.g., the parent-child relationship). Third, children may feel motivated to "regulate exposure to marital emotion" so that they directly intervene in, or actively withdraw from, the immediate vicinity of the conflict. The impact of the conflict on children is determined by the extent to which one or more of these aspects of emotional security is adversely affected and how well children can manage to regulate emotional disruption.

Initial tests of this perspective by Davies and Cummings (1998) found that exposure to marital conflict led to differences in how emotionally secure children felt, and that these in turn explained the initial impact of conflict on children's emotional and behavioral problems. Specifically, children who felt sad, angry, or scared and who regarded the conflict episode as an immediate and potentially longer term threat to the quality of other family relationships (e.g., parent-child relationship) showed heightened symptoms of emotional and behavioral distress.

More recently, Harold, Shelton, Goeke-Morey, and Cummings (2002) integrated the two perspectives offered by Grych and Fincham (1990; cognitive-contextual framework) and Davies and Cummings (1994; emotional security hypothesis). They showed that children's cognitions and emotions work in concert to the extent that the emotional reactions children have to their parents' marital arguments explain the impact that their cognitive appraisals have on their symptoms of psychological distress. These results highlight the mental architecture that underlies the link between marital conflict and child adjustment. Moreover, the findings underscore the importance of considering the child's perspective in accounting for the effects of marital conflict on children's development. By employing a prospective, longitudinal design, these analyses were among the first to identify marital conflict as a potential causative agent in the development of children's emotional and behavioral problems (see also Grych et al., 2003; Harold and colleagues, 1997, 2002, 2004).

A Familywide Model of Interparental Conflict and Its Effects on Children

Building on the proposal that children's understanding of interparental conflict is an important factor in determining its impact on their psychological development, Harold and colleagues (1997) offer a familywide model suggesting that *both* interparental and parent-child conflict exert adverse effects on children's psychological development. Importantly, however, these authors propose that how children perceive their parents to behave toward each other (i.e., marital conflict) determines how they expect their parents to behave toward them (parent-child conflict), which in turn affects their symptoms of psychological distress. What is significant about this approach is that it combines traditional explanations aimed at accounting for the effects of interparental conflict on children (i.e., the spillover of negative affect from the marital relationship to the parent-child relationship; Erel &

Burman, 1995) with more recent theoretical perspectives emphasizing the importance of considering children's cognitive representations of conflict for explaining effects on development.

Collectively, these theoretical models highlight the importance of considering the child's perspective in understanding how exposure to conflict between parents adversely affects his or her psychological well-being. By highlighting the active role that children's subjective evaluations of interparental conflict play in determining its effects on their well-being, we may better understand why some children seem relatively unaffected by interparental conflict while others go on to develop long-term, clinically significant emotional and behavioral problems (Harold, Pryor, & Reynolds, 2001).

FAMILY PROCESSES IN FIRST-FAMILY AND STEPFAMILY HOMES

Some research has indicated that conflict between partners in stepfamilies is more overt (with regard to expressed levels of criticism and anger) than in first marriages; children living in these families therefore may be more likely to be exposed to interadult conflict (Fine, 2001; e.g. Hetherington, 1993). Children living in stepfamilies also report higher levels of family conflict compared to children in first-family households, with links, in turn, to children's adjustment problems (Barber & Lyons, 1994; Kurdek & Fine, 1993). Likewise, in a comparison of single-parent, first-marriage, and stepfamily homes, there were no significant differences in adolescent adjustment as a function of family type; rather, differences in adjustment were found as a function of adolescent perceptions of the level of family conflict (Borrine, Handal, Brown, & Searight, 1991). Collectively, these findings underscore the importance of considering the child's perspective when investigating children's adjustment across family types. Most recently, a study identified that interadult conflict about children accounted for an increase in externalizing problems in children, after controlling for the effects of family type (Jenkins, Simpson, Dunn, Rasbash, & O'Connor, 2005). This is consistent with research highlighting the mediating role of children's appraisals of self-blame in the relationship between interparental conflict and later behavior problems (Grych et al., 2003). However, whether the processes identified to account for the relationship between interadult conflict and children's psychological adjustment in first-family households are also relevant to explaining this link in stepfamilies remains relatively unexplored (Fine, 2001).

THE PRESENT STUDY

The present study evaluated a theoretical model linking children's perceptions of interparental conflict to their internalizing symptoms (depressive symptoms and anxiety) and externalizing problems (aggressive behavior

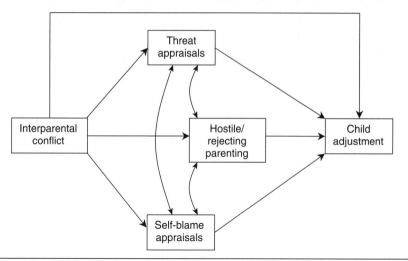

Figure 11.1 Proposed Theoretical Model.

and hostility) among a sample of children living in stepparent and first-family households. The proposed theoretical model assessed the relative role of children's attributions of threat and self-blame relating to couple relationship conflicts and their associated appraisals of rejection relating to the parent-child relationship in accounting for variation in their internalizing symptoms and externalizing problems (see Figure 11.1). Models were tested separately for a group of 325 British children from continuously married homes and a group of 48 children living in stepparent households. Few studies have considered the relative role of children's social cognitions (attributions) relating to the couple relationship and children's experience of negative parenting within the same analysis, and none have looked at this pattern of relations among children living in first-marriage versus stepparent households.

SAMPLE

The sample for the present study was derived from a 3-year longitudinal study of 387 schoolchildren, parents, and teachers living in the United Kingdom (83% response from total sample contacted). The study focused on children's experiences of family life and their socioemotional development. Given the primary focus on interparental conflict investigated in these analyses, children from all family types other than two-parent families were excluded from the present study. Participating children lived in homes where both a male and a female guardian were resident and at least one of these adults was the child's biological parent. The present study uses data collected from 373 children (and their teachers) living in Wales who had complete information on the study variables of interest at the first assessment (1999). The first-family group contained 325 children who lived with both of their biological, married parents. The stepparent group contained 48 children who lived with one biological parent and a stepparent (87.5% lived with mother and stepfather, 12.5% lived with father and stepmother). In the larger study, 45 children reported that they lived with their mother and father but that they also had half-siblings. These children, while living in a blended family form, are not considered as part of the first-family group or the stepparent group in these analyses.

Of the first families, 92% of children had between one and five siblings (median = 1). Of the stepfamilies, 94% of children had between one and five siblings (median = 1) and 75% also had between 1 and 6 half-siblings (median = 2). Children were recruited through nine schools and were between 11 and 13 years old (mean age = 11.69, SD = .47) in the first year of the study. The total sample consisted of approximately equal numbers of boys (48.5%) and girls (51.5%). The total sample was predominantly White European (97.3%), with a smaller proportion who described their ethnicity as Indian, Sri Lankan, or Pakistani (2.6%). Preliminary analyses indicated that families who completed the study at all time points did not significantly differ from families who participated only in the first or second year of the study on any variables measured.

After receiving permission from area schools, parents were informed about the study by summaries sent through the mail and presentations at parent-teacher meetings. Parents provided written consent for their child to participate in a study investigating the relationship between adolescent experiences of family life and their socioemotional development. Participating children completed their questionnaires at school. Questionnaires contained measures relating to family interaction, parent-child relations, interparental conflict, psychological health, and family economics. Children sat apart from one another while the confidential nature of the study was explained. They were asked to answer questions relating to the interadult relationship and the parent-child relationship for those parents (or guardians) they lived with. As part of an overall debriefing, researchers and children discussed the benefits of conflict resolution and problem solving in relationships. No child raised concerns during or following participating in the study. Teachers also completed questionnaires assessing children's psychological functioning. Parents were sent questionnaires in the mail, including separate envelopes for each respondent, instructions for completion, and a prepaid return envelope. Parents' questionnaires contained measures relating to conflict occurring between parents, parenting, parent and child psychological health, and economic conditions. No payment was made to families, but parents were informed that a summary booklet outlining key research findings would be distributed to all families upon completion of the study.

Children's reports of interparental conflict were measured using the Conflict Properties subscale of the Children's Perceptions of Inter-parental Conflict scale (CPIC; Grych, Seid, & Fincham, 1992). This subscale consists of 17 items, which aim to represent the frequency, intensity, and resolution of interparental conflict. It includes statements such as "I never see my parents arguing" (frequency), "My parents get really angry when they argue" (intensity), and "When my parents argue they usually make it up right away" (resolution). Response options are "true," "sort of true," and "false." Internal consistency scores for this subscale were good in both groups (first-family, $\alpha = .90$; stepfamily, $\alpha = .92$).

Appraisals of threat and self-blame were assessed using the Perceived Threat and Self-Blame subscales of the CPIC (Grych et al., 1992). Response options are "true," "sort of true," and "false." The Threat subscale contains 12 items, such as "When my parents argue I worry what will happen to me." One item, "When my parents argue I'm afraid one of them will get hurt," was omitted due to concerns raised during the process of obtaining ethical approval. The Self-Blame subscale contains 9 items, including "It is usually my fault when my parents argue." Derived internal consistency estimates for threat and self-blame were acceptable in both groups (blame: first family, $\alpha = .84$; stepfamily, $\alpha = .85$; threat: first family, $\alpha = .82$; stepfamily, $\alpha = .77$).

The quality of parent-child relations was assessed using the Acceptance/Rejection subscale of the Children's Report of Parent Behavior Inventory (CRPBI; Margolies & Weintraub, 1977). The 15 items assess parental acceptance and closeness to the child and were coded for study purposes to capture low levels of acceptance and high levels of rejection. Response options ranged from 1 "true" to 3 "not true." The Acceptance subscale contains 8 items relating to warmth and provision of reassurance, for example, "Often speaks of the good things that I do." The Rejection subscale has 7 items and includes "Almost always complains about what I do" and "Isn't very patient with me." Children's reports for mothers' and fathers' behavior on both subscales had good internal consistency in both groups (mother: first family, $\alpha = .86$; stepfamily, $\alpha = .85$; father: first family, $\alpha = .89$; stepfamily, $\alpha = .87$). These were combined to provide an overall index of adolescent appraisals of parent-child rejection (first family, $\alpha = .92$; stepfamily, $\alpha = .90$).

Psychological adjustment was assessed in the following ways:

- *Internalizing symptoms:* Because children tend to be the best reporters of their own internalized states (Achenbach, 1991a), two self-report scales were used to assess internalizing symptoms. The Children's Depression Inventory (Kovacs, 1981) is a 26-item measure of depressive symptoms. One item regarding suicidal thoughts was omitted because of concerns raised during the process of receiving ethical approval. This measure had good internal consistency in both groups at Time 1 (first family, $\alpha = .87$; stepfamily, $\alpha = .87$). The second measure was the Anxious/Depressed subscale of the Youth Self-Report Form of the Child Behavior Checklist (Achenbach, 1991a). The subscale had good internal consistency in both groups (first family, $\alpha = .84$; stepfamily, $\alpha = .85$). A combined estimate of internalizing symptoms had good internal consistency in both groups (first family, $\alpha = .90$; stepfamily, $\alpha = .88$).

- *Externalizing problems:* Externalizing problems were assessed using the Aggression subscale of the Youth Self-Report (Achenbach, 1991a) and the trait hostility measure of antisocial behavior (Buss & Durkee, 1957). The Aggression subscale had good internal consistency in both groups (first family, $\alpha = .85$; stepfamily, $\alpha = .81$). Items from the trait hostility measure include "If I have to use physical violence to defend myself I will." The internal consistency in the current sample for this measure was good (first family, $\alpha = .81$; stepfamily, $\alpha = .84$). The third measure of externalizing behavior was the Aggression subscale of the Teacher Report Form of the Child Behavior Checklist (Achenbach, 1991b). This measure also demonstrated good internal consistency for both groups (first family, $\alpha = .93$; stepfamily, $\alpha = .96$). A combined estimate of externalizing problems had good internal consistency in both groups (first family, $\alpha = .88$; stepfamily, $\alpha = .93$).

Statistical analyses were conducted in three primary stages. First, mean score comparisons were conducted for all primary variables among children living in first-family and stepparent households. Second, intercorrelations between all primary variables for each group were assessed and compared. Third, path analysis using maximum likelihood structural equation modelling (LISREL 8.12; Jöreskog & Sörbom, 1996) was conducted to test the empirical validity of each proposed theoretical model.

MEAN COMPARISONS AND CORRELATION ANALYSIS

Comparison of mean scores derived for children living in first-family households ($N = 325$) and stepparent households ($N = 48$) were assessed for all primary variables. Children living in stepparent households scored significantly higher in comparison to children in first-family households on measures relating to their experience of hostile and rejecting parenting ($t = 2.13, p < .05$) and symptoms of externalizing problems ($t = 2.50, p < .05$). There was a trend for higher levels of internalizing symptoms ($t = 1.93, p < .10$; see Table 11.1). These results are informative in that they show higher rates of psychopathology among children living in stepparent

Table 11.1
Means, Standard Deviations, and Group-Level Differences

Study Variables	First Families		Stepparent Families		
	Mean	SD	Mean	SD	T
Family process variables					
Interparental conflict	26.20	7.04	28.32	8.15	1.71
Threat appraisals	20.30	5.24	21.36	4.86	1.32
Self-blame appraisals	12.18	3.44	13.04	4.11	1.38
Parent-child rejection	39.90	9.16	42.93	9.20	2.14*
Adjustment problems					
Internalizing symptoms	15.47	10.33	18.55	10.31	1.93**
Externalizing problems	34.30	13.89	41.21	18.37	2.50*

Notes: First families ($N = 325$); Stepparent families ($N = 48$).

*$p < .05$; **$p < .10$.

households compared to those living in first-family households and significantly higher scores for children's perceptions of family relationships (parent-child relations).

Correlational analysis revealed an interesting pattern of bivariate relationships across groups (see Table 11.2). For children living in first-family households, significant correlations were apparent between interparental conflict and children's attributions of threat and self-blame, as well as their experience of negative parent-child relations and each index of psychological adjustment. Appraisals of threat, self-blame, and negative parenting were also significantly correlated with internalizing symptoms and externalizing problems. For children living in stepparent households, a significant correlation was apparent between interparental conflict and threat appraisals but not with self-blame appraisals, and between interparental conflict and each index of psychological adjustment. Interestingly, only one

Table 11.2
Intercorrelations between All Primary Theoretical Constructs

	1	2	3	4	5	6
Study Variable						
Interparental conflict	—	.43**	.20	.34*	.42**	.29*
Threat appraisals	.57**	—	.40**	.27	.34*	.13
Self-blame appraisals	.37**	.39**	—	.21	.23	.00
Parent-child rejection	.46**	.36**	.43**	—	.52**	.36*
Internalizing symptoms	.38**	.42**	.36**	.53**	—	.34*
Externalizing problems	.38**	.22**	.40**	.40**	.33**	—

Notes: First families ($N = 325$) appear below the diagonal; stepparent families ($N = 48$) above the diagonal.

*$p < .05$; **$p < .01$.

of four correlations between threat and self-blame appraisals and internalizing symptoms and externalizing problems appeared statistically significant (threat and internalizing), with appraisals of negative parenting significantly associated with each index of adjustment.

Two conclusions may be derived from these results. First, a mediational hypothesis as outlined by Baron and Kenny (1986) is testable for each group in relation to the association between interparental conflict and internalizing symptoms and externalizing problems. Second, the operating mechanism(s) for children living in first-family households may involve appraisals of threat, self-blame, and negative parenting. In contrast, for children living in stepparent households, only threat appraisals and negative parenting appear relevant to adjustment problems. However, conclusions relating to this pattern of relationships can be established only in the context of full multivariate analysis.

Path Analysis and Tests of Indirect Effects

Two sets of analyses were run for each subgroup linking interparental conflict, appraisals of threat and self-blame, and negative parenting to internalizing symptoms and externalizing problems. Comparisons were then conducted to establish the significance of indirect pathways across all models and subgroup comparisons considered.

Internalizing Symptoms

For children living in first-family households, interparental conflict was significantly associated with appraisals of threat, self-blame, and negative parenting. In turn, threat and negative parenting were associated with children's internalizing symptoms. Importantly, the initially significant association between interparental conflict and internalizing symptoms was no longer significant when threat, self-blame, and negative parenting were simultaneously considered in the analysis, suggesting mediation of this initial relationship (see Baron & Kenny, 1986). It is important to point out, however, that although the conditions necessary for tests of mediation as outlined by Baron and Kenny are apparent in the present analysis, it is not necessary for a significant direct effect to exist between two variables in order to carry out a mediational analysis. An independent variable can have an indirect effect on a dependent variable even if they are not correlated, if the independent variable influences a third (or intervening) variable, which in turn affects the dependent variable (MacKinnon, Lockwood, Hoffman, West, & Sheets, 2002). This method also allows for the assessment of the significance of indirect pathways, thereby allowing the relative contribution of one or more pathways to be compared in accounting for the initial association between an independent and a dependent variable. For the present analysis, significant indirect pathways were apparent between interparental conflict and internalizing symptoms through appraisals of threat ($\beta = .13, p < .05$) and negative parenting ($\beta = .18, p < .01$), but not through appraisals of self-blame ($\beta = .03, p > .10$). This pattern of results is consistent with past longitudinal research highlighting the respective role of children's appraisals of threat, self-blame, and negative parenting and internalizing and externalizing problems among children living in first-family households (Grych et al., 2003; Harold et al., 2007).

For children living in stepparent households, interparental conflict was again related to children's appraisals of threat and negative parenting, but not appraisals of self-blame. Contrary to results for children living in first-family households, negative parenting but not appraisals of threat or self-blame was related to internalizing symptoms. Once again the initially significant association between interparental conflict and internalizing symptoms was no longer significant when each hypothesized mediating variable was considered, suggesting that negative parenting, not attributions of threat or self-blame emanating from parents' marital arguments, explains this initial association for children living in stepparent households. The magnitude of the indirect effect from interparental conflict to internalizing symptoms through negative parenting also appeared statistically significant ($\beta = .14, p < .05$). These results are important because they suggest that the operating mechanisms for children living in first-family households involve their active appraisals of threat relating to parents' marital arguments *and* experiences of negative parenting in accounting for variation in internalizing symptoms, whereas for children living in stepparent households, experiences of negative parenting, not attributions relating to interparental conflict, explained effects on symptoms (see Figure 11.2, Panels A and B).

Externalizing Problems

With one exception (the path between interparental conflict and self-blame appraisals), tests of a model for externalizing problems revealed the same pattern of standardized coefficients linking interparental conflict to children's appraisals of threat, self-blame, and negative parenting for both groups (see magnitude of coefficients in previous section and correlations presented in Table 11.2). However, effects varied in relation to the criterion variable considered. For children living in first-family households, significant effects were apparent from self-blame appraisals and negative parenting, but not threat appraisals, to externalizing problems. Interestingly, the relationship between interparental conflict and externalizing problems remained significant when each of the proposed mediating variables was considered. Tests of indirect effects revealed significant pathways through parenting ($\beta = .10, p < .01$) and self-blame attributions ($\beta = .10, p < .05$), suggesting that interparental conflict exerts both direct and indirect effects

Panel A

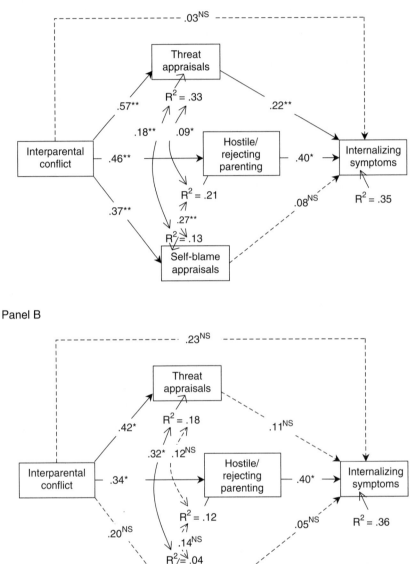

Panel B

Figure 11.2 Maximum Likelihood Estimation of Proposed Theoretical Model for Internalizing Symptoms among Children Living in First-Family (Panel A) and Stepparent (Panel B) Households ($^*p < .05$; $^{**}p < .01$).

on children's behavior problems for children living in first-family households. This finding concurs with previous longitudinal research (Harold et al., 1997, 2004).

For children living in stepparent households, effects were consistent with those relating to internalizing symptoms in that only negative parenting was significantly associated with externalizing problems. Contrary to the finding for children in first-family households, the initial association between interparental conflict and externalizing problems was not significant when the proposed mediators were included in the same analysis, suggesting that appraisals of negative parenting, not attributions of threat and self-blame relating to parents' marital arguments, mediate this relationship for children living in stepparent households. Tests of indirect effects revealed a significant pathway through parenting ($\beta = .11, p < .05$). This finding replicates that noted for internalizing symptoms (see Figure 11.3, Panels A and B).

In summary, these results suggest that for children living in first-family households, children's appraisals of negative parenting and their perceptions of threat and self-blame, respectively, are linked to their internalizing symptoms and externalizing problems. For internalizing symptoms, negative parenting and appraisals of threat jointly mediate the initial association with interparental conflict. For externalizing problems, negative parenting and appraisals of self-blame partially mediate effects from interparental conflict, suggesting the presence of both direct and indirect effects when this index of adjustment is considered. For children living in stepparent households, negative parenting but not appraisals of threat or self-blame relating to interparental conflict explained effects on both internalizing symptoms and externalizing problems.

DISCUSSION

The aim of this study was to investigate the relative role of children's appraisals of threat and self-blame emanating from parents' marital arguments, their feelings of hostile and rejecting parenting, and their internalizing symptoms and externalizing problems among a sample of children living in first-family and stepparent households.

Derived results are broadly consistent with Hetherington's transactional model (Hetherington et al., 1998) in explaining differences in children's adaptation to marital transition in so far as they highlight the role of the parent-child relationship as a mediator of the effects of couple conflict on children's psychological health. In addition, these findings highlight how analyzing the mechanisms that characterize family processes has the potential to elucidate how children living in different family constellations are affected by interadult conflict. Results of this study showed that for adolescents living in stepfamily homes, appraisals of parent-child rejection

Panel A

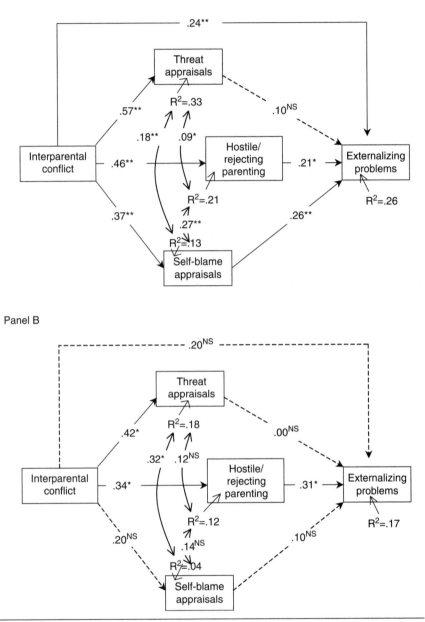

Figure 11.3 Maximum Likelihood Estimation of Proposed Theoretical Model for Externalizing Problems among Children Living in First-Family (Panel A) and Stepparent (Panel B) Households (*$p < .05$; **$p < .01$).

mediated the effects of interparental conflict on adjustment outcomes. This provides support for a spillover hypothesis, typically tested in the context of intact first-family households, in which marital conflict is related to less effective parenting behavior, emotional unavailability, and rejection of the child (Engfer, 1988; Erel & Burman, 1995; Kaczynski et al., 2006). It has been suggested that experiencing rejection and withdrawal of the parent may be a particularly salient dimension of parenting to young adolescents (Fauber, Forehand, Thomas, & Wierson, 1990), with children who experience parental rejection appearing vulnerable to internalizing symptoms and behavior problems (Kaczynski et al., 2006). For adolescents from recently divorced homes, a primary concern may be to maintain a close bond with their custodial parent, with increased sensitivity to behaviors indicative of rejection and withdrawal (Fauber et al., 1990). Indeed, irrespective of when divorce or separation has occurred, what characterizes the majority of children living in stepfamily homes is that they have already experienced life with their biological parents, separation or divorce of their parents and a period of time in a single-parent home before the remarriage (Hetherington, Stanley-Hagan, & Anderson, 1989). Such a sequence of transitions may account, at least in part, for child concerns with the quality of the parent-child relationship. It is noteworthy therefore that the present study found higher levels of reported parent rejection by children living in stepfamily homes compared to first-family homes. For children living in first-family homes, a dual pathway model appears to explain effects; that is, these children were affected directly via their appraisals of threat and self-blame in the context of their parent's conflict, and indirectly via the spillover of negative behavior expressed in the parent-child relationship. These findings are consistent with earlier work comparing family processes in intact and divorced families in which parent behavior did not fully mediate the effects of marital conflict on children living in intact families (Fauber et al., 1990). Few studies however, have tested the mediating roles of parenting behavior *and* children's appraisals about the interparental relationship, concurrently. In one investigation, children's emotional security about parenting partially mediated links between emotional security about the marital relationship and children's psychological adjustment (Harold et al., 2004): another study found that when assessed simultaneously, only children's self-blame attributions for parents' marital arguments, not appraisals of negative parenting, affected long-term academic attainment (Harold et al., 2007).

The finding that threat attributions mediated the relationship between interparental conflict and internalizing symptoms in the first-family but not the stepfamily group is consistent with previous work by Gerard, Buehler, Franck, and Anderson (2005). They found a stronger association between children's appraisals of interparental conflict and threat appraisals for children living in intact families compared with children from divorced families. Our additional finding that self-blame appraisals mediated effects of conflict on externalizing problems in first-family but not stepparent homes is interesting. There was no absolute difference in levels of self-blame in response to interparental conflict between these groups (or in levels of threat appraisals). It is possible that for children living in first-family homes who are exposed to interparental conflict, the activation of appraisals of threat and self-blame has direct implications for their psychological adjustment because the relationship between their biological parents is particularly salient to them and their feelings of emotional security in the context of the interparental relationship. For stepfamilies, this appears not to be the case. Children's appraisals of threat and responsibility for couple conflict were not related to their appraisals of parent rejection or to their psychological adjustment. Instead, interparental conflict exerted effects on psychological adjustment via the parent-child relationship only. This finding should not be interpreted to suggest that children's social cognitions or attributions relating to conflict between couples in stepparent households are negated in terms of relevance to well-being; rather, the specific mechanism through which couple conflict exerts effects on well-being for children in stepparent households is the parent-child relationship. This mechanism, however, may relate more to the salience of a reconfigured caregiver relationship whereby children's attention is directed toward establishing relations that offer security and stability, a process consistent with the recognized role of parenting and parent-child attachment in the early years (see Waters & Cummings, 2000). Longitudinal research is needed to more adequately test this hypothesis as children grow and adapt, or not, within remarried or blended family contexts over time. Addressing this challenge represents one of the primary limitations of the present study.

The present study was unable to differentiate children in stepfamilies based on time since parental remarriage. Previous research indicates that in the years that follow the formation of a stepfamily via remarriage, the affective quality of mother-child relations improves, and the relationship that children form with a stepfather varies as a function of their age, with positive relationship formation occurring for young children and less so for adolescents (Hetherington et al., 1998). Yet in at least one study that compared family functioning in non-stepfamilies and established stepfamilies (average length of remarried relationship was 9 years), there were no substantive differences in the pattern of results that characterized parent-adolescent relationships across family type (O'Connor et al., 1998). One explanation for these findings that the authors proposed was that the processes that characterize nondivorced families come to be fostered in stepfamilies. It is possible, therefore, that links between children's appraisals of the adult relationship and the parent-child relationship with psychological adjustment vary as a function of the length of time they have been a member of that stepfamily.

An additional limitation of the present study relates to the cross-sectional attributes of the analyses presented. By not including an estimate of initial levels of children's emotional and behavior problems on their subsequent psychological adjustment, or of relations with interparental conflict and cognitive appraisals of family functioning, the conclusions that can be drawn about the processes that underlie links between parental conflict and child adjustment are limited (see Harold et al., 2004). The use of cross-sectional analysis and child report across measures of family functioning was necessitated by the relatively small number of stepfamilies available. However, recent research has highlighted the relevance of child reports of interparental conflict and documented consistent effects of child and parent reports of marital conflict on children's appraisals of threat and self-blame (e.g., Grych et al., 2003). Moreover, it can be argued that child reports of interparental conflict more accurately captures conflict behaviors to which children have been exposed; previous research shows a distinction between children's reports of parents' conflict behavior and the threat and level of self-blame they experience or attribute to such behavior (Bickham & Fiese, 1996; Grych et al., 1992, 2000).

Finally, the present study assessed adolescents' appraisals of their relationship with their custodial parents (parent and stepparent) with whom they spent most of their time. It would have been interesting to have also assessed children's relationship with their other parents (e.g., father and stepmother or partner) to more accurately reflect the complexities of family life for these children (Fine, 2001). An investigation of child appraisals of their relationships with other family members that may themselves be characterized by conflict, or in some way act to moderate custodial parent-child relationships, is an important avenue to pursue.

CONCLUSION

The present study highlights the processes through which exposure to frequent, intense, and poorly resolved interparental conflict affects the psychological adaptation of children living in first families and stepparent families. Specifically, children's appraisals of conflict behaviors occurring between their parents were shown to exert effects on adjustment via the parent-child relationship (in both first-family and stepfamily homes) and via threat and self-blame appraisals (in first-family homes only). The apparent differences in the mediating mechanisms through which conflict exerted effects on children's adjustment suggests that intervention efforts for stepfamilies characterized by discordant relationships should focus on the co-occurrence of children's appraisals of conflict behavior between parents and their experience of their parents as rejecting and hostile. That is, children's awareness of interadult conflict as frequent, intense, and poorly resolved appears directly related to their appraisal of the quality of the parent-child relationship. In first families, there remains a clear need to consider how early adolescents' subjective interpretations of interparental conflict as it relates to them (threat, self-blame appraisals) *and* their experience of the parent-child relationship informs their psychological adjustment (e.g., Grych et al., 2003; Harold et al., 1997). Therefore, for children living in first-family households, an appreciation of multiple pathways through which children are affected by couple conflict holds the most promise for developing efficacious intervention programs (Grych, 2005).

The findings from the present study underscore the need to inform parents about the effects of couple conflict on children and how problems in the marital relationship engender child appraisals of parents as more hostile and rejecting. With a continued emphasis on the child's perspective as the primary mechanism through which he or she is adversely (or otherwise) affected by conflict occurring between parents comes the opportunity to support children who experience marital conflict and family transitions. In a recent overview of the impact of social policy relating to interparental conflict, Emery (2001) was optimistic that the cumulative effects of policy initiatives and educational interventions seeking to foster interparental cooperation and discourage conflict could ultimately produce a cultural change in family processes. With this objective in mind, recognizing and acting on the processes through which children are affected by family experiences, and in particular family change and transition, is a necessary step if we are to realistically address the needs of children at a time of such significant structural change in the landscape of modern family life.

REFERENCES

Achenbach, T. M. (1991a). *Manual for the Youth Self-Report and 1991 profile*. Burlington: University of Vermont, Department of Psychiatry.

Achenbach, T. M. (1991b). *Manual for the Teachers Report Form and 1991 profile*. Burlington: University of Vermont, Department of Psychiatry.

Amato, P. R. (2001). Children of divorce in the 1990s: An update of the Amato and Keith (1991) meta-analysis. *Journal of Family Psychology, 15*, 355–370.

Amato, P. R., & Keith, B. (1991). Parental divorce and the well-being of children: A meta-analysis. *Psychological Bulletin, 110*, 26–46.

Avenevoli, S., Sessa, F. M., & Steinberg, L. (1999). Family structure, parenting practices, and adolescent adjustment: An ecological examination. In E. M. Hetherington (Ed.), *Coping with divorce, single parenting and remarriage: A risk and resiliency perspective* (pp. 65–90). Mahwah, NJ: Erlbaum.

Barber, B. L., & Lyons, J. M. (1994). Family processes and adolescent adjustment in intact and remarried families. *Journal of Youth and Adolescence, 23*, 421–436.

Baron, R. M., & Kenny, D. A. (1986). The moderator-mediator distinction in social psychological research: Conceptual, strategic and statistical considerations. *Journal of Personality and Social Psychology, 51*, 1173–1182.

Bickham, N. L., & Fiese, B. H. (1996). Extension of the Children's Perception of Inter-Parental Conflict Scale for use with late adolescents. *Journal of Family Psychology, 11*, 246–250.

Borrine, M. L., Handal, P. J., Brown, N. Y., & Searight, H. R. (1991). Family conflict and adolescent adjustment in intact, divorced and blended families. *Journal of Consulting and Clinical Psychology, 59*(5), 753–755.

Bowlby, J. (1969). *Attachment and loss: Vol. 1. Attachment.* New York: Basic Books.

Buss, A., & Durkee, A. (1957). An inventory for assessing different kinds of hostility. *Journal of Consulting Psychology, 21*, 343–349.

Conger, R. D., Ge, X., Elder, G. H., Lorenz, F. O., & Simons, R. L. (1994). Economic stress, coercive family process, and developmental problems of adolescents. *Child Development, 65*, 341–361.

Cox, M. J., Paley, B., & Harter, K. (2001). Inter-parental conflict and parent-child relationships. In J. Grych & F. Fincham (Eds.), *Child development and inter-parental conflict* (pp. 249–272). New York: Cambridge University Press.

Cummings, E. M., & Davies, P. T. (2002). Effects of marital conflict on children: Recent advances and emergent themes in process-oriented research. *Journal of Child Psychology and Psychiatry, 43*, 31–63.

Dadds, M. R., Atkinson, E., Turner, C., Blums, G. J., & Lendich, B. (1999). Family conflict and child adjustment: Evidence for a cognitive-contextual model of intergenerational transmission. *Journal of Family Psychology, 13*, 194–208.

Davies, P. T., & Cummings, E. M. (1994). Marital conflict and child adjustment: An emotional security hypothesis. *Psychological Bulletin, 116*, 387–411.

Davies, P. T., & Cummings, E. M. (1998). Exploring children's emotional security as a mediator of the link between marital relations and child adjustment. *Child Adjustment, 69*, 124–139.

Davies, P. T., Harold, G., Goeke-Morey, M., & Cummings, E. M. (2002). Child emotional security and inter-parental conflict. *Monographs for the Society for Research in Child Development, 67*(3), vii–viii.

Downey, G., & Coyne, J. C. (1990). Children of depressed parents: An integrative review. *Psychological Bulletin, 108*, 50–76.

Emery, R. E. (1982). Inter-parental conflict and the children of discord and divorce. *Psychological Bulletin, 92*, 310–330.

Emery, R. E. (2001). Interparental conflict and social policy. In J. Grych & F. Fincham (Eds.), *Interparental conflict and child development* (pp. 417–439). New York: Cambridge University Press.

Emery, R. E., Fincham, F. D., & Cummings, E. M. (1992). Parenting in context: Systematic thinking about parental conflict and its influence on children. *Journal of Consulting and Clinical Psychology, 60*, 909–912.

Engfer, A. (1988). The interrelatedness of marriage and the mother-child relationship. In R. A. Hinde & J. Stephenson-Hinde (Eds.), *Relationships within families* (pp. 104–118). Oxford: Clarendon Press.

Erel, O., & Burman, B. (1995). Interrelatedness of marital relations and parent-child relations: A meta-analytic review. *Psychological Bulletin, 118*, 108–132.

Fauber, R., Forehand, R., Thomas, A., & Wierson, M. (1990). A mediational model of the impact of marital conflict on adolescent adjustment in intact and divorced families: The role of disrupted parenting. *Child Development, 61*, 1112–1123.

Fine, M. (2001). Conflict in stepfamilies. In J. Grych & F. Fincham (Eds.), *Interparental conflict and child development: Theory, research and application* (pp. 363–384). New York: Cambridge University Press.

Gerard, J. M., Buehler, C., Franck, K., & Anderson, O. (2005). In the eyes of the beholder: Cognitive appraisals as mediators of the association between interparental conflict and youth maladjustment. *Journal of Family Psychology, 19*, 376–384.

Goldberg, W. A., & Easterbrooks, M. A. (1984). The role of marital quality in toddler development. *Developmental Psychology, 20*, 504–514.

Grych, J. H. (2005). Inter-parental conflict as a risk factor for child maladjustment: Implications for the development of prevention programmes. *Family Court Review, 43*, 97–108.

Grych, J. H., & Fincham, F. D. (1990). Marital conflict and children's adjustment: A cognitive-contextual framework. *Psychological Bulletin, 108*, 267–290.

Grych, J. H., Fincham, F. D., Jouriles, E. N., & McDonald, R. (2000). Inter-parental conflict and child adjustment: Testing the mediational roles of appraisals in the cognitive-contextual framework. *Child Development, 71*, 1648–1661.

Grych, J. H., Harold, G. T., & Miles, C. J. (2003). A prospective investigation of appraisals as mediators of the link between inter-parental conflict and child adjustment. *Child Development, 74*, 1176–1193.

Grych, J. H., Raynor, S. R., & Fosco, G. M. (2004). Family processes that shape the impact of inter-parental conflict on adolescents. *Development and Psychopathology, 16*, 649–665.

Grych, J. H., Seid, M., & Fincham, F. D. (1992). Assessing marital conflict from the child's perspective. *Child Development, 63*, 558–572.

Harold, G. T., Aitken, J., & Shelton, K. H. (2007). Inter-parental conflict and children's academic attainment: A longitudinal analysis. *Journal of Child Psychology and Psychiatry, 48*, 1223–1232.

Harold, G. T., & Conger, R. D. (1997). Marital conflict and adolescent distress: The role of adolescent awareness. *Child Development, 68*, 330–350.

Harold, G. T., Fincham, F. D., Osborne, L. N., & Conger, R. D. (1997). Mom and Dad are at it again: Adolescent perceptions of marital conflict and adolescent psychological distress. *Developmental Psychology, 33*, 333–350.

Harold, G. T., & Murch, M. A. (2005). Inter-parental conflict and children's adaptation to separation and divorce: Implications for family law. *Child and Family Law Quarterly, 17*, 185–205.

Harold, G. T., Pryor, J., & Reynolds, J. (2001). *Not in front of the children? How conflict between parents affects children.* London: One-Plus-One Marriage and Partnership Research.

Harold, G. T., Shelton, K. H., Goeke-Morey, M. C., & Cummings, E. M. (2002). Relations between inter-parental conflict, child emotional security, and adjustment in the context of cognitive appraisals. In P. Davies, G. Harold, M. Goekey-Morey, & E. M. Cummings (Eds.), Child emotional security and inter-parental conflict. *Monographs for the Society for Research in Child Development, 67*(3), vii–viii.

Harold, G. T., Shelton, K. H., Goeke-Morey, M. C., & Cummings, E. M. (2004). Marital conflict, child emotional security about family relationships and child adjustment. *Social Development, 13*, 350–376.

Hetherington, E. M. (1989). Coping with family transitions: Winners, losers, and survivors. *Child Development, 60*, 1–14.

Hetherington, E. M. (1993). An overview of the Virginia Longitudinal Study of Divorce and Remarriage with a focus on early adolescence. *Journal of Family Psychology, 7*, 39–56.

Hetherington, E. M., Bridges, M., & Insabella, G. M. (1998). What matters, what does not? Five perspectives on the association between marital transitions and children's adjustment. *American Psychologist, 53*, 167–184.

Hetherington, E. M., Henderson, S. H., & Reiss, D. (1999). Adolescent siblings in stepfamilies: Family functioning and adolescent adjustment. *Monographs of the Society for Research in Child Development.*

Hetherington, E. M., Stanley-Hagan, M., & Anderson, E. R. (1989). Marital transitions: A child's perspective. *American Psychologist, 44*, 303–312.

Jenkins, J., Simpson, A., Dunn, J., Rasbash, J., & O'Connor, T. G. (2005). Mutual influence of marital conflict and children's behavior problems: Shared and nonshared family risks. *Child Development, 76*(1), 24–39.

Jöreskog, K., & Sörbom, D. (1996). *Lisrel 8: Structural equation modelling with the SIMPLIS command language.* Hillsdale, NJ: Erlbaum.

Kaczynski, K. J., Lindahl, K. M., Malik, N. M., & Laurenceau, J.-P. (2006). Marital conflict, maternal and paternal parenting, and child adjustment: A test of mediation and moderation. *Journal of Family Psychology, 20*, 199–208.

Kerig, P. (1998). Moderators and mediators of the effects of inter-parental conflict on children's adjustment. *Journal of Abnormal Child Psychology, 26*, 199–212.

Kovacs, M. (1981). Rating scales to assess depression in school-aged children. *Acta Paedo-Psychiatrica, 46*, 305–315.

Kurdek, L., & Fine, M. (1993). The relation between family structure and young adolescent's appraisals of family climate and parenting behavior. *Journal of Family Issues, 14*, 279–290.

Long, N., Forehand, R., Fauber, R., & Brody, G. H. (1987). Self-perceived and independently observed competence of young adolescents as a function of parental marital conflict and recent divorce. *Journal of Abnormal Child Psychology, 15*, 15–27.

MacKinnon, D. P., Lockwood, C. M., Hoffman, J. M., West, S. G., & Sheets, V. (2002). A comparison of methods to test mediation and other intervening variable effects. *Psychological Methods, 7*, 83–104.

Margolies, P. J., & Weintraub, S. (1977). The revised 56-item CRPBI as a research instrument: Reliability and factor structure. *Journal of Clinical Psychology, 33*, 472–476.

O'Connor, T. G., Hetherington, E. M., & Reiss, D. (1998). Family systems and adolescent development: Shared and non-shared risk and protective factors in nondivorced and remarried families. *Development and Psychopathology, 10*, 353–375.

Paley, B., Conger, R. D., & Harold, G. T. (2000). Parents' affect, adolescent cognitive representations, and adolescent social development. *Journal of Marriage and the Family, 62*, 761–776.

Parentlineplus. (2005). *A new stepfamily can be one step too far for children, says new report.* Retrieved June, 29, 2005, from www.parentlineplus.org.uk/.

Pryor, J., & Rogers, B. (2001). *Children in changing families: Life after parental separation.* Oxford: Blackwell.

Rivett, M., Howarth, E., & Harold, G. (2006). Watching from the stairs: Towards evidence based practice in work with child witnesses of domestic violence. *Clinical Child Psychology and Psychiatry, 11*, 103–125.

Serot, N. M., & Teevan, R. C. (1961). Perception of the parent-child relationship and its relation to child adjustment. *Child Development, 32*, 373–378.

Towle, C. (1931). The evaluation and management of marital status in foster homes. *American Journal of Orthopsychiatry, 1*, 271–284.

Waters, E., & Cummings, E. M. (2000). A secure base from which to explore close relationships. *Child Development, 71*, 164–172.

CHAPTER 12

The Distribution of Household Tasks in First-Marriage Families and Stepfamilies Across Europe

LAURENT SNOECKX, BRITT DEHERTOGH,
and DIMITRI MORTELMANS

IN THIS CHAPTER, we look at the family dynamics of the division of household tasks in Europe. Since the 1990s, this has been a hot topic among family researchers as a result of the increasing (policy) importance of reconciling work and family life in virtually all industrialized societies. Because of the steep increase in family instability and the "new risks" people have to meet (Beck, 1994), implicated by recent changes in family trajectories, we want to throw more light on the dynamics in stepfamilies. We examine the household task division in stepfamilies compared to first-marriage partnerships. As Shelton and John (1993) state, first-order marriages no longer represent the variety of family forms in Western societies since the 1960s. Household labor research must move beyond the group of first-married couples to meet with the present complex reality of different and shifting family forms. In their extensive review of the literature on stepfamilies, Ganong and Coleman (2004) point out that the limited number of studies on the division of labor in stepfamilies has produced contrasting results. Some studies have shown that women in stepfamilies do less household work than in first marriages; others found that the division is more equal. Moreover, none of the studies included a cross-national comparative perspective. Our goal is to examine the division of labor from an international perspective. As we want to take a look at this housework division cross-nationally, we use a multilevel approach on the European Social Survey data from 2004–2005 (second wave).

The allocation of household tasks is situated within the triad of family, labor market, and state. Therefore, its changing patterns are linked to the radical social and economic changes after World War II in nearly all Western societies. The standard of living in these countries increased due to industrialization and modern technology, and households shifted from household labor to market activity to enjoy its benefits (Blossfeld & Drobnic, 2001). This resulted in an enormous increase of female participation in the labor market and a shift from the single- to the dual-earner family as the norm. From that moment on, the Western family substantially changed, and new demographic trends arose. In this second demographic transition (Lesthaeghe & Neels, 2002; Van de Kaa, 1994), individual autonomy and female emancipation are central processes. The second demographic transition is characterized by an upward accelerating divorce trend, a rising age of marriage, and a rise in new family forms, such as premarital cohabitations (that eventually lead to "paperless marriages" and a rise in extramarital births), single-parent families (most of them headed by women), remarriages, and stepfamilies (Lesthaeghe, 1995).

Because of the widespread existence of dual-earner families, there is often a conflict between the time spent in the labor market and the time spent in the family. Especially for women, it has been difficult to reconcile the competing demands of labor market work and work inside the home, such as the care for children and other domestic jobs. Indeed, the gendered division of labor stopped at the door of most households (Cooke, 2004). For men, the breadwinner role remains rather constant in most industrialized countries, although an increasing number of men take on more responsibilities in caring and domestic tasks, especially in the case of dual-earner families (Goldscheider & Waite, 1991; Kalleberg & Rosenfeld, 1990). In spite of the general increase of men's contribution to household labor in the past decades, housework primarily remains unequally divided, at the expense of women (Batalova & Cohen, 2002; Bianchi, Milkie, Sayer, & Robinson, 2000; Coltrane, 2000). Women spend more time in housework, such as doing laundry, cooking, cleaning, and taking care of the children, than men do (Nordenmark, 2004). Depending on how household work is defined, there are small differences in the housework that women report doing, but general studies indicate that they perform twice as much household work as men and almost two thirds of the total housework load (for an overview, see Nordenmark, 2004; Shelton & John, 1993).

It is clear that the presence of children affects the division of household tasks. However, there are other factors that influence the gendered division of housework for a couple: employment status, income and educational attainment, sex-role attitudes, and other relational experiences. How these determinants affect the gender disparity in household tasks can be conceptualized in three core approaches in recent sociological research: time availability, relative resources, and gender ideology perspective. However, the balance between work and family demands is not only determined by family characteristics but is also mitigated by institutional state characteristics and cultural factors such as equal career opportunity policies and the provision of child care facilities and the prevailing gender ideology (Batalova & Cohen, 2002; Fuwa, 2004). Recent research therefore pays more attention to the "nesting" (Blumberg, 1984) of these household patterns in broader social, cultural, and institutional contexts (Batalova & Cohen, 2002; Geist, 2005; Hook, 2006). We elaborate on the influence of these micro and macro determinants on the division of household labor.

If we want to understand which processes and determinants are responsible for the allocation of household tasks at the micro and macro levels, we have to examine both classic first-marriage families and stepfamilies in different countries. In addition to earlier household distribution research that either focused on the disparities between couples with different marital statuses (Demo & Acock, 1993; Ishii-Kuntz & Coltrane, 1992; Shelton & John, 1993; South & Spitze, 1994; Sullivan, 1997) or included cross-national comparisons (Baxter, 1997; Fuwa, 2004; Geist, 2005; Kamo, 1994; Sanchez, 1993, 1994), we examine both aspects in this contribution. We first elaborate on the influence of micro and macro determinants on the gendered division of household tasks. Thereafter, we discuss the divergence of the household task division between first marriages and stepfamilies.

A GENDERED DIVISION OF HOUSEHOLD TASKS

Micro Determinants

Different factors are formulated to explain the gender disparity in household task division. They are often conceptualized in three theoretical approaches that focus on different determinants: time availability, relative resources, and gender-role attitudes (Coleman, Ganong, & Fine, 2000; Shelton & John, 1993; South & Spitze, 1994). The combination of the three perspectives gives support to a holistic view of people's behavior by combining economic (time and resources) and cultural (gender ideology) explanations.

The first explanation assumes that the allocation of household work is a rational process wherein partners maximize utility by assigning household tasks according to the number of working hours and potential earnings in paid employment (Becker, 1981). This time availability argument is mostly operationalized by the number of working hours of women. Since women in most cases work fewer hours or get paid less than their partners, they spend more hours on housework (Bianchi et al., 2000; Shelton & John, 1996;

South & Spitze, 1994). For men, the opposite is found: Their number of working hours has a negative effect on the relative share of their housework participation.

A second approach stresses the importance of relative resources in the partners' bargaining process regarding household task allocation (Batalova & Cohen, 2002; Geist, 2005; Hook, 2006; Ishii-Kuntz & Coltrane, 1992). The starting point is the assumption that housework is unpleasant. The partner with the higher relative status and income has more negotiating power and will be able to reduce his or her own share of household work. These relative resources are often operationalized by using the woman's earnings or educational attainment, measured either as absolute or relative (in comparison with her partner). The more a woman contributes to the household income and the higher her degree, the smaller her share of housework will be. For men, the opposite holds.

A final approach focuses on gender-role ideology and states that spouses who adhere more to egalitarian gender attitudes divide the household labor more equally (Batalova & Cohen, 2002; Geist, 2005; Hook, 2006; Ishii-Kuntz & Coltrane, 1992). People are assumed to be socialized into female and male gender roles, thereby adopting values and opinions about the appropriate allocation of household labor within the family (Coltrane, 2000; Geist, 2005; Ishii-Kuntz & Coltrane, 1992; Kane & Sanchez, 1994). Internalization of more equal gender roles leads to a more balanced division of tasks.

MACRO DETERMINANTS

Next to the influence of individual or couple economic and cultural characteristics, the impact of macro-level factors such as parental leave arrangements, child care availability, and overall gender ideology is important to fully understand household labor allocation dynamics. The embeddedness of families in institutional and sociocultural frameworks brings cross-national variation into the gendered household labor division (Batalova & Cohen, 2002; Fuwa, 2004; Geist, 2005; Hook, 2006). Cross-national differences in household labor distribution within families can thus be attributed to varying individual characteristics (due to compositional differences across countries) and to varying institutional (structural) and cultural country characteristics.

Many scholars have already pointed to the interrelation between institutional policies and cultural country characteristics (Inglehart, 1990; Orloff, 1993; Rindfuss, Brewster, & Kavee, 1996; Sainsbury, 1994; Treas & Widmer, 2000). When looking at this interplay with reference to the allocation of household work, a woman-friendly policy emerges from initial gender equality values, and these values will be promoted by pursuing a gender equality policy (e.g., availability of paternity leave, child care arrangements, gender-neutral wages). In other words, state policies internalize gender ideology, thereby promoting these values to citizens via policy initiatives. In fact, as Treas and Widmer (2000) state, a country's policy is successful only when citizens and public opinion adhere to the state's ideology.

As shown in earlier research (Batalova & Cohen, 2002; Fuwa, 2004; Geist, 2005; Hook, 2006), both structural economic (e.g., parental leave or gross domestic product [GDP]) and cultural (e.g., gender equality values) macro characteristics affect the allocation of household work within the family, ir-respective of the type of family. Structural country characteristics such as gender-equalizing work and family policies may influence the division of household labor because they change the benefits of specialization and af-fect the intracouple bargaining processes (Hook, 2006). Cultural macro characteristics can influence the allocation of household labor by processes of socialization, since people adhere to socially constructed gender norms. Therefore, the role of husband and wife within the family is influenced by the societal opinions about these gender roles.

THE DIVISION OF HOUSEHOLD LABOR IN FIRST-MARRIAGE FAMILIES AND STEPFAMILIES

There are substantive reasons to believe that there is a difference in the household task distribution between first-marriage families and stepfami-lies. Changes in family structure are likely to generate changes in family processes, so it would not be surprising if classic first-order marriages and new stepfamilies differ in their distribution of household labor (Demo & Acock, 1993). Most of the research that has focused on the relationship between marital status and household labor division indicates that women are inclined to take up less housework when entering a second relationship, whereas remarried men spend more time on housework than do men in first marriages, although evidence is mixed (e.g., Demo & Acock, 1993; Ishii-Kuntz & Coltrane, 1992; Pyke & Coltrane, 1996; Sullivan, 1997).

Scholars have put forward different hypotheses to explain the relation-ship between marital status and the division of household labor. In these considerations, role performance, negotiation processes, and prior relation-al experiences are central. Cherlin's (1978) incomplete institution hypothesis states that there is more role ambiguity in new families because of the absence of normative guidelines for role performance. Because of the lack of institutionalized procedures to handle problems, there is more bargain-ing and open communication between spouses in remarriage families (Ishii-Kuntz & Coltrane, 1992). Precisely because of this lack of institutional rules and gender norms for the conduct of stepfamilies, there is more inter-action and conversation about the housework division between partners, which leads to a more egalitarian household labor division (Coltrane, 2000;

Gupta, 1999). Related to this incomplete institution hypothesis, Sullivan (1997) stresses the importance of open communication and bargaining in the selection of a new partner and maintenance of the relation. He states that, to explain the division of housework, it is necessary to develop more sophisticated models than rational partner choice that put forward interactive processes and gendered perceptions of an equal division of household labor. This is consistent with research pointing to the socializing impacts of prior relational experiences (Demo & Acock, 1993; Ishii-Kuntz & Coltrane, 1992) because of the evident impact of the biographies of the partners in their ideas and discussions on equal household task division (Sullivan, 1997).

Another process that combines these views is West and Zimmerman's (1987) concept of "doing gender." The basic idea of this gender-role approach is that individuals behave according to their own internalized roles and others' expectations to make cognitive sense of the world (Bittman, England, Sayer, Folbre, & Matheson, 2003). This approach stresses the active role of people in producing gender roles by organizing everyday (inter)action, in this case the allocation of household labor (Berk, 1985; Koelet, 2005; Shelton & John, 1993; South & Spitze, 1994). In addition to the classic socialization approach wherein rigid gender roles are to some degree ascribed to people, this theory emphasizes that gender roles can be conceptualized as "a routine accomplishment embedded in everyday interaction" (South & Spitze, 1994, p. 329; West & Zimmerman, 1987, p. 125). Remarriers would consider it less necessary to adopt clear marital roles than first-married spouses, due to the socializing impacts of their prior marital experience (Coltrane & Ishii-Kuntz, 1992, 2000; Demo & Acock, 1993; Sullivan, 1997) and the availability of multiple role identities (Coltrane, 2000). According to this view, household labor is a more important source for first marriers to construct the roles of "wife" and "husband" than for partners in stepfamilies.

By joining the three core approaches (time availability, relative resources, and gender roles) with the perspective of doing gender, the different explanations for the division of housework in stepfamilies can again be divided in two main groups. On the one hand, an economic view states that the available time from work and the economic resources are the factors that influence housework division between stepfamily members. On the other hand, a cultural view tries to explain the differences in attitudes toward gender equality that are socialized during the life course. Societal gender norms and prior relational experiences have an impact on the task division in families. The question is whether we can find differences in household labor division between stepfamilies and first marriages, and if we do, whether cultural or economic determinants (or both) on the micro and macro level have an effect on the division.

Data

We used data from the second wave of the European Social Survey (ESS) from 2005. The ESS is a large-scale project collecting data on attitudes, values, and behavioral patterns throughout Europe. With high-quality standards on data collection, the ESS offers very recent representative data for 17 countries. Participating countries in the second wave are Austria, Belgium, Germany, Norway, Finland, Sweden, Denmark, Poland, Portugal, Spain, Greece, Slovenia, Estonia, Switzerland, United Kingdom, Czech Republic, and Luxembourg. Other countries, such as France and Iceland, have also participated, but the data were not available at the time of this study. In the second wave, information on the behavior of both partners concerning household tasks was gathered. This survey is unique because it creates a household grid detailing the age, gender, and relationship to the respondent for every family member surveyed. An important note is that the information was given by the respondent; because the ESS is a survey of individuals and not families or couples, we have information on partners and children only through the respondent. We made a selection of heterosexual unions, with children living in the household. The final data set contains 7,018 individuals.

Before elaborating on the construction of several other variables from the ESS, we must define the two most crucial concepts: household tasks and stepfamilies. In defining these concepts, we were led by theoretical considerations and the availability of measurement instruments in the data.

Household tasks are limited to housework such as cooking, cleaning, and doing laundry. Tasks that involve child care in any way are not included. We used two questions on the proportion of housework (in categories) the respondent and the partner carry out. To make a comparison between the proportions, we divided the proportion of the women by the proportion of the men. This calculation resulted in a ratio of female task completion to male task completion. Using a ratio instead of the absolute male involvement is crucial because it takes the contracting out of housework into account. As expected, the ratio was right-skewed, with a much higher female contribution. Therefore, and for more theoretical reasons, we chose to dichotomize the dependent variable into a category of more female contribution and one of equal or more male contribution. Families with at least an equal division can be easily compared with those with more traditional task divisions.

Stepfamilies are couples with children of one of the partners from a former marriage or relationship. The children live in the home of the biological parent and the new partner, either full or part time. A problem we had to deal with in the data was the definition of the relationship between the respondent and the children in the household. In the grid, no distinction is made between biological and stepchildren. All children who lived in the household were registered. Moreover, there is no question in the survey on the number of biological children. We solved the problem by looking at the age of the oldest child and the duration of the new relationship. Couples with inhabiting children older than the duration of the relationship were marked as stepfamilies. An important shortcoming of this definition is that we are unable to distinguish between stepfamilies in which the respondent is the biological parent or the stepparent of the children.

The covariates can be divided into two groups. First, economic variables are included. To measure time availability, we use the working hours of both partners. Respondents were asked to note how many hours a week they worked, housework and voluntary work not included. The educational level of the partners was used as a measure of relative resources. We simplified the covariate by reducing the number of categories to three: primary, secondary, and tertiary education. A final economic (relative resources) indicator was the income partners provided. Only the proportion of income the respondent and the partner respectively supplied was available in the data. The proportion is registered as a categorical variable (not as a percentage). For that reason, we combined both proportions into one: the proportion of female contribution to the household income compared to the male contribution. We distinguished three possibilities according to the univariate dispersion: the woman contributes less than the man, both bring in approximately equal amounts, or the woman contributes more.

The second group of covariates contains cultural indicators such as gender equality and religious values. The ESS holds many attitudes and values toward different subjects but lacks a consistent gender equality scale. However, one question in the survey did ask whether a woman should be prepared to cut down on paid work for the sake of the family. Although this only partly covers the concept of gender equality, in terms of the division of housework the question provides us with a good indicator of the preferred gender balance between work and family. We recoded the scale into a categorical variable with three values: a positive attitude toward gender equality, a neutral attitude, and a negative attitude. To introduce religion as a cultural indicator, we used a 10-point scale of how religious people judge themselves.

Next to cultural and economic resources, two control variables were added. First, we assumed that there would be a difference in task division between rural and nonrural areas. Using a self-reported question on degree of urbanization of the domicile, a categorical variable was created. Furthermore, the age of the children is also important in understanding task division. For that reason, we made a variable that told us if there were children under the age of 3, between 3 and 12, or older than 12.

Differences between countries are studied in terms of structural and cultural domains. We chose to include economic and female power measurements. The gross domestic product ($) per capita (GDP), taking purchasing power into account, was selected to give an indication of the economic welfare of a nation. To measure the political and economic power of women, we used the figures provided by the Organization for Economic Cooperation and Development of the proportion of female ministers in a country. We assume that a higher proportion indicates a more equal gender climate in the country (Directorate General of Human Rights, 2006). In many Western nations, women do get elected into parliament but are still excluded from the executive branch of government. The proportion of women in executive power (variable wommin) can therefore be regarded as a good indicator of female political power (and consequently also economic power). In several other studies the Gender Empowerment Measure (GEM) is used; this is a composition of four separate figures giving a view on the amount of economic and political power women have. We chose not to use the GEM for two important reasons. First, only the proportion of women in parliament is included as a measure of political power in the GEM; however, female participation in parliament is a poor indicator. A second argument is that there is no GEM available for one of the countries (Luxembourg).

METHOD

The first step in the analysis is to explore the data and look at differences between stepfamilies and first marriages in terms of time availability, relative resources, and gender-role attitudes. Next, we examine the household task division for stepfamilies and first marriages in every country. After the exploration of the three theoretical approaches and housework division for each country, we link both parts in a multilevel analysis. We use multilevel models (logit estimation) to examine whether the individual housework division differs between countries according to economic and cultural features. The advantage of multilevel models, with macro variables on level 2 (country level) and micro indicators on level 1 (individual level), is that the variance explained by both levels is separated (Stier, 2006). A disadvantage of a multilevel logit model is that it is impossible to determine the variance explained by the first level, since binary variables do not have real variance. It is accepted that an estimation of the variance on level 1 can be used for all models (Snijders & Bosker, 1999). Because it gives us no additional information, we look only at the variance explained on level 2. The variance partitioning coefficient (VPC) gives the percentage of variance on level 2. The differences in variance on level 2 were too small to apply random slopes. Therefore, we assume the effect of the GDP and the proportion of women ministers have a similar direction in all countries. A final remark is that we checked for high associations between the level 1 variables and between the level 2 variables in our model. However, none of the variables had to be excluded.

Five models were estimated. The first model is the intercept-only model. The initial –2LL (in the intercept-only model) is compared to the –2LL of the more complex models to determine how well these models fit (Snijders & Bosker, 1999). Adding the variable on first marriages or stepfamilies gives us the second model. In the third model, we included all individual variables on level 1. Because some variables were not relevant, we excluded them in a fourth model. In the final model, we included macro variables in addition to the individual characteristics. The multilevel models did not allow the inclusion of interaction effects to measure the differential influence of individual characteristics on the household division across both types of families.

RESULTS

Time Availability, Relative Resources, and Gender-Role Attitudes in Stepfamilies in National Context

In this section we determine whether stepfamilies differ from first marriages with respect to the dimensions of time availability, relative resources, and gender role attitudes. Tables 12.1 and 12.2 show the percentages and frequencies for the 17 ESS countries in total and separately.

The overall relative resources of women are higher in stepfamilies (Table 12.1); the proportion of women who have attained secondary education is higher, and their earnings equal or exceed the partner's income more often. Only the proportion of women with a tertiary degree is represented slightly more in the group of first marriages. In almost all of the countries educational attainment at the primary, secondary, and tertiary level differs between the two types: there are more women with primary and tertiary education completed among the first marriages; in stepfamilies, we find a higher proportion of women who have completed secondary education.

The proportion of women in stepfamilies who earn as much as their partner is higher in most countries. For the first-marriage families, the group of women who earn less than their partner is larger. It is rare for women to contribute more to the household income than their partner. In most countries, stepfamilies have higher proportions of female high earners; in four countries, we record higher proportions for the first marriages (Czech Republic, Germany, Denmark, and Norway).

The next dimension we considered is working hours. On average, women in stepfamilies work an hour longer per week than women in first marriages. However, we find contrasting patterns. In Germany, Finland,

Table 12.1

Percentage of Relative Resources

Country	Family Type	Female Educational Attainment			Relative Income		
		Primary	Secondary	Tertiary	Less	Equal	More
Austria	First marriage	15.5 (73)	79.7 (376)	4.9 (23)	73.3 (316)	15.8 (68)	10.9 (47)
	Stepfamily	23.4 (11)	68.1 (32)	8.5 (4)	54.5 (2)	27.3 (12)	18.2 (8)
Belgium	First marriage	4.4 (13)	57.0 (170)	38.6 (118)	68.8 (201)	21.9 (64)	9.2 (27)
	Stepfamily	FTL (3)	FTL (16)	FTL (8)	FTL (12)	FTL (9)	FTL (6)
Switzerland	First marriage	1.0 (4)	89.5 (375)	9.5 (40)	85.8 (351)	21.9 (64)	9.3 (38)
	Stepfamily	FTL (1)	FTL (32)	FTL (5)	FTL (26)	FTL (9)	FTL (6)
Czech Republic	First marriage	0 (0)	88.6 (468)	11.4 (60)	67.3 (341)	18.1 (92)	14.6 (74)
	Stepfamily	0 (0)	90.5 (76)	9.5 (8)	59.5 (50)	26.2 (22)	14.3 (12)
Germany	First marriage	3.0 (14)	76.4 (360)	20.6 (97)	78.9 (366)	12.1 (56)	9.1 (42)
	Stepfamily	5.6 (4)	78.9 (56)	15.5 (11)	60.0 (42)	31.4 (22)	8.57 (6)
Denmark	First marriage	1.2 (3)	61.2 (153)	37.6 (94)	56.0 (140)	28.4 (71)	15.6 (39)
	Stepfamily	0 (0)	87.0 (40)	13.0 (6)	65.2 (30)	26.1 (12)	8.7 (4)
Estonia	First marriage	0.3 (1)	61.5 (179)	38.1 (111)	63.9 (184)	20.1 (58)	16.0 (46)
	Stepfamily	0 (0)	78.6 (55)	21.4 (15)	54.3 (38)	24.3 (17)	21.4 (15)
Spain	First marriage	33.8 (116)	50.7 (174)	15.5 (53)	76.1 (261)	17.2 (59)	6.7 (23)
	Stepfamily	FTL (4)	FTL (8)	FTL (6)	FTL (9)	FTL (7)	FTL (2)
Finland	First marriage	3.9 (12)	48.2 (147)	47.8 (146)	64.5 (196)	27.0 (82)	8.6 (26)
	Stepfamily	2.3 (1)	54.5 (24)	43.2 (19)	47.7 (21)	40.9 (18)	11.4 (5)
United Kingdom	First marriage	2.5 (4)	71.2 (114)	26.2 (42)	81.1 (254)	10.9 (34)	8.0 (25)
	Stepfamily	FTL (0)	FTL (21)	FTL (9)	63.0 (34)	18.5 (10)	18.5 (10)
Greece	First marriage	31.6 (163)	59.3 (306)	9.1 (47)	77.8 (395)	15.2 (77)	7.1 (36)
	Stepfamily	FTL (5)	FTL (15)	FTL (2)	FTL (17)	FTL (3)	FTL (2)
Luxembourg	First marriage	39.1 (127)	43.4 (141)	17.5 (57)	78.7 (262)	12.0 (40)	9.3 (31)
	Stepfamily	38.9 (21)	44.4 (24)	16.7 (9)	55.4 (34)	19.6 (11)	25 (14)

Table 12.1 (Continued)

Country	Family Type	Female Educational Attainment			Relative Income		
		Primary	Secondary	Tertiary	Less	Equal	More
Norway	First marriage	0.6 (2)	50.6 (162)	48.7 (156)	66.5 (212)	23.2 (74)	10.3 (33)
	Stepfamily	0 (0)	59.7 (40)	40.3 (27)	61.2 (41)	29.9 (20)	9.0 (6)
Poland	First marriage	10.3 (53)	74.1 (380)	15.6 (80)	59.5 (303)	21.4 (109)	19.1 (97)
	Stepfamily	FTL (5)	FTL (12)	FTL (1)	FTL (8)	FTL (4)	FTL (6)
Portugal	First marriage	62.9 (214)	27.9 (95)	9.1 (31)	70.2 (238)	21.5 (73)	8.3 (28)
	Stepfamily	FTL (21)	FTL (7)	FTL (2)	FTL (19)	FTL (9)	FTL (2)
Sweden	First marriage	8.6 (22)	48.6 (124)	42.7 (109)	64.1 (164)	28.9 (74)	7.0 (18)
	Stepfamily	17.9 (14)	47.4 (37)	34.6 (27)	60.3 (47)	23.1 (18)	16.7 (13)
Slovenia	First marriage	24.7 (60)	62.5 (152)	12.7 (31)	39.7 (94)	38.0 (90)	22.4 (53)
	Stepfamily	FTL (3)	FTL (8)	FTL (2)	FTL (5)	FTL (4)	25 (3)
Total	First marriage	14.6 (883)	64.1 (3,878)	21.4 (1,293)	70.1 (4,277)	19.0 (1,159)	10.9 (666)
	Stepfamily	12.5 (95)	66.5 (504)	21.0 (159)	58.4 (454)	26.4 (205)	15.2 (118)

Note: Number of respondents shown in parentheses.
FTL = Frequency too low to interpret percentages.

Table 12.2

Percentage of Time Available and Gender-Role Attitudes

Country	Family Type	Gender Equality			Female Work Hours	
		Negative	Neutral	Positive	Mean	SD
Austria	First marriage	21.2 (99)	28.3 (132)	50.4 (235)	21.8	18.0
	Stepfamily	19.6 (9)	32.6 (15)	47.8 (22)	20.8	17.5
Belgium	First marriage	37.1 (111)	17.4 (52)	45.5 (136)	21.5	19.0
	Stepfamily	FTL (11)	FTL (5)	FTL (11)	FTL	FTL
Switzerland	First marriage	65.2 (275)	20.1 (85)	14.7 (62)	15.4	16.4
	Stepfamily	FTL (20)	FTL (12)	FTL (6)	FTL	FTL
Czech	First marriage	63.8 (337)	20.5 (108)	15.7 (83)	29.9	20.1
Republic	Stepfamily	50 (42)	20.2 (17)	29.8 (25)	26.5	21.9
Germany	First marriage	54.2 (254)	22.2 (104)	23.7 (111)	18.0	18.1
	Stepfamily	48.6 (34)	21.4 (15)	30 (21)	20.1	20.5
Denmark	First marriage	14.5 (36)	17.7 (44)	67.9 (169)	31.4	14.0
	Stepfamily	10.9 (5)	17.4 (8)	71.7 (33)	26.3	17.9
Estonia	First marriage	57.5 (164)	24.6 (70)	17.9 (51)	31.1	18.0
	Stepfamily	58.6 (41)	22.8 (16)	18.6 (13)	29.2	19.6
Spain	First marriage	59.9 (206)	18.3 (63)	21.8 (75)	15.7	19.6
	Stepfamily	FTL (9)	FTL (4)	FTL (6)	FTL	FTL
Finland	First marriage	21.6 (66)	30.8 (94)	47.5 (145)	28.4	17.7
	Stepfamily	18.2 (8)	22.7 (10)	59.1 (26)	29.4	19.4
United	First marriage	49.5 (157)	25.9 (82)	24.6 (78)	18.6	17.4
Kingdom	Stepfamily	34.5 (19)	38.2 (21)	27.3 (15)	17.2	18.2
Greece	First marriage	47.6 (246)	24.0 (124)	28.4 (147)	14.7	20.4
	Stepfamily	FTL (9)	FTL (5)	FTL (9)	FTL	FTL
Luxembourg	First marriage	66.7 (222)	16.6 (55)	16.6 (55)	16.4	17.5
	Stepfamily	64.3 (36)	14.3 (8)	21.4 (12)	22.8	22.1
Norway	First marriage	24.7 (79)	28.2 (90)	47.0 (150)	26.2	15.6
	Stepfamily	17.9 (12)	28.4 (19)	53.7 (36)	24.1	15.4
Poland	First marriage	56.4 (287)	19.8 (101)	23.8 (121)	23.3	22.5
	Stepfamily	FTL (13)	FTL (2)	FTL (1)	FTL	FTL
Portugal	First marriage	70.8 (243)	15.1 (52)	14.0 (48)	21.0	20.3
	Stepfamily	FTL (24)	FTL (3)	FTL (3)	FTL	FTL
Sweden	First marriage	17.1 (44)	27.2 (70)	55.6 (143)	31.2	15.8
	Stepfamily	11.5 (9)	28.2 (22)	60.3 (47)	31.8	16.6
Slovenia	First marriage	46.1 (111)	23.7 (57)	30.3 (73)	30.2	21.0
	Stepfamily	FTL (5)	FTL (4)	FTL (4)	FTL	FTL
Total	First marriage	49.6 (3,075)	22.3 (1,382)	28.1 (1,745)	22.54	19.6
	Stepfamily	41.0 (320)	23.6 (184)	35.4 (276)	23.81	19.8

Note: Number of respondents shown in parentheses.
FTL = Frequency too low to interpret percentages.

Luxembourg, and Sweden, the mean working hours are higher. However, in most cases the standard deviation of the working hours is as high as the mean itself, which is an indication of a strong dispersion of working hours. Therefore, it is difficult to make a conclusion about the working hours of women in stepfamilies.

With respect to gender-role attitudes, stepfamilies are more gender-equal than first marriages. Both in the total proportions and for the separate countries, there is a clear tendency of a more equal role attitude.

In conclusion, we can state that stepfamilies are more gender-equal, their relative resources are higher, and the time availability for women is lower. However, the overall picture is not the same for every country. Within countries, significant differences and reversed patterns are found. We were unable to find recurring patterns per country on the dimensions, nor was it possible to detect differences according to the welfare regime (Esping-Andersen, 1990) or other structural or cultural cleavages in Europe.

Household Task Division of Stepfamilies in National Context

Our second aim is to look at the housework between stepfamilies and first marriages. Table 12.3 shows the percentages and the number of people (in parentheses) in households with large female or male contribution. As expected, the percentages of stepfamilies and first marriages in which the

Table 12.3

Percentage of Household Task Division and the Difference between Family Types

Country	Family Type					Difference between Family Types
	Stepfamilies		First Marriage			
	Women Do More	Equal or Men Do More	Women Do More	Equal or Men Do More		
Austria	81.4 (48)	18.6 (11)	85.8 (442)	14.2 (73)		4.5
Belgium	83.3 (25)	16.7 (5)	85.4 (269)	14.6 (46)		2.1
Czech Republic	82.6 (71)	17.4 (15)	76.7 (477)	23.3 (145)		−5.9
Denmark	70.2 (33)	29.8 (14)	70.4 (183)	29.6 (77)		0.2
Estonia	74.3 (52)	25.7 (18)	81.3 (248)	18.7 (57)		7.0
Finland	67.4 (31)	32.6 (15)	71.4 (237)	28.6 (91)		4.0
Germany	81.3 (61)	18.7 (14)	85.6 (423)	14.4 (71)		4.3
Greece	FTL (32)	FTL (0)	95.2 (298)	4.8 (30)		D
Luxembourg	74.5 (41)	25.5 (14)	83.0 (289)	17.0 (59)		8.5
Norway	70.6 (48)	29.4 (20)	77.2 (254)	22.8 (75)		6.6
Poland	72.2 (13)	27.8 (5)	83.9 (475)	16.1 (91)		11.7
Portugal	FTL (32)	FTL (2)	94.6 (402)	5.4 (23)		D
Slovenia	FTL (16)	FTL (3)	81.0 (272)	19.0 (34)		D
Spain	71.4 (15)	28.6 (6)	85.3 (313)	14.7 (54)		13.9
Sweden	51.3 (40)	48.7 (38)	63.4 (166)	36.6 (96)		12.1
Switzerland	87.5 (35)	12.5 (5)	89.7 (394)	10.3 (45)		2.2
United Kingdom	75.9 (44)	24.1 (14)	81.1 (270)	18.9 (63)		5.2

Note: Number of respondents shown in parentheses.
D = The difference cannot be calculated; FTL = Frequency too low to interpret percentages.

man does an equal share or more of the housework are very low. In all countries, the majority of the families have a traditional housework pattern. When we look at the first marriages, the Scandinavian countries (Norway, Sweden, Finland, and Denmark) have the highest number of families with larger male contribution. Two southern European countries, Greece and Portugal, have the most traditional division; in more than 90% of the families, the woman does the housework.

Next, we focus on stepfamilies and their differences from first marriages. Again, the Scandinavian countries experience the most equality in housework division. To examine the difference in household task division between the two types of families, we subtracted the percentage of equal or more male contribution in stepfamilies from first marriages. In the last column of the table, positive differences mean that the household task division in stepfamilies is more equal or there is a higher male contribution. A negative remainder tells us that the household task division in stepfamilies is less equal. For some of the countries, the number of respondents was too low to calculate percentages. In all of the countries except for the Czech Republic, we found a positive difference. Although the percentages are still in favor of more female contribution, housework in stepfamilies is more often equally divided than in first marriages.

THE INFLUENCE OF INDIVIDUAL ECONOMIC RESOURCES AND CULTURAL VALUES ON HOUSEHOLD TASK DIVISION

In this section, we explain the differences between stepfamilies and first marriages by looking at individual economic and cultural features. In Table 12.4 the second and the third multilevel models are shown. Model 2 displays the intercept and the effect of living in a first marriage or a stepfamily on the household task division. Living in a stepfamily gives the respondents 1.3 times more chance of having an equal division or more male task execution. This is in line with our expectations and the results in Table 12.1.

Adding the individual variables to the model implies that we can examine the influence of cultural and economic indicators separately. The first thing to be noticed is that the Exp(B) of the stepfamily category decreases but is still significant. This means that a part of the difference between the family types can be explained by individual characteristics. The variance to be explained on level 2 decreases by entering the level 1 variables (from 10.5% to 7.3%), indicating that part of the country differences can be attributed to the different individual characteristics within countries.

None of the cultural variables seems to be relevant in explaining the difference. Religiosity has no significant effect on the household task division, and neither does the attitude toward gender equality. People who have

Table 12.4

Multilevel Results for Individual Effects on the Household Task Division

Individual Effects	Model 2 Exp(B) (*p*-value)	Model 3 Exp(B) (*p*-value)
Intercept	0.193 (.000)	0.136 (.000)
Stepfamily (0 = first marriage)	1.346 (.002)	1.275 (.002)
Religiosity		0.991 (.548)
Gender equality—negative (0 = neutral)		0.979 (.849)
Gender equality—positive (0 = neutral)		1.265 (.062)
Working hours, man		0.974 (.000)
Working hours, woman		1.022 (.000)
Education level, man—secondary (0 = primary)		1.179 (.089)
Education level, man—tertiary (0 = primary)		1.348 (.001)
Education level, woman—secondary (0 = primary)		1.402 (.001)
Education level, woman—tertiary (0 = primary)		1.435 (.021)
Income, woman—equal (0 = less)		1.745 (.000)
Income, woman—more (0 = less)		2.077 (.000)
Young child—3 to 12 years old (0 = 0–3)		1.091 (.627)
Young child—over 12 years old (0 = 0–3)		0.947 (.731)
Urbanization—town (0 = countryside)		1.131 (.317)
Urbanization—city (0 = countryside)		1.023 (.897)
−2LL	4816.9	3608.09
VPC	10.5%	7.3%

Note: Model 2 (intercept-only): −2LL = 4835.55; VPC = Variance partitioning coefficient (10.9%).

positive attitudes toward gender equality have a higher chance of living in an equally divided household, but the significance level slightly exceeds the alpha level of .05 (*p* = .062). The economic variables are much more important. The working hours of both men and women influence the task division. Although the effects are very small, a rise in working hours of men implies a higher chance of having a more traditional task division. If women work more hours, the chances of a balanced household task division are slightly higher. A higher education for men and women results in higher odds on a more equal division. Women have almost 1.5 times more chance of having a partner who does an equal amount of housework or more if they attained a tertiary-level diploma. This also holds for highly educated men. The largest effect is to be found with the relative income of the woman compared to the man. If she earns an equal share or more than the man, the chances for equal division of household labor are nearly doubled. Urbanization and having young children have no influence.

The conclusion we can make is that the economic variables are the most important in explaining the difference between stepfamilies and first marriages in the division of household tasks. A higher education, more working hours for the woman, fewer working hours for the man, and a higher relative share in the household income are significant elements in understanding the household task division of stepfamilies.

DOES THE NATIONAL CONTEXT MATTER?

Model 5 adds the country-level variables to explain possible differences between countries. To insert the country variables on level 2, we deleted the nonsignificant level 1 indicators. Because there were too many categorical variables in Model 3, it was impossible to fit the level 2 model without removing others (the model no longer converges with too many variables). In Model 4 we therefore reestimated the values for level 1. The effects remained almost the same. Table 12.5 shows that there is hardly an improvement of the model when the level 2 terms are included. Still, both the macro variables are significant. A higher GDP in the country and more female ministers give a very slight increase in the chances of having an equal or more male task division. The estimations approach the value of no influence.

From the results in Table 12.5, we can infer that country differences are of much less importance than individual differences. Even though there are some contrasts between Scandinavian countries, southern countries, and the others in Table 12.3, they hardly contribute to a multilevel approach.

Table 12.5
Multilevel Results for Individual and Country Effects on Household Task Division

Individual Effects	Model 4 Exp(B) (p-value)	Model 5 Exp(B) (p-value)
Intercept	0.134 (.000)	0.061 (.000)
Stepfamily (0 = First marriage)	1.296 (.004)	1.292 (.003)
Gender equality—negative (0 = neutral)	0.972 (.799)	0.979 (.843)
Gender equality—positive (0 = neutral)	1.271 (.056)	1.267 (.062)
Working hours, man	0.975 (.000)	0.975 (.000)
Working hours, woman	1.022 (.000)	1.023 (.000)
Education level, man—secondary (0 = primary)	1.197 (.053)	1.201 (.048)
Education level, man—tertiary (0 = primary)	1.370 (.000)	1.362 (.000)
Education level, woman—secondary (0 = primary)	1.412 (.000)	1.427 (.000)
Education level, woman—tertiary (0 = primary)	1.451 (.015)	1.453 (.015)
Income, woman—equal (0 = less)	1.738 (.000)	1.741 (.000)
Income, woman—more (0 = less)	2.050 (.000)	2.066 (.000)
GDP		1.010 (.028)
Wommin		1.017 (.005)
$-2LL_0$	3622.64	3622.53
VPC	7.5%	4.4%

Note: Model 1 (intercept-only): $-2LL_0 = 4835.55$.
GDP = Gross domestic product; VCP = Variance partitioning coefficient (10.9%); Wommin = Female ministers.

Neither is the economic welfare of a country nor the political power of women of major influence to the process of household task division.

CONCLUSION

Stepfamily couples differ in household task division from first marriages in most European countries. In general, the overall household task division, independent of family type, is clearly less traditional in Scandinavian countries and more traditional in southern European countries. We see that in all countries, except for the Czech Republic, stepfamilies show a more equal task division. With this study on recent and representative European data (ESS), we have been able to confirm earlier findings on national surveys: that in stepfamilies the balance of power is more equal than in traditional families.

How can we explain these findings? To meet the increasing (policy) importance of the work-life balance and the variety of family forms in Western societies, many scholars have studied household task division over the past decades. Much is known about the gendered division of housework, but the research focused mostly on married couples. Only recently has the task division of cohabiting couples and stepfamilies become a subject of study. Nevertheless, we have a substantive body of literature at our disposal on factors that influence the segregation of housework, on the micro and the macro levels. Our goal was to combine the micro and macro perspectives. Therefore, we merged two bodies of literature. On the one hand, we adopted traditional research on the effects of individuals' and partners' characteristics on household labor division (time availability, relative resources, and gender-role attitudes). These include macro-level factors such as women-friendly policies and equal gender norms. On the other hand, we considered theoretical insights on the role-based differences between first marriages and stepfamilies. The mixture suggested two main approaches of housework task division: an economic and a cultural approach.

First, we looked for possible differences in economic and cultural characteristics between stepfamilies and first marriages. For most countries, we found that stepfamilies show more equal gender attitudes and that women in stepfamilies are slightly higher educated, have a higher relative income, and work more hours compared to women in first-marriage families. However, it is clear that there are several country differences.

The next step in explaining household task segregation is to use a multivariate model to determine whether these characteristics have an influence. The results of our models show that economic variables are the most important in explaining the difference between stepfamilies and first marriages in the division of household tasks. Relative resources and time availability concepts are significant elements in understanding the household task division of stepfamilies. Higher earnings, more working hours, and a slightly higher education result in women doing less housework in stepfamilies. Even though we expected the attitude toward gender equality to have an important effect, in the multivariate model it hardly contributed. Although national characteristics such as GDP and the number of female ministers do show a (small) effect on the household task distribution, country characteristics seem to be of less importance.

These findings indicate that the division of household tasks is primarily the subject of decision processes within the family that are affected by intertwining economic circumstances, such as partners' time availability within the household, the share of income contribution, and the educational level. So it seems that the structural differences between first-marriage families and stepfamilies are the main cause of the different domestic divisions of labor, not the cultural preferences. We are aware of the limitations of the measurement instrument of gender-role attitudes. Yet the results clearly point in the direction of the importance of economic resources.

For future research on stepfamilies, we recommend a longitudinal or retrospective perspective. If we want to learn more about the household task division in stepfamilies, information about the task division and economic and cultural characteristics in former relationships might give us new insights. How the division differs between types of relationships can obviously benefit from life course research. About one thing we can be certain: Stepfamilies have a more balanced housework division than first marriages, and therefore are more similar to cohabiting relationships than to first marriages. Maybe the current household task division of the stepfamily is becoming the household task division of the classic family in the future.

REFERENCES

Batalova, J. A., & Cohen, P. N. (2002). Premarital cohabitation and housework: Couples in cross-national perspective. *Journal of Marriage and the Family, 64,* 743–755.

Baxter, J. (1997). Gender equality and participation in housework: A cross-national perspective. *Journal of Comparative Family Studies, 3,* 220–247.

Beck, U. (1994). *Risk society: Towards a new modernity.* London: Sage.

Becker, G. (1981). *A treatise on the family.* Cambridge, MA: Harvard University Press.

Berk, S. F. (1985). *The gender factory: The apportionment of work in American households.* New York: Plenum Press.

Bianchi, S. M., Milkie, M. A., Sayer, L. C., & Robinson, J. P. (2000). Is anyone doing the housework? Trends in the gender division of household labor. *Social Forces, 79,* 191–228.

Bittman, E., England, P., Sayer, L., Folbre, N., & Matheson, G. (2003). When does gender trump money? Bargaining and time in household work. *American Journal of Sociology, 109,* 186–214.

Blossfeld, H.-P., & Drobnic, S. (2001). *Careers of couples in contemporary societies: From male breadwinner to dual earner families.* Oxford: Oxford University Press.

Blumberg, R. L. (1984). A general theory of gender stratification. *Sociological Theory, 2,* 23–101.

Cherlin, A. (1978). Remarriage as an incomplete institution. *American Journal of Sociology, 84,* 634–650.

Coleman, M., Ganong, L., & Fine, M. (2000). Reinvestigating remarriage: Another decade of progress. *Journal of Marriage and the Family, 62,* 1288–1307.

Coltrane, S. (2000). Research on household labor: Modeling and measuring the social embeddedness of routine family work. *Journal of Marriage and the Family, 62,* 1208–1264.

Coltrane, S., & Ishii-Kuntz, M. (1992). Men's housework: A life course perspective. *Journal of Marriage and the Family, 54,* 43–57.

Cooke, L. P. (2004). The gendered division of labor and family outcomes in Germany. *Journal of Marriage and the Family, 66,* 1246–1259.

Demo, D. H., & Acock, A. C. (1993). Family diversity and the division of domestic labor: How much have things really changed? *Family Relations, 42,* 323–331.

Directorate General of Human Rights. (2006). *Steering Committee for the Equality between Women and Men: Sex-disaggregated statistics on the participation of women and men in political and public decision-making in Council of Europe member states, situation as at 1 September 2005.* Strasbourg, France: Council of Europe.

Esping-Andersen, G. (1990). *The three worlds of welfare capitalism.* Princeton, NJ: Princeton University Press.

Fuwa, M. (2004). Macro-level gender inequality and the division of household labor in 22 countries. *American Sociological Review, 69,* 751–767.

Ganong, L. H., & Coleman, M. (2004). *Stepfamily relationships: Development, dynamics, and interventions.* New York: Kluwer Academic/Plenum Press.

Geist, C. (2005). The welfare state and the home: Regime differences in the domestic division of labour. *European Sociological Review, 21,* 23–41.

Goldscheider, F. K., & Waite, L. J. (1991). *New families, no families? The transformation of the American home.* Berkeley: University of California Press.

Gupta, S. (1999). The effects of transitions in marital status on men's performance of housework. *Journal of Marriage and the Family, 61,* 700–711.

Hook, J. L. (2006). Care in context: Men's unpaid work in 20 countries, 1965–2003. *American Sociological Review, 71,* 639–660.

Inglehart, R. (1990). *Culture shift in advanced industrial countries.* Princeton, NJ: Princeton University Press.

Ishii-Kuntz, M., & Coltrane, S. (1992). Remarriage, stepparenting and household labor. *Journal of Family Issues, 13,* 215–233.

Kalleberg, A. L., & Rosenfeld, R. A. (1990). Work in the family and in the labor market: A cross-national, reciprocal analysis. *Journal of Marriage and the Family, 52,* 331–346.

Kamo, Y. (1994). Division of household work in the United States and Japan. *Journal of Family Issues, 3,* 348–378.

Kane, E. W., & Sanchez, L. (1994). Family status and criticism of gender inequality at home and at work. *Social Forces, 4,* 1079–1102.

Koelet, S. (2005). *Standvastige verschillen: Een analyse van theoretische benaderingen over de verdeling van het huishoudelijke werk van vrouwen en mannen op basis van tijdsbudgetonderzoek* [Steady differences: An analysis of theoretical perspectives on the division of household tasks between women and men, based on time research]. Unpublished doctoral dissertation, Vrij Universiteit, Brussels, Belgium.

Lesthaeghe, R. (1995). The second demographic transition in Western countries: An interpretation. In K. O. Mason & A.-M. Jensen (Eds.), *Gender and change in industrialized countries* (pp. 17–62). Oxford: Clarendon Press.

Lesthaeghe, R., & Neels, K. (2002). From the first to the second demographic transition: An interpretation of the spatial continuity of demographic innovation in France, Belgium, and Switzerland. *European Journal of Population, 18,* 325–360.

Nordenmark, M. (2004). Does gender ideology explain differences between countries regarding the involvement of women and of men in paid and unpaid work? *International Journal of Social Welfare, 13,* 233–243.

Orloff, A. S. (1993). Gender and the social rights of citizenship: State policies and gender relations in comparative perspective. *American Sociological Review, 58,* 303–328.

Pyke, K., & Coltrane, S. (1996). Entitlement, obligation, and gratitude in family work. *Journal of Family Issues, 17,* 60–82.

Rindfuss, R. R., Brewster, K. L., & Kavee, A. L. (1996). Women, work, and children: Behavioral and attitudinal change in the United States. *Population and Development Review, 22,* 457–482.

Sainsbury, D. (1994). *Gendering welfare states.* Thousand Oaks, CA: Sage.

Sanchez, L. (1993). Women's power and the gendered division of domestic labor in the third world. *Gender and Society, 3,* 434–459.

Sanchez, L. (1994). Marital resources, family structure resources and husband's housework participation: A cross-national comparison. *Journal of Family Issues, 3,* 379–402.

Shelton, B. A., & John, D. (1993). Does marital status make a difference? Housework among married and cohabiting men and women. *Journal of Family Issues, 14,* 401–420.

Shelton, B. A., & John, D. (1996). The division of household labor. *Annual Review of Sociology, 22,* 299–322.

Snijders, T., & Bosker, R. (1999). *Multilevel analysis: An introduction to basic and advanced multilevel modeling.* London: Sage.

South, S. J., & Spitze, G. (1994). Housework in marital and nonmarital households. *American Sociological Review, 59,* 327–347.

Stier, H. (2006, November 3–4). *Conceptualization and measurements of institutional contexts: A review.* Paper presented at the second Workshop on the Economic and Social Consequences of Partnership Dissolution, Cologne, Germany.

Sullivan, O. (1997). The division of housework among "remarried" couples. *Journal of Family Issues, 18,* 205–223.

Treas, J., & Widmer, E. D. (2000). Married women's employment over the life course: Attitudes in cross-national perspective. *Social Forces, 4,* 1409–1436.

Van de Kaa, D. J. (1994). The second demographic transition revisited: Theories and expectations. In H. Beets, H. van den Brekel, R. Cliquet, G. Dooghe, & J. De Jong Gierveld (Eds.), *Population and family in the low countries 1993: Late fertility and other current issues* (pp. 81–126). Amsterdam: Swets and Zeitlinger.

West, C., & Zimmerman, D. C. (1987). Doing gender. *Gender and Society, 2*, 125–151.

CHAPTER 13

Communication in Stepfamilies: Stressors and Resilience

TAMARA D. AFIFI

THE INCREASING number of divorces, remarriages, and stepfamilies over the past 4 decades, combined with the complexity of the family dynamics created by these changes and their implications for families, has given rise to volumes of research on the effects of divorce and remarriage on children and adults in the United States and other Western countries (see Coleman, Ganong, & Fine, 2000; Dunn, 2004; Pryor & Rodgers, 2001). In particular, researchers have devoted a considerable amount of attention to studying the effects of divorce and remarriage on children's well-being and adjustment (e.g., Amato, 2001; Amato & Keith, 1991; Amato & Sobolewski, 2001; Booth & Amato, 2001; Rodgers & Rose, 2002; White & Gilbreth, 2001). Other research has focused on the psychological and relational consequences of divorce and remarriage for marital relationships (e.g., Kurdek & Fine, 1991), parent-child relationships (e.g., Afifi & Schrodt, 2003a; Lye, 1996; Taanila, Laitinen, Moilanen, & Jarvelin, 2002), and stepparent-stepchild relationships (e.g., Henry & Lovelace, 1995).

Researchers have made an important shift from a predominant focus on the individual to also looking at the different dyads in the stepfamily. Family systems theory (Minuchin, 1974; Satir, 1972) has become a theoretical hallmark for scholars interested in understanding the interplay of stepfamily relationships. Its basic tenets have provided researchers with the foundation to examine how stepfamily members' behaviors influence one another and the stepfamily as a whole. The notion of boundaries, or rules and norms that define appropriate behavior and membership within and outside of the family (Broderick, 1994), has also become a focus of much of the stepfamily literature (e.g., Stewart, 2005; Taanila et al., 2002). For instance, researchers have now documented quite extensively the difficulties that can ensue when triangulation, or loyalty conflicts that result when a covert coalition is formed uniting two family members against another family member, exists in a stepfamily (Baxter, Braithwaite, & Bryant, 2006; Coleman, Fine, Ganong, Downs, & Pauk, 2001; Schrodt & Afifi, in press). Scholars have noted the challenges that result when the boundaries between custodial parents and children become blurred after a divorce and children become their parents' social support system (emotional parentification) and/or take on additional roles and household tasks that were once assumed by the parent (instrumental parentification; Alexander, 2003; Biblarz & Gottainer, 2000; Jurkovic, Thirkeild, & Morrell, 2001). In particular, researchers have noted the difficulties that stepfathers experience when attempting to enter a family in which cohesive and relatively impermeable boundaries have been created around the custodial mother and her children (e.g., Baxter et al., 2006; Coleman et al., 2001; Golish, 2003). In this sense, scholars have begun to examine the constellation of relationships that constitute stepfamilies and how family members' behaviors and actions affect one another.

Researchers have also made significant advances in understanding the processual nature of divorce, remarriage, and stepfamily formation. They have emphasized the importance of longitudinal work for studying these phenomena as processes. Perhaps one of the most important discoveries in the divorce literature is that it may not be the divorce per se that is harmful to children's well-being as much as the degree of interparental conflict between parents and the extent to which children recognize the conflict and become enmeshed in it over time (Amato & Afifi, 2006; Amato & Sobolewski, 2001; Booth & Amato, 2001; Jekielek, 1998). Another primary finding has been that children vary considerably in how they respond to divorce and remarriage (Hetherington, 1993, 1999). Some children suffer considerable long-term effects of divorce; others experience improved well-being because they were removed from a conflict-ridden home and/or have a loving relationship with their new stepparent. The results also show more dramatic short-term effects of divorce on children, but that many of these effects dissipate over time (see Amato, 2001; Amato & Keith, 1991). Likewise, research has shown that it takes several years for a stepfamily to form and for stepfamily members to build close relationships (Bray & Harvey, 1995; Hetherington, 1999). Children may still be grieving the end of their parents' marriage and their previous family form when their parents are ready to get remarried (Ganong & Coleman, 1994). Unlike first-marriage families, stepfamilies lack a history from which to develop their relationships and must negotiate the family rituals, relationships, and routines in their "new" family with those of their "old" family (Braithwaite, Baxter, & Harper, 1998).

Although researchers studying stepfamilies have been incredibly productive and important advancements in the understanding of stepfamily life have been made, additional research is necessary that more closely examines the systemic and multifaceted nature of stepfamily life and the factors that promote healthy stepfamily functioning. Researchers often conceptualize stepfamilies from a systems perspective but fail to operationalize the relationships within them in a concurrent manner. For example, researchers might discuss the difficulty that stepparents experience attempting to bridge a preexisting bond between the custodial parent and a child. However, they might interview or survey only the child in the family instead of gathering information from multiple family members (e.g., the custodial parent, the child, and the stepparent or the stepparent-stepchild dyad). Gathering the perspectives of multiple family members is important, in part, because research suggests that family members often have divergent perspectives on the behaviors and relationships in their stepfamily (Coleman et al., 2001; Golish, 2003). Of course, many scholars do not integrate fully a systems approach in their work because it is time-consuming to collect the sample, very complex to analyze, and difficult to understand and report in a parsimonious manner. Nevertheless, recent advancements in multilevel modeling make the complexity and layers of relationships in stepfamilies easier to analyze and interpret.

As Coleman et al. (2000) contend, even though recent research has provided more complex conceptualizations of stepfamilies and has employed more sophisticated methodological designs and statistical techniques, the research still tends to adopt a deficit approach to stepfamilies. That is, researchers have a tendency to examine the behaviors, actions, and processes that are problematic in stepfamilies, especially in comparison to first-marriage families, at the expense of the behaviors, actions, and processes that foster growth and resilience (Coleman et al., 2000; Golish, 2003; Kelley, 1992; Visher & Visher, 1993). For instance, researchers know quite a bit about the fragility of the stepparent-stepchild relationship and the factors that contribute to it, especially in comparison to "blood" or "original" family relationships, but they still know very little about the factors that facilitate strong stepparent-stepchild relationships. An extensive body of research is available that examines the impact of the stepfamily structure on children's well-being compared to first-marriage families and single-parent families (e.g., Barrett & Turner, 2005; MacDonald & DeMaris, 1995). As a whole, these findings paint a rather bleak picture of stepfamily life, with children from stepfamilies fairing consistently worse than children from first-marriage families and the stepparent-stepchild relationship as one that is rife with problems.

Although it is true that stepfamilies face a considerable amount of stress in their development, the current research does not capture adequately the stepfamily as a social unit and the behavioral processes that contribute to the successful orientation of stepfamily life. As Visher and Visher (1993) pointed out, researchers need to examine more within-group variance by adopting a "normative-adaptive" approach to their research. That is, scholars should examine the factors that make some stepfamilies function better than others. What behaviors help create healthy stepfamily relationships? One way that scholars have attempted to answer this question is by applying a "risk and resiliency" approach to their research (see Hetherington, 1999; Kelly & Emery, 2003; Rodgers & Rose, 2002). In essence, scholars attempt to understand the factors that place children and adults at risk after a divorce and remarriage, as well as the factors that protect them and potentially even make them stronger. Assuming such an approach may shed light on why there is so much variation in children's responses to divorce and remarriage.

The purpose of this chapter is to identify some of the behavioral patterns that researchers have discovered about stepfamily relationships and how the research can be advanced by conceptualizing stepfamilies from a holistic perspective—a perspective that includes the notion of process, risk and resiliency, and systems dynamics. More specifically, I focus on the interpersonal behaviors, or interpersonal communication, in stepfamilies that foster and inhibit the development and maintenance of stepfamily relationships.

Why focus on interpersonal communication in stepfamilies? Communication is the embodiment of a family because it is the primary way through which meaning (or reality) is created and maintained among its members (Fitzpatrick & Ritchie, 1993). Interpersonal communication is also a primary way that scholars are able to understand and analyze the complexity of relationships in stepfamilies and the interdependency of people's behaviors. Communication includes "any instance of the creation of symbols in some medium in such a fashion that other people can notice the symbols and make sense of them" (p. 568). Within a stepfamily, communication scholars are interested primarily in the verbal and nonverbal messages among members and the people outside of the stepfamily that influence them. They are also interested in the cognitive processes by which the messages are created and interpreted and the environmental and societal factors that shape their meaning. In the sections that follow, I examine some of the research on communication and interpersonal relationships in stepfamilies and the implications that it can have for understanding stepfamilies from a holistic perspective.

THE PROCESSUAL AND MULTIDIMENSIONAL NATURE OF STEPFAMILIES

Most research has tended to view stepfamilies as equivalent to one another and as developing along one linear, developmental path toward becoming a family (Braithwaite, Olson, Golish, Soukup, & Turman, 2001). Scholars tend to depict the formation of stepfamily relationships as a unitary model based on prescriptive, chronological stages (Braithwaite et al., 2001). As Braithwaite et al. argue, these developmental stage models are limiting because they are prescriptive in nature, oversimplify the developmental processes of stepfamilies, and fail to recognize the processual and diverse nature of stepfamily development. In response to the limitations of stage models, Baxter, Braithwaite, and Nicholson (1999) developed a process view of stepfamily formation. They interviewed stepparents and stepchildren, asking them to reflect back on the first 4 years of the development of their stepfamily. They identified five developmental trajectories that the stepfamilies followed in their development: accelerated, prolonged, stagnating, declining, and high-amplitude turbulent. The different pathways depicted the changes in the levels at which the family members "felt like a family." The accelerated trajectory reflected intense movement toward feeling like a family, whereas the prolonged family felt like a family, but it took them longer to reach that point. The declining trajectory began with stronger feelings of cohesion, but this dropped dramatically by the end of the 4-year period. The stagnating group was consistently low in their feeling like a family throughout the 4 years. Finally, the high-amplitude group was characterized by sporadic increases and decreases in their levels of feeling like a family. As this study by Baxter et al. illustrates, stepfamilies do not follow a single trajectory in their development as a stepfamily. These authors contend that scholars need to better differentiate the paths that stepfamilies take in the process of becoming a family. Stepfamilies have different trajectories and timetables for development, with corresponding levels of functioning.

Using the same data, Braithwaite et al. (2001) took the five trajectories developed by Baxter et al. (1999) and examined how the stepfamilies experiencing the different developmental trajectories discursively represented the issues they were facing in their development. Braithwaite et al. discovered that issues of boundaries, solidarity, and willingness to adapt to change surfaced in all of the family types. Applying more of a risk and resiliency approach, the authors noted that families that were successful in their ability to "feel like a family" were able to develop and maintain flexible boundaries between households. Families that were unable to successfully negotiate their family ties had boundaries that "became extremely rigid and impermeable, demarcating bloodlines and generations" (Braithwaite et al., 2001, p. 241). More specifically, parents and children from their original family had a tendency to align with one another, creating distance from their new stepfamily members. They also found that families that let their bonds and roles within the family develop naturally, instead of adhering to the "myth of instant love" that Visher and Visher (1993) describe, were better able to establish close relationships over time. Finally, they discovered that families that were open and willing to confront conflict directly and that were willing to adapt to change were able to manage the uncertainty and fluctuation of emotions that were associated with developing a stepfamily.

Other research (e.g., Schrodt, 2006) has distinguished among various stepfamily types and made important comparisons in their communication patterns and levels of functioning. Because stepfamilies are often very complex in the configuration of their relationships and the stressors they face, some researchers have attempted to simplify or deconstruct them along various relational dimensions to make them more understandable and to better predict stepfamily functioning. For example, Schrodt surveyed 586 stepchildren and established a typology of five types of stepfamilies: bonded, functional, ambivalent, evasive, and conflicted. The stepchildren in the bonded and functional stepfamily types reported less dissension and avoidance and more involvement and expressiveness than stepchildren in the other three family types. They also reported experiencing fewer adverse mental health symptoms than stepchildren from the three family types experiencing more difficulty adapting. The family members in the bonded and functional stepfamilies were also perceived by the stepchildren to be more communicatively competent than the family members in the other stepfamily types.

Still other scholars (e.g., Golish, 2003; Kelley, 1992; Knaub, Hanna, & Stinnett, 1984; Schultz, Schultz, & Olson, 1991) have attempted to identify relational processes in stepfamilies according to the perceived strength of the stepfamily. For instance, Golish interviewed stepchildren, parents, and stepparents from 30 stepfamilies and found that the families faced similar challenges, regardless of their strength. However, how they managed these challenges, particularly how they communicated about them, differed according to the strength of the family. Families that were considered strong tended to use more skills, such as open communication, family problem solving, humor, empathy, and adaptability, compared to families that had greater difficulty adjusting to stepfamily life. Similarly, the stepfamily members that Kelley interviewed mentioned that the strengths of their family were flexibility, respect, patience, support systems, communication, fun, and humor. When Knaub et al. asked closed-ended questions in their study, they discovered that strong stepfamilies perceived that they had support from others, were secure financially, and did not seek outside professional help. However, when these researchers asked open-ended questions, stepfamilies responded that the characteristics of their strength were communication, sensitivity, support, security, flexibility, family solidarity, and compromise. As these studies suggest, communication as a whole appears to be vital to the creation and maintenance of a strong stepfamily.

There are also patterns of relating that distinguish "dysfunctional" stepfamilies from "functional" stepfamilies. Dysfunctional stepfamilies or stepfamilies that have sought clinical treatment have been found to have less involvement by the stepparent, more communication patterns that exclude the stepparent from the family, and more parent-child coalitions than step-families that have not sought clinical treatment (Anderson & White, 1986; Bray, 1992). Clinical stepfamilies also tend to have more negative conflict patterns, less problem solving, more marital difficulties, more unrealistic expectations, and less cohesiveness than nonclinical stepfamilies (Anderson & White, 1986; Bray, 1992, 1999; Brown, Green, & Druckman, 1990). As Bray (1999) notes, clinical stepfamilies also have more destructive (e.g., coercion, conflict, hostility, dogmatism) and less constructive (e.g., warmth, under-standing, other-orientation, responsiveness, affection) parent-child interac-tion than nonclinical stepfamilies. Although many stepfamilies that have not sought counseling may be considered dysfunctional and many stepfa-milies that have sought counseling may be functional, the differences in communication patterns between clinical and nonclinical samples are quite consistent across studies.

The sheer complexity of the composition of stepfamilies may also influ-ence the relationships within them. Research has found that individuals in complex stepfamilies (where both spouses have children from a previous relationship) tend to report greater stress than individuals in simple stepfa-milies (where one spouse has a child or children from a previous relation-ship; e.g., Clingempeel, 1981; Pasley & Ihinger-Tallman, 1984; Schultz et al., 1991). Schultz et al. found that couples in complex stepfamilies reported more stressors, fewer strengths, and less positive agreement about the stres-sors and strengths in their family than couples in simple stepfamilies. In particular, couples in simple stepfamilies had significantly more strengths in the categories of conflict resolution and communication than couples in complex stepfamilies. As the name implies, complex stepfamilies often face more complexities in parenting and managing boundaries within and out-side the family than simple stepfamilies because each relationship brings with it a different set of expectations, standards, rituals, and roles (Schultz et al., 1991).

Even though scholars have begun to move away from family structure as the primary indicator of family functioning in favor of family processes, family structure can still influence the communication patterns in stepfami-lies. Different stepfamilies also have different patterns of behavior and ways of relating that influence the trajectory of their development. Examin-ing variance within stepfamilies may help explain why stepfamilies, and their individual members, function at different levels.

WITHIN-FAMILY DIFFERENCES AND MULTIPLE POINTS OF VIEW

Just as there are differences among stepfamilies in terms of their relational patterns and functioning, there are also differences among individuals within the same stepfamily. As Dunn (2004) points out, children within the same family often report vastly different ways of coping with their parents' divorce and remarriage. In fact, she notes that there is greater variance within stepfamilies in terms of how children adapt to their parents' divorce than there is across families. Siblings from the same stepfamily often cope with the divorce and remarriage differently. For instance, Hetherington (1988) has found in her research that siblings and stepsiblings respond differently to their stepfamily environment and that their responses also vary by the sex of the child. Parents may also communicate with their children in different ways, influencing why children within the same family experience their relationship with their parents differently. For instance, O'Connor, Dunn, Jenkins, and Rasbash (2006) surveyed and interviewed 404 children in 171 families; the sample consisted of equal numbers of first-marriage, single-mother, stepfamily, and complex stepmother stepfamilies. They found substantial within-family variation in parent-child relationship quality, with the greatest variation in complex stepmother families. The largest proportion of this variance could be accounted for by differential treatment by the parents due to differences in the siblings' biological relatedness to them and other variables that were individually related (e.g., child aggressiveness). As these authors point out, many of their results support the family systems perspective, that there are family-level processes that influence the patterns of relationships within families.

Individuals' perceptions about the difficulties and strengths within their family also depend on their orientation or standpoint within the family. For instance, children, stepparents, and parents may have different perspectives on their stepfamily because of their position in the family and history with one another. Golish (2003) found that, compared to parents, stepchildren tended to have a more pessimistic view of the state of their stepfamily. The stepparent's viewpoint was also more closely aligned to the stepchild's than was the view of the parent, who had a more optimistic perception of the problems in the family. Kurdek and Fine (1991) also discovered that mothers had a more optimistic perspective of their stepfamily and reported greater satisfaction with the (step)parent-child relationships than did stepfathers. Parents may be inclined to downplay potential problem areas in their stepfamily, and thus refrain from talking about them, for fear of conflict (Ganong & Coleman, 1994) and in hopes of a brighter future (Bray & Kelly, 1998; Golish, 2003). To acknowledge and talk about the extent of the problems in one's new family may prompt a fear that the marriage is in jeopardy, even if it is not. Children also tend to report that their parent discloses more negative information about their former spouse to their children than the parent thinks he or she does (Afifi, Coho, & McManus, 2008; Afifi, McManus, Hutchinson, & Baker, 2007). These findings are not surprising, given that children, in general, tend to have more negative interpretations of their parental relationship than their parents have (see Sillars, Koerner, & Fitzpatrick, 2005).

Different perceptions of family relationships and family functioning are a natural part of family life and also may be the result of personality differences of individual family members. However, perceptions that are too disparate may signal that family members' needs are not being met or that conflicts are left unresolved, which can produce dissatisfaction (Coleman et al., 2001). For instance, Coleman et al. found that when they interviewed multiple family members from the same family, many of them had different perceptions of the same conflict episodes. When family members let the conflict fester and were unable or unwilling to assume each other's perspectives and compromise, the conflicts were left unresolved, producing further division among them. Fine, Coleman, and Ganong (1998) discovered that there was considerable variability in how stepfamily members perceived the role of the stepparent in the family. Stepchildren were more likely than the parents or stepparents to indicate that they preferred the stepparent to function as a friend rather than as a parental figure. In addition, they found that the *consistency* among family members in their perceptions of the stepparent role was positively associated with stepfamily members' interpersonal adjustment. Banker and Gaertner (1998) found that the more stepchildren were likely to perceive their stepfamily as one group, the more this was associated with perceptions of stepfamily harmony. Therefore, the degree to which family members share similar perspectives about what their family should be like, the roles that each family member should assume, and how they should communicate with one another may influence adaptation.

Individuals within the same family may even differ in their perceptions of who is considered a part of their family. That is, people may disagree on what constitutes their family boundaries or who is considered "in" and "out" of their stepfamily (Braithwaite et al., 2001; Caughlin et al., 2000; Schmeeckle, Giarrusso, Feng, & Bengtson, 2006). When individuals feel closer to someone, especially when stepchildren feel closer to their stepparent, they are more likely to consider that person to be an integral part of their family (Schmeeckle et al., 2006). Family members often use communication as a way to demarcate boundaries within their family (Baxter et al., 2006; Coleman et al., 2001; Golish & Caughlin, 2002). For instance, stepchildren may avoid talking about certain topics with their stepparent as a way to signal to the stepparent that he or she is not yet a part of the family. Loyalty conflicts can ensue when parents and children are confused or disagree about how much the stepparent should be integrated into the family (Coleman et al., 2001).

In addition to creating and maintaining boundaries from a family systems theory perspective, family members also foster what Petronio (1991,

2000, 2002) refers to as "privacy boundaries." Privacy boundaries are meta-phorical boundaries that people place around themselves, the relationships within the family, and the family itself in an effort to control personal infor-mation that they deem private (Petronio, 2002). The more that people trust others and feel close to them, the more likely they are to create open or more permeable privacy boundaries (Petronio, 2002). Therefore, when stepfamily members trust each other and feel a sense of solidarity, they are more likely to disclose personal information to one another. However, significant life events such as divorce and remarriage can alter the rules for privacy boun-daries within families (Petronio, 2002). For example, parents have to adjust and align their privacy rules with one another after divorce so that they re-frain from denigrating one another's character in front of their children (Afifi, 2003). When one or both of the parents violate these rules or disagree about them, it can create conflict and stress within various levels of the fam-ily system. Likewise, the parents (custodial and noncustodial) and steppar-ents need to be in agreement about the privacy rules within and across families.

As the aforementioned research illustrates, it is important for researchers and practitioners to consider multiple perspectives within the stepfamily. The congruence or incongruence in family members' perspectives on their family may influence their ability to adapt to divorce and remarriage. Although congruence in family members' perspectives about their family may not be a desirable goal, recognizing that these differences exist can pro-vide additional information about the family's ability to adapt to stepfamily life.

"Relation-Shipping" in Stepfamilies

Although research has been conducted on stepfamilies as a whole, much of the relational research on stepfamilies has focused on various dyads (e.g., parent-child, stepparent-stepchild) and the communication processes that characterize them. Within this research, most of the emphasis resides on the problems, stress, and conflict in these relationships. For example, as Coleman et al. (2001) contend, stepfamily researchers and clinicians assume that conflict is ubiquitous in stepfamilies and that it is always destructive, inhibiting stepfamily relationships from developing. As these authors found, however, conflict can be productive *and* destructive in stepfamilies; it is how the conflict is managed that is essential to stepfamily functioning. They found that families that spent time together and held family meetings tended to successfully prevent and negotiate their conflicts. In contrast, loy-alty conflicts, especially children's feelings of being caught between their custodial parent and stepparent, were divisive forms of family conflict. Sim-ilar to previous research (e.g., Kelley, 1992), these authors also found that stepfathers frequently felt like "outsiders" because of the preexisting ties between the custodial mother and her children. This often resulted in the parent and child forming a coalition against the stepparent. Children also attempted to create divisions between their custodial parent and the new stepparent by pitting one against the other. Most research (Afifi, 2003; Cissna, Cox, & Bochner, 1990; Kelley, 1992) suggests that in an attempt to combat this latter type of loyalty conflict from occurring, many parents and stepparents form a united front by communicating the importance and permanence of the marital bond to the children. Other research (Baxter et al., 2006) has found that children find their relationships with their parent and stepparent to be the most fulfilling and the least conflicted when there is open communication among all of them.

A significant amount of research has focused on the difficulty that stepparents encounter upon entering a new stepfamily because of the previously established relationships that exist within it. To understand why stepparents report feeling like outsiders, one needs to understand the process that parents and children experience together after a divorce. Research has been devoted to understanding how the relationships between parents and children change as a result of divorce and remarriage. In particular, research has examined how the relationships between parents and children change in the period after a divorce and before remarriage occurs. The majority of the research suggests that the quality of the parent-child relationship tends to suffer after a divorce (Hetherington, Cox, & Cox, 1982; Lye, 1996; Tein, Sandler, & Zautra, 2000; Wallerstein & Kelly, 1980). Children whose parents divorce tend to have less close and less satisfactory relationships with their parents than children whose parents remain married (Afifi & Schrodt, 2003a). Research also indicates that interaction between parents and their children changes dramatically after a divorce. Specifically, children have less contact with their noncustodial parent following a divorce, which often results in the noncustodial parent having fewer and lower-quality conversations with their children, more permissive parenting, and greater difficulty maintaining their relationship with their children (see Amato, 2000; Esposito, 1995; Stephens, 1996). In addition, custodial parents have been found to exhibit a diminished capacity to parent their children after a divorce (Forehand, Thomas, Wierson, & Brody, 1990; Hetherington et al., 1982; Tein et al., 2000; Wallerstein & Kelly, 1980). In particular, there is a diminution in monitoring and attention to one's children, less time communicating with them, inconsistency in discipline, a decline in affection and warmth, and parentification, or children assuming too much of a parental role in the family, which have all been associated with children's poor physical and mental health symptoms and adaptation difficulties (Biblarz & Gottainer, 2000; Koerner, Jacobs, & Raymond, 2000). In contrast, there is a growing body of research that suggests that the bond between custodial mothers and children, especially mothers and daughters, often becomes more cohesive after a divorce (see Amato, 2000; Aquilino, 1994; Arditti, 1999; Orbuch, Thorton, & Cancio, 2000). Custodial mothers often disclose sensitive information about the divorce and the other parent to their adolescent children, which can bring them closer together, but simultaneously harm the children's physical and mental health (Afifi, Afifi, Coho, & Morse 2008; Afifi et al., 2007; Koerner et al., 2000; Koerner, Wallace, Lehman, Lee, & Escalante, 2004; Koerner, Wallace, Lehman, & Raymond, 2002). The dramatic shifts in the communication between custodial parents and their children, and changes in the power and roles that they assume after the divorce, make it especially difficult for new stepparents to enter into a stepfamily.

Stepparents have been found to have difficulty forming cohesive relationships with their stepchildren. After a divorce, children often assume more power in the family hierarchy and may feel threatened by a stepparent, who is perceived as vying for power with them (Golish, 2003). Stepparents can be viewed as a threat to the child's existing relationship with the parent and resources within the family (Fine, Kurdek, & Hennigen, 1992). Unlike other types of family relationships, the step relationship is an involuntary one, and some stepchildren may have little desire to form a close relationship with their stepparent (Ganong, Coleman, Fine, & Martin, 1999). In fact, the stepparent-stepchild relationship is generally considered to be the most stressful, conflict-ridden, and avoidant, least involved, and least affectionate relationship within the stepfamily (Golish & Caughlin, 2002; Hetherington, 1988; Hetherington & Clingempeel, 1992; Schwebel, Fine, & Renner, 1991). As Ganong et al. (1999) point out, because of the potential for stress and conflict in this relationship, it is often identified by researchers and practitioners as a risk factor for the success of the stepfamily.

Part of the reason why stepparents experience difficulty is because there is typically a great deal of ambiguity surrounding their parental role (e.g., Baxter, Braithwaite, Bryant, & Wagner, 2004; Fine & Kurdek, 1994; Weaver & Coleman, 2005). Many practitioners and researchers (e.g., Fine et al., 1998; Kelley, 1992; Whitsett & Land, 1992) suggest that stepparents should form warm and nurturing relationships or friendships with their stepchildren before attempting to parent them. However, stepparents are often too removed in their parenting, which can also adversely affect stepparent-stepchild relationships (Hetherington, 1988, 1999). In fact, Hetherington's (1988) research has shown that stepparents tend to become more disengaged in their parenting over time. The parental role of the stepparent also depends on other key factors, such as the sex of the child and the age of the child, how long it has been since the divorce, and when the stepfamily is formed, that influence its effectiveness (Hetherington, 1999).

There is a host of research about the stressors that surround the stepparent-stepchild relationship, but little information is available on how stepparents actually create warm and cohesive relationships with their stepchildren. In an effort to address this issue, Ganong et al. (1999) interviewed family members from 17 stepfamilies and identified 31 strategies that stepparents use to develop affinity with their stepchildren. They found that stepparents who engaged in affinity-maintaining behaviors instead of reducing them to fulfill other roles had closer relationships with their stepchildren over time. As the family systems literature would suggest, they also found that the success or failure of the stepparents' affinity-seeking attempts was influenced by third parties (e.g., custodial parent, noncustodial parent, siblings). They discovered that when children were able to think of the nonresidential parent and the stepparent as fulfilling separate roles in their life, they were better able to form close relationships with both of them without the cognitive dissonance that this might otherwise produce. The parent also had to be able to allow the stepparent and stepchild enough space and time to form their own relationship, independent of the parent-child bond. In stepfamilies where the stepparent-stepchild relationship was struggling, there was competition for affection with the noncustodial parent and the stepparents' personalities were too dominating, creating an environment in which children were unable to recognize the stepparents' affinity-seeking attempts. Other research (e.g., Fine, Voydanoff, & Donnelly, 1993; Henry & Lovelace, 1995) has found that warmth, flexibility, and effectiveness in stepparent-stepchild communication are associated with adolescents' satisfaction with the stepparent-parent relationship and adolescents' well-being.

As researchers have begun to demonstrate, the strength of the stepchild-stepparent relationship depends on the other individuals and relationships in the stepfamily. For instance, little research has examined the impact that the nonresidential parent has on stepparent-stepchild relational quality (e.g., MacDonald & DeMaris, 2002; Marsiglio, 1992; Yuan & Hamilton, 2006). Yet the extent to which the stepparent's opinions and parenting practices are effective probably depends in part on the involvement of the nonresidential parent in the children's lives (MacDonald & DeMaris, 2002). For example, MacDonald and DeMaris found that stepchildren whose biological father frequently interacted with them and was actively involved in parenting decisions had the most trouble with their stepparent relationship when the stepparent strongly demanded conformity in household rules. However, when interaction with the biological father was infrequent, the stepparent's conformity had a more positive influence on the child. In a similar manner, the strength of the mother-child bond tends to have an impact on the quality of the stepparent-stepchild relationship (Yuan & Hamilton, 2006). For instance, Yuan and Hamilton found that the relationships among mother involvement, stepfather involvement, and adolescent well-being were interactive. Feeling close to a mother or feeling close to a stepfather independently contributed to the child's well-being, but feeling close to both the mother and the stepfather fostered even greater child well-being.

In essence, recent research suggests that the various dyads within the family do not exist in isolation from one another, but interact with one another to influence the strength of specific relationships within the stepfamily and the stepfamily as a whole. The stepfamily consists of a web of relationships, with communication serving as the means through which family members relate to each other. Unfortunately, much research still tends to be limited to the individual or dyad within the stepfamily rather than several family members as the unit of analysis. This is due to cost, difficulty gathering the sample, statistical complications, and the impracticality of interviewing or surveying multiple people. Yet, as the aforementioned research illustrates, it is imperative that researchers conceptualize and operationalize stepfamily relationships as interrelated and interactive. How the stepparent and stepchild relate to one another is influenced by the child's bonds with the noncustodial parent and the custodial parent. Likewise, how noncustodial parents are able to successfully maintain their relationship with their children is dependent on how well they get along with the custodial parent. It can be difficult for new spouses to create a cohesive and unified front to their children (Cissna et al., 1990) when the children are attempting to form alliances with their parent against the stepparent. As these basic examples illustrate, stepfamilies comprise interlocking relationships that influence, and are influenced by, one another.

This web of relationships tends to change over time as the stepfamily begins to feel like a family (Braithwaite et al., 2001). With time, most stepfamily members learn to communicate effectively with one another and build cohesive relationships. What remains to be tested is how stepfamily members, both in isolation and in conjunction with other members of the family, create and maintain positive stepfamily bonds. Researchers have an understanding of the communication processes that undermine stepfamily relationships, but additional research is necessary that examines the communication patterns that build healthy stepfamilies.

CONCLUSION AND SUGGESTIONS FOR FUTURE RESEARCH

Researchers have begun to tackle the larger complexities that surround stepfamily relationships. As they do, some of the seeming inconsistencies in the divorce and remarriage literature begin to make sense and new challenges begin to unfold. In addition to uncovering the interrelationships within the stepfamily, scholars are linking these relationships with those outside of the custodial stepfamily to the noncustodial parent. They are beginning to understand the role of the noncustodial parent in conjunction with the relationships within the custodial family and the difficulties that exist when attempting to maintain healthy stepfamily relationships. They are also starting to explore the stepchild–step-grandparent relationship, where even more layers of relationships and communication patterns emerge (e.g., Christensen & Smith, 2002; Ganong, Chapter 17, this volume). The nuances in stepfamily relationships can reveal important intergroup similarities and differences that, in turn, could help explain the varying levels of resiliency of stepfamilies and their individual members.

Research needs to continue to explore the multifaceted nature of stepfamily relationships, and stepfamilies as a whole, and how stepfamily members' behaviors affect one another. Important insights can be gleaned by examining the various combinations of individuals and relationships in stepfamilies and how they influence each other. Research should also examine how stepfamily members cope together as a group. For instance, the research on stress and coping in divorced families, single-parent families, and stepfamilies continues to focus on how individuals cope with divorce and stepfamily life in isolation from other stepfamily members. However, it has been shown that family members' stress and coping abilities affect one another (e.g., Coyne & Smith, 1994; Coyne, Wortman, & Lehman, 1988; Lyons, Mickelson, Sullivan, & Coyne, 1998). For example, Larson and Gilman (1999) found that single mothers' stress can be transferred indirectly to their adolescent children. Children's ability to communicate about divorce and remarriage stressors is related to how their parents communicate about it with them (Afifi, Huber, & Ohs, 2006). The family also often copes with divorce and remarriage together as a social unit. As Afifi, Hutchinson, and Krouse (2006) contend, family scholars would benefit from applying the literature on small groups to examine the norms, power differentials, and compliance-gaining attempts that influence family members' ability to cope with divorce and remarriage. As they found in their group and individual interviews with custodial parents, stepparents, and stepchildren from 60 families, the extent to which the family coped together as a social unit and its effectiveness depended on the appropriate level of responsibility and ownership for the stressors. Sometimes stressors should be shared and coped with communally as a group. At other times, however, individuals are better off coping with stressors alone, avoiding undue strain on other individuals and relationships within the family. For instance, financial stress may be better coped with alone by the parent, whereas stressors related to family routines and everyone contributing around the household might be best addressed by the entire family. Research has shown that the type and severity of the stressor affect the types of coping strategies that people use (Gottlieb & Gignac, 1996; Lakey & Cohen, 2000). Future research could examine how specific divorce and remarriage stressors influence the ways family members cope and whether or not individuals cope alone or as a family unit and the effectiveness of the communal nature of these strategies.

More longitudinal research on stepfamilies is necessary to track their progression. Hetherington's (1999) research has made important strides showing that stepfamilies, and the relationships in them, change significantly over time. As Hetherington notes, much of the research has been conducted on stepfamilies that have been formed relatively recently, instead of following stepfamilies over a longer period of time. Researchers often compare long-established first-marriage families to stepfamilies that are in the early stages of their formation, with dire conclusions drawn about stepfamily relationships (Hetherington, 1999). After a period of stabilization, certain family processes and cognitions may approximate those of first-marriage families. For instance, Afifi and Schrodt (2003b) found that the uncertainty that characterizes stepfamily relationships begins to fade and approaches that of first-marriage families after approximately 6 years. Longitudinal research would help identify the processes that foster risk and resilience in stepfamilies during and after their initial formation. The first few years are crucial to stepfamily formation, but researchers, practitioners, and family members need a better understanding of what communication characteristics help maintain healthy, long-term stepfamily relationships.

Additional studies need to be devoted to examining the positive behaviors in stepfamilies that make them function effectively. In particular, research needs to be devoted to deciphering the ways of interacting that help family members successfully integrate their previous family bonds, roles, and rituals with those in their new family so that all family members feel valued and appreciated. Interventions should also be designed to educate parents, children, and stepparents on how to communicate with one another about the stressors that often accompany divorce and remarriage. For instance, parents often have a difficult time communicating about one another to their children. This issue is commonly identified by parents and adolescents as extremely stressful and one that pervades other stressors in the family (Afifi et al., in press). If researchers and practitioners can educate family members to communicate with one another more effectively about their stressors, even if it is just the stressor involving the parents' relationship, the family members can better adapt to the divorce and remarriage process. In particular, interventions are needed that use behavioral modification to change the ways that parents talk about their stress with their adolescents. Parents are often unaware of how much information, and what type of information, they are disclosing about the divorce and remarriage process with their adolescents (Afifi et al., 2006, in press). Interventions could be designed so that parents and adolescents interact with one another about their stressors and then watch themselves on videotape (using video recall procedures). They could then be taught how to communicate more effectively, incorporating the researcher's suggestions into their discussions and modifying their behavior accordingly. The researcher could then follow up with them weeks and months after the process to see if the ideas are actually being implemented at home. Such efforts should improve stepfamilies' relationships.

REFERENCES

Afifi, T. D. (2003). "Feeling caught" in stepfamilies: Managing boundaries turbulence through appropriate communication privacy rules. *Journal of Social and Personal Relationships, 20,* 729–755.

Afifi, T. D., Afifi, W. A., Coho, A., & Morse, C. (2008). *Adolescents' anxiety and physiological reactions to their parents' negative disclosures about the other parent in divorced and non-divorced families.* Manuscript submitted for publication.

Afifi, T. D., Coho, A., & McManus, T. (2008). *Custodial parents' divorce disclosures and their impact on parent-adolescent relational quality and adolescents' physical and mental health.* Manuscript submitted for publication.

Afifi, T. D., Huber, F., & Ohs, J. (2006). Parents' and adolescents' communication about divorce related stressors and its impact on their ability to cope positively with divorce. *Journal of Divorce and Remarriage, 45,* 1–30.

Afifi, T. D., Hutchinson, S., & Krouse, S. (2006). Toward a theoretical model of communal coping in post-divorce families and other naturally occurring groups. *Communication Theory, 16,* 378–409.

Afifi, T. D., McManus, T., Hutchinson, S., & Baker, B. (2007). Parental divorce disclosures, the factors that prompt them, and their impact on parents' and adolescents' well-being. *Communication Monographs, 74,* 78–103.

Afifi, T. D., & Schrodt, P. (2003a). "Feeling caught" as a mediator of adolescents' and young adults' avoidance and satisfaction with their parents in divorce and non-divorced households. *Communication Monographs, 70,* 142–173.

Afifi, T. D., & Schrodt, P. (2003b). Uncertainty and the avoidance of the state of one's family in stepfamilies, postdivorce single-parent families, and first-marriage families. *Human Communication Research, 29,* 516–532.

Alexander, P. C. (2003). Parent-child role reversal: Development of a measure and test of an attachment theory model. *Journal of Systemic Therapies, 22,* 31–43.

Amato, P. R. (2000). The consequences of divorce for adults and children. *Journal of Marriage and the Family, 62,* 1269–1287.

Amato, P. R. (2001). Children of divorce in the 1990s: An update of the Amato and Keith (1991) meta-analysis. *Journal of Family Psychology, 15,* 355–370.

Amato, P. R., & Afifi, T. D. (2006). Feeling caught between parents: Adult children's relations with parents and subjective well-being. *Journal of Marriage and the Family, 68,* 222–236.

Amato, P. R., & Keith, B. (1991). Parental divorce and the well-being of children: A meta-analysis. *Psychological Bulletin, 110,* 26–46.

Amato, P. R., & Sobolewski, J. M. (2001). The effects of divorce and marital discord on adult children's psychological well-being. *American Sociological Review, 66,* 900–921.

Anderson, J. Z., & White, G. D. (1986). An empirical investigation of interaction and relationship patterns in functional and dysfunctional nuclear families and stepfamilies. *Family Process, 25,* 407–422.

Aquilino, W. S. (1994). Impact of childhood family disruption on young adults' relationships with parents. *Journal of Marriage and the Family, 56,* 295–313.

Arditti, J. A. (1999). Rethinking relationships between divorced mothers and their children: Capitalizing on family strengths. *Family Relations, 48,* 109–119.

Banker, B. S., & Gaertner, S. L. (1998). Achieving stepfamily harmony: An intergroup-relations approach. *Journal of Family Psychology, 12,* 310–325.

Barrett, A. E., & Turner, R. J. (2005). Family structure and mental health: The mediating effects of socioeconomic status, family process, and social stress. *Journal of Health and Social Behavior, 46,* 156–169.

Baxter, L. A., Braithwaite, D. O., & Bryant, L. (2006). Types of communication triads perceived by young-adult stepchildren in established stepfamilies. *Communication Studies, 57,* 381–400.

Baxter, L. A., Braithwaite, D. O., Bryant, L., & Wagner, A. (2004). Stepchildren's perceptions of the contradictions in communication with stepparents. *Journal of Social and Personal Relationships, 21,* 447–467.

Baxter, L. A., Braithwaite, D. O., & Nicholson, J. (1999). Turning points in the development of blended family relationships. *Journal of Social and Personal Relationships, 16,* 291–313.

Biblarz, T. J., & Gottainer, G. (2000). Family structure and children's success: A comparison of widowed and divorced single-mother families. *Journal of Marriage and the Family, 62,* 533–548.

Booth, A., & Amato, P. R. (2001). Parental predivorce relations and offspring postdivorce well-being. *Journal of Marriage and the Family, 63,* 197–212.

Braithwaite, D. O., Baxter, L. A., & Harper, A. M. (1998). The role of rituals in the management of the dialectical tension of "old" and "new" in blended families. *Communication Studies, 49,* 101–120.

Braithwaite, D. O., Olson, L., Golish, T. D., Soukup, C., & Turman, P. (2001). "Becoming a family": Developmental processes represented in blended family discourse. *Journal of Applied Communication Research, 29,* 221–247.

Bray, J. H. (1992). Family relationships and children's adjustment in clinical and nonclinical stepfather families. *Journal of Family Psychology, 6,* 60–68.

Bray, J. H. (1999). From marriage to remarriage and beyond: Findings from the Developmental Issues in Stepfamilies research project. In D. M. Hetherington (Ed.), *Coping with divorce, single parenting, and remarriage* (pp. 253–272). Mahwah, NJ: Erlbaum.

Bray, J. H., & Harvey, D. M. (1995). Adolescents in stepfamilies: Developmental family interventions. *Psychotherapy, 32,* 122–130.

Bray, J. H., & Kelly, J. (1998). *Stepfamilies: Love, marriage, and parenting in the first decade.* New York: Broadway Books.

Broderick, C. (1994). *Understanding family process.* Newbury Park, CA: Sage.

Brown, A. C., Green, R., & Druckman, J. (1990). A comparison of stepfamilies with and without child-focused problems. *American Journal of Orthopsychiatry, 60,* 556–566.

Caughlin, J. P., Golish, T. D., Olson, L. N., Sargent, J. E., Cook, J. S., & Petronio, S. (2000). Family secrets in various family configurations: A communication boundary management perspective. *Communication Studies, 51*, 116–134.

Christensen, F. B., & Smith, T. A. (2002). What is happening to satisfaction and quality of relationships between step/grandparents and step/grandchildren? *Journal of Divorce and Remarriage, 37*, 117–133.

Cissna, K. N., Cox, D. E., & Bochner, A. P. (1990). The dialectic of marital and parental relationships within the stepfamily. *Communication Monographs, 37*, 44–61.

Clingempeel, G. (1981). Quasi-kin relationships and marital quality in stepfamilies. *Journal of Personality and Social Psychology, 41*, 890–901.

Coleman, M., Fine, M. A., Ganong, L. H., Downs, K. J. M., & Pauk, N. (2001). When you're not the Brady Bunch: Identifying perceived conflicts and resolution strategies in stepfamilies. *Personal Relationships, 8*, 55–73.

Coleman, M., Ganong, L., & Fine, M. (2000). Reinvestigating remarriage: Another decade of progress. *Journal of Marriage and the Family, 62*, 1288–1307.

Coyne, J. C., & Smith, D. A. F. (1994). Couples coping with a myocardial infarction: Contextual perspective on patient self-efficacy. *Journal of Family Psychology, 8*, 43–54.

Coyne, J. C., Wortman, C. B., & Lehman, D. R. (1988). The other side of social support: Emotional overinvolvement and miscarried helping. In B. H. Gottlieb (Ed.), *Marshalling social support: Formats, processes, and effects* (pp. 305–330). Newbury Park, CA: Sage.

Dunn, J. (2004). Understanding children's family worlds: Family transitions and children's outcome. *Merrill-Palmer Quarterly, 50*, 224–235.

Esposito, S. A. (1995). Cohesion and adaptability in the non-custodial father-child relationship: The effects of interaction quality. *Journal of Divorce and Remarriage, 23*, 21–37.

Fine, M. A., Coleman, M., & Ganong, L. H. (1998). Consistency in perceptions of the stepparent role among stepparents, parents, and stepchildren. *Journal of Social and Personal Relationships, 15*, 810–828.

Fine, M. A., & Kurdek, L. A. (1994). Parenting cognitions in stepfamilies: Differences between parents and stepparents and relations to parenting satisfaction. *Journal of Social and Personal Relationships, 11*, 95–112.

Fine, M. A., Kurdek, L. A., & Hennigen, L. (1992). Perceived self-competence, stepfamily myths, and (step)parent role ambiguity in adolescents from stepfather and stepmother families. *Journal of Family Psychology, 6*, 69–76.

Fine, M. A., Voydanoff, P., & Donnelly, B. W. (1993). Relations between parental control and warmth and child well-being in stepfamilies. *Family Psychology, 2*, 222–232.

Fitzpatrick, M. A., & Ritchie, L. D. (1993). Communication theory and the family. In P. G. Boss, W. J. Doherty, R. LaRossa, W. R. Schumm, & S. K. Steinmetz (Eds.), *Sourcebook of family theories and methods: A contextual approach* (pp. 565–585). New York: Plenum Press.

Forehand, R., Thomas, A. M., Wierson, M., & Brody, G. (1990). Role of maternal functioning and parenting skills in adolescent functioning following parental divorce. *Journal of Abnormal Psychology, 99*, 278–283.

Ganong, L., & Coleman, M. (1994). *Remarried family relationships*. Thousand Oaks, CA: Sage.

Ganong, L., Coleman, M., Fine, M., & Martin, P. (1999). Stepparents' affinity-seeking and affinity-maintaining strategies with stepchildren. *Journal of Family Issues, 20*, 299–327.

Golish, T. D. (2003). Stepfamily communication strengths: Understanding the ties that bind. *Human Communication Research, 29*, 41–80.

Golish, T. D., & Caughlin, J. P. (2002). "I'd rather not talk about it": Adolescents' and young adults' use of topic avoidance in stepfamilies. *Journal of Applied Communication Research, 30*(1), 78–106.

Gottlieb, B. H., & Gignac, M. A. M. (1996). Content and domain specificity of coping among family caregivers of persons with dementia. *Journal of Aging Studies, 10*, 137–155.

Henry, C. S., & Lovelace, S. G. (1995). Family resources and adolescent family life satisfaction in remarried family households. *Journal of Family Issues, 16*, 765–786.

Hetherington, E. M. (1988). Parents, children, and siblings six years after divorce. In R. Hinde & J. Stevenson-Hinde (Eds.), *Relationships within families*. New York: Oxford University Press.

Hetherington, E. M. (1993). An overview of the Virginia Longitudinal Study of Divorce and Remarriage with a focus on early adolescence. *Journal of Family Psychology, 7*, 39–56.

Hetherington, E. M. (1999). Family functioning and the adjustment of adolescent siblings in diverse types of families. In E. M. Hetherington, S. H. Henderson, & D. Reiss (Eds.), Adolescent siblings in stepfamilies: Family functioning and adolescent adjustment. *Monographs of the Society for Research in Child Development, 64*, 1–25.

Hetherington, E. M., & Clingempeel, W. G. (1992). Coping with marital transitions: A family systems perspective. *Monographs of the Society for Research on Child Development, 57*(2/3, Serial No. 227).

Hetherington, E. M., Cox, M., & Cox, R. (1982). Effects of divorce on parents and children. In M. Lamb (Ed.), *Nontraditional families: Parenting and child development* (pp. 233–259). Hillsdale, NJ: Erlbaum.

Jekielek, S. (1998). Parental conflict, marital disruption, and children's emotional well-being. *Social Forces, 76*, 905–936.

Jurkovic, G. J., Thirkeild, A., & Morrell, R. (2001). Parentification of adult children of divorce: A multidimensional analysis. *Journal of Youth and Adolescence, 30*, 245–258.

Kelley, P. (1992). Healthy stepfamily functioning. *Families in Society: Journal of Contemporary Human Services, 73*, 579–587.

Kelly, J. B., & Emery, R. E. (2003). Children's adjustment following divorce: Risk and resiliency perspectives. *Family Relations, 52*, 352–362.

Knaub, P. K., Hanna, S. L., & Stinnett, N. (1984). Strengths of remarried families. *Journal of Divorce, 7*, 41–55.

Koerner, S. S., Jacobs, S. L., & Raymond, M. (2000). When mothers turn to their adolescent daughters: Predicting daughter's vulnerability to negative adjustment outcomes. *Family Relations, 49*, 301–309.

Koerner, S. S., Wallace, S., Lehman, S. J., Lee, S.-A., & Escalante, K. A. (2004). Sensitive mother-to-adolescent disclosures after divorce: Is the experience of sons different from that of daughters? *Journal of Family Psychology, 18*, 46–57.

Koerner, S. S., Wallace, S., Lehman, S. J., & Raymond, M. (2002). Mother-to-daughter disclosure after divorce: Are there costs and benefits? *Journal of Child and Family Studies, 11*, 469–483.

Kurdek, L. A., & Fine, M. A. (1991). Cognitive correlates of satisfaction for mothers and stepfamilies in stepfather families. *Journal of Marriage and the Family, 53*, 565–572.

Lakey, B., & Cohen, S. (2000). Social support theory and measurement. In S. Cohen, L. G. Underwood, & B. H. Gottlieb (Eds.), *Social support measurement and intervention: A guide for health and social scientists* (pp. 29–52). New York: Oxford University Press.

Larson, R. W., & Gillman, S. (1999). Transmission of emotions in the daily interactions of single-mother families. *Journal of Marriage and the Family, 61*, 21–37.

Lye, D. N. (1996). Adult child-parent relationships. *Annual Review of Sociology, 22*, 79–103.

Lyons, R. F., Mickelson, K., Sullivan, J. L., & Coyne, J. C. (1998). Coping as a communal process. *Journal of Social and Personal Relationships, 15*, 579–607.

MacDonald, W. L., & DeMaris, A. (1995). Remarriage, stepchildren, and marital conflict: Challenges to the incomplete institutionalization hypothesis. *Journal of Marriage and the Family, 57*, 387–399.

MacDonald, W. L., & DeMaris, A. (2002). Stepfather-stepchild relationship quality. *Journal of Family Issues, 23*, 121–137.

Marsiglio, W. (1992). Stepfathers with minor children living at home: Parental perceptions and relationship quality. *Journal of Family Issues, 13*, 195–214.

Minuchin, S. (1974). *Family and family therapy.* Cambridge, MA: Harvard University Press.

O'Connor, T. G., Dunn, J., Jenkins, J. M., & Rasbash, J. (2006). Predictors of between-family and within-family variation in parent-child relationships. *Journal of Child Psychology and Psychiatry, 47*, 498–510.

Orbuch, T. L., Thorton, A., & Cancio, J. (2000). The impact of marital quality, divorce and remarriage on the relationships between parents and their children. *Marriage and Family Review, 29*, 221–244.

Pasley, K., & Ihinger-Tallman, M. (1984). Stress in remarried families. *Family Perspectives, 16*, 181–190.

Petronio, S. (1991). Communication boundary management: A theoretical model of managing disclosure of private information between marital couples. *Communication Theory, 1*, 311–335.

Petronio, S. (2000). The boundaries of privacy: Praxis of everyday life. In S. Petronio (Ed.), *Balancing the secrets of private disclosures* (pp. 37–49). Mahwah, NJ: Erlbaum.

Petronio, S. (2002). *Boundaries of privacy: Dialectics of disclosure.* Albany: State University of New York Press.

Pryor, J., & Rodgers, B. (2001). *Children in changing families: Life after parental separation.* Oxford: Blackwell.

Rodgers, K. B., & Rose, H. A. (2002). Risk and resiliency factors among adolescents who experience marital transitions. *Journal of Marriage and the Family, 64*, 1024–1037.

Satir, V. (1972). *Peoplemaking*. Palo Alto, CA: Science and Behavior Books.

Schmeeckle, M., Giarrusso, R., Feng, D., & Bengtson, V. L. (2006). What makes someone family? Adult children's perceptions of current and former stepparents. *Journal of Marriage and the Family, 68*, 595–610.

Schrodt, P. (2006). A typological examination of communication competence and mental health in stepchildren. *Communication Monographs, 73*, 309–333.

Schrodt, P., & Afifi, T. (in press). Communication processes that predict young adults' feelings of being caught and their associations with mental health and family satisfaction. *Communication Monographs*.

Schultz, N. C., Schultz, C. L., & Olson, D. H. (1991). Couple strengths and stressors in complex and simple stepfamilies in Australia. *Journal of Marriage and the Family, 53*, 555–564.

Schwebel, A. I., Fine, M. A., & Renner, M. A. (1991). A study of perceptions of the stepparent role. *Journal of Family Issues, 12*, 43–57.

Sillars, A., Koerner, A., & Fitzpatrick, M. A. (2005). Communication and understanding in parent-adolescent relationships. *Human Communication Research, 31*, 102–128.

Stephens, L. S. (1996). Will Johnny see Daddy this week? An empirical test of three theoretical perspectives of postdivorce contact. *Journal of Family Issues, 17*, 466–494.

Stewart, S. D. (2005). Boundary ambiguity in stepfamilies. *Journal of Family Issues, 26*, 1002–1029.

Taanila, A., Laitinen, E., Moilanen, I., & Jarvelin, M. R. (2002). Effects of family interaction on the child's behavior in single-parent and reconstructed families. *Family Process, 41*, 693–708.

Tein, J., Sandler, I. N., & Zautra, A. J. (2000). Stressful life events, psychological distress, coping, and parenting of divorced mothers: A longitudinal study. *Journal of Family Psychology, 14*, 27–41.

Visher, E. B., & Visher, J. S. (1993). Remarriage families and stepparenting. In F. Walsh (Ed.), *Normal family processes* (2nd ed., pp. 235–253). New York: Guilford Press.

Wallerstein, R. S., & Kelly, J. B. (1980). *Surviving the breakup*. New York: Basic Books.

Weaver, S. E., & Coleman, M. (2005). A mothering but not a mother role: A grounded theory study of the nonresidential stepmother role. *Journal of Social and Personal Relationships, 22*, 477–497.

White, L., & Gilbreth, J. G. (2001). When children have two fathers: Effects of relationships with stepfathers and noncustodial fathers on adolescent outcomes. *Journal of Marriage and the Family, 63*, 155–167.

Whitsett, D., & Land, H. (1992). Role strain, coping, and marital satisfaction of stepparents. *Families in Society: Journal of Contemporary Human Services, 73*, 79–92.

Yuan, A. A. V., & Hamilton, H. A. (2006). Stepfather involvement and adolescent well-being: Do mothers and nonresidential fathers matter? *Journal of Family Issues, 27*, 1191–1213.

INFLUENCES AND RELATIONSHIPS BEYOND THE HOUSEHOLD

CHAPTER 14

Kinship in Stepfamilies

GRAHAM ALLAN, SHEILA HAWKER,
and GRAHAM CROW

SOME OF the key questions asked by researchers into stepfamily life concern the processes by which stepfamilies become recognized by themselves and by others as families. In the main, the focus of these research questions concerns the sense of unity that is—or is not—generated within households with dependent children when a stepparent moves in. The creation of "normal family life" frequently appears to be a key goal of the adults involved, though it is an aspiration that can prove difficult to achieve, in the long run as well as more immediately (Ribbens McCarthy, Edwards, & Gillies, 2003). As other chapters in this collection attest, the different loyalties, experiences, and commitments of both the children and the adults in the household frequently make the forging of a sense of family a complex and difficult process, with no guarantee of success. The research literature discusses how stepfamily practices, in Morgan's (1996) sense, can differ from the practices found in families where the parental pair remain living together. In particular, the two classic problems of (a) stepfamily boundaries being more permeable than those constructed in "biological"[1] families and (b) how much of a parent a stepparent should attempt to be have to be confronted by nearly all stepfamily households. The different negotiations (Finch & Mason, 1993) these matters entail can

[1] Throughout this chapter we have drawn on the distinction between stepfamilies and "biological" families. Like the alternative terms used by our respondents to describe their family relationships—most commonly, "blood," "real," and "natural"—the term "biological" contains a number of questionable assumptions. While in this chapter we have not placed the term "biological" in quotation marks throughout, it should be understood that we are referring to cultural notions of biological connection, which may or may not reflect a demonstrable genetic one.

323

be both fraught and extensive, with successful resolution frequently dependent on a level of cooperation from those outside the household as well as those in it.

This chapter is concerned with aspects of family solidarity and membership, though its focus is different from the majority of research examining stepfamily unity. Our principal interest lies with "family as kinship" rather than "family as household." In other words, we seek to analyze the character of the nonhousehold stepkin relationships that members of stepfamilies have. This perspective on family complements a "family as household" perspective by emphasizing cultural understandings of family connection and the extent to which different "others" are, and are not, recognized as belonging to one's family. The chapter is principally concerned with adult kin relationships rather than aspects of parenting or stepparenting dependent children. Put simply, our focus is on the extent to which stepkin are recognized as kin and incorporated into the domain of family. Given the importance of kinship networks within standard constructions of kinship, we assess the degree to which a sense of family membership extends to individuals who are involved in what we term "stepkin networks."

This is not a topic about which there has been a great deal of research. As a result, the chapter is somewhat exploratory. We draw on material from a qualitative study of stepfamily kinship undertaken in England to illustrate the analysis developed. Of course, kinship systems are not uniform. Even within a society different families will develop different kinship practices, depending on their family biographies, material circumstances, and the like. Even more so, it cannot be assumed that kinship practices will be common across societies, even when those societies have shared heritages and/or a similar economic standing. Consequently, the conclusions drawn from this study do not necessarily apply to the kinship systems manifested in other countries. However, the issues addressed in the chapter—and by the respondents in the study—are ones that are likely to be of relevance elsewhere.

In line with the methodology of the study, but also to facilitate the posing of questions about the construction of stepfamily kinship, we draw on a case study perspective. The material included is not intended to be wholly representative of the ways stepfamily kinship is ordered, but rather to illustrate the different influences there are on relational outcomes. Certain uniformities in practice are highlighted, but so too is the variation in the development of these relationships. Given the commonly recognized lack of normative consensus over many relationship issues within stepfamily households, it would be somewhat surprising if stepfamily kinship did not also reflect diverse practice.

FAMILY AS KINSHIP

In his classic study, *American Kinship: A Cultural Account*, David Schneider (1968) argues that the idea of "diffuse, enduring solidarity" is central to American understandings of family relationships. It is this sense of diffuse and enduring solidarity that distinguishes kinship from other (nonfamily) forms of relationship. In turn, in American culture, the basis of this "diffuse, enduring solidarity" rests on people's beliefs about the role of nature and law in the construction of family relatedness. Nature is signified by people's ideas of "blood" connection; law is encapsulated in ideas of marriage as well as adoption. Similarly, these elements of blood and marriage are central to understandings of kinship connection in other Western societies. In general, when people construct their genealogies and define their kinship, these criteria are the ones that are routinely applied (Allan, 2008).

Of course, Schneider was writing in the 1960s. The demography of family life has altered very significantly since that time. In particular, changes in union formation and dissolution have had an impact on the continuing centrality of marriage within family life. With increased cohabitation, higher levels of divorce, and higher proportions of children born outside wedlock, marriage in many Western societies is, in Cherlin's (2004) terms, tending to become increasingly "de-institutionalized." Compared to the past, marriage is of reduced consequence socially, even though it is still legally privileged in most jurisdictions. Similarly, ideas about the importance of legitimacy in childbearing have given way to a greater acceptance that parenting responsibilities are independent of marital status. Almost inevitably these shifts in the demography of family construction will gradually percolate into people's understandings of kinship, though with what consequences is at this stage uncertain. Nonetheless, it seems likely that blood connection will become increasingly significant in comparison to partnership connection. Not only are partnerships, including marriage, increasingly fragile, but the accepted power of DNA testing makes beliefs about blood connection the more compelling.

There is a further feature of kinship that is important in sustaining the "diffuse, enduring solidarity" that characterizes it: its network properties. Typically kinship does not just involve a series of discrete and separate relationships. Kinship entails a network of relationships that tie people together collectively. This does not mean that different people, even in the same family, have identical kinships, merely that there is a degree of overlap that helps sustain and pattern the individual kinship ties involved in each person's kinship network. That is, the network properties of kinship normally result in individual relationships being influenced by, and in turn influencing, the other ties incorporated into the kinship network. Thus, for example, news and gossip about different family members routinely passes through the network, with some people acting as "kin-keepers" for the network more widely. Similarly, family rituals and celebrations serve to bring the network together at different times and cement family connection. In such ways the network characteristics of kinship serve to distinguish family ties from other forms of personal relationship and provide a sense of collective family identity.

Although kinship may be characterized by "diffuse, enduring solidarity," the manner in which such solidarity is expressed is not fixed or determined. There are broad normative agreements about appropriate ways of patterning different types of kin relationships—in particular, governing which ties warrant most priority—but the specifics of how different relationships are ordered varies widely in practice. It is conventionally understood, for example, that there should be solidarity between siblings, but exactly what this entails depends on their individual circumstances. As Finch and Mason (1993) have argued, kinship ties should be understood as "negotiated," with the history of the relationships, the different situations of those involved, and the respective character of their other responsibilities all playing a part in framing the nature of their current exchanges. Such negotiations should not be seen as being only between the two individuals in a given relationship. The network of kin ties provides a context for these negotiations, to different degrees facilitating information flows as well as interactional opportunities.

These issues around "family as kinship" are of consequence for understanding stepfamilies. As with kinship in biological families, many different patterns of kinship connection are possible. However, whereas in biological families, the collective sense of family is often reinforced through the tacit operation of kinship dynamics, in stepfamilies their operation is usually more open to questioning and less taken for granted. The kinship solidarity that exists between stepfamily members within a household is itself often problematic; when, for example, does a stepfather come to be regarded as a member of one's kinship? The degree to which the kin of a stepfamily member are considered to be members of one's own kinship raises further issues that are not readily resolvable in terms of conventional kinship beliefs. Yet these issues are of consequence. As suggested, it is the kinship integration of others outside a particular dyad, as much as those within it, that serves to generate a common sense of family membership.

CASE STUDY DATA

As noted, stepkin relationships have not been widely examined. As a basis for discussion, we draw on case study material taken from research into stepfamily kinship conducted in England between 1998 and 2000.[2] The

[2] The research on which this paper is based was funded by the Economic and Social Research Council in the UK (Award number R000237504). We are grateful for their support.

material included from this research is intended to be illustrative of some of the principles that underlie stepfamily kinship, though clearly the extent to which these relationships are organized in equivalent ways in different societies is an open question. The research was concerned primarily with the ways different kin relationships were negotiated and managed within stepfamily networks. Information was collected through semi-structured interviews with respondents who were or had been members of stepfamilies or who had close kin who were. The study was based on interviews with 80 respondents, 30 of whom had a kinship link with at least one other respondent in the sample.[3]

Respondents were recruited either through screening letters and telephone calls to selected localities in a southern English town, or else through snowballing techniques using third parties as intermediaries.[4] The respondents occupied a range of positions within stepfamily networks. Some were stepparents; some stepchildren; some were stepaunts; others were step-grandparents. Many had varied experiences of being in a stepfamily; they might, for example, have been a stepdaughter for some period of their life, while now being a stepmother, a stepaunt, and/or a step-grandmother. Equally, some had belonged to a stepfamily in the past, and others had become part of a stepfamily only relatively recently. The respondents ranged in age from 16 to 79. For the study, this diversity among the respondents meant that as well as collecting data from different perspectives we could also obtain accounts that detailed how individual step relationships had altered over time. Table 14.1 provides further details of the sample.

The respondents were interviewed once, in interviews typically lasting between 60 and 90 minutes. All but seven of the interviews were tape-recorded and then transcribed in full. In seven cases respondents preferred that the interview was not tape-recorded. Notes were taken during these interviews and then written up as fully as possible immediately afterward. The interviews were all organized around the construction of a kinship genogram (McGoldrick & Gerson, 1985). These were mapped out during

---

[3] The 30 respondents who had a kinship link to at least one other respondent in the sample were members of 13 separate kin groupings. There were 11 dyads—5 married or cohabiting couples; 3 parent-child or stepparent-stepchild dyads; and 3 sibling, sibling-in-law, or half-sibling dyads. There were also 2 sets of four "linked" respondents, involving different constellations of family (and ex-family) ties.

[4] Thirty-four respondents were obtained through letters sent to all the households of three small, economically diverse areas of a town in southern England. A further 30 respondents were recruited through snowballing. Five of those interviewed as a result of the letters then introduced us to a further 7 respondents who had a kin connection to them. Similarly, 7 of those initially snowballed introduced us to 9 of their kin. (One linked sibling pair both lived in our selected areas and agreed independently to be interviewed in response to our letter.) Although the achieved sample of 80 cannot be regarded as representative of stepfamily experience more widely, it was sufficiently diverse to allow us to capture a range of different stepfamily experiences.

Table 14.1
Age, Gender, and Partnership Status of Respondents

	Male		Female	
Age	Married/Cohabiting	Divorced/Single	Married/Cohabiting	Divorced/Single
16–30	3	5	6	7
31–40	5	1	18	2
41–50	2	0	13	1
51–80	6	2	6	3

the interview, and throughout provided a basis for the discussion. Geno-grams proved to be an extremely useful methodological tool in the project. As well as enabling details of a wide range of kin to be collected, they allowed comparisons to be made between different relationships. More-over, they provided an active, visual focus to which respondents readily turned when they were expressing complex or critical commentaries about their different kin and stepkin relationships. It appeared that the genograms helped ease the process of interviewing for the respondents and enabled them to convey more readily the characteristics and subtleties of their vari-ous kin relationships.

As well as details of their own relationships with the people included in the genogram, respondents also provided information about the relation-ships some of those in the genogram had with one another. For example, parents discussed the type of relationship their children had with their dif-ferent grandparents, and spouses reported on each other's relationships within their kinship network. This was a quite deliberate strategy on our part. We wanted respondents to reflect on the different relationships within their kinship network, partly to enable comparison with their own relation-ships, but also because this would enable us to obtain a better understand-ing of how stepkinship was constructed within their kinship networks. However, for this chapter we have prioritized the accounts given by respondents of their own relationships, while still paying heed to the ac-counts they gave of other ties in their networks.

A CASE STUDY: MARK BURTON

Mark was 26 at the time of the interview and living alone. Figure 14.1 pro-vides a simplified portrayal of his genogram. His biological parents, Michael and Ann, separated when he was less than a year old. He lived with his mother and her parents, Pop and Nana, briefly until Ann married Tom Wellington. Ann and Tom had two children, Phil and Heather, ages 20 and 18 at the time of the interview. Michael had lived in different parts of the country as a result of his work in the Armed Forces, but had maintained regular fortnightly contact with Mark throughout his childhood. Michael

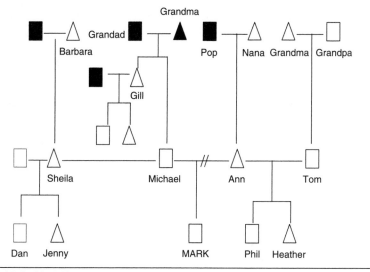

Figure 14.1 Mark Burton.

had married Sheila when Mark was 14. Sheila had two children from a pre-vious marriage, Dan and Jenny, now ages 25 and 20, who until recently lived with their mother and Michael.

From the beginning of the interview, Mark made it clear that he regarded his closest family to be Ann, Tom, Phil, and Heather, the members of the household in which he had grown up, together with his grandparents. These were the people who were his family and whom he felt most at home with. He said, "Yup, what happened was parents divorced when [I was] very young, and my mother remarried very quickly, to Tom who's always been 'Dad' to me." Although Mark had not changed his surname from Burton (i.e., Michael's surname), at various stages in the interview he em-phasized that he had always thought of Phil and Heather as full siblings and of Tom's parents, Grandpa and Grandma, as full grandparents. He had always been treated by them as a grandson and was still very close to them. Indeed, in the course of the interview Grandpa rang him up to make ar-rangements to go out together.

INTERVIEWER: Now Tom's parents, you were very young when your mum and—

MARK: That's Grandma and Grandpa.

INTERVIEWER: Right. And they were in effect your stepgrandparents. But did they feel like stepgrandparents?

MARK: No, no, we spent a lot of time with them. Still do see them though, saw them on Sunday, you know we see them a lot really.

INTERVIEWER: So they're your grandparents?

MARK: Yes. There's no real distinction on that side of the family, if you like everything that side [referring to the Wellington part of the genogram] is family.

This sense of who his family is was pervasive throughout the interview. He clearly perceived a strong boundary around the Wellington family group and included himself as a full member. In contrast, his relationship with his biological father was quite different. As noted, Michael's work had taken him to different parts of the country, but he had still visited Mark very regularly every 2 weeks when he was younger.

MARK: Yes, every 2 weeks. Visited every 2 weeks, every second Sunday.
INTERVIEWER: Right and always you went?
MARK: Well he always came to visit me usually.
INTERVIEWER: In your home?
MARK: Yes . . . We'd go out for a day or something.

Later in the interview Mark added, ''With the exception of once or twice, I don't think I've ever been driven over there, he was always coming over this way.'' This pattern began to change when Mark was in his midteens as a result, according to Mark, of three factors: his father's marriage to Sheila, Mark's increasingly independent social life as a teenager, and a very serious car crash that had left Michael partially disabled. Indeed, once Mark learned to drive, the pattern changed again, with Mark now visiting Michael and Sheila, albeit somewhat less frequently, at their home some 60 miles away rather than his father driving to see him.

Thus, in Mark's portrayal, Michael came into his world rather than him (Mark) going into Michael's. Interestingly this pattern seemed to continue even after Mark started driving to Michael and Sheila's home. For example, he said that he had never actually stayed at Michael and Sheila's, despite getting on well with Sheila's son, Dan.

INTERVIEWER: Of course you and Dan are almost the same age.
MARK: Yes.
INTERVIEWER: So did you start then to go and stay with them?
MARK: No, never stayed with them.
INTERVIEWER: Never have?
MARK: I have always been a bit hesitant if you know what I mean.
INTERVIEWER: You didn't want to do that?
MARK: No, not really. That is very definitely McDonald [Sheila's surname] family, this is really—friends, if you know what I mean. It's a different . . .
INTERVIEWER: So for you it's a different—role?
MARK: Yes.

At other times in the interview, Mark also indicated a hesitancy about his involvement with or incorporation into his (biological) father's new family. This was not a consequence of "traditional" stepfamily problems; he described Sheila as "very nice" and appeared to have an entirely cordial, though not strong, relationship with her. As in the dialogue just quoted, though, he implied that with Michael's marriage to Sheila and sharing a home with her two children, Michael's kinship location had shifted. It was as if Michael had been removed that much further from the orbit of Mark's family Wellington into Sheila's family McDonald. As discussed later, Mark did not see this as problematic; instead, he rather welcomed it as a solution to the complexity of his "unclear" (Simpson, 1998) family circumstances.

One of the ways Mark expressed his commitment to his biological father while still asserting his full membership in the Wellington family was through using the language of friendship rather than family to describe his relationship with Michael.

INTERVIEWER: And your relationship with [Michael], is it a good, close relationship?

MARK: Yes, more like we're friends really. . . . It's more like a—friends really.

Similarly, in discussing his relationship with Dan, Sheila's son, he drew on the language of friendship as a contrast to family.

INTERVIEWER: So do you feel that Dan—when you talk about this side [McDonalds] as friends—does Dan feel more like a brother?

MARK: Er—Dan feels like a good close family member, yeah.

INTERVIEWER: . . . like a brother, of course it's different for everybody anyway

MARK: Yeah. I wouldn't, I mean it may be wrong of me but I wouldn't put Dan in the [pause] how would you say it—friend of special consideration—I don't know.

INTERVIEWER: Special friend?

MARK: Special friend, something like that. . . . Except we don't, as I said because of time and everything, we don't see each other a lot, I've got other friends I see a lot more.

In contrast, Mark felt no ambiguity about his relationships with his grandparents, all of whom he had had strong bonds with, though three of the six were now dead. Like Tom's parents, Ann's parents had lived nearby and been important to him throughout his life. Michael's parents lived over 100 miles away, but Mark had had regular contact with them throughout his childhood. Indeed, not only had Michael taken him to visit them on some of his contact visits, but Ann had been active in sustaining this relationship as well as Mark's relationship with his paternal aunt, Gill. Granddad and Grandma sometimes came to stay with Ann and Tom, and, according to Mark, Ann and Gill had remained good friends despite her separation from Michael. In addition, Mark had frequently stopped off at Granddad and Grandma's on his way to and from university in the north of England. He said of his three sets of grandparents:

MARK: And in some respects it's much easier with grandparents.
INTERVIEWER: In what way?
MARK: Well it's easy to have a more normal relationship with grandparents, 'cause grandparents usually see, you know, a couple of dozen times a year perhaps, maybe not even that, a dozen times a year for a day or something and therefore you can have quite a normal grandparent-type relationship with stepgrandparents or whatever.

In contrast to these ties, Mark had no real relationship with Sheila's mother, Barbara, having met her on only a small number of occasions.

Mark was alluding to the difficulty he experienced having two fathers. As noted, he regarded his stepfather, Tom, as his "dad" and used a friendship analogy to characterize his relationship with Michael. In part, this reflected his everyday experience growing up, but it was also a reflection of his sense of who had taken on more parental responsibility. He was very aware of Tom's commitment to him and that Tom had never differentiated between Mark and his two biological children. He was also aware that Michael, despite being in a well-paid job, had contributed relatively little maintenance. Tom, by contrast, had been very generous, among other things paying for expensive private education. At the end of the interview, Mark was quite forthcoming about the tensions he felt around these relationships. He reported that when Michael married Sheila he (Mark) wanted to stop his regular access visits. For him, this seemed to offer something of a watershed, an opportunity for Michael to become more "embedded" in his new family and for Mark's family relationships to become more normative and "ordered." When he was asked if his relationship with Michael had ever caused any trouble with Ann and Tom, Mark replied:

Caused more aggro with me actually, the number of occasions I thought "This is it, I've had enough." . . . Once or twice I said "That's it, don't want any more to do with it." . . . [Mum] was responsible for keeping the links open. Had it been up to me I'd probably . . . [have kicked] it into touch, just lose it really. . . .

He ended the interview with a reflection that captured well his views of how family should be:

> I think you've got to pick one side of the family for being family, you can't have two families I don't think. You've got one group of a family, and the other group are going to be friends. . . . You've got to put your flag in the, on this level you've got to put your flag in the ground one side.

Mark's case, is, of course, not typical. No single case example could be typical. Each stepfamily has a unique history, developing from the specifics of the circumstances through which it was constructed. So too, over time individual stepfamily members actively generate their own constellation of family relationships, containing differences as well as similarities with others in a seemingly similar position. In Mark's case, his age at the time of his stepfamily's formation, the birth of half-siblings when he was still quite young, and the parenting role his stepfather assumed from early on are among the myriad factors that shaped his understanding of his location within his kinship network. Yet though not typical, Mark's account of his family connections provides a ready framework for examining key issues in the construction of nonhousehold stepfamily kinship. In developing this analysis, we focus in turn on different categories of stepfamily relationship, starting with nonresidential stepmothers.[5]

NONRESIDENTIAL STEPMOTHERS

From his statements quoted earlier, it is evident that Mark did not regard his stepmother, Sheila, as part of his family. She was clearly his father's partner rather than a member of Mark's own family. Because she was his father's partner, he developed a cordial, essentially positive relationship with Sheila, but it appeared to go no further than this. His contact with her was limited to those occasions when he visited his father. He had never stayed with her in the house that was clearly perceived the McDonald home. Moreover, although he had a friendship with Tom, his stepbrother, he was not involved with Sheila's family more widely. For instance, although he had met Sheila's mother on occasion, he did not have a significant relationship with her. In all these ways, it was evident that Sheila lay

---

[5] Throughout this chapter we use the U.K. terms "residential" and "nonresidential," rather than the North American terms "custodial" and "noncustodial," to refer to a parent with whom a child does or does not usually live. Of course, this distinction has become less straightforward over time as families and courts work out more flexible domestic arrangements for maintaining parental relationships following separation and divorce.

outside Mark's understanding of family. It is possible, of course, that this might change in the future, perhaps especially if Mark has children who come to regard Sheila as a grandmother figure, but as things were, Mark's relationship with Sheila was not perceived as a kinship one.

The majority of nonresidential stepmother-stepchild ties in the study took a broadly similar form to the relationship between Mark and Sheila. Especially once the child was an adult, the ties tended to be cordial but not particularly close. However, not all nonresidential stepmother-stepchild relationships are like this. Some children (of whatever age) have no relationship at all with their father's new partner. Principally this occurs when contact between the father and the child is either very limited or nonexistent following a divorce, a pattern that was more frequent in the past, when notions of a "clean break" held sway. In our sample there were a number of cases like this. In contrast, in a small number of other cases the relationships were much closer, with the stepchild coming to see the nonresidential stepmother as a family member despite their never having shared a household. Usually this was a consequence of the stepmother—and sometimes the stepchild—having demonstrated high levels of support and loyalty over a number of years, together with the child having a strong relationship with his or her father.

Overall, the pattern of nonresidential stepmother-stepchild relationships is influenced by a range of factors. Included among the most important are the relationship the child has with the father; the history of involvement of the child in the domestic arrangements of the nonresidential home, the relationship between the stepchild and any of his or her half-siblings, the types of support the stepmother has provided, and the length of time her partnership with the father has existed. Indeed, time, along with life course phase, can have its own consequences for the pattern of stepfamily solidarities. Not only can different dynamics and different perspectives develop in adulthood compared to childhood, but, as important, the birth of third-generation children may see the stepmother take on a grandmother role that modifies perceptions of the kinship connection between her and her (now parental) stepchild. This is unlikely to happen where the relationship between the stepmother and stepchild was previously negative, but, along with the increasingly sustained length of the relationship, participation of the stepmother in the grandchild's family-relevant experiences is likely to foster a sense of collective kinship.

We have focused on stepmothers and ignored stepfathers. In large part this is because nonresidential stepfathers are less common in childhood than nonresidential stepmothers, though this is changing to the extent that children are now more likely to spend time with both parents, in line with recent policy initiatives on parenting after separation and divorce. However, it is reasonable to assume that the same range of factors would pattern stepchildren's relationships with nonresidential stepfathers as pattern their relationships with nonresidential stepmothers.

A factor not considered explicitly here are the relationships that develop when a parent remarries after the child is already an adult. Generally such relationships appear not to be understood as kinship ones, except when an evident grandparental role develops over time. This issue is considered briefly in the next section, which focuses on step-grandparenthood.

STEP-GRANDPARENTS

Exactly who is a step-grandparent, and when they are regarded as such, are more complex issues than the attribution of biological grandparenthood. Until quite recently, remarriage was the defining criterion of step relations, though now, with the increase in cohabitation, the designation of this status is more complex. Further complexities arise when a son or daughter has been involved in a series of partnerships (as well as when the grandparents themselves have divorced and repartnered).

Two basic types of step-grandparental relationship can be identified. The first (referred to here as Type 1) involves the parents of a stepparent and that stepparent's stepchildren. The second form (Type 2) arises when a biological grandparent has remarried or repartnered. We will consider Type 2 step-grandparental ties briefly, but our main focus is on those step-grandparental relationships that develop as a consequence of repartnering in the middle generation.

Research has shown that grandparental relationships are neither uniform nor static (Gauthier, 2002; Rosenthal & Gladstone, 2000). They vary quite widely, with the same grandparents having different relationships with different grandchildren and, perhaps more important, with different sets of grandchildren. Moreover, these relationships change over time, as the generations age and their circumstances alter (Kemp, 2005; Silverstein & Marenco, 2001). Importantly too, grandparental relationships, like other kin ties, are influenced by the character of the ties sustained between the grandparents and the parents. This becomes particularly relevant when parents separate or divorce. In these instances the character of the relationship between grandchildren and their nonresidential parent's parents is likely to be affected by any tension that develops between the residential parent, on the one hand, and the nonresidential parent and his or her parents, on the other.

Notwithstanding the general diversity of grandparental relationships, what is evident in most relationships with biological grandchildren is the uniformity with which the perceived biological connection of blood is central to the understanding of grandparenting. The patterning of individual relationships may vary, yet the existence of a "natural" commitment, and consequently involvement, is largely unquestioned (Allan, 1996; Hodgson, 1992). Indeed, in our study, even when such involvement was absent, its absence was seen as needing explanation, thereby indicating its cardinal significance. While circumstances, feelings, and family culture may enter into the expression of this solidarity, its existence is largely taken as a natural feature of familial life.

Type 1 Step-grandparents

As with biological grandparents, there is diversity in the relationships maintained between Type 1 step-grandchildren and step-grandparents. Some, like Mark with Grandma and Grandpa, are very close, being seen in virtually all respects as equivalent in kinship terms to biological grandparents. However, in our study, as elsewhere, this was by no means the dominant pattern; most step-grandparents were viewed quite differently from biological grandparents. Indeed, in the majority of cases, step-grandchildren and step-grandparents were of relatively little consequence in each other's lives. In this, Mark's relationship with Sheila's mother was more typical than his relationship with Grandma and Grandpa. Although most respondents in our study recognized a mediated kin tie—step-grandparents were the parents of either their mother's or father's partner, and step-grandchildren were the children of their child's partner—this kin tie was not defined as full membership in their own kin universe. There was little sense of commonality or obligation and limited involvement except through the intermediary second generation (Coleman, Ganong, & Cable, 1997). Usually, they remained on the boundaries of each other's kinship.

The particular circumstances in which different relationships develop affect their structure (Attias-Donfut & Segalen, 2002). For example, the length of time the stepfamily has existed generally influences the ways the ties develop, as do the ages of the children when it was formed. Of consequence too is the degree to which the step-grandparents are routinely involved in the family's and child's life, which in turn depends in part on the quality of the relationship between the step-grandparents, their child, and their child's partner (Ganong & Coleman, 1998; Schmeeckle, Giarrusso, Feng, & Bengtson, 2006). In the case study, Mark's experiences with his respective step-grandparents are clearly illustrative of these broad processes. Mark's step-grandparents, Grandma and Grandpa, had been important grandparental figures throughout his childhood and were fully incorporated into his family experiences. Mark's commitment to and sense of kinship with them can be understood as a direct consequence of this history. But equally, the absence of any real involvement between Mark and Sheila's mother, Barbara, meant that Mark never regarded Barbara (somewhat like Sheila) as family, instead defining her as just "Sheila's mother." Step-grandparental relationships can also be influenced by the demography of grandparenting.

For example, the number of biological grandchildren a step-grandparent has, whether any of these grandchildren live in the same household as the step-grandchildren, and the role the step-grandchildren's biological grandparents play in their lives can all have an impact on the step-grandparental relationship.

A more kinship-relevant relationship may develop between a step-grandparent and a step-grandchild if the child was still dependent at the time the new partnership was formed. Even here, though, there is considerable variation, in part shaped by the issue of residence. Just as the step-grandchildren in the study needed to be young if any kinship element was to emerge, so too the children usually needed to be part of the stepparent's household for the step-grandparents to have become active in their lives (Cherlin & Furstenberg, 1994). Normally a nonresidential stepparent's parents had little involvement with their child's stepchildren, as was the case with Mark and Barbara. Indeed, generally they did not even meet that frequently. Principally this is because contact between the stepparent and his or her parents and between the stepparent and his or her stepchildren living outside the household is generally organized so as not to overlap. In other words, when a child spends time with a nonresidential parent, that time is typically set aside for servicing and sustaining the parent-child relationship, rather than involving "outsiders," which, in kinship terms, is how step-grandparents are normally perceived. If other kin ties outside the household are to be involved during these contact times, precedence would routinely be given to biological grandparents (or aunts, uncles, and cousins) on the nonresidential parent's side rather than to the step-grandparents (or other step relatives).

Thus, overall, Type 1 step-grandparental relationships are normally seen as quite distinct in kinship terms from grandparental relationships. Even allowing for the variation in the latter, this form of step-grandparenthood does not usually entail the same type of commitment, solidarity, or sense of kinship that biological grandparental ties typically do. Certainly among our sample only a subset of Type 1 ties between step-grandparents and step-grandchildren were considered at all pertinent to the kinship domain: those cases where the stepchild was young and living in the household with the stepparent at the time the stepfamily was formed. Mark's situation is a clear illustration of such a case, although it is atypical in the strength of the kinship solidarity expressed. However, even within these parameters, step-grandparents and step-grandchildren did not necessarily see themselves as kin. Usually they were conscious that their relationships were different from the ones they sustained with their biological grandchildren or grandparents. Indeed in our study, Type 1 ties between step-grandparents and step-grandchildren were generally only construed as kinship when a stepparent had taken on parental responsibility for infants or very young children—where, in effect, they had in some sense replaced the biological parent in the child's life from an early age.

Thus, normally there was an evident demarcation between "real" grandparents (i.e., those connected by a blood tie) and Type 1 step-grandparents. Even if the former, like most of the latter, played only a small part in their grandchild's day-to-day life, the sense of enduring solidarity and shared heritage was quite distinct from the emphasis on contingency present in the accounts given by our respondents of these Type 1 relationships. Emotionally, biological grandparents were commonly perceived—by grandparents, parents, and grandchildren—as having a common bond and self-evident connection with their grandchildren, however difficult it was to define such solidarity with any precision. Although there were counterexamples, in the large majority of cases these grandparents "naturally" took an interest in their grandchildren and cared about them. In contrast, and again with counterexamples such as Mark, step-grandparents were usually not seen, by any of the generations involved, to be committed to their step-grandchildren in the same way and were not thought of as having the same level of interest or right to involvement in their lives. Thus, in contrast to blood grandparenthood, Type 1 step-grandparent relationships generally entailed limited interest, minimal recognition of commonality, and little personal commitment. In this, the two sets of relationships were defined according to different frameworks, the one firmly rooted in the realm of kinship, but the other being seen as largely peripheral to it, defined as kin of a parent's partner rather than kin of one's own (Simpson, 1998).

Type 2 Step-grandparents

Type 2 step-grandparenthood occurs when a biological grandparent remarries or otherwise repartners. In some of these cases, the relationship between the step-grandparent and step-grandchildren is very limited, frequently as a result of a poor relationship between the parent and grandparent following the parental divorce. In particular, where fathers have had little contact with their children after separation, neither they nor their new partner is likely to be active in the grandchildren's lives. In some other cases too, the relationship between Type 2 step-grandparents and step-grandchildren lies outside a grandparental frame. In the study, this was usually a consequence of either a relatively recent repartnering or because of continuing conflict between the stepparent and the stepchild (i.e., the step-grandchildren's parent).

However, in nearly three quarters of cases of Type 2 step-grandparental ties discussed by our respondents, the relationship between the first and third generation took a clear grandparental form. Most markedly, where a step-grandparent had been a residential stepparent during the parent's own childhood, he or she usually formed part of a grandparental "package" with the biological grandparent, and they were treated as if they were biological grandparents. Even if the stepparent-stepchild relationship was problematic in earlier life phases, these stepparents were normally, though not always, assigned the status of honorary biological grandparents, especially from the perspective of the grandchildren, who in some cases were not even very aware that a step relationship existed. From their perspective, the grandparent and step-grandparent acted as grandparents do: generally visiting together, giving gifts jointly, and routinely being referred to in grandparental terms. As indicated earlier, this recognition of the kinship properties of Type 2 step-grandparents was rarely evident with Type 1 step-grandparents.

STEPSIBLINGS

Relationships between stepsiblings also vary depending on their circumstances, but overall, like step-grandparents, these people are not generally understood as being family members. The case example of Mark again provides a good illustration of this. Whereas Mark clearly regarded his half-siblings, Phil and Heather, as key members of his family, his relationships with Sheila's children, Dan and Jenny, were more distant. He appeared to have very little to do with Jenny, aside from meeting her when he went to visit his father. And of course, in the early part of Michael's relationship with Sheila, Michael visited Mark rather than Mark visiting him. Thus, in addition to their significant age difference, contact between Mark and Jenny was quite limited until Mark began to drive to Michael and Sheila's house.

These same factors applied in Mark's relationship with Dan, except they were similar in age. Mark's responses to questions about Dan show an evident ambivalence. It is almost as though he is uncomfortable saying that Dan is not part of his family, but equally has some problem saying that he is. He describes him as "a good close family member" to begin with, but then hesitates in calling him a brother, ending up solving this dilemma by calling him a friend: "Yeah. I wouldn't, I mean it may be wrong of me but I wouldn't put Dan in the [pause] how would you say it—friend of special consideration—I don't know." This ambivalence captures well the general uncertainty surrounding the kinship qualities of stepsibling ties where a good relationship exists. They tend to be seen as not quite family but still family-relevant.

Of course, it needs to be recognized here that Mark also sought to distance his family connection with his father while still presenting their relationship positively, also referring to his father in "friend" terms. The key to this lies in the way Mark constructed his family as the Wellington family rather than the McDonald family, with Dan (and Michael) belonging to the latter. Crucially in kinship terms, Mark's involvement with the McDonalds was only through his "weak" network tie (Granovetter, 1983). In effect, the absence of other family relationships between the Wellingtons and the McDonalds (aside from the link through Michael) providing network strength to the connection between Mark and Dan rendered their relationship less familylike. Related to this, the fact that Mark was incorporated only to a very limited degree in McDonald family rituals and celebrations also served to undermine his perception of Dan as family.

Other adult stepsibling relationships in the sample were influenced by similar considerations. Some, of course, were, in personal relationship terms, essentially nonexistent. In particular, in cases where a child had no further contact with a parent, usually the father, following parental divorce, there would be no likelihood of a personal tie developing between that child and any stepsiblings formed through the parent's repartnering. There may be knowledge that that parent had repartnered and now had stepchildren, but no relationship followed at the stepsibling level. In cases where a relationship with the nonresidential repartnered parent continued, there was likely to be contact with stepsiblings, but in the majority of cases, as with Mark and Jenny, this was limited. Factors such as age differences, geographical separation, and visiting patterns tended to restrict the extent to which a family-relevant connection developed. The relationship with the stepparent also seemed to be of consequence. The more positive this tie was, and consequently the more the stepson or stepdaughter was included in family events, the more likely that there would be interaction between the stepsiblings in adulthood.

Often, though, as in childhood, routine visits by adult stepsiblings to the parent's/stepparent's home were orchestrated to avoid overlap. That is, parents and stepparents tended to have their children visit at different times, so in practice, the opportunities for the stepsiblings to meet were comparatively limited. This is a different pattern from that commonly organized when (full or half-) siblings visit, in which case a parent may specifically arrange for other siblings to be there part of the time. With stepsiblings, especially those who have never shared a home in childhood, this happens far less frequently. Of course, when the stepsiblings lived near their parent's/stepparent's home, they were more likely to meet stepsiblings in passing, both at the parental home and in the locality, but generally this did not reflect a particularly significant relationship. As with biological siblings, parents may pass on news of stepsiblings and their families, but this tended to reflect superficial interest more than high levels of commitment or solidarity.

Aside from access visits, most stepsiblings do not live together during their childhood, and such access visits may sometimes be arranged so that residential children are visiting their own nonresidential parent when the nonresidential stepchild is visiting. Even when stepsiblings do share a home, it may be for quite a short period of their life, especially if the remarriage or repartnering occurred when one or the other was already in later adolescence. There may also be a significant age difference between them. However, when stepsiblings do spend their childhood in the same household, it is likely that different solidarities will develop; in these circumstances, their sense of family connection is likely to be stronger. In our sample, we had only one respondent, Ruth, who had lived with a stepsibling in childhood. (There were six other cases where a parent or stepparent reported on relationships between children and stepchildren who were currently coresiding or had coresided in the past. However, in all but one of these cases the children were still young and living in the parental/stepparental household.) Ruth expressed a strong sibling solidarity with her stepbrother, though the situation was confounded by her father's adoption of her stepbrother, who had no continuing contact with his biological father. Although no generalizations are warranted from this one case, it was noticeable that the sense of kinship portrayed for this relationship was markedly different from those reported by stepsiblings who had not been brought up in the same household.

CONCLUSION: KINSHIP SOLIDARITY AND COMMITMENT

Many analysts have focused on the difficulties that members of stepfamilies can experience in attempting to construct a viable sense of family. A wide range of factors, including the different kinship biographies of those involved, militate against the creation of the unity and connection commonly understood as central components of biological families. Generally these analyses of solidarity within stepfamilies focus on relationships developed and sustained within the household. This is a relatively narrow conception of what family involves, though one which is understandable given the within-household issues and divisions that can arise in stepfamilies, especially in their initial phases.

However, cultural constructions of family are premised on more than just the relationships within a particular household, important though these relationships are. Family is also about kinship. It involves people's shared connections to related others not necessarily living in the same household. In other words, it entails membership of a broader kinship network in which there is mutual recognition of common membership. Moreover, the significance of the kinship networks lies in their operating as networks. For genealogically closer kin especially, news and information about others flows through the network, thereby keeping people current, albeit differentially and sometimes at a distance, in each other's lives. Moreover, opportunities for interaction are often partially engineered through the agency of intermediaries who help coordinate visits and other activities involving different family members. Similarly, family rituals and ceremonies, including birthdays and religious festivities, bring closer kin together and consolidate their shared feeling of family. Such mundane network activity helps generate, as well as express, the shared commitment and solidarity that family signifies.

Our argument has been that these processes are generally far less constitutive of stepfamily kinship. The routine practices of kinship within stepfamilies do not serve to bind step relationships in the ways they do biological kin ties. Indeed, the operation of kinship within stepfamilies often serves to signify difference and boundaries rather than commonality. Even if stepchildren and stepparents come to define themselves as family, and the degree to which this happens is of course variable, it does not follow that the kin of either also define their relationships with, respectively, the stepparent or the stepchild in this way. Especially where the core stepfamily relationships are or were nonresidential, it is unlikely that they will do so. As important, the extent to which they will interact with one another in family settings will be quite limited.

Consider birthday celebrations as a simple illustration of family rituals that serve to demarcate family membership. If the event is, say, a stepfather's birthday, it is quite feasible that the stepfather's parents, siblings, and children may be involved in the birthday celebration. His stepchildren may also participate, depending on their age, residence, and the closeness of their tie. However, unless the stepchild is young (i.e., still a child) and living with the stepfather, it is far less likely that these same kin of the stepfather will be involved in the stepchild's birthday in any significant way. In a similar vein, it is unlikely for the reasons discussed earlier that any of a stepparent's kin would arrange to be present when stepchildren visit their parent and stepparent's home. It is the absence of stepkin from mundane involvement in the contexts in which such family practices are enacted that serves to mark them off as nonfamily. That is, their noninclusion in each other's family life is not coincidental; it is structured into family organization and signifies family boundaries and difference.

As emphasized throughout this chapter, there is much variation in the detailed ways that different relationships between stepkin develop. Moreover, relationships are not static; they can change significantly over time. There has been comparatively little research conducted into stepkinship. The growing body of research into stepfamily relationships has been predominantly concerned with the management of relationships within stepfamily households. Even where research attention is directed at stepfamily relationships outside the household, it tends to focus most on stepparent-stepchild relationships in adulthood rather than examining the wider set of stepkin ties. As a consequence, this chapter has relied heavily on a single study carried out in England, the conclusions of which may or may not mirror the organization of stepfamily kin relationships in other Western cultures. However, given the similarities found in other aspects of stepfamily practices, it seems likely that the general thrust of the findings will have wider applicability.

With certain exceptions, there seems little to indicate that stepkin in general play a particularly significant part in people's lives. One exception is with long-standing Type 2 step-grandparents, where the step-grandparent is fully part of the grandparent package. A second exception can occur as a result of the stepfamily being formed when a child is very young and residing with a stepparent who fulfills a strong parental role in his or her life. In such cases, stepkin connections are likely to be stronger when there are half-siblings born in the stepfamily close in age to the residential stepchildren. Overall, though, in other stepfamily formations, stepkin ties appear not to be recognized as being within the realm of "family as kinship." Although an indirect linkage will be acknowledged, this is rarely constructed as one in which normative conventions of "real" kinship apply.

There is, for example, little sense of obligation or responsibility and, importantly, little sense of connection in these cases. The "diffuse, enduring solidarity" that Schneider (1968) identified as the hallmark of American kinship is certainly absent in the majority of instances. Most stepkin do not appear to participate in the routine family and kinship practices that help constitute an individual's construction of family. Instead, these are people who, on an everyday level, lie outside the symbolic boundaries of family and kinship. Their existence does not consolidate the kinship network, but rather serves to demarcate ideas of family solidarity within step relationships. That is, they tend to signify the different kinship networks within which the stepfamily members are involved and thus are effectively "qualifiers" in the construction of family solidarity. In biological families, despite the coming together of two kin sets, kinship practices tend to be integrative. As we have argued, it is less clear that this is so with stepkin relationships. With most stepkin practices, it appears to be the absence of connection that is implicitly reinforced.

REFERENCES

Allan, G. (1996). *Kinship and friendship in modern Britain.* Oxford: Oxford University Press.

Allan, G. (2008). Flexibility, friendship, and family. *Personal Relationships, 15,* 1–16.

Attias-Donfut, C., & Segalen, M. (2002). The construction of grandparenthood. *Current Sociology, 50,* 281–294.

Cherlin, A. (2004). The deinstitutionalization of American marriage. *Journal of Marriage and the Family, 66,* 848–861.

Cherlin, A., & Furstenberg, F. (1994). Stepfamilies in the United States: A reconsideration. *American Review of Sociology, 20,* 359–381.

Coleman, M., Ganong, L., & Cable, S. M. (1997). Beliefs about women's intergenerational family obligations to provide support before and after divorce and remarriage. *Journal of Marriage and the Family, 59,* 165–176.

Finch, J., & Mason, J. (1993). *Negotiating family responsibilities.* London: Routledge.

Ganong, L. H., & Coleman, M. (1998). An exploratory study of grandparents' and stepgrandparents' financial obligations to grandchildren and stepgrandchildren. *Journal of Social and Personal Relationships, 15,* 39–58.

Gauthier, A. (2002). The role of grandparents. *Current Sociology, 50,* 295–307.

Granovetter, M. (1983). The strength of weak ties: A network theory revisited. *Sociological Theory, 1,* 201–233.

Hodgson, L. G. (1992). Adult grandchildren and their grandparents: The enduring bond. *International Journal of Aging and Human Development, 34,* 209–225.

Kemp, C. L. (2005). Dimensions of grandparent-adult grandchild relationships: From family ties to intergenerational friendships. *Canadian Journal on Aging, 24,* 161–177.

McGoldrick, M., & Gerson, R. (1985). *Genograms in family assessment.* London: Norton.

Morgan, D. H. J. (1996). *Family connections.* Cambridge, England: Polity Press.

Ribbens McCarthy, J., Edwards, R., & Gillies, V. (2003). *Making families: Moral tales of parenting and step-parenting.* Durham, England: Sociologypress.

Rosenthal, C., & Gladstone, J. (2000). *Grandparenthood in Canada.* Ottawa, Ontario, Canada: Vanier Institute of the Family.

Schmeeckle, M., Giarrusso, R., Feng, D., & Bengtson, V. L. (2006). What makes someone family? Adult children's perceptions of current and former stepparents. *Journal of Marriage and the Family, 68,* 595–610.

Schneider, D. (1968). *American kinship: A cultural account.* Englewood Cliffs, NJ: Prentice-Hall.

Silverstein, M., & Marenco, A. (2001). How Americans enact the grandparent role across the family life course. *Journal of Family Issues, 22,* 493–522.

Simpson, B. (1998). *Changing families.* Oxford: Berg.

CHAPTER 15

Children in Stepfamilies: Relationships with Nonresident Parents

JAN PRYOR

Contrary to popular impressions . . . when the former spouse remains active in the child's life, stepfamily life . . . does not seem to suffer.
—Furstenberg and Nord (1985, p. 893)

THE DYNAMICS of stepfamily relationships, particularly for children, have changed significantly in the past 6 decades. Perhaps most challenging and perplexing for children is whether they can, or should, maintain relationships with both their resident and nonresident parents, and if so, how to do this. Until relatively recently, this dilemma did not exist. Either a parent was lost through death, in which case there was no choice to be made, or the nonresident parent was absent from the children's lives. The latter situation may have removed a dilemma, but it put the children in the position of experiencing "ambiguous loss"—where the person missing from their lives is not dead, but neither is he or she accessible to them.

For many children this loss is amplified by the criticism and reviling of their absent parent by the parent with whom they live. They suffer, in this case, the double burden of missing and continuing to love the person who may simultaneously be being denigrated by their other parent. This parent may be experiencing rejection, anger, or guilt; at the very least, his or her relationship with the nonresident parent has deteriorated to the point that cohabitation is no longer tenable.

Into this mix comes the fact that, after their parents' divorce, children are likely to enter a stepfamily household, when one or both parents repartner. It is estimated that 33% of children in the United States will spend some time in a stepfamily before the age of 18 (Bumpass, Raley, & Sweet, 1995) and that 66% of children with a nonresident parent will gain a stepfather in their life (White & Gilbreth, 2001). In Japan, 25% of marriages are remarriages for one or both of the partners (Nozawa, 2006); in the United Kingdom 30% of marriages in 1993 were remarriages for one or both partners; in Australia the figure is 34%; and in New Zealand the figure was 34% in 2005 (Statistics, 2007b). Furthermore, many partners in stepfamilies cohabit rather than marry; in Australia 53% of stepfamilies were in cohabiting households, and 72% cohabited before marrying (De Vaus & Qu, 2003).

The introduction, and sometimes intrusion, of another parenting figure brings with it another layer of dilemmas when children may have to pit the feelings they have for their nonresident parent against those for the new person with whom they will now live. As many chapters in this book attest, families deal with these issues in diverse and more or less successful ways.

The likelihood of a nonresident parent being absent from a child's life is changing. Until recently, statistics indicated that contact between nonresident fathers and their children decreases over time and is very likely to cease altogether (Furstenberg & Nord, 1985; Seltzer, 1991). Recent studies suggest, however, that increasing numbers of men are wanting and in many cases achieving not just regular contact, but involved parenting relationships with their children (Pryor & Rodgers, 2001). This is reinforced, in turn, by the assumption (or presumption, in some jurisdictions) of shared responsibility for children after parental separation. The rights talk that has predominated in this regard is increasingly being replaced by a discourse about parents' joint responsibilities for their children's well-being. At the same time, research is indicating that contact and involvement with nonresident parents may be beneficial for children after divorce (Amato & Gilbreth, 1999). These factors have been effective in encouraging men not just to see their children on weekends and to entertain them, but to have day-to-day, ordinary experiences with them that encompass parenting behaviors such as preparing meals and taking children to school. However, until very recently most extant research has not distinguished between contact with children in lone-parent households and contact with those living in stepfamilies.

Does the finding that involvement with a nonresident parent is beneficial apply in stepfamilies, when a parent repartners? As the epigraph, written 23 years ago, suggests, there was a cautious acknowledgment that it might not *hurt* children to stay in touch with their nonresident parent after a stepfamily has formed. Research is now asking whether contact and involvement by this parent might in fact benefit children and the stepfamilies they live in, and if so, under what conditions. It is also addressing the question of what dynamics play out among the relationships a child sustains or not between resident parent, stepparent, and nonresident parent. In this chapter, I discuss recent data on contact between children and nonresident parents and outline the factors that inhibit or encourage contact. I address the impact on contact of either or both parents repartnering and review recent studies that have examined the comparative and unique contributions of contact with nonresident parents.

HOW MUCH CONTACT DO CHILDREN HAVE WITH NONRESIDENT PARENTS?

Studies that address the amount of contact that children have with nonresident parents have tended to focus on nonresident fathers, since even today the majority of children live primarily with their mother. In Australia in 2003, for example, 82% of nonresident parents were men (Australian Bureau of Statistics (ABS, 2006), and in New Zealand 81.8% of lone-parent households were headed by women (Statistics, 2007b), suggesting that about the same numbers of nonresident parents are men.

The measurement of contact between children and nonresident parents is far from straightforward. Argys, Peters, Cook, Garasky, Nepomnyaschy, and Sorenson (2007) note that even using nationally representative samples with similar age and ethnic distributions, reported levels of contact vary significantly. Reported levels of contact also differ by reporter. In most studies, mothers' estimates of contact are collected. Where estimates are gathered from both resident and nonresident parents, it is almost always the case that resident parents report lower levels of nonresident parent contact than do nonresident parents (Argys et al., 2007; Blackwell & Dawe, 2003). Interestingly, Argys does not report instances of children's estimates of contact; in a nonrepresentative sample of children in stepfamilies where estimates were taken from resident and nonresident parents and children, children's and nonresident parents' reports of frequent contact (once a week or more) were similar to each other and lower than those of resident parents (Pryor, 2004).

Increasingly, too, contact is maintained not just by face-to-face meetings but also by phone, mail, e-mail, and texting. These can be significant channels for maintaining the relationship a child has with a parent he or she is not living with and is not able to see frequently. Argys et al. (2007) reports that in the National Longitudinal Study of Youth (NLSY) 97 sample, 10% of children had contact with nonresident parents only by cards, letters, or phone. Indeed, texting may be a means of maintaining a relationship that would otherwise be awkward face-to-face. Cooksey and Craig (1998) suggest that communication by phone and letter may foster communication about what is happening for the child more than visits, which might tend to focus on activities. There appears to be a positive correlation, however, between direct and indirect contact (Blackwell & Dawe, 2003; Cooksey & Craig, 1998). In other words, if a child has a lot of direct contact with the nonresident parent, they are also likely to have high levels of indirect contact (phone, texting, e-mail etc).

Overall, contact between children and their nonresident parent is both complex and changing. However, it is possible to discern a trend toward increasing involvement of nonresident parents in the lives of their children.

DIFFERENCES BETWEEN NONRESIDENT FATHERS AND NONRESIDENT MOTHERS

The few studies that have examined the differences in contact between non-resident fathers and nonresident mothers have all reported that children see more of their nonresident mother than of their nonresident father (ABS, 2006; Australian, 2006; Furstenberg & Nord, 1985; Stewart, 1999). In their 1981 sample, Furstenberg and Nord found that 64% of nonresident mothers and 40% of nonresident fathers had seen their children in the prior month and that 7% of mothers and 42% of fathers had not seen their children in the prior year.

More recent figures from Australia, in 2003, show a similar pattern: 65% of nonresident mothers and 53% of nonresident fathers reported seeing their children every other week, while 14% of nonresident mothers and 36% of nonresident fathers never saw their children (ABS, 2006). Using a 1987–1988 sample from the National Survey of Families and Households in the United States, Stewart (1999) found that in-person visits were at similar levels for mothers and fathers, but that nonresident mothers were more likely than nonresident fathers to communicate by phone and letter and to have spent extended time with their children.

There are some differences in the living arrangements of nonresident mothers and fathers that are likely to be important in this regard. In an Australian survey, it was found that 86% of nonresident mothers live in a family, but only 60% of nonresident fathers do; 32% of nonresident fathers are living alone, compared with only 9.7% of mothers (ABS, 2006). Furthermore, in many cases the children of nonresident mothers were not living with their father but with other family members. Men who are living alone may be involved in a lifestyle that does not easily fit with spending time with children; they may not have appropriate accommodation for them, for example.

OVERNIGHT VISITS

An important aspect of contact is whether or not children stay overnight with their nonresident parent. Furstenberg and Nord (1985) found that 20% of nonresident fathers and 42% of nonresident mothers never had their children stay with them overnight; in Australia in 2003, 52% of children never stayed with their nonresident father, and 36% of those living with their father never stayed with their nonresident mother (ABS, 2006). This is likely to be very significant for fostering the relationship between children and the parents they do not live with, since staying overnight provides the opportunity for parenting that involves ordinary activities such as preparing meals, getting children ready for bed, and preparing them for school in the morning.

WHAT FACTORS ARE ASSOCIATED WITH CHILDREN'S CONTACT WITH NONRESIDENT PARENTS?

Just as understanding the levels of contact between children and their parent living outside their household is complex, so too are the factors that impact the frequency of contact. There is, though, reasonable consensus among studies about the influences that bear on this. The repartnering of either parent, as a factor potentially influencing contact, is considered in a separate section.

THE RELATIONSHIP BETWEEN CHILDREN'S BIOLOGICAL PARENTS

The extent to which parents can cooperate in coparenting their children after separation is found consistently to be related to contact between children and their nonresident parent. Parents who communicate effectively and have at least a degree of positive regard for their ex-partner are likely to foster, or at least not to impede, the relationship of the child with the other parent. Studies in Australia (Funder, Harrison, & Weston, 1993), the United Kingdom (Dunn, Cheng, O'Connor, & Bridges, 2004; Flouri, 2006), and the United States (Arditti & Bickley, 1996; Sobolewski & King, 2005; Whiteside & Becker, 2000) all report a positive association between the quality of the interparental relationship and contact with nonresident parents. Some also find a negative association between conflict and frequency of contact (Whiteside & Becker, 2000); others, though, do not (Buchanan & Maccoby, 1996; Sobolewski & King, 2005). Flouri found that interparental conflict predicted not contact, but level of involvement between children and nonresident parents; it was also predictive of outcomes for children. This suggests that although conflicted parents may be able to sustain contact between children and nonresident parents, the quality of that relationship is compromised by disagreement and has an impact on children's well-being, possibly via the quality of the relationship.

In their English sample of formerly married parents, Maclean and Eekelaar (1997) found that where contact was maintained between children and nonresident parents over time, 58% of the parental relationships *improved* over time. So did 48% of formerly cohabiting parents, and 31% of parents who had never lived together. In many instances these relationships had been quite conflicted immediately after separation. This finding highlights that caution is necessary in assuming causality between conflict and contact and the need to examine the course of conflict over time between parents. It may be that ongoing contact between children and parents living outside the household fosters the reduction of conflict and an increase in cooperation between parents. Indeed, time usually acts to reduce the negative aspects of separation and divorce for adults and for children.

PARTNERSHIP STATUS AT THE TIME OF CHILDREN'S BIRTH

Remaining in contact with a nonresident child is a major aspect of commitment to that child by a parent, and it might be expected that the status of the interparental relationship at the child's birth will reflect that commitment. This is elegantly demonstrated in the U.K. study by Maclean and Eekelaar (1997), in which they noted a continuum of contact from those fathers who were not living with their child's mother at the time of birth, through those who were cohabiting, to those who were married. Continuing contact was found for 35% of the never-together group, 45% for the cohabiting group, and 69% of the formerly married group. Conversely, no contact was reported for 39% of the never-together group, 14% of the formerly cohabiting group, and 5% for the formerly married parents. Seltzer (1991) and Cooksey and Craig (1998) report similar patterns in the United States, although Cooksey and Craig found no differences in contact between formerly cohabiting and formerly married nonresident parents.

PAYMENT OF CHILD SUPPORT

There are consistent findings both in the United Kingdom (Blackwell & Dawe, 2003; Maclean & Eekelaar, 1997) and the United States (Whiteside & Becker, 2000) that payment of child support by nonresident parents is associated with the frequency of contact with children. Although the direction of effects has not been unraveled, it is likely both that having to pay support encourages contact and also that those fathers who seek contact are more likely than not to pay child support.

AGE AND GENDER OF CHILDREN

The age of children in itself is not consistently associated with frequency of contact (Aquilino, 2006; Blackwell & Dawe, 2003; Cooksey & Craig, 1998); however, their age at the time their parents separated is. Maclean and Eekelaar (1997) found that fathers were more likely to stay in contact with their nonresident children the longer they had lived with them, and Aquilino reported that if children was separated from their father at birth, levels of contact and support were very low. The corollary of this is the finding that the longer parents had been separated, the lower the levels of contact (Blackwell & Dawe, 2003; Flouri, 2006). Not surprisingly, the age of children is associated with their ability to talk on the phone with their nonresident parents, with younger children less able to do this and hence maintain indirect contact (Cooksey & Craig, 1998). Age at time of separation is, of course, confounded with the length of time the parent and child lived together before separation, a factor that may be more important.

Gender is not a predictor of contact with nonresident parents (Aquilino, 2006; Cooksey & Craig, 1998; Flouri, 2006; Stewart, 1999). However, boys are less likely than girls to talk on the phone to their father (Cooksey & Craig, 1998).

DISTANCE BETWEEN HOMES

Not surprisingly, the farther away a nonresident parent lives from his children, the lower the level of both direct and indirect contact (Cooksey & Craig, 1998). Blackwell and Dawe (2003), however, found that in the United Kingdom distance had less impact on levels of phone calls and letters than on levels of direct contact.

DOES CONTACT CHANGE WHEN PARENTS REPARTNER?

The majority of research has focused on children's relationships with nonresident parents without distinguishing between nonresident (and resident) parents who have repartnered and those who have not. Yet parental separation and divorce is usually the first of at least two transitions between household types for children, since the majority of adults repartner within 5 years of divorce.

When a resident parent repartners, the dynamics of the interparental relationship are likely to change, and, as we have seen, this relationship is associated with levels of contact for the child and the nonresident parent. The parent who repartners is likely to feel supported by the new partner in his or her parenting, while at the same time focusing energy on the new relationship. This may lead to reduced quality of relationship with the ex-partner. In turn, the nonresident parent may feel a sense of threat about being replaced by the stepparent of the same sex, living day to day in the same household with their child. Both factors may contribute to a reduction in contact levels for the child and the nonresident parent.

Repartnering by nonresident parents is also likely to have an impact on the dynamics of their relationship with their child. They will be investing more energy in their new household, especially if they are in a parenting role with children of their new partner that conflicts with the relationship with their own child; or they may have children with their new partner.

When the resident parent repartners, children may experience a conflict of loyalties between parenting figures of the same sex, which may impact their contribution to the contact they have with the other parent. On the one hand, the introduction of a new parenting figure into the household may lead them to seek increased contact with their nonresident parent as a reaction to their resident parent's new partner. On the other hand, they may withdraw from the nonresident parent because of the confusion involved in maintaining the two relationships.

Partnering by Residential Parents: The Evidence

Reports about the potential impact when a residential parent repartners are evenly divided in their findings. Four studies, using samples a decade apart, found that the repartnering of resident mothers had no impact on the frequency and quality of contact between children and nonresident parents (Dunn et al., 2004; Flouri, 2006; Maclean & Eekelaar, 1997; Manning & Smock, 1999). Conversely, two reports based on recent samples (ABS, 2006; Blackwell & Dawe, 2003) and one based on data collected a decade earlier (Aquilino, 2006) indicate that resident mothers' repartnering was related to contact between children and their nonresident parent. However, in the later samples maternal repartnering was associated with reduced contact, whereas the longitudinal data used by Aquilino showed that when resident mothers repartnered, both contact with and support from nonresident fathers increased. In Blackwell and Dawe's sample, contact decreased only if the mother repartnered *and* had another child.

The younger children are when parents repartner, the more likely they are to have diminishing contact with their nonresident parent, since they will have spent a shorter time living in the same household with him or her. The young people in Aquilino's (2006) sample were between 13 and 19 when their parents repartnered and, as Aquilino suggests, may have found stepfamily life complicated in their mother's households and so turned to their nonresident father for support. In Mclean and Eekelaar's (1997) sample, the repartnering of formerly married parents made a minimal difference to contact; however, the age of the child at divorce did: Contact decreased more if the children were younger at separation than if they were older. The strength of a nonresident father-child relationship seems to be very dependent on the length of time they have lived together.

Overall, the available evidence suggests that children's contact with nonresident parents does not necessarily decrease when resident parents repartner, and may even increase. The factors that influence increased or decreased contact need further investigation. In particular, changes in the nature of the coparenting relationship merit further investigation.

Partnering by Nonresident Parents: The Evidence

As with resident parents, the evidence for changing levels of contact when nonresident parents repartner is at best equivocal. Some studies using recent data (ABS, 2006; Blackwell & Dawe, 2003) indicate that when nonresident parents repartner, contact is reduced, especially if the nonresident parent has subsequent children. Stewart (1999) reported lower levels of both contact and involvement with nonresident parents when they repartnered. However, Flouri (2006) reported reduced frequency of contact but not of involvement in her U.K. sample. On the other hand, both Cooksey and Craig (1998) and Aquilino (2006) reported *increased* involvement with nonresident parents who are married, and both studies suggest that there is an association between remarriage and family orientation. Remarried fathers demonstrate an orientation to family life that is matched by their continuing relationships with their nonresident children.

Two factors appear to be particularly important. First, Seltzer (1991), Maclean and Eekelaar (1997), and Aquilino (2006) all found that the status of the parents' relationship at the birth of the child is predictive of level of contact between the child and the nonresident parent. If parents are not living together or are cohabiting but not married, contact between nonresident parents and children is less frequent. This suggests that nonresident parents who were not married to the child's other parent had a lower level of commitment to their children, and probably spent less time living with them.

Second, Cooksey and Craig (1998) found an association between the children with whom a nonresident parent is living and contact with his or her nonresident children. Specifically, living with stepchildren does not reduce contact, but living with new biological children does. However, using the same data from the National Survey of Families and Households, Aquilino (2006) did not find this association.

Clearly there is a great deal of diversity in the ways family dynamics play out when parents repartner. The impact of residential parents' repartnering appears to be negligible or even positive in regard to contact between children and their nonresident parent, especially if the child is an adolescent at the time of repartnering. Because the majority of stepfamilies are stepfather households, we might expect, then, that the formation of a stepfamily will not reduce contact. The picture is more complex for nonresident parents who repartner. Some, especially those who marry, appear to maintain involvement with biological nonresident children; for others, involvement with a new partner and coresident children seems to crowd out their involvement with their nonresident children. For children in

stepfamilies, then, nonresident parent partnership status may be more salient for ongoing contact than the fact that they are living in a stepfamily.

DOES THE RELATIONSHIP WITH NONRESIDENT PARENTS MATTER FOR CHILDREN?

Given the common finding that children want to see more of their nonresident parent than they usually do (Pryor & Rodgers, 2001), we might assume
that the apparent rise in levels of contact is a good thing in its own right
(with obvious caveats, such as the presence of abuse). When the evidence
for advantages of contact is examined, however, the findings are at best
equivocal (Amato, 1993; King, 1994). There is surprisingly little support for
the benefits of contact in itself for children's well-being. When this became
apparent, scholars looked at the possible role of the affective quality of the
relationships between children and their nonresident parent. Again, the
evidence is mixed; some studies report some benefits (Amato & Riviera,
1999; Buchanan & Maccoby, 1996), while others find no relationship between closeness and well-being (Furstenberg, Morgan, & Allison, 1987).

A meta-analysis of studies that have investigated the nonresident parent-
child relationship has suggested that the most important factor is the extent
to which the parent can be involved with the child in an active parenting
role (Amato & Gilbreth, 1999). This includes monitoring, support, and involvement with school life rather than contact that is based on entertain-
ment and gift giving. More recent studies, though, especially those that
examine children in stepfamilies, suggest that contact does have links with
well-being (Dunn et al., 2004). It is notable, too, that involvement may have
a cultural component that changes the nature of the relationship between
contact and well-being. In Chinese families in Hong Kong, for example,
contact with nonresident fathers is linked with lower well-being for children because Chinese fathers tend to exhibit discipline-oriented and
problem-oriented patterns of parenting (Lau, 2004). In African American
families, children tend not to benefit from contact with their father (Thomas,
Farrell, & Grace, 1996).

Overall, research that has examined facets of nonresident parent-child
relationships including levels of contact, feelings of closeness, and quality
of involvement indicates that although the first two may have advantages
and some links with well-being, the quality of the involvement appears to
have the most measurable benefits for children.

Importantly, though, most of the research that has taken place examining the impact of the relationship between the child and the nonresident
parent has not distinguished between children living in lone-parent households and those living in stepfamilies. It has also focused, in the main, on
nonresident fathers since the majority of nonresident parents are men. In

the previous section I noted that the repartnering of resident parents does not appear to have an impact on the levels of contact between children and nonresident parents, especially for children who are older at the time their parent repartners. Feelings of closeness might, though, be affected by a child's relationship with another parent of the same sex (usually the step-father). On the one hand, they may feel less close to their nonresident parent as the relationship with the resident stepparent develops, especially if the nonresident parent is relatively absent in their life. Or they may move closer to their nonresident parent if they experience the stepparent as an intrusion in their life. Opportunities for the nonresident parent to remain an active and involved parent may thus either decrease or increase when another parenting figure enters a child's life. The age of the child at the time the stepfamily is formed is likely to be salient; stepparents are less likely to become involved in the parenting of older children and adolescents and more likely to be involved with younger stepchildren. Children who are younger when their biological parents separate and when a step-family is formed will also have spent less time with their nonresident parent than older children, reducing the likelihood of having formed a close relationship.

What does the research say? In the past 10 to 15 years several studies have examined the impact of nonresident parents on children in stepfamilies in several countries, including the United States (Berg, 2003; Falci, 2006; King, 2006; Schenck et al., 2006; Vogt Yuan & Hamilton, 2006; White & Gilbreth, 2001), the United Kingdom (Dunn et al., 2004; Flouri, 2006), and New Zealand (Pryor, 2004). All report, to a greater or lesser degree, links between the relationship between the child and the nonresident parent and the child's well-being. And, similar to those studies that did not distinguish children in stepfamilies from those in lone-parent families, the majority found that it was the quality of the relationships rather than the contact level that was salient. Quality is measured in various ways; in many cases closeness was assessed as a measure of quality, often using a single item (Berg, 2003; Falci, 2006; King, 2006). A more comprehensive measure was used by White and Gilbreth (six items assessing the quality of the relationship). Schenk et al. (2006) assessed the degree to which 12-year-olds felt they mattered to their nonresident father using a seven-item measure. It was notable, though, that in our New Zealand study discussed later, we found that closeness to nonresident parents, measured by a single item, was more strongly predictive of well-being than comprehensive measures of the quality of the relationship.

Two studies (Dunn et al., 2004; Flouri, 2006) found that the salient factor was contact level rather than the quality of the relationship. It was notable that Dunn and colleagues found that the relationship between the child and the nonresident parent was more relevant for children in lone-parent households than for those living in stepfamilies. One study (Vogt Yuan & Hamilton, 2006) reported that levels of conflict between adolescents and their nonresident parents was the variable that was predictive of well-being, and that closeness and contact were not.

STEPPARENTS AND NONRESIDENT PARENTS: EITHER, BOTH, OR NEITHER?

When children's biological parents repartner, they are in a situation where they usually have at least three potential parenting figures in their lives, two of the same sex—usually a stepfather and a nonresident father. White and Gilbreth (2001) have suggested three possible models to predict whether or not nonresident parents remain important for children in stepfamilies. An *accumulation* model suggests that both fathers are important for well-being and that children can add parenting figures to their lives. The *substitution* model indicates that children substitute one parent for the other—most often the stepfather takes the place of the nonresident father—and that children can involve only one fathering figure in their lives. The *loss* model suggests that children lose significant relationships with any fathering figures when they enter a stepfamily because their nonresident father becomes irrelevant and the stepfather does not fulfill a parenting role.

An interesting question is whether or not the quality of relationships children have with the parenting figures is related. If a child has a positive relationship with a stepparent, does he or she also have a positive relationship with a nonresident parent? If so, this would suggest that the quality of the relationships children have with parenting figures is at least partially an indication of the children's ability to sustain relationships (and conversely, to foster negative relationships with parenting figures). If there is no correspondence between the quality of the two relationships, this indicates that they are quite independent of each other and that other factors will determine the quality of each relationship. If they are negatively related, the indication is that children cannot sustain positive relationships with two parents of the same sex; if one relationship is positive, the other is negative. This last situation supports the substitution model. The few studies that reported correlations between measures of relationships with stepfathers and nonresident fathers found either no relationship (Schenck et al., 2006; White & Gilbreth, 2001) or partial support for a positive relationship (Dunn et al., 2004). Our study, discussed later, found moderate support for positive associations between the two relationships.

Valerie King (2006) has extended the three models proposed by White and Gilbreth (2001) to suggest five hypotheses regarding the importance for the children's well-being of children's relationships with nonresident parents and stepparents. The first is the *additive* hypothesis, similar to the cumulative model, which predicts that closeness to both father figures will lead to the highest levels of well-being. The second is the *redundancy* hypothesis, suggesting that it doesn't matter which father a child is close to and that being close to a second father is redundant in terms of well-being so long as he or she is close to one of them. The third, the *primacy of biology* hypothesis, predicts that what is important is being close to the biological father and that being close to a stepfather adds little in terms of well-being. The fourth, the *primacy of residency* hypothesis, suggests the opposite: that closeness to the residential stepfather confers well-being with little added benefit from feeling close to the nonresident parent. The final hypothesis suggested by King is the *irrelevance* model, suggesting that neither father is important for children's well-being because relationships with mothers or other resources are more significant.

There are five studies that have addressed these questions in regard to stepfather families; I will describe the findings of each in turn. First, Dunn and her colleagues (2004) found that contact, but *not* the quality of the relationships, with nonresident parents was associated with low levels of externalizing in their sample of 10-year-olds. The relationships with stepfathers did not predict well-being in the sample. These findings offer support for the substitution model and for the primacy of biology hypothesis: The nonresident parents continued to exert an influence on their children's well-being, but the stepparents did not.

White and Gilbreth (2001) found evidence in support of the accumulation model, with relationships with both stepfathers and nonresident fathers being associated with adolescents' outcomes. They noted, too, that although the quality of the relationships with the two fathers was not correlated, they were almost identical.

Falci's (2006) findings in adolescents also supported the accumulation model. High levels of closeness to both stepfathers and nonresident fathers in her study were associated with low levels of distress. She also found that in stepfamilies closeness to mothers was not related to levels of distress. Similarly, Berg's (2003) study of adolescents showed an accumulation model, whereby both stepfathers and nonresident fathers contributed to levels of self-esteem. King's (2006) findings are a little more complex, but nonetheless support a cumulative model. She found that the optimal combination for the adolescents in her study was a close relationship with both stepfathers and nonresident fathers, but that close relationships with stepfathers alone was almost as beneficial, offering partial support for the substitution model and the primacy of residency hypothesis. Those young people who were worst off did not have close relationships with either their stepfather or their nonresident father, refuting the loss model suggested by White and Gilbreth (2001). King also found, along with Falci (2006), that closeness to resident mothers did not make a significant contribution to adolescent well-being.

Finally, Schenck and her colleagues (2006) found that mattering to non-resident fathers was associated with children's internalizing behavior, and that mattering to stepfathers was related to both internalizing and externalizing behavior. The cumulative model is again supported, although like King (2006) they found that for school-based problems the redundancy hypothesis seemed to be accurate; mattering to one or the other father was sufficient to reduce problems at school.

Two studies have addressed these complex dynamics in resident step-mother families. Berg (2003) included a group of stepmother families in her study and found that although young people reported being closer to nonresident mothers than to nonresident fathers, their feelings of closeness to stepmothers contributed the most variance to their self-esteem. A recent study by King (2007) found that adolescents reported similar levels of closeness to stepmothers and nonresident mothers when levels of contact were taken into consideration. Closeness to resident fathers in these families was the strongest predictor of both internalizing and externalizing behaviors, and closeness to nonresident mothers was also a significant but somewhat weaker predictor. Closeness to stepmothers predicted neither kinds of behavior. These findings are contrary to those of Berg's, but support an accumulation model—38% of these adolescents said they were close to both stepmothers and nonresident mothers. It is important to note, though, that different outcomes were used in these studies, and it is possible that there are differential patterns for each parenting figure. There is a paucity of research involving stepmother households; it seems, however, that the dynamics among parent-child relationships in these families may differ from those in stepfather households.

These findings offer consistent support for the accumulation model of the roles of fathering figures in children's lives, and also for King's (2006) additive hypothesis. It is notable, too, that in many instances the quality of the relationship with nonresident parents was primarily related to internalizing or affective aspects of well-being, whereas the relationship with stepfathers was primarily related to externalizing behaviors.

THE RESILIENCE IN STEPFAMILIES STUDY

This study was carried out in 2004 in Wellington, New Zealand. Three members in each of a total of 90 stepfamilies completed questionnaires (focal child, resident parent, and stepparent). Nonresident parents also completed questionnaires in 32 cases; their data are not reported here. All children were between the ages of 9 and 15 years, and there were 50 girls and 40 boys in the final sample. There were 60 stepfather families and 30 stepmother families. The income and education levels of the families were somewhat higher than average for New Zealand, and most of the families were Pakeha (New Zealand European). Two-thirds of the families had been together for longer than 2 years.

All respondents completed identical measures of the quality of the following relationships: child–resident parent, child-stepparent, and child–nonresident parent. The scales used were the Security Scale (Kerns, Klepac, & Cole, 1996) and the Warmth and Hostility Scale (Melby et al., 1993). Respondents also completed the Strengths and Difficulties Questionnaire in relation to the children's well-being (Goodman, 1997). Subscales of prosocial behavior, externalizing, anxiety, and peer problems are used in the analyses here. Children also completed a measure of self-concept developed in New Zealand (Williams & McGee, 1991) and single-item measures of how close they felt to each of the three parents.

We had measures of frequency of contact with the nonresident parent provided by resident parents, the children themselves, and nonresident parents. Eighty percent of the children in the sample saw their nonresident parent at times; resident parent accounts indicated that 39% saw that parent once a week or more, 40% once or twice a month, and 21% every 3 to 6 months. Measures of the involvement of the nonresident parent (provided by both resident and nonresident parents) were for involvement in health, school, activities, and discipline. With the exception of discipline, the nonresident parents reported that they had significantly higher levels of involvement than resident parents attributed to them. For consistency and because only 32 nonresident parents completed interviews, the reports of the resident parents are used in the following analyses.

Analyses were carried out to examine the relative contributions to children's well-being of the relationships the children had with stepparents and nonresident parents. Only children who did have contact with their nonresident parent were included. Tables 15.1 and 15.2 show the levels of closeness, security, and warmth or hostility the children reported for each parent, and the correlations among the relationship variables for those parents.

For the closeness and security variables, the means for the resident parent and the stepparent were significantly different. The children's feelings of warmth toward their nonresident parent were higher than those for either the resident parent or the stepparent. This suggests that relationships

Table 15.1

Means and Standard Deviations (in parentheses) of Relationship Variables: Children's Assessments

Relationship Variables	To Resident Parent	To Stepparent	To Nonresident Parent
Closeness (1 item)	3.5 (0.8)	3.0 (0.8)	3.3 (1.0)
Security (15 items)	48.8 (7.1)	43.6 (7.5)	47.1 (8.5)
Warmth/hostility (13 items)	43.4 (5.5)	40.9 (5.8)	46.2 (4.8)

Table 15.2
Correlations Among Relationship Variables: Children's Perceptions

Relationship Variables	Closeness		Warmth		Security	
	Stepparent	Resident Parent	Stepparent	Resident Parent	Stepparent	Resident Parent
Closeness Nonresident parent	.221*	.136	.218*	.201	.049	−.151
Warmth Nonresident parent	.058	.062	.210	.233*	−.104	−.071
Security Nonresident parent	.014	.114	−.029	.174	.001	.289*

*Denotes significant correlation.

as seen by the children were not as close, warm, or trusting with their stepparent as with their biological parent. Scores were, nonetheless, above the middle of the range, suggesting that the children enjoyed moderately close relationships with their stepparent. (Stepparents rated this relationship as somewhat less close and warm than did stepchildren.) The children also reported a warm relationship with their stepparent and felt high levels of closeness and trust.

ASSOCIATIONS AMONG RELATIONSHIPS WITH NONRESIDENT PARENTS, RESIDENT PARENTS, AND STEPPARENTS

Table 15.2 indicates that children's feeling close to nonresident parents was positively related to feeling close to and enjoying a warm relationship with their stepparent, indicating that the children in this group were able to accumulate parenting relationships in their lives. They did not appear to feel close to one parent at the expense of another. Also, warmth and security in relation to their nonresident parent were positively associated with the same variables in their relationship with their resident parent. It is notable that there were no significant negative associations among relationship variables with their parenting figures, and the warmth scores for nonresident parents and stepparents were positively associated, although the correlation did not reach significance. Overall, the pattern suggests that both within and outside of the stepfamily household, relations with the three parenting figures were positively associated.

Which Parent Matters for What Outcome?

To examine the comparative contributions of stepparents and nonresident parents to children's well-being, hierarchical regressions were carried out. Outcome variables assessed by children and their resident parent were used. Child gender, kind of stepfamily (stepmother or stepfather), level of contact with the nonresident parent, and the equivalent child–resident parent variable were controlled for in the regressions. The outcomes that were considered were prosocial behavior, externalizing behavior, anxiety, troubles with peers (all assessed by children and parents), and children's perceptions of their strengths (self-concept scale).

When warmth/hostility variables were entered as predictors in the initial analyses, only one regression revealed a significant main effect. Warmth/hostility in the relationship between the child and the nonresident parent predicted 5.1% of the variance in child-assessed anxiety ($\beta = -.260$, S.E. $= .058$, $p < .034$). Neither child–resident parent nor child-stepparent warmth/hostility scores were significant predictors.

When security variables for each relationship (assessed by the children) were entered as predictors, one regression showed a significant main effect. Security in the child-stepparent relationship predicted 6.5% of the variance in children's perceptions of strengths ($\beta = .315$, S.E. $= .071$, $p < .012$).

When closeness ratings were entered, however, six outcomes were predicted significantly by child-parent variables. Table 15.3 shows the findings.

In all six outcomes that were predicted by assessments of closeness, the relationship with the nonresident parent was a significant predictor. Closeness to stepparents predicted self-concept, as did the sense of security in that relationship. It is notable that for two outcomes (peer problems and externalizing), both child and parent assessments were predicted by the child's feelings of closeness to the nonresident parent.

Overall, warmth/hostility and closeness to the nonresident parent dominated in predicting behavioral outcomes for these children in stepfamilies. In contrast, the relationships with stepparents were salient for self-concept, with security and feelings of closeness being significant predictors. These findings are similar to those of Berg (2003), who used self-esteem as an outcome and found that closeness to stepmothers was the primary predictor, and King (2007) who measured externalizing and internalizing behaviors and found that closeness to nonresident parents was the main predictor. Strikingly, in the Resilience in Stepfamily Study, it was *feeling close* to both nonresident parents and stepparents that was salient for these children, rather than more behaviorally based measures of trust and warmth/hostility.

WHAT ARE THE MOST IMPORTANT ASPECTS OF THE RELATIONSHIP BETWEEN THE CHILD AND THE NONRESIDENT PARENT?

It is clear from the findings reported so far that the closer a child in a stepfamily feels to the nonresident parent, the less likely he or she is to have behavior problems. It may be, however, that feeling close in itself is not as important as either frequency of contact with or, given Amato and

Table 15.3

Closeness Variables: Significant Predictors of Outcomes as Measured by Children and Parents

Outcome Variable	Significant Predictor	Percent Variance	β	Standard Error	P
Peer problems Child assessment	Closeness to nonresident parent	18.4	-.518	.252	.000
Peer problems Parent assessment	Closeness to nonresident parent	7.6	-.334	.273	.02
Perception of strengths Child assessment	Closeness to stepparent	13.3	-.326	.571	.002
	Closeness to nonresident parent	5.9	.292	.489	.016
Prosocial behavior Child assessment	Closeness to nonresident parent	12.2	.420	-.197	.001
Externalizing behavior Child assessment	Closeness to nonresident parent	7.5	-.330	.222	.016
Externalizing behavior Parent assessment	Closeness to nonresident parent	10.3	-.390	.239	.006

Gilbreth's findings of the importance of involved parenting (Amato & Gilbreth, 1999), the involvement of the nonresident parent in the child's life.

We were able to examine these questions using measures of frequency of contact between children and their nonresident parent and of involvement by the nonresident parent in areas of child health, discipline, activities, and schooling. Because child and parent reports of frequency of contact were highly correlated (.8), we used child reports for that measure and reports by mothers on nonresident parent involvement. Involvement levels in health, schooling, and activities were highly correlated, but involvement in discipline was not, so a composite variable of the first three was computed for simplicity of analysis. Similarly, for simplicity two outcome variables were computed, one representing prosocial behavior and self-concept, the other externalizing behavior and peer problems. Figure 15.1 depicts the relationships found.

Frequency of contact was highly correlated with the child's feelings of closeness to the nonresident parent. Contact was also strongly correlated with the nonresident parent's involvement in health, schooling, and general activities. A modest but significant relationship was found between involvement and closeness (and security). Strikingly, however, only the

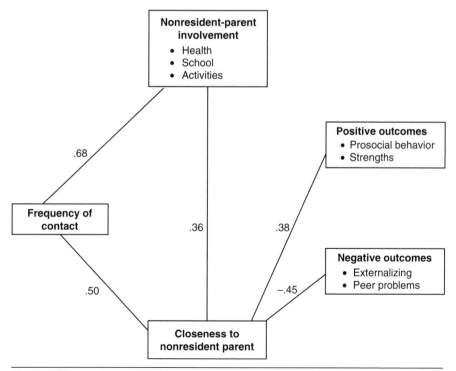

Figure 15.1 Relationships among Frequency of Contact, Involvement, Child–Nonresident Parent Closeness, and Well-being in Children in Stepfamilies.

child's feelings of closeness were related to child outcomes. Neither frequency of contact nor involvement, even at the univariate level, was associated with outcomes. This pattern of findings only partially supports Amato and Gilbreth's (1999) meta-analysis reporting that parenting behaviors were the most salient for children's well-being. The vast majority of the studies Amato and Gilbreth considered, however, did not differentiate between children living in lone-parent households and those in stepfamilies; recall that Dunn et al. (2004) found that contact with a nonresident parent was important particularly in lone-parent families rather than stepfamilies.

DISCUSSION AND CONCLUSION

The scholarly community has moved, in 23 years, from its cautious conclusion that involvement of a parent no longer living with a child might not cause suffering, to active examination of the roles of nonresident parents in the lives of children living in stepfamilies. This reflects, in part, the change in the ways families organize their lives after divorce to include contact with nonresident parents, and in turn is encouraged by jurisdictions that emphasize the desirability of ongoing responsibilities for both parents after they divorce.

A spectacular rise in awareness of children's rights, principally through the United Nations Convention on the Rights of the Child, has also made a significant contribution to this change. Article 9(3) states:

> States' parties shall respect the right of the child who is separated from one or both parents to maintain personal relationships and direct contact with both parents on a regular basis, except if it is contrary to the child's best interests.

Although the Convention has not been ratified by the United States, its influence is pervasive worldwide and is likely to have permeated into the awareness of those working with families after divorce. Perhaps most compellingly, children themselves are eloquent in voicing their desire to maintain a relationship with their nonresident parent.

These changes bring to the fore the tension described by Edwards, Gillies, and Ribbens McCarthy (1999) between the perspective that "children need biological families" and the view that "children need social families." Awkwardly for stepfamilies, unlike most first families, both perspectives are salient, and this puts in place the day-to-day challenges of balancing the need for stepfamilies to function as units and the desirability for children to maintain relationships with at least three parenting figures.

The finding that repartnering by biological parents does not, overall, reduce levels of contact between children and nonresident parents is somewhat surprising given the expected change in family dynamics that repartnering brings about. Given the wide range of ways in which children and their nonresident parents can stay in contact (text, phone, e-mail), we might surmise that ongoing communication that includes these modes would not be challenged so directly as face-to-face contact by the introduction of a new parenting figure into a child's life. More significantly, perhaps, it is likely that nonresident parents are more diligent than in the past in their efforts to stay in touch with children. Awareness of the rights and responsibilities of biological parents has increased, as has the understanding of the benefits for children of ongoing relationships with—especially—their father. Given that the major predictor of contact between children and nonresident parents is the quality of the relationship between biological parents, we might assume, too, that repartnering is not having a major impact on that relationship where contact levels do not change.

One possible explanation for this may be that, increasingly, people repartner more than once. In the United Kingdom the number of people divorcing who had a previous divorce doubled between 1981 and 2006 (National Statistics, United Kingdom, n.d.). In a recent study of new stepfamilies (see Chapters 6 and 7), over half of the children in a community sample of stepfamilies had lived in another stepfamily household before the present one. These statistics suggest the possibility that where adults have experienced multiple partnerships, the demise of subsequent relationships may not involve the strongly negative emotions that a first dissolution would. This may enable more relaxed relationships between ex-partners. It is notable that very few studies report the number of previous relationships parents have had.

Taken together, these changes suggest that it is neither as difficult nor as unusual as in the past for children to sustain relationships with both their nonresident parent and their stepparent. Research to date suggests that not only may stepfamily life not suffer, it might benefit, at least in regard to children's well-being. Robertson (this volume) found that most stepfathers thought that children's contact with nonresident parents either had no negative impact (the "does not seem to suffer" position) or was beneficial and helped the child. A recent paper by Marsiglio (2007) explored a trend for stepfathers to see themselves as allies of nonresident fathers (Marsiglio & Hinojosa, 2007). The research reviewed and reported in this chapter supports the conclusion that, with obvious caveats, children benefit measurably from close relationships with both their nonresident parent and their stepparent.

A question that arises in response to the findings here is why, in contrast to Amato and Gilbreth's (1999) meta-analysis, children's reports of *feeling close* to nonresident parents dominated as a predictor of well-being. In the Resilience in Stepfamilies study, neither frequency of contact nor levels of nonresident parent involvement were directly related to favorable outcomes other than through feelings of closeness, and other studies reviewed reported that a single item measuring closeness predicted the outcomes they measured. This suggests, in stepfamilies at least, the relative lack of importance of specific aspects of the relationship, such as contact and areas of involvement in children's lives, and the primacy of *affective* factors—in this case, how close the child feels to the parent he or she does not live with. A similar construct is that of mattering, measured by Schenck et al. (2006).

In stepfamilies the day-to-day, hands-on, involved parenting is done primarily by the resident parent but also by the stepparent, especially if children are young. This is in contrast to lone-parent households, where, it would seem, the practical involvement of a nonresident parent in a child's life would matter more than in a stepfamily. For children in stepfamilies, what might be most salient is a sense of being loved, of mattering, and of being close to the parent the child does not live with. This does not, of course, mean that contact and involvement are not important—as we have seen, they are both strongly linked with feelings of closeness. But in the end, it is being acknowledged and loved by the other parent that appears to benefit children, no matter how that is manifest. There is much to learn about the nuances of the relationship between the child and the nonresident parent in stepfamilies, including the challenges family members face and how they resolve them, the ways contact is best maintained to foster closeness, and the experiences and feelings of nonresident parents who are maintaining the relationships with their children who live in a household with two other parents.

REFERENCES

Amato, P. (1993). Children's adjustment to divorce: Theories, hypotheses, and empirical support. *Journal of Marriage and the Family, 55*, 23–28.

Amato, P., & Gilbreth, J. G. (1999). Nonresident fathers and children's well-being: A meta-analysis. *Journal of Marriage and the Family, 61*, 557–573.

Amato, P., & Riviera, F. (1999). Paternal involvement and children's behavior problems. *Journal of Marriage and the Family, 61*, 375–384.

Aquilino, W. S. (2006, November). The noncustodial father-child relationship from adolescence to young adulthood. *Journal of Marriage and the Family, 68*, 929–946.

Arditti, J., & Bickley, P. (1996). Fathers' involvement and mothers' parenting stress postdivorce. *Journal of Divorce and Remarriage, 26*(1/2), 1–23.

Argys, L., Peters, E., Cook, S., Garasky, S., Nepomnyaschy, L., & Sorensen, E. (2007). Measuring contact between children and nonresident fathers. In S. Hofferth & L. Casper (Eds.), *Handbook of measurement issues in family research* (pp. 375–398). Mahwah, NJ: Erlbaum.

Australian Bureau of Statistics (ABS). (2006). *Children living apart from one parent.* Retrieved January 28, 2007, from www.abs.gov.au/AUSSTATS/abs@nsf/ 7d12b0f6763c78caca257061001cc588/5a3e290eb5b1ca2571b0001032d8!

Berg, E. C. (2003). The effects of perceived closeness to custodial parents, stepparents and nonresident parents on adolescent self esteem. *Journal of Divorce and Remarriage, 40*(1/2), 69–86.

Blackwell, A., & Dawe, F. (2003). *Non-resident parental contact*. London: Office for National Statistics.

Buchanan, C. M., & Maccoby, E. E. (1996). *Adolescents after divorce*. Cambridge, MA: Harvard University Press.

Bumpass, L., Raley, R. K., & Sweet, J. (1995). The changing character of stepfamilies: Implications of cohabitation and non-marital child bearing. *Demography, 32*, 425–436.

Cooksey, E. C., & Craig, P. H. (1998). Parenting from a distance: The effects of paternal characteristics on contact between nonresidential fathers and their children. *Demography, 35*(2), 187–200.

De Vaus, D. L., & Qu, X. (2003, February). *Does premarital cohabitation affect the chances of marriage lasting?* Paper presented at the Eighth Australian Institute of Family Studies Conference: Steps Forward for families: Research, Practice and Policy, Melbourne, Australia.

Dunn, J. H., Cheng, H., O'Connor, T. G., & Bridges, L. (2004). Children's perspectives on their relationships with their nonresident fathers: Influences, outcomes, and implications. *Journal of Child Psychology and Psychiatry, 45*(3), 553–566.

Edwards, R. V., Gillies, V., & Ribbens McCarthy, J. (1999). Biological parents and social families: Legal discourses and everyday understandings of the position of stepparents. *International Journal of Law, Policy and the Family, 13*(1), 78–105.

Falci, C. (2006). Family structure, closeness to residential and nonresidential parents, and psychological distress in early and middle adolescence. *Sociological Quarterly, 47*, 123–146.

Flouri, E. (2006). Non-resident fathers' relationships with their secondary school age children: Determinants and children's mental health outcomes. *Journal of Adolescence, 29*(4), 525–538.

Funder, K. M., Harrison, M., & Weston, R. (1993). *Settling down: Pathways of parents after divorce*. Melbourne: Australian Institute of Family Studies.

Furstenberg, F. F., Morgan, S. P., & Allison, P. D. (1987). Paternal participation and children's well-being after marital dissolution. *American Sociological Review, 52*, 695–701.

Furstenberg, F. F., & Nord, C. W. (1985). Parenting apart: Patterns of childrearing after marital disruption. *Journal of Marriage and the Family, 47*, 893–904.

Goodman, R. (1997). The Strengths and Difficulties Questionnaire: A research note. *Journal of Child Psychology and Psychiatry, 38*, 581–586.

Kerns, K. A., Klepac, L., & Cole, A. (1996). Peer relationship and preadolescents' perceptions of security in the child-mother relationship. *Developmental Psychology, 32*(3), 457–466.

King, V. (1994). Nonresident father involvement and child wellbeing: Can dads make a difference? *Journal of Family Issues, 15*, 78–96.

King, V. (2006). The antecedents and consequences of adolescents' relationships with stepfathers and nonresident fathers. *Journal of Marriage and the Family, 68*, 910–928.

Lau, Y. K. (2004). Nonresident parents' participation in nonresidential parenting in a Chinese context. *Journal of Divorce and Remarriage, 40*(3/4), 149–159.

Maclean, M., & Eekelaar, J. (1997). *The parental obligation: A study of parenthood across households*. Oxford: Hart.

Manning, W. D., & Smock, P. J. (1999). New families and nonresident father-child visitation. *Social Forces, 78*(1), 87–116.

Marsiglio, W., & Hinojosa, R. (2007, August). Managing the multifather family: Stepfathers as father allies. *Journal of Marriage and the Family, 69,* 845–862.

Melby, J. R., Conger, R., Book, R., Rueter, M., Lucy, L., Repinski, D., et al. (1993). *The Iowa Family Interaction Rating Scales* (2nd ed.). Iowa City: Iowa State University Center for Family Research in Rural Mental Health.

National Statistics, United Kingdom. (n.d.). Retrieved January 6, 2007, from http://www.statistics.gov.uk/CCI/nugget.asp?ID=170&Pos=1&ColRank=2&Rank=1000.

Nozawa, S. (2006). *Stepfamilies in Japan: Strain and support.* Tallahassee: Florida State University.

Pryor, J. (2004). *Resilience in stepfamilies.* Wellington, New Zealand: Ministry of Social Development.

Pryor, J., & Rodgers, B. (2001). *Children in changing families: Life after parental separation.* Oxford: Blackwell.

Schenck, C. E., Braver, S. L., Wolchik, S. A., Saenz, D., Cookston, J. T., & Fabricious, W. (2006). *Do I matter to my (step- and non-residential) dad? The relation between perceived mattering and adolescent mental health problems.* Manuscript submitted for publication.

Seltzer, J. A. (1991). Relationships between fathers and children who live apart: The father's role after separation. *Journal of Marriage and the Family, 53,* 79–101.

Sobolewski, J. M., & King, V. (2005). The importance of the coparental relationship for nonresident fathers' ties to children. *Journal of Marriage and the Family, 67*(5), 1196–2012.

Statistics, New Zealand. (2007a). *Divorce rate lowest for 22 years.* Wellington, New Zealand: Author.

Statistics, New Zealand. (2007b). *2001 Census data: Families and households highlights.* Retrieved January 28, 2007, from www.stats.govt.nz/census/2001-census-data/2001-families-households/highlights.htm.

Stewart, S. D. (1999). Nonresident mothers' and fathers' social contact with children. *Journal of Marriage and the Family, 61,* 894–907.

Thomas, G. M. P., Farrell, M. P., & Grace, M. (1996). The effects of single-mother families and nonresident fathers on delinquency and substance abuse in Black and White adolescents. *Journal of Marriage and the Family, 58*(4), 884–895.

Vogt Yuan, A. S., & Hamilton, H. A. (2006). Stepfather involvement and adolescent well-being: Do mothers and nonresidential fathers matter? *Journal of Family Issues, 27*(9), 1191–1213.

White, L., & Gilbreth, J. G. (2001). When children have two fathers: Effects of relationships with stepfathers and non-custodial fathers on adolescent outcomes. *Journal of Marriage and the Family, 63,* 155–167.

Whiteside, M. F., & Becker, B. J. (2000). Parental factors and the young child's post-divorce adjustment: A meta-analysis with implications for parenting arrangements. *Journal of Family Psychology, 14*(1), 5–26.

Williams, S., & McGee, R. (1991). Adolescents' self-perceptions of their strengths. *Journal of Youth and Adolescence, 20,* 325–337.

CHAPTER 16

The Diversity of Stepmothers: The Influences of Stigma, Gender, and Context on Stepmother Identities

MARILYN COLEMAN, JESSICA TROILO,
and TYLER JAMISON

Speaking from the land of the stepparent, I tell you—this business of being evil is hard. It is very hard. Being a stepmother is the hardest thing I have ever done. And what rewards there are, are small. No one pats me on the head for having given up the pleasures of endive and champagne and tuna steaks for spaghetti sauce and hamburgers. That's what mothers do. Except, of course, they get to be the mom.

—Maureen McHale, a stepmother and author, in an online article
for a stepmother web site

As Maureen McHale's online message attests, being a stepmother is not easy. Women throughout the world are socialized to be mothers. Early socialization includes playing with dolls, no matter how crudely constructed. Girls are taught that good mothers sacrifice their own needs for the needs of their children, that women find their greatest satisfaction and fulfillment as mothers, and that motherhood will be their future identity. Mothers in Western countries have responsibility for their children until they are considered adults, but Japanese mothers consider themselves to have lifelong responsibility for their children. Urban Indian mothers are increasingly

369

responsible for their children's upbringing as children look up to them rather than their more distant, authoritarian fathers, and Chinese mothers closely monitor their daughters because they are the ones responsible for assuring their daughter's chastity before marriage.

Young girls expect and are expected to grow up to be mothers. What that entails varies from country to country, but almost invariably the responsibility for children's well-being is primarily theirs. What they do not expect and plan for is to grow up and become stepmothers. And yet enormous numbers of women throughout the world find themselves assuming the ambiguous role of stepmother. These are the women who may do a lot of mothering but, as McHale mused, they don't get to be the mom.

Stepmothers are women who live with partners who have children from previous relationships. They may share a household with their partner and stepchildren most of the time (residential stepmother), or they may share their household with stepchildren anywhere from a few days a year to nearly half of the time (nonresidential stepmother). Some nonresidential stepmothers have no contact with their stepchildren and may have never even met them. This situation is more likely when women marry men who have lost contact with their children following divorce.

DEMOGRAPHY OF STEPMOTHERHOOD

Data on the numbers of stepmothers are as ambiguous and mysterious as the reported roles that stepmothers assume. In the United States, the 2000 census indicated that 4.4 million children, or 8% of all children, were stepchildren, but according to a special census report, only 17% of the 4.4 million stepchildren were living with stepmothers in 2001 (Kreider & Fields, 2005). By admission of their own staff, however, the census may have identified only about two thirds of stepchildren. Whether a child was identified as a stepchild or not depended on who filled out the census form (Kreider, 2003). If stepparents filled out the form, the children were identified as stepchildren, and they were considered a stepfamily household. If biological parents filled out the form, the children were not identified as stepchildren, and the household was not identified as a stepfamily.

In addition to the 8% of all American children who have been identified as stepchildren, an additional 2.5% are adopted (Kreider, 2003). Somewhere between 42% and 50% of all formal adoptions in the United States are by stepparents or relatives, and although these children and parents no longer identify themselves as members of a stepfamily, the relationships are not biological ones, and sometimes stepfamily dynamics remain in force. It is also known that informal adoptions are common among some cultures (e.g., African Americans, Hispanics), which would raise the numbers of stepfamilies in the United States even higher. All of these data are difficult to verify, but they are more solid than the data on the number of children who visit their biological father and his partner (their nonresidential stepmother) on a regular or irregular basis. According to Stewart (2001), the vast majority (80%) of stepmothers in the United States are nonresidential.

In Australia, among coresident stepfamilies, 12% are stepmother households. Another 4% are blended-family households (both members of the couple bring children from previous relationships to the household; Qu & Weston, 2005). About 31% of Australian men and 33% of Australian women who remarry have children from previous relationships. It also is estimated that in 85% of Australian couples with nonresident stepchildren under age 18, the stepparent is a stepmother. In the United Kingdom, the census reports that 10% of all married or cohabiting family households with dependent children are stepfamilies, and over 80% of them are stepfather households (U.K. Office of National Statistics, 2001). Approximately 2.5 million children grow up in stepfamilies in the United Kingdom, but these data reflect households only (Vaitilingam, 2004). In Finland and Austria about 15% of women enter a second union by age 35, and about half of those women have children from previous relationships. The number of Finnish men who have children from previous relationships is not clear; it is believed that they underreport their number of children, especially those men who have little contact with them (Vikat, Thomas, & Prskawetz, 2003). In Sweden 27% of women remarry by age 35, and 77% remarry over the life course. In Norway, Switzerland, Finland, and Austria, 15% to 17% remarry by age 35. One of the lower rates of remarriage is in Belgium, where only 7% of women remarry by age 35. We can only speculate that similar numbers of men who are fathers remarry. In all former socialist countries, most of the women who formed second unions had children. This was less true of women in Western countries who remarried (Prskawetz, Vikat, Philipov, & Engelhardt, 2002). Approximately 12% of Danish children live in stepfamilies (Danmarks Statistik, 1995). In Canada, 60% of children who had experienced their parents' divorce by the time they were 10 had also experienced the remarriage of at least one parent; 30% of mothers had remarried, 30% of fathers had remarried, and in 40% of cases, both parents had remarried (Marcil-Gratton, 1998). Finally, we know that the divorce rate tripled in France and Holland between 1970 and 1990 and doubled in Belgium (Goode, 1993). It more than doubled in China between 1985 and 1995, and by 2005 the rate had tripled (Fan, 2007). These increases in divorce rates are no doubt accompanied by increases in rates of residential and nonresidential stepfamilies, but figures are not available.

As the numbers of divorcing couples with children increase, so does the number of stepmothers. The fact that we know so little about the number and percentage of stepmothers in these various countries signifies both problems of identifying children who may visit but not live with their father (census surveys allot children to only one household, even if the child spends equal time in two households) and perhaps the lack of importance generally allotted to nonresidential stepmothers. If they are not considered an important person in the lives of children, there is no need to go to extra effort to identify them. Stepmothers may be in the unenviable position of being both ignored and stigmatized.

STEPMOTHER STIGMA

Of all the various roles in families, perhaps the one carrying the most stigma is that of the stepmother. Forever linked with the stepmother in the minds of most is the term "wicked." The concept of the wicked stepmother has a long history that can be traced to ninth-century China (Wald, 1981), and stories of wicked stepmothers exist in nearly every culture. Various versions of "Snow White," "Hansel and Gretel," "Cinderella," and "Sleeping Beauty" are known throughout the world, and nearly all popular magazine articles about stepmothers begin with this theme. Why is this so?

According to the psychiatrist Bruno Bettelheim (1976), the fantasy of the wicked stepmother and the child's triumph over her allowed an outlet for "Oedipal anguish." If daughters competed with mothers for the attention of the father/husband, the fairy tale tended to reduce the child's guilt. The child split his or her mother into two figures: the wonderful, loving pre-Oedipal mother and the mean, wicked Oedipal stepmother. The stepmother ended up getting what she deserved—usually death. Bettelheim postulated that the wicked stepmother stereotype was stronger than other stereotypes about stepfamilies because stepmothers tended to spend a great deal of time in the home with their stepchildren. Stepfathers were more likely to spend their days in the workplace, so there was less opportunity for them to interact with and thwart their stepchildren. It was seldom the stepfather who made children eat their vegetables for lunch, take naps, and pick up their toys. Because stepfathers interacted less with their stepchildren, the argument was that they had less opportunity to upset them. Bettelheim's argument has weakened, however, by the exponential increase in the numbers of nonresidential stepmothers, who now far outnumber those who reside with their stepchildren. Yet these nonresidential stepmothers are just as stigmatized as residential ones, if not more so.

A more recent stigmatization that has been associated with stepmothers (and stepfamilies in general) comes from the work of Daly and Wilson (1999), Canadian evolutionary psychologists who are sometimes called the new social Darwinists. In their book *Darwinism Today: The Truth about Cinderella,* they argued that having a stepparent is the most powerful risk factor for severe maltreatment of children yet discovered. Evolutionary psychologists theorize that stepmothers (and stepfathers) want their own children to thrive, so they neglect, abuse, and sometimes kill their stepchildren to remove them from competition for resources with their biological children. In a rejoinder to Daly and Wilson, Mary Ann Mason (2000) pointed out that Darwinian views have been used through time to provide support for marginalizing and oppressing people. Poverty has thus been explained as the result of the poor being unfit to be anything other than poor, and higher education has been touted as wasted on women because the demands of reproduction retard the evolution of their intellectual and emotional capabilities. Darwinian explanations have also been used to target Jews, people of color, homosexuals, and others as inferior because of biological differences. According to Mason, Daly and Wilson are now using social Darwinism to marginalize and stigmatize stepparents. They are inferior parents not because they differ biologically from the predominant culture, but because they do not share their genetic makeup with their stepchildren.

Although Daly and Wilson (1999) identified stepfathers as more likely than stepmothers to abuse stepchildren, in reality it is biological mothers, and not stepparents of either sex, who represent the greatest risk for maltreatment of children (U.S. Department of Health and Human Services, Administration on Children, Youth and Families, 2004). Yet, despite evidence to the contrary, the stigma of the cruel and abusive stepmother remains strong, while biological mothers continue to enjoy the positive stereotyping long associated with motherhood (Nielsen, 1999).

What difference does the stereotype of the wicked stepmother make to stepfamilies and to societies in general? Why are fairy tales not written off as silly, old-fashioned stories for children that have little relevance for real people or modern-day stepmothers? One reason they have not been ignored is that these stereotypes still have general cultural meaning. *Merriam-Webster's Online Dictionary* defines *stepchild* as "one that fails to receive proper care or attention." The media also, and on a regular basis, has used "stepchild" to denote something negative: "The team's defense was beaten like a red-headed stepchild"; "Software is the stepchild of the computer business." The first author was recently dismayed to see "Stepmonsters Watch Out!" as the headline for a newspaper article relaying her research on the nuances of intergenerational obligations between adult children and their stepparents. The underlying assumption is that the relationship between stepmothers and stepchildren is at best contentious, and at worst, stepchildren are beaten or neglected by their wicked stepmothers.

The stigma of being wicked or seen as a stepmonster, therefore, permeates stepmothers' thoughts and behaviors and is sometimes internalized as a part of their personal identity (Salwen, 1990). Stepmothers, for example, have reported that they have avoided disciplining their stepchildren to avoid the wicked stepmother stereotype (Weaver & Coleman, 2005).

THE INFLUENCE OF THE MYTH OF MOTHERHOOD ON STEPMOTHER IDENTITIES

As a result of stigma, stepmothers are often reluctant to reveal their status, which is not surprising; the stigmatized often attempt to avoid stigma. Many stepmothers initially describe themselves in terms of what they are *not*. First of all, they do *not* want to be identified as wicked stepmothers. Second, most stepmothers reject the notion that they should be a replacement for their stepchildren's biological mother. This may sound relatively easy, but it is not. The cultural significance of womanhood is intimately tied to the mothering role (Braverman, 1989), and all mothers grapple with what Braverman referred to as the *myth of motherhood*. According to Hays (1996), women are defined by this myth whether they are mothers or not. The myth of motherhood contends that mothers are either all good (e.g., self-sacrificing, loving, patient) or all bad (e.g., controlling, cold, rejecting). The *good mother* is characterized by her natural ability to nurture and her unique pleasure in sacrificing her well-being, if necessary, for the good of the child. It is the mother and only the mother who is suitable to care for her child.

The myth of motherhood is deeply embedded in most industrialized cultures. It is reflected in how we think about mothers and how we stereotype them. In an American investigation of the content of stereotypes about mothers, the influence of the myth of motherhood was quite evident (Ganong & Coleman, 1995). Stereotypic content about married mothers was universally positive (e.g., always on call, children come first, generous, not a failure at marriage, protective, warm), reflecting an idealization of mothers that is impossible to attain. Stepmothers, on the other hand, were seen as unskilled, uninterested in child rearing, not family oriented, and not skilled at marriage. In general, the stereotypes related to stepmothers were as wholly negative as the stereotypes related to mothers were idealistically positive.

The ideals associated with the myth of motherhood appear to influence the way many stepmothers approach their roles. Stepmothers do not have the necessary biological connection that is part of the myth of motherhood, yet they are expected, as females, to relate to their stepchildren in a nurturing manner. Levin (1997b) has discussed this in some detail, concluding that traditional female roles have had a unique and powerful influence on the identity development of stepmothers. She asserted that the tasks typically associated with the female role (e.g., housework and child care) tended to be imposed on stepmothers by their spouse and stepchildren. The performance of some of these tasks, especially those related to child care, involve closeness and nurturance and require that the stepmother have frequent, intimate contact with her stepchildren. The closeness of this imposed female role, however, was incongruent with the distance from stepchildren that stepparents were expected to maintain (Dainton, 1993). Thus, many stepmothers constantly negotiate physical and emotional closeness and distance in their attempts to be both good women and good stepmothers. Because men's family roles are narrower and consistent regardless of family structure, stepfathers do not face this incongruence. That is, the cultural conceptualization of good fathers (and stepfathers) allows for less emotional closeness and more distant involvement with children. Men can fulfill their primary family duties simply by providing financially and acting as a protector for the family (Andrews, Luckey, Bolden, Whiting-Fickling, & Lind, 2004). If they are nurturing and emotionally engaged, it is seen as a bonus.

Levin (1997b) suggested that generally, at least initially, the traditional female role superseded the role of stepmother and ultimately determined how the stepmother behaved in the family. In clinical samples, Visher and Visher (1980) found that over the course of therapy, stepmothers, consistent with traditionally gendered female roles, often related feelings of responsibility for the emotional well-being of their family. In fact, most stepmothers perceived that they sacrificed their needs and negated their feelings in order to reduce overall family conflict. Their inability to control family conflict in spite of their sacrifices left many of them feeling like failures as women.

The involvement of stepmothers with their stepchildren, however, was related to the attitudes and beliefs that biological mothers held about mothering (Levin, 1997b; Nielsen, 1999). If the mothers identified strongly with possessive, exclusive notions of motherhood, stepmothers had little chance of developing close relationships with their stepchildren. In fact, unless the biological mother actually *endorsed* the development of a relationship between her children and their stepmother, the stepmother had little or no chance of forging bonds with her stepchildren.

This lack of connection and agency in the stepparent-stepchild relationship was described by Jones (2004) as a limitation of being a stepmother. Many of the women in her sample of participants in a stepmothers' self-help group expressed frustration with what Jones called *caregiving without authority*. Stepmothers in the group provided varying degrees of hands-on care but often found that their authority as parents was undermined by their spouse or, more often, by the children's biological mother. When biological mothers undermined or rejected stepmothers as active parents, it added confusion for stepmothers about their roles as women and caretakers (Nielsen, 1999).

The power that mothers typically derive from within their family is another gender-related factor that complicates the lives of stepmothers. Kranichfeld (1987) described women as strategists who seek and use social power to control their family, to shape the lives of their children, and to maintain family cohesion. Their power was described as vertical in that they influence their bond with their children over the life span, and marital transitions are unlikely to disrupt it. Men's family power is horizontal; men influence the marital relationship, but compared to women, their bonds with their children are less close and they have less influence with them. Because biological mothers have this enduring vertical power, stepmothers can have only as much influence over their stepchildren as the biological mother will allow. If men control the power within the marital relationship and the biological mother controls the vertical power with the children, the stepmother is left with virtually no power at all, at least within the family. This powerlessness has left some stepmothers feeling inadequate for the first time in their lives (Morrison & Thompson-Guppy, 1985). Although most stepmothers are employed outside the home and may exert power in their work environment, having no power in the typical feminine domain (the home) may leave them depressed or feeling disappointed in their abilities to perform feminine tasks. Those who try to exert power within the home are often rebuffed. Those who do not try to exert power sometimes report feeling like outsiders in their own home, anxious and depressed (Doodson & Morley, 2006).

STEPMOTHER TYPOLOGIES

If stepmothers cannot or feel they should not fulfill the role of mother with their stepchildren, what identity can they assume within their stepfamily? Researchers have found that the roles with which stepmothers have identified are diverse and often complex (Church, 1999; Erera-Weatherly, 1996; Weaver & Coleman, 2005). Although the body of literature is not large, some scholars have used typologies to describe various roles and behaviors of stepmothers. Typologies are generally devised to make the complexity of stepfamilies easier to understand (Ganong & Coleman, 2004). The ones reported here are based on Canadian stepmothers' definitions of family and their attitudes toward stepparenting (Church), Israeli stepmothers' attitudes toward stepparenting (Erera-Weatherly), role identities of midwestern U.S. nonresidential stepmothers (Weaver & Coleman, 2005), Norwegian women's strategies for creating a family unit with nonbiological members (Levin, 1997a), and U.S. stepdaughters' perceptions of their stepmother's roles (Crohn, 2006).

Church (1999) devised a typology of stepmothers by identifying five notions of kinship shared by stepmothers: *nuclear, extended, couple, no family,* and *biological.* In spite of stepmothers generally espousing avoidance of the biological mother's role, 23 women (22%) in Church's sample ascribed to the nuclear model, openly idealizing the re-creation of a nuclear family with them in the mother role. These stepmothers avoided publicly referring to themselves as stepmothers and instead attempted to appear as their stepchildren's mother. One stepmother even reported dyeing her hair to more closely match her stepdaughter's and increase the chances that they would be mistaken as genetically related. These stepmothers typically did not consider their husband's former spouse to be a good mother, and some indicated that they wished the biological mother would die so that they could assume the mother role in a reconstructed nuclear family. Unfortunately, Church did not indicate how many stepmothers in her sample were residential and how many were nonresidential, but she did report that significantly more of those enacting the role of mother (i.e., nuclear stepmothers) were residing with their stepchildren.

The majority of the stepmothers in Church's (1999) study were focused on the couple relationship, either as the foundation for a broad, inclusive family network (extended model, 27%) or as the central and singular focus of the family (couple model, 30%). Extended stepmothers differed from nuclear stepmothers in that they assumed some of the mothering duties but neither defined themselves as mothers nor wanted to interfere with biological mothers' relationships with their children. They were labeled extended stepmothers because they had broad definitions of family that included children, stepchildren, parents of stepchildren, former and current in-laws, and others. In fact, they generally considered the biological mother to be a good mother and aspired to have a cordial relationship with her. Their main frustration was dealing with family members and others who did not share their broad definitions of family.

Although women whom Church (1999) identified as couple model stepmothers placed similar primacy on the couple relationship, they did not identify their stepchildren as kin and they did not want to have anything to do with the stepchildren's mother. In general, these stepmothers were less likely than other stepmothers to have preschool-age stepchildren when they remarried, which may have made it easier for them to be a nonparent, particularly since these stepchildren lived elsewhere. Many identified themselves as friends to their stepchildren, but others were more ambivalent. Church reported that about a third of these stepmothers were new to stepmotherhood and planned to have children of their own in the future. She hypothesized that couple model stepmothers might change their ideas about kinship over time.

Three stepmothers saw themselves as outsiders (no family model, 3%) and not related to anyone in the stepfamily (Church, 1999). They considered their relationships with their stepchildren as problematic and felt like their husband was not supportive. Their expectations for their role in the stepfamily originally had been positive, but they gradually withdrew because they felt unappreciated and viewed as wicked and evil regardless of their behavior. They did not believe that they had been given a chance, and all of their descriptions of their stepfamily experiences were negative.

Some stepmothers who also had children of their own emphasized their role as biological mother over their role as stepmother (biological model, 17%; Church, 1999). These stepmothers focused primarily on themselves and their biological children, essentially viewing the household as containing two separate families: she and her children, her husband and his children. Church indicated that half of these stepmothers even neglected to include their husband when asked to name who was in their family. The relationship these stepmothers had with their stepchildren depended on how much they liked the children, and they had no desire to be a mother to them. This model often created conflict between the stepmother and her husband, especially when the husband wanted her to serve as a mother to his children. Conflict also arose when the husband favored his children over hers. Guilt was often a companion to these women because they felt as though they should love their stepchildren, and if they did not, they were not "good women."

Each of these models reflected a different conceptualization of the stepmother role, and Church (1999) noted that identifying with one of these kinship models was often a developmental process. For example, the couple model was sometimes a starting point from which stepmothers evolved into an extended or biological model. Over time, developing closer relationships with stepchildren or giving birth to their own children changed stepmothers' definitions of family as well as their roles in their family.

Five stepparent styles were identified by Erera-Weatherly (1996): *biological parent*, *super good stepmoms*, *detached*, *uncertain*, and *friendship*. The biological parent style was adopted only by stepfathers; none of these Israeli stepmothers identified themselves as replacements for the biological mother. Super good stepmoms were very conscientious about avoiding the wicked stepmother label. They described actively trying to distance themselves from the stereotype by taking their stepchildren places, buying them things, and spending a lot of time with them. Detached stepmothers were primarily nonresidential stepmothers who withdrew from the stepchildren, often after failed attempts at one of the more active styles of stepparenting (e.g., super good or friend). Uncertain stepparents were primarily stepfathers who lacked previous experience in parenting and did not know how to interact with children. The final category, friendship, described those women who genuinely accepted and cared about their stepchildren but did not try to act like the children's mother. They also tried to help their husband develop relationships with the stepchildren.

The myth of motherhood dominated how nonresidential stepmothers studied by Weaver and Coleman (2005) conceptualized their family roles. These women's identities included (a) *mothering but not mother* roles, such as *friend, responsible and caring adult, provider of emotional support*, and *mentor*; (b) *other-focused* roles, such as *liaison* and *facilitator*; and (c) *outsider* roles, including *role by relation* and *involved outsider*.

The mothering but not mother roles were developed in reaction to the myth of motherhood. These women were careful to at least give voice to avoidance of infringing on the biological mother's roles. Although they identified themselves as friends, responsible and caring adults, and so on, their descriptions included actions that most would identify as behaviors of typical mothers. The difference between the roles was difficult to tease out, but included behaviors such as discipline (a responsible and caring adult disciplines, a friend does not). Although an observer would probably have great difficulty distinguishing these roles, the women were adamant that they were distinguishable constructs.

Other-focused roles were those that emphasized the needs and reactions of others, and they were generally performed on behalf of the husband. The liaison role included providing a buffer and keeping the lines of communication open between their husband and his ex-wife. Arranging child visits often was a part of this role. The role of facilitator involved helping the husband with parenting skills, and it also included explaining to their stepchildren their father's behavior in an attempt to improve relationships. An additional important facet of this role was making the stepchildren feel welcome when they visited.

Outsider roles were manifested as role by relation, meaning that they either had a distant role or no role at all (their identity was as the wife of the children's father), or involved outsider. The latter role was slightly more involved in that they were present when the stepchildren visited but they did not participate in activities with their husband and the stepchildren. Regardless of which role the women took, they had mixed feelings about it, often accompanied by guilt.

Levin (1997a) posited that stepfamilies approach the construction of their family in different ways, often revealing different values or ideals about family roles in general. She noted four common patterns of step-family formation: *reconstruction, wait-and-see, innovation,* and *functional involvement*. Stepmothers played different roles in each of the four patterns. The stepfamilies that she described as reconstructors idealized the nuclear family and did their best to re-create it. In these stepfamilies, the stepmother replaced or reconstructed the role of a biological mother. Stepfamilies in the wait-and-see category were more flexible and tried a variety of behaviors in search of what felt comfortable. The entire family engaged in this process of trial and error, and stepmothers often adopted a variety of role identities before determining which was the best fit for their stepfamily. Some of these stepmothers ended up playing the role of the biological mother, but unlike the reconstructors, it was a role they assumed after trying several others rather than one they attempted from the beginning.

A third group, innovators, were stepfamily members, usually the adults, who tended to believe that the nuclear family model had not worked well in their previous family and were eager to attempt something completely new (Levin, 1997a). For example, one innovator couple divided their living space. The stepmother basically viewed her role as being a single mom, and she and her children lived in quarters within the household that were separate from those of her husband and his child, who occasionally visited. This stepfamily also had a common space they shared in the house. The decision to live this way was an attempt to offset the nuclear family model, which they described as starting out physically close and then drifting apart. They felt that their model—starting out physically and emotionally distant—might then lead to closeness and more satisfaction.

The functional involvement model described stepmothers who took on many of the same tasks and responsibilities as a biological mother but denied fulfilling the mother role (Levin, 1997a). These stepmothers generally prepared meals, transported children to activities, and provided emotional support for their stepchildren, engaging in what most would define as mothering behaviors, even if they saw their nonresidential stepchildren only occasionally. This resulted in a dilemma that has been described as "mothering but not a mother" (Weaver & Coleman, 2005, p. 483).

Unfortunately, Levin (1997a) did not describe the percentage distribution of stepfamilies into each model. It also was not entirely clear if all members of the family had to agree on a particular model for it to work or if the decisions on how the family would function were primarily those of the remarried couple. In summarizing, however, she did explain that the family patterns were not always consistent across family members, and it was sometimes necessary to redefine the family due to changes in personal preference or practical arrangements. These changes and inconsistencies, however, often resulted in conflict and role confusion. For example, one woman in Levin's study revealed that redefining the family became necessary when she felt that reconstructing the mother role had caused her to *become* a wicked stepmother. She initiated a role change from that of the mother (i.e., reconstruction pattern) to a much more flexible mode of behavior (i.e., the wait-and-see pattern). Similar to Church's (1999) was Levin's view that roles within stepfamilies may change and evolve over time.

A stepmother typology developed by Crohn (2006) was based on labels that stepdaughters used to describe their stepmother. Crohn sampled 19 young adult women who self-identified as having positive relationships with both their mother and stepmother. She found some common themes among how stepdaughters described their stepmother. The results suggested that stepdaughters experienced varying amounts of "warmth, control functions, attachment, perceived status (more or less equal), and topic avoidance and disclosure" (p. 130) with their stepmother, leading to descriptions of a continuum of roles: *my father's wife, peer-like girlfriend, older close friend, type of kin,* and *like another mother.* The two stepdaughters who identified their stepmother as "my father's wife" described their relationship as polite but not particularly close. Contact with the stepmother was almost exclusively in the presence of the biological father. These stepdaughters perceived themselves to be equal in status with their stepmother, whom they viewed as disengaged. The stepmothers in this category probably resembled those Church (1999) referred to as the couple model and Erera-Weatherly (1996) labeled as detached. These stepdaughters were not interested in developing much of a relationship with their stepmother, so stepmothers who maintained their distance were appreciated.

Stepmothers who were described as peer-like girlfriends by three participants in Crohn's (2006) study were characterized by closeness to the stepdaughters based on commonality and shared activities (e.g., shopping). These stepmothers frequently confided in their stepdaughter about personal problems, which made the stepdaughters uncomfortable. They dealt with their discomfort by not self-disclosing in turn, an attempt to establish a hierarchical boundary (or at least a privacy boundary) in the relationship. The older close friend group (eight participants) involved a greater sense of closeness than the previous two groups. These stepmother-stepdaughter relationships were highlighted by friendship, yet the gap between generations was also distinguished. That is, a boundary hierarchy was maintained similar to well-functioning parent-child relationships (Nock, 1998). This appears to be the relationship that would have been preferred by stepdaughters who identified their relationship with their stepmother as peer-like girlfriends. Other types of kin (five participants) relationships were very similar to the older close friend group, but elicited such labels as cousin, sister, or aunt instead of friend. For both friend and kin groups, stepdaughters felt that their stepmother was an important source of encouragement, and some stepdaughters even credited their stepmother with helping them make major decisions, such as going to college out of state or taking a risk in a new job. Finally, the one stepmother who was identified as like another mother was reported as giving a great deal of nurturance and support to her stepdaughter. The stepmother's love and attention was viewed as a welcome change from the biological mother's absence and lack of warmth.

Crohn's (2006) findings suggested that stepdaughters can be satisfied with a variety of stepmother roles, depending somewhat on the expectations stepdaughters have and perhaps on their needs and desires. Crohn also noted that some stepmothers manifested more than one style, but as she did not interview the stepmothers of these young women, we do not know which types of relationships the stepmothers found satisfying, or even if they would describe their relationships with their stepdaughter similarly.

Just as parent-child relationships are bidirectional (the child and parent are each influenced by the behavior of the other; Bronfenbrenner, 1976), relationships between stepmothers and stepchildren must also be bidirectional. A stepmother who wishes to serve as "another mother" to a stepdaughter who views her as "my father's wife," for example, will find herself in an untenable situation. If she is able to assume what Levin (1997a) labeled a wait-and-see attitude, she may be able to try other behaviors until she finds something that is acceptable to both her stepdaughter and herself. Stepmothers who are less flexible, however, may finally withdraw from their stepdaughter when their efforts to mother are continually rebuffed.

STEPFAMILY CONTEXT

Although stepmother typologies provide an emerging picture of stepmother identity and the underlying struggle for clarity in poorly defined roles, the context within which stepmothers attempt to establish their identities within their family is critical to their success. Researchers (e.g., Erera-Weatherly, 1996) have suggested that some of the difficulty stepmothers experience in carrying out their roles can be attributed to their dependence on others (e.g., stepchildren, husband, biological mother). For example, loyalty to their biological mother may encourage stepchildren to resist forming relationships with their stepmother regardless of any attempts the stepmother makes to form relationships with their stepchildren (Kheshgi-Genovese & Genovese, 1997).

Erera-Weatherly (1996) found that any change in the roles stepmothers might enact will be influenced by the stepchildren, the nonresidential parent, and the residential parent. She reported that stepchildren were directly involved in shaping the stepparent role. For example, stepparents who were rejected by their stepchildren often reduced their involvement and assumed distant relationships with their stepchildren. Nonresidential parents also influenced how positively or problematically the stepparent-stepchild relationship developed. For example, when nonresidential parents were actively involved, lived close to their children, and described their parent-child relationships as positive, the stepparent tended to be detached and not play a parental role. On the other hand, when the nonresidential parent was not actively involved in raising the child but was a positive parent, the stepparent-stepchild bond was generally warm and close. Residential parents also played a part in the formation of the stepparent-stepchild relationship, sometimes serving as a source of stress for the stepparent. One stepfather in Erera-Weatherley's study commented, "They [the stepchildren] see me through her [the stepchildren's mother's] eyes" (p. 166).

Stepparents generally reported that their relationships with their stepchildren would always be overshadowed by the relationship between the residential parent and his or her children. As a result, the stepmother identity may be actively negotiated by other stepfamily members as they position her to adopt certain roles and behaviors. Dedaic (2001) explored how a stepdaughter constructed and maintained her stepmother's identity through communication at the dinner table. The stepdaughter vacillated between inclusion and exclusion of the stepmother, at times maintaining "we-ness" that included the stepmother, and at other times using "we-ness" to describe only herself and her father. We-ness refers to the grouping of individuals in an exclusive way. For example, an exchange ensued about the stepmother (Annamaria) needing an apron. The stepdaughter began by saying, "Annamaria needs . . ." and then corrected herself, stating, "We need to get Annamaria an apron." In her final statement, the stepdaughter established her and her father as an exclusive "we," positioning Annamaria outside of the group. Analysis of these specific communication techniques revealed an overall fluctuation between the stepmother's efforts to define her role and the stepdaughter's acceptance or denial of the stepmother's position in the family.

THE CONTEXT OF STEPCHILD RESIDENCE

Some scholars have suggested that the roles available to nonresidential stepmothers may be more ambiguous than those available to residential stepmothers (Ambert, 1986; Fine, 1995). Both types of stepmothers, however, have reported feeling ambivalent about being stepparents, although about twice as many nonresidential stepmothers (54%) as residential stepmothers (30%) report feeling ambivalent about their stepmother roles (Ambert, 1986). Therefore, when discussing role ambiguity, it is crucial to make a distinction between stepmothers who live full time with their stepchildren and those whose contact may range from several days a week to limited or sporadic.

Residential stepmothers have higher expectations for their physical and emotional involvement with their stepchildren than nonresidential stepmothers, even those who do not view themselves as replacements for biological mothers (Orchard & Solberg, 1999). Residential stepmothers also are more likely than nonresidential stepmothers to believe that their stepchildren view them rather positively (Ambert, 1986). On the other hand, nonresidential stepmothers neither believe that their stepchildren view them positively, nor do they view their stepchildren positively (Ambert, 1986; Knox & Zusman, 2001). In fact, most perceive that their marriage would be happier without stepchildren.

There is some evidence that the differences in how residential and nonresidential stepmothers perceive their roles and relationships with their stepchildren may be related to how stepmothers entered their stepfamily. For instance, residential stepmothers generally are caring for stepchildren because of the biological mother's inability to do so due to addiction or psychological disorder and occasionally because the biological mother died (Cherlin & Furstenberg, 1994). These circumstances almost force them to take a traditional mothering role, especially if the children are young. Canadian residential stepmothers in Ambert's (1986) study reported feeling appreciated because they were helping to raise their husband's children. They also felt closer to their husband, more in control over their family situations, and less worried about the influence and criticism of the ex-wife. In fact, many reported feeling superior to their husband's former spouse.

In contrast to residential stepmothers, nonresidential stepmothers generally are involved with their stepchildren on a part-time basis (Nielsen, 1999), and it has fairly consistently been found that they view their experiences rather negatively (Ambert, 1986; Doodson & Morley, 2006). Although nonresidential stepmothers often participated in household labor to a greater extent than their husband when the stepchildren visited, they did not feel appreciated for this extra work, and many reported a growing dissatisfaction with their situation (Guisinger, Cowan, & Schuldberg, 1989). Perhaps the most telling evidence of nonresidential stepmothers' negative experiences was reflected in the advice that Doodson and Morley reported nonresidential stepmothers gave to other women: "Do not become stepmothers."

Contributing to nonresidential stepmothers' negative experiences has been their perceived lack of control over their roles in their stepfamily and over their stepchildren (Ambert, 1986; Doodson & Morley, 2006; Weaver & Coleman, 2005). Some have reported feeling uncomfortable and unable to be natural with their stepchildren but have been constrained by the biological mother in their ability to make changes to improve their situation (Doodson & Morley, 2006). Other stepmothers have reported that because there are few or no role expectations, their roles were in a constant state of change. The roles they did adopt were often dependent on the needs of others rather than a reflection of the roles they preferred to adopt (Weaver & Coleman, 2005). That is, nonresidential stepmothers would feel obligated to parent their stepchildren when no biological parent was around, but would retreat when biological parents were available. This on-again/off-again parenting likely contributed to their perceived lack of control over their stepparenting roles and contributed to their feelings of anxiety, stress, and depression.

Many nonresidential stepmothers have negatively assessed their husband's relationship with his former spouse (Doodson & Morley, 2006; Knox & Zusman, 2001), and some have reported feeling that their husband was too quick to concede to the former spouse's demands, particularly those concerning the stepchildren. For example, two stepmothers interviewed by

Doodson and Morley resented their husband's former spouse for not allowing the husband to have adequate time with his children during holidays. A majority of nonresidential stepmothers (83%) have also reported that their husband's financial responsibility to his first family intruded on their lifestyle (Knox & Zusman, 2001). These stepmothers resented their husband's first family, experienced significantly less marital satisfaction, and were more likely to think about divorce. The larger the husband's financial responsibility was, the more negative these stepmothers reported feeling.

Discipline of the stepchildren has also been a source of nonresidential stepmothers' discontent. Some felt that their husband was too strict with the children (Doodson & Morley, 2006), whereas others felt that the biological mother was too lenient (Weaver & Coleman, 2005). In both cases, nonresidential stepmothers did not feel that they had the authority to challenge or establish rules of discipline. The nonresidential stepmothers in Weaver and Coleman's study perceived little, if any, control over *any* decisions regarding their stepchildren (e.g., child rearing, discipline, length of and schedule for visitation, changes in residence). Decisions were either made without their input or were overridden by the biological mother. One stepmother even reported that she had no say in a decision that resulted in her stepchildren moving in with her full time!

Weaver and Coleman (2005) reported a number of factors that influenced the types of roles that were available to nonresidential stepmothers. Because the biological mothers were primarily responsible for child rearing, stepmothers positioned themselves in secondary roles that did not disrupt the mother-child relationship. Stepmothers also viewed their roles as dependent on their husband's expectations and on their stepchildren's needs, wants, age, and developmental stages. Those who had children of their own reported that their own children influenced the stepmother roles they assumed. They did not want to damage their relationships with their own children by their attempts to maintain equity between their children and stepchildren. Those who had emotionally needy stepchildren were especially worried that the stepchildren's successful attempts to engage them in their problems would upset their own children. One stepmother expressed concern and discomfort when her stepdaughter continuously referred to her as "Mom." Extended family also influenced the role enactment of some stepmothers. They reported feeling evaluated by extended family members, particularly their husband's family. Others reported confusion about what outside family members expected of them.

AGENCY

Despite the complex nature of their roles, most stepmothers actively seek to develop and maintain a satisfactory identity in the stepfamily. They address the ambiguity of their role through a number of strategies, some of which involve renegotiating interpersonal relations and others focusing on individual identity management. Stepmothers use agency in creating and recreating their roles; as one identity or role fails, they try a different one. Erera-Weatherly (1996) discussed this process of rotating through roles to find a comfortable fit, noting that stepmothers who actively engage in different roles fare better than those who choose one static role and stick with it. The active negotiation of identity gives more power to the stepmother role.

Barbara Waterman (2001), a therapist and stepmother to twin girls, addressed identity when she described two basic elements of parenting: *being* and *doing*. She referred to *being* as feminine and maternal (i.e., being a mother) and described it as a merger or feeling of "oneness," sometimes referred to by mothers as occurring soon after childbirth. She described *doing* as a process that followed being and involved more masculine tasks, such as moving the child away from oneness with the mother and toward recognition of others and a sense of the world as separate from the self. In contrast to biological mothers, Waterman suggested that stepmothers may engage in these tasks in a different developmental sequence. They may, for example, choose to take a doing role, that is, to stepmother rather than to mother, though they may eventually move into a being role (i.e., mothering). Waterman warned, however, that the stepchild's father delimits the stepmother's ability to take either a being or doing role. If he is unwilling to share his power and include her in a parenting role, she will be thwarted regardless of her mothering desires.

Women who feel unappreciated or thwarted as stepmothers often feel they lack social support as they struggle with their identity, especially their identity as a stepmother. Some have turned to the Internet for support in dealing with troublesome issues. Christian's (2005) evaluation of an online support group revealed two narratives that assisted her sample of stepmothers in resolving the conflict between the *good mother* and the *wicked stepmother*. One narrative evaluated biological mothers as *incompetent or mentally unstable*. The second narrative described the *stepmother as martyr*, in which the stepmother was the healthier maternal influence on the stepchildren. These narratives appeared to function as ways for stepmothers to both avoid negative labels associated with stepmotherhood and to assign themselves more positive roles in their family. As Christian explained, the myth of the wicked stepmother, like other narratives, places characters at polar ends of *good* and *evil*. In some ways, the wickedness of stepmothers is necessary to uphold the sanctity of biological motherhood. For stepmothers in the online group, positioning biological mothers in a negative role left the positive position open for themselves. They constructed the narratives of the incompetent biological mother and the stepmother as martyr to defuse the negative aspects of the stepmother role, rewriting the fairy tale to allow themselves to triumph over evil.

The myth of the wicked stepmother, however, is only one of many subtle influences that guide identity construction in stepmothers. The conflicting myths of *instant love* and *the evil stepmother* not only stigmatize stepmothers, but also force them to employ a variety of identity-management strategies to accommodate competing expectations (Dainton, 1993). The instant love myth assumes that stepmothers, like all mothers, should feel instantly attached to their stepchildren, resulting in a natural desire to nurture and invest in the children. By comparison, the wicked stepmother is characterized as wild and cruel, a force of evil that children must endure. The contradictory nature of these myths forces stepmothers to carefully negotiate their role in the stepfamily, and context becomes an important indicator for how they should behave.

Stepmothers employ various identity-management strategies in different contexts (Dainton, 1993). In private settings with her family present, a stepmother sometimes employs corrective strategies in different contexts, such as *self-promotion* (e.g., displaying competence in mothering) and *ingratiation* (acting in positive or helpful ways) to improve her status as a respectable member of the family. In public, she often uses *passing* as a way to defuse negative perceptions about herself as a stepmother. For example, during introductions she might refer to the child as "my daughter" rather than "my stepdaughter" to avoid claiming her status as a stepmother. These strategies are motivated, in part, by the expectations of her stepfamily. In the home, stepchildren are likely to demand a distinction between their biological mother and their stepmother. In public, however, they too may work to avoid the stigma of being labeled a stepfamily member. As a result, stepchildren may accept the stepmother calling them son or daughter in public, but not at home. Because the stepmother role is defined by both internal and external expectations, identity management requires a great deal of flexibility.

Aside from these identity-management strategies, researchers have found preliminary evidence that stepmothers play a unique and positive role in many stepfamilies. In the few studies examining the contributions stepmothers have made to families, the roles of kin-keeper, carpenter, liaison, and facilitator show promise in terms of highlighting positive attributes of stepmother involvement in families. Research on mothers and grandmothers has shaped the notion that women are the kin-keepers of families (e.g., Connidis, 1989; Kranichfeld, 1987), the ones who maintain family relationships across distance and between generations. Although stepmothers are rarely identified as kin-keepers, some evidence suggests that they can, and sometimes do, serve a similar function in stepfamilies, especially older stepmothers. Vinick and Lanspery (2000) interviewed stepmothers with grown stepchildren and found that, despite initial struggles with competition and conflict, stepmothers frequently acted as carpenters in the stepfamily; they helped to repair and rebuild strained postdivorce relationships between their husband and their husband's adult children. Weaver and Coleman (2005) described stepmothers implementing similar roles, although the stepchildren in their study were minors. The liaison role involved the stepmother mediating contact between her husband and his ex-spouse. The stepmother also kept the biological mother informed about issues concerning the children and/or organized the logistics between families (e.g., who would pick up the children, making arrangements for vacation or other special visits). Stepmothers assuming facilitator roles helped build and maintain healthy relationships between their husband and his children by making suggestions to him about parenting, explaining his behavior to his children, and reinforcing to the children that they are important in their father's life. More attention needs to be devoted to studying stepmothers' identity construction and management, especially some of the unique roles that have been described here.

COPING STRATEGIES

The use of narratives has been one way that stepmothers cope with the stress of living with the stepmother myth (Christian, 2005; Jones, 2004). Jones described narratives as "the central means by which people construct, describe, and understand their experiences" (p. 130). Narratives provide a medium through which stepmothers connect to each other's common experiences and also effect change in their own life. Narrative therapies have been used to facilitate the construction of more satisfying or authentic personal stories. Through a process of telling and retelling stories, stepmothers in Jones's study were able to create narratives that promoted a sense of personal agency, meaning, and satisfaction with their roles.

Christian (2005) argued that stepmothers' self-esteem and family relationships suffer under the negative influence of perceiving themselves as a wicked stepmother. Both Christian (2005) and Jones (2004) suggested that women who seek community with other stepmothers may find it easier to cope with the stigma of their role. From her investigation of an online support group, Christian concluded that one distinct advantage of using online support was the anonymity it allowed its members. For women who are struggling to avoid negative interactions with their spouse and stepchildren, full disclosure of their feelings may endanger these relationships. Through a virtual support system, stepmothers can vent without fear of perpetuating the negative stereotypes that accompany their role. On the other hand, Jones found that face-to-face participation in regular self-help group meetings allowed stepmothers to engage in a process of transforming their stories. From a clinical perspective, narrative transformation involves a therapist assisting with the gradual deconstruction of a story and uncovering underlying beliefs and patterns. This process provides an opportunity to build a more satisfactory story. In a group setting, this process is characterized by the input of supportive, similar others. As participants in Jones's group showed, revisiting the same stories over time provided both validation for present struggles and the support to effect change. Participating in either face-to-face or online support groups has been shown to be an active, healthy strategy for stepmothers to gain confidence and share experiences (Christian, 2005; Jones, 2004). The following quotes from a stepmothers' online message board help illustrate the support:

> . . . just wanted to follow up with your stepson. . . . I know things can be difficult with him, but keep plugging away. You will make progress eventually. (Goinggrey, n.d.)

> I think I am evil, too. It is refreshing to know that there are others out there who feel the same as I. I was beginning to think I was alone and something was wrong with me. (Amanda, n.d.)

> I am new to the board. This is a great site. I am a newlywed with a Blended family (My son & a teenage stepdaughter). I've read over a few postings and I find it fascinating and a relief that I am not the only [one] going through these challenges. (Lynette, n.d.)

STEPMOTHER RESEARCH: WHAT WE NEED TO KNOW

Although stepmothers have recently gained more attention from researchers, there is still little that we can definitively say about their experiences in stepfamilies. The body of existing literature on stepmothers primarily illustrates the complexity of balancing roles and establishing a satisfactory identity. Research with carefully identified samples could aid our understanding of the process used in adopting and discarding role identities. We know that residential stepmothers have experiences that are vastly different from those of nonresidential stepmothers, yet researchers often do not distinguish between them when describing their samples.

Some researchers (e.g., Church, 1999; Erera-Weatherly, 1996; Levin, 1997b) have indicated that stepmothers may change their role strategies over time, yet this speculation is based on retrospective rather than longitudinal studies. Even small, qualitative studies that extend over 3 to 5 years could greatly enhance our understanding of these changes. Phenomenological studies of stepmothers' lived experiences could yield valuable information in this regard as well. Studies of stepmothers guided by theoretical approaches are limited in number. Symbolic interaction could be used to study how stepmothers parent, similar to Marsiglio's (2004) work on stepfathers' paternal identities. Although family systems theory has been used in some stepfamily research, it could be more often utilized to guide work on understanding how the family system adjusts to the addition of a stepmother. Although Weaver and Coleman (2005) used feminist theory in their study of nonresidential stepmothers, because gender socialization and gender norms influence the stepmother role, feminist theory could be more widely applied to the study of stepmothers. Finally, the benefits derived from constructing stepmother narratives, as was the case with the stepmothers in Jones's (2004) study, suggest that postmodern theories may be useful in guiding stepmother experiences.

Crohn's (2006) study of how stepdaughters viewed their stepmother was enlightening. A second step in that research would be to investigate the congruence between the views of stepdaughters and stepmothers regarding stepmother roles. Little is known about how the husbands of stepmothers view the roles their wives take in the stepfamily. We know that context is important, but examining it from various stepfamily members' perspectives could provide enormously useful data. Especially needed are studies examining how *satisfied* stepmothers differ from those who express frustration, even rage, with their position. What contextual factors contribute to their success or failure? Considerable research has been devoted to identifying problems, but much less is known about the circumstances leading to stepmothers feeling good about their contributions. Are these circumstances related to the individual attributes and attitudes of the stepmother, or are they related to her relationships with others in the stepfamily system?

Although clinicians offer suggestions about what stepmothers should do, there is little research on how and where stepmothers receive support either inside or outside the family. Christian's (2005) use of an online support group suggests that stepmothers may be receiving support from sources outside of their immediate relations or even their geographic community. Understanding the nature of these support networks has important implications, particularly for practitioners.

There is evidence that stepmothers, at least those in Western cultures, experience similar problems in determining how to structure their role in the family. We need to continue to explore the effects of culture on stepmothers' role development nonetheless. The studies reported here are primarily of middle-class women regardless of locale. Broadening samples to include social class and racial diversity could prove informative. This book should help establish a dialogue between stepfamily researchers and clinicians throughout the world. We can and should learn from each other and use that information to enhance the lives of stepfamilies.

REFERENCES

Amanda. (n.d.). *Am I a wicked stepmother?* Message posted to http://roughdraft .typepad.com/dotmoms/2005/01/am_i_a_wicked_s.html#comments.

Ambert, A. M. (1986). Being a stepparent: Live-in and visiting stepchildren. *Journal of Marriage and the Family, 48,* 795–804.

Andrews, A. B., Luckey, R., Bolden, E., Whiting-Fickling, J., & Lind, K. A. (2004). Public perceptions about father involvement: Results of a statewide survey. *Journal of Family Issues, 25,* 603–633.

Bettelheim, B. (1976). *The uses of enchantment: The meaning and importance of fairy tales.* New York: Random House.

Braverman, L. (1989). Beyond the myth of motherhood. In M. McGoldrick, C. M. Anderson, & F. Walsh (Eds.), *Women in families* (pp. 227–241). New York: Norton.

Bronfenbrenner, U. (1976). Who cares for America's children? In V. C. Vaughan & T. B. Brazelton (Eds.), *The family: Can it be saved?* (pp. 3–32). Chicago: Year Book Medical Publishers.

Cherlin, A., & Furstenberg, F. (1994). Stepfamilies in the United States. *Review of Sociology, 20,* 359–381.

Christian, A. (2005). Contesting the myth of the "wicked stepmother": Narrative analysis of an online stepfamily support group. *Western Journal of Communication, 69,* 27–47.

Church, E. (1999). Who are the people in your family? Stepmothers' diverse notions of kinship. *Journal of Divorce and Remarriage, 31,* 83–105.

Connidis, I. A. (1989). Sibling ties. In I. A. Connidis (Ed.), *Family ties and aging* (pp. 71–86). Toronto, Ontario, Canada: Butterworths.

Crohn, H. M. (2006). Five styles of positive stepmothering from the perspective of young adult stepdaughters. *Journal of Divorce and Remarriage, 46,* 119–134.

Dainton, M. (1993). The myths and misconceptions of the stepmother identity: Descriptions and prescriptions for identity management. *Family Relations, 42,* 93–98.

Daly, M., & Wilson, M. (1999). *Darwinism today: The truth about Cinderella.* New Haven, CT: Yale University Press.

Danmarks Statistik. (1995). *Statistics on persons in Denmark: A register-based statistical system* (Eurostat and Danmarks Statistik). Luxembourg, Denmark.

Dedaic, M. N. (2001). Stepmother as electron: Positioning the stepmother in a family dinner conversation. *Journal of Sociolinguistics, 5,* 372–400.

Doodson, L., & Morley, D. (2006). Understanding the roles of non-residential stepmothers. *Journal of Divorce and Remarriage, 45,* 109–130.

Economic and Social Research Council. (2004). *Seven ages of man and woman.* Swindon, UK: Vaitilingam, R.

Erera-Weatherly, P. (1996). On becoming a stepparent: Factors associated with the adoption of alternative stepparenting styles. *Journal of Divorce and Remarriage, 25,* 155–174.

Fan, M. (2007, April 9). Chinese slough off old barriers to divorce: Breakups skyrocket alongside an embrace of individualism. *Washington Post,* p. A8.

Fine, M. A. (1995). The clarity and content of the stepparent role: A review of the literature. *Journal of Divorce and Remarriage, 24,* 19–34.

Ganong, L. H., & Coleman, M. (1995). The content of mother stereotypes. *Sex Roles, 32*, 495–512.

Ganong, L. H., & Coleman, M. (2004). *Stepfamily relationships: Development, dynamics, and interventions.* New York: Kluwer Academic/Plenum Press.

Goinggrey. (n.d.). *Am I a wicked stepmother?* Message posted to http://roughdraft .typepad.com/dotmoms/2005/01/am_i_a_wicked_s.html#comments.

Goode, W. J. (1993). *World changes in divorce patterns.* New Haven, CT: Yale University Press.

Guisinger, S., Cowan, P., & Schuldberg, D. (1989). Changing parent and spouse relations in first years of remarriage of divorced fathers. *Journal of Marriage and the Family, 51*, 445–456.

Hays, S. (1996). *The cultural contradictions of motherhood.* New Haven, CT: Yale University Press.

Jones, A. C. (2004). Transforming the story: Narrative applications to a stepmother support group. *Families in Society: Journal of Contemporary Social Services, 85*, 129–138.

Kheshgi-Genovese, A., & Genovese, T. (1997). Developing the spousal relationship within stepfamilies. *Families in Society, 78*, 255–264.

Knox, D., & Zusman, M. E. (2001). Marrying a man with "baggage": Implications for second wives. *Journal of Divorce and Remarriage, 35*, 67–79.

Kranichfeld, M. L. (1987). Rethinking family power. *Journal of Family Issues, 8*, 42–56.

Kreider, R. M. (2003). *Adopted children and stepchildren: 2000* (CENSR-6RV; Census 2000 Special Reports). Washington, DC: U.S. Census Bureau.

Kreider, R. M., & Fields, J. (2005). *Living arrangements of children: 2001* (P70–104; Household Economic Studies). Washington, DC: U.S. Census Bureau.

Levin, I. (1997a). Stepfamily as project. *Marriage and Family Review, 26*, 123–133.

Levin, I. (1997b). The stepparent role from a gender perspective. *Marriage and Family Review, 26*, 177–190.

Lynette. (n.d.). *Am I a wicked stepmother?* Message posted to http://roughdraft.type-pad.com/dotmoms/2005/01/am_i_a_wicked_s.html#comments.

Marsiglio, W. (2004). When stepfathers claim stepchildren: A conceptual analysis. *Journal of Marriage and the Family, 66*, 22–39.

Mason, M. A. (2000). Was Cinderella right? The new social Darwinism targets stepparents. In M. Coleman & L. Ganong (Eds.), *Handbook of contemporary families: Considering the past, contemplating the future* (pp. 432–450). Thousand Oaks, CA: Sage.

Max-Planck Institute for Demographic Research. (2002, October). *Pathways to stepfamily formation in Europe: Results from the FFS* (Working Paper WP 2002–046). Rostock, Germany: Prskawetz, A., Vikat, A., Philipov, D., & Engelhardt, H.

Max-Planck Institute for Demographic Research. (2003, January). *Childrearing responsibility and stepfamily fertility in Finland and Austria* (Working Paper 2003–001). Rostock, Germany: Vikat, A., Thomas, E., & Prskawetz, A.

Morrison, K., & Thompson-Guppy, A. (1985). Cinderella's stepmother syndrome. *Canadian Journal of Psychiatry, 30*, 521–529.

Nielsen, L. (1999). Stepmothers: Why so much stress? A review of the research. *Journal of Divorce and Remarriage, 30*, 115–148.

Nock, S. (1998). Too much privacy? *Journal of Family Issues, 19,* 101–118.

Orchard, A. L., & Solberg, K. B. (1999). Expectations of the stepmother's role. *Journal of Divorce and Remarriage, 31,* 107–123.

Qu, L., & Weston, R. (2005). Snapshot of families with stepparent-child relationships. *Family Trends, 70,* 36–37.

Salwen, L. V. (1990). The myth of the wicked stepmother. *Women and Therapy, 10,* 117–125.

Statistics Canada. (1998). *Growing up with Mom and Dad: The intricate life course of Canadian children.* Ottawa, Ontario: Marcil-Gratton, N.

Stepchild. *Merriam-Webster's Online Dictionary.* (n.d.). Retrieved March 19, 2007, from www.m-w.com/.

Stewart, S. D. (2001). Contemporary American stepparenthood: Integrating cohabiting and nonresident stepparents. *Population Research and Policy Review, 20,* 345–364.

U.K. Office of National Statistics. (2001). *Stepfamilies.* Retrieved April 7, 2007, from www.statistics.gov.uk/CCI/nugget.asp?ID=1164&Pos=&ColRank=1&Rank=358.

U.S. Census Bureau. (2000). *Households and families.* Washington, DC: U.S. Department of Commerce.

U.S. Department of Health and Human Services, Administration on Children, Youth, and Families. (2004). *Child maltreatment.* Washington, DC: U.S. Government Printing Office.

Vinick, B. H., & Lanspery, S. (2000). Cinderella's sequel: Stepmothers' long-term relationships with adult children. *Journal of Comparative Family Studies, 31,* 377–384.

Visher, E., & Visher, J. (1980). *Stepfamilies: Myths and realities.* Secaucus, NJ: Citadel Press.

Wald, E. (1981). *The remarried family: Challenge and promise.* New York: Family Service Association of America.

Waterman, B. (2001, August). *Doing to being: Psychological factors influencing women's experiences of stepmothering.* Paper presented at the annual convention of the American Psychological Association, Psychoanalytic Division, San Francisco.

Weaver, S. E., & Coleman, M. (2005). A mothering but not a mother role: A grounded theory study of the nonresidential stepmother role. *Journal of Social and Personal Relationships, 22,* 477–497.

CHAPTER 17

Intergenerational Relationships in Stepfamilies

LAWRENCE GANONG

MOST STEPFAMILY researchers and clinicians have focused their attention on stepfamilies with young children and adolescents, generally ignoring older stepfamilies (Ganong & Coleman, 2004). Of course, family structure alterations are not limited to younger adults with minor-age children; stepfamilies exist throughout the life course. In fact, as adults in most industrialized nations live longer, healthier lives, many stepfamilies are not formed until the adults are in the second half of life (U.S. Bureau of the Census, 1995; Wu & Penning, 1997). Older stepfamilies are quietly growing in number in most industrialized nations, and their issues and concerns increasingly will be important and relevant for policy makers, practitioners, and researchers.

DEMOGRAPHIC TRENDS

Recent demographic trends in industrialized nations have increased the relevance of understanding intergenerational relationships in stepfamilies. Although many demographic changes are occurring in these societies, three are particularly pertinent: (1) increased longevity, (2) decreased fertility, and (3) increases in marital transitions throughout the life course.

LONGER LIFE SPANS

In many industrialized nations, older adults are the most rapidly growing segment of the population. For example, by the year 2030 approximately 20% of the U.S. population will be age 65 and older (U.S. Bureau of the Census, 1993).

Life expectancies in most industrialized nations have been increasing for decades, and projections are that they will continue to increase (Vaupel & Kistowski, 2005). In most of these societies there are greater numbers of three- and four-generation families than ever before (Uhlenberg & Kirby, 1998). Becoming a grandparent has become a normative part of the life course, and most children can expect to have relationships with grandparents and even great-grandparents throughout most, if not all, of their childhood years. For instance, in the United States in 2000 about 75% of all people age 65 and older were grandparents, and approximately 66% of all children had four living grandparents throughout their childhood (Uhlenberg & Kirby, 1998).

FEWER CHILDREN

Women in the industrialized nations of Europe, the Pacific Rim, and North America have had fewer children over the past several decades than earlier cohorts (Pinnelli, 1995; Uhlenberg & Kirby, 1998). This means that families are smaller, with fewer children per adult. Consequently, although there are more grandparents and great-grandparents now than ever before, they have fewer grandchildren on average than they did just a few generations ago. For instance, American women ages 60 to 64 near the end of the twentieth century had about half the number of grandchildren on average than did women 100 years earlier (Uhlenberg & Kirby, 1998).

The demographic combination of longer life span and lower rates of reproduction gradually has transformed the shape of multigenerational families from resembling triangles (i.e., a few elders at the "top" of the family tree being supported by larger numbers of offspring and even larger numbers of grandchildren) to resembling a pole (i.e., the numbers of elders, their children, and grandchildren are nearly the same; Bengtson, 2001). Consequently, multigenerational families no longer have many more young people than older people; instead, as the generation born immediately after World War II reaches age 65, there will be only slightly more younger family members than older ones, a situation that likely will continue into the foreseeable future.

DISSOLUTIONS AND REPARTNERING

Changes in marriage rates and relationship stability also have affected family structures in maturing societies. In some European societies, for instance, fewer adults marry than was true in the past (de Jong Gierveld, 2004; Jensen, 1998; Pinnelli, 1995), and those who do are less likely to remain married until one spouse dies than they were two generations ago (e.g., U.K. Marriage, Divorce and Adoption Statistics, 2000). As a result, the number of older adults who have been divorced has increased. For example, in the United States the number of women older than 65 who were ever divorced increased 650% between 1960 and 1990 (Taeuber, 1992), and since 1990, the number of divorced older adults has increased 4 times faster than the older U.S. population as a whole (Fowler, 1995). In 1998, 25% of adults ages 65 to 74 had been divorced. Cohabitation rates also have grown rapidly in most industrialized societies over the past few decades (Allen, Hawker, & Crow, 2004), and separation and dissolution of cohabiting relationships have equaled, and in some societies surpassed, divorce rates (Allen et al., 2004). Therefore, growing numbers of older adults will have been in one or more cohabiting relationships throughout their lives. Consequently, it is common for adults and their children to have experienced several household living arrangements due to serial cohabitation or serial marriages of the adults before the children reach adulthood (Allen et al., 2004; Bumpass, Sweet, & Castro Martin, 1990).

Remarriage across the life course is widespread. For example, so many divorced people in the United States remarry that nearly half of all marriages are remarriages for one or both spouses (Bumpass et al., 1990). Over 10% of these remarriages represent at least the third marriage for one or both partners (U.S. National Center for Health Statistics, 1993). In many remarriages one or both adults have children from prior relationships, and an estimated 10% of U.S. children experience at least two divorces of their custodial parent before they turn 16 (Furstenberg, 1988).

In the relatively near future a large number of individuals will have been members of a stepfamily. Among the generation born in the years following World War II will be unprecedented numbers of individuals who are step-parents. Consequently, step-grandparents are more prevalent in number than ever before. For instance, nearly 40% of families in the United States have a step-grandparent (Szinovacz, 1998). By 2030, Americans will have 1 step-grandchild for every 1.7 biological grandchild (Wachter, 1997). Step-grandparents reside in complex intergenerational families: Some have both stepchildren and children of their own; some may have children and step-children from several relationships; and some have adult stepchildren but no genetic or adopted children. Moreover, they may be remarried, cohabiting, or in what is known as "live apart together" relationships, in which separate households are maintained, yet the individuals consider themselves to be a couple and live together periodically (de Jong Gierveld & Peeters, 2003).

TYPES OF INTERGENERATIONAL STEP RELATIONSHIPS

Intergenerational relationships exist within a context of many other family ties. For example, adult stepchildren could have four generations of stepfamily members with whom they interact (e.g., parents and stepparents, grandparents and step-grandparents, children and stepchildren, and grandchildren and step-grandchildren).

To better understand the complexity of intergenerational step relationships, it makes sense to consider when they began. Long-term step relationships that have existed since the childhood of the youngest generation differ in many ways from step relationships that started when members of the youngest generation were independent adults. Obviously, some adult-onset step relationships can exist for decades, such as when a middle-aged parent remarries when his or her children are young adults. But these later life relationships generally differ from long-term stepparent-stepchild relationships that began when the stepchildren were dependent minors. There are fewer opportunities for coresidence and prolonged contact over time; emotional bonds may not be as strong; and there are fewer opportunities to exchange resources (e.g., money, emotional support, gifts) from older to younger generations (White, 1994b). These factors likely contribute to differences between long-term step relationships and those that formed later in life.

STEP-GRANDPARENTS AND STEP-GRANDCHILDREN

Despite their prevalence, step-grandparent–step-grandchildren relationships have seldom been studied, and the functions expected of step-grandparents are largely unexplored and unknown (Ganong & Coleman, 2004). Normative expectations for relationships between step-grandparents and stepchildren often are unclear (Bornat, Dimmock, Jones, & Peace, 1999), although such norms gradually may be developing in many societies (Ganong & Coleman, 1999).

Step-grandparents are a heterogeneous group. A person becomes a step-grandparent in one of three ways, and these different paths to the role represent quite different circumstances that affect subsequent step-grandparent–step-grandchild relationships (Ganong & Coleman, 2004). These three pathways to step-grandparenthood may be distinguished based on who is remarrying or repartnering: (1) In *the later life step-grandparenthood* model, an *individual* remarries or repartners with a person who has grandchildren already; (2) in *the inherited step-grandparenthood* model, an individual's *adult son or daughter* is the person who is marrying or repartnering with someone who already has children; and (3) in the *long-term step-grandparenthood* model, the remarriage or repartnering of the grandparent and step-grandparent occurs years before step-grandchildren are born; in fact, the parents of the step-grandchildren were likely to have been children themselves when the remarriage or repartnering of the older generation began. It seems likely that the pathways into the relationships and the contexts within which such relationships are formed affect how intergenerational relationships between step-grandparents and step-grandchildren are defined and how those relationships are enacted.

LATER LIFE STEP-GRANDPARENTHOOD

Marrying or cohabiting with someone who has grandchildren creates a situation somewhat similar to that of becoming a nonresidential stepparent to minor-age children. In this context, the new spouse or partner is often a relative stranger to most of the extended family members when the remarriage or repartnering begins and, in fact, may rarely or never come in contact with adult stepchildren and step-grandchildren. For example, in Figure 17.1, Ann (age 67) was an unmarried and childless woman who married Tom (age 70) in 1995. Tom's son, Joe, was 50 when his father remarried, and Joe's only child, Sue, was 25. Ann and Tom live in Florida, where they met after they had both moved there to retire. Joe lives 3,500 miles away in California, and Sue lives in Chicago, a 3-hour flight to visit either her parents or her grandfather.

It is highly likely that Tom will not identify himself as a middle-aged stepchild, nor will he think of Ann as his stepmother. Instead, he might mention his *father's wife*, or he might say that Ann is the *woman who married his father*. Adult stepchildren who acquire a stepparent later in life do not think of themselves, nor do they want to identify themselves, as members

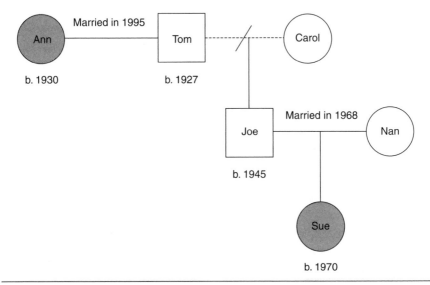

Figure 17.1 Pathways to Step-Grandparenthood: Later Life Step-Grandparent. *Note:* Sue was 25 years old when Ann married Tom and became Sue's step-grandmother.

of a stepfamily (Bornat et al., 1999). This rejection of step-kin labels is not necessarily a reflection of the relationship quality between the older stepparent and grown stepchild, but may be a reflection of the stigma and discomfort that people associate with stepfamily position labels (Bornat et al., 1999; Ganong & Coleman, 2004). Although there is little research on this, it is highly unlikely that later life step-grandparents would be defined as kin by step-grandchildren and their parents (Ganong & Coleman, 2006). Instead, it is more likely that a new spouse or cohabiting partner of a grandparent will be seen as a family friend or acquaintance rather than a member of the family or kin network (Ganong & Coleman, 2006). It is also likely that later life step-grandparents will not see themselves as fulfilling any type of grandparent role. Even when they see each other regularly it is probable that step-grandparent–step-grandchild relationships formed later in life will not develop into emotionally close relationships; Cherlin and Furstenberg (1986) found that the older grandchildren were at remarriage, the less likely they were to regard step-grandparents as important as genetic grandparents.

INHERITED STEP-GRANDPARENTHOOD

The second pathway to step-grandparenthood is comparable to grandparenthood in that the older adult does nothing to acquire this new status. Instead, an individual "inherits" step-grandchildren when a grown son or daughter becomes a stepparent by marrying someone with children from a prior relationship. The step-grandparent not only acquires a son- or daughter-in-law; he or she acquires step-grandchildren as well. For example, in Figure 17.2, Ann became a step-grandmother when her son Joe married Nan, who had a 10-year-old daughter from a prior marriage, Sue.

The nature of inherited step-grandparent–step-grandchild relationships is likely to vary, depending on a number of factors, such as distance, genders of the older and middle generations, ages of the step-grandparent and step-grandchild, and perhaps the number of genetic grandparents that children have and the number of grandchildren older adults have. It seems reasonable to hypothesize that these relationships will be closer if (a) they live near each other and have frequent contact, (b) the middle-generation stepparent and the older step-grandparent are women, (c) the step-grandchildren are younger when their parent remarries or repartners, (d) the step-grandchildren live with the step-grandparent's offspring, and (e) the step-grandchildren have few or no genetic grandparents available to them and the step-grandparents have few or no genetic grandchildren available to them.

Contact

Proximity and frequent contact present more chances for step-grandparents to build affinity with step-grandchildren by doing nice things for them,

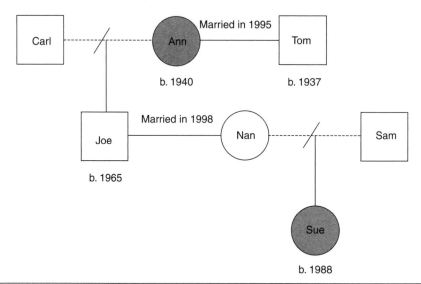

Figure 17.2 Pathways to Step-Grandparenthood: Inherited Step-Grandparent.
Note: Ann and Tom had been married 3 years when Joe married Nan and became a stepfather to Sue. Sue was 10 when Ann became her step-grandmother.

giving gifts, and bonding with them over time (Clawson & Ganong, 2002). For instance, stepparents who intentionally engaged in affinity-seeking and -maintaining behaviors developed emotionally closer relationships with minor-age stepchildren than did stepparents who engaged in no affinity strategies or who stopped such behaviors after marriage (Ganong, Coleman, Fine, & Martin, 1999). It is also probable that step-grandparents who engage in such affinity-seeking and affinity-maintaining behaviors will have closer relationships with step-grandchildren. Spending time together in rewarding activities is an important way for relationships to grow closer, so proximity and contact are important.

Gender and Kin-Keeping

Women in general maintain kin ties in families (McGraw & Walker, 2004), and stepmothers, despite negative stereotypes about them, also tend to function as kin-keepers (Schmeekle, 2007; Vinick, 1999; Weaver & Coleman, 2005). Although stepfathers have an easier adjustment in younger stepfamilies than do stepmothers (Ganong & Coleman, 2004), the fact that women mediate the relationships between members of the adjacent generations (Schmeekle, 2007; Vinick, 1999; Weaver & Coleman, 2005) makes it likely that stepchildren's relationships with step-grandparents differ depending on whether the older adults are step-maternal or step-paternal grandparents. This has rarely been investigated; however, in one British study the gender of the stepparents was not related to the amount of contact between step-grandchildren and step-grandparents (Lussier, Deater-Deckard, Dunn, & Davies, 2002).

Step-Grandchild Age

Younger stepchildren are more likely to accept stepparents' extended family members as new relatives (Cherlin & Furstenberg, 1986). Stepfamilies also are more likely to try to re-create a nuclear family when children are young, which means that parents and stepparents would encourage step-grandchildren to relate to their step-grandparents as grandparents.

Step-Grandchild Residence

Whether or not the step-grandchild lives with the offspring of the step-grandparent also may affect the relationship. Parents of residential stepparents may be more likely to have contact with their step-grandchildren than parents of nonresidential stepparents (Lussier et al., 2002). Nonresidential stepparents may themselves have minimal interaction with their stepchildren (e.g., weekends only or maybe short summer visits and holidays, if they don't live nearby), so the opportunity for step-grandparents to form relationships with their step-grandchildren may be quite limited.

Available Grandchildren

Giles-Sims (personal communication, 2003) found in her case studies of grandmothers that relationships with step-grandchildren varied depending on whether or not the step-grandmother had genetic grandchildren. One step-grandmother with no genetic grandchildren readily adopted a grandparent role; another, who had genetic grandchildren, tried to treat the step-grandchild and grandchildren the same but felt guilty because she did not feel as close to her step-grandchildren.

Kinship Definitions

In addition to these demographic predictors, it might be that how the middle generation defines the family and how they perceive extended family relationships greatly affect the nature of step-grandparent–step-grandchild relationships. For example, if Joe and Nan in Figure 17.2 attempt to re-create a nuclear family and live as if they were a first-married family, they will likely encourage Sue, Nan's daughter, to call Joe "Daddy" and to call his parents and stepfather "Grandpa" and "Grandma." Moreover, Sue would be encouraged to regard the older-generation adults as grandparents and to expect to be treated as if she were a genetic grandchild. On the other hand, if Joe and Nan operationalize a different model of stepfamily living, Sue might be encouraged to think of her stepfather as a friend she can count on, and his parents and stepparent would be added members to her new kin and social support network (in a positive scenario). Or she might consider

Joe as an unwanted intruder into her family, and his extended family might be ignored. Or their overtures to Sue might be rejected, or there might be little encouragement from anyone for the extended stepkin network to develop any type of relationship with Sue.

Henry, Ceglian, and Ostrander (1993) proposed a developmental model for step-grandparents that applies primarily to inherited step-grandparents. This model began with tasks related to adjusting to an adult offspring's divorce and subsequent changes in extended family relationships. Henry et al. proposed tasks related to accepting an adult offspring's new romantic relationship with someone who had children from a prior union. They described ways that inherited grandparents could try to build relationships with the new spouse and their new step-grandchildren. This developmental model has not been empirically examined, but Sanders and Trygstad (1989) found that acceptance of the middle-generation remarriage by the step-grandparents and step-grandchildren was a predictor of subsequent relationships between step-grandparents and step-grandchildren. If either the step-grandparents or the step-grandchildren were upset about or didn't support the remarriage, it was less likely that a good relationship would develop between them.

A final comment about inherited step-grandparenthood: The prior discussion has centered primarily on remarriage of the middle generation rather than on cohabiting. Although it may be true that the step-grandparent–step-grandchild dynamics in cohabiting step relationships are similar to those of remarried couples, stepfamilies are still somewhat of an incompletely institutionalized family system in the United States, and cohabiting couples are even less institutionalized and more marginalized (Cherlin, 1978). In less conservative societies, such as New Zealand, Australia, and most European countries, the relational dynamics among remarried and repartnered cohabiting families may be more similar. In the United States, however, it would be logical to speculate that few families would see the parents of cohabiting stepcouples as step-grandparents, with the possible exception of African American families (Crosbie-Burnett & Lewis, 1993). Instead, they might be seen as friends of the de facto stepchildren, or maybe just as acquaintances. This clearly is an area needing further study.

LONG-TERM STEP-GRANDPARENTS

In the final pathway to step-grandparenthood, an older stepparent becomes a step-grandparent when an adult stepchild whom the older stepparent helped raise becomes a parent (see Table 17.1 and Figure 17.3). Many of the factors that are potentially important to this type of step-grandparenthood are related to the relationship between the oldest and middle-generation stepkin. The age of the child when the step relationship began and the

Table 17.1
Pathways to Becoming a Step-Grandparent

Later Life Step-Grandparenthood		
	Grandchild's (G3) birth	Remarriage of G1
Child (G3)	G3 is born	G3 becomes a **step-grandchild**
Adult child (G2)	G2 becomes a parent	G2 becomes an **adult stepchild**
Parent (G1)	G1 becomes a grandparent	G1 gets remarried, relation to G2 and G3 does not change
Stepparent (SG1)	Not in family yet	SG1 becomes a **step-grandparent** to G3
Inherited Step-Grandparenthood		
	Child's (G3) Birth	Remarriage of G2
Child (G3)	G3 is born	G3 becomes a **stepchild** and **step-grandchild**
Adult child (G2)	Not in family yet	G2 gets remarried, becomes a **stepparent to G3**
Parent (G1)	Not in family yet	G1 becomes a **step-grandparent** to G3
Long-Term Step-Grandparenthood		
	Remarriage of G1	Child's (G3) Birth
Child (G3)	Not born yet	G3 becomes a **grandchild (G1)** and **step-grandchild (SG1)**
Adult child (G2)	Becomes a **stepchild**	Becomes a **parent to G3**
Parent (G1)	Remarries SG1	G1 becomes a **grandparent** to G3
Stepparent (SG1)	Remarries G1, becomes a **stepparent**	SG1 becomes a **step-grandparent** to G3

emotional closeness and quality of the step relationship may be particularly relevant to how middle-generation stepchildren perceive the connections between their children and their stepparents. Given that the middle generation serves as gatekeepers to children, limiting or freely granting grandparents' access to them (Kornhaber, 1996), the quality of the relationships between the step-grandparents and the middle generation may be pivotal.

For instance, in a long-term stepparent-stepchild relationship, particularly one that began when the stepchild was a preadolescent and lived with the stepparent, it is probable that step-grandparent–step-grandchild relationships will resemble grandparent-grandchild relationships in most, if not in all, ways, especially when stepparent-stepchild relationships have been generally positive. There is evidence, however, that long-term step-grandparents can function as grandparents even when stepparent-stepchild relationships have been affectively neutral or even emotionally distant. In a small, in-depth study of adult stepchild–older stepparent relationships, Clawson and Ganong (2002) found that adult stepchildren reconsidered their negative judgments about older stepparents when they saw how close their children felt toward the older step-grandparents. Clawson and Ganong concluded that close and loving relationships between long-term

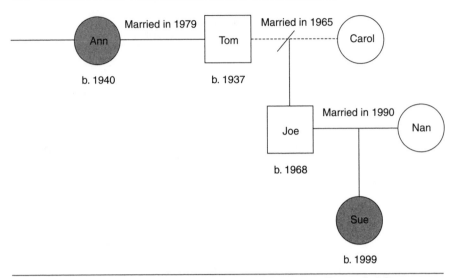

Figure 17.3 Pathways to Step-Grandparenthood: Long-term Remarried Step-Grandparent. *Note:* Ann and Tom had been married 20 years when Sue was born, making Ann a step-grandmother, Joe had lived with Tom since he was 3 years old, and he had lived with Ann since she joined the household when she was 11 years old.

step-grandparents and their step-grandchildren helped facilitate the development of closer relationships between step-grandparents and their adult stepchildren, even years into the relationship.

The cultural norm of having multiple grandparents is one reason why long-term step-grandparents' relationships may be similar to genetic grandparent-grandchild ties. In Western cultures people expect children to have multiple grandparents, and, given increases in life spans, many children now have great-grandparents as well. All of these grandparents are given names to identify them and to distinguish them from the other grandparents. So children in families in which there are no step relationships in the prior few generations may have a Grandpa and Grandma, a Nanna and Poppa, and a Big Grandma and Big Grandpa, all of whom are loved and recognized as grandparents who have legitimate claims to the grandchildren's affections. It is relatively easy for long-term step-grandparents to be named and recognized as one of the cast of grandparents a child might have. For example, in Figure 17.3, Sue has three grandparent figures on her father's side: Tom and Carol, her divorced grandparents; and Ann, her long-term step-grandmother who helped raise Sue's father. Sue may have additional grandparents and step-grandparents on her mother's side of the family, as well as great-grandparents. If intergenerational relationships are positive, Sue will have little difficulty identifying these older adults by unique names.

Stepparents face a cultural norm that says a child cannot have more than two parents; this normative barrier is absent for long-term step-grandparents (and potentially for other types of step-grandparents as well). Step-grandchildren are therefore less likely to experience loyalty conflicts between grandparents and step-grandparents, are less confused about having multiple grandparents, and are able to more readily accept that they can relate to multiple adults in grandparent roles. This is especially true for step-grandchildren who have always known their step-grandparents, such as in long-term step-grandparenthood situations. Children may eventually become aware that Poppa is a step-grandparent rather than a genetic grandparent, but if their parents do not make the step relationship an issue, step-grandchildren do not make clear distinctions about how their relationships with long-term step-grandparents are different from their relationships with their grandparents.

Of course, jealous genetic grandparents can interfere, or hostile relationships between adult stepchildren and their stepparents can hinder the development of stepparent–step-grandchild relationships, despite the presence of helpful cultural norms. For example, Carol could try to undermine Ann's relationship with Sue (Figure 17.3). Although there is a growing literature on loyalty conflicts among stepchildren (e.g., Afifi, 2003; Afifi & Schrodt, 2003; Clingempeel, Colyar, & Hetherington, 1994), similar work with step-grandchildren has not been done. There are other factors that may influence those relationships as well (e.g., distance, and perhaps sex of the adult stepchild and older stepparent). However, even though cultural beliefs about stepparents make stepparenting harder, cultural beliefs about grandparents may ease the transition for step-grandparents.

RESEARCH ON STEP-GRANDPARENTS AND STEP-GRANDCHILDREN

Researchers have not distinguished between these different types of step-grandparents. Consequently, it is rarely clear in studies how long step-grandchildren have known their step-grandparents (e.g., all their lives, 2 years), and sometimes it is not clear how much contact they have had (e.g., daily, never met them). The early studies on intergenerational step relationships have been largely exploratory and rudimentary, yet they have reported that some step-grandparents play an important part in the lives of their step-grandchildren. Although relationships between later life and inherited step-grandchildren and step-grandparents are typically less involved than grandparent-grandchildren ties, many step-grandchildren think of their step-grandparents as valuable resources and see step-grandparent relationships as important (Henry, Ceglian, & Matthews, 1992; Sanders & Trygstad, 1989). Sanders and Trygstad found that children rated their grandparents as more involved with them than their step-grandparents; even so, 48% of step-grandchildren viewed the step-grandparent relationship as either important or extremely important, and 63% wanted more contact with the step-grandparents.

GRANDPARENTS AND GRANDCHILDREN IN STEPFAMILIES

Although clinicians have focused some attention on grandparents (Kalish & Visher, 1981; Visher & Visher, 1996), only a few stepfamily researchers have studied grandparent-grandchild bonds.

GRANDPARENTS WHO REMARRY OR REPARTNER LATER IN LIFE

On the surface, the later life remarriage or repartnering of a grandparent might be expected to have little effect on relationships with genetic or adopted grandchildren. For example, in Figure 17.1, Tom was Sue's grandfather before his remarriage, and he remains her grandfather after his remarriage.

However, later life unions have the potential for residual effects on grandparent-grandchild and parent-child relationships (see Table 17.2). Some scholars have found inheritance issues to be important and sources of

Table 17.2
Types of Grandparents in Stepfamilies

Later Life Remarried/Repartnered Grandparenthood		
	Grandchild's (G3) Birth	Remarriage or Other Union of G1
Child (G3)	G3 is born	G3 is still **grandchild;** becomes a **step-grandchild to G1's partner**
Adult child (G2)	G2 becomes a parent	G2 is still an **adult child;** becomes an **adult stepchild**
Parent (G1)	G1 becomes a grandparent	G1 gets remarried, **relation to G2 and G3 does not change**
Complex Stepfamily Grandparenthood		
	Grandchild's (G3) Birth	Remarriage or Other Union of G2
Child (G3)	G3 is born	G3 becomes a **stepchild** and **step-grandchild**
Adult child (G2)	G2 becomes a parent	G2 gets remarried, may become a **stepparent; is a parent to G3**
Parent (G1)	G1 becomes a grandparent	G1 is a grandparent to G3; may become a **step-grandparent**
Grandparenthood in Long-Term Stepfamilies		
	Remarriage of G1	Child's (G3) Birth
Child (G3)	Not born yet	G3 becomes a **grandchild (G1)** and **stepgrandchild (SG1)**
Adult child (G2)	Becomes a **stepchild**	Becomes a **parent to G3**
Parent (G1)	Remarries or cohabits	G1 becomes a **grandparent** to G3

concern in later life stepfamilies (Bornat et al., 1999), so it is likely that grandparents forming new partnerships later in life is of significant interest to younger kin. There also may be concerns about who will provide physical caregiving when older adults form new romantic unions (Bornat et al., 1999; Kuhn, Morhardt, & Monbrod-Framburg, 1993).

The previous marital and relationship history of the grandparent may be relevant; how grandchildren and adult children respond to the new union is likely to be related to whether the grandparent was widowed, divorced, or separated from the other genetic grandparent, how long the grandparent had been single, the number of prior relational transitions the grandparent had experienced, and whether he or she had maintained close relationships with younger kin (Ganong & Coleman, 2004). The nature of the new relationship—remarriage, cohabiting, or "live apart together"—might also make a difference in how younger generations relate to older couples partnering later in life. In a Dutch study cohabiters and "live apart together" couples had weaker ties with children than remarried adults had (de Jong Gierveld & Peeters, 2003). There may also be gender dynamics at work in the acceptance of these new unions and the development of relationships (Schmeekle, 2007; Vinick, 1999), although findings about gender and intergenerational relationships in stepfamilies have been mixed (Mills, Wakeman, & Fea, 2001; Szinovacz, 1997).

Characteristics of the grandparents' new partner also may be relevant. Prior marital history (i.e., number, type of relationships, years single before the later life union), number of children and grandchildren, physical health status, income, age, and other factors may all be relevant in predicting the nature of grandparent-grandchild and parent-child relationships after later life remarriage or cohabitation. If the grandparent remarries a person with grandchildren, he or she becomes a later life step-grandparent and a stepparent to an adult stepchild. These new family statuses may not be recognized by the new stepkin, but they will not be ignored by the younger genetic kin, who might see the stepkin as possible threats to family wealth (through inheritance) or to the quality of their relationships with their parent or grandparent. Evidence for this is mostly anecdotal, however. Kuhn and colleagues (1993) contended that older stepfamilies formed from later life remarriages must deal with many of the same issues as younger stepfamilies, including, presumably, maintaining genetic kinship ties. This contention has not been examined empirically.

COMPLEX STEPFAMILY GRANDPARENTS

The older adults whose adult son or daughter remarried or repartnered with someone who had children were described earlier in this chapter as *inherited step-grandparents*. Some of these individuals also are grandparents if their son or daughter had reproduced either before the new union or after its formation. For instance, in Figure 17.2, if Joe had children before his remarriage to Nan, or if he and Nan had a baby together, then Ann would be both an inherited step-grandmother to Sue and a grandmother to Joe's children (not shown on the figure). Stepfamily households in which both adults bring children from prior unions are often called complex stepfamilies, so this type of grandparenthood is labeled the *complex stepfamily grandparent*. These grandparents may have grandchildren living with their offspring or with their former daughter- or son-in-law, or the grandchildren may be grown and on their own.

The maintenance of the grandparent-grandchild relationship after remarriage or repartnering of the middle-generation offspring may be dependent on (a) when the grandchildren were born, (b) who has physical custody of the grandchildren (if they are young), (c) the quality of the relationships between the oldest and middle-generation adults, and (d) the amount of contact between grandparents and grandchildren.

When the Grandchild Was Born

The timing of the birth of grandchildren in complex stepfamily grandparenthood is important. If the grandchild was born to the new remarriage or repartnering union, then the complexity of the extended family is quite different than if the grandchild was born into a prior union of the adult offspring. If the grandchild was born to the remarried or repartnered child and his or her new spouse or partner, then grandparent-grandchild relationships likely will be similar to grandparent-grandchild relationships in first-marriage families. From the grandchild's perspective there may be little or no difference between his or her family and an extended family of once-married adults (except for the possible presence of half-siblings from a previous union of one or both of the parents). From the grandparent perspective, there also is no difference. However, if the grandchild was born to the adult offspring's prior union, then the nature of the grandparent-grandchild relationship is likely to be dependent on a number of factors, including where the child lives (with the grandparents' child or former child-in-law), what the custody arrangement is, and how well the grandparents get along with the middle-generation adults.

Physical Custody of the Grandchild

Most grandparents probably want to continue to maintain ties with their grandchildren after their children divorce or separate, but because the relationships between grandparents and young grandchildren are mediated by the adults of the middle generation (Kornhaber, 1996), where the grandchildren live predicts how often and when grandparents interact with grandchildren. After divorce, the parent with physical custody of the children typically regulates grandparents' access to them (Johnson, 1992). Because mothers most often have physical custody of young children, maternal grandparents are more likely to be involved with grandchildren than paternal grandparents, in part because mothers often serve as gatekeepers. Even when the involvement of maternal and paternal grandparents is similar immediately following divorce, over time paternal grandparents have significantly less contact with grandchildren, and they provide less social and emotional support to them (Johnson, 1992). Paternal grandparents may see their grandchildren only when the children are visiting their son. Given the evidence that some remarried fathers "substitute" stepchildren with whom they live for their nonresidential biological children (Manning & Smock, 2000), paternal grandparents may have a hard time maintaining relationships with grandchildren after their son remarries or repartners if the grandchildren live most of the time with their mother. In fact, when sons substitute sets of children, there may be pressure on paternal grandparents to do the same. Of course, grown grandchildren are able to maintain ties with grandparents without parental mediation, although they may be affected by parents' relationships with grandparents.

In Western societies, when married or cohabiting offspring with minor-age children find themselves single again, grandparents often provide them with financial support, child care, emotional support, advice, and even a place to live (Johnson, 1992). This support is then reduced when the offspring remarries or repartners (Bray & Berger, 1990; Cherlin & Furstenberg, 1986; Clingempeel, Colyar, Brand, & Hetherington, 1992; Gladstone, 1989), a phenomenon called the *latent function hypothesis*.

Quality of Relationships

The roles of grandparents may need to be renegotiated when an adult child separates or divorces and then remarries or cohabits with a new partner. In first-marriage families grandparents generally follow the lead of the middle-generation adults for how they should function (Cherlin & Furstenberg, 1986; Kornhaber, 1996), but this is harder to do when the middle-generation couple is no longer together and may, in fact, disagree with each other about how much and in what ways they want grandparents involved. It is imperative that the oldest and middle-generation adults get along if grandparents are to maintain relationships with grandchildren after middle-generation adults remarry or repartner.

Relationships between former in-laws are hard to maintain for a lot of people after divorce because (a) the interactions become cold and impersonal, (b) they feel ill at ease with each other, or (c) they engage in hostile behavior (e.g., yelling, accusing; Ambert, 1988). In fact, some grandparents take sides and reject not only their former in-laws but their grandchildren as well (Ambert, 1988). In the United States, grandparents have reacted to their lack of control over whether or not they see their grandchildren by pushing for laws that are designed to give them the legal right to see their grandchildren after offspring divorce. Maintaining positive relationships with former in-laws may be a cheaper and more effective way of ensuring continuing contact than litigation. More research is needed on how grandparents negotiate their ties with former children-in-law who have physical custody of their grandchildren.

Maintaining Contact

Maintaining contact has been found to be an important factor affecting normative beliefs about intergenerational obligations (Coleman, Ganong, Hans, Sharp, & Rothrauff, 2005; Ganong & Coleman, 1998). Regular contact may be interpreted as an indication of relationship closeness.

Although geographical distance between grandparents and grandchildren is related to frequency of contact for grandparents in general, Bornat and colleagues (1999) did not find distance to be related to grandparent-grandchild relationships. The advent of technology such as e-mail, cell phones, and computer-assisted calling may mediate the effects of distance for maintaining intergenerational relationships (Hughes & Hans, 2004).

Bridges or Walls?

Clinicians have long asserted that grandparents can be either helpful or harmful to remarried adult children's attempts at developing and maintaining a positive stepfamily life: They can build bridges or they can build walls (Visher & Visher, 1996). They build bridges by accepting the remarriage, offering assistance when requested, and otherwise allowing the next generations to develop in their own ways. On the other hand, they can build walls by criticizing a new stepparent's attempts to help raise their grandchildren, by taking sides when former spouses argue over finances or child rearing, by actively trying to break up a child's new marriage (or the remarriage of a former son- or daughter-in-law), by refusing to accept into their family new step-grandchildren or a new son- or daughter-in-law, by using money and inheritance as weapons to punish or to divide younger generations, and by clearly favoring genetic grandchildren, particularly children born into the remarriage, over step-grandchildren (Kalish & Visher, 1981). Grandparents usually have little or no control when a child or former child-in-law divorces and remarries, so some try to exert control in ways that are destructive to the remarriage or to the establishment of a functional stepfamily. Although researchers have found that grandparents are perceived by grandchildren to be important sources of emotional support for them after a parental remarriage (Kennedy & Kennedy, 1993; Mills et al., 2001), overall there has been little research on relationships between grandchildren and complex stepfamily grandparents.

GRANDPARENTS IN LONG-TERM STEPFAMILIES

In long-term stepfamilies, the grandparents are the biological parents who had minor-age children from prior unions when they remarried or repartnered and who remained in this long-term relationship at least until their children grew up and reproduced. The intergenerational relationships among grandparents in long-term stepfamilies are likely to be similar to grandparent-grandchild relationships in ever-married nuclear families, if the grandparent helped raise the grandchildren's parent and maintained an emotionally close relationship with him or her over the years (Clawson & Ganong, 2002; Ganong & Coleman, 1999). Having helped raise the middle generation implies taking care of them financially, emotionally, and physically when the children were young, and then aiding them in various ways as they transitioned into young adulthood. Maintaining contact with non-residential children and helping them when possible also are important for grandparents in long-term stepfamilies who did not live with their children when the children were young (Coleman et al., 2005; Ganong & Coleman, 1998). Although a few scholars have conducted studies of grandparents and grandchildren in long-term stepfamilies, little is known about these relationships.

RELATIONSHIPS AMONG ADULT STEPCHILDREN AND OLDER STEPPARENTS

The availability of several large, longitudinal data sets that extended data collection from birth or early childhood into adulthood (e.g., the British National Child Development Survey) or that followed adolescents into adulthood (e.g., U.S. Panel Study of Income Dynamics) has contributed to increases in research examining relationships between adult stepchildren and their stepparents and parents. The focus of many of these investigations was the long-term effects of parents' remarriages on adult offspring (39 such studies were conducted between 1990 and 1999 alone; Coleman, Ganong, & Fine, 2000). Although the effects of parental remarriage are beyond the scope of this chapter, there also was research on intergenerational relationships: early home leaving, coresidence with parents, closeness of relationships with parents and stepparents, and exchanges of resources.

HOME LEAVING

In several studies in the United Kingdom, Australia, and the United States, researchers have reported that adolescents who lived in stepparent households left the household at younger ages on average than did adolescents living with both parents (e.g., Aquilino, 1991a; Goldscheider & Goldscheider, 1998; Kiernan, 1992). Apparently, these stepchildren left to set up their own household because they were less likely to attend school or join the military than were children in nuclear family households. Early home leaving may be more prevalent for stepdaughters than stepsons (Aquilino, 1991a), although not all studies have found gender differences (Hill, Yeung, & Duncan, 1996).

Early home leaving has generally been attributed to the more stressful atmosphere in step households (e.g., Cooney & Mortimer, 1999; Kiernan, 1992) or to conflict with parents and stepparents (Young, 1987). The presence of stepsiblings as a significant predictor of home leaving suggests that greater stepfamily complexity might contribute as well (Aquilino, 1991a). More children in the household and the resulting financial demands might lead stepfamily households to encourage home leaving. Goldscheider and Goldscheider (1998) found evidence suggesting that members of stepparent households (adults and adolescents) had greater expectations for early independence of adolescents than did members of other types of households. Other researchers found that both parents and stepparents thought that they had fewer obligations to financially support children than did parents in first-marriage families (Aquilino, 2005; Marks, 1995), which may indicate a greater willingness in stepfamilies to encourage young adults to strike out on their own.

Crosbie-Burnett and colleagues (2005), assuming that all stepchildren who left the household early were pushed out by the parent and stepparent or left voluntarily due to highly stressful conditions, proposed a number of explanations for adult stepchild extrusion, including: (a) insecure attachments between stepchild and parent and between stepchild and stepparent, (b) greater power in the hands of the presumably extruding stepparent, and (c) extruding the stepchild because of the stepparent's beliefs that such action would reduce the stepparent's stress or would otherwise increase the likelihood of improving the quality of stepfamily living. In a commentary on this essay, Ganong and Coleman (2005) cautioned against unidirectional explanations; they favored research designs that utilize bidirectional models of influence (stepchildren affecting the adults as well as vice versa). They also criticized research models of stepfamily living that assume stepchildren are members of only one household (increasingly in the United States stepchildren spend some time with both biological parents after divorce), and they questioned whether early home leaving was always due to negative reasons. For example, one factor that has not been examined is the possibility that earlier home leaving by adolescent and young adult stepchildren involves moving in with their other parent or other relatives (Ganong & Coleman, 2005). In addition to needing further research on the reasons for earlier home leaving, it would be helpful to have longitudinal studies of the effects of home leaving on parent-child and stepparent-stepchild relationships.

CORESIDENCE

It is not unusual for adult offspring to reside in a multigenerational household with their parents; sometimes the older generation has taken in the younger to assist them during rough financial times, and sometimes the younger adult shares his or her residence with aging parents, sometimes to provide care and sometimes for financial reasons (Cohen & Casper, 2002). Research findings about adult children sharing a residence with older parents and stepparents have been mixed. One researcher reported that adult children were less likely to live in a remarried parent's home (Aquilino, 1991b), but in another study, only adults who grew up with a father and stepmother were less likely to take older parents into their home than were individuals from nuclear families; there were no differences in coresidence when children had grown up with a mother and stepfather (Szinovacz, 1997). Differences between young adults from father-stepmother and nuclear family households disappeared when closeness to parents and demographic variables were considered. In yet another study, adults who had a stepfather were not significantly less likely to share a residence with their mother than were young adults whose parents were still married (White & Rogers, 1997). In these studies, differences in intergenerational closeness have been the main factor used to explain differences in coresidence between stepchildren and adult children of married parents.

CLOSENESS TO PARENTS AND STEPPARENTS

Remarried parents have less contact with their adult children than do first-married parents (Aquilino, 1994; Bulcroft & Bulcroft, 1991; de Jong Gierveld & Peeters, 2003; Lawton, Silverstein, & Bengtson, 1994), and parents in cohabiting and "live apart together" relationships have less frequent weekly contact with adult children than do remarried parents (de Jong Gierveld & Peeters, 2003). Frequency of contact between adult children and their parents is often assumed to be an indicator of emotional closeness, although not all studies have found a strong connection between contact and perceived closeness (White, 1992).

Some studies have reported strong gender effects. For instance, in a U.S. longitudinal study, mothers' remarriages had positive effects on closeness of relationships with adult children for mothers, nonresidential fathers, and stepfathers, but fathers' remarriages had negative effects on their relationships (White, 1994a; White & Wang, 2001). White also found that daughters were more negatively affected by parental remarriage than were sons, a finding consistent with several studies of minor-age stepchildren.

Not all studies have reported these gender effects, however. Aquilino (1994), using the same data set as did White (1994a), found that remarriage of custodial parents had only slight effects on relationship quality and children's contact with custodial parents, and the effects were similar for mothers and fathers. Mothers' remarriage did reduce contacts with nonresidential fathers, but custodial fathers' remarriage had large negative effects on relationship quality with nonresidential mothers and on contact frequency. Sons and daughters did not react differently to parental remarriage (Aquilino, 1994). Cooney, Hutchinson, and Leather (1995) found that maternal remarriage was related to children's limited intimacy with both parents, but paternal remarriage contributed to mother-son intimacy.

It is hard to know what the mixed findings on gender and adult child-parent relationships mean. In an unusual qualitative longitudinal design, Schmeekle (2007) found that traditional gender practices in raising children had residual effects on adult stepchild-stepparent and parent-child relationships in stepfamilies. Gendered practices in relating to offspring as adults also affected relationship closeness, not only among stepfamily household members but also among nonresidential parents and the entire stepfamily. Her study illustrated the complex nature of gender effects in stepfamilies (e.g., stepmothers were kin-keepers, but parents and stepparents, regardless of sex, served as relationship gatekeepers for their own kin). It may be that egalitarian stepfamily couples relate to children and stepchildren in different ways than do more traditionally gendered couples, which results in divergent long-term relationship dynamics. More research is needed to determine the relevance of gender on relationship outcomes.

Most of the studies on parent–adult child and stepparent–adult stepchild closeness have utilized reports of either parents or stepparents in large data sets. Adult children and stepchildren may have different views about these relationships, however, so researchers should make efforts to obtain their perspectives as well (Aquilino, 1999; Schmeekle, 2007). Small-scale qualitative designs could add immeasurably to what is known about relationship quality between children and adults in stepfamilies. For instance, fathers in Vinick's (1999) in-depth study of 36 long-term remarried couples illustrated how they made attempts at rectifying disengaged relationships with nonresidential children from whom they had drifted away, and other qualitative studies have started to reveal the important kin-keeping roles played by older stepmothers (Schmeekle, 2007; Vinick, 1998). Little is known about the long-term family processes in stepmother households (see Coleman, Troilo, and Jamison, this volume, for a review of stepmother research), and how they might differ from those of stepfather households, so additional research, whether retrospective or longitudinal designs, would be enormously helpful. The longitudinal design used by Schmeekle is a good example of employing qualitative methods to assess gendered dynamics in stepfamilies from the stepchildren's perspectives.

RESOURCES EXCHANGED

Although not all studies report differences between first-marriage and re-marriage families in resources exchanged between adult children and parents and stepparents (e.g., Eggebeen, 1992), and the differences often were not large, most researchers have reported that, on average, remarried parents provide less financial and instrumental support to adult (step)children than do parents in first marriages (White, 1992, 1994b). Mothers who are remarried may give some type of support as much as do married mothers (Amato, Rezac, & Booth, 1995; Marks, 1995; Spitze & Logan, 1992), and they exchange more resources with children than do remarried fathers (Amato et al., 1995; White, 1994a).

Conversely, adult children who lived in stepfamilies exchange less support on average with parents and stepparents than do adults from nuclear families (Pezzin & Schone, 1999; White, 1994b). For instance, Amato et al. (1995) found that even though remarried mothers gave as much to their adult children as did married mothers, they received less support from children than did married mothers.

With rare exceptions, studies of resource exchanges between adult children and parents and stepparents have compared members of step households to those from first-marriage households and single-parent households. This ignores the possibility that adult stepchildren may have adults from two households (e.g., remarried or repartnered mother and re-married or repartnered father) with whom they may exchange resources. Given the small differences often found between household types (e.g., White, 1994b, found that 47% of adult children from first-marriage families received help from parents compared to 41% from stepfather households and 38% from stepmother households), it is likely that adult stepchildren may receive as much support as those from ever-married parents if both households are included. Of course, this also means that some adult step-children have three or four older adults living in two households for whom they might need to provide support, so researchers must be careful when studying intergenerational aid in stepfamilies to accurately assess the demands and resources available to people in complex stepfamilies.

CONCLUSION

Flying below the radar screen, intergenerational relationships in aging stepfamilies have grown rapidly in most industrialized societies, and older stepfamilies and their issues will soon be confronting practitioners and policy makers in large numbers. Although there has been an explosion of informative research in the past 15 years, there are many areas remaining to be investigated. Researchers need to differentiate between types of step-grandparents and grandparents, noting when stepfamilies formed.

Longitudinal studies of grandparents and step-grandparents are needed. Researchers should be aware that there are multiple perspectives to be considered when studying intergenerational relationships in stepfamilies, and each generation should be included, if not in every study, in the body of work that is accumulating. Qualitative methods should continue to be employed because they offer great insights into family processes.

Future studies could examine the development of step relationships, or they could investigate patterns of how bridges and walls are constructed by either step-grandparents or grandparents. A number of questions are pertinent: What resources are exchanged between stepkin? How are responsibilities to stepkin negotiated? What are stepchildren's concerns about aging stepparents? How does the death of a parent affect intergenerational relationships between stepkin? How are inheritance issues resolved in stepfamilies? How do cohabiting stepfamilies in later life differ from remarried intergenerational stepfamilies? What are the effects of serial parental relationships on parent-child bonds? What roles do gender expectations play in the development and maintenance of intergenerational relationships in stepfamilies? The list of unaddressed and underaddressed questions could go on and on. Much remains to be known about intergenerational relationships in stepfamilies. To paraphrase Robert Browning's positive note on aging: In this area of study, "the best is yet to be."

REFERENCES

Afifi, T. (2003). "Feeling caught" in stepfamilies: Managing boundary turbulence through appropriate communication privacy rules. *Journal of Social and Personal Relationships, 20*, 729–755.

Afifi, T., & Schrodt, P. (2003). Uncertainty and the avoidance of the state of one's family in stepfamilies, postdivorce single-parent families, and first-marriage families. *Human Communication Research, 29*, 516–532.

Allen, G., Hawker, S., & Crow, G. (2004). Britain's changing families. In M. Coleman & L. Ganong (Eds.), *Handbook of contemporary families* (pp. 302–316). Thousand Oaks, CA: Sage.

Amato, P. R., Rezac, S. J., & Booth, A. (1995). Helping between parents and young adult offspring: The role of parental marital quality, divorce, and remarriage. *Journal of Marriage and the Family, 57*, 363–374.

Ambert, A. (1988). Relationships with former in-laws after divorce: A research note. *Journal of Marriage and the Family, 50*, 679–686.

Aquilino, W. S. (1991a). Family structure and home-leaving: A further specification of the relationship. *Journal of Marriage and the Family, 53*, 999–1010.

Aquilino, W. S. (1991b). Predicting parents' experiences with coresident adult children. *Journal of Family Issues, 12*, 323–342.

Aquilino, W. S. (1994). Impact of childhood family disruption on young adults' relationships with parents. *Journal of Marriage and the Family, 56*, 295–313.

Aquilino, W. S. (1999). Two views of one relationship: Comparing parents' and young adult children's reports of the quality of intergenerational relations. *Journal of Marriage and the Family, 61,* 858–870.

Aquilino, W. S. (2005). Impact of family structure on parental attitudes toward the economic support of adult children over the transition to adulthood. *Journal of Family Issues, 26,* 143–167.

Bengtson, V. (2001). Beyond the nuclear family: The increasing importance of multi-generational bonds. *Journal of Marriage and the Family, 63,* 1–16.

Bornat, J., Dimmock, B., Jones, D., & Peace, S. (1999). Stepfamilies and older people: Evaluating the implications of family change for an aging population. *Aging and Society, 19,* 239–261.

Bray, J. H., & Berger, S. H. (1990). Noncustodial father and paternal grandparents' relationships in stepfamilies. *Family Relations, 39,* 414–419.

Bulcroft, K. A., & Bulcroft, R. A. (1991). The timing of divorce: Effects on parent-child relationships in later life. *Research on Aging, 13,* 226–243.

Bumpass, L., Sweet, J., & Castro Martin, T. (1990). Changing patterns of remarriage. *Journal of Marriage and the Family, 52,* 747–756.

Cherlin, A. (1978). Remarriage as an incomplete institution. *American Journal of Sociology, 84,* 634–650.

Cherlin, A., & Furstenberg, F. (1986). *American grandparenthood.* New York: Basic Books.

Clawson, J., & Ganong, L. (2002). Adult stepchildren's obligations to older stepparents. *Journal of Family Nursing, 8,* 50–73.

Clingempeel, W. G., Colyar, J. J., Brand, E., & Hetherington, E. M. (1992). Children's relationships with maternal grandparents: A longitudinal study of family structure and pubertal status effects. *Child Development, 63,* 1404–1422.

Clingempeel, W. G., Colyar, J. J., & Hetherington, E. M. (1994). Toward a cognitive dissonance conceptualization of stepchildren and biological children loyalty conflicts: A construct validity study. In K. Pasley & M. Ihinger-Tallman (Eds.), *Stepparenting: Issues in theory, research, and practice* (pp. 151–174). Westport, CT: Greenwood Press.

Cohen, P. N., & Casper, L. M. (2002). In whose home? Multigenerational families in the United States, 1998–2000. *Sociological Perspectives, 45,* 1–20.

Coleman, M., Ganong, L., & Fine, M. (2000). Reinvestigating remarriage: Another decade of progress. *Journal of Marriage and the Family, 62,* 1288–1307.

Coleman, M., Ganong, L., Hans, J., Sharp, E. A., & Rothrauff, T. (2005). Filial obligations in post-divorce stepfamilies. *Journal of Divorce and Remarriage, 43*(3/4), 1–27.

Cooney, T. M., Hutchinson, M. K., & Leather, D. M. (1995). Surviving the breakup? Predictors of parent-adult child relations after parental divorce. *Family Relations, 44,* 153–161.

Cooney, T. M., & Mortimer, J. T. (1999). Family structure differences in the timing of leaving home: Exploring mediating factors. *Journal of Research on Adolescence, 9,* 367–393.

Crosbie-Burnett, M., & Lewis, E. A. (1993). Use of African-American family structures and functioning to address the challenges of European-American postdivorce families. *Family Relations, 42,* 243–248.

Crosbie-Burnett, M., Lewis, E. A., Sullivan, S., Podolsky, J., Mantilla de Souza, R., & Mitrani, V. (2005). The case of extrusion in stepfamilies. In V. Bengtson, A. Acock, K. Allen, P. Dilworth-Anderson, & D. Klein (Eds.), Sourcebook of family theory and methods (pp. 213–230). Thousands Oaks, CA: Sage.

de Jong Gierveld, J. (2004). Remarriage, unmarried cohabitation, living apart together: Partner relationships following bereavement or divorce. Journal of Marriage and the Family, 66, 236–243.

de Jong Gierveld, J., & Peeters, A. (2003). The interweaving of repartnered older adults' lives with their children and siblings. Aging and Society, 23, 187–205.

Eggebeen, D. J. (1992). From generation unto generation: Parent-child support in aging American families. Generations, 16, 45–49.

Fowler, D. G. (1995). Profile of older Americans. Washington, DC: U.S. Department of Health and Human Services, Administration on Aging.

Furstenberg, F. F. (1988). Child care after divorce and remarriage. In E. M. Hetherington & J. D. Aresteh (Eds.), Impact of divorce, single parenting, and stepparenting (pp. 245–261). New York: Erlbaum.

Ganong, L., & Coleman, M. (1998). Attitudes regarding filial responsibilities to help elderly divorced parents and stepparents. Journal of Aging Studies, 12, 271–290.

Ganong, L., & Coleman, M. (1999). Changing families, changing responsibilities: Family obligations following divorce and remarriage. Hillsdale, NJ: Erlbaum.

Ganong, L., & Coleman, M. (2004). Stepfamily relationships: Development, dynamics, and intervention. New York: Springer.

Ganong, L., & Coleman, M. (2005). Leaving whose home? When stepchildren leave is it always extrusion? In V. Bengtson, A. Acock, K. Allen, P. Dilworth-Anderson, & D. Klein (Eds.), Sourcebook of family theory and methods (pp. 233–236). Thousands Oaks, CA: Sage.

Ganong, L., & Coleman, M. (2006). Responsibilities to stepparents acquired in later life: Relationship quality and acuity of needs. Journal of Gerontology: Social Sciences, 61B, S80–S88.

Ganong, L., Coleman, M., Fine, M., & Martin, P. (1999). Stepparents' affinity-seeking and affinity-maintaining strategies with stepchildren. Journal of Family Issues, 20, 299–327.

Gladstone, J. (1989). Grandmother-grandchild contact: The mediating influences of the middle generation following marriage breakdown and remarriage. Canadian Journal of Aging, 8, 355–365.

Goldscheider, F., & Goldscheider, C. (1998). The effects of childhood family structure on leaving and returning home. Journal of Marriage and the Family, 60, 745–756.

Henry, C. S., Ceglian, C. P., & Matthews, D. W. (1992). The role behaviors, role meanings, and grandmothering styles of grandmothers and stepgrandmothers: Perceptions of the middle generation. Journal of Divorce and Remarriage, 17, 1–22.

Henry, C. S., Ceglian, C. P., & Ostrander, D. L. (1993). The transition to stepgrandparenthood. Journal of Divorce and Remarriage, 19, 25–44.

Hill, M. S., Yeung, W.-J. J., & Duncan, G. J. (1996). Timing of childhood events and early-adult household formation. In J. Graber & J. S. Dubas (Eds.), Leaving home: Understanding the transition to adulthood (pp. 87–107). San Francisco: Jossey-Bass.

Hughes, R., & Hans, J. (2004). Understanding the effects of the Internet on family life. In M. Coleman & L. Ganong (Eds.), *Handbook of contemporary families* (pp. 506–520). Thousand Oaks, CA: Sage.

Jensen, A. M. (1998). Partnership and parenthood in contemporary Europe. *European Journal of Population, 14*, 89–99.

Johnson, C. L. (1992). Divorced and reconstituted families: Effects on the older generation. *Generations, 16*, 17–20.

Kalish, R. A., & Visher, E. (1981). Grandparents of divorce and remarriage. *Journal of Divorce, 5*, 127–140.

Kennedy, G. E., & Kennedy, C. E. (1993). Grandparents: A special resource for children in stepfamilies. *Journal of Divorce and Remarriage, 19*, 45–68.

Kiernan, K. (1992). The impact of family disruptions in childhood on transitions made in young adult life. *Population Studies, 46*, 213–234.

Kornhaber, A. (1996). *Contemporary grandparenting.* Thousand Oaks, CA: Sage.

Kuhn, D. R., Morhardt, D. J., & Monbrod-Framburg, G. (1993). Late-life marriage, older stepfamilies, and Alzheimer's disease. *Families in Society, 74*, 154–162.

Lawton, L., Silverstein, M., & Bengtson, V. (1994). Affection, social contact, and geographic distance between adult children and their parents. *Journal of Marriage and the Family, 56*, 57–68.

Lussier, G., Deater-Deckard, K., Dunn, J., & Davies, L. (2002). Support across two generations: Children's closeness to grandparents following parental divorce and remarriage. *Journal of Family Psychology, 16*, 363–376.

Manning, W. D., & Smock, P. J. (2000). "Swapping families": Serial parenting and economic support for children. *Journal of Marriage and the Family, 62*, 111–122.

Marks, N. (1995). Midlife marital status differences in special support relationships with adult children and psychological well-being. *Journal of Family Issues, 16*, 5–28.

McGraw, L., & Walker, A. J. (2004). Gendered family relations: The more things change, the more they stay the same. In M. Coleman & L. Ganong (Eds.), *Handbook of contemporary families* (pp. 174–191). Thousand Oaks, CA: Sage.

Mills, T. L., Wakeman, M. A., & Fea, C. B. (2001). Adult grandchildren's perceptions of emotional closeness and consensus with their maternal and paternal grandparents. *Journal of Family Issues, 22*, 427–455.

Pezzin, L. E., & Schone, B. S. (1999). Parental marital disruption and intergenerational transfers: An analysis of lone elderly parents and children. *Demography, 36*, 287–297.

Pinnelli, A. (1995). Women's condition, low fertility, and emerging union patterns in Europe. In K. Mason & A. M. Jensen (Eds.), *Gender and family change in industrialized countries* (pp. 82–101). Oxford: Clarendon.

Sanders, G. F., & Trygstad, D. W. (1989). Stepgrandparents and grandparents: The view from young adults. *Family Relations, 38*, 71–75.

Schmeekle, M. (2007). Gender dynamics in stepfamilies: Adult stepchildren's views. *Journal of Marriage and the Family, 69*, 174–189.

Spitze, G., & Logan, J. (1992). Helping as a component of parent-adult child relations. *Research on Aging, 14*, 291–312.

Szinovacz, M. (1997). Adult children taking parents into their homes: Effects of childhood living arrangements. *Journal of Marriage and the Family, 59*, 700–717.

Szinovacz, M. (1998). Grandparents today: A demographic profile. *Gerontologist, 38,* 37–52.

Taeuber, C. M. (1992). *Sixty-five plus in America* (Current Population Reports P23–178). Washington, DC: U.S. Department of Commerce, Economics, and Statistics Administration.

Uhlenberg, P., & Kirby, J. B. (1998). Grandparenthood over time: Historical and demographic trends. In M. Szinovacz (Ed.), *Handbook on grandparenthood* (pp. 23–39). Hartford, CT: Greenwood.

U.K. Marriage, Divorce, and Adoption Statistics. (2000). *Marriage, divorce, and adoption statistics* (ONS, Series FM2. No. 26). London: HMSO.

U.S. Bureau of the Census. (1993). *Statistical abstract of the United States: 1993* (113th ed.). Washington, DC: Author.

U.S. Bureau of the Census. (1995). *Statistical abstract of the United States: 1995* (115th ed.). Washington, DC: Author.

U.S. National Center for Health Statistics. (1993). *1988 marriages: Number of the marriage by bride by groom* [Computer program]. Washington, DC: NCHS Computer Center.

Vaupel, J. W., & Kistowski, K. G. (2005). Broken limits to life expectancy. *Aging Horizons, 3,* 6–13.

Vinick, B. (1998, December). *Older stepfamilies: Views from the parental generation.* Report to the AARP-Andrus Foundation.

Vinick, B. (1999, November). *Factors affecting family support to older men in the normative aging study: Divorce and remarriage.* Paper presented at the annual meeting of the Gerontological Society of America, San Francisco.

Visher, E. B., & Visher, J. S. (1996). *Therapy with stepfamilies.* New York: Brunner/Mazel.

Wachter, K. W. (1997). Kinship resources for the elderly. *Philosophical Transactions of the Royal Society of London Biological Sciences, 352*(13631), 1811–1817.

Weaver, S. E., & Coleman, M. (2005). A mothering but not a mother role: A grounded theory study of the nonresidential stepmother role. *Journal of Social and Personal Relationships, 22,* 477–497.

White, L. (1992). The effects of parental divorce and remarriage on parental support for adult children. *Journal of Family Issues, 13,* 234–250.

White, L. (1994a). Growing up with single parents and stepparents: Long-term effects on family solidarity. *Journal of Marriage and the Family, 56,* 935–948.

White, L. (1994b). Stepfamilies over the life course: Social support. In A. Booth & J. Dunn (Eds.), *Stepfamilies: Who benefits? Who does not?* (pp. 109–138). Hillsdale, NJ: Erlbaum.

White, L., & Rogers, S. J. (1997). Strong support but uneasy relationships: Coresidence and adult children's relationships with their parents. *Journal of Marriage and the Family, 59,* 62–76.

White, L., & Wang, H. (2001). *Acquiring stepparents in adulthood: Effect on child's relationships with parents.* Unpublished manuscript.

Wu, Z., & Penning, M. J. (1997). Marital instability after midlife. *Journal of Family Issues, 18,* 459–478.

Young, C. (1987). Young people leaving home in Australia: The trend toward independence. *Australian Family Formation Project Monograph No. 9.* Melbourne: Australian Institute of Family Studies.

CLINICAL AND LEGAL ISSUES

CHAPTER 18

A Clinician's View of "Stepfamily Architecture": Strategies for Meeting the Challenges

PATRICIA L. PAPERNOW

LIVING IN what we blithely but inaccurately call "blended families" creates intense challenges for our patients and for the clinicians involved with them. Whether stepfamily issues appear as the primary focus for therapy or as background to other concerns, expert help can make a significant difference in meeting these challenges successfully. Unfortunately, all too often, clinicians use a first-time family map to address stepfamily issues. The results are as frustrating, debilitating, and potentially dangerous as trying to navigate the streets of New York City using a map of Boston.

This chapter begins by laying out the differences between first-time families and stepfamilies. Five major challenges created by "stepfamily architecture" are outlined. Drawing on current research and the author's 30 years of clinical experience, specific strategies for meeting these challenges are described. The Stepfamily Cycle, a model of normal stepfamily development, provides a picture of how stepfamilies meet these challenges over time. The chapter ends with a brief description of a three-level approach to clinical assessment and intervention.

Portions of this chapter have been adapted from "Stepfamilies Clinical Update," by Patricia Papernow, 2006, *Family Therapy Magazine, 5*(3), pp. 34–42.

WHERE STEPFAMILIES START

Middle Ground

A concept called "middle ground" developed by Dr. Sonia Nevis (Nevis & Warner, 1983) helps to illuminate the ways stepfamilies differ from first-time families. Middle ground refers to areas of agreement in a relationship where there are easy paths to joint action, often with little thought or discussion needed. Over time, thickening middle ground in a relationship makes living together easier and calmer. On the other hand, very thick middle ground can make life too predictable and boring. When middle ground in a relationship is thin, there are few areas of easy agreement, and many differences require resolution before joint action is possible. Thin middle ground can make life more exciting as well as more anxiety-provoking. It also requires more skills in listening, managing anxiety, and conflict resolution.

The preview is that new stepfamilies start with their thick middle ground in the parent-child relationship and their thin middle ground in the new adult stepcouple and stepparent-stepchild relationships. Furthermore, middle ground in new step relationships has to be forged, in the presence of that thicker parent-child middle ground.

First-Time Couples

Couples in first-time families have time alone together without children to experience the shared middle ground they brought to the relationship. In their first year or two together, maybe Ed and Janie (Figure 18.1) sing each other the show tunes they both love. They bring each other to their favorite hiking places. They have time to feel their chemistry together without attending to children's needs. First-time couples also have time to build awareness of each other's values and preferences and vulnerabilities. In addition, there is time to resolve some of their differences before children

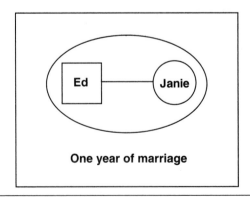

One year of marriage

Figure 18.1 First-Time Couple.

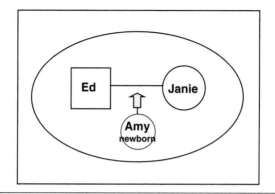

Figure 18.2 First-Time Family First Child.

arrive on the scene. In first-time couples, much middle ground accrues, almost unconsciously, over time: Perhaps Janie and Ed develop harmonies to
those show tunes. Perhaps they evolve an easy division of labor as they prepare meals or set up camp. What began as uncharted territory evolves into
well-defined, easily traveled paths of daily living.

CHILDREN IN A FIRST-TIME FAMILY

Children in a first-time family enter into the couple's already established
ground (Figure 18.2). Usually both adults are in love with their baby, which
in itself provides a source of connection. Maybe the adults begin singing
show tunes as lullabies; Amy learns the words as soon as she starts talking.

Ed and Janie take Amy hiking in a backpack. A few years later, a second
child, Tommy, is born into this ever-thickening family ground (Figure 18.3).
Both children grow up exploring the outdoors with their parents; both
know all the words to "our songs."

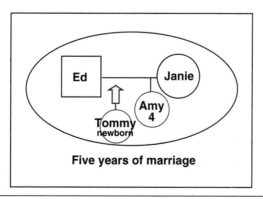

Figure 18.3 First-Time Family Second Child.

Over time the family's middle ground becomes a rich tapestry of habits and understandings, some consciously created and much accrued without awareness. Some is forged out of active negotiation over disagreements and some grows out of more subtle accommodation. As inevitable differences emerge, first-time couples can struggle with them for a while and then return to comfortable middle ground for rest and recovery.

FROM DIVORCE OR DEATH TO SINGLE-PARENT FAMILY

Divorce, or death, requires multiple major and minor alterations in rhythms of daily living, creating many ruptures in comfortable middle ground. Children become part of at least one, and often two, single-parent homes (Figure 18.4). Ideally, each parent maintains some routine that provides some comfort and stability. Maybe Mom keeps the bedtime ritual of singing show tunes as lullabies; Dad keeps singing in the car. Both parents cook familiar food, and both keep hiking with the children.

Over time, each single-parent family begins to accrue its own new middle ground. Perhaps Friday night becomes "Snuggle Night" at Ed's. Everyone changes into their pajamas after supper and all snuggle on the couch to eat popcorn and watch a movie together. Ed, who has always liked to cook, teaches Amy to make pancakes. Because it's the kids' favorite meal, Amy makes a pancake dinner on Wednesday night overnights at Daddy's. The children are now part of what Connie Ahrons (1987) calls a "binuclear family." Important for our story, discipline in single-parent families tends to loosen and adult-child boundaries become less firm as single parents and their children hunker down into a kind of foxhole mentality.

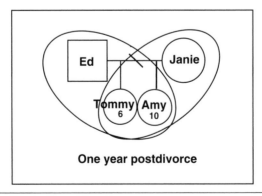

Figure 18.4 Two Single-Parent Families.

Source: "Binuclear Family" (pp. 225–256), by C. R. Ahrons and L. Wallisch, in *Remarriage and Stepparenting: Current Research and Theory*, K. Pasley and M. Ihinger-Tallman (Eds.), 1987, New York: Guilford Press.

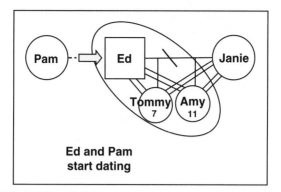

Figure 18.5 New Stepcouple.

NEW STEPFAMILY

The new stepcouple in Figure 18.5 begins their lives together in a radically different architecture than the first-time couple in Figure 18.1. Pam, the new stepparent, enters as an outsider to an already established system. Areas of easy functioning and agreement about everything from whether sugar cereal is a breakfast food or an afternoon treat to what constitutes a "loud" noise lie within the *parent-child* unit, *not* within the new adult couple. For every member of this extended family, the new stepfamily structure beginning to take shape in Figure 18.5 creates a very different experience than the first-time family structure in Figures 18.1 through 18.3. Two vignettes illustrate this.

First Vignette

Perhaps Pam discovers that Ed and his children drink Coke with meals and eat pancakes for Wednesday night dinners. Worried for their health, she prepares a nice healthy fish meal with milk. Amy bursts into tears, "How could you!" Tommy pushes his food around on his plate. Pam is hurt, the kids are upset, and Ed is caught between his partner and his children. If things go well, Pam says to Ed later, "Gee, that was tough. What happened there?" Ed expresses his compassion for Pam and talks with the children about their feelings. Together Ed and Pam figure out what to do. If things do not go well, Pam insists that Ed discipline the kids. Ed resists (or complies), and tension builds.

Second Vignette

As the adult couple becomes more serious, Ed invites Pam to join him and his kids for a Friday night Snuggle Night. When the movie begins, Pam of course expects to snuggle with her new honey on the couch. Amy, feeling a little scared and displaced, goes to sit between them. Pam is startled. Ed, who is pleased to have both his girls with him on the couch, sees no problem, leaving Pam a bit hurt.

Later, when the children are in bed, Pam raises the issue with Ed. If she is skilled, she says something like, "Gee, what happened there when Amy got between us?" Ed, if he is skilled, will respond with something like, "You know, I should have thought of this. Let me tell you about Snuggle Night." Together they may decide to keep Friday night a dad-kid night and to plan adult snuggling for another time. On the other hand, if she is less skilled, Pam may open with, "Your daughter is manipulative." Ed may respond defensively with "She's just being a kid," leaving Pam feeling invisible and frustrated and Ed feeling torn and confused. On the next Snuggle Night, the strain increases.

When Amy goes to her mom's house, she may talk with Janie, Ed's ex-wife, about "that witch, Pam." If Amy is lucky, her mom responds, "Tough to have someone new in the mix, huh? Want to talk about it?" If she is unlucky, Mom reacts with "Your father always was self-centered." Meanwhile, Janie may begin to feel anxious about being replaced by Pam in her children's lives. If things go well, Janie handles these feelings with some grace and generosity. If not, she may begin saying nasty things about Pam to the children.

In both of these vignettes, this new stepfamily is beginning to feel the effects of stepfamily architecture.

STEPFAMILY ARCHITECTURE

Five major challenges are created by stepfamily architecture:

1. *Insider/outsider* roles are stuck and intense.
2. Children bring *losses and loyalty binds*.
3. *Parenting tasks* polarize the adults.
4. *New family culture* must be forged out of multiple differences.
5. *Ex-spouses* are part of the new family.

These five challenges exist in all forms of stepfamilies: When only one adult brings children, they form a simple stepfamily, as we see with Ed and Pam in Figure 18.6 after a year of marriage. When both adults bring children, two different parent-child systems come together to form a double or complex stepfamily, as we see in Figure 18.7. Note that Figure 18.7 is a lesbian-headed family. The dynamics discussed here apply whether the adult couple is gay or straight. They also apply whether the stepcouple is married or not. Indeed, stepcouples have many good financial, logistical, and emotional reasons not to marry.

Figure 18.8 shows a new stepfamily formed by death. Here, too, the same dynamics are at work as the stepparent joins an already established parent-child unit. The three lines connecting the widowed father and son tell us that the two have become especially close after the death of the mother.

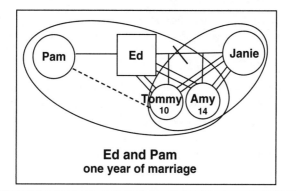

Figure 18.6 Stepfamily: Early Stages.

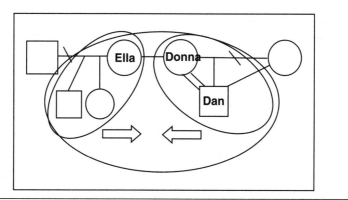

Figure 18.7 Double Stepfamily.

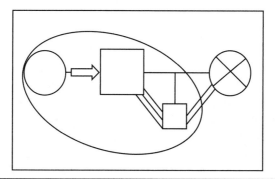

Figure 18.8 Death of Previous Parent.

Adoptive and foster families, however, begin with a very different structure, in that the child joins an *already established* adult couple.

INSIDER/OUTSIDER ROLES ARE STUCK AND INTENSE

In a healthy first-time family, insider/outsider positions rotate: sometimes Mom is close to one child, leaving Dad out for a while; the next hour or year or day, Dad is "in" and Mom is "out." Nonetheless, in a first-time couple, the adult couple starts out and remains the primary insider unit.

In Figure 18.6 we see Ed and Pam after a year of marriage. Ed, the original parent, is the *stuck insider*. He remains much closer to his children, and to his ex-wife, Janie, than to Pam, the stepparent. Stepparents like Pam are the *stuck outsiders* to all of these relationships. Even after a year of marriage, the thicker middle ground of the original parent-child relationships (and to some extent, the ex-spouse relationship) constantly trumps the thinner middle ground of the new stepcouple and stepparent-stepchild relationships, often leaving the stepparent feeling invisible and alone.

In the double family in Figure 18.7, the stuck roles abruptly switch back and forth. During most of their week, Ella, whose two children live full time with her, functions as the stuck insider, while Donna is the stuck outsider. When Donna's son, Dan, visits on weekends and vacations, mother and son connect intensely. Now Ella feels left out and upset, and Donna is caught between her partner's needs and her son's.

CHILDREN BRING LOSSES AND LOYALTY BINDS

In first-time families, as we saw, children entered their parents' established middle ground, and the family's ground continued to thicken over time. Children enter stepfamilies very differently, through a series of losses. Adults experience their new relationship as a gain. However, as we saw in our Snuggle Night vignette, for children the entry of a stepparent may bring yet more loss and yet another set of unwelcome changes (Cartwright, 2005, 2006; Cartwright & Seymour, 2002; Koerner, Rankin, Kenyon, & Korn, 2004).

Multiple opportunities for parent-child misattunement are created in the gap between Dad and Pam's joy at having found each other and Amy's feelings of loss and anxiety as her daddy snuggles with Pam. As Ed is tucking his daughter in, Amy says, "I hate Pam." What she means is "I need you. I am scared that I am losing you." Parental ability to listen and empathize is critical to helping children through this transition. Amy needs her dad to respond, "Tell me more." However, from his position in the family architecture, Ed is as likely to retort, "But Pam is a nice person," deepening Amy's loneliness and anxiety, as well as her dad's sense of confusion and inadequacy. The Faber and Mazlish (1999) classic *How to Listen So Kids Will Talk and Talk So Kids Will Listen* is extremely useful in guiding parents to provide the empathy that will support their children through these transitions.

The entry of a stepparent into a child's life also seems to create almost genetic *loyalty binds*. "If I like my stepmom, I am disloyal to my mom." "If I like my stepdad, I am disloyal to my dad." Because these loyalty binds seem to be part of the human condition, we often see them even in very collaborative divorces. When ex-spouses, or grandparents, badmouth an adult in a child's life, these binds can become unbearably painful. The death of a parent can also intensify loyalty binds for children, as the entry of a stepparent may raise the fear of losing even the memory of a lost parent.

We often find that a child who appears especially "distant" or "resistant" is, like Amy in Figures 18.5 and 18.6, especially close to the parent in the other household. For Amy, moving toward Pam will create a much more painful loyalty bind than for her brother, Tommy. Because Tommy's loyalty binds will resolve more quickly and easily than Amy's, he is more available for a relationship with Pam.

PARENTING TASKS POLARIZE THE ADULTS

Stepfamily architecture creates significant challenges to a primary task of the adults in any family: parenting. Figure 18.9 helps to illuminate the dilemma. This chart, adapted from the work of Daniel Amen (2000), tells us that parenting ranges from loving to hostile, and from firm to permissive, creating four parenting styles. Three of these four line up nicely with a huge body of parenting research by Diana Baumrind and her colleagues (1967, 1989, 1991a, 1991b; Darling & Steinberg, 1993).

The upper left *loving and firm* quadrant describes Baumrind's *authoritative* parenting. Authoritative parenting is loving, warm, and attuned to

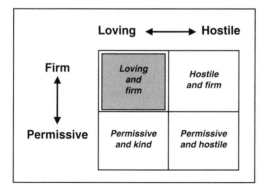

Figure 18.9 Parenting Styles.

Source: From *New Skills for Frazzled Parents: The Instruction Manual That Should Have Come with Your Child*, by D. G. Amen, 2000, Newport Beach, CA: MindWorks Press. Adapted with permission.

children's feelings and needs. Authoritative parents are also firm; they make developmentally appropriate demands for maturity, such as "You have a right to be angry at all these changes. Want to talk about it?" followed later by "I do think you're old enough to say, 'I'm mad' and talk to me rather than screaming and calling me names." Research shows, unequivocally, that authoritative parenting produces the best results for children on every measure imaginable (Baumrind, 1967, 1989, 1991a, 1991b; Dornbusch, Ritter, Liederman, Roberts, & Fraleigh, 1987).

The upper right *hostile and firm* quadrant aligns with Baumrind's *authoritarian* parenting. Authoritarian parents provide clear limits and structure, but without sufficient warmth or emotional attunement. They may make inappropriately harsh or unrealistic demands of children. The lower left *loving and permissive* quadrant describes Baumrind's *permissive* parenting. Permissive parents are warm and caring but not firm. They do not provide enough structure, and they make insufficient demands for mature behavior. Authoritarian and permissive parenting styles produce significantly less optimal results for children. Finally, *permissive and hostile* parents offer a very unstable and unpredictable environment for children, who can count on neither enough warmth and connection nor enough predictable structure.

Stepfamily architecture pulls the adult stepcouple to opposite parenting styles (Papernow, 2006a). Parents come to the new family with a more intense emotional connection to their own children than stepparents do. Remember, too, that discipline has often lapsed during single parenting, pulling insider parents to the lower left, *permissive* quadrant. Stepparents have neither a history nor a heart connection with their stepchildren. Remember also that stepchildren's losses and loyalty binds often engender indifference toward, and even outright rejection of, their stepparent. This further lowers stepparents' tolerance of their stepchildren's behavior. For these reasons, stepfamily architecture pulls stepparents to the upper right, *authoritarian* quadrant of parenting behavior.

Especially for couples with poor interpersonal skills, this difference can result in painful cycles of polarization. We saw the seeds of this in our Snuggle Night vignette when Pam said, "Your daughter is manipulative," and Ed replied, "But she's just a kid." Indeed, research shows that parents consistently describe stepparents as negatively biased and too harsh and demanding. Stepparents describe parents as blindly optimistic and too permissive.

NEW FAMILY MIDDLE GROUND MUST BE FORGED OUT OF MULTIPLE DIFFERENCES

We turn now to the impact of stepfamily architecture on the task of creating a new stepfamily middle ground, carving out paths to joint action around rules, mess, money, food, and so on. In a first-time family, by the time children reach the ages of Amy and Tommy in Figure 18.6, much of family life no longer needs discussion. In a new stepfamily, suddenly everything needs discussion and requires negotiation. Even breakfast suddenly becomes a negotiation over whether sugar cereal is a dessert or a breakfast food. And, as we have seen, the adult couple charged with leading the negotiation is constantly divided by stepfamily architecture. Furthermore, they have not had enough time to establish much comfortable middle ground to retreat to for rest and regrouping.

Ex-Spouses Are Part of the New Family

Last, but not least, stepfamily boundaries extend beyond the household to include at least one other parent who affects, and is affected by, what happens inside the stepfamily. Rules and expectations may differ significantly between the households. The ex-spouse may be involved in arrangements for everything from homework assignments to doctor's appointments to vacation planning to when to serve the Thanksgiving meal. In addition, as we will see, a jealous or anxious ex-spouse, or a hostile ex-spouse relationship, can intensify children's loyalty binds and significantly impact their adjustment.

NORMAL STEPFAMILY DEVELOPMENT: MEETING THE CHALLENGES OVER TIME

The Stepfamily Cycle (Papernow, 1984, 1996) provides a picture of how stepfamilies meet the challenges posed by stepfamily architecture. The Stepfamily Cycle describes Early, Middle, and Later Stages of normal stepfamily development. In the Early Stages, the thick middle ground lies in the preexisting parent-child relationships, and insider/outsider roles remain extremely stuck. Children's losses and loyalty binds are most intense, and cultural differences abound. The structure begins to shift in the Middle Stages, as children's losses begin to ease, differences begin to be resolved, and middle ground begins to develop in step relationships. In the Later Stages, we see a mature stepfamily with solid middle ground in both stepcouple and stepparent-stepchild relationships. Often a family moves forward on one issue, while remaining in Early Stages on another. Different family members may also move at different paces.

Early Stages: Getting Started (or Getting Stuck)

Fantasy: The Invisible Burden

All new relationships engender fantasies. Stepfamily members bring their own particular set: loving stepparent-stepchild relationships, a new family that heals previous wounds, a stepparent who provides discipline and order for grateful children, children as thrilled as the adults, a nuclear blended family, an ex-spouse who fades into the background.

The developmental task in this stage is to remain open enough to experience and education so that fantasies can be replaced with more realistic expectations. Remember that relinquishing wishes for loving step relationships and an instant family can involve substantial grief. Clinicians (and family members) must approach with compassion and gentleness.

Immersion: "Something's Wrong Here. It Must Be Me (or You)"

In the Immersion Stage, the realities of stepfamily architecture begin to make themselves felt. Unexpected cultural differences begin to emerge. Children who had seemed initially pleased may begin to feel more abandoned by their parent's new relationship. As stepparents become more involved in their lives and children's loyalty binds tighten, they may become more rejecting of stepparents. Insider/outsider forces become more obvious. For stepparents, the feelings of isolation, jealousy, and loneliness of the outsider position begin to mount. The reality of the ex-spouse's presence becomes more obvious. As children and stepparents become more unhappy and ex-spouses exert their influence, parents begin to feel more caught in their stuck insider positions. The adults often experience the children's and ex-spouse's behavior very differently, further dividing stepparents and parents.

The challenge in the Immersion Stage is to bear the painful feelings created by stepfamily architecture with compassion and curiosity rather than turning to shame and blame. When an easily shamed stepparent pairs with a blaming parent who holds tightly to unrealistic fantasies, stepfamilies can become mired in this stage.

Awareness: Mapping the Territory

In this stage, stepfamily members begin to make more sense of their feelings, gaining clarity about the impact of their family structure and increasing their understanding of the other positions in the family architecture. Families that move more quickly from the shame, blame, and confusion of the Immersion Stage into the curiosity and compassion of the Awareness Stage progress more quickly developmentally.

In the Immersion Stage, Pam may be saying to herself, "What is wrong with me that I can't ever get it right!" In the Awareness Stage, Pam may say, "It's not that I'm inadequate. It's that I'm always the outsider!" As one stepparent said, "It's like there's this biological force field" (Papernow, 1996, p. 122). In the Immersion Stage, Pam is asking herself, "What's wrong with me (or the kids) that they don't like my cooking?" Now she can say, "That was painful!" Moving into the Awareness Stage also involves becoming more curious about the other positions in the family architecture: "Oops! Looks like fish didn't work at all. I wonder what made this so difficult for the kids?"

In the Immersion Stage, Ed may be saying, "What is wrong with Pam that she got so upset?" or "What is wrong with my children that they can't be nice to Pam?" or "What's wrong with me that I can't keep everyone happy?" In the Awareness Stage, parents can articulate, "I feel torn between the people I love because their needs are really different and there's only one of me!" In the Awareness Stage, family members can also begin to reach for understanding of other family members' experience: "Gee, I can see that was really painful for Pam and tough for the kids. I wonder what happened and what would help?"

MIDDLE STAGES: REORGANIZING THE FAMILY

In the Middle Stages, the family begins to reorganize, and middle ground begins to grow in step relationships.

Mobilization: Airing Differences

In the Mobilization Stage, stepfamily members begin to air their differences more openly. Sometimes an overwhelmed child starts acting out. Often it is the stepparent who, as the outsider adult, feels most uncomfortable and initiates a push for change, as when Pam started driving the food issue. In families with poor interpersonal skills, this can be an extremely rocky and difficult period. Couples who resort easily to blaming and fighting can become stuck in the Mobilization Stage. Couples who communicate constructively about their differences are more likely to move from Awareness to Action with considerably less struggle.

Action: Going into Business Together

In the Action Stage, stepfamily members begin to resolve differences and forge some resolution. When families move into Action based on solid understanding of the needs of all family members, patches of easy middle ground begin to form. Pam and Ed have agreed to leave pancakes as the special Wednesday night dinner, although Ed has agreed to require milk rather than Coke and to add more vegetables to the children's meals. Friday Snuggle Night is now clearly established as a night for Ed and his kids. Pam spends that evening with friends. She and Ed have a separate date night each week.

Pam, always frugal, and Ed, who is used to spending liberally, still differ about money. However, they have developed a "three-pot" system, which enables them to function fairly smoothly despite their differences. Using a formula that considers Ed's larger salary and greater people numbers, they contribute proportionately to a house pot from which they pay their mortgage and other joint expenses. Ed pays his child support out of his individual pot and spends as he sees fit on his children. Pam and Ed each pay their own individual expenses out of their individual pots.

Conversation continues about Pam's concerns that Ed is "spoiling" his kids, and Ed has begun to consider giving the children a set allowance. If they are skilled, the couple will handle this as an Awareness issue, with curiosity and calm conversation. If not, they may slip back into Immersion, with at least one member going silent, or lurch into pitched battle (Mobilization).

The drive for "blended bliss" propels some couples to move too quickly into Action, forming a tight boundary around the couple and setting a host of new rules and expectations. Prematurely moving into Action asks too much change too fast of children. As children rebel, or become depressed, parents begin waffling on the new rules, leaving stepparents feeling betrayed and unsupported. Equally injurious, parents may ally with their new partner, leaving children feeling abandoned and disconnected. In stepfamilies, "a step at a time saves nine" (Papernow, 1996, p. 174).

LATER STAGES: MATURE STEPFAMILY

By the Later Stages, we see a mature stepfamily with large areas of middle ground in step relationships. The family now has a sense of how "we" do things.

Contact: Intimacy and Authenticity in Step Relationships

In the Contact Stage, stepfamilies finally get their honeymoon (Papernow, 1996, pp. 198–212). The adult stepcouple has now forged satisfying resolutions to many of their differences or found a way to live well enough with them (as in the three-pot money system). The family enjoys substantial areas of thickening middle ground with many paths to easy joint action. Although stepparents may or may not have become primary disciplinarians, they often have substantial input into parenting decisions.

In this stage, stepparents have become close enough to know their stepchildren well and to care deeply about them. Yet they remain distant enough to be considerably less reactive than parents around such issues as drugs, sex, and career planning. This combination makes for a special kind of "intimate outsider" role (Papernow, 1996, p. 201) with some (though often not all) of their stepchildren. This intimate outsider role is extremely satisfying and nourishing for both stepparents and stepchildren.

Resolution: A Solid Sense of "We-ness"

In the Resolution Stage, there is solid middle ground in the adult couple and in stepparent-stepchild relationships (Papernow, 1996, pp. 212–230).

One stepchild may remain distant, but even that has become part of the easy middle ground of the family. Insider/outsider relationships have not entirely disappeared, but they have softened considerably. The family has developed a solid sense of how "we" do things. Whether or not the stepparent has entered a full parental role, the adults have forged agreements about how they handle most child issues. As when any two cultures join, some differences remain. However, there are many easy paths to joint action, even concerning a difficult ex-spouse or a particularly distant stepchild.

In the Resolution Stage, new issues, such as college expenses, a child's wedding, or the birth of a grandchild, may reactivate children's losses and loyalty binds and the adults' insider/outsider pulls as well as temporarily increasing strain with the ex-spouse. However, these differences now arise in the context of solid, secure step relationships. The family can now retreat to their own thick middle ground for rest and regrouping.

MATURE STEPFAMILY ARCHITECTURE

Figure 18.6 shows Ed and Pam in the Early Stages of their new stepfamily after a year of marriage. Middle ground in their step relationships is very thin. The stepparent, Pam, occupies a stuck outsider role. The parent, Ed, is the stuck insider. Amy's tight relationship with her mother creates an intense loyalty bind that requires her to keep her distance from Pam. Even in the Early Stages, Tommy is freer than his sister to move toward his new stepmother.

In Figure 18.10 we see a mature stepfamily in the Later Stages. Ed and Pam have forged an intimate, caring relationship and consider themselves a team on most family issues. Ed's children have been supported well enough so that their losses have resolved and loyalty binds have eased. Ed still spends some time alone with each of his children, including some

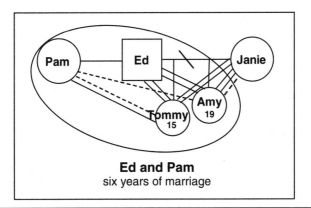

Ed and Pam
six years of marriage

Figure 18.10 Mature Stepfamily: Later Stages.

vacation time. Parent-child relationships remain closer than stepparent-stepchild relationships. However, Tommy and his stepmother enjoy a nourishing "intimate outsider" (Papernow, 1996, p. 201) relationship. He confides in his stepmother about girl problems. Pam parents Tommy equally with Ed. She coaches her stepson's soccer team and travels with him to away games. Although Amy remains especially close to her mother, her loyalty bind has loosened enough so that she and her stepmother have a pleasant, though still more distant relationship. In matters regarding her stepdaughter, Pam gives input, but Ed retains final say and he remains the disciplinarian. This, too, has become an ordinary part of the family dynamic.

This particular stepfamily maintains its three-pot money system. Pam still prefers "healthier" food than Ed and his children do. However, the family has developed its own solid, easy middle ground regarding food, money, dealing with Ed's ex-spouse, and a host of other issues. Somehow, and nobody remembers when, Snuggle Night became a family movie night. Pam plays volleyball some Wednesday nights, partly to leave special time for Ed and Tommy to have dinner together. Working out Amy's college expenses created some short-term tension with Janie, which has now been resolved.

TIME: HOW LONG WILL IT TAKE?

Becoming a stepfamily is a process, not an event. In this author's clinical experience, the fastest families require 2 to 3 years to get to the Action Stage, where joint action becomes more regular and reliable. This time frame aligns with the findings of James Bray (1999) and Mavis Hetherington (2003) that stepfamilies require 2 to 3 years to get comfortable. The faster families come to their new families with more realistic expectations. They are able to provide support for both children and the new adult stepcouple. They are more likely to handle their differences with an attitude of learning and realistic problem solving rather than arguing over right and wrong.

In this author's experience, moderately paced families may take 4 or 5 years to gain a foothold in the Action Stage. The slowest families can remain stuck for 6 or more years. These slower families often harbor more unrealistic expectations they cannot relinquish. They often have poor interpersonal skills. Insider/outsider dynamics may trigger overwhelming old family-of-origin issues. Slow and moderately paced families may become mired in Immersion, with one or both members of the adult couple lost in silent shame. They may get stuck in the Mobilization Stage, blaming each other and arguing, or they may move too quickly to the Action Stage, creating a radically new regimen that backfires when the stepparent moves in too vigorously.

In all cases, progress requires completing the tasks of the Awareness Stage: getting to know each other, understanding each other's differences, and realistically addressing the needs of all family members for security and connection. With this base, families can move into effective Action. From the Action Stage on, daily living requires considerably less work and attention. Most stepfamilies need only a couple more years to mature into the deeper sense of "we-ness" of the Later Stages.

STRATEGIES THAT MEET THE CHALLENGES AND SUPPORT STEPFAMILY DEVELOPMENT

Several decades of research and 30 years of clinical experience provide considerable guidance for specific strategies that support stepfamily development and that help meet the challenges of stepfamily architecture.

NORMALIZE THE EFFECTS OF STEPFAMILY ARCHITECTURE

Normalizing the intense feelings created by stepfamily architecture can begin to free energy and attention from straining for the impossible to successfully meeting challenges. It can help enormously to understand that stuck insiders and outsiders, multiple differences among family members, and children's loyalty binds and losses are the normal result of stepfamily architecture, not signs of failure. Providing language for the painful feelings these challenges create also helps move stepfamilies from the confusion of the Immersion Stage to the greater clarity of the Awareness Stage. Stepparents need to hear that the outsider position makes a lot of stepparents feel invisible, left out, and jealous. To parents we can say, "This thing called 'stepfamily architecture' makes you the stuck insider. Lots of parents in stepfamilies feel torn between the people they love and confused about whose needs to meet when. Sound familiar?" When apparently minor differences evoke intense reactions, we can offer: "Stunning, isn't it, that even an apparently small thing like sugar cereal exposes such painful differences? It may feel as if you are failing at being a family. But it's actually just that you live in a stepfamily." Likewise, the parenting styles chart (Figure 18.9) helps stepfamily members visually grasp how stepfamily architecture works to divide the adults on parenting issues.

It is supportive for both children and adults to know that most stepchildren feel overwhelmed, sad, and angry about the changes in their lives and that many stepkids feel something called a "loyalty bind." Children's need for time alone with their parents and time to get to know their stepparents slowly may feel "un-familylike" to many. Clinicians can acknowledge that it is unlike a first-time family; however, it is normal, necessary, and very helpful in a stepfamily.

GENTLY EXPLORE FANTASIES

The confusion, pain, and shame of early stepfamily life can be overwhelming. Visions of blended families clash painfully with stuck insider/outsider roles, resistant grieving children, polarized parenting struggles, overwhelming differences, and interfering ex-spouses. Clinging to what cannot be ensures continued frustration and failure. However, because relinquishing fantasies often requires grieving for what cannot be, they must be approached gently and compassionately: "It makes so much sense that you want your wife to love your children. What parent wouldn't want that? And, as you've noticed, it doesn't work that way in stepfamilies. What's that like to hear?"

SPEND TIME IN ONE-TO-ONE RELATIONSHIPS: COMPARTMENTALIZING WORKS BETTER THAN BLENDING

The term "blended family" implies that stepfamilies develop best by spending time together as a whole family. However, when the whole stepfamily gathers, insider/outsider pulls become most intense, children feel the most discomfort, and struggles over differences and polarization around parenting styles emerge most acutely. For this reason, it is wise to keep family time brief and low-key in a new stepfamily. In fact, *one-to-one time*, or "compartmentalizing," works much better than blending to ease insider/outsider tensions, diminish children's losses, and manage the differences of early stepfamily life.

Carving out one-to-one time for the *new couple* provides space to build new middle ground without competing with the thicker parent-child ground. One-to-one stepcouple time also moves the stepparent into an insider position and enables the insider parent to pay full attention to a new partner without contending with children's feelings.

Using the first-time family as a model, many clinicians have mistakenly advocated for couple time without attention to the needs of children. In fact, research is showing that very tight stepcouple relationships create considerable stress for stepchildren (Cartwright, 2005, 2006; Cartwright & Seymour, 2002; Moore & Cartwright, 2005), as well as poorer outcomes, especially for female stepchildren (Clingempeel, Ievoli, & Brand, 1984). Regular *parent-child* alone time is critical to provide the consistent warmth and caring that research shows improves children's adjustment to both divorce and remarriage (Nicholson, Phillips, Peterson, & Battistutta, 2002; Rodgers & Rose, 2000). Wise stepcouples balance the needs of the adult couple with the needs of the children as Ed and Pam did when they established a separate date night for themselves, leaving Snuggle Night and Wednesday Pancake Night as parent-child events, at least initially.

Stepparent-stepchild alone time, without the parent, gives this new relationship space to develop, free of competition from the thicker ground of the preexisting parent-child relationship. Finally, the outsider position is exhausting. *Stepparents* need time away from the new family to pursue their own easy middle ground with friends and colleagues.

PROACTIVELY LOOSEN CHILDREN'S LOYALTY BINDS

Coaching adults to proactively loosen children's loyalty binds is critical in supporting stepfamily development. Age-appropriate "loyalty bind talks" help loosen children's loyalty binds. Ed might say to his children, "It can be kind of confusing to have both a mom and a stepmom. I want you to know that your mom's place in your heart, and your place in hers, is permanent. Like the mountains. Like the sun. I love Pam. You do not have to love her. I hope you will come to like her. But even then, it will be a totally different place in your heart." Likewise, Pam can say, "Your mom will always be your mom. Your mom's place in your heart is permanent. I will never ever take that place. Humans have big hearts. Sometime, I hope there will be room in your heart for me. But, even then, it will be a totally different place from your mom's."

Like sex education, loyalty bind talks need to be revisited as children mature and cognitive understanding increases. They often need repeating at major transition times, such as when the couple moves in together or decides to marry.

SET REALISTIC EXPECTATIONS OF STEPPARENTS AND STEPCHILDREN

Expecting love between stepparents and stepchildren is a setup for failure. It is important, however, to require civility and respect between stepparents and stepchildren. Ed can say, "You didn't choose Pam, I did. You do not have to love each other, or even like each other. But you do have to be civil and decent to each other." Parents must hold stepparents, as well as children, accountable for respectful behavior.

Research shows that preteen and early adolescent girls have the most significant adjustment challenges in a new stepfamily (Clingempeel, Brand, & Ievoli, 1984). As stated earlier, my own clinical experience is that children, especially girls, with a tight relationship with the parent in the other house experience the tightest loyalty binds. Like Ed's daughter, Amy, in Figure 18.6, these children may prefer a more distant stepparent-stepchild relationship for the long term. Within the same family, another child, often the youngest, may, like Amy's brother Tommy, be more immediately available to the new stepparent Yet a third child in the same family may track a course somewhere between. Likewise, some stepparents are eager for a relationship with their stepchildren, whereas others prefer less involvement. Thus, there is no single model for stepparent-stepchild relationships. As Margaret Crosbie-Burnett (1984) states, the relationship that works is one that is "mutually suitable" for each particular stepchild-stepparent pair. Remember that even in the Later Stages, Pam and Amy had a friendly but somewhat distant relationship in which Ed remained the primary parent, while Pam had assumed a more parental role with Tommy.

Follow Research-Based Guidelines for Parenting and Stepparenting

Research establishes that *most stepchildren cannot accept even an authoritative parenting role from stepparents* in the Early Stages of stepfamily development. Children in stepfamilies do best when control and discipline remain in the hands of the original parent, not the stepparent (Bray, 1988, 1999; Bray & Kelly, 1998; Hetherington, 1987, 1993; Hetherington & Kelly, 2002), at least in the Early Stages. A helpful model is for stepparents to have *input*, with the original parent retaining *final say* (Papernow, 1996). Bray's research suggests a "monitoring" role for stepparents: expressing concern and encouragement ("How was the soccer game?") and reporting problems to the parent ("Looks like Tommy didn't do his math homework"). Until or unless children become ready to accept the stepparent in a parenting role, David Mills (1984) offers the model of a babysitter or adult friend who "enforces the rules of the house," especially in the parent's absence.

Again, research shows that *authoritative*, loving, and firm parenting assures the best outcomes not only on most important measures of well-being in first-time families (Baumrind, 1967, 1991a, 1991b), but also for children in divorce and remarriage (Dunn, 2004; Nicholson et al., 2002). Children benefit, therefore, when stepparents can help parents to move up on the parenting styles chart (Figure 18.9) from the permissive quadrant to firmer, more authoritative parenting. In addition, children benefit when parents can help stepparents to gain more empathy and move from the upper right, authoritarian "hostile and firm" quadrant to being more caring and understanding of children's needs.

It is important to note that, in practice, communication about parenting often proves hazardous in stepcouples. Parents are often extremely sensitive to criticism about their parenting and about their children. Stepparents, already exhausted and alienated by their outsider status and their stepchildren's rejection, do not welcome requests for compassion. Success requires the ability to raise these concerns with caring and compassion. (See "Level II. Interpersonal Skills" under "Clinical Assessment and Intervention.")

REGULATE THE AMOUNT OF CHANGE

Thin middle ground in new step relationships often drives an urge to quickly establish a complete set of new rules and rituals. However, stepfamilies actually speed things up by slowing things down. Dashing prematurely into the Action Stage with a complete new set of rules and expectations does not preserve enough familiar routine to maintain sufficient stabilizing middle ground for children. On the other hand, no change at all leaves stepparents without a voice in their own home, and often mired in the Immersion Stage. *Two or three changes at a time* work well. In a double stepfamily, equalize the amount of change required of each set of children.

Money is a central area of negotiation for new stepfamilies. The blended family ideal leads many stepcouples to pool their money early on, before the new couple has enough time to resolve their differences. However, if Pam feels $20 is plenty for a pair of shoes, whereas $100 seems quite normal for Ed and his children, conflict will abound while middle ground in the couple remains too thin to settle the issue. For many stepfamilies, a three-pot system like Ed and Pam's finesses some of these struggles. Joint expenses are paid out of a joint pot to which each adult contributes in an agreed-upon formula. Each adult also maintains a separate account, from which each pays his or her own individual expenses and, for Ed, his children's expenses. It is critical that clinicians relinquish any bias toward a "right" way for stepfamilies to divide expenses. Research establishes that money is a complex issue in remarried families (Ganong & Coleman, 1999). What is right is what works.

Holidays come with powerful expectations for family bonding via familiar traditions and equally acute disappointment when inevitable differences arise. Successful holidays in stepfamilies actually require considerable upfront negotiation and compromise about multiple details. Everything from where the Christmas stockings should be hung to what they contain may need discussion. Even the best resolutions require sacrifice and change from all involved at a time when many family members are already tired of adjusting to change. Prematurely attempting to blend holidays may risk creating bad memories, which will then need to be undone for the family to go forward. Sometimes spending the first few major holidays apart can pave the way for more success down the road.

LOWER CONFLICT WITH THE "OTHER" PARENT

Over the past several decades, an ever-expanding body of research demonstrates that adult conflict seriously compromises children's mental health, whether in a first-time family or postdivorce (Hobart, 1987; Porter & O'Leary, 1980; Roseby & Johnston, 1998; Wierson, Forehand, & McCombs, 1998).

Voluminous research establishes that postdivorce parental conflict is the "most robust" (Doolittle & Deutsch, 1999) predictor of children's postdivorce maladjustment (Amato, 1993; Grych & Fincham, 1990; Johnston & Roseby, 1997; Kline, Johnston, & Tschann, 1991; Radovanovic, 1993; Tschann, Johnston, Kline, & Wallerstein, 1989). It is critical that clinicians actively intervene to lower conflict between ex-spouses (Papernow, 2002). Wittman's (2001) excellent book, *Custody Chaos, Personal Peace*, is a terrific resource for patients who like to read. Clinicians need to ensure that adults handle decisions about scheduling, and all other issues, out of children's earshot. Teach your clients that badmouthing the other parent hurts children. The aim is to help ex-spouses to develop what Mary Whiteside (1988) calls "a repertoire of courteous and respectful patterns of co-parenting exchanges."

Children can tolerate most differences between their households as long as the adults remain neutral about them. When Amy says "But Mommy lets us drink Coke all the time," Ed can respond, "Yup. You're right. In Mommy's house you drink Coke with all your meals. In Daddy's house we drink milk now. When you grow up you can decide which you think is better." What will be damaging to children is, "Your mom never did care about your teeth."

For some ex-spouses, the entry of a stepparent raises the specter of losing their children to their ex-spouse's new partner. An anxious ex-spouse is much more likely to behave badly than a secure one. Providing reassurance can help. Ed can say to his ex-wife, "Whatever the conflict between us, I don't want you to worry even a second that Pam will ever replace you as the kids' mother. I hope she will add to their lives, but just the way a teacher or a coach might, never in competition with you. And just so you know, here is what we are saying to Amy and Tommy about having a mom and a stepmom. And it is what we believe. We are telling them that your place in the kids' hearts and in their lives is special and permanent."

If conflict remains very high between ex-spouses, arrange morning drop-off at school by one parent and afternoon pick-up by the other. Lower opportunities for negotiation and conflict by setting the parenting plan in stone in the divorce agreement, with exact dates and times of both weekly and holiday schedules over several years. Teach the principle that either parent can ask for a change in the schedule; however, if they cannot agree, the original schedule determines the outcome.

One of the most painful situations for a parent occurs when an ex-spouse says something toxic or untrue to a child. In this case, pure neutrality, or, "But your Mommy loves you," leaves the child without validation for his or her experience. Adults must validate the child's reality without tightening his or her loyalty bind. First, affirm the child's experience in a neutral, simple way: "Yes, Mommy does say those things about me sometimes. She is mad at me. Sometimes when people are upset, they say a lot of things they feel are true, but aren't." Then turn the focus to the *child's* feelings: "That's an awful thing to hear about your dad. How confusing inside. It must be hard to know who to believe! Want to say more?"

Establish Boundaries between Households

Shifting to the other side of the coin, very friendly ex-spouse relationships also pose challenges in stepfamilies. Ed's chatty evening conversations with his ex-wife, Janie, about the day's events may have become part of their normal postdivorce routine. However, these chats may feel quite intrusive to Ed's new partner, Pam. Again, stepfamily architecture makes Pam's and Ed's experiences of these conversations very different.

A "Dutch door" between ex-spouses is a helpful concept (Papernow, 2002, p. 8). The top half of the door remains open to facilitate conversations about the children. But the bottom half of the door now needs to close, drawing a firm boundary around more personal issues and personal time. It will be important to help Ed to communicate this change to his ex-wife with utmost kindness and care.

Whether ex-spouses are "Cooperative Colleagues" or "Fiery Foes" (Ahrons, 1994), some boundaries between children's households are necessary. In terms of discipline, ex-spouses need to know that they cannot make disciplinary decisions for each other. If Janie grounds Amy for coming home late, Amy is grounded at her mother's house, but not at her father's unless Janie has asked and Ed has agreed. A metaphor that works well here, for both adults and children, is that having two houses is like having two different teachers: "In Mrs. Smith's class you have to raise your hand even to sharpen your pencil. In Mr. Jones's class you can walk around any time." Likewise, ex-spouses cannot make plans for their children on the other parent's time without express permission.

CLINICAL ASSESSMENT AND INTERVENTION

Whether step issues appear as the primary issue for treatment or as background to other concerns, well-informed, skilled clinicians can make the difference between stalled development and successful transition to mature stepfamilydom. However, the complexity and intensity of the issues created by stepfamily architecture can overwhelm even the most experienced practitioner. Indeed, step systems often comprise some of the most challenging cases in a therapist's practice. When stepfamily members appear in the clinical setting, it is helpful to think about assessment and intervention on three levels: psychoeducational, interpersonal, and intrapsychic. I call these "What," "How," and "Why."

LEVEL I. PSYCHOEDUCATION: WHAT DO MY CLIENTS NEED TO KNOW ABOUT STEPFAMILY ARCHITECTURE?

The mental health field has amassed substantial information about many arenas of human functioning: chronic illness, trauma, grief, adolescence, parenting, childhood development, alcoholism, and so on. Communicating what to expect, what works, and what does not in each of these areas is a vital part of good clinical practice.

Assessing Psychoeducational Needs

Assessment on the "What" level involves identifying the strengths and gaps in the client's information base and determining the next piece of information that might be useful: What knowledge does this client have about insider/outsider issues, children's losses and loyalty binds, parenting versus stepparenting roles, multiple differences, and conducting constructive relationships with ex-spouses? What would be the most useful piece of information to share next?

What strategies is this family using to meet the challenges of stepfamily living? Have they established one-to-one time throughout the family? Are the adults attuned to the children's experience? Do the adults need help talking about loyalty binds with children? Are they taking change a few steps at a time? Do they need coaching about how to lower conflict with an ex-spouse? What could they learn next?

Providing Psychoeducation to Stepfamily Members

Psychoeducation helps stepfamily members to shift their energy and attention from straining to make the impossible happen, such as trying to quickly blend into a smoothly running family, rushing children's adjustment, or attempting to install a stepparent in a parenting role. It enables them to devote their energy to things that work, such as supporting both the step and the parent-child relationships in the family by carving out one-to-one time for all.

However, much of the information we have to impart about stepfamily functioning can be disappointing and even heartbreaking. My supervisees often complain that their stepfamily clients are "resistant" to corrective information. The news that stepfamilies do not blend, and that stepparents cannot immediately step into a parenting role, provides substantial relief for some. For others, however, this information requires facing a significant and unexpected loss of beliefs, dreams, and wishes. Furthermore, it is important to remember that exposing "wrong ideas" always risks shaming the recipient of even the most well-meaning correction.

For these reasons, skillful psychoeducation requires not only a solid base of current information, but the ability to lead with compassion, not criticalness. Before you differ with or correct even the most wrongheaded idea, practice the fundamental skill of *joining*. Joining is simply operationalized compassion. Do not share corrective information until you can convey what you do understand about your clients' experience. For instance, a frustrated stepparent complains, "My husband's children are brats. I can't believe they are so disrespectful." The stepparent will be more receptive to educational input if the clinician can begin with: "It is so painful to be ignored and treated badly. That phrase 'blended family' doesn't quite set you up for this, does it?" When there is full connection, the therapist can go on: "Turns out kids are often not ready for stepparents. Would it be okay to talk about why that is?" Now the patient may be open to information about children's losses and loyalty binds and the importance of one-to-one time.

The skillful clinician presents information a piece at a time, pausing to check for impact: "What is it like to hear this from me?" Any resistance is met first with more joining. Psychoeducation does not proceed until an empathic connection is reestablished. Furthermore, what appears easy and logical to the clinician may be beyond reach for our clients. Check the viability of any action suggestions with, "On a scale of one to ten—one is a cinch and ten is really hard—how do-able does this feel?" Extra support, or a different strategy, will be necessary for anything above a four or five.

LEVEL II. INTERPERSONAL SKILLS: HOW ARE MY CLIENTS COMMUNICATING ABOUT THESE CHALLENGES?

Meeting the challenges of the divisive differences and polarizing pulls of stepfamily architecture requires excellent interpersonal skills. When stepfamily members come with good enough communication skills, a session or two that provides some solid information is often sufficient, combined with a few realistic strategies, such as one-to-one time and loyalty bind talks. The couple or individual may then return a while later for another short-term consultation. More commonly, however, troubled step systems come with poor skills for handling the differences and disappointments that abound in early stepfamily life.

Assessing Interpersonal Skills

On the "How" level, the clinician shifts attention to the interpersonal dynamics that are critical to developmental success. Good enough interpersonal skills enable couples to build their "insider" connection with each other, despite the difference in their experience of the family. When inevitable differences arise, the assessment question is: How does this stepfamily member or subsystem communicate? Do they respond with, "Tell me more about how you see this," or do they argue over who is right and who is wrong? Can they name their feelings (sad, mad, glad; I like it; I don't like it), or do they label each other ("stupid," "lazy," "manipulative")?

Can they make a clean request: "It would really help me if you'd ask Amy to say hello to me when she walks into the room." Or do they accuse? "If you weren't such a wimp, your daughter wouldn't be so manipulative and rude." Can they give negative input with some grace and caring: "I know you love your daughter and that you want the best for her. I do think she's ready to handle her anger without throwing a temper tantrum. What do you think?" Or do they attack? "I can't believe you let her get away with that again." Are adults responsive to children's losses: "All these changes are tough, huh?" Or do they quickly attempt to talk children out of their feelings: "But this new house is much nicer than our old one!" Do they give each other enough support and positive feedback to maintain the 5-to-1 positive-to-negative ratio necessary for well-being (Gottman, 1993, 1994)?

Teaching Interpersonal Skills

Because interpersonal skills are so crucial to managing the challenges of stepfamily architecture, working on this level is an essential part of clinical intervention. This holds whether the client is an individual parent, stepparent, child, or ex-spouse, or a stepcouple, parent-child pair, or dueling set of ex-spouses. Empathy and curiosity enable stepfamily members to sustain connection across the polarizing gaps created by stepfamily architecture. Calm communication enables new stepfamilies to understand their differences well enough to resolve them and begin building new middle ground together.

Conversely, when stepfamily members criticize, withdraw, attack, or defend, the differences open into great divides, deepening the cycles of disconnection and despair. Again, attention to interpersonal skills is as vital in individual work as in couples work. When a stepparent complains that a parent won't accept input, the clinician empathizes, but then explores *how* this patient brings up sensitive issues.

These are overwhelmed systems. Picking one or two skills and teaching them well helps create hope rather than adding to the overwhelm. For instance, "soft/hard/soft" teaches clients to begin and end with something "soft" when introducing something "hard." This skill operationalizes the "soft startup" that marital research (Gottman & Silver, 1999) identifies as critical to successful couple relationships. It eases communication about parenting issues, across insider/outsider gaps, and between ex-spouses. Some ways to soften "hard" information are acknowledging positive intentions, giving positive feedback, beginning with what you do understand even when you don't agree (i.e., "joining"), and expressing empathy or caring. Stepparent to parent: "I know you've been working hard with Amy about saying hello to me. Would you remind her again? I know it's difficult for her. It really helps me." Parent to stepparent: "I get that it is totally irritating when my kids leave their stuff everywhere. I promise I'll keep working on them about this. And I really need you to use a kinder tone. I do understand that you'd like to wring their necks sometimes!"

For clients who like to read, I recommend *Difficult Conversations* (Stone, Patton, Heen, & Fisher, 1999) or *Why Marriages Succeed or Fail* (Gottman, 1994). *How to Talk So Your Kids Will Listen and Listen So Your Kids Will Talk* (Faber & Mazlish, 1999) remains a first-class, step-by-step primer for parents who want to learn how to respond more empathically to their children.

LEVEL III. INTRAPSYCHIC DYNAMICS: WHY IS THIS PARTICULAR ISSUE OR SKILL SO HARD FOR THIS PARTICULAR PATIENT?

On the "Why" level, the clinician's attention turns to individual psychodynamics: *Why* is this particular place in stepfamily architecture, or this particular interpersonal skill, *especially* challenging for this patient? "Papernow's Bruise Theory of Feelings" provides a useful metaphor for many patients: If you bump your arm in a place where the flesh is healthy, it hurts. However, if you already have a bruise there, it hurts much more. If the bruise is deep, even a slight touch will elicit a very strong response.

All intimate living involves disappointments and differences that can potentially reactivate old bruises. The disruptive schisms and unwelcome surprises of stepfamily architecture can deliver especially hard wallops. For instance, a stepparent who occupied the outsider position in his or her family of origin will find this position in the stepfamily architecture especially painful. The insider position will be much more anxiety-provoking for parents who grew up with family members whom they could not please. Children who come to their new stepfamily with significant losses (adoption, death of a parent, chronic illness of a parent) will feel the loss of parental attention more acutely.

Individually trained clinicians may feel inclined to begin here. However, beginning at the intrapsychic level ignores the fact that stepfamily architecture creates powerful feelings in the sanest of us. Turning prematurely to individual dynamics to explain a stepparent's jealousy, a parent's anxiety, a child's sense of loss, or an ex-spouse's insecurity is shaming and destructive. It is also ineffective. Often psychoeducation and improving interpersonal skills will resolve the issues. Prematurely moving to the intrapsychic level without meeting these basic needs for guidance and information is a mistake and a disservice.

Assessing Intrapsychic Dynamics in Stepfamilies

While working on the first two levels, store away bits of data that may (*or may not*) be indications of intrapsychic issues. Start a genogram that tracks each family member's position in his or her own family-of-origin. Notice especially stubborn areas of resistance to psychoeducation. Note repetitive patterns of intense triggering or numbing.

When, *despite work on the first two levels,* information doesn't stick, interpersonal skills won't hold, emotional arousal levels remain high, or patients consistently become defensive or withdrawn, it is time to begin looking to the intrapsychic level. Often the clue is a feeling of "looping" over and over the same territory with very little change.

For instance, Sarah, a stepmother, reports feeling painfully jealous and abandoned during visitation weeks. The therapist begins with psychoeducation, normalizing the intense feelings created by her stuck outsider position. Sarah is also coached to express her pain with less blame so that she can evoke her husband's compassion rather than his defensiveness. The therapist has helped Sarah to find small "insider" moves she can request from her husband, Brian, that will help her feel their connection when his children are present (a discrete hug, playing footsie under the table, a date night the night before kid weeks). Sarah is encouraged to spend one-to-one time with each stepchild and to pursue her friendships outside the house during some portion of the children's visits. Often even a few of these moves ease the problem. However, Sarah continues to feel overwhelmed by feelings of rejection and jealousy during visitations. *Now* it is time to shift to exploring old bruises.

Adrian, a parent in a new stepfamily, is deeply upset that his new partner, Maria, is not being a mother to his children. Every attempt to provide psychoeducation about the ways first-time families and stepfamilies differ feels like a struggle. Research-based information about parenting versus stepparenting has been rejected as "un-familylike." No amount of joining seems to make a dent in Adrian's disappointment that Maria is not "stepping up" to parent his children. *Now* it is time to explore the intrapsychic level of Adrian's difficulties.

Exploring "Old Bruises": Shifting to Intrapsychic Work with Stepfamily Members

Work on the intrapsychic level begins, always, with the skill of joining, *fully* acknowledging the power of stepfamily architecture. With Sarah, the clinician might begin joining her with, "Sarah, as we all know, your outsider position makes intense feelings that are nobody's favorites. It is so hard to live in a family where you are a stuck outsider. Nobody would like this." And, "It seems as though there is something about this stepparent position that is especially painful for you. I am wondering—who were the insiders and the outsiders in the family where you grew up?" Sarah reveals that she was an outsider to an exclusive relationship between her mother and an adored and cruel older brother. Father was an absent workaholic. "Wow. No wonder this is so painful. You're getting kicked smack in an old bruise, aren't you!"

In Adrian's case, the therapist might open with, "All parents want the best for their children. Of course you'd like your partner to love your children the way you do. That makes so much sense, doesn't it? The fact that it's not possible in this kind of family is not great news, is it? Nobody would like this. And yet it seems an especially bitter pill for you. I am wondering, is there something about where you come from that makes it especially painful to watch an adult who does not love a child? Would it be okay to tell me something about what parenting was like in the family you came from?" With some gentle exploration, we discover that Adrian's own parents were extremely distant and disconnected. It appears that his own pain is being reactivated by watching Maria.

Sometimes awareness and compassionate exploration is enough to heal the old experience and separate it from the new. If the injury is substantial, treatment that goes beyond talking, to address the subcortical level on which the pain is stored, may be most effective, for example, Eye Movement Desensitization and Reprocessing (EMDR) (Shapiro, 2001), Internal Family Systems (Schwartz, 1995), or Sensorimotor Therapy (Ogden, Minton, & Pain, 2006). In couple's therapy, some individual intrapsychic work may be necessary within the couples' session, or with another therapist, to heal the bruise sufficiently to make progress possible in the stepfamily. If there is a significant trauma history, I find that conjoint individual therapy with a skilled trauma therapist is a prerequisite to untangling these interactions.

CONCLUSION

Although stepfamily architecture makes "blending" a cruel fantasy, stepfamilies able to meet the challenges posed by stepfamily architecture do form satisfying, nourishing family systems. Clinicians working with an accurate blueprint of stepfamily architecture and the challenges it creates, using evidence-based strategies for meeting these challenges, can play a significant role in helping stepfamily members to create families that work for all involved.

REFERENCES

Ahrons, C. R. (1994). *The good divorce: Keeping your family together when your marriage comes apart.* New York: HarperCollins.

Ahrons, C. R., & Wallisch, L. (1987). Parenting in the binuclear family: Relationships between biological and stepparents. In K. Pasley & M. Ihinger-Tallman (Eds.), *Remarriage and stepparenting: Current research and theory* (pp. 225–256). New York: Guilford Press.

Amato, P. R. (1993). Children's adjustment to divorce: Theories, hypotheses, and empirical support. *Journal of Marriage and the Family, 55*, 23–38.

Amen, D. G. (2000). *New skills for frazzled parents: The instruction manual that should have come with your child*. Newport Beach, CA: MindWorks Press.

Baumrind, D. (1967). Child care practices anteceding three patterns of preschool behavior. *Genetic Psychology Monographs* (75), 43–88.

Baumrind, D. (1989). Rearing competent children. In W. Damon (Ed.), *Child development today and tomorrow* (pp. 349–378). San Francisco: Jossey-Bass.

Baumrind, D. (1991a). Effective parenting during the early adolescent transition. In P. Cowan & E. M. Hetherington (Eds.), *Advances in family research* (Vol. 2, pp. 111–163). Hillsdale, NJ: Erlbaum.

Baumrind, D. (1991b). Parenting styles and adolescent development. In J. Brooks-Gun, R. Lerner, & A. C. Petersen (Eds.), *Encyclopedia of adolescence* (pp. 746–758). New York: Garland Press.

Bray, J. H. (1988). Children's development during early remarriage. In E. M. Hetherington & J. Arasteh (Eds.), *The impact of divorce, single-parenting and stepparenting on children* (pp. 279–298). Hillsdale, NJ: Erlbaum.

Bray, J. H. (1999). From marriage to remarriage and beyond: Findings from the Developmental Issues in Stepfamilies Research Project. In E. M. Hetherington (Ed.), *Coping with divorce, single parenting and remarriage: A risk and resiliency perspective* (pp. 253–273). Mahwah, NJ: Erlbaum.

Bray, J. H., & Kelly, J. (1998). *Stepfamilies: Love, marriage, and parenting in the first decade*. New York: Broadway Books.

Cartwright, C. (2005). Stepfamily living and parent-child relations: An exploratory investigation. *Journal of Family Studies, 11*(2), 267–283.

Cartwright, C. (2006). You want to know how it affected me? Young adults' perceptions of the impact of parental divorce. *Journal of Divorce and Remarriage, 44*, 125–144.

Cartwright, C., & Seymour, F. (2002). Young adults' perceptions of parents' responses in stepfamilies: What hurts? What helps? *Journal of Divorce and Remarriage, 37*, 123–141.

Clingempeel, W. G., Brand, E., & Ievoli, R. (1984). Stepparent-stepchild relationships in stepmother and stepfather families: A multimethod study. *Family Relations 33*(3), 465–472.

Clingempeel, W. G., Ievoli, R., & Brand, E. (1984). Structural complexity and the quality of stepfather-stepchild relationships. *Family Process, 23*, 547–560.

Crosbie-Burnett, M. (1984). The centrality of the step relationship: A challenge to family theory and practice. *Family Relations, 33*(3), 459–464.

Darling, N., & Steinberg, L. (1993). Parenting style as context: An integrative model. *Psychological Bulletin, 113*(3), 487–496.

Doolittle, D. B., & Deutsch, R. (1999). Children and high conflict divorce: Theory, research and intervention. In R. Galatzer-Levy & L. Kraus (Eds.), *The scientific basis of child custody decisions* (pp. 425–440). New York: Wiley.

Dornbusch, S. M., Ritter, P. L., Liederman, P. H., Roberts, D. F., & Fraleigh, M. J. (1987). The relation of parenting style to adolescent school performance. *Child Development, 58*, 1244–1257.

Dunn, J. (2004). Understanding children's family worlds: Family transitions and children's outcomes. *Merrill-Palmer Quarterly, 50*, 224–235.

Faber, A., & Mazlish, E. (1999). *How to talk so kids will listen and listen so kids will talk.* New York: Avon Books.

Ganong, L., & Coleman, M. (1999). *Changing families, changing responsibilities: Family obligations following divorce and remarriage.* Mahwah, NJ: Erlbaum.

Gottman, J. M. (1993). A theory of marital dissolution and stability. *Journal of Family Psychology, 7*(11), 57–75.

Gottman, J. M. (1994). *Why marriages succeed or fail: What you can learn from the break-through research to make your marriage last.* New York: Simon & Schuster.

Gottman, J. M., & Silver, N. (1999). *The seven principles for making marriage work.* New York: Three Rivers Press.

Grych, J. H., & Fincham, F. D. (1990). Marital conflict and children's adjustment: A cognitive-contextual framework. *Psychological Bulletin, 111*(3), 434–454.

Hetherington, E. M. (1987). Family relations six years after divorce. In K. Pasley & M. Ihinger-Talman (Eds.), *Remarriage and stepparenting: Current research and theory* (pp. 185–205). New York: Guilford Press.

Hetherington, E. M. (1993). An overview of the Virginia Longitudinal Study of Divorce and Remarriage with a focus on early adolescence. *Journal of Family Psychology, 7*, 39–56.

Hetherington, E. M. (2003). Intimate pathways: Changing patterns in close relationships across time. *Family Relations, 52*, 318–331.

Hetherington, E. M., & Kelly, J. (2002). *For better or for worse: Divorce reconsidered.* New York: Norton.

Hobart, C. (1987). Parent-child relations in remarried families. *Journal of Family Issues, 8*, 259–277.

Johnston, J. R., & Roseby, V. (1997). *In the name of the child: A developmental approach to understanding and helping children of conflicted and violent divorce.* New York: Simon & Schuster.

Kline, M., Johnston, J. R., & Tschann, J. M. (1991). The long shadow of marital conflict: A model for children's postdivorce adjustment. *Journal of Marriage and the Family, 53*, 297–309.

Koerner, S. S., Rankin, L. A., Kenyon, D. B., & Korn, M. (2004). Mothers re-partnering after divorce: Diverging perceptions of mothers and adolescents. *Journal of Divorce and Remarriage, 41*(1/2), 25–38.

Mills, D. (1984). A model for stepfamily development. *Family Relations, 33*, 365–372.

Moore, S., & Cartwright, C. (2005). Adolescents' and young adults' expectations of parental responsibilities in stepfamilies. *Journal of Divorce and Remarriage, 43*, 109–128.

Nevis, S., & Warner, E. D. (1983). Conversing about Gestalt couple and family therapy. *Gestalt Journal, 6*(2), 40–50.

Nicholson, J., Phillips, M., Peterson, C., & Battistutta, D. (2002). Relationship between the parenting styles of biological parents and stepparents and the adjustment of young adult stepchildren. *Journal of Divorce and Remarriage, 36*(3/4), 57–76.

Ogden, P., Minton, M., & Pain, C. (2006). *Trauma and the body: A sensorimotor approach to psychotherapy.* New York: Norton.

Papernow, P. L. (1984). The Stepfamily Cycle: An experiential model of stepfamily development. *Family Relations, 33*(3), 355–363.

Papernow, P. L. (1996). *Becoming a stepfamily: Patterns of development in remarried families.* Hillsdale, NJ: Analytic Press.

Papernow, P. L. (2002). Post-divorce parenting: A baker's dozen of suggestions for protecting children. *Family Mediation Quarterly, 1*(2), 6–10.

Papernow, P. L., (2006a, May–June). Clinical update: Stepfamilies. *Family Therapy Magazine, 5*(3), 34–42.

Papernow, P. L. (2006b). *Stepfamilies* (AAMFT Consumer Update No. I105). Alexandria, VA: American Association of Marriage and Family Therapists.

Porter, B., & O'Leary, K. D. (1980). Marital discord and child behavior problems. *Journal of Abnormal Child Psychology, 80,* 287–295.

Radovanovic, H. (1993). Parental conflict and children's coping styles in litigating separated families: Relationships with children's adjustment. *Journal of Abnormal Child Psychology, 14,* 55–60.

Rodgers, K., & Rose, H. (2000). Risk and resiliency factors among adolescents who experience marital transitions. *Journal of Marriage and the Family, 64,* 1024–1037.

Roseby, V., & Johnston, J. R. (1998). Children of Armageddon: Common developmental threats in high-conflict divorcing families. *Child and Adolescent Psychiatry Clinics of North America, 7*(2), 295–309.

Schwartz, R. C. (1995). *Internal family systems therapy.* New York: Guilford Press.

Shapiro, F. (2001). *Eye movement desensitization and reprocessing (EMDR): Basic principles, protocols and processes.* New York: Guilford Press.

Stone, D., Patton, B., Heen, S., & Fisher, R. (1999). *Difficult conversations: How to discuss what matters most.* New York: Penguin.

Tschann, J. M., Johnston, J. R., Kline, M., & Wallerstein, J. S. (1989). Family process and children's functioning during divorce. *Journal of Marriage and the Family, 51,* 431–444.

Whiteside, M. F. (1988). Remarried systems. In L. Combrinck-Graham (Ed.), *Children in family contexts: Perspectives on treatment* (pp. 135–160). New York: Guilford Press.

Wierson, M., Forehand, R., & McCombs, A. (1998). The relationship of early adolescent functioning to parent-reported and adolescent-perceived interparental conflict. *Journal of Abnormal Child Psychology, 16*(6), 707–718.

Wittman, J. P. (2001). *Custody chaos, personal peace: Sharing custody with an ex who is driving you crazy.* New York: Penguin.

CHAPTER 19

Research on Interventions for Stepfamily Couples: The State of the Field

SARAH W. WHITTON, JAN M. NICHOLSON,
and HOWARD J. MARKMAN

HIGH RATES of remarriage in most Western countries (around 40% of all new marriages; Kreider, 2005) have resulted in many adults living in households that include children from a previous relationship. For example, 10% of U.S. fathers and 2% of U.S. mothers live with their partner's child (Kreider & Fields, 2005). Many couples in stepfamilies are happy in their relationships; others struggle with the challenges inherent in forming a stepfamily. Research suggests that living in a stepfamily confers an elevated risk for negative couple outcomes, including high rates of conflict and divorce. Unfortunately, clinical interventions to prevent or treat couple relationship problems in the context of a stepfamily are extremely limited. Much of the early clinical work with stepfamilies focused on stepparent-stepchild relationships and parenting, with little or no attention to the couple's relationship (reviewed by Lawton & Sanders, 1994). On the other hand, general couple interventions that are effective in promoting healthy relationships (e.g., Halford, Markman, Kline, & Stanley, 2003) may be of limited efficacy when applied to couples in stepfamilies if they do not address stepfamily-specific factors that confer additional risks.

In this chapter, we present a brief overview of the factors associated with couple functioning in stepfamilies, which may represent appropriate targets for clinical interventions. Next, we review the existing research on clinical stepfamily interventions, describing the content and formats of the interventions, assessing the methodological quality of program evaluations, and summarizing existing findings regarding effectiveness of different program components and formats. We conclude with specific clinical and research recommendations about future interventions to *promote healthy couple relationships* within stepfamilies. In the following chapter (Chapter 20, this volume), two studies evaluating the impact of stepfamily interventions on child outcomes are described and recommendations are made for research on *promoting healthy child adjustment* within stepfamilies.

MARITAL FUNCTIONING AND DIVORCE IN REMARRIAGE AND STEPFAMILIES

Remarried couples are more likely than first-marriage couples to divorce (Booth & Edwards, 1992; Tzeng & Mare, 1995), and remarried women are 2 times more likely to divorce than remarried men (Tzeng & Mare, 1995). It appears that the presence of children from previous unions may place remarriages at greater risk (Booth & Edwards, 1992; White & Booth, 1985). For example, recent U.S. Census data indicate higher rates of divorce in remarriages for women with children (40% to 44%) than for women without children (32%; Bramlett & Mosher, 2002). Similarly, in a large national sample, couples with children present prior to marriage were 50% more likely to divorce (Tzeng & Mare, 1995). Given that 80% of children in stepfamilies live with their biological mother (Kreider & Fields, 2005), the heightened risk that children confer may help explain the higher divorce rates for remarried women than men.

Despite their higher incidence of divorce, remarried couples are not notably less satisfied with their marriages. In a large national U.S. sample, no differences in self-reported marital satisfaction were found between first marriages and remarriages (Ishii-Kuntz & Ihinger-Tallman, 1991). A meta-analysis of 16 studies showed that although marital satisfaction was slightly higher in first marriages than remarriages, the effect size was small (Vemer, Coleman, Ganong, & Cooper, 1989). However, satisfaction does appear to decline more rapidly for remarried couples (Booth & Edwards, 1992), which may be related to the presence of stepchildren. Bringing children into a remarriage is associated with lower marital satisfaction (White & Booth, 1985), increasing levels of marital distress over time (Kurdek, 1991), and greater frequency of marital disagreements and perceptions that the couple may separate (Stewart, 2005). Having children from multiple past or current relationships may have an additive negative effect on marital quality. Couples in complex stepfamilies (i.e., families with children from current and past relationships or from both spouses' previous relationships) report lower relationship satisfaction than couples in simple stepfamilies (Hobart, 1991; Schultz, Schultz, & Olson, 1991).

In sum, remarried couples with stepchildren have a heightened risk for declining satisfaction and divorce. Next, with an eye toward informing interventions, we explore potential explanations for the increased risk by describing factors associated with stepfamily couple outcomes.

COUPLE RELATIONSHIP FACTORS

Couple Communication and Conflict Patterns

Destructive couple conflict and ineffective problem solving are strong predictors of marital distress and divorce for all couples (e.g., Clements, Stanley, & Markman, 2004). Unfortunately, deficits in these areas may be common among stepfamily couples. Observational studies have shown remarried couples to be more negative and less supportive, to show more negative escalation, and to have poorer problem-solving skills than couples in first marriages (Bray & Berger, 1993; Hetherington et al., 1999; Prado & Markman, 1999). These differences have been found during the early stages of remarriage (Bray & Berger, 1993; Hetherington & Clingempeel, 1992) and in well-established stepfamilies (Bray & Kelly, 1998). In contrast, stepfamily couples in a recent Australian study were observed to be much *less* negative than first-marriage couples, but they were also less positive and more likely to withdraw from discussions (Halford, Nicholson, & Sanders, 2007). Similarly, stepfamily couples have self-reported that they avoid discussion of sensitive topics more than do first-marriage couples (Afifi & Schrodt, 2003; Ganong & Coleman, 1989).

Although more research is required to clarify the specific characteristics of communication in stepfamily couples, there is clear evidence of elevated rates of ineffective communication, which in turn predicts relationship dissatisfaction. Poor couple communication is moderately associated with distress in remarriages, just as in first marriages (Allen, Baucom, Burnett, Epstein, & Rankin-Esquer, 2001; Hetherington & Clingempeel, 1992). High negativity in remarriages has also predicted decreased satisfaction 1 year later, fully accounting for associations between stepfamily problems and subsequent marital satisfaction (Beaudry, Boisvert, Simard, Parent, & Blais, 2004). These results suggest that it is how couples communicate about disagreements, rather than the mere presence of disagreements, that is important to marital health in stepfamilies (Stanley, Blumberg, & Markman, 1999). Clinically, this suggests the application to stepfamilies of couples interventions that improve couples' conflict resolution skills.

Commitment to Marriage

Individuals with low commitment to the institution of marriage, who are more accepting of divorce as an appropriate solution to marital unhappiness, are at heightened risk for decreases in marital quality (Amato & Rogers, 1999) and divorce (Amato, 1996). Low commitment to marriage may be a problematic area for remarried and stepfamily couples. Divorcing a previous partner predicts an increase in the belief that divorce is an appropriate solution to marital distress (Amato & Booth, 1991; Segrin, Taylor, & Altman, 2005). Accordingly, remarried individuals report lower commitment to the institution of marriage and greater willingness to leave the marriage than do first-marrieds (Booth & Edwards, 1992). Moreover, among remarried couples, those with stepchildren report more favorable attitudes toward divorce (White & Booth, 1985) and show stronger links between marital dissatisfaction and instability (van Eeden-Moorefield & Pasley, this volume). These differences may explain why remarriages more frequently end in divorce despite levels of satisfaction similar to those in first marriages. Remarried couples, especially those with children, may tolerate less marital unhappiness, family conflict, or child distress before choosing to divorce.

Conversely, high commitment levels, associated with relationship happiness and longevity in all couples (e.g., Bui, Peplau, & Hill, 1996), may play a protective role in stepfamilies. Couples in long-term stepfamilies said that commitment was key to their success in building a stable family (Bray & Kelly, 1998).

Stepfamily Expectations

Formation of a stepfamily brings together individuals who have different family histories, including family traditions and methods for handling family difficulties (e.g., Visher & Visher, 1979). More so than couples entering first marriages with no preexisting children, partners entering a stepfamily may have different expectations about household rules, family members' roles, and patterns for interacting with children, which can be a major source of conflict and maladjustment (Fine & Kurdek, 1994; Webber, Sharpley, & Rowley, 1988). Also, stepparents with no prior parenting experience, or whose experiences involve children of a different age or temperament, may have expectations that are developmentally inappropriate or ineffective for their partner's children. Moreover, couples entering a stepfamily often have unrealistic expectations of how quickly relationships will develop between family members. Belief in the myth of "instant love" often leads to hurt and feelings of rejection in stepparents (Nelson & Levant, 1991) and lower family and marital satisfaction in both spouses (Kurdek & Fine, 1991). In general, unrealistic and discrepant expectations are a common source of conflict for stepfamily couples and have prospectively predicted family distress (Bray & Kelly, 1998; Hetherington & Kelly, 2002).

PARENTING AND CHILD-RELATED FACTORS

Consensus on Child Rearing

According to a national poll, the most frequently reported issue that couples argue about in remarriages is children (Stanley, Markman, & Whitton, 2002). Compared to first-married couples, remarried couples report more conflict around children and parenting (Henry & Miller, 2004; Hobart, 1991) and lower levels of parenting satisfaction (Ishii-Kuntz & Ihinger-Tallman, 1991). These difficulties are evident in both simple and complex stepfamilies (Hetherington et al., 1999), but may be exacerbated in complex stepfamilies (Schultz et al., 1991).

Conflict over child rearing has demonstrated moderate associations with marital quality in stepfamilies, just as in first marriages, and is linked with decreases in men's marital positivity over time (Hetherington et al., 1999). In contrast, stepfather support of mothers' decisions about the child strongly predicts marital quality (Orleans, Palisi, & Caddell, 1989). Results of a longitudinal study of stepfamilies indicate that developing a consensus on parenting and child-related issues is necessary to building a strong marriage and stepfamily (Bray & Kelly, 1998).

Biological Parent-Child Relationships

Parent-child relationships tend to become strained after parental divorce and remarriage, with lower relationship quality and more conflict (Ruschena, Prior, Sanson, & Smart, 2005). Compared to first marriages and continuously single mothers, stepfamilies show lower levels of mother-adolescent interaction and parental supervision and higher levels of mother-adolescent disagreement (Demo & Acock, 1996). During stepfamily formation, remarried mothers tend to be more negative and less positive toward their children, monitor children's behavior less, and have less control over their children than nondivorced or divorced single mothers (Bray & Berger, 1993; Hetherington & Clingempeel, 1992), and children in stepfamilies display greater negativity toward their mothers (Hetherington & Clingempeel, 1992).

Maintaining quality parent-child relationships may be important to healthy couple functioning in stepfamilies, as positive parent-child relations are associated with marital satisfaction and positivity (Bray, 1999; Hetherington & Clingempeel, 1992). For example, positive mother-child interactions are related to more positive couple interactions and to stepfathers' marital satisfaction (Bray & Berger, 1993). In fact, the impact of parent-child relationships on marital functioning and stability may be greater for stepfamilies than for nondivorced families (Hetherington & Clingempeel, 1992; White & Booth, 1985).

Parent-child relationships are also important to consider in terms of child outcomes. Poor parent-child relationships may account for most of the association between stepfamily status and psychological distress among adolescents (Falci, 2006). In stepfamilies, parent-child coercion and negativity have been associated with lower general well-being, social competence, and academic competence in stepfamily children (Hetherington & Clingempeel, 1992; Nicholson et al., 2002), while parental warmth, monitoring, and involvement promote children's social and psychological well-being.

Stepparent-Stepchild Relationships

Relationships between stepparents and stepchildren can be quite conflicted and negative (e.g., Bray & Berger, 1993; Hetherington & Clingempeel, 1992). Men tend to be less affectionate, warm, and involved and more distant, coercive, and angry with their stepchildren than with their biological children (Hetherington et al., 1999). Stepchildren tend to reciprocate with less warmth toward their stepfather (Bray & Berger, 1993; Hetherington & Clingempeel, 1992). Often feeling rebuffed by children, stepfathers generally grow less involved with them over the first 2 years after remarriage (Bray & Kelly, 1998). Many stepparents adopt a disengaged style of parenting, characterized by low levels of support, negativity, and control (Crosbie-Burnett & Giles-Sims, 1994; Hetherington & Clingempeel, 1992).

Stepparent-stepchild relationship quality appears to exert a greater influence on the couple's marital well-being than does the biological parent-child relationship (Fine & Kurdek, 1995), and healthy stepparent-stepchild relationships predict marital satisfaction 3 years later (Guisinger, Cowan, & Schuldberg, 1989). The stepparent-stepchild relationship is also central to child well-being. Even when controlling for the child's relationship quality with the biological mother, stepparent-stepchild relationship quality is associated with lower internalizing and externalizing symptoms (King & Sobolewski, 2006; White & Gilbreth, 2001). However, the optimal type of stepparent relationship for marital and child outcomes is not straightforward and likely depends on the stage of stepfamily development. After 6 months of remarriage, couples reported greater marital satisfaction when stepfathers were not expected to assume a parental role or form close relationships with their stepchildren; however, 2 years later, marital adjustment was better when stepfathers had closer relationships to their stepchildren (Bray & Berger, 1993). Based on the available evidence, some suggest that the optimal developmental process involves an initial stage in which the stepparent focuses on developing a warm, mutually respectful relationship with the child while avoiding a disciplinary role (Bray & Kelly, 1998; Ganong, Coleman, Fine, & Martin, 1999).

EXTERNAL FACTORS

Relations with Former Partners

Because most remarriages are formed following divorce rather than death, remarried couples typically must continue having interactions with at least one spouse's former partner. In fact, 10 years after divorce, over half of adults surveyed reported contact with their former spouse (Fischer, De Graaf, & Kalmijn, 2005). This contact is often hostile, particularly during the first year (Fischer et al., 2005). Around two thirds of divorced adults with shared children report a moderate to high amount of conflict with their ex-spouse, usually centering around visitation, child support, parenting practices, and money (Bonach, 2005). Remarriage reduces, but does not eliminate, hostile and friendly contact between former spouses (Fischer et al., 2005).

Developing workable rules for dealing with former spouses is a central task of couples in newly formed stepfamilies (Bray & Kelly, 1998). Continued emotional attachment or conflict with an ex-spouse has been negatively associated with remarriage intimacy and satisfaction (Buunk & Mutsaers, 1999; Knox & Zusman, 2001). Remarried couples often have conflict over how one spouse interacts with his or her former partner, which is associated with marital distress (Buunk & Mutsaers, 1999). In addition, conflict between mothers and nonresidential fathers has been associated with lower adolescent well-being (Demo & Acock, 1996) and child difficulty adjusting to remarriage (Ganong & Coleman, 2004). Biological parents fighting with or denigrating the other parent is distressing and angering to children (Cartwright & Seymour, 2002). Cooperative coparenting, though uncommon, predicts higher father-child contact and relationship quality (Sobolewski & King, 2005).

Social Support versus Isolation

Remarriages are characterized by greater social isolation than first marriages, especially if both partners were previously married (Booth & Edwards, 1992). Spouses in remarriages tend to be involved in fewer social groups that can provide support (Forste & Heaton, 2004), have less contact with their parents and in-laws (Booth & Edwards, 1992), and receive support from fewer members in their family of origin (Kurdek, 1989b). Mothers perceive less support from their own kin when they gain stepchildren (Harknett & Knab, 2007), and stepparents receive less instrumental support from their family than do adoptive or biological parents (Ceballo, Lansford, Abbey, & Stewart, 2004). These factors clearly impact marital outcomes. Across types of couples, dissatisfaction with social support is linked with relationship distress (Kurdek, 1989a). Poor social integration increases the risk for divorce (Booth, Edwards, & Johnson, 1991), and, among remarried women, lack of perceived support from family and friends predicts poor marital quality (Knox & Zusman, 2001).

SUMMARY

Couples' communication skills, commitment, expectations for stepfamily development, parenting and coparenting skills, relations with former partners, and social support are all linked with stepfamily couple outcomes. As such, they represent appropriate targets for clinical interventions. In the next section, we explore the extent to which these risk and protective factors are being considered in the development of clinical interventions for stepfamily couples and evaluate the existing data regarding the effectiveness of such programs.

CLINICAL INTERVENTIONS FOR STEPFAMILIES

A major objective of this chapter is to review the research on clinical interventions to prevent or treat couple relationship problems in the context of stepfamilies. Very few studies evaluate any type of intervention designed specifically for stepfamilies, and existing programs tend to target multiple aspects of stepfamily functioning. Therefore, we have reviewed *all* types of stepfamily interventions that have been empirically evaluated, including those targeting the whole family, the couple, or specific problem behaviors in one family member. Our goal was to gain a complete picture of what existing data tell us about the potential of clinical interventions to improve or maintain couple functioning in stepfamilies. This chapter updates Lawton and Sanders's (1994) brief review of stepfamily intervention evaluations by including more recent studies and unpublished dissertations, and differs from Adler-Baeder and Higginbotham's (2004) review, which described the content of all available educational programs for stepfamily couples, with little attention to evidence of effectiveness.

To locate articles describing empirically evaluated stepfamily programs, we searched electronic databases (PsycInfo, Academic Search Premier) using search terms that included combinations of the family terms stepfamily, remarriage, stepfather, stepmother, and stepchild with the following program terms: prevention, marriage education, intervention, and program. We also searched the reference section of each obtained article for additional studies. All studies that reported program evaluation data (including subjective reports of participant satisfaction) were included in the review.

Twenty programs were identified, as summarized in chronological order in Table 19.1.

In this section, we highlight the major findings from this review. We start by describing the quality of research design to provide a context for

Table 19.1

Summary of Existing Empirical Evidence on Stepfamily Intervention Outcomes

Authors (Year)	Intervention	Participants	Content	Method	Measures	Results
Messinger, Walker, & Freeman (1978)	4-session discussion group for couples	22 couples contemplating remarriage, or remarried with stepchild(ren)	Nondirective group discussions about common stepfamily challenges: myths, stepfathering, relations with ex-spouse, child loyalty conflicts	Pilot study No control group	Subjective evaluations Clinician case descriptions	Positive evaluation of program Perceived improvement in understanding of experience and guidelines to work on remarriage issues
Pill (1981)	6-session family life education group for couples	6 couples in stepfamilies	Education on stepfamily challenges and development, stepparenting Coparenting with ex-spouse Strengthening couple	Postevaluations No control group	Questionnaires on perceived change in target areas	Positive evaluation of program Perceived change in expectations, skills, and support
Brady & Ambler (1982)	4-session education group for couples	33 couples	Education about stepfamily life and parenting, change maladaptive expectations	Pre-post design Randomized control group	Questionnaires: family environment (standardized), beliefs about stepparent role (author's own) Interview evaluation	Treatment effect on only 1 of 10 family environment scales (conflict) Both groups reduced nonadaptive beliefs Positive evaluation

(continued)

463

Table 19.1 (*Continued*)

Authors (Year)	Intervention	Participants	Content	Method	Measures	Results
Stroup (1982)*	8-session structured family group therapy; 1st group had 4 couple & 4 family sessions; 2nd group had 8 family sessions.	7 stepfamilies with no serious psychopathology, no other current treatment.	Build family cohesion, problem solving, communication, forgiveness, stepfamily issues, "ghosts" of past family	Pre-post alternative treatment comparison design	Standardized questionnaires: family environment, marital adjustment. Family sculpture scale.	No group differences. Both showed gains on family environment and closeness, and marital adjustment.
Nadler (1983)	6-session psychodynamic and behavioral group for couples	31 couples (of 60 couples attending group)	Information on stepfamily challenges and development, communication and problem-solving skills training	Postevaluations No control group	Written and verbal reports of perceived changes in target areas	>75% reported improvement in parenting, relations with child and spouse, communication, understanding of stepchild's position
Cuddeby (1984)*	4-session stepparent education group for couples	24 couples with stepchild(ren) in home	Discussion of stepfamily issues, training in communication, conflict resolution, and parenting skills	Pre-, postinterventions and 4-week follow-up Control group	Standardized questionnaires: stepfamily knowledge and family environment	Treatment effect on all target areas, especially stepfamily knowledge at postintervention Improvement on conflict maintained at follow-up

464

	Intervention	Sample	Content	Design	Measures	Results
Ellis (1984)	6-session education group for couples	9 cohabiting or remarried couples with residential stepchild(ren)	Education and discussion focused on realistic family model, strengthening couple, normalizing experience	Postintervention and 6–8 week follow-up evaluations. No control group	Qualitative evaluation by discussion	All reported improved marital relationship and parenting. High satisfaction with group
Webber, Sharpley, & Rowley (1988)	6-session education group for couples	29 couples with stepchildren (includes recent cohabitors to married 7 years)	Problem-solving discussions, skill building to strengthen couple relationship and increase constructive stepparent-stepchild behavior	Pre-post design. No control group	Standardized questionnaires: marital adjustment, self-esteem, problem inventories	Increased marital satisfaction and self-esteem. Decreased perceived problems in all areas except relations with former partner
Mandell & Birenzweig (1990)	6-session family life education and therapeutic group for couples and children	3 stepfamilies of <5 years	Education on stepfamily development, role clarification, problem-solving skills	Pilot study. No control group	Subjective evaluations. Clinician observations	Positive program evaluation. Perceived reduction in stress and improved hope

(continued)

Table 19.1 (*Continued*)

Authors (Year)	Intervention	Participants	Content	Method	Measures	Results
Nelson & Levant (1991)	4-session group for parents in stepfamilies (only one parent attends the group)	14 biological parents or step-parents (average of 6–7 years remarried) 20 in comparison group	Demonstration and practice of communication skills (listening, responding, self-awareness) and parenting skills (rules, family meetings, consequences)	Pre-post design Comparison group	Standardized questionnaires: child and parent report of parent behavior and communication skills, family environment	Increased positive communication with child but no decrease in negative parenting communication

No change in child perceptions of parenting or in focal parent and spouse perceptions of family variables |
| Bielenberg (1991) | 6-session preventive, education group for couples | 15 stepfamily couples (premarriage or newly married) with no serious problems | Information and discussion of stepfamily formation, building couple relationship, coparenting with ex-spouse, creating roles, and helping children adjust | Pre-, postinterventions and 2-month follow up-data No control group | Standardized questionnaires: family environment, general health, parenting social support, coping | No change in family cohesion Improved social support, anxiety, and insomnia at postintervention and follow-up Improved coping at postintervention only |

Study	Program	Sample	Content	Design	Measures	Results
Duncan & Brown (1992)	Self-directed education program for stepfamilies	3 stepfamilies	6 booklets to guide home-based family strength building. Each includes information and strength-building family activities	Pre-post design. No control group	Family strength questionnaire (author's own), qualitative interview	Positive evaluation. All 3 families had increased family strength scores from pre- to post-intervention
Higbie (1994)*	8-session education group for couples	22 couples (remarried or planning marriage) with stepchild(ren)	Education on stepfamily development, stepparenting, strengthening couple, communication, helping children adjust, financial decisions	Pre-, postinterventions & 6-week follow-up. Randomized control group in an 8-week support group	Standardized questionnaires: family environment, couple satisfaction, stepfamily knowledge. Author's own: family behavior frequency, program evaluation	Improvement in favorability of self, knowledge of stepfamily issues, couple time. No treatment effect on family cohesion or adaptability or couple satisfaction
Fausel (1995)	6-session stress-inoculation group for couples	52 couples in stepfamilies (married <2 yrs or planning to marry)	Education on stepfamily formation, skills for stress management, parenting, coparenting with ex-spouse, communication, protecting couple relationship	Pre-post design. No control group	Standardized questionnaires: clinical stress. Informal evaluation	62% had lower stress scores at post- than at pretest. Positive program evaluation

(continued)

Table 19.1 (*Continued*)

Authors (Year)	Intervention	Participants	Content	Method	Measures	Results
Gibbard (1998)*	8-session education group for couples	13 couples in stepfamilies	Information on stepfamily challenges and complexity, guides for stepparenting, communication skills, building couple strength, coparenting with ex-spouse	Pre-post design No control group	Standardized questionnaires: marital satisfaction, family environment	Improvement in satisfaction with children, child-rearing conflict, and family cohesion, expressiveness, and conflict Improvements in some but not all areas of marital satisfaction
Nicholson & Sanders (1999)	8-module behavioral family intervention: one group therapist-directed, one group self-directed	42 stepfamilies with a 7- to 12-year-old residential child with conduct problems	Stepfamily education, training in positive and cooperative parenting skills, problem-solving and communication skills, family activities (integrating stepparent)	Pre-post design Randomized control and alternative treatment groups	Standardized self-report, interview, and diary measures of child behaviors and symptoms and parenting conflict	Both treatment groups had reduced child behavior problems, child internalizing symptoms, and couple parenting conflict

| Henderson (2001)* | 5-session court-ordered education group for couples with adjudicated adolescents | 30 cohabiting or remarried couples with a stepchild convicted of a crime | Information on stepfamily formation, strengthening couple relationship, family communication, building (step)parent-child bond, helping children adjust | Pre-post design. Randomized control group | Standardized questionnaires: family environment. Informal follow-up interview | Improvement in family cohesion but not adaptability. Majority informally reported improved couple relationship and parenting |
| Trone (2002)* | Educational 30-minute video of normative stepfamily development | 132 stepfather families with ≥1 residential (or part-time) child 14–17 years old | Information on stepfamily developmental stages, changes in family structure | 4 groups: 1 treatment and 1 control group for those with preintervention data, and 1 treatment and 1 control group for those without preintervention data | Standardized questionnaires: stepfamily adjustment | No pre- to posttest changes tested. At posttest, treatment group had higher family adjustment than control group. Completing questionnaire prior to video strengthened treatment effect |

(continued)

Table 19.1 (*Continued*)

Authors (Year)	Intervention	Participants	Content	Method	Measures	Results
Michaels (2000; 2006)	5-session prevention and education group for couples	8 couples remarried <5 years without serious marital or mental health problems	Education and group discussion on normalizing experience, building marital satisfaction, building positive stepparent-stepchild relationships, effectively dealing with noncustodial parent	Posttreatment evaluation only No control group	Questionnaire (author's own) and focus group to assess any perceived changes since started group	Positive change reported in understanding of stepfamily experience, family interactions, children's behavior, coparenting, and marital quality
Forgatch, DeGarmo, & Beldavs (2005); DeGarmo & Forgatch (2007)	13-session parent management training (not group format)	110 recently married (<2 years) stepfather families with a child in Kindergarten through third grade showing early signs of conduct problems	Parent training: noncoercive discipline, skill encouragement, effective monitoring, problem solving, positive involvement Strategies for resolving stepfamily issues Optional couple enhancement	Pretreatment, 6-12- and 24-month data Randomized control group	Standardized, multimethod (self-report, observed, and interview) data on parenting and child behavior	Large treatment effect on couple, effective parenting, and effective stepfathering, which were linked with reduced child noncompliance and problem behaviors

*Unpublished dissertation.

evaluating the studies' findings regarding program effects. We then highlight themes regarding preventive versus therapeutic programs, common program content areas, and program formats. However, the first and most notable finding is the extremely small number of empirically evaluated stepfamily interventions. Despite an extensive clinical literature on what therapists can do to help stepfamilies (e.g., Papernow, 1994; Visher & Visher, 1979, 2003) and growing empirical evidence regarding the factors associated with positive stepfamily outcomes that are good candidates for interventions (reviewed earlier), there are strikingly few empirically tested interventions.

QUALITY OF PROGRAM EVALUATION

As a whole, the stepfamily intervention studies suffered from a number of methodological problems. First, sample sizes were generally very small. The average sample size was 29.8; two samples consisted of only three families, and six studies had samples smaller than 10. This severely limits generalizability of findings and power to detect treatment effects. Almost universally, authors described difficulties recruiting stepfamily members to participate in their programs. At times, the poor response to recruitment efforts prevented researchers from including control groups (e.g., Stroup, 1982). Perhaps for this reason, only nine studies (45%) included any type of comparison group. Of these, only six randomly assigned participants to active versus control conditions (see Column 5, "Method," in Table 19.1). This further limits the usefulness of findings, leaving it unclear whether observed changes in participants could be attributed to the intervention. There was also a general lack of follow-up data. Only five studies included any follow-up; four of these were fairly short term, occurring within 2 months of the program's end (Bielenberg, 1991; Cuddeby, 1984; Ellis, 1984; Higbie, 1994). The other assessed outcomes at 6 and 12 months postintervention (Forgatch, DeGarmo, & Beldavs, 2005). It is particularly unfortunate that no studies followed participants long enough to assess intervention effects on divorce rates.

The measures used to evaluate interventions were also problematic. Several studies relied solely on subjective participant evaluations or consumer satisfaction ratings (Ellis, 1984; Mandell & Birenzweig, 1990; Messinger, Walker, & Freeman, 1978). Others used nonstandardized measures, often created by the authors themselves (e.g., Brady & Ambler, 1982; Duncan & Brown, 1992; Michaels, 2000). In addition, rarely was the same variable or measure included in more than one study, making it difficult to summarize or compare results across studies. Future research could benefit from a standard set of outcome variables, assessed with common measures. Finally, accessibility of the studies was limited, as 30% (6) were unpublished dissertations. Despite a recent increase in the availability of dissertations online, many remain difficult and at times costly to obtain.

In sum, the identified studies generally suffered from small samples, lack of control groups, and inconsistent use of standardized measures. (Two notable exceptions are the Nicholson and Sanders [1999] and Forgatch et al. [2005] studies, which used large samples, randomized control groups, and standardized measures collected from multiple raters.) Nevertheless, together the studies provide a picture of the types of stepfamily programs being developed and preliminary information on the effectiveness of different program types, contents, and formats. As we review the major findings, we specify which results were demonstrated in contrast to controls and which were more tentative, based on small, uncontrolled trials.

PREVENTION AND TREATMENT PROGRAMS

Eighty-five percent (17) of the identified interventions were prevention programs, designed to prevent the development of marital or family discord or psychological distress in stepfamily members. Intervention designers appear to be heeding the call of clinicians for a preventive approach to helping stepfamilies (Ganong & Coleman, 1989; Stanton, 1986; Visher & Visher, 1979). These clinicians have long proposed that the risks stepfamilies face for poor marital and child outcomes result from the challenges inherent in forming a stepfamily, rather than intrapersonal or interpersonal deficits among their members. Consequently, it is believed that most stepfamilies need education rather than therapy (Visher & Visher, 1979) and that the provision of information about normal stepfamily development might prevent problems by preparing stepfamily members for the expectable family stages they will encounter and by normalizing their difficult experiences (Papernow, 1984). Accordingly, most prevention programs we identified were closely focused on psychoeducation about common stepfamily challenges, realistic expectations for family relationships, and normative stepfamily development (see Column 4, "Content," in Table 19.1).

For preventive interventions that were evaluated compared to control groups, participants in active treatment demonstrated greater reductions in family conflict (Brady & Ambler, 1982; Cuddeby, 1984) and greater knowledge of stepfamily issues (Cuddeby, 1984; Higbie, 1994). However, although two controlled trials showed positive treatment effects on family environment (Cuddeby, 1984; Trone, 2002), three did not (Brady & Ambler, 1982; Higbie, 1994; Nelson & Levant, 1991). Several evaluations of prevention programs indicated improvements in marital satisfaction among participants (Ellis, 1984; Gibbard, 1998; Stroup, 1982; Webber et al., 1988), but the only study to assess couple satisfaction compared to a control group found no treatment effect (Higbie, 1994). The lack of consistent program effects on perceived family environment and couple satisfaction mirrors the general finding that effects of premarital education programs on self-reported relationship quality are typically not evident at posttreatment but emerge over time (Markman, Floyd, Stanley, & Storaasli, 1988). Future research with long-term follow-up data is needed to detect potential long-term stepfamily intervention effects on perceived couple and family relationship quality.

In addition to the prevention programs, we identified three programs designed to treat existing problems in stepfamilies, all of which targeted child conduct problems. Henderson (2001) assessed an educational group for stepfamily couples who were parents of an adolescent recently convicted of a crime. Nicholson and Sanders (1999) and Forgatch et al. (2005) evaluated behavioral child management training programs delivered to parents and stepparents of children displaying oppositional or conduct behavior problems. Although Henderson's findings were mixed, the other two studies demonstrated strong treatment effects in comparison to controls, including improved parenting, reduced child behavior problems (Forgatch et al., 2005; Nicholson & Sanders, 1999), and reduced couple conflict over parenting (Nicholson & Sanders, 1999).

CONTENT OF PROGRAMS

As a whole, the content of the evaluated stepfamily intervention programs was relatively well-grounded in the clinical and empirical literature, addressing many of the factors associated with couple outcomes in stepfamilies. Nearly all preventive and treatment programs included *education about stepfamilies*, presenting information on typical stepfamily development and common challenges that stepfamilies face. Consistent with empirical evidence that unrealistic expectations for stepfamily development predict poor couple and family outcomes (Bray & Kelly, 1998; Hetherington & Kelly, 2002), this content was aimed at normalizing the stepfamily experience and helping families have realistic expectations for stepfamily life. Couples receiving educational material on stepfamily life reported subjective improvements in their understanding of the stepfamily experience (Messinger et al., 1978; Michaels, 2000), more realistic expectations (Pill, 1981), and greater hopes for creating a successful stepfamily (Mandell and Birenzweig, 1990). Compared to couples in control groups, those who attended educational groups reported greater stepfamily knowledge (Cuddeby, 1984; Higbie, 1994).

Ten interventions (50%) included a component specifically focused on *strengthening or protecting the couple relationship*. This content may be particularly important for stepfamily couples, whose relationship is newer than preexisting parent-child relationships and who may have little unplanned time alone together without children (e.g., Papernow, 1984). Couples entering the programs were eager to get help with maintaining their relationships; they ranked couple health as very important and rated sessions on building a successful marriage very helpful (e.g., Michaels, 2000). Noncontrolled studies indicated that participants perceived improvements in their couple relationship (Ellis, 1984; Gibbard, 1998; Henderson, 2001; Webber et al., 1988). Only one study compared couple outcomes to a control group, finding a significant treatment effect on the amount of time spent alone as a couple but not on couple satisfaction (Higbie, 1994).

Over half of the programs included content focused on building *communication and problem-solving skills*. These components are likely crucial to intervention effectiveness, given the strong associations between communication patterns and couple health in remarriages (e.g., Allen et al., 2001). Compared to controls, participants in two programs with communication skills training demonstrated improvements in self-rated family communication (Nelson & Levant, 1991) and conflict (Cuddeby, 1984). Unfortunately, no controlled studies specifically assessed *couple* communication skills. In noncontrolled studies, participants reported improved marital satisfaction (Gibbard, 1998; Stroup, 1982; Webber et al., 1988) and family environment (Stroup, 1982), although the lack of comparison groups leaves it unclear whether the changes were due to the treatment. Consumer satisfaction with communication skills training was high (e.g., Michaels, 2000), rated in one study as the most helpful program component (Gibbard, 1998), echoing findings from general marriage education research (Markman & Halford, 2005; Stanley, 2001).

The majority of programs included a component on *parenting and stepparenting*. Some programs provided information on parenting, such as appropriate methods of child discipline and the importance of mutual support between spouses in their disciplining (e.g., Brady & Ambler, 1982; Bray & Kelly, 1998; Cuddeby, 1984; Pill, 1981). Information and guidelines for stepparenting were often included, such as recommendations to slowly involve the stepparent in discipline, after a warm stepparent-stepchild relationship has been established (e.g., Gibbard, 1998; Pill, 1981). This content is consistent with evidence that child and marital adjustment is better when mothers were primary disciplinarians and stepfathers played a less active role during first 6 months of remarriage (Bray & Berger, 1993; Ganong et al., 1999). Other programs supplemented this information with active training and practice in parenting skills (Fausel, 1995; Forgatch et al., 2005; Nelson & Levant, 1991; Nicholson & Sanders, 1999), as is suggested by evidence that competent parenting is associated with marital satisfaction and more positive (step)parent-child relations (e.g., Bray, 1999; Fine & Kurdek, 1995; Hetherington & Clingempeel, 1992). Compared to control groups, these programs demonstrated positive effects on parenting (Forgatch et al., 2005) and stepparenting skills (DeGarmo & Forgatch, 2007), positive parent-child communication (Nelson & Levant, 1991), and child behavior and emotional well-being (Forgatch et al., 2005; Nicholson & Sanders, 1999). To address the high levels of conflict over child rearing among stepfamily couples, Nicholson and Sanders's program also included *cooperative parenting skills training* to help spouses develop skills for supporting one another's parenting. Compared to controls, couples receiving this treatment showed significant reductions in parenting conflict (Nicholson & Sanders, 1999).

Dealing with children's nonresidential parent was addressed in half of the programs. Some interventions emphasized ending emotional ties with former partners and completing mourning over the past relationship, which can interfere with coparenting and with the new marriage (Bielenberg, 1991; Ellis, 1984; Stroup, 1982). The majority provided strategies for creating a nonhostile, businesslike coparenting relationship (Fausel, 1995; Messinger et al., 1978; Michaels, 2000; Nadler, 1983; Pill, 1981) and for resolving visitation issues (Ellis, 1984; Gibbard, 1998; Messinger et al., 1978; Webber et al., 1988), such as difficult child transitions between households (Nadler, 1983). Very few studies evaluated treatment effects on relations with ex-partners; the one study that did found no improvements in those relations (Webber et al., 1988). However, consumer satisfaction was high for sessions on dealing with noncustodial parents, and participants informally reported increased understanding of how maintaining positive relations with their ex-spouse can benefit the children (Michaels, 2000).

PROGRAM FORMAT

The vast majority of stepfamily interventions were offered in group settings (see Column 2, "Intervention," in Table 19.1). Thirteen were groups for couples only. Others held simultaneous child and parent groups (Mandell & Birenzweig, 1990), some group meetings for couples only and other meetings for all family members (Stroup, 1982), or groups that only one parent (either step- or biological) from each family attended (Nelson & Levant, 1991). Many studies reported that participants liked the group format, which helped them to see that other families were struggling with similar issues and that their problems were normal reactions to the stresses of stepfamily development (e.g., Higbie, 1994). Participants reported that listening to other couples in the groups helped them become aware of how similar the stepfamily experience can be across families (Michaels, 2000) and made them feel less isolated (Pill, 1981). This is important, given the social isolation many stepfamilies face (Forste & Heaton, 2004) that is linked to couple distress (Booth et al., 1991). Furthermore, leaders reported that group work was more effective than working with individual couples (Ellis, 1984).

The two interventions designed to treat child disruptive behavior disorders (Forgatch et al., 2005; Nicholson & Sanders, 1999) used a more traditional therapeutic format, in which therapists met with individual families to provide active skills training in effective parenting strategies. In Forgatch et al.'s intervention, children were brought into specific sessions for rehearsal of parenting skills. As described earlier, these treatments demonstrated strong effects on parenting and child outcomes compared to controls.

Two studies described self-directed interventions for stepfamilies. Duncan and Brown's (1992) program provided families with booklets containing information on stepfamily strengths and home-based strength-building family activities. Although program evaluation was very limited, families showed increased family strength scores from pre- to post-intervention. A self-directed version of Nicholson and Sanders's (1999) behavioral family intervention for child behavior problems included an initial therapist meeting to explain program aims and content, followed by weekly modules mailed to the family of readings and activities focused on a specific intervention content area. Interestingly, the self-directed version was equally as effective in reducing child behavior problems and parenting conflict as the therapist-directed version, although power to detect differences between conditions was limited. These results are promising for future use of self-directed programs for stepfamilies, which may be important because couples preparing for remarriage are more likely to use self-help materials than attend counseling (Ganong & Coleman, 1989).

One unique intervention comprised only a 30-minute educational video viewed by all stepfamily members, which provided normative information on stepfamily development and functioning (Trone, 2002). Families who received this minimal intervention had more positive perceived family adjustment than families who did not.

CONCLUSION AND RECOMMENDATIONS

Based on this review, clinical research on stepfamily interventions is still in its infancy. Only a small number of programs for stepfamilies have been evaluated, many in uncontrolled trials with small samples. Unfortunately, the similarity of these findings to those of Lawton and Sanders (1994) suggests that the field has not progressed significantly in the past 13 years. However, it is encouraging that two large randomized clinical trials emerged (Forgatch et al., 2005; Nicholson & Sanders, 1999), both evaluating stepfamily-based behavioral treatments for child behavior problems. In addition, evaluation data from a new prevention-oriented version of the Nicholson and Sanders program are presented in the next chapter. Hopefully these studies will lead the way to additional large-sample, controlled clinical trials of other stepfamily interventions, particularly couples-focused programs, which are more prevalent but less well examined.

As a whole, these studies provide a foundation and some direction for the development of future interventions to promote healthy couple relationships within stepfamilies. In particular, they provide preliminary evidence for the effectiveness of preventive, educational programs delivered to couples in group formats. This method is consistent with most existing relationship education programs, which are typically preventive, group-based couple interventions. A preventive approach may be particularly important for maintaining relationship health in stepfamilies, given clinical (Papernow, 1994) and empirical (Bray & Berger, 1993) evidence that couple satisfaction in stepfamilies declines rapidly. Couples interventions tend to be most effective early in relationships, when relationship satisfaction is high (van Widenfelt, Hosman, Schaap, & van der Staak, 1996). Preventive relationship education programs also carry less stigma than therapy, which may be particularly important to stepfamilies, who often already feel stigmatized by society (Coleman, Ganong, & Cable, 1996). There is a clear need for stepfamily preparation services; most couples do not prepare for remarriage (Ganong & Coleman, 1989) and report having little to no awareness about normative stepfamily development (Nelson & Levant, 1991) or about things they could do to facilitate healthy family formation (Ganong et al., 1999).

Although relationship education programs are supported by growing evidence of their effectiveness in preventing relationship distress and dissolution (Markman & Halford, 2005), and this review suggests their appropriateness for couples in stepfamily contexts, these programs in their current forms may not address many of the unique needs of stepfamily couples. We believe that the next step in the field is modification and augmentation of existing relationship education programs to better meet stepfamily couple needs. This stance is consistent with an increasing call for tailoring relationship education programs to address the specific issues that place certain couples at high risk for distress and divorce (Halford et al., 2003), with close attention to the context in which couples live (Karney & Bradbury, 2005). In support of this approach, two of the programs reviewed with strong treatment effects were theory-driven modifications of existing, empirically supported treatments (Forgatch et al., 2005; Nicholson & Sanders, 1999). Based on the empirical literature, there are several ways in which relationship education could be modified for stepfamily couples.

First, the creation of relationship education programs solely for stepfamily couples may be important. Their participation in programs designed for first-marriage couples may heighten feelings of differentness and reinforce notions that stepfamilies should try to look exactly like first-marriage families, which is associated with poor stepfamily outcomes. Our review indicated that couples value being in groups with other stepfamily couples, which normalizes their experience of stepfamily processes and reduces their sense of social isolation, a risk factor for stepfamily couple distress (e.g., Knox & Zusman, 2001). Also, interventions serving only stepfamily couples would allow for the presentation of information about normal stepfamily development, which our review suggests is effective in increasing realistic expectations and reducing family conflict. Trone's (2002) finding that an intervention consisting *solely* of information on stepfamily dynamics was associated with improved perceptions of stepfamily functioning is compelling evidence of the potency of education for couples in stepfamily contexts. Inclusion of such education will likely be an important modification to existing couples interventions to make them better suited to the needs of stepfamily couples.

Second, the current review suggests the importance of including intervention components on parenting skills, which demonstrated strong treatment effects in improving parenting and stepparenting, as well as child functioning, in two controlled trials (Forgatch et al., 2005; Nicholson & Sanders, 1999). Unfortunately, the only available evidence regarding the influence of the parenting interventions on stepcouple outcomes is that they reduce couple conflict about parenting (Nicholson & Sanders, 1999). However, given that parent-child relationships, stepparent-stepchild relationships, and couple agreement in parenting are strong predictors of marital quality (e.g., Hetherington et al., 1999), parent training will likely confer benefits to overall couple functioning. Further, the beneficial effects of parent training on parenting and child outcomes alone warrant their inclusion in future interventions.

Results of the current review also support the use of communication skills training, a standard component of most relationship education, with stepfamily couples. Communication skills training was evaluated positively by couples in several studies and demonstrated improvements in self-reported family communication and conflict. Moreover, marriage educators have noted that improving communication in couples who are at high risk for relationship deterioration (a group that includes couples in stepfamilies) can help maintain relationship satisfaction (Halford et al., 2003). Future programs may increase the effectiveness of communication training by applying these skills to stepfamily-relevant issues, such as negotiation of new roles and relationships of family members. In addition, recent evidence that stepfamily couples may exhibit high rates of withdrawal but not hostility (Halford et al., 2007) suggests that communication interventions for stepfamily couples should place particular emphasis on reducing withdrawal and avoidance. Participants attending a program that stressed the need for remarried couples to disclose feelings and not avoid the discussion of problems reported improved skills in this area (Nadler, 1983).

In addition, inclusion of treatment components to improve relations with the couple's former partners, particularly by creating businesslike coparenting relationships, may provide added benefit to couples programming. Although our review did not reveal assessments of the effectiveness of these treatment components, they received high participant satisfaction ratings (e.g., Michaels, 2000). Further, strained relations with former spouses are linked with poor remarriage (Buunk & Mutsaers, 1999) and child outcomes (Demo & Acock, 1996).

Although the existing interventions address many of the risk factors present in remarried couples and stepfamilies, interventions may benefit from targeting additional risk factors. Foremost among these is the low commitment to marriage and favorable attitudes toward divorce character- izing many remarriages. Commitment to marriage may be required to en- dure the turmoil of early stepfamily development until things settle down. In general, commitment promotes pro-relationship behavior and inhibits destructive behavior at times of crisis, helping couples stay together through difficult times (e.g., Rusbult & Buunk, 1993). Some relationship ed- ucation programs include sessions focused on the importance of commit- ment to staying married for weathering the ups and downs of married life (Stanley et al., 1999); these may be particularly important for stepfamily couples.

In closing, the development of preventive education programs for step- family couples is an important public health initiative, given the growing number of couples who live in stepfamily homes and the specific challenges they face. We hope that this chapter provides not only a description of the current state of the field of stepfamily intervention outcome research, but also provides some guide to the types of program formats and content that may be most beneficial to this population, and the type of well-designed research that is needed to evaluate newly developed programs.

REFERENCES

Adler-Baeder, F., & Higginbotham, B. (2004). Implications of remarriage and step- family formation for marriage education. *Family Relations, 53,* 448–458.

Afifi, T. D., & Schrodt, P. (2003). Uncertainty and the avoidance of the state of one's family in stepfamilies, postdivorce single-parent families, and first-marriage fam- ilies. *Human Communication Research, 29,* 516–532.

Allen, E. S., Baucom, D. H., Burnett, C. K., Epstein, N., & Rankin-Esquer, L. A. (2001). Decision-making power, autonomy, and communication in remarried spouses compared with first-married spouses. *Family Relations, 50,* 326–334.

Amato, P. R. (1996). Explaining the intergenerational transmission of divorce. *Journal of Marriage and the Family, 58,* 628–640.

Amato, P. R., & Booth, A. (1991). The consequences of divorce for attitudes toward divorce and gender roles. *Journal of Family Issues, 12,* 306–322.

Amato, P. R., & Rogers, S. J. (1999). Do attitudes toward divorce affect marital qual- ity? *Journal of Family Issues, 20,* 69–86.

Beaudry, M., Boisvert, J.-M., Simard, M., Parent, C., & Blais, M.-C. (2004). Communication: A key component to meeting the challenges of stepfamilies. *Journal of Divorce and Remarriage, 42*, 85–104.

Bielenberg, L. T. (1991). A task-centered preventive group approach to create cohesion in the new stepfamily: A preliminary evaluation. *Research on Social Work Practice, 1*, 416–433.

Bonach, K. (2005). Factors contributing to quality coparenting: Implications for family policy. *Journal of Divorce and Remarriage, 43*, 79–104.

Booth, A., & Edwards, J. N. (1992). Starting over: Why remarriages are more unstable. *Journal of Family Issues, 13*, 179–194.

Booth, A., Edwards, J. N., & Johnson, D. R. (1991). Social integration and divorce. *Social Forces, 70*, 207–225.

Brady, C. A., & Ambler, J. (1982). Use of group educational techniques with remarried couples. *Family Therapy Collections, 2*, 145–157.

Bramlett, M. D., & Mosher, W. D. (2002). Cohabitation, marriage, divorce, and remarriage in the United States. *National Center for Health Statistics, 23*, 1–32.

Bray, J. H. (1999). From marriage to remarriage and beyond: Findings from the Developmental Issues in Stepfamilies Research Project. In E. M. Hetherington (Ed.), *Coping with divorce, single parenting, and remarriage: A risk and resiliency perspective* (pp. 253–271). Mahwah, NJ: Erlbaum.

Bray, J. H., & Berger, S. H. (1993). Developmental issues in Stepfamilies Research Project: Family relationships and parent-child interactions. *Journal of Family Psychology, 7*, 76–90.

Bray, J. H., & Kelly, J. (1998). *Stepfamilies: Love, marriage and parenting in the first decade.* New York: Broadway Books.

Bui, K. V. T., Peplau, L. A., & Hill, C. T. (1996). Testing the Rusbult model of relationship commitment and stability in a 15-year study of heterosexual couples. *Personality and Social Psychology Bulletin, 22*, 1244–1257.

Buunk, B. P., & Mutsaers, W. (1999). The nature of the relationship between remarried individuals and former spouses and its impact on marital satisfaction. *Journal of Family Psychology, 13*, 165–174.

Cartwright, C., & Seymour, F. (2002). Young adults' perceptions of parents' response in stepfamilies: What hurts? What helps? *Journal of Divorce and Remarriage, 37*, 123–141.

Ceballo, R., Lansford, J. E., Abbey, A., & Stewart, A. J. (2004). Gaining a child: Comparing the experiences of biological parents, adoptive parents, and stepparents. *Family Relations, 53*, 38–48.

Clements, M. L., Stanley, S. M., & Markman, H. J. (2004). Before they said ''I do'': Discriminating among marital outcomes over 13 years. *Journal of Marriage and the Family, 66*, 613–626.

Coleman, M., Ganong, L. H., & Cable, S. M. (1996). Perceptions of stepparents: An examination of the incomplete institutionalization and social stigma hypotheses. *Journal of Divorce and Remarriage, 26*, 25–48.

Crosbie-Burnett, M., & Giles-Sims, J. (1994). Adolescent adjustment and stepparenting styles. *Family Relations, 43*, 394–399.

Cuddeby, G. W. (1984). The effects of stepparent education on perceived family cohesion, organization, and conflict. *Dissertation Abstracts International, 45*, 1072.

DeGarmo, D. S., & Forgatch, M. S. (2007). *Efficacy of parent training for stepfathers: From playful spectator and polite stranger to effective stepfathering.* Manuscript under review.

Demo, D. H., & Acock, A. C. (1996). Singlehood, marriage, and remarriage: The effects of family structure and family relationships on mothers' well-being. *Journal of Family Issues, 17,* 388–407.

Duncan, S. F., & Brown, G. (1992). RENEW: A program for building remarried family strengths. *Families in Society, 73,* 149–158.

Ellis, A. J. (1984). Second time around: A preventive intervention for remarried couples. *Australian Journal of Sex, Marriage, and Family, 5,* 139–146.

Falci, C. (2006). Family structure, closeness to residential and nonresidential parents, and psychological distress in early and middle adolescence. *Sociological Quarterly, 47,* 123–146.

Fausel, D. F. (1995). Stress inoculation training for stepcouples. *Marriage and Family Review, 21,* 137–155.

Fine, M. A., & Kurdek, L. A. (1994). Parenting cognitions in stepfamilies: Differences between parents and stepparents and relations to parenting satisfaction. *Journal of Social and Personal Relationships, 11,* 95–112.

Fine, M. A., & Kurdek, L. A. (1995). Relation between marital quality and (step)parent child relationship quality for parents and stepparents in stepfamilies. *Journal of Family Psychology, 9,* 216–223.

Fischer, T. F. C., De Graaf, P. M., & Kalmijn, M. (2005). Friendly and antagonistic contact between former spouses after divorce: Patterns and determinants. *Journal of Family Issues, 26,* 1131–1163.

Forgatch, M. S., DeGarmo, D. S., & Beldavs, Z. G. (2005). An efficacious theory-based intervention for stepfamilies. *Behavior Therapy, 36,* 357–365.

Forste, R., & Heaton, T. B. (2004). The divorce generation: Well-being, family attitudes, and socioeconomic consequences of marital disruption. *Journal of Divorce and Remarriage, 41,* 95–114.

Ganong, L. H., & Coleman, M. (1989). Preparing for remarriage: Anticipating the issues, seeking solutions. *Family Relations, 38,* 28–33.

Ganong, L. H., & Coleman, M. (2004). *Stepfamily relationships: Development, dynamics, and interventions.* Boston: Kluwer Academic/Plenum Press.

Ganong, L. H., Coleman, M., Fine, M., & Martin, P. (1999). Stepparents' affinity-seeking and affinity-maintaining strategies with stepchildren. *Journal of Family Issues, 20,* 299–327.

Gibbard, S. D. (1998). The effectiveness of an eight-week psychoeducational seminar on family environment and marital satisfaction in stepfamilies. *Dissertation Abstracts International, 58,* 4184.

Guisinger, S., Cowan, P. A., & Schuldberg, D. (1989). Changing parent and spouse relations in the first years of remarriage of divorced fathers. *Journal of Marriage and the Family, 51,* 445–456.

Halford, K., Nicholson, J., & Sanders, M. (2007). Couple communication in stepfamilies. *Family Process, 46,* 471–483.

Halford, W. K., Markman, H. J., Kline, G. H., & Stanley, S. M. (2003). Best practice in couple relationship education. *Journal of Marital and Family Therapy, 29,* 385–406.

Harknett, K., & Knab, J. (2007). More kin, less support: Multipartnered fertility and perceived support among mothers. *Journal of Marriage and the Family, 69*, 237–253.

Henderson, H. J. (2001). Impact of a court-ordered psychoeducational course on stepfamily adaptability and cohesion. *Dissertation Abstracts International, 62*, 472.

Henry, R. G., & Miller, R. B. (2004). Marital problems occurring in midlife: Implications for couples therapists. *American Journal of Family Therapy, 32*, 405–417.

Hetherington, E. M., & Clingempeel, W. G. (1992). Coping with marital transitions: A family systems perspective. *Monographs of the Society for Research in Child Development, 57*, 1–242.

Hetherington, E. M., Henderson, S. H., Reiss, D., Anderson, E. R., Bridges, M., Chan, R. W., et al. (1999). Adolescent siblings in stepfamilies: Family functioning and adolescent adjustment. *Monographs of the Society for Research in Child Development, 64*.

Hetherington, E. M., & Kelly, J. (2002). *For better or for worse: Divorce reconsidered*. New York: Norton.

Higbie, D. R. (1994). Empowering stepfamilies: Evaluation of an educational curriculum for stepfamily couples. *Dissertation Abstracts International, 54*, 4038.

Hobart, C. (1991). Conflict in remarriages. *Journal of Divorce and Remarriage, 15*, 69–86.

Ishii-Kuntz, M., & Ihinger-Tallman, M. (1991). The subjective well-being of parents. *Journal of Family Issues, 12*, 58–68.

Karney, B. R., & Bradbury, T. N. (2005). Contextual influences on marriage. *Current Directions in Psychological Science, 14*, 171–174.

King, V., & Sobolewski, J. M. (2006). Nonresident fathers' contributions to adolescent well-being. *Journal of Marriage and the Family, 68*, 537–557.

Knox, D., & Zusman, M. E. (2001). Marrying a man with "baggage": Implications for second wives. *Journal of Divorce and Remarriage, 35*, 67–79.

Kreider, R. M. (2005). Number, timing, and duration of marriages and divorces: 2001. *Current Population Reports, U.S. Census Bureau*, 70–97.

Kreider, R. M., & Fields, J. (2005). *Living arrangements of children: 2001* (Current Population Reports, P70–104). Washington, DC: U.S. Census Bureau.

Kurdek, L. A. (1989a). Relationship quality for newly married husbands and wives: Marital history, stepchildren, and individual-difference predictors. *Journal of Marriage and the Family, 51*, 1053–1064.

Kurdek, L. A. (1989b). Social support and psychological distress in first-married and remarried newlywed husbands and wives. *Journal of Marriage and the Family, 51*, 1047–1052.

Kurdek, L. A. (1991). Predictors of increases in marital distress in newlywed couples: A 3-year prospective longitudinal study. *Developmental Psychology, 27*, 627–636.

Kurdek, L. A., & Fine, M. A. (1991). Cognitive correlates of satisfaction for mothers and stepfathers in stepfather families. *Journal of Marriage and the Family, 53*, 565–572.

Lawton, J. M., & Sanders, M. R. (1994). Designing effective behavioral family interventions for stepfamilies. *Clinical Psychology Review, 14*, 463–496.

Mandell, D., & Birenzweig, E. (1990). Stepfamilies: A model for group work with remarried couples and their children. *Journal of Divorce and Remarriage, 14*, 29–41.

Markman, H. J., Floyd, F. J., Stanley, S. M., & Storaasli, R. D. (1988). Prevention of marital distress: A longitudinal investigation. *Journal of Consulting and Clinical Psychology, 56,* 210–217.

Markman, H. J., & Halford, W. K. (2005). International perspectives on couple relationship education. *Family Process, 44,* 139–146.

Messinger, L., Walker, K. N., & Freeman, S. J. (1978). Preparation for remarriage following divorce: The use of group techniques. *American Journal of Orthopsychiatry, 48,* 263–272.

Michaels, M. L. (2000). Stepfamily Enrichment Program: A preliminary evaluation using focus groups. *American Journal of Family Therapy, 28,* 61–73.

Michaels, M. L. (2006). Stepfamily Enrichment Program: A preventive intervention for remarried couples. *Journal for Specialists in Group Work, 31,* 135–152.

Nadler, J. H. (1983). Effecting change in stepfamilies: A psychodynamic/behavioral group approach. *American Journal of Psychotherapy, 37,* 100–112.

Nelson, W. P., & Levant, R. F. (1991). An evaluation of a skills training program for parents in stepfamilies. *Family Relations, 40,* 291–296.

Nicholson, J. M., Phillips, M. E., Peterson, C. C., & Battistutta, D. (2002). Relationship between the parenting styles of biological parents and stepparents and the adjustment of young adult stepchildren. *Journal of Divorce and Remarriage, 36,* 57–76.

Nicholson, J. M., & Sanders, M. R. (1999). Randomized controlled trial of behavioral family intervention for the treatment of child behavior problems in stepfamilies. *Journal of Divorce and Remarriage, 30,* 1–23.

Orleans, M., Palisi, B. J., & Caddell, D. (1989). Marriage adjustment and satisfaction of stepfathers: Their feelings and perceptions of decision making and stepchildren relations. *Family Relations, 38,* 371–377.

Papernow, P. L. (1984). The stepfamily cycle: An experiential model of stepfamily development. *Family Relations, 33,* 355.

Papernow, P. L. (1994). Therapy with remarried couples. In G. Wheeler & S. Backman (Eds.), *On intimate ground: A Gestalt approach to working with couples* (pp. 128–165). San Francisco: Jossey-Bass.

Pill, C. J. (1981). A family life education group for working with stepparents. *Social Casework, 62,* 159–166.

Prado, L. M., & Markman, H. J. (1999). Unearthing the seeds of marital distress: What we have learned from married and remarried couples. In M. J. Cox & J. Brooks-Gunn (Eds.), *Conflict and cohesion in families: Causes and consequences* (pp. 51–85). Hillsdale, NJ: Erlbaum.

Rusbult, C. E., & Buunk, B. P. (1993). Commitment processes in close relationships: An interdependence analysis. *Journal of Social and Personal Relationships, 10,* 175–204.

Ruschena, E., Prior, M., Sanson, A., & Smart, D. (2005). A longitudinal study of adolescent adjustment following family transitions. *Journal of Child Psychology and Psychiatry, 46,* 353–363.

Schultz, N. C., Schultz, C. L., & Olson, D. H. (1991). Couple strengths and stressors in complex and simple stepfamilies in Australia. *Journal of Marriage and the Family, 53,* 555–564.

Segrin, C., Taylor, M. E., & Altman, J. (2005). Social cognitive mediators and relational outcomes associated with parental divorce. *Journal of Social and Personal Relationships, 22,* 361–377.

Sobolewski, J. M., & King, V. (2005). The importance of the coparental relationship for nonresident fathers' ties to children. *Journal of Marriage and the Family, 67,* 1196–1212.

Stanley, S. M. (2001). Making a case for premarital education. *Family Relations, 50,* 272–280.

Stanley, S. M., Blumberg, S. L., & Markman, H. J. (1999). Helping couples fight for their marriages: The PREP approach. In R. Berger & M. T. Hannah (Eds.), *Preventive approaches in couples therapy* (pp. 279–303). New York: Brunner/Mazel.

Stanley, S. M., Markman, H. J., & Whitton, S. W. (2002). Communication, conflict and commitment: Insights on the foundations of relationship success from a national survey. *Family Process, 41,* 659–675.

Stanton, G. W. (1986). Preventive intervention with stepfamilies. *Social Work, 31,* 201–206.

Stewart, S. D. (2005). Boundary ambiguity in stepfamilies. *Journal of Family Issues, 26,* 1002–1029.

Stroup, M. (1982). A preliminary study comparing two structured group treatments for stepfamilies: Couple/family treatment and family treatment. *Dissertation Abstracts International, 43,* 941.

Trone, C. L. (2002). The effect of normative stepfamily information on level of perceived stepfamily adjustment. *Dissertation Abstracts International, 63,* 2078.

Tzeng, J. M., & Mare, R. D. (1995). Labor market and socioeconomic effects on marital stability. *Social Science Research, 24,* 329–351.

van Widenfelt, B., Hosman, C., Schaap, C., & van der Staak, C. (1996). The prevention of relationship distress for couples at risk: A controlled evaluation with 9-month and 2-year follow-ups. *Family Relations, 45,* 156–165.

Vemer, E., Coleman, M., Ganong, L. H., & Cooper, H. (1989). Marital satisfaction in remarriage: A meta-analysis. *Journal of Marriage and the Family, 51,* 713–725.

Visher, E. B., & Visher, J. S. (1979). *Stepfamilies: A guide to working with stepparents and stepchildren.* New York: Brunner/Mazel.

Visher, E. B., & Visher, J. S. (2003). The remarried family: Characteristics and interventions. In G. P. Sholevar (Ed.), *Textbook of family and couples therapy: Clinical applications* (pp. 523–538). Washington, DC: American Psychiatric Publishing.

Webber, R. P., Sharpley, C. F., & Rowley, G. L. (1988). Living in a stepfamily. *Australian Journal of Sex, Marriage, and Family, 9,* 21–29.

White, L. K., & Booth, A. (1985). The quality and stability of remarriages: The role of stepchildren. *American Sociological Review, 50,* 689–698.

White, L. K., & Gilbreth, J. G. (2001). When children have two fathers: Effects of relationships with stepfathers and noncustodial fathers on adolescent outcomes. *Journal of Marriage and the Family, 63,* 155–167.

CHAPTER 20

The Prevention and Treatment of Children's Adjustment Problems in Stepfamilies

JAN M. NICHOLSON, MATTHEW R. SANDERS, W. KIM HALFORD,
MADDY PHILLIPS, and SARAH W. WHITTON

CHILDREN WHO live in stepfamilies are more likely than peers raised in intact two-parent families to experience a range of behavioral and emotional difficulties. There is evidence that a number of challenges inherent in the stepfamily context contribute to children's adjustment difficulties. In this chapter we first summarize the stepfamily-specific factors that have been found to be associated with child adjustment. Next we present two studies that have evaluated the effectiveness of interventions designed to treat (Study 1) or prevent (Study 2) adjustment problems for 7- to 12-year-old children living in stepfamilies. The two studies are contrasted, their effects compared, and the challenges of clinical research and practice with stepfamilies are discussed. Recommendations are provided regarding future child-focused stepfamily research and intervention.

THE ADJUSTMENT OF CHILDREN AND YOUNG PEOPLE LIVING IN STEPFAMILIES

Children of all ages can have significant difficulties adjusting to living in a stepfamily (Coleman, Ganong, & Leon, 2006). About 30% of adults who

Research reported here was funded by the National Health and Medical Research Council of Australia (grants: 951290, 954213, 390136) and a Griffith University PhD scholarship (MP). Ethical clearance was obtained from the relevant university committees. Correspondence should be directed to Associate Professor Jan M. Nicholson.

have lived in a stepfamily during their childhood recalled their parent's re-marriage as being more stressful than when their parents initially got divorced (Ahrons, 2007). Research indicates that children living in stepfa-milies have a range of behavioral and emotional adjustment problems. In two meta-analyses, conducted 14 years apart, children in stepfamilies were consistently found to have poorer psychological well-being than children from intact two-parent families (Ganong & Coleman, 1993; Jeynes, 2007).

The adverse impact of living in a stepfamily appears to be broad and long-lasting, influencing a wide range of outcomes for children and young people. Children in stepfamilies are more likely than those from intact fam-ilies to have disruptive behavior problems and to engage in drug and alco-hol use, fighting, early sexual activity, and criminal behavior (Breivik & Olweus, 2006; Carlson, 2006; Ganong & Coleman, 2004; Hetherington et al., 1999; Kirby, 2006; Nicholson, Fergusson, & Horwood, 1999). They are also more likely to exhibit internalizing symptoms, have lower self-esteem, and report psychological distress than children in intact families (Barber & Lyons, 1994; Carlson, 2006; Falci, 2006). In terms of academic problems, chil-dren in stepfamilies are more likely to receive poor grades in school, score lower on standardized tests, miss more days of school, and leave school at an earlier age than children in intact families (Ganong & Coleman, 2004; Nicholson et al., 1999). Young children in stepfamilies also have a sevenfold increased risk for being physically abused compared children who live with two biological parents (Daly & Wilson, 1996).

Although these patterns are largely consistent across studies, some cau-tion is warranted. The differences reported were typically small, averaging only 0.2 standard deviations (Jeynes, 2007), and the majority of stepchildren fall within normal ranges for adjustment. Nonetheless, around one quarter experience problems—a rate that is double the risk for children in intact families (Bray & Berger, 1993; Hetherington, Bridges, & Insabella, 1998). A twofold increase in risk for adjustment problems is noteworthy and war-rants the allocation of resources toward this group in terms of prevention and intervention efforts.

FACTORS INFLUENCING CHILDREN'S ADJUSTMENT IN STEPFAMILIES

It is possible that differences in the adjustment of children from stepfamilies when compared with children from intact families arise from factors other than exposure to a stepfamily. For example, several studies have found that the adjustment of children in stepfamilies differs little from that of children living in single-parent families (e.g., Breivik & Olweus, 2006; Falci, 2006). It may be that the children who end up living in stepfamilies are initially different from their peers in important ways. This selection effects hypothesis would suggest, for example, that children born into single-parent families or children whose parents divorce (and who are therefore selected into the group likely to enter a stepfamily) may already be at risk for adjustment problems as a result of these earlier family circumstances.

In one of the few studies to investigate this, Nicholson and colleagues (1999) used longitudinal data to examine the adjustment at age 16 of young people who had lived in a stepfamily after the age of 6. As expected, children who had lived in stepfamilies fared significantly worse than their peers at age 16 on a range of measures, including offending, substance use, early school leaving, and early and unsafe sexual practices. However, these young people also differed significantly from their peers at age 6 (i.e., prior to living in a stepfamily) in terms of their family socioeconomic circumstances, the number of adverse family life events and family mobility experienced, and behavioral and emotional adjustment. After adjusting for these early life differences, effects at age 16 remained but were reduced. This study therefore provides partial support for a selection effect: that much of the difference in long-term outcomes between children raised in stepfamilies and their non-stepfamily peers is due to factors not specific to living in a stepfamily. However, there were small and significant adverse effects on children's adjustment that were not accounted for and appeared to be due to the effects of living in a stepfamily.

We have previously presented reviews of the stepfamily research and clinical literatures to identify the stepfamily-specific factors that may impact adversely on children's adjustment (Lawton & Sanders, 1994; Nicholson & Sanders, 1999), and more descriptive information is provided in other chapters in this volume. In particular, the previous chapter (Whitton, Nicholson, & Markman, this volume) summarized the factors associated with couple adjustment in stepfamilies, and many of these factors are also implicated in children's adjustment.

However, it is also important to understand the impact of living in a stepfamily from the perspective of a child whose parent has repartnered. It is our experience in working with stepfamilies that stepparents have a poor appreciation of the challenges faced by children. Parents may have some understanding of what is affecting their children, but often this understanding is not well formulated, and parents may have difficulty explaining their concerns to their partner. For this reason, educating stepfamily couples about the emotions and struggles experienced by children during stepfamily development is an important component of interventions. By presenting couples with an evidence-based overview of the stepfamily circumstances that present challenges to children, both parents and stepparents can gain a better understanding of their children's behavior, and consequently are better placed to decide appropriate ways of responding to their child. The following are key points that we present to parents and stepparents for consideration in the first session of our intervention programs.

TRANSITIONS AND LOSSES

Children whose parents remarry experience a number of changes that can affect healthy development. Remarriage may involve moving to a new house, with associated disruptions to children's schools, social networks, and activities. Remarriage also impacts existing relationships between the child's biological parents. When a former partner moves into a new relationship, there is often a renewal in conflict and changes to arrangements around visitation (Visher & Visher, 1989). For example, the nonresident parent may feel displaced by the stepparent's role in the child's life and become more openly critical of the new couple and the stepparent in particular. While access arrangements may have previously been flexible, the new couple may prefer more regulated arrangements to make it easier to plan family and couple activities. But the nonresident parent may be resistant to such changes. Exposure to hostility between parents and using the child to convey messages between households can be particularly harmful for children (Johnston, Kline, & Tschann, 1989).

Children also experience a number of losses as a result of parental remarriage. Prior to remarriage, when parents are single, children may take on a number of adultlike roles within the family. These can include responsibilities for younger siblings, chores around the house, and being a confidant of the parent. Indeed, children raised in single-parent families have reported a loss of their childhood through the need to assume roles of responsibility within the family (Wallerstein & Corbin, 1989). While the addition of a second adult to the household can relieve the burden on children, this also brings losses in terms of the special roles that children previously held.

This can be further exacerbated if the new partner brings other children to the relationship. Children may be jealous of the time that their parent spends with these children and resent the inclusion of "outsiders" in family activities. For some children, the addition of stepsiblings displaces them from their previous position as the oldest or youngest in the family. Children can be sensitive to differential treatment. Those who reside full-time in the household may feel that visiting children receive special treatment, and children who visit may feel excluded from things that occur during their absences. Resentments also develop when children are expected to share rooms or possessions with new stepsiblings, and there can be a loss of privacy as well as disruptions to previously established routines. Rules and expectations around children's behavior will change to accommodate

the different needs of the extended family, which can lead to further inse-
curities and experiences of loss for children.

Loss of family identity and sense of belonging are also common for children in stepfamilies. Family boundaries become blurred, and there can be
considerable variation, even within families, as to who is regarded as being
a member of the family. As described by Papernow (this volume), activities
and traditions that characterized the family may be lost. New routines and
traditions need to be established to provide opportunity for developing a
new sense of family identity. This needs to be balanced by the maintenance
of some previous routines to provide children with security and to protect
existing family relationships.

PARENT-CHILD RELATIONSHIPS

Added to these losses are the disruptions that occur to the parent-child relationship. When parents establish a new relationship they typically devote
time to getting to know their new partner and that partner's children. This
takes time and attention away from existing children and can further accen-
tuate children's fears about being replaced in the lives of their parents. The
birth of a joint child to the new relationship may provide the family with a
shared focus, but will also take parental time away from other children. The
persistence of children's feelings of hurt and betrayal have been documented in studies of young adults' reflections on how remarriage altered
their relationship with their parent (Cartwright & Seymour, 2002).

Parenting styles may change after remarriage. When single, parents face
many challenges in managing household responsibilities, ensuring an adequate family income, and caring for their children. Single parents can be
somewhat indulgent, viewing children's distress and misbehavior as a natural consequence of adjusting to parental separation. Compared to parents
in other family circumstances, single parents tend to be more lax and inconsistent in their discipline (Hetherington, 1987; Hetherington, Cox, & Cox,
1982). These patterns appear to change with parental remarriage, with studies suggesting that mothers have elevated rates of coercive and inconsistent
discipline, at least in the early stages of remarriage (Hetherington, 1987; Vuchinich, Hetherington, Vuchinich, & Clingempeel, 1991). Reasons for this
may include changes in expectations around children's behavior, new
household rules, and the influence of the stepparent.

STEPPARENT-STEPCHILD RELATIONSHIPS

Relationships between stepparents and stepchildren are widely acknowledged as one of the most difficult aspects of stepfamily formation. For many

children, parental remarriage brings a loss of hope that their parents will get back together again. Some children may be actively hostile to the new stepparent in the hope that he or she will leave, allowing their parents to reconcile. Children's acceptance of the new stepparent is particularly problematic when the stepparent is seen to be the cause of parental separation. Even children who previously got along well with the stepparent when he or she was in a dating relationship with the parent can find coresidence to be challenging, and relationships often deteriorate in the early stages of living together.

Stepparent-stepchild relationships are further complicated by a lack of clarity over the role of the stepparent (Keshet, 1990). Some stepparents have no prior child-rearing experiences, or their experience may be limited to children of a different age or temperament. This can lead to unrealistic expectations for their partner's children, frustration, and the adoption of overly harsh strategies for dealing with child misbehavior (Whitsett & Land, 1992). Additionally, children may react badly to a stepparent who tries to take an active role in discipline early in the relationship. Acceptance of a stepparent's parenting role tends to be more difficult for older than younger children, and can be undermined if the parent is not consistently seen to support the stepparent (see Papernow, this volume, for an excellent illustration of these problems).

The stepparent-stepchild relationship is further hampered by loyalty conflicts (Visher & Visher, 1989). Children may feel that they are being disloyal to their other parent if they like the new stepparent, and some will be upset by concerns that the stepparent is trying to replace their parent. Jealousies may also exist, with children resentful of the closer relationship the stepparent has with his or her own children.

COPARENTING ROLES

One area of stepfamily functioning that is particularly challenging to children's adjustment is the way the parent and stepparent jointly approach the tasks of child rearing (coparenting). In biological two-parent families, it is well-established that children's behavioral and emotional adjustment is optimized when both parents have warm, affectionate relationships with the child, are interested and involved in the child's daily life, and combine this with clearly articulated, developmentally appropriate expectations for the child's behavior, with rules and expectations consistently applied (Baumrind, 1991; Maccoby & Martin, 1983). This authoritative parenting style (characterized by high warmth and high control) is associated with better long-term outcomes for children and adolescents when compared to other alternatives: parenting that is authoritarian (low warmth, high control), permissive (high warmth, low control), or disengaged (low warmth, low control).

However, in stepfamilies it is less clear what combinations of parenting styles are optimal (Nicholson, Phillips, Peterson, & Battistutta, 2002) or even possible. For young children (i.e., infants and toddlers) it may be possible for both parent and stepparent to be authoritative in their approach, and having one or both parents using an authoritative parenting style appears protective against later adjustment problems (Nicholson et al., 2002). However, older children, particularly adolescents, are likely to reject a stepparent's attempts to discipline them (the "You can't tell me what to do, you're not my father" reaction). It has been widely recommended by clinicians working with stepfamilies that stepparents should not attempt a disciplinary role until they have established a warm, mutually respectful relationship with the child (Papernow, this volume). Essentially, the stepparent is advised to initially develop a permissive role with the child (also termed "friendlike"), which may evolve over time into one that is more authoritative.

For the stepparent to successfully withdraw from the disciplinary role, the biological parent must be responsible for balancing discipline with warmth. This can be challenging, however. As noted earlier, the single parenthood phase that typically precedes stepfamily formation is characterized by parental laxness. Thus, when the parent becomes more firm and consistent, this further contributes to the child's perceptions of adverse changes since the arrival of the stepparent.

Many stepfamily couples struggle to find mutually acceptable parenting styles, to the detriment of children. A common pattern is for stepparents to move quickly into a disciplinary role. Often this is underpinned by beliefs that the biological parent has been too indulgent, that the children are out of control, and that they need a firm hand. Initially this role may have the implicit or explicit support of the parent. However, the consequences include children rebelling against the stepparent, the biological parent feeling that the stepparent is too harsh or doesn't understand, and parental undermining of the stepparent. This leads to a negatively escalating cycle, with the stepparent becoming more authoritarian, the parent becoming more permissive, increasing conflict over child rearing, and increasing child behavior problems.

In summary, the introduction of a stepparent into the household causes disruptions to many aspects of children's daily lives. Children can experience losses in terms of their family roles and relationships with biological parents. At the same time, they are expected to make adjustments to accommodate the needs of new family members whom they didn't choose and may not even like. There may be increased exposure to conflict within the household and between households. Development of positive relationships can be undermined by premature attempts by the stepparent to adopt a disciplinary role with the child. Children's behavioral and emotional adjustment can be further threatened when the biological parent and step-parent are inconsistent with each other and when they undermine each other's parenting.

At the commencement of our clinical work with stepfamilies, we present each parent-stepparent couple with a list, written from a child's perspective, of the possible factors that may impact on adjustment (see Table 20.1). Each factor is verbally described, and the couple is asked to identify which of these may be impacting their child. The resulting subset, combined with other information collected from preintervention assessments, provides a

Table 20.1
Factors Influencing the Adjustment of Children in Stepfamilies*

Fears of Being Replaced or Unloved
Being hurt by Mom wanting to spend time alone with stepdad
Feeling sad when stepdad appears more loving toward his own children
Feeling jealous of Mom spending time with stepchildren

Grief over Losing Original Family
Feeling sad about Mom and Dad not getting back together
Resentment at stepdad for causing the divorce

Loyalty Conflicts
Feeling compelled to stick up for Mom when Dad is criticizing her
Feeling upset that stepdad is trying to replace Dad
Being afraid that liking stepdad will make Dad angry
Being anxious about saying the wrong things when asked about the other household

Uncertainty over Family Relationships
Being afraid of being expected to love stepdad and his kids
Being unsure what stepdad can and can't do
Being confused when stepdad is sometimes nice and at other times is cross

Uncertainty about the Future
Hearing Mom and stepdad fight and being afraid the new family will break up
Feeling it is pointless getting to know the stepdad because he will leave, just like Dad did
Worrying about being responsible for family fights

Exposure to Conflict
Feeling upset by Mom and Dad saying bad things about each other
Feeling caught in the middle passing messages between parents

Changes in Roles and Status
Losing that special feeling of not being the youngest or oldest anymore
Resentment of the stepdad taking over
Feeling rejected when Mom confides in stepdad and not me

Feeling Invaded
Feeling resentful over having to share room or possessions with stepsiblings

Changes in Rules and Expectations
Resentment about changes in what is expected and what is okay
Being uncertain about whether I will get yelled at
Being confused when Mom overrides what stepdad says

*Examples written for biological mother/stepfather family.

shared context for introducing specific intervention strategies in subsequent sessions (Sanders & Lawton, 1993).

This brief review has implications for the development of stepfamily interventions to treat children's adjustment problems or to prevent the development of adjustment problems. A central focus should be on strategies for providing children with consistency and stability, minimizing exposure to conflict, and ensuring that parents and stepparents develop mutually agreed-upon, complementary child-rearing roles. It is also clear from this brief review that the participation of both parent and stepparent in an intervention program is essential. The extent to which effective change can be achieved from a focus on only the parent-child or stepparent-stepchild relationship is likely to be limited given the interactive nature of these roles.

DESIGNING CHILD-FOCUSED INTERVENTIONS FOR STEPFAMILIES

In designing appropriate interventions for addressing child-focused problems in stepfamilies, one approach is to first consider the interventions that are known to be effective for improving children's adjustment in general, and whether these can be adapted to address stepfamily-specific factors (Lawton & Sanders, 1994). For child-focused interventions, the strongest evidence for efficacy comes from the field of behavioral parent training, also referred to as behavioral family intervention (Sanders, Gooley, & Nicholson, 2000). The main focus is the relationship between parents and children. This is the environmental context that is most proximal to and influential on development during the early years of life. The key underlying principle is that children's behavior can be modified by altering the way that parents interact with their child (Forehand & McMahon, 1981; Patterson, 1982; Patterson, DeBaryshe, & Ramsey, 1989; Sanders, 1999). Using a structured skills-focused format, typically ranging from 4 to 12 sessions, parents are provided with information on the causes of their child's behavior problems and learn strategies for promoting appropriate prosocial behavior and noncoercive methods for responding to disruptive and noncompliant behaviors. This approach provides parents with specific strategies for developing a parenting style consistent with authoritative parenting.

Early work in this field was conducted with children displaying clinically significant levels of oppositional or conduct-disordered behavior problems. Behavioral family interventions have been shown to be effective in reducing these behavior problems, with studies conducted by different research groups (Dishion & Patterson, 1992; Hahlweg, Heinrichs, Kuschel, & Feldmann, in press; Leung, Sanders, Leung, Mak, & Lau, 2003; Markie-Dadds & Sanders, 2006b; Stallman & Ralph, 2007; Webster-Stratton, 1996), across a range of delivery modalities (i.e., individual, group, self-directed learning; Markie-Dadds & Sanders, 2006a; Morawska & Sanders, 2006, 2007; Sanders, Bor, & Morawska, 2007) and across different service delivery contexts (Turner & Sanders, 2006; Zubrick et al., 2005). Components have been added to improve effectiveness for families with comorbid difficulties, such as marital distress (Dadds, Schwartz, & Sanders, 1987) or parental depression (Sanders & McFarland, 2000). In light of this evidence, we selected behavioral family intervention as an appropriate foundation, to be tailored to address the additional factors relevant to stepfamilies.

Two studies were conducted to evaluate the effectiveness of a modified behavioral family intervention for the parents and stepparents of elementary school-age children. The first program was for stepfamilies of children presenting with clinically significant behavioral disorders. The second program was for stepfamilies seeking a preventive intervention to promote healthy stepfamily functioning. In this study, the focus child did not necessarily meet clinical diagnostic criteria for a behavioral disorder. Both interventions were conducted with parent-stepparent couples, and the focus child was seen for assessment purposes only. Data were collected from each parent, stepparent, and focus child using a range of previously validated questionnaire, interview, and observational methods. Participants were assessed at preintervention, postintervention, 6 months later, and 12 months later (Study 2 only). In both studies, two formats of the intervention were compared: therapist-delivered versus self-directed. In Study 1, the effects of these interventions were compared to no intervention using a wait-list control. Program content, format, and the evaluation designs are summarized in Table 20.2.

TREATING CHILD BEHAVIOR PROBLEMS
IN STEPFAMILIES

INTERVENTION

The intervention program was a behavioral stepfamily intervention delivered as a therapist-directed (TD) or self-directed (SD) program. As shown in Table 20.2, it consisted of 8 sessions (or modules) delivered over 10 weeks. Content covered knowledge and skills in five areas, four of which were identified earlier: understanding the causes of children's behavior problems in stepfamilies, effective parenting strategies, coparenting, and the development of stepfamily identity and cohesion. A module on stepfamily communication and problem solving was also included due to the evidence that stepfamily couples presenting for therapy have higher rates of overt conflict, higher rates of unresolved problems, and poorer problem-solving skills than couples in other families (Brown, Green, & Druckman, 1991; Hoge, Andrews, & Robinson, 1990; Vosler & Proctor, 1991).

Table 20.2

Intervention Strategies and Evaluation Design Used in the Treatment (Study 1) and Prevention (Study 2) Programs

Common Difficulties Identified in Stepfamilies	Intervention Strategies	Study 1 Treatment		Study 2 Prevention	
		TD	SD	TD	SD
Lack of stepfamily knowledge	Written educational materials	✓	✓	✓	✓
	Review assessment data and goal setting	✓	✓	✓	✓
	Contact with other stepfamilies	✓		✓	✓
Lack of parenting skills and confidence	Enhancing relationships with children	✓	✓	✓	✓
	Managing problem behaviors	✓	✓	✓	✓
Disagreements over coparenting roles	Developing complementary parent and stepparent roles	✓		✓	✓
	Setting rules and expectations	✓	✓	✓	✓
	Joint, regular reviews of parenting	✓	✓	✓	✓
	Avoiding interference and criticism of partner's parenting	✓	✓	✓	✓
Couple relationship difficulties	Caring behaviors and quality time			✓	✓
	Emotional communication skills	✓	✓	✓	✓
	Problem-solving communication skills	✓	✓	✓	✓
Lack of family identity and shared history	Planned family activities and family traditions	✓	✓	✓	✓
	Family meetings for decision making and planning	✓	✓	✓	✓
Other difficulties	Problem solving for other problems (e.g., ex-spouses, finances)	✓	✓	✓	✓
Program format	Individual (I) or group (G)	I	I	G	G then I
	Number of sessions (or weeks)	8	8	6	1 then 5
	Total therapist contact time (hours)	12	½	12	2
	Active skills training	✓		✓	✓
Assessments	Pre-intervention	✓	✓	✓	✓
	Postintervention	✓	✓	✓	✓
	6 months after completion	✓		✓	✓
	12 months after completion			✓	✓

TD = Therapist-directed; SD = Self-directed.

The informational content of the two forms of the program was identical. All participants received extensive written materials providing information about stepfamilies, recommended activities, and recording sheets to monitor progress. The two versions differed in terms of the amount of therapist contact received, and only those in the TD condition received active skills training.

PARTICIPANTS AND EXPECTED OUTCOMES

Participants were 70 stepfamily couples with a child age 7 to 12 years meeting clinical diagnosis for Oppositional Defiant Disorder (ODD) or Conduct Disorder (CD; *DSM-III*, American Psychiatric Association, 1994). The focus child resided with the couple for at least 5 days per week. Participating children were an average age of 9.5 years, and 64% were male. On average, parents were 34 years old, had been separated from the child's other biological parent for 6 years, and had been living with the stepparent for 3.5 years. Stepparents were an average of 35 years old and 81% were male. Half the couples were legally married (the remainder cohabiting), and 41% had a joint child. Families were large (average family size was 4.9 children), and parents were well-educated (61% had completed high school, and half of these had some post–high school education). Participating families were randomly allocated at the end of the preassessment to one of two intervention conditions or wait-list control.

Key outcomes of interest were child behavior problems, parenting behaviors, and coparenting conflict. It was hypothesized that relative to wait-list controls, participants receiving either active intervention would show greater improvements from pre- to postintervention on the key outcomes, which would be maintained at 6-month follow-up. Additionally, it was hypothesized that relative to those receiving the self-directed intervention, families in the therapist-directed intervention who received the active skills training would show greater improvements at postevaluation and better maintenance of treatment gains at 6-month follow-up. Data were collected over a 5-year period, and results have been reported previously (Nicholson & Sanders, 1999). Here we provide a summary of the main findings, including previously unpublished data.

RESULTS

Sample Recruitment and Retention

Recruitment for the intervention study was undertaken concurrently with a larger study of family functioning in stepfamilies. Families were recruited through media outreach (80%), school newsletter advertisements (12%), and referrals (8%). Recruitment took more than 4 years to complete and proved extremely difficult. Of the 299 families who contacted the research team, 62% failed to meet eligibility criteria; most commonly, the child was outside the target age range, the couple was not currently residing together, or the children were not resident full time in the family. A further 7% were unable to be recontacted, and 15% met eligibility criteria but either declined participation, failed to attend assessment, or dropped out after one assessment session.

Retention over time was also challenging. Of the 70 families allocated to an intervention or control, preassessments were not completed by 14%, and 26% dropped out during the intervention or wait-list period. Analyses revealed that a higher proportion of those who dropped out were from complex stepfamilies (30%) compared to those who completed intervention (4%). All stepmother families allocated to the self-directed intervention failed to complete the program, whereas two thirds of stepmother families allocated to therapist-directed intervention completed the program. Of those who completed either program, 14% of TD and 50% of SD families declined to participate in the 6-month follow-up assessments. After these sample losses, data were available at pre- and postevaluation for 42 families: 14 from TD, 12 from SD, and 16 from the wait-list control. Follow-up data were provided by 12 families from TD and 6 families from SD.

Children's Adjustment

Child behavioral problems were measured by parent and stepparent reports on the Child Behavior Checklist (CBCL; Achenbach & Edelbrock, 1983), and by diary records of problem occurrences, the Parent Daily Report (PDR; Chamberlain & Reid, 1987). *DSM-III* criteria were used in interview to classify children as having no diagnosis, ODD, or CD. We also assessed children's depression and self-esteem using child reports on the Child Depression Inventory (CDI; Kovacs, 1981) and the Self-Esteem Inventory (SEI; Coopersmith, 1981).

All participating children met criteria for a diagnosis of ODD or CD at preassessment and had elevated rates of behavioral problems. Children also showed elevated rates of depression and moderate levels of self-esteem. Figures 20.1 and 20.2 show the mean scores on the measures of children's adjustment at pre- and postintervention and follow-up by group: therapist-directed (TD), self-directed (SD), and wait-list control (WL). Parent and stepparent report data are presented in Figure 20.1 and child report data in Figure 20.2. The figures show the data for all 42 children with complete data at both pre- and postintervention, and for the 18 children assessed at 6-month follow-up. Multivariate (MANOVA) or univariate analyses of variance (ANOVA) methods were used to test for differences by intervention and by time (pre-post). Statistical analysis of data at follow-up was not conducted due to low sample numbers.

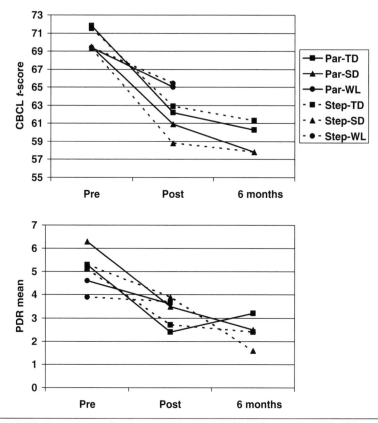

Figure 20.1 Parent- and Stepparent-Reported Child Behavior Checklist Mean *t*-scores and Number of Child Behavior Problems per Day (PDR).

Analyses revealed no significant differences in outcomes between children whose parents and stepparents participated in TD, SD, and WL conditions at either pre- or postintervention. As shown in the figures, child adjustment scores showed improvements from pre- to postintervention for all groups ($p<.001$), with the exception of child depression (which had a high degree of variance). For those in the intervention groups who completed follow-up, scores on all measures appeared to remain constant or to deteriorate somewhat from postevaluation, but were better than those reported at preintervention. An interaction effect of intervention-by-time was evident only for CBCL scores ($p < .05$). According to parent and stepparent reports, children of those who attended the TD and SD groups showed significantly greater reductions in overall behavior problems from pre- to postintervention when compared to those in the control group.

The proportion of children meeting diagnostic criteria for CD or ODD was compared for those in the two intervention groups versus control. As shown in Figure 20.3, for those families in either active intervention

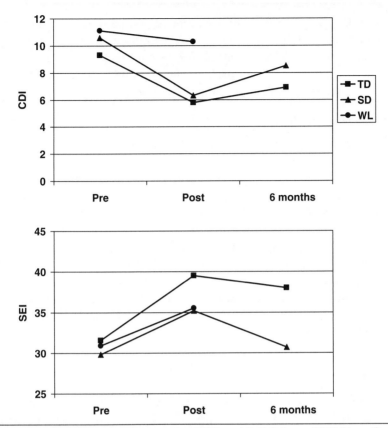

Figure 20.2 Child-Reported Depression (CDI) and Self-Esteem (SEI) Mean Scores.

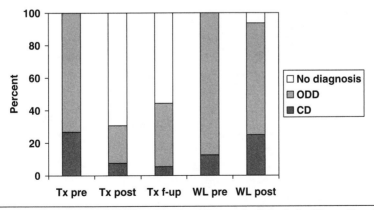

Figure 20.3 Proportion of Children Meeting Diagnostic Criteria for Oppositional Defiant Disorder and Conduct Disorder.

condition, the proportion of children meeting either diagnosis was greatly reduced from pre-intervention (100%) to postintervention (31%), with an increase to follow-up (44%). In contrast, for the control group, the reduction in those meeting diagnosis from pre-intervention (100%) to postintervention (94%) was negligible and not statistically significant.

Parenting and Coparenting

Coercive parenting (verbal negativity, angry affect, or sad affect) was assessed by observation of structured interaction tasks for parent and child and stepparent and child. Positive involvement with the child was assessed on the Family Involvement Scales (FIS; Santrock, Sitterle, & Warshak, 1988), designed for use with stepfamilies to assess involvement in routine activities and low-frequency important events. Conflict in the couple over parenting was assessed on the Parent Problems Checklist (Dadds & Powell, 1991), which lists common areas of disagreement in parenting. No significant changes over time were found for parenting behaviors. However, conflict over parenting (Figure 20.4) reduced from pre- to postintervention for parents and stepparents in the two intervention groups ($p < .001$), but not for controls ($p = .10$).

DISCUSSION

Parents and stepparents receiving either active intervention reported significant reductions in child behavior problems from pre- to postintervention, with corresponding reductions in parent-stepparent conflict over parenting. However, parenting behaviors remained unchanged. Families assigned to the wait-list control also showed some significant improvements in children's behavior, but not parenting conflict. These improvements were less

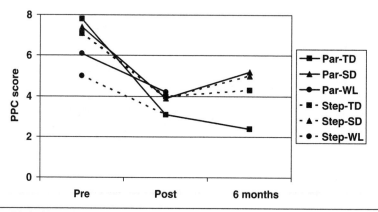

Figure 20.4 Mean Number of Parent- and Stepparent-Reported Areas of Conflict over Parenting.

strong than those achieved by the intervention families. Improvements for intervention families appeared to be partially maintained at the 6-month follow-up, although sample losses precluded formal statistical testing.

Contrary to predictions, there were no significant differences in outcomes for those allocated to therapist-directed versus self-directed intervention. While the small sample numbers resulted in a lack of power for detecting group differences, there were no trends in the data to indicate the superiority of one intervention over the other. These findings suggest that self-directed parenting interventions should be considered as a potentially cost-efficient alternative to more intensive therapist-led interventions for stepfamilies. Such approaches may also be more popular, as indicated by our wait-list families. When offered the intervention of their choice at the end of the wait-list period, two thirds selected the self-directed approach.

One surprising finding in this study was the lack of change on measures of parenting. Previous studies of behavioral family interventions have consistently produced reductions in coercive parenting (Sanders et al., 2000), which have been attributed as the reason for improvements in children's behavior. It is possible that the observational assessment protocol used here was, for some reason, not effective in eliciting the sorts of behaviors typically observed in parents of children with behavior problems. Baseline levels of coerciveness during the observation task were low, and there was little room for improvement as a result of the intervention. It may be that parenting was influenced by the intervention, but that the measures used did not sufficiently capture this change. This suggests that alternative measures of parenting may need to be considered for research with stepfamilies.

Several practical issues arose during this study that have implications for future interventions and research with stepfamilies. A key concern was the considerable difficulties that were encountered in recruiting participants to the study. As has been recommended by other stepfamily researchers (e.g., Pasley, 1988), we sought to recruit a sample of stepfamilies that was relatively homogeneous in order to aid with the interpretation of findings. Initially we attempted to recruit participants who were similar in terms of the structural characteristics of stepparent gender, stepfamily complexity, and length of time together. This was quickly found to be impractical in terms of the amount of time that would be required to recruit the sample and the number of families who were seeking participation but failed to meet selection criteria. Even after these restrictions were dropped, two thirds of the families who contacted our team seeking an intervention failed to meet our remaining selection criteria (age and residential status of child, child behavior problems). Thus, it appears that a research-driven desire to restrict the sample had poor compatibility with the wide range of family characteristics among stepfamilies seeking help.

Once families entered the study, retention was also problematic. This included retention difficulties from the initial contact through the preassessment, which was conducted over two sessions a week apart, to the commencement of the intervention, which was usually another week later. High levels of family distress and dysfunction were apparent. For 14% of families, either the couple separated or the focus child was moved out of the family home before intervention commenced. Based on our contact with these families, it seemed that they were often reluctant to identify a need for assistance and delayed seeking professional help (Nicholson & Sanders, 1999). Problems were relatively entrenched and families were often in crisis at the time of presentation.

PREVENTION OF CHILD ADJUSTMENT PROBLEMS IN STEPFAMILIES

INTERVENTION

Our next study was designed to address the limitations identified in Study 1. We aimed to provide stepfamilies with a preventive program delivered in the relatively early stages of stepfamily formation. Given the importance of parent-stepparent conflict over parenting and the high rates of couple separation in the first study, we selected additional evidence-based intervention components to address the couple relationship (see Table 20.2). Relationship education programs for couples (see Whitton et al., this volume) have been shown to be effective in promoting healthy couple relationships (Halford, Markman, Stanley, & Kline, 2003) and can be tailored to address the specific issues and circumstances of high-risk populations such as remarried couples (Halford, Moore, Wilson, Dyer, & Farrugia, 2004). Modules were included that focused on developing healthy couple relationships (including spending quality time together) and positive communication skills, and there was an extended focus on problem solving and conflict resolution. Additionally, to promote social support and to normalize stepfamily experiences (Whitton et al., this volume), we elected to use a group-based approach for the therapist intervention. As the aim of the study was prevention, long-term follow-up of outcomes was planned, and it was judged to be inappropriate to employ a nonintervention control group for the study. Therefore, the effects of therapy were compared across the two versions: therapist- and self-directed.

The additional components used in this program were derived from an efficacious behavioral intervention for couples (the Prevention and Relationship Enhancement Program, PREP; Halford et al., 2003). The therapist-directed version (the Stepfamily Prevention and Relationship Enhancement Program; Step-PREP) involved 6 weekly 2-hour group sessions conducted with four to eight couples. Each session involved some didactic input, group discussion, and active skills training. Application of skills and knowledge was encouraged through the use of structured homework tasks. Couples also completed weekly readings from a popular Australian self-help text for stepfamilies (*Living in a Stepfamily*, Webber, 1994).

The self-directed version (Self-Regulatory Prevention and Relationship Enhancement Program; Self-PREP) had the same content. To improve families' sense of engagement and to assist undertaking program activities at home, two changes were made to the previous self-directed program. There was an initial group meeting to discuss the format of the program and identify strategies for maximizing gains from participation, and therapists conducted a midprogram telephone call to each couple to review progress.

PARTICIPANTS AND EXPECTED OUTCOMES

Participants were 73 couples recruited using outreach methods similar to those for Study 1. Included couples were in a committed relationship, and at least one partner had a child age 7 to 12 from a former relationship who lived with the couple for 2 or more days per week. Couples were excluded if they presented with significant relationship distress and if either partner was currently in treatment for a psychological disorder. Participating children were an average age of 9.6 years, and there were equal proportions of boys and girls. On average, parents were 38 years old, had been separated from the child's other biological parent for 5.3 years, and had been in a committed relationship with the stepparent for 2.6 years. Stepparents were an average of 39 years old, and 69% were male. Sixteen couples maintained separate households (22%), 33 were cohabiting (45%), and 24 were married (33%). Families were large (average family size was 3.7 children), 14% had a joint child, and parents were well-educated (67% had completed high school, and 75% of these had post–high school education). Compared to the sample for Study 1, these parents and stepparents were older and more highly educated, were presenting earlier in their relationships (by an average of nearly a year), and included noncohabiting couples.

The intervention aimed to prevent couple relationship and child adjustment problems and to improve coparenting and communication skills. Efficacy was compared across therapist-directed and self-directed versions. It was hypothesized that the active skills training and opportunities for social support provided by the group intervention would be associated with better outcomes than in the self-directed program. As the program aimed to prevent the development of problems, it was hypothesized that differences between the two programs would increase over time. That is, few differences were expected at postintervention, and it was expected that differences would become increasingly apparent at the 6- and 12-month follow-ups.

Results from this study have not been reported previously. Only the findings related to children's adjustment are reported here; couple relationship outcomes are being prepared for separate publication.

RESULTS

Sample Recruitment and Retention

Again, recruitment was primarily through media outreach (70%), program promotion through schools (18%), and referrals (11%), and was conducted over a 3-year period. It became clear part way through recruitment that rates of dropout during intervention were higher for families allocated to the self-directed program. To achieve approximately equal numbers of participants with complete pre-post data, the randomization schedule was altered from an equal probability of selection to allocate a slightly higher proportion of families to Self-PREP (a 1:1.3 ratio).

Of the 73 families who completed the preassessments and were allocated to intervention (Step-PREP $N = 32$; Self-PREP $N = 41$), 66 (90.4%) completed the program and provided data at postintervention. Noncompletion was lower for families allocated to Step-PREP (3%) compared to Self-PREP (15%). Further losses to 12-month follow-up were similar for both groups, at 36% and 34%, respectively. Reported analyses are based on the 20 Step-PREP and 23 Self-PREP families who provided data at all four assessments.

Children's Adjustment

Children's behavior problems were assessed by parent and stepparent reports on the Eyberg Child Behavior Inventory (ECBI; Eyberg & Pincus, 1999), which has psychometric properties comparable to the measure used in Study 1. Although clinically significant levels of child behavior problems were not a requirement for participation, participating children had elevated rates of behavior problems at preassessment. Child depression and self-esteem were assessed as for Study 1, and children in this study had fewer depressive symptoms and better self-esteem than those in Study 1.

Figures 20.5 and 20.6 show the mean scores on the measures of children's adjustment at pre- and postintervention and 6-month and 12-month follow-up by group: therapist-directed Step-PREP (TD) or self-directed Self-PREP (SD). For child behavior, there were no significant effects for time or intervention condition and no time-by-condition interactions. There were significant time effects for child depression, $F(3,37) = 5.85$, $p = .002$, and self-esteem, $F(3,37) = 4.98$, $p = .005$, with no significant effects for intervention condition and no time-by-condition interactions. These results indicated reductions in depressive symptoms and improvements in children's self-esteem for those in either intervention.

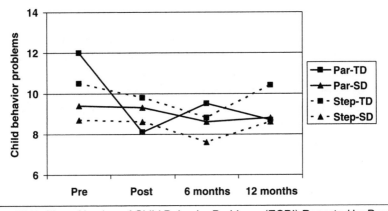

Figure 20.5 Mean Number of Child Behavior Problems (ECBI) Reported by Parents and Stepparents.

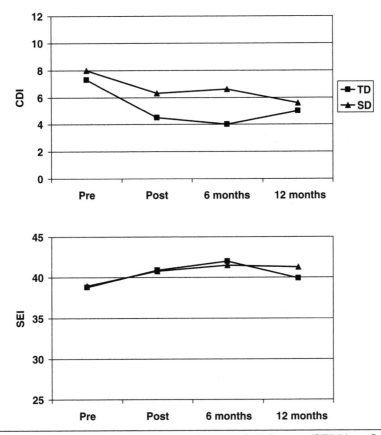

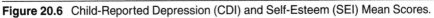

Figure 20.6 Child-Reported Depression (CDI) and Self-Esteem (SEI) Mean Scores.

Parenting and Coparenting

Two self-report measures of parenting were collected. Coercive discipline practices were assessed using the Parenting Scale (PS; Arnold, O'Leary, Wolff, & Acker, 1993), and parenting self-efficacy was assessed using the Parenting Sense of Competence Scale (PSOC; Johnston & Mash, 1989). Involvement and coparenting conflict were assessed as for Study 1. Mean scores on these measures are shown in Figures 20.7 and 20.8.

Parents (but not stepparents) allocated to the Step-PREP intervention reported significantly less effective parenting in terms of coerciveness and self-efficacy than parents allocated to Self-PREP, and these differences remained evident at all assessment points. The analyses revealed significant time effects for coercive parenting for both parents, $F(3,38) = 4.14$, $p = .012$, and stepparents, $F(3,38) = 3.48$, $p = .025$, and significant time effects for parenting self-efficacy for parents, $F(3,39) = 4.81$, $p = .006$, but not stepparents,

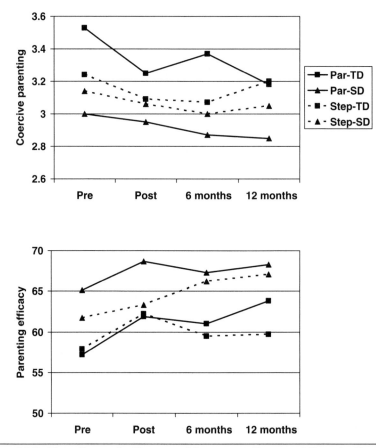

Figure 20.7 Mean Scores for Parent and Stepparent Reports of Coercive Parenting (PS) and Parenting Efficacy (PSOC).

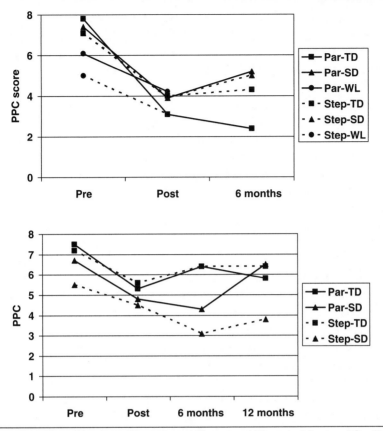

Figure 20.8 Mean Number of Parent- and Stepparent-Reported Areas of Conflict over Parenting from the Parenting Scale (PS) and the Parenting Sense of Competence Scale (PSOC).

$F(3,39) = 1.87$, $p = .151$. There were also significant time effects for parent- and stepparent-reported conflict over parenting, $F(3,39) = 3.92$, $p = .015$. There were no significant effects for parent or stepparent level of involvement with the focus child. For all analyses there were no significant effects for intervention condition and no time-by-condition interactions. These results indicated that both interventions were associated with reductions in coercive parenting behaviors and coparenting conflict for parents and stepparents, and with improved parenting self-efficacy for parents but not stepparents.

DISCUSSION

These results showed that families who completed all four assessments, regardless of intervention condition, reported improvements over time in children's adjustment (depression and self-esteem), parenting coerciveness, parenting conflict, and parenting self-efficacy, with the last significant for parents but not stepparents. Although children showed elevated rates of conduct problems at baseline, these were not significantly reduced over time, despite the use of the same intervention strategies as were employed in Study 1.

Contrary to expectations (but consistent with Study 1), there were no differences in parent or child outcomes according to intervention condition. Unfortunately, in the absence of data from a comparable no-intervention control group, the possibility that the observed changes would have occurred in the absence of an intervention cannot be excluded. Around a third of the sample from both interventions was lost at follow-up, and this also raises the possibility that full data were provided only by those families whose adjustment was maintained or improved over time.

Step-PREP was designed (and marketed to participating families) as a preventive intervention that aimed to prevent problems in children's adjustment, parenting, and the couple relationship. It was anticipated that intervention effects would become increasingly apparent over time and that differences between groups would also increase over time. There was no evidence to support these predictions. Rather, as shown in Figures 20.7 and 20.8, the largest reported improvements in outcomes tended to occur between the pre- and postassessments, with maintenance or some relapse occurring at 6- and 12-month follow-ups. These findings are consistent with Study 1, which also found improvements from pre- to postintervention. However, the practical challenges encountered and the inconclusive nature of the findings raise more questions than are answered. These issues are discussed next in relation to both studies.

ISSUES AND FUTURE DIRECTIONS IN CHILD-FOCUSED STEPFAMILY INTERVENTIONS

The two studies presented here aimed to improve the behavioral and emotional adjustment of children living in stepfamilies. They were designed to address a number of the limitations identified by our earlier review of stepfamily intervention research (Lawton & Sanders, 1994) and that are still evident in much of the stepfamilies research today (Whitton et al., this volume). In particular, the interventions were founded on strategies that had been previously shown to be effective (with non-stepfamily samples), which were tailored to the demonstrated needs and circumstances of stepfamilies. Additionally, both studies employed measures that had been validated and widely used before, and the study designs included randomization to intervention condition and attempts to collect long-term follow-up data. These studies are two of only three evaluations of stepfamily interventions to have employed a randomized, repeated-measures design with long-term follow-up, the other being a child-focused treatment study (Forgatch, DeGarmo, & Beldavs, 2005; see review in Whitton et al., this volume). As such, they represent a significant addition to the existing evidence base on stepfamily interventions. Implications of the research are considered in terms of intervention content, delivery format, program reach, methods of measurement, and long-term impact.

PROGRAM CONTENT

The majority of previous stepfamily interventions have included information and/or skills training in the following areas: (a) stepfamily development, (b) couple relationship skills, (c) parenting and stepparenting skills, and (d) communication and problem solving (Whitton et al., this volume). The interventions evaluated here also covered these areas, but differed in their focus on strategies for developing skills that had previously proved successful. Unlike many other stepfamily interventions, we used modifications of existing interventions for child behavior problems and prevention of couple distress that have been empirically demonstrated to be effective, rather than creating our own intervention or using components of the untested stepfamily interventions that have proliferated. Additionally, our content modifications were based on strong theory and available evidence about what types of strategies are helpful for this population. Forgatch and colleagues (2005) have conducted the only other evaluation of an existing evidence-based approach and found strong effect sizes (see Whitton et al., this volume). Together, these studies suggest that such an approach holds promise for future stepfamily interventions.

DELIVERY FORMAT

An important finding across both studies was the similarity in outcomes obtained for families receiving the therapist-directed and self-directed interventions. These findings suggest that self-directed programs may offer an effective, less costly, and possibly more acceptable alternative to clinic-based interventions. Other evidence from the field of parent and couple education also supports the potential value of self-directed programs. A series of studies examining the efficacy of the Triple P Positive Parenting Program (Sanders & Markie-Dadds, 1996), a form of behavioral family intervention, has consistently shown that a 10-session self-directed variant can be effective. For example, a self-help parent workbook (Markie-Dadds, Sanders, & Turner, 2000), delivered either alone (Markie-Dadds & Sanders, 2006b) or in combination with brief weekly telephone consultations, has been shown to improve parenting skills and reduce conduct problems in parents of disruptive toddlers (Morawska & Sanders, 2006), oppositional preschool-age children (Markie-Dadds & Sanders, 2006b), and disruptive teenagers (Stallman & Ralph, 2007), and when applied as a population-wide intervention (Hahlweg et al., in press). The intervention effects appear to be maintained up to 3 years postintervention (Sanders et al., 2007).

A second example is Couple CARE (Halford, Moore, et al., 2006), a six-unit, self-directed program that consists of three components: a DVD that introduces key concepts and models core relationship skills, a participant guidebook that provides structured exercises for the couple to apply the ideas covered in the DVD, and a series of telephone calls with a relationship educator who coaches and supports the couple. A controlled trial showed that couples engage well with the program and are highly satisfied with the content, and the program enhances couples' relationship satisfaction, at least in the short term (Halford et al., 2004).

Most existing relationship interventions are offered in face-to-face sessions (Halford et al., 2003). Although this format appeals to some, the majority of couples do not participate (Simons, Harris, & Willis, 1994), and stepfamilies are particularly unlikely to attend such face-to-face programs (Halford, O'Donnell, Lizzio, & Wilson, 2006). Many adults prefer self-directed programs that can be undertaken at times and places that suit participants (Christensen & Jacobson, 1994). For stepfamilies the cost of child care while attending face-to-face session is likely to be a barrier to attendance that can be circumvented by offering programs to complete at home. Moreover, in geographically large countries like the United States, Canada, and Australia, distance can make attendance difficult, and flexible delivery programs may help to overcome the tyranny of distance.

However, therapist-delivered interventions may have some advantages over self-directed approaches in terms of participant satisfaction, motivation, and sustainability. For example, in both studies presented here, ratings of client satisfaction with the intervention were significantly more positive for those who received the therapist-directed intervention. Mean satisfaction scores on a 7-point scale were 1.5 points higher for parents ($p < .005$) and 1.0 point higher for stepparents ($p < .05$) who received individual therapy when compared to those who received the self-directed intervention in Study 1, and 0.9 point higher for both parents and stepparents ($p < .001$) in the group intervention compared to those who received self-directed intervention in Study 2.

Additionally, dropouts over time were higher in both studies for those allocated to the self-directed intervention. In Study 1, 50% of those who received the self-directed intervention declined to participate in the follow-up assessment, compared to a refusal rate of only 14% for the therapist-directed participants; dropouts were highest for complex stepfamilies and stepmother families in the self-directed intervention. Though not systematically assessed, it appeared that there were three main reasons for dropout:

The family was currently experiencing problems; the parent or stepparent reported that the family had received no benefit from the intervention; or the couple had separated. All three stepmother families allocated to the self-directed group declined participation due to a lack of benefit from the program. In Study 2, differential dropout occurred between pre- and post-intervention, with 15% of families in the self-directed intervention dropping out compared to 3% of those in the therapist-directed intervention. In all cases, a lack of perceived benefits from the program was cited as the reason for dropout.

Thus, it seems that some caution may be warranted when considering the potential benefits of self-directed programs for stepfamilies. It is possible that families are less likely to persist with such programs, and such approaches may be of limited utility for complex or stepmother families. For those families who do complete a self-directed approach, there also appears to be a heightened risk (at least when the presenting problem is clinically significant child behavior problems) that initial gains will not be maintained well over time.

In Study 2 a group-based approach was employed. Group interventions are the most common delivery format for stepfamilies (Whitton et al., this volume). They are thought to have advantages over individual programs by normalizing stepfamily experiences and providing participants with social support through the group. Although none of the families participating in our study identified social support as a reason for seeking intervention, a quarter subsequently reported this to be a benefit they had received (Nicholson, Phillips, Whitton, Halford, & Sanders, 2007). We found no evidence to suggest that this approach was any more (or less) beneficial than our other delivery methods. In the absence of other evidence, a group-based approach appears to be a cost-effective alternative to individual therapy.

PROGRAM REACH

In both studies presented here, we encountered significant problems recruiting stepfamilies into the research. Recruitment problems have been reported in almost all previous stepfamily intervention studies, which may account for the very slow progress that has been made in this field in the past 12 to 15 years. It is essential in evaluation research to obtain sufficiently large samples to ensure that the study has adequate power for detecting the time-by-condition interaction effects that demonstrate the superiority of one condition over an alternative. Of those programs reviewed in the previous chapter (Whitton et al., this volume), the study by Forgatch and colleagues (2005) found the strongest intervention effects and also had the largest sample size ($N = 110$). A key concern in conducting evaluation studies with small samples is the risk of erroneously concluding that an intervention was not effective, when in fact the study design was insufficiently powered to detect effects. Lack of adequately powered studies in the stepfamily area may be one reason why the results from intervention studies have appeared to be so poor.

It is not clear why the recruitment of stepfamilies for research continues to be problematic. Stepfamilies are becoming an increasing proportion of all families. The difficulties these families encounter are now widely recognized, as is the need for specialist services and programs that are sensitive to the unique challenges faced by these families. In light of this, it is puzzling that intervention research with stepfamilies continues to be plagued by recruitment problems.

In terms of clinical intervention services, one possible explanation may lie in the sensitivity of stepfamily members to showing any signs that all may not be well in the family. Adults who enter a new couple relationship may face considerable opposition—from their children, extended family, ex-spouses, and friends. Presenting a united and happy front may therefore be a key coping strategy in the face of such opposition. In addition, a couple's satisfaction with their relationship may initially remain high in the face of a number of challenges. It is possible that declines occur rapidly after a threshold level of problems (in terms of intensity or duration or both) has been exceeded. This would explain why many of the families who participated in Study 1 were highly distressed upon initial presentation and subsequently separated or removed the child from the home before therapy was able to commence. More research is needed into the developmental course and stability of stepfamily relationships to improve our understanding of how distress develops, the trigger points for separation, and the optimal timing for intervention.

In terms of preventive services, stepfamily interventions face the same challenges of other preventive services: how to convince individuals of the value of prevention. This requires overcoming the perception "If it's not broken, don't fix it." Qualitative data collected at intake for Study 2 also indicated that men were more reluctant participants than women and were more likely to cite that their primary reason for attending was "because my wife wanted me to" (Nicholson et al., 2007). Participation of both parent and stepparent was a requirement for our programs, and we would argue that this is essential for effective intervention. To improve the extent to which preventive programs are able to effectively reach stepfamily couples, consideration is required of the strategies that best market these approaches. In particular, more research is needed into the strategies that are effective for conveying messages about the importance of prevention, and how to target the specific concerns and reluctance of men.

Another challenge related to program reach concerns the extent to which programs such as those evaluated here can be disseminated broadly.

Our programs involved the application of specialist intervention techniques, delivered by master's- or PhD-qualified psychologists. In addition to skills in behavioral and couple interventions, our staff also had advanced knowledge of stepfamily development. These conditions limit the extent to which our intervention materials may be successfully used by other professionals. Two areas of further research and program development are required.

First, we need to know more about who benefits from less intensive forms of interventions. In an environment where families are time-poor and there are limited amounts of specialist services available, it is important to be able to correctly identify those who are able to make and sustain gains from self-directed approaches so that more intensive methods can be prioritized for those who need greater support and specialist expertise. Second, the fields of family and couples interventions more broadly are moving increasingly toward investigation of alternative, interactive technologies such as Web-based programs (Larson, Newell, Topham, & Nichols, 2002). These approaches may have particular benefits for stepfamilies, enabling privacy and the convenience of working from home at one's own pace, but with access to expertise as required.

Finally, it is also important to consider the match between stepfamilies on presentation and the services available. Clinicians working with stepfamilies have long stressed the importance of having a sound understanding of normative stepfamily development and avoiding applying implicit beliefs about how families should function based on nuclear family models. A survey of 267 members of an American stepfamily association who had accessed a family intervention revealed that half of those who found therapy to be unhelpful cited the therapist's lack of training and knowledge about stepfamilies as the key problem (Pasley, Rhoden, Visher, & Visher, 1996). If our belief is correct, that stepfamily couples are reluctant to identify themselves as having problems, then the provision of a service that does not match expectations may impede further help seeking, and the opportunity to provide assistance may be lost.

METHODS OF MEASUREMENT

Past evaluation studies have been criticized for measurement approaches that have focused on participant satisfaction or have employed nonstandardized author-developed measures (Lawton & Sanders, 1994; Whitton et al., this volume). One of the challenges has been the lack of clearly agreed-upon measures of stepfamily functioning. The studies presented here have illustrated the value of using measures that enable comparisons across studies. We were able to compare the adjustment of children in our studies against clinical and general populations. The use of some common measures in both studies also enabled comparison of the severity of problems across the two samples. For example, this allowed us to confirm that we had been successful in recruiting a more well-adjusted sample for the prevention trial in Study 2.

The challenge of using stepfamily-specific measures was also illustrated. We selected the Family Involvement Scales (Santrock et al., 1988) as an appropriate measure of the extent to which parents and stepparents were involved in daily and infrequent but important aspects of their children's lives. As expected, parents scored significantly higher than stepparents on the FIS at all time points. However, scores on this measure remained unchanged over time and seemed impervious to the effects of intervention. While it is possible that our interventions were not successful in impacting parent or stepparent involvement, this seems improbable as this was a major focus of the intervention content and is a core component of enhancing effective parenting. More research is needed to identify measures of stepfamily functioning that are capable of reflecting changes in stepfamily functioning over time.

The need for careful selection of measures is particularly important when issues of participant burden are considered. The interventions described here are similar to most stepfamily interventions in targeting a wide range of possible problems. Measurement of effects therefore also needs to be wide-ranging and should extend beyond the targets of intervention to ensure that there are no inadvertent adverse consequences. For example, although the focus of our interventions was on children's behavioral problems, we also measured other aspects of adjustment. Results showed that improvements were also evident on these outcomes, which had not been explicitly predicted.

For stepfamilies who are sensitive about the potential stigma of seeking help and whose lives are often complex and busy, there is a need to ensure a good balance between collecting quality evidence and not overburdening participants. For example, observational methods have typically been regarded as a gold standard for assessing changes in parenting following intervention. However, in Study 1, this process did not elicit the expected high levels of coercive parenting, and there were no changes in parenting over time. In contrast, the self-report parenting measures in Study 2 provided clear evidence of changes in parenting over time and therefore appear to offer a better and less burdensome approach. This is not to suggest that all observational methods are inappropriate for use in stepfamilies research. In data reported elsewhere from Study 2, we found that observations of couple problem-solving discussions led to the identification of a distinctive pattern of couple communication that differentiated couples in stepfamilies from those entering first marriages (Halford, Nicholson, & Sanders, 2007).

LONG-TERM IMPACT AND MAINTENANCE

There is a need to consider whether short programs really are sufficient for addressing complex problems in stepfamilies. Three quarters of the programs reviewed in the previous chapter were six or fewer sessions in length, and this may be insufficient for ensuring long-term effects. Even in Study 1, which was 8 sessions in length, some initial treatment gains were not well maintained over time.

Stepfamilies are dynamic entities that progress through a series of developmental changes. Adults and children in stepfamilies report higher levels of life events and family changes than adults and children in other types of families. Family structures change as new children are born to the couple and older children change residential arrangements. Patterns of parenting and stepparenting develop and change over time as relationships become established and as children grow and move into new developmental stages. Additionally, relationships with those external to the family, particularly children's nonresidential parents, can be quite variable over time.

Our interventions aimed to provide parents and stepparents with the communication and problem-solving skills that would facilitate their ability to manage new and emerging challenges. However, additional strategies may be needed. For example, it may be useful to provide booster or maintenance sessions targeted at key developmental periods when risks for relapse are greatest. The key challenge, of course, is identifying such times, as the timing of stepfamily development seems to be nonlinear and highly variable.

THE IMPORTANCE OF CONTROL GROUP DATA

Finally, the studies presented here clearly illustrated the importance of employing a control group. Collection of control group data in Study 1 enabled us to conclude that although children in the control group also improved, the improvements were greater for those who received an active intervention. In Study 2, the absence of such data prevented us from reaching strong conclusions about the study's findings. The data may be interpreted as indicating that parents and children who received the interventions showed improvements over time, but these improvements cannot be attributed to the effects of the intervention. The rationale for not collecting control group data in Study 2 was based on the expected timing of change following intervention. As this was a prevention study, we expected that few changes would be evident at postintervention, but that these would increasingly emerge over the subsequent 12-month period. As such, it was judged to be unethical to have a control group who received no intervention over this long observation period. Contrary to expectations, we found that the largest changes occurred from pre- to postintervention, and as such, a wait-list control group would have been feasible and informative.

CONCLUSION

These studies have added to the evidence base regarding clinical and preventive interventions for stepfamilies. They indicate that well-designed, empirically based interventions can have positive impacts on the behavior and well-being of children, improve the parenting practices employed in stepfamilies, and reduce parent-stepparent conflict over parenting. Of particular importance, though the interventions focused primarily on children's externalizing behaviors, internalizing problems also appeared to improve. Even though the children themselves were not involved in the delivery of the interventions, improvements were found on children's self-reports of their adjustment. The families participating in this research all had children between 7 and 12 years old at intake. As it is generally accepted that older children and adolescents in stepfamilies have greater adjustment difficulties (Bray, 1999), this work needs to be extended to this older group.

Promising areas for further study include the investigation of alternative delivery formats and the potential gains that may arise from the use of booster and maintenance sessions. Also, research into understanding what motivates individuals to seek help may assist with better program targeting and outreach in the future (Nicholson et al., 2007).

REFERENCES

Achenbach, T. M., & Edelbrock, C. S. (1983). *Manual for the Child Behavior Checklist and Revised Child Behavior Profile*. Burlington: University of Vermont.

Ahrons, C. R. (2007). Family ties after divorce: Long-term implications for children. *Family Process, 46*(1), 53–65.

American Psychiatric Association. (1994). *Diagnostic and statistical manual of mental disorders* (4th ed.). Washington, DC: Author.

Arnold, D. S., O'Leary, S. G., Wolff, L. S., & Acker, M. M. (1993). The Parenting Scale: A measure of dysfunctional parenting in discipline situations. *Psychological Assessment, 5*, 137–144.

Barber, B. L., & Lyons, J. M. (1994). Family processes and adolescent adjustment in intact and remarried families. *Journal of Youth and Adolescence, 23*(4), 421–436.

Baumrind, D. (1991). The influence of parenting style on adolescent competence and substance use. *Journal of Early Adolescence, 11*(1), 56–95.

Bray, J. H. (1999). From marriage to remarriage and beyond: Findings from the Developmental Issues in Stepfamilies Research Project. In E. M. Hetherington (Ed.), *Coping with divorce, single parenting, and remarriage: A risk and resiliency perspective* (pp. 253–271). Mahwah, NJ: Erlbaum.

Bray, J. H., & Berger, S. H. (1993). Developmental issues in Stepfamilies Research Project: Family relationships and parent-child interactions. *Journal of Family Psychology, 7*(1), 76–90.

Breivik, K., & Olweus, D. (2006). Adolescents' adjustment in four post-divorce family structures: Single mother, stepfather, joint physical custody and single father families. *Journal of Divorce and Remarriage, 44*(3), 99–124.

Brown, A. C., Green, R. J., & Druckman, J. (1991). A comparison of stepfamilies with and without child-focused problems. *Annual Progress in Child Psychiatry and Child Development, 60*(4), 556–566.

Carlson, M. J. (2006). Family structure, father involvement, and adolescent behavioral outcomes. *Journal of Marriage and the Family, 68*(1), 137–154.

Cartwright, C., & Seymour, F. (2002). Young adults' perceptions of parents' response in stepfamilies: What hurts? What helps? *Journal of Divorce and Remarriage, 37*, 123–141.

Chamberlain, P., & Reid, J. B. (1987). Parent observation and report of child symptoms. *Behavioral Assessment, 9*, 97–109.

Christensen, A., & Jacobson, N. S. (1994). Who (or what) can do psychotherapy: The status and challenge of nonprofessional therapies. *Psychological Science, 5*, 8–14.

Coleman, M., Ganong, L. H., & Leon, K. (2006). Divorce and postdivorce relationships. In A. L. Vangelisti & D. Perlman (Eds.), *Cambridge handbook of personal relationships* (pp. 157–173). New York: Cambridge University Press.

Coopersmith, S. (1981). *SEI Self-Esteem Inventories.* Palo Alto, CA: Consulting Psychologists Press.

Dadds, M. R., & Powell, M. B. (1991). The relationship of interparental conflict and global marital adjustment to aggression, anxiety, and immaturity in aggressive and nonclinic children. *Journal of Abnormal Child Psychology, 19*, 553–567.

Dadds, M. R., Schwartz, S., & Sanders, M. R. (1987). Marital discord and treatment outcome in behavioural treatment of child conduct disorders. *Journal of Consulting and Clinical Psychology, 55*(3), 396–403.

Daly, M., & Wilson, M. I. (1996). Violence against stepchildren. *Current Directions in Psychological Science, 5*(3), 77–81.

Dishion, T. J., & Patterson, G. R. (1992). Age effects in parent training outcome. *Behavior Therapy, 23*, 719–729.

Eyberg, S. M., & Pincus, D. (1999). *Eyberg Child Behavior Inventory and Stutter-Eyberg Student Behavior Inventory—Revised: Professional manual.* Odessa, FL: Psychological Assessment Resources.

Falci, C. (2006). Family structure, closeness to residential and nonresidential parents, and psychological distress in early and middle adolescence. *Sociological Quarterly, 47*(1), 123–146.

Forehand, R. L., & McMahon, R. J. (1981). *Helping the noncompliant child: A clinician's guide to parent training.* New York: Guilford Press.

Forgatch, M. S., DeGarmo, D. S., & Beldavs, Z. G. (2005). An efficacious theory-based intervention for stepfamilies. *Behavior Therapy, 36*, 357–365.

Ganong, L. H., & Coleman, M. (1993). A meta-analytic comparison of the self-esteem and behavior problems of stepchildren to children in other family structures. *Journal of Divorce and Remarriage, 19*, 143–163.

Ganong, L. H., & Coleman, M. (2004). *Stepfamily relationships: Development, dynamics, and interventions.* New York: Kluwer Academic/Plenum Press.

Hahlweg, K., Heinrichs, N., Kuschel, A., & Feldmann, M. (in press). Therapist assisted self-administered bibliotherapy to enhance parental competence: Short- and long-term effects. *Behavior Modification*.

Halford, W. K., Markman, H. J., Stanley, S., & Kline, G. (2003). Best practice in relationship education. *Journal of Marital and Family Therapy, 29*, 385–406.

Halford, W. K., Moore, E. M., Wilson, K. L., Dyer, C., & Farrugia, C. (2004). Benefits of a flexible delivery relationship education: An evaluation of the Couple CARE program. *Family Relations, 53*, 469–476.

Halford, W. K., Moore, E. M., Wilson, K. L., Dyer, C., Farrugia, C., & Judge, K. (2006). *Couple commitment and relationship enhancement*. Brisbane: Australian Academic Press.

Halford, W. K., Nicholson, J. M., & Sanders, M. R. (2007). Couple communication in stepfamilies. *Family Process, 46*, 471–483.

Halford, W. K., O'Donnell, C., Lizzio, A., & Wilson, K. L. (2006). Do couples at high-risk of relationship problems attend pre-marriage education? *Journal of Family Psychology, 20*, 160–163.

Hetherington, E. M. (1987). Family relations six years after divorce. In K. Pasely & M. Ihinger-Tallman (Eds.), *Remarriage and stepparenting: Current research and theory* (pp. 185–205). New York: Guilford Press.

Hetherington, E. M., Bridges, M., & Insabella, G. M. (1998). What matters? What does not? Five perspectives on the association between marital transitions and children's adjustment. *American Psychologist, 53*(2), 167–184.

Hetherington, E. M., Cox, M., & Cox, R. (1982). Effects of divorce on parents and children. In M. E. Lamb (Ed.), *Nontraditional families: Parenting and child development* (pp. 233–288). Hillsdale, NJ: Erlbaum.

Hetherington, E. M., Henderson, S. H., Reiss, D., Anderson, E. R., Bridges, M., Chan, R. W., et al. (1999). Adolescent siblings in stepfamilies: Family functioning and adolescent adjustment. *Monographs of the Society for Research in Child Development, 64*(4), 222.

Hoge, R. D., Andrews, D. A., & Robinson, D. (1990). Patterns of child and parenting problems within six family types. *Canadian Journal of Behavioural Science, 22*(2), 99–109.

Jeynes, W. H. (2007). The impact of parental remarriage on children: A meta-analysis. *Marriage and Family Review, 40*(4), 75–102.

Johnston, C., & Mash, E. J. (1989). A measure of parenting satisfaction and efficacy. *Journal of Clinical Child Psychology, 18*, 167–175.

Johnston, J. R., Kline, M., & Tschann, J. M. (1989). Ongoing postdivorce conflict: Effects on children of joint custody and frequent access. *American Journal of Orthopsychiatry, 59*(4), 576–592.

Keshet, J. K. (1990). Cognitive remodeling of the family: How remarried people view stepfamilies. *American Journal of Orthopsychiatry, 60*(2), 196–203.

Kirby, J. B. (2006). From single-parent families to stepfamilies: Is the transition associated with adolescent alcohol initiation? *Journal of Family Issues, 27*(5), 685–711.

Kovacs, M. (1981). Rating scales to assess depression in school-aged children. *Acta Paedopsychiatrica, 46*, 305–315.

Larson, J. H., Newell, K., Topham, G., & Nichols, S. (2002). A review of three comprehensive premarital assessment questionnaires. *Journal of Marital and Family Therapy, 28,* 233–239.

Lawton, J. M., & Sanders, M. R. (1994). Designing effective behavioral family interventions for stepfamilies. *Clinical Psychology Review, 14,* 463–496.

Leung, C., Sanders, M. R., Leung, S., Mak, R., & Lau, J. (2003). An outcome evaluation of the implementation of the Triple P-Positive Parenting Program in Hong Kong. *Family Process, 42,* 531–544.

Maccoby, E. E., & Martin, J. A. (1983). Socialization in the context of the family: Parent-child interaction. In P. H. Mussen & E. M. Hetherington (Eds.), *Handbook of child psychology* (Vol. 4, pp. 1–101). New York: Wiley.

Markie-Dadds, C., & Sanders, M. R. (2006a). A controlled evaluation of an enhanced self-directed behavioral family intervention for parents of children with conduct problems in rural and remote areas. *Behaviour Change, 23*(1), 55–72.

Markie-Dadds, C., & Sanders, M. R. (2006b). Self-directed Triple P (Positive Parenting Program) for mothers with children at-risk of developing conduct problems. *Behavioural and Cognitive Psychotherapy, 34*(3), 259–275.

Markie-Dadds, C., Sanders, M. R., & Turner, K. M. T. (2000). *Every parent's family workbook.* Brisbane, Queensland, Australia: Families International.

Morawska, A., & Sanders, M. R. (2006). Self-administered behavioral family intervention for parents of toddlers: Pt. I. Efficacy. *Journal of Clinical and Consulting Psychology, 74*(1), 10–19.

Morawska, A., & Sanders, M. R. (2007). Are parent-reported outcomes for self-directed or telephone-assisted behavioral family intervention enhanced if parents are observed? *Behavior Modification, 31*(3), 279–297.

Nicholson, J. M., Fergusson, D. M., & Horwood, L. J. (1999). Effects on later adjustment of living in a stepfamily during childhood and adolescence. *Journal of Child Psychology and Psychiatry, 40*(3), 405–416.

Nicholson, J. M., Phillips, L. E., Peterson, C., & Battistutta, D. (2002). Relationship between the parenting styles of biological parents and stepparents and the adjustment of young adult stepchildren. *Journal of Divorce and Remarriage, 36,* 57–76.

Nicholson, J. M., Phillips, M., Whitton, S. W., Halford, W. K., & Sanders, M. R. (2007). Promoting healthy stepfamilies: Couples' reasons for seeking help and perceived benefits from intervention. *Family Matters, 77,* 48–57.

Nicholson, J. M., & Sanders, M. R. (1999). Randomized controlled trial of behavioral family intervention for the treatment of child behavior problems in stepfamilies. *Journal of Divorce and Remarriage, 30*(3/4), 1–23.

Pasley, K. (1988). Contributing to the field of investigation. *Journal of Family Psychology, 1,* 452–456.

Pasley, K., Rhoden, L., Visher, E. B., & Visher, J. S. (1996). Successful stepfamily therapy: Clients' perspectives. *Journal of Marriage and the Family, 22,* 343–357.

Patterson, G. R. (1982). *A social learning approach: Coercive family processes* (Vol. 3). Eugene, OR: Castalia.

Patterson, G. R., DeBaryshe, B. D., & Ramsey, E. (1989). A developmental perspective on antisocial behavior. *American Psychologist, 44,* 329–335.

Sanders, M. R. (1999). Triple P-Positive Parenting Program: Towards an empirically validated multilevel parenting and family support strategy for the prevention of behaviour and emotional problems in children. *Clinical Child and Family Psychology Review, 2,* 71–90.

Sanders, M. R., Bor, W., & Morawska, A. (2007). Maintenance of treatment gains: A comparison of enhanced, standard, and self-directed Triple P-Positive Parenting Program. *Journal of Abnormal Child Psychology, 35,* 983–998.

Sanders, M. R., Gooley, S., & Nicholson, J. M. (2000). *Early intervention in conduct problems in children.* Adelaide: Australian Early Intervention Network for Mental Health in Young People.

Sanders, M. R., & Lawton, J. M. (1993). Discussing assessment findings with families: A guided participation model of information transfer. *Child and Family Behavior Therapy, 15,* 5–35.

Sanders, M. R., & Markie-Dadds, C. (1996). Triple P: A multilevel family intervention program for children with disruptive behaviour disorders. In P. Cotton & H. Jackson (Eds.), *Early intervention and prevention in mental health* (pp. 59–85). Melbourne: Australian Psychological Society.

Sanders, M. R., & McFarland, M. L. (2000). The treatment of depressed mothers with disruptive children: A controlled evaluation of cognitive behavioral family intervention. *Behavior Therapy, 31*(1), 89–112.

Santrock, J. W., Sitterle, K. A., & Warshak, R. A. (1988). Parent-child relationships in stepfather families. In P. Bronstein & C. Pape Cowan (Eds.), *Fatherhood today: Men's changing roles in the family* (pp. 144–165). New York: Wiley.

Simons, M., Harris, R., & Willis, P. (1994). *Pathways to marriage: Learning for married life in Australia.* Adelaide: University of South Australia, Centre for Research in Education and Work.

Stallman, H. M., & Ralph, A. (2007). Reducing risk factors for adolescent behavioural and emotional problems: A pilot randomised controlled trial of a self-administered parenting intervention. *Australian e-Journal for the Advancement of Mental Health, 6*(2), www.auseinet.com/journal/vol6iss2/stallman.pdf.

Turner, K. M. T., & Sanders, M. R. (2006). Help when it's needed first: A controlled evaluation of brief, preventive behavioral family intervention in a primary care setting. *Behavior Therapy, 37,* 131–142.

Visher, E. B., & Visher, J. S. (1989). Parenting coalitions after remarriage: Dynamics and therapeutic guidelines. *Family Relations, 38*(1), 65–70.

Vosler, N. R., & Proctor, E. K. (1991). Family structure and stressors in a child guidance clinic population. *Families in Society, 72*(3), 164–173.

Vuchinich, S., Hetherington, E. M., Vuchinich, R. A., & Clingempeel, W. G. (1991). Parent-child interaction and gender differences in early adolescents' adaptation to stepfamilies. *Developmental Psychology, 27*(4), 618–626.

Wallerstein, J. S., & Corbin, S. B. (1989). Daughters of divorce: Report from a 10-year follow-up. *American Journal of Orthopsychiatry, 59*(4), 593–604.

Webber, R. (1994). *Living in a stepfamily: A stepparent's handbook.* Melbourne: Australian Council for Educational Research.

Webster-Stratton, C. (1996). Early intervention with videotape modeling: Programs for families with children with oppositional defiant disorder or conduct disorder.

In E. D. Hibbs & P. S. Jensen (Eds.), *Empirically based strategies for clinical practice* (pp. 435–474). Washington, DC: American Psychological Association.

Whitsett, D. P., & Land, H. M. (1992). Role strain, coping, and marital satisfaction of stepparents. *Families in Society, 73*(2), 79–92.

Zubrick, S. R., Ward, K. A., Silburn, S. R., Lawrence, D., Williams, A. A., Blair, E., et al. (2005). Prevention of child behavior problems through universal implementation of a group behavioral family intervention. *Prevention Science, 6,* 287–304.

CHAPTER 21

Legal Structures and Re-Formed Families: The New Zealand Example

BILL ATKIN

BACKGROUND

THE CHANGING patterns of family life, especially in the West, have given rise to some of the most significant issues in lawmaking over the past 5 decades. Few, if any, legal systems have escaped the need to wrestle with the implications of differing lifestyles and values.

Often the law has reacted to events; it rarely leads. It can, rightly or wrongly, stand in the way of change, for instance if divorce laws remain tight or, more controversially, if marriage laws remain closed to same-sex couples. Sometimes the law's resistance is based on a genuine desire to protect the vulnerable; to take clear-cut examples, incest is unlikely to be legalized, nor underage sexual relations (although one may debate what is the appropriate age). On the other hand, the law is sometimes shaped by tradition and a worldview that has been overtaken by social circumstances. For example, the law has often ignored the phenomenon of unmarried cohabitation or else left it to the courts to conjure up imaginative ways of settling disputes. Some legal systems now place married and unmarried couples on much the same basis, while others still privilege marriage.

Special thanks to Esther Watt and Bevan Marten, former research assistants, whose ongoing help and encouragement are greatly appreciated.

When families break up, there is a range of legal issues to be addressed. In some cases, there is a formal dissolution of a marriage (and now add civil unions or civil partnerships where such exist), but in contrast to former years, divorce is no longer such a major item. Instead, the economic resolution of the relationship and the well-being of the children dominate.

The re-forming of families may occur, of course, at any time. Sometimes, the breakup of a family coincides with repartnering, and hence the legal issues relating to the winding up of the first family can be intertwined with the formation of the new one. For example, the finding of new accommodation for the former parties is one thing if you are on your own, quite another thing if you have already repartnered and your new partner has children. Who occupies the family home? Should it be sold so that each party can leave with some capital for setting up new homes? Often, all this takes time. The process of winding up a family may take months or years, during which time repartnering may occur, shifting the ground on which the parties are negotiating. In other cases, family re-formation may occur much later on, after settlement of the legal issues surrounding the first family. A different set of issues may then arise. Further, the second family may also break up, and there can be issues concerning the relationship between the first and second, maybe even a third family. We can discern from this that, even if the legal issues relating to the first family have been sorted out, the consequences of the first family continue to follow the second and subsequent ones. The parental relationships with the children involved do not cease, not even when the children reach the age of majority (i.e., full legal independence), for parents will still have an interest in their children's welfare into adulthood and beyond the parents' deaths.

THE ISSUES FOR LEGAL POLICY SPARKED BY FAMILY RE-FORMATION

One of the key players in family re-formation is the new partner, especially when there are children. Yet, the place of stepparents in most countries' law of family re-formation is rather inconclusive. Some people talk of the invisibility of stepparents or the ambiguous nature of the law. Lynn Wardle (1993, p. 384) ascribes to the stepfamily the phrase the "new family" but says that its legal rights and responsibilities are "awkward and contradictory," part of "the schizophrenic American concept of family relations." The image is not restricted to American law; indeed, it emerges in most jurisdictions from uncertainty in society itself about stepparenthood and underlying policy concerns.

What are some of the issues raised for legal policy by the phenomenon of stepfamilies?

- How should law and policy take account of reconstituted families? Turning a blind eye is not really an option. Just as the existence of de facto relationships and same-sex unions forces itself upon the system in some way or another, re-formed families inevitably do the same. In contrast, one could develop a coherent code that provides logically and consistently for all situations. However, whether politically this is ever likely to be achieved is doubtful. Furthermore, it may be undesirable to treat all stepfamilies the same. Wardle (1993, p. 387) talks about the variety of stepfamilies and the undesirability of stifling them with legal stereotypes. Anders Agell (1993, p. 419) does not believe in a special statute for stepparenthood but prefers to rely on the general law to deal with the issues that arise. The reality is that in most jurisdictions the law develops a bit like Topsy, making provision for stepparents in some contexts and not in others.

- To what extent should priority be given to the first family over the second? Traditionally, following the notion that marriage is for life, a first family was given priority, particularly when it came to issues of finance. To leave your first family and found another was frowned upon and not to be encouraged. For example, the first principle in Section 43 of the Family Law Act 1975 of Australia, which governs the operation of the Family Court, is "the need to preserve and protect the institution of marriage as the union of a man and a woman to the exclusion of all others voluntarily entered into for life." In other words, lifelong marriage, by definition not serial marriage, let alone unmarried cohabitation, is the preferred model for family life. However, given readily obtained divorce, this hardly reflects legal realities. One of the principal legal consequences of divorce is the freedom it gives the parties to remarry, and this freedom brings us back head-on to the question of priorities between first and second families. To what extent should the law smooth the path for family transformation?

- The fact that the second family is likely in some sense to be a stepfamily raises a further priority question. To what extent should biological links be favored over social reality? Legal systems usually treat natural parenthood as a life sentence, unless there has been a legal adoption. Indeed, natural children have inheritance rights, and this has trickle-down effects on the way issues of care and responsibility are handled.

- How should the law determine lines of responsibility with respect to children? John Eekelaar (1991) distinguishes between two types of responsibility: (1) the practical exercise of responsibility, which may be carried out by a variety of people, and (2) the responsibility that arises automatically from being a natural or adoptive parent. Responsibility in both senses will often coincide, because most natural and adoptive parents are the ones who, in practice as well as in theory, are responsible for their children. Where they do not coincide, responsibility in the second sense is "nakedly ideological" (p. 45). Stepparents will often have practical responsibility in the first sense, but to what extent is this reinforced or hindered by the law? What should legal policy be in this regard?

- Let us sharpen this a little more. Andrew Bainham (1999, p. 43) asks us to "scrutinise carefully the circumstances under which social parents are actually allowed to become legal parents" or to have some formal legal standing with respect to a child. He goes on to put stepparents at the top of the list. By legal standing, we mean recognition in law of the relationship between child and stepparent, granting formal authority to the stepparent to act in the role of a parent. Legal policy therefore must determine how and when it is going to give the new parental figure legal standing, especially as the stepparent is often in the legal background. In doing so, however, the law must take into account other persons in the child's life. Unless there is a healthy shared parenting arrangement, the absent or nonresident parent from the first family may struggle to maintain a good relationship with the children, and this is one of the most fraught and fought over areas of family law. Bainham advances the view that "we should be vigorously defending the parental status of the divorced parent in these cases and not pretending that a stepparent is a parent" (p. 43). On this view the continuing, if residual, role of the nonresident parent should not be undermined by too readily granting parental authority to the stepparent.

- There is a further angle to this, which also takes us back to the balance between biology and social reality. Some cultures, particularly indigenous peoples, focus more on the wider family or the local tribal community than parents. For example, in some cultures, grandparents are as important as parents, if not more so. The concentration on the responsibility of parents ignores these other value systems and other realities. From one point of view, the indigenous perspective strengthens the biological links within the family, but from another it widens our horizons in a way that could more easily find a place for stepparents than conventional legal wisdom has done.

- To what extent should the answers to some of these questions vary depending on whether the stepfamily is intact or has in its turn ceased? Legal policy may in some instances want to reinforce an ongoing family, but take a very different view once that family breaks up. Carol Rogerson (2001, pp. 153–154) argues that these situations should be kept separate, and that issues of postseparation custody and access should also be analyzed separately from financial support.

MORE FUNDAMENTAL QUESTIONS

The issues just discussed arise frequently in the context of family law and policy. Lurking behind them is another set of fundamental questions that we should briefly address:

- What do we understand by "family"? Writing 20 years ago, Brenda Hoggett (1987, cited by Bainham, 1999, p. 43), now Baroness Hale, the distinguished first female member of the judicial branch of the House of Lords, stated that "the step-relation is not the same as the 'normal' family and perhaps we should not pretend that it is." This was written when talking about the dubious desire to exclude the other natural parent or to shore up some insecurity in the new family, but it suggests that the stepfamily is not a real family, or is a second-rate family that is not to be treated quite the same way as the classic married man and woman with children. Most legal commentators would opt for an inclusive rather than an exclusive definition of family. In New Zealand, this is reflected in the statute establishing the Families Commission. The first two subsections of section 10 of the Families Commission Act of 2003 read as follows:

  (1) In the exercise and performance of its powers and functions, the Commission must have regard to the kinds, structures, and diversity of families.
  (2) In this section, family includes a group of people related by marriage, civil union, blood, or adoption, an extended family, 2 or more persons living together as a family, and a whanau or other culturally recognized family group. [Whanau is the indigenous Maori word for "family," meaning the wider family group rather than a narrower "nuclear" family of parents and children.]

  Although this definition relates to a body established to conduct research and advocate on behalf of families, it is nevertheless suggestive of a more general approach to families, and while step relations are not expressly mentioned, they are surely embraced within the notion of diversity.

- Another, allied question is the place of marriage in legal policy. Traditionally, of course, marriage was the predominant paradigm, but in many jurisdictions this is no longer the situation. Recognition of de facto relationships and the creation of civil unions and partnerships have introduced a new paradigm. Nevertheless, when it comes to the legal rights and responsibilities of new partners, the law is sometimes slow to adjust to the new paradigm. Whether it should do so and exactly how are matters of debate.
- What about the children? Much of the focus of discussion up to this point has been on the adults: the new partners or spouses, their legal

status, the place of the former spouse or partner, and so on. There can be genuine adult questions that arise on family re-formation, for instance (as already mentioned and to be discussed again later) questions about property and housing. Further, if the second relationship ends, another set of legal issues arises as the parties sort out their lives. However, the adult focus can sometimes belie the impact of family reconstitution on the children, especially minor children. While adult children may have their own legal questions about their parents' new partners, for example the effect on inheritance, it is the care of minor children that is most acute for legal policy. This resolves itself into the core question of how the law is to treat the relationship between the minor child and the new spouse or partner, in other words, that between the stepchild and the stepparent.

It is trite to say that the welfare and best interests of the minor child are the paramount consideration in family law policy. The United Nations Convention on the Rights of the Child, ratified by all nations except Somalia and the United States, has become a touchstone against which child laws are now evaluated, and Article 3 states that the child's best interests must be "a primary consideration." While the use of "a" rather than "the" may be queried, for present purposes we can be assured that a staunch child focus rather than an adult focus is demanded. The Supreme Court of Canada in *Chartier v. Chartier* (1999, 1 SCR 242, paragraph 21), a leading case on the role of stepparents, made this clear when it said that the focus is on best interests and "not on biological parenthood, or the legal status of children."

Interestingly, the UN Convention does not further address the issue of step relationships. There is emphasis in several articles (e.g., Articles 3(2), 5, 9(3), and 18) on parents, with references in some places also to legal guardians and those "legally responsible" for the child. This does not actually take us very far. Frustratingly, "parent" is not defined, but the context assumes natural or adoptive parents, not social parents. The reference to those "legally responsible" for the child is a general one and begs the question as to who ought to be legally responsible. Different legal systems will answer this in different ways. Article 5 mentions "members of the extended family or community as provided for by local custom," but this little avails the stepparent. Article 9(3) provides for "the right of the child who is separated from one or both parents, to maintain personal relations and a direct contact with both parents on a regular basis, except if it is contrary to the child's best interests." The importance of this is that, in general, the law should not exclude the absent natural parent from contact with the child, even where the stepparent has effectively replaced the natural parent in the upbringing of the child.

Two further points affecting legal policy arise from the Convention. First, under Article 12 the child has a right to express views on the matters affecting him or her. It follows that legal mechanisms designed to tackle some of the issues that we have identified need to provide for the child's views to be heard and taken account of. Without this, the adult focus will reemerge as the driver of law and policy. Article 12 uses the phrase "due weight in accordance with the age and maturity of the child," and this could be used as a pretext to play down the child's views. However, even young children can express opinions, preferences, and indications that can be highly relevant to a legal process determining the legal standing of a social parent. The child may not appreciate any or all of the legal implications at stake but can give plenty of clues about how positive or negative the relationships with the parent figures are.

Second, Article 2 states that children's rights must be applied "without discrimination of any kind." This suggests that it should not matter what race, sex, or age the child is, nor should it matter whether the child's parents are married or unmarried, what their race is, nor their sexual orientation. What matters instead are the child's best interests.

THE FUNCTION OF THE LAW: A BIT PLAYER

We have identified a range of challenges that legal policy faces because of family re-formation. What role does the law play in these circumstances? Most repartnering occurs quite naturally, and in general in a liberal democracy the people involved do not look over their shoulders to see what the law says; for the most part, people simply get on with their lives. Nevertheless, there are times when the law can become crucial. This is often when human affairs start to unravel and people become disputatious. The law may be needed to establish markers to help resolve the problems.

Several relevant functions of the law can be listed:

- Authorization: The law gives official or formal authority to people to act in specific ways. In the context of family re-formation, it may be critical to know who has the authority to make longer term and day-to-day decisions about a child. More specifically, does a stepparent have any legal authority with respect to a stepchild? The stepparent may act de facto as someone in charge of the child, but will this hold sway in the community, for instance with the child's school or doctor?
- Upholder of rights: Authorization gives a person certain rights, but there is another sense in which the law upholds rights. The child has rights, as already discussed. Others may have a right to have contact with a child. The practical enforcement of such rights may not always be easy, but the law nevertheless provides the foundation for the claim and follow-up action.

- Imposer of duties: The law both gives and takes. Those caring for children have obligations to maintain appropriate standards of care. Even noncarers may have duties—for example, to pay financial support.
- Protective function: The law protects those to whom duties are owed. The law will, for example, empower the state to step in where a child is suffering from poor parenting, whether by biological or social parents. In other ways, the law will place barriers in the way of harmful action, such as the ban on incestuous marriages and sexual activity.
- Symbolic function: The law should reflect the value system of the country in question. In this sense, the law serves an important symbolic function by giving its imprimatur to the current mores. Although fashions change, the law should not shift with every whim. Perhaps fortunately, the slowness of both the legislative and the judicial procedures means the law usually plays catch-up. What the law says or fails to say on stepparents may make an important statement about the place of reconstituted families in that society.
- Dispute resolution: The earlier points relate to the substantive law, the rules used to regulate society, the "dos and don'ts," the "mays and the musts." Another important function of the law is dispute resolution. This may take many forms. The conventional trial and adjudication ought to be a last resort form of resolution. Instead, the law is increasingly providing mechanisms such as mediation to facilitate the parties' reaching their own solutions. These mechanisms are more often likely to be valuable in the wind-up of a first family rather than in the creation of a fresh one.

The law does not re-create families, nor is it a panacea when things go wrong. In fact, it is a bit player, but in that role it can be obstructive or facilitative. Legal policy has to determine when to encourage and when to discourage. On incest, it may be obstructive—that is easy for most to agree to—but on the place of step relatives it is far less easy to decide what the appropriate direction should be.

THE NEW ZEALAND EXAMPLE

The many issues outlined earlier are tackled in a variety of ways in different jurisdictions. It is impossible to catalogue every approach. For this reason, it is useful to concentrate on one country, and the balance of this chapter considers the law of New Zealand. There are other reasons for this. New Zealand is a small and reasonably compact nation of 4 million people. The English common law has largely shaped its heritage, but recently it has felt less encumbered by its past. Although the country has become increasingly multicultural, it has developed a reasonable level of consensus on most issues. It could be described as a largely secular liberal democracy, with a significant indigenous population whose views sometimes challenge the prevailing Western orthodoxy. New Zealand has sometimes been seen as a social laboratory, and this has been reflected in the law. While there are some parallels with neighbor Australia, New Zealand may be closer to Canada and Scandinavia in its general approach.

Much of the focus of the discussion that follows is on child-adult relationships. First, however, we dispose of some distinctly adult matters.

THE HOUSE AND OTHER THINGS

When two people enter into a new relationship after the ending of earlier ones, they will have to decide where to live and whether to pool their finances and income. Much will depend on individual circumstances, including the number of children who have to be taken into account. Two adults living together will have far fewer needs than two adults and, say, three children, even if the children are in the household only some of the time. For the most part, these matters are for the people themselves to work out, but legal advice may be warranted in some situations. One concern is that the parties may not enter the new relationship on a roughly equal basis; one may have a stronger capital base than the other, quite possibly as a result of the division of the property of the earlier relationship. That party may want some reassurance that his or her capital will be preserved and not dissipated, should the new relationship fail, leading to a fresh division of property. There may also be a desire to ensure that the interests of the children of the first relationship are protected, even if those children are now adult and independent.

In New Zealand, the law on property division is, bar some small exceptions, the same for married and unmarried couples, including same-sex couples and those in civil unions (created by the Civil Union Act, 2004). "Relationship property," formerly called "matrimonial property," is prima facie divided equally when the parties separate (see the Property (Relationships) Act, 1976. This is sometimes called "deferred community," in contrast to the "community property" regimes of civil law jurisdictions). Each party is free therefore to take his or her half, subject to postponements caused, for example, by one party's right to occupy the family home. When a party repartners, his or her property from the earlier relationship will remain his or her "separate property" and not fall subject to further division. However, anything that is put into the family home or chattels or devoted in some way to the new family will lose its separate property status and become relationship property. This could be quite unfair if the other person has kept his or her property separate in both the popular and legal meanings of the word. Take an example. Following her divorce with Mr. Smith, Mrs. Smith uses her half-share to buy a house. She starts a de facto relationship with Mr. Jones, but they separate 4 years later. Mr. Jones had kept his property untouched in investments. Under the 1976 Act, Mr. Jones is entitled to half of Mrs. Smith's "half share."

Can anything be done about this potential unfairness? Under New Zealand law, two tactics should be considered. Both tactics assume that the property is worth enough to make the effort worthwhile. First, the parties to the second relationship can enter into an agreement "contracting out" of the equal division rules. These are sometimes called prenuptial agreements or settlements, which is hardly appropriate for civil unions or de facto relationships; furthermore, an agreement may be entered into after the new relationship has begun. There are two fishhooks to this strategy. The new partner must be willing to sign the agreement, and as part of the process must, according to the law, receive independent legal advice. If the agreement is reciprocal—for example, it preserves as separate the property both have owned at the start of the relationship—then agreement may be readily achieved. However, it is far less likely if the other party is advised that he or she is forfeiting a claim that he or she might otherwise have. The other potential difficulty is that the courts can set an agreement aside if its enforcement would cause serious injustice. Thus, the agreement may come unstuck, but the attitude of the courts to agreements of the kind outlined, especially if they essentially preserve what the parties entered the relationship with, is in general to uphold them.

The other strategy is to place property into a family trust. A trust is a distinct legal entity, and the property it owns is not property belonging to the individuals from whom it was transferred. For a variety of reasons, family trusts have become very popular in New Zealand. Figures from the 2006 census indicate that 12.3% of privately occupied dwellings are owned by a family trust. There is potential unfairness if relationship property is diverted to a trust during the course of a marriage, civil union, or relationship, but there can be less objection if this is done before any cohabitation occurs. Thus, the court has power to award compensation in the former situation, but not the latter. The party who wishes to protect his or her home should therefore ensure that it is transferred to a trust before repartnering, not after its commencement.

One may perhaps regard this discussion with a cynical eye. It implies a somewhat negative view of human nature and a less than sanguine attitude toward the survival chances of subsequent relationships. On the other hand, it reflects the reality of many family rearrangements. "Once bitten, twice shy" is true for enough people that legal approaches that assist the move to new patterns of life are surely beneficial and not destructive.

THE MEANING OF "STEPPARENT"

The law tends to focus on the parties who make up stepfamilies, in particular stepchildren and stepparents, rather than stepfamilies themselves. In

New Zealand, the legal meaning of these terms has been changing over the past dozen years. Oddly, the change has involved a broadening and a narrowing at the same time, but has also gone around in circles. The same meaning is not standard in all pieces of legislation.

The Earlier Formula

The classic statement of the conventional definition of a stepparent is in *Sample v. Sample* (1973, 1 NZLR 584, 586), where Justice Mahon said, "The expression 'stepparent' . . . must bear the ordinary meaning of a spouse by a subsequent marriage of the child's parent." This excludes the wife's husband if, as in that case, the couple had been married before the child was born—there was no *subsequent* marriage. The upshot was that the husband, under the law as it then stood, could not be forced to pay maintenance as a stepparent. The definition also excludes de facto relationships, a point reinforced by Justice John Hansen in *Dixon v. Hatcher* (2000, 19 FRNZ 627), where, under a now repealed law, the de facto partner was denied access to the child, partly because he was not in law a "stepfather." The definition of "stepparent" in Section 4 of the Australian Family Law Act of 1975, like the Mahon definition, requires a formal marriage; however, that section adds a rider that the person must have treated "the child as a member of the family formed with the parent."

The Mahon formula has the virtue of simplicity. One simply asks whether the natural parent has subsequently married. The new spouse is a stepparent. No inquiry is necessary into the extent to which the spouse was actually involved in the parenting itself.

Child Support Definition

The first inroad into the Mahon formula in New Zealand is found in the Child Support Act of 1991, a statute that pays scant attention to stepfamilies. Nevertheless, under Section 99, the court may make a stepparent declaration, that is, a declaration declaring a person to be a stepparent for the purposes of paying child support. There is no need for the stepparent to be married to a natural parent of the child. This circumstance is merely one of the factors that the court must have regard to. Thus, a stepparent may exist in a de facto relationship, and in this sense the definition of stepparent is noticeably widened. On the other hand, the mere fact of married or unmarried cohabitation with a natural parent is not enough. Obviously, stepparent status does not flow automatically under the Child Support Act as it does under the Mahon formula but depends on a court declaration. The court must take into account other factors, in particular the extent to which the person had assumed responsibility for the maintenance of the child. In other words, the focus is on the parenting done by the alleged stepparent, and in particular the financial contribution to the child's upbringing.

There have been very few stepparent declarations under the Child Support Act. An application was denied in *BPS v. MNS* (1998, NZFLR 289), a case in which the mother became pregnant through what might be described as donor insemination by natural means, artificial means having failed. The husband had initially played a full parental role in the child's life, but the parties separated not long afterward. The husband endeavored to exercise access, but this became impossible and he gave up trying. In short, the husband had had no contact with the child for 6 out of the child's 7½ years of life. The wife applied for the stepparent declaration long after the separation, her admitted motive being that the money would enable her to return to the workforce. On the Mahon formula, there is no way that the man could be a stepparent. However, the Child Support Act provisions, as already pointed out, differ markedly from Mahon. Justices Doogue and Goddard held that the question of the man's status as a stepparent had to be determined at the date of the court hearing, not at some other time, such as the date of separation. Given his lack of involvement with the child for so long, they held that it would be wrong to declare him a stepparent.

A stepparent declaration was also denied in *DS v. GW* (2006, NZFLR 925), where a man had continued to fulfill a parenting role even after he discovered that he was not the child's father. The judge took the view that the man had done his bit: "Enough is enough. . . . It is now the father's turn" (paragraph 64). If this approach is correct, it narrows the scope for stepparent declarations to very few situations indeed.

Contrast these two cases with *A v. R* (1999, NZFLR 249). Here, two women had lived in a relationship for 14 years. One of them was birth mother to three children conceived through donor insemination. The women separated, and the birth mother sought a stepparent declaration against the other. Justice Hammond granted the declaration, being influenced by the extent to which the woman acted as a parent, but also by the facts that the women had regarded their relationship as one in the nature of marriage and the partner had been a court-appointed guardian. Again, this is a far cry from Mahon. First, Mahon would never have contemplated a lesbian partner's being a stepparent. Second, he would not have been concerned to analyze the actual parenting and material support that the partner had given.

As an aside, the law has now been changed, so that the lesbian partner is regarded in law as one of the child's legal parents. She will therefore be liable under the Child Support Act as a "parent," without the need for a stepparent declaration (see Section 18, Status of Children Act, 1969, as amended in 2004).

DEFINITION IN THE CARE OF CHILDREN ACT, 2004

The Care of Children Act uses the phrase "spouse or partner of a parent" rather than "stepparent," and defines it in Section 8 to mean, "in relation to a child, a person who is not the child's parent but

1. who is or has been married to, or in a civil union or de facto relationship with, a parent of the child; and
2. who shares responsibility for the child's day-to-day care with the parent.

The definition is important for several reasons, for instance because a person falling within the definition has an automatic right to apply for a parenting order and may also be appointed a guardian by agreement between the parties. Compared to the Mahon formula, we are no longer limited to subsequent marriages, and thus, a same-sex or opposite-sex partner at any time, whether married or not, may count. However, the "spouse or partner of a parent" must share responsibility for the child's care. What exactly does this mean? It differs from the Child Support Act, where the emphasis is on contributing to the child's maintenance, that is, material and financial support. Responsibility for care suggests some level of participation in the child's parenting without necessarily any financial involvement. For example, the nonemployed partner may come under the Care of Children Act but may well fall outside the Child Support Act. To what extent must the person be responsible for the child's care? Would some transport on the weekend to parties or sports games be enough? Would taking the whole family away on vacation be enough? These are questions that may yet have to be tested before the courts.

A further difficulty with the definition is that it is cast in the present tense. If the parties have separated, as happened in the child support cases discussed earlier, and the natural parent has assumed care of the child, is the ex-cohabitant still sharing responsibility for the child's day-to-day care? The answer to this may depend on the facts. The ex-cohabitant may in some instances be looking after the children several days a week by arrangement with the parent. That is rather different from the scenario in which the person has intermittent contact, which may, as in *BPS*, be a point of tension. It is suggested that a person who did share care of the child may no longer do so and thus, though once being a "spouse or partner of a parent," will have lost that status. This creates considerable volatility in the legal concepts.

The Return of the Step Language

The statutory flirtation with "spouse or partner of a parent" was somewhat short-lived, although the words remain in the Care of Children Act. In 2005, Parliament passed an amendment to the Interpretation Act of 1999 by inserting a definition of "stepparent":

> For the purposes of an enactment, the relationship of step-parent, stepson, stepdaughter, or any other relationship described by a word containing the prefix "step," may be established by civil union or by de facto relationship as well as by marriage. (Section 29B)

(Note: The hyphen in "stepparent" and not in the other words is how the legislation is drafted.)

The legislative history of this provision is checkered. At one point, the parliamentary select committee was advised to use the awkward Care of Children Act language. For reasons that are not explained, the select committee resurrected "step" terminology and wanted the Care of Children Act brought into line. The latter did not occur, but the definition in the Interpretation Act just quoted was eventually passed. It applies to any statutory reference that is not otherwise defined in the relevant statute. It is significant that it simply extends the Mahon formula to civil union and de facto partners and, despite some proposals to the contrary, does not in any way take into account the extent to which the spouse or partner was involved in the actual parenting. The extension to civil union and de facto partners was part of a wider process whereby discrimination on the basis of marital status was removed from legislation unless there was good reason for not doing so.

CHILD CARE

Different Notions of a "Parent"

Who has rights and responsibilities for children when families are rearranged? This is a central matter for the law to grapple with. Bainham (1999, pp. 28–31) draws out some helpful distinctions, and in so doing suggests that the legal and social meanings differ. In the legal sense, "parentage" refers to genetic origins, a child's natural parents. Bainham uses "parenthood" for the social role of parents that various people play, including stepparents, foster parents, and adoptive parents, and as such parenthood carries no legal status with it. "Parental responsibility," as a legal concept, is the formal authority possessed by someone in relation to a child. "Parental responsibility" is a phrase used typically in English law. What is important to appreciate are the differences between official status as a natural or birth parent, acting de facto as a parent, and having formal standing with respect to the child. On family re-formation, the natural parents continue to be recognized as such, unless there is an adoption. The stepparent who acts de facto as a parent may well have no legal standing, although anyone acting in loco parentis, officially or unofficially, will have a duty to provide at least basic care. Individual legal systems may have procedures that enable the stepparent to gain legal standing, but typically this is only after the procedure has been activated.

In New Zealand, the 2004 Care of Children Act is the primary source of the law relating to parenting. In some instances where there has been child abuse or neglect, the Children, Young Persons and Their Families Act of 1989 comes into play. We shall put that Act to one side, except to note that it defines "parent" to include stepparent, "but only if the stepparent shares responsibility for the day-to-day care of the child with a parent of the child" (Section 2(1)). Also, the key piece of legislation dealing with the status of the child, that is, who the child's legal parents are, is the 1969 Status of Children Act. With the exception of situations where assisted reproductive technologies have been used, the Act is designed to grant parental status to the child's genetic parents. The conventional wisdom is that a child has a maximum of two parents, a mother and a father, by definition excluding a stepparent. However, the question has been raised why a child could not have more than two parents, either to cover donation of gametes or the stepparent situation (e.g., Bainham, 1999, p. 44; New Zealand Law Commission, 2005). In terms of practical politics, this is unlikely to be picked up in the near future because of the predominance of the so-called nuclear family model. Nevertheless, it has the virtue of inclusion, rather than exclusion, of key parental figures.

Guardianship

Under the Care of Children Act, the notion of guardianship is fundamental to New Zealand child law. It is similar to "parental responsibility" in some other jurisdictions. A guardian has the core responsibility for a child's upbringing. Usually the parents are a child's guardians, but this is not always so. Other people can be appointed guardians by the Family Court and thus have legal responsibility for a child's life (Section 27). This may be very sensible in cases where the child is being brought up by persons other than the parents, such as a stepparent. As a guardian, the stepparent can legitimately be involved in the child's schooling, religious upbringing, medical treatment, and so forth. Appointment as a guardian does not remove any guardianship rights possessed by the other natural parent(s), but Section 16(5) calls on all guardians to act jointly. Thus, it cannot be assumed that guardianship gives the stepparent the right to act unilaterally.

An application to the court to be appointed a guardian is never certain of success. Although Section 27 is itself barren of guidance, the court must decide with the child's welfare and best interests as the paramount consideration and must give the child an opportunity to express his or her views (Sections 4–6).

Appointment by Agreement

A new and somewhat controversial procedure enables a child's two natural or adoptive parents to appoint a stepparent as an additional guardian on a largely do-it-yourself basis (Sections 21–25). The procedure for appointing a stepparent as a guardian is shrouded in a number of qualifications. How often it will be used will be interesting to watch. Typically, agreement all around will be required. This assumes a degree of amiability between the stepparent and the ex-partner, or at least sufficient goodwill to support the appointment. The stepparent must:

- have shared the parenting of the child for at least a year;
- must not have been involved in proceedings under the Care of Children Act; the former Guardianship Act; or the Children, Young Persons, and Their Families Act;
- must not have been a respondent in proceedings under the Domestic Violence Act, 1995;
- must not have been convicted of a child abuse offense or of a child pornography offense.

As part of this process, various declarations must accompany the form appointing a stepparent as a guardian, including a declaration that the appointing parties believe that the proposed guardian does not have convictions of the kind just described. The latter's criminal record must also be lodged. The parties must state whether they believe that the appointment is conducive to the child's welfare and best interests—they are hardly likely to deny it—and whether all reasonable steps have been taken "to ascertain and consider" the child's views. But, if the child is hostile to the appointment, there is no mechanism to acknowledge those contrary views or anything about the content of the child's views. There is a further problem with the process. A person may have wrongly been a respondent under the Domestic Violence Act. Or a person may have been involved in proceedings under the Children, Young Persons and Their Families Act as a family member who attended a family group conference. Why these should exclude one from appointment is unexplained.

Assuming that there are no hitches along the way and that the documentation is all in order, the appointment as guardian takes effect as soon as it has been approved by a Family Court registrar. The latter's role is, one assumes, purely administrative. The registrar, "having made all reasonable inquiries," must be satisfied that the form and declarations, accompanied by the criminal record, "have been properly completed and appear to be in order." There is nothing to suggest that the registrar's inquiries have to dig into the substance of the documentation. Arguably, it will suffice if inquiries reveal as a matter of form that the documentation is in order.

There has been criticism of the new procedure (see Watt, 2006). In particular, it is not clear that the new system sufficiently vets the child's welfare and best interests, nor takes adequate account of the child's views. Watt proposes "a tax-payer funded inquiry by an independent assessor into whether the appointment is in the child's best interests" (p. 125). On the other hand, in England under Section 4A of the Adoption and Children Act of 2002, a stepparent may be given parental responsibility entirely by agreement, with none of the qualifications found in the New Zealand procedure, although the stepparent must be married to one of the parents. Cretney, Masson, and Bailey-Harris (2003, p. 562) appear to favor the soft English line, even querying why the nonresident parent should have to consent. They argue that such consent gives that parent "bargaining chips" and may make it hard to obtain agreement.

Whatever the precise merits and demerits of the appointment-by-agreement system, it is a clear legislative recognition of the place of stepparents in the diversity of New Zealand families.

OTHER PROCEDURES, INCLUDING PARENTING ORDERS: A POTENTIAL PROBLEM

A stepparent, as "a spouse or partner of a parent," has an automatic right to ask for a child to be placed under the guardianship of the court (an important residual power for the protection of a child), to apply for the removal of a guardian and to apply for a parenting order (Care of Children Act, 2004, Sections 31(2)(d), 29(2)(e), 47(1)(c)). A parenting order is the mechanism by which the court can grant one or more parties day-to-day care of a child or contact.

As discussed earlier, "a spouse or partner of a parent" must in the present tense share responsibility for the child's day-to-day care. Thus, whether a stepparent can actually apply may depend on the facts of each case and the way day-to-day care is carried out. One can well imagine a situation in which a stepparent has been heavily involved in a child's life for many years, but, on separation from the birth parent, the latter takes the children, leaving the stepparent with little or no contact. Should the stepparent not automatically have a right to apply for a parenting order to ensure some degree of contact? One way this problem can be alleviated is if the stepparent is also a guardian, who would have an automatic right to apply for various orders. The wider importance of being a guardian has already been pointed out: It gives the stepparent legal authority to act in guardianship matters with respect to the upbringing of a child. Now, it might rescue the position of the stepparent on relationship breakdown. If the relationship between the child and the stepparent was strong, it may also rescue the position of the child, whose welfare must always be paramount.

STEPPARENT ADOPTION

One way of ensuring that the stepparent has full legal authority with respect to the child is through a stepparent adoption. In European jurisdictions, a distinction is often drawn between full and simple adoption, the latter being closer to guardianship or "parental responsibility" (Sosson, 1993, pp. 398–400). Our focus is on adoption that involves a complete transfer of parental status and responsibility to the adoptive parties.

Stepparent adoption has not had a good press. An English judge, Lord Justice Cumming-Bruce, put it starkly:

> It is quite wrong to use adoption law to extinguish the relationship between the protesting father and the child, unless there is some really serious factor which justifies the use of the statutory guillotine. The courts should not encourage the idea that after divorce the children of the family can be reshuffled and dealt out like a pack of cards in a second rubber of bridge. (*Re B (a minor)*, [(1975)] Fam 127, 143)

Adoption is a drastic move because of the knockout effect it has on the other natural parent. Its use may be better restricted to situations in which the other natural parent has died or has disappeared. However, even in these situations, adoption may not be appropriate. In the New Zealand case of *Parker v. Pearce* (1987, 4 NZFLR 150), where the mother had died, the judge refused to grant an adoption in favor of the father's new wife largely because of the effect on the mother's family, especially the children's grandparents. One matter that concerned the father and his wife was their desire to change the children's surname. Surnames can be a problem in family reformation, but most jurisdictions will have mechanisms short of adoption to allow for a change, if desired. In this case, the judge thought that the parties had overstated the point, which "is generally approached by families with realism" (156).

The New Zealand Law Commission (2000, paragraph 375) has recommended that a judge hearing a stepparent adoption application should be required to consider the degree of contact with the natural parent and wider family, whether guardianship would be a better option, and whether the stepparent had lived with the child for at least 3 years. One other quirk in stepparent adoptions is that the natural parent as well as the stepparent must adopt the child, and people often regard it is odd to have to adopt their own child. The law in England has sensibly been changed to avoid this (Adoption and Children Act, 2002, Sections 46(3)(b), 51(2)).

CHILD SUPPORT

The New Zealand Child Support Act (1991) is firmly rooted in the conventional nuclear family model. It is set up to ensure that liable parents are assessed according to a strict formula to pay child support for their children. One of its express objects is "to ensure that obligations to birth and adopted children are not extinguished by obligations to stepchildren" (Section 4(i)). Thus, with the rarely used exception already discussed allowing a court to declare someone a stepparent, a liable parent will be a child's legal parent, usually the child's biological or adoptive parent.

The New Zealand approach is unusual in the sense of including stepparent obligations in its explicit child support legislation. In England, although there is power under the 1989 Children Act to order financial relief against a stepparent (see especially paragraph 4 of Schedule 1) and also, in relation to "a child of their family" in Section 52 of the Matrimonial Causes Act (1973), the child support legislation is said to represent "an overt disregard for step-family situations" (Edwards, Gillies, & McCarthy, 1999, p. 86) and "an attempt to undermine a possible social obligation" (Maclean & Eekelaar, 1997, p. 47). The position in Australia is similar, with residual stepparent obligations relegated to the Family Law Act of 1975, where Section 66D states, somewhat blatantly, that any stepparent duty "is a secondary duty subject to the primary duty of the parents of the child to maintain the child" and "does not derogate from the primary duty of the parents to maintain the child." In contrast, Canada, especially since the Supreme Court's decision in *Chartier v. Chartier* (1999, 1 SCR 242) and the publication of child support guidelines, has imposed significant obligations on stepparents, "arguably more extensive than in any other jurisdiction" (Rogerson, 2001, p. 151). Rogerson notes that there is very little analysis of why stepparents should have financial obligations. She argues for "a more nuanced, less rigid approach," with greater emphasis on the assessment and apportionment of liability rather than the threshold for liability, even if this is at the expense of predictability and certainty (Rogerson, 2001, p. 156).

Despite questions regarding the liability of stepparents, there is another important way in which the step relationship impacts the New Zealand scheme. The child support formula has built into it a living allowance, which takes account of new family obligations (Section 30). These obligations, up to a maximum of four dependent children, result in a reduction in the amount of child support payable. A "dependent child" is one "who is maintained as a member of [the liable parent's] family" and "in respect of whom the [liable parent] either is the sole or principal provider of ongoing daily care for the child or shares ongoing daily care of the child substantially equally with another person." This definition is certainly wide enough to cover stepchildren who are part of the liable parent's new family. Perhaps the noncustodial natural parent should be paying for these children. The reality is, however, that this will often not be the situation, or payments will be at an inadequate level.

What if the stepparent is part of the family *receiving* support? For example, the custodian's new partner, that is, a stepparent, may be providing handsomely for the receiving family, and the liable parent may consider that this is a good reason to modify the amount to be paid. It is possible to argue for a "departure" from the set payment formula, but the courts have tended not to look generously on these arguments, which depend on the existence of "special circumstances." The Court of Appeal in the leading decision in *Lyon v. Wilcox* (1994, 3 NZLR 422, 432) said that there was nothing special about a stepfather's acting as a child's father figure: "It is very common for the child of one parent to become a member of the family of another parent or spouse." Thus, the true position of the stepfamily was ignored. The liable parent's stepfamily is recognized through the living allowance, but the custodian's stepfamily is largely excluded from consideration.

INHERITANCE

A step relationship is one that may continue for life. The issues are not simply about young children but also adult stepchildren. Typically the legal issues that arise later in life are concerned with inheritance. This grudging approach in the child support legislation is largely carried through to inheritance laws. Although a stepchild may be provided for in a will, often this is not so. Where does this leave the excluded stepchild? Broadly speaking, the stepchild gains little.

Where the deceased has left no will, various family members are entitled to share in the estate, but stepchildren are not included (Administration Act, 1969). Family members may apply under the Family Protection Act (1955) for a share of the estate if they were excluded from the will or for a larger share if they were treated poorly under the will (or, rarely, on an intestacy). Stepchildren may apply but only so long as they were dependent on the deceased, that is, "were being maintained wholly or partly or were legally entitled to be maintained wholly or partly by the deceased immediately before his death" (Family Protection Act, 1955, Section 3(1)(d)). The position in England is broadly similar, except that the step relationship can be established only through marriage or civil partnership, and the test is either one of maintenance by the deceased or having been treated by the deceased as a child of the family (Inheritance (Provision for Family and Dependants) Act, 1975, Section 1(1)).

Given that under the 1991 Child Support Act stepparents generally have no legal liability for their stepchildren, the references to a legal entitlement to be maintained may be practically meaningless. The chance of a stepchild's making a claim under the Act will depend on actual maintenance by the deceased. This need not be limited by age. For example, a 30-year-old with an intellectual disability may have been maintained by the deceased at the time of death.

Enough has been said to indicate that under these provisions, stepchildren are treated very differently from biological and adopted children and that they are likely to be successful only in rare situations.

An adult stepchild who had been involved in the deceased's life possibly up until death may make a claim under the Law Reform (Testamentary

Promises) Act of 1949, an Act that has no restrictions on the class of people who may apply but that has other criteria that must be satisfied. These criteria are (a) that the claimant had rendered services to the deceased and (b) that there had been a promise that in return, the claimant would be recognized in the will.

In the leading case of *Re Welch* (1990, 3 NZLR 1), the stepson and his wife lived with the deceased at various points early in their marriage. They continued to enjoy a close relationship with the claimant's mother and the stepfather, who treated him as his own son. The stepfather had indicated that the claimant would inherit most of the estate, but in fact he died intestate. The High Court awarded the stepson a significant part of the estate, but the Court of Appeal reduced it to $20,000, a figure upheld by the Privy Council, where it was said, "It appears to their Lordships that some straining of the scope of the Act is required to bring within the concept of services the natural incidents and consequences of life within a close family group, such as existed in this case" (p. 7). In other words, a stepchild will usually struggle to get anything much under a testamentary promises claim. The tenor of the Privy Council's judgment is that even $20,000 may not have been warranted. On the other hand, if the stepson in *Re Welch* had been adopted, his legal position would have been remarkably better because he would have been treated as a biological child.

The *Welch* saga raises the question of how parents provide for their natural children and their stepchildren. With successive relationships, people are often likely to be concerned about preserving some of their assets for their natural children rather than their stepchildren. What may well happen is that a new partner, whether married or unmarried, will be entitled to half of the relationship property. If the partners co-own the family home as joint tenants, then the survivor automatically gets the whole of the home. The survivor will probably provide for the survivor's children but not the deceased's. Thus, in this scenario the stepchildren of the person who died first may end up rather better off. As discussed earlier (see "The House and Other Things"), a device such as a family trust may be desirable.

CONCLUSION

The law's recognition of stepfamilies has been volatile and often built on shifting sands. In some areas, especially where money or property is involved, recognition is sparse. On the other hand, where the issues have more to do with hands-on parenting, there is much more acceptance of the position of stepparents. Are we comfortable living with a degree of incoherency? Or should there be a sustained attempt to create a consistent set of policies and legal rules?

REFERENCES

Administration Act 1969 (NZ).

Adoption and Children Act 2002 (England and Wales).

Agell, A. (1993). Step-parenthood and biological parenthood: Competition of coop-eration. In J. Eekelaar & P. Šarčević (Eds.), *Parenthood in modern society: Legal and social issues for the twenty-first century* (pp. 407–420). Dordrecht, The Netherlands: Martinus Nijhoff.

A v. R, NZFLR (New Zealand Family Law Reports) 249 (1999).

Bainham, A. (1999). Parentage, parenthood and parental responsibility. In A. Bainham, S. D. Sclater, & M. Richards (Eds.), *What is a parent? A socio-legal analysis* (pp. 25–46). Oxford: Hart.

BPS v. MNS, NZFLR (New Zealand Family Law Reports) 289 (1998).

Care of Children Act 2004 (NZ).

Chartier v. Chartier, 1 SCR (Supreme Court Reports, Canada) 242 (1999).

Children, Young Persons, and Their Families Act 1989 (NZ).

Children Act 1989 (England and Wales).

Child Support Act 1991 (NZ).

Civil Union Act 2004 (NZ).

Cretney, S., Masson, J., & Bailey-Harris, R. (2003). *Principles of family law* (7th ed.). London: Thomson Sweet and Maxwell.

Dixon v. Hatcher, 19 FRNZ (Family Reports of New Zealand) 627 (2000).

Domestic Violence Act 1975 (NZ).

DS v. GW, NZFLR (New Zealand Family Law Reports) 925 (2006).

Edwards, R., Gillies, V., & McCarthy, J. R. (1999). Biological parents and social fami-lies' legal discourses and everyday understandings of the position of step-parents. *International Journal of Law, Policy and the Family, 13*, 78–105.

Eekelaar, J. (1991). Parental responsibility: State of nature or nature of the state? *Journal of Social Welfare and Family Law*, 37–50.

Families Commission Act 2003 (NZ).

Family Law Act 1975 (Australia).

Family Protection Act 1955 (NZ).

Hoggett, B. (1987). *Parents and children: The law of parental responsibility* (3rd ed.). London: Sweet and Maxwell.

Inheritance (Provision for Family and Dependants) Act 1975 (England and Wales).

Law Reform (Testamentary Promises) Act 1949 (NZ).

Lyon v. Wilcox, 3 NZLR (New Zealand Law Reports) 422 (1994).

Maclean, M., & Eekelaar, J. (1997). *The parental obligation: A study of parenthood across households*. Oxford: Hart.

Matrimonial Causes Act 1973 (England and Wales).

New Zealand Law Commission. (2000). *Adoption and its alternatives: A different ap-proach and new framework* (Report 65). Wellington, New Zealand: Author.

New Zealand Law Commission. (2005). *New issues in parenthood* (Report 88). Well-ington, New Zealand: Author.

Parker v. Pearce, 4 NZFLR (New Zealand Family Law Reports) 150 (1987).

Property (Relationships) Act 1976 (NZ).

Re B (a minor), Fam (Family Reports, England) 127 (1975).

Re Welch, 3 NZLR (New Zealand Law Reports) 1 (1990).

Rogerson, C. (2001). The child support obligations of step-parents. *Canadian Journal of Family Law, 18,* 9–157.

Sample v. Sample, 1 NZLR (New Zealand Law Reports) 584 (1973).

Sosson, J. (1993). The legal status of step-families. In J. Eekelaar & P. Šarčević (Eds.), *Parenthood in modern society: Legal and social issues for the twenty-first century* (pp. 395–405). Dordrecht, The Netherlands: Martinus Nijhoff.

Status of Children Act 1969 (NZ).

United Nations Convention on the Rights of the Child.

Wardle, L. D. (1993). The evolving rights and duties of step-parents: Making new rules for new families. In J. Eekelaar & P. Šarčević (Eds.), *Parenthood in modern society: Legal and social issues for the twenty-first century* (pp. 375–393). Dordrecht, The Netherlands: Martinus Nijhoff.

Watt, E. (2006). The DIY procedure for appointing step-parents as additional guardians. *New Zealand Family Law Journal, 5,* 118–127.

CHAPTER 22

How Relevant Are U.S. Family and Probate Laws to Stepfamilies?

SARAH E. C. MALIA

As MANY as 1 in 3 American children will spend some portion of their childhood years living with a stepparent (Seltzer, 1994). Although many stepparents and stepchildren form close, enduring bonds, the role of stepfamily relationships generally is invisible in the law (Mason, 1998; Mason, Harrison-Jay, Svare, & Wolfinger, 2002). Despite a recognized need for stepfamily legal reforms (Bartlett, 1999), U.S. family law and probate law have failed to keep pace with societal changes (Gary, 2000; Romesberg, 1999; Wendel, 2005). Statutes and court decisions regarding stepparent rights and obligations vary greatly, and policy makers generally remain biased toward a traditional nuclear family ideology (Ganong, Coleman, Fine, & McDaniel, 1998; Mahoney, 1999; Young, 1998). Although legislatures and courts slowly are recognizing diverse family forms, critics argue that legal reform has been sporadic and piecemeal (Gary, 2000). Legal changes affecting stepfamilies have occurred indirectly as a result of policy shifts involving nonstepparent interested third parties, such as grandparents (Mason, Fine, & Carnochan, 2001). Generally, U.S. legal policy has insufficiently accommodated diverse family forms and relationships (Gary, 2000; Hans, 2002; Malia, 2005).

American cultural beliefs about what constitutes a proper family exert a subtle, yet powerful influence on how family members perceive themselves

Special thanks to Ms. Amy Massengill for her gentle reminders and assistance in transcribing notes and Drs. Julia and James Malia for their steadfast support.

and expect to be regarded by others, which in turn may affect family conduct and functioning (Ganong & Coleman, 1997; Marsiglio, 2004). Traditionally in the United States, the structure of the ideal immediate family is *nuclear*, meaning two legal parents and their child(ren). Two prevailing cultural perspectives of stepfamilies, both deficit-based, have been identified by family scholars: (1) as incomplete institutions to be ignored (Cherlin, 1978) and (2) as stigmatized groups, less functional and more problematic than nuclear families (Ganong & Coleman, 1997). In contrast to a deficit perspective, which scholars have argued hinders stepfamily development and functioning (Ganong & Coleman, 1997; Mason et al., 2002), a normative-adaptive perspective of families acknowledges and honors diverse functional family relationships and forms (Ganong & Coleman, 1997). Such an approach emphasizes social and economic mutual interdependency among members as the central underlying characteristic of being a family rather than legal or blood ties (Gary, 2000; Younger, 1996). This chapter is informed by the normative-adaptive perspective of stepfamilies in terms of its emphasis on legal reform and a more flexible and inclusive notion of family (Kavanagh, 2004; Young, 1998).

In this chapter I discuss (a) U.S. federal and state policies and rules affecting stepfamilies, focusing on custody and divorce rules under family law and default inheritance rules under probate law (trusts and estates); (b) related policy reform efforts proposed by social science researchers and legal commentators; and (c) social science research concerning child development, divorce, and stepfamily relationships. Summarized research demonstrates the importance of developing empirically derived policy reform strategies that would balance various stepfamily members' interests while promoting children's welfare and strengthening diverse family forms and relationships. The crux of the policy debate is the tension between honoring the parental rights of the nonresidential or noncustodial parent (usually the biological father) and recognizing and legitimizing stepparent-stepchild relationships.

Some caveats need to be mentioned. First, as many of the issues addressed in this chapter are state-specific, it is important that individuals and families who wish to plan for such challenges seek the counsel of legal representation familiar with the particular laws of their domicile state (Giarmarco, 2006). Second, *U.S.* is used as a descriptive adjective in this chapter, depending on the context, to refer to (a) the sum total of U.S. policy, which includes both state and federal common law (court case decisions) and statutory rules and regulations, or (b) federal law alone. Third, the extant legal definition of *stepfamily* in the United States is limited to a valid marriage between a man and a woman in which one or both spouses have child(ren) from different, prior relationship(s). Unless noted otherwise, the scope of the discussion focuses on married stepfamilies and their ex-partners and extended relatives. But other "nontraditional" family forms—such as cohabiting families (with opposite- or same-sex partners and parents) and grandparents rearing grandchildren—face related issues and problems, and the policy arguments articulated here have been applied and are applicable to their family situations.

Fourth, it should be noted that residential stepfathers, not stepmothers, predominate in the United States (Mnookin & Maccoby, 2002); thus, legal polices affecting residential stepparents are likely to be most relevant for stepfathers. Nonetheless, based on the assumption that stepparent policies in theory are salient for all stepfamilies, inclusive references to *stepparents* generally are used when not citing specific research. Public policies reflect cultural expectations for stepfamily members, diverse household arrangements exist, and good policy making does not discriminate based on gender (Malia, 2005).

Finally, it is outside the scope of this chapter to articulate fully the extent to which legal rules may impact stepfamily roles and behavior. It is commonly accepted that stepfamily members in the United States can be oblivious to or consciously ignore official legal parameters in their every-day lives (Malia, 2005). For example, divorced parents often arrange and readjust informal custody or visitation agreements over time that depart widely from the official parenting plan approved by the court (Fox & Blanton, 1995). On the other hand, once a court order involving a step-family member has been issued (e.g., in divorce or postdivorce proceed-ings), the court will not necessarily waive its enforceability, even if the recipient arguably has done so (Gregory, Swisher, & Wolf, 2001) by mak-ing or acquiescing to informal changes or failing to seek an enforcement action in a timely manner. In essence, the state is the third "member" of any marriage, past or present; the court's independent role reflects the state's "power to regulate *all* the incidents of the marital relationship" (Gregory et al., 2001, p. 31) because it controls the legal status of persons as being married or not. More apparent probably in daily life, private stepfamily affairs regularly collide with societal institutions' restricted definitions of family and protocols for authorized consent and consulta-tion (Mason et al., 2002). Such institutions include schools, camps, doc-tors' offices, and insurance and financial companies.

U.S. FAMILY AND PROBATE LAW TRADITIONS

In the United States, much of the law affecting stepfamilies is state-driven, although directly or indirectly modified at times by federal law. This is true for both family and probate law. Metaphorically, the United States is made up of 50 smaller "countries" (states) pieced together with federal rules in a patchwork quilt. U.S. jurisdictions generally adopted British common law (up to the nation's official inception) and were heavily influenced by British jurisprudential traditions. The law of the State of Louisiana provides a notable exception; it is based instead on the Napoleonic Code. Typically, non-Louisiana legal practitioners are not well versed in Louisiana rules and procedures and consider the state particularly "foreign," legally speaking. *State family law* governs domestic relations, including establishing the requirements for valid marriages and divorces, legally recognizing parent-child relationships, and regulating parental rights and child custody and support issues (Malia, 2005). State and federal family law policy distinctions affecting stepfamilies are addressed further in subsequent sections. But parental rights are paramount when considering stepfamily policy issues and thus are discussed first, followed by an overview of inheritance and probate law.

PARENTAL RIGHTS DOCTRINE AND PARENTHOOD AS AN EXCLUSIVE STATUS

Legal parental rights in the United States encompass considerable authority to direct the care, control, and upbringing of a child; for instance, parents have the power to make decisions regarding their child's religious education and participation, medical treatments, residence, and school selection (Skinner & Kohler, 2002). Family law resists formal recognition of nontraditional caregivers such as stepparents, regardless of their psychological or functional roles in a child's life (Bartlett, 2001), largely because of robust legal precedent that protects and seeks to maintain legal parents and responsible parenting on the part of biological or adoptive nuclear parents (Bartlett, 1999; Malia, 2005). Two basic tenets of U.S. family law are used in determining parental rights. The first rule, the *parental rights doctrine*, gives biological parents fundamental rights, such as an entitlement of procreation and making parental decisions for their children (Malia, 2005; Skinner & Kohler, 2002). The second rule, *parenthood as an exclusive status*, establishes that the law recognizes a maximum of two parents for a child at any one time (Bartlett, 2001). Unless a legal adoption occurs severing parental ties, in contrast to marriage, parenthood is a life sentence and beyond (see Atkin, this volume).

The first tenet, the *parental rights doctrine*, is based on a line of U.S. Supreme Court cases (e.g., *Meyer v. Nebraska*, 1923; *Santosky v. Kramer*, 1982; *Troxel v. Granville*, 2000). They demonstrate that fit parents' fundamental due process rights to make personal decisions regarding the rearing of their children are not easily overcome by third parties, such as grandparents, stepparents, or the government (Skinner & Kohler, 2002). The U.S. Constitution implicitly protects a family's right to integrity and autonomy, that is, freedom from government interference. If the government infringes on this privacy right, then it must provide the family with due process (Romesberg, 1999). *Fit parents* are defined legally as those who adequately care for their children's needs and do not neglect, abuse, or abandon their children (Mahoney, 1997). A person or agency challenging a parent's fitness bears the burden of overcoming the court's presumption that parents are fit and act in the best interests of their children (Ramsey & Abrams, 2001).

Classifying parental rights as private and fundamental requires U.S. courts to apply *strict scrutiny*, the highest standard of protection in individual constitutional rights analysis (also used to protect against government violations and limitations regarding free speech, voting rights, and interstate travel). Thus, state intervention or government regulation is proper only if there is a compelling state interest—such as public safety or children's welfare—met through least restrictive means (Ramsey & Abrams, 2001; Skinner & Kohler, 2002). In contrast, government interference must only be substantially related to an important state purpose to satisfy the *intermediate scrutiny standard* applied in particular constitutional rights cases (e.g., regulatory discrimination against illegitimate children). Most commonly applicable, the lowest level of constitutional rights protection is utilized for determining whether government interference meets the *reasonable rational basis standard* (e.g., in cases concerning government taxes, welfare guidelines, and regulations on commerce; Ramsey & Abrams, 2001).

The second tenet, *parenthood as an exclusive status,* is reinforced in several ways (Skinner & Kohler, 2002; Young, 1998). U.S. law consistently has pronounced that a child cannot have more than two parents, each with full parental rights and duties that are shared with no one else. Family law provides for dissolving and re-creating families through divorce, remarriage, and adoption, and establishing each new parental or spousal family unit entails legally nullifying a preexisting family (Malia, 2005). But marital status changes alone do not signify shifts in parental rights and duties (Skinner & Kohler, 2002). Contemporary U.S. and British legal discourses are dominated by the notion of *shared parenting* or *coparenting* (i.e., joint legal and/or physical custody between ex-spouses or ex-partners who share biological ties with a child). This is despite observed difficulties in coparenting being put into practice due to separate current living arrangements, ongoing conflicts, and likely new relationships (Edwards, Gillies, & McCarthy, 1999; Mnookin & Maccoby, 2002). The U.S. legal assumption of exclusive parenthood prohibits the recognition of multiple parental figures within stepfamilies and other family forms (Malia, 2005; Skinner & Kohler, 2002). One exception, perhaps unsurprisingly, is a Louisiana statutory rule that allows a stepfather to qualify as a legitimate father while requiring the biological father to pay child support (see LA Civil Code Annotated Article

184, cited in Romesberg, 1999), effectively permitting a child to have more than two parents with legal parental rights. Documentation could not be located regarding the extent to which this statute is employed or its effects on families.

In sum, the parental rights doctrine establishes the legal priority of biological ties, and the premise of exclusive parenthood recognizes only one legal set of parents at a time (Malia, 2005). As such, these two basic tenets of family law result in legal ambiguity for stepparents who may function as parental figures (Skinner & Kohler, 2002), particularly those who are in residence with their stepchildren. While courts must apply the *strict scrutiny* standard in such cases, there are established *compelling* child welfare reasons that allow the state to limit or overturn parental rights. These include mandatory school attendance, child labor prohibitions, essential health care provision, and child endangerment prohibitions (Skinner & Kohler, 2002). Perhaps a similar compelling governmental interest argument can be used to justify legal recognition of stepparent-stepchild relationships, particularly those characterized by mutual interdependency (Malia, 2005). The legal challenge, therefore, is to determine how the law may honor a psychological attachment that may exist between a stepparent and stepchild while not denying the biological parents' constitutional and legal rights to their child (Hans, 2002; Malia, 2005).

PROBATE LAW AND INHERITANCE OVERVIEW

The U.S. stepfamily policy debate spills over into state probate law because inheritance rights attach themselves to legally recognized marital spouses and parent-child relationships (Wendel, 2005). *Trusts and estates law* covers the means and estate planning tools available for protecting and transferring individuals' property and interests during their lifetime and upon death (e.g., with tax-planning trusts, durable powers of attorney for financial and health care matters, wills, and account beneficiary designations). Although used in this chapter in a more generic sense, *probate law* technically refers to a subsection of trusts and estates governing will execution, validity, and interpretation; the estate administration process for fiduciaries (e.g., executors); and default state rules for probate property inheritance when individuals die *intestate*, or without a will. Intestacy laws usually do not recognize unrelated persons (Giarmarco, 2006), such as step relations or domestic partners. However, assets payable by beneficiary designation to a person or trust (e.g., life insurance and retirement account proceeds) or passing to a surviving joint owner are not part of a deceased person's probate estate and therefore are not subject to intestacy rules (Giarmarco, 2006; Quinn, 2007). Instead, such nonprobate assets generally are transferred in a manner consistent with basic contract principles of law. When unmarried couples do not utilize estate planning, they in particular risk abdicating considerable control and autonomy to third parties by relying on most states' default laws for such matters as burial wishes and priority among persons to act as guardians, conservators, health care patient advocates, and estate executors (Giarmarco).

When a person in the United States dies without a will, the state where the deceased person was a resident (and where he or she owned real property) steps in. It designates who takes or inherits the person's probate property, in what order, and how much each family beneficiary or creditor receives (Cahn, 2004; Wendel, 2005). Although the details of each state's intestate provisions vary greatly between jurisdictions, the hierarchical order of beneficiaries essentially is the same (Wendel). The surviving spouse, if any, takes first priority. If the deceased person has surviving biological or adopted children or offspring of any degree, the offspring either directly inherit their respective shares along with the surviving spouse, or, after the surviving spouse receives an initial lump-sum amount, the estate balance then is divided between the spouse and offspring (Andersen, 2003; Wendel). A deceased person's legal offspring or progeny are called the *decedent's issue* and includes any children, grandchildren, and other direct descendants.

Establishing a legally recognized parent-child relationship is a prerequisite for a person to qualify as an offspring entitled to an inheritance. Traditionally, probate law has recognized two methods of establishing a parent-child relationship: (1) naturally, via shared biological, genetic material at birth (the predominant approach), or (2) artificially, via legal adoption (Wendel, 2005). Regardless of the parents' marital status, a child can inherit from and through his or her natural or adopted parents, and each parent can inherit from and through the child (Cahn, 2004). As a corollary, terminating parent-child relationships usually includes complete severance of inheritance rights between the child and natural parent(s). The legal significance of a parent-child relationship applies in both directions. Thus, if neither a spouse nor legal offspring survives a deceased person, then states' intestacy schemes designate the nearest degree of maternal and paternal relatives who are qualified to inherit (Wendel, 2005). Traditionally and as a default rule still in most state jurisdictions, unadopted stepchildren are not able to inherit from or through their stepparents (Cahn, 2004). Even stepparents who make a will may be limited by other inheritance laws that guarantee a share of the estate for a surviving spouse or legal offspring (Mahoney, 1997).

STATE VERSUS FEDERAL FAMILY LAW POLICIES AND THE STEPPARENT-STEPCHILD DERIVATIVE MODEL

Both federal and state law set policies that influence stepfamilies. State law governs traditional probate and family law matters regarding marriage, divorce, adoption, and inheritance, while federal law covers a wide range of general welfare benefits and programs that affect the lives of most people, including stepfamily members (Mason, 1998). Overall, state and federal policies clash in their treatment of stepfamilies, based on two competing models and differing policy goals and interests. State policies usually follow a *stranger model*, treating residential stepparents as legal strangers to their stepchildren, with no rights or duties during or after marriage. Federal policies often reflect a *dependency model*, assuming residential stepparents in fact are supporting their stepchildren; accordingly, such policies limit welfare benefits that stepchildren otherwise would be eligible to receive (Malia, 2005; Mason, 1998).

State Policies Assume Stepparents Are Strangers

The rights and responsibilities of stepparents vis-à-vis their stepchildren are a key policy issue for intact stepfamilies (Fine, 1997). A residential stepparent in the United States generally has fewer rights than does a legal guardian or foster parent (Mason, 1998). Even if the custodial parent wishes to grant his or her spouse authority to act on the child's behalf, a stepparent cannot validly sign permission slips or make decisions that can be honored, for instance, by schools or medical personnel (e.g., about a child's class field trip participation or medical treatment) unless authorized by legal documentation (Chambers, 1990; Skinner & Kohler, 2002). Additionally, depending on the jurisdiction and situation, state laws determine whether stepchildren are eligible for benefits connected to their stepparent (such as workers' compensation; Ramsey & Abrams, 2001) and stepparents' responsibilities relative to any damage that may be caused by their stepchildren. Thus, the law is mixed regarding the primacy of biological ties. However, stepparents' preferences and rights remain subordinate to even noncustodial legal parents' (Fine, 1997; Malia, 2005).

Federal Policies Assume Stepchildren Are Dependents

In contrast to most state policies that tend to delimit stepparents' rights and guard the rights of biological parents, U.S. federal policy recognizes the presence of a residential stepparent relative to stepchildren's eligibility for a wide variety of benefits available to dependent children (Duran-Aydintug & Ihinger-Tallman, 1995; Mason, 1998). Stepchildren may be considered stepparents' dependents for income tax purposes as well as employee benefits guidelines (e.g., health insurance) and for such programs as Temporary Assistance to Needy Families and Social Security (Mason) and Higher Education Resources and Student Assistance (Mahoney, 1997). Thus, federal and state approaches differ greatly because of divergent policy purposes, goals, and scope. Federal social welfare regulations focus on general family needs and trends, recognizing and assuming that many stepparents voluntarily provide financial support (Fine, 1997; Mahoney, 1997) and thus help conserve government resources by limiting and reallocating benefits eligibility (Malia, 2005).

DE FACTO PARENT OR IN LOCO PARENTIS DOCTRINE

State courts developed the common law doctrine of *in loco parentis* ("in the place of a parent"; also known as a *functional, psychological*, or *de facto parent* or a *parent by estoppel*) to resolve the issue of when parental rights and obligations should be imposed (Gary, 2000; Skinner & Kohler, 2002). A stepparent serving as a de facto parent is someone who has voluntarily and willingly taken on the role of the biological parent in a child's life (Skinner & Kohler, 2002), commonly evidenced by a shared residence and significant caretaking role (Romesberg, 1999). A de facto parent basically has the same rights and responsibilities as the biological parents (Fine, 1997). For instance, de facto parents can physically discipline their stepchildren, but they also are subject to the same physical and sexual abuse legal prohibitions (Fine, 1997). De facto or in loco parentis status is not automatic; it is determined by the stepparent's intent. Such intent could be stated explicitly, or it could result implicitly from an action of assuming parental duties, such as providing substantial financial support or taking over custodial responsibilities (Skinner & Kohler, 2002).

De facto parent status, however, generally is not based on the actual quality of the stepparent-stepchild relationship, and stepparents may terminate their in loco parentis role (prior to a related legal suit) at their discretion, even though there might have been promises to provide future support (Mahoney, 1997; Malia, 2005). The de facto parent doctrine is similar in style and effect to the rights created by common-law marriages, a now defunct doctrine in the United States (Romesberg, 1999). Both doctrines judicially establish binding familial relationships (complete with inheritance rights) without a formal, state-sanctioned procedure. Ultimately, though, such traditional theories do not provide satisfactory results because courts may manipulate common law precedent, resulting in inconsistent and uncertain family responsibilities and rights (Romesberg, 1999).

FINANCIAL SUPPORT OBLIGATIONS

In most states, stepparents are not required to financially support their spouse's children, although most voluntarily choose to provide contributions

(Fine, 1997; Mahoney, 1997). In contrast, with or without marriage, all biological parents are obligated by statute and legal precedent to adequately support their children (Ramsey & Abrams, 2001), including in Louisiana, where a stepfather also may have a recognized parental role (Romesberg, 1999). Only a few states (e.g., Missouri) have enacted statutes that specifically impose on stepparents a child support obligation, but this duty ends if the child does not reside with the stepparent or the marriage ends (Malia, 2005). Other state courts sometimes rely on the de facto parent doctrine to impose subsequent responsibility on stepparents to support their stepchildren (Hans, 2002; Skinner & Kohler, 2002), particularly if a child otherwise would be dependent on state support (Gary, 2000). Thus, with regard to financial obligations, there are some exceptions to the *parenthood as an exclusive status* rule in that states may allow more than two adults to hold parental status for the purpose of imposing a duty to support. Yet the logistics of enforcing financial obligations of stepparents as well as the implications of such an expanded parental status in the United States remain unclear (Malia, 2005; Ramsey & Abrams, 2001).

Derivative Relationships Model

In general, then, if death or divorce severs marital ties between a child's legal parent and stepparent, state common law and statutes nearly uniformly abolish any vague legal connection between the stepparent and his or her stepchild (Mahoney, 1997; Skinner & Kohler, 2002). This is despite some exclusions to the exclusive parent rule with de facto parent status and support obligations. Most American lawmakers perceive stepparent-stepchild relationships as based on a *derivative relationships model*; that is, step relationships exist only as long as the marriage lasts and do not need to be protected. Critics argue that the derivative model ignores various and complex relationships, expectations, and emotions involved with stepfamilies (Malia, 2005; Skinner & Kohler, 2002). Such a legal assumption can have serious financial and emotional impact on stepchildren when they are not eligible to receive support or other benefits or suddenly have limited or no contact with a close stepparent in the event of marital dissolution. If stepparents have not adopted their stepchildren, the stepparents usually have to rely on the biological parents' consent to have continued access to their stepchildren (Hans, 2002). Additionally, in the event of the death of a stepparent, many jurisdictions disallow a stepchild not only intestate inheritance rights but also the right to bring a negligence suit for the accidental death of a stepparent (Mason, 1998; Skinner & Kohler, 2002). Step relationship quality and potentially close emotional ties are considered irrelevant.

LOSSES ASSOCIATED WITH DEATH OR DIVORCE OF PARENTS IN STEPFAMILIES

Divorce or death of a biological parent in a stepfamily poses certain risks for children who were under their care. Financial risks dominate, apart from the evident emotional and psychological losses associated with death or divorce (Malia, 2005). As previously noted, stepparents in the United States are not legally obligated to financially support stepchildren after their marriage to the child's legal parent ends. This general rule holds even for the few states that require stepparents to support residential stepchildren during the marriage (Fine, 1997). The risks associated with severed financial and emotional ties and loss of contact with the stepparent are not fully understood but probably are important, especially for families that have developed close stepparent-stepchild bonds. The potential loss of a stepparent either through divorce or in addition to the death of the biological custodial parent could be devastating for children, particularly in instances where they do not have contact or support with a nonresidential biological parent (Malia, 2005). In recognition of such family situations, all states now have provisions that allow third parties, such as stepparents, to petition for visitation rights. In contrast, though, only about half of the states have passed legislation that permits a third party to file for legal and physical custody (Hans, 2002; Skinner & Kohler, 2002). Despite third-party statutes, however, many stepparents who wish to maintain contact with their stepchildren have difficulty establishing the legal right (standing) to even bring their visitation or custody requests to court, much less have their requests granted (Levine, 1996; Malia, 2005).

VISITATION AND CUSTODY ISSUES

U.S. state courts typically follow a three-step process with stepparents' visitation or custody requests (Hans, 2002; Malia, 2005). The stepparent must (1) establish that he or she has *standing*, or a legal right to bring his or her petition before the court (through a third-party statute or showing of de facto parent status); (2) defeat the legal preference given to biological and adoptive parents (i.e., show a compelling reason, such as potential harm to the child or that a child protection agency has established the legal parent to be unfit); and (3) present evidence that satisfies the *child's best interests standard* (e.g., demonstrate that the stepparent provides such things as a good, healthy environment, stability, and continuity for the child and that the child wishes to be with him or her). Although the process of attaining a custody or visitation court decision is relatively clear, the criteria courts use to make decisions at each stage remain ambiguous and largely left to each judge's discretion (Hans, 2002; Malia, 2005).

In the case of divorce, custody almost always goes to the biological parent rather than a stepparent (Skinner & Kohler, 2002). Courts prefer to defer to the legal parent's right to decide who can associate with his or her child, but stepparents' visitation requests are subject to a case-by-case weighing process based on the child's best interests standard (Ramsey & Abrams, 2001). In the event of the residential biological parent's death, state courts usually grant custody to the noncustodial biological parent, even if the stepparent-stepchild relationship is of longer standing and close, once again reflecting the legal primacy of biological parenthood (Skinner & Kohler, 2002). Thus, stepparents must demonstrate extraordinary circumstances to be granted custody of stepchildren. They must prove their parental fitness, the other parent's unfitness, and that placement with them (the stepparent) is in the best interest of the child (Ramsey & Abrams, 2001). Visitation rights are a simpler matter for the courts than custody disputes because visitation requests overall are less intrusive on parental authority and therefore are more likely to be granted than custody requests (Hans, 2002; Malia, 2005).

In summary, although U.S. federal and state policies differ in their underlying assumptions about stepfamily functioning, stepparents legally remain quasi-strangers to their stepchildren with potential support obligations and few, if any, rights. Family law protocol, however, may be irrelevant if biological parents and stepparents are able to reach consensual private agreements and do some estate planning.

ESTATE PLANNING AND CONTRACTING: AVAILABLE OPTIONS BUT WITH COSTS

By operation of law in the United States, binding marital support obligations and property rights generally devolve upon the spouses at the time of marriage (Gregory et al., 2001), similar to establishing parent-child relationships through childbirth or adoption. Married and cohabiting stepfamilies in the United States may utilize private contractual marital agreements and estate planning devices to expand, modify, or waive their family and property rights and duties, including clarifying support, child visitation and custody, and inheritance arrangements (Gregory et al., 2001; Mahoney, 1997). See Malia (2007a, 2007b) for concrete suggestions applicable to stepfamilies regarding marital contracting and estate planning within current legal limitations. Stepfamilies, in any case, are strongly encouraged to put negotiated agreements in writing (Malia, 2005) to clarify expectations and minimize future disputes.

Private Autonomy and Its Costs

Estate plans and marital agreements empower parties to privately control and negotiate, at their convenience, many important aspects of their own marriage and family (Gregory et al., 2001). The emphasis on contractual freedom in the United States reflects and advances core American values of privacy, individual autonomy, and self-reliance. For instance, legal commentators have observed that "the preferences of legislators, judges, bureaucrats, experts, and academics, with all their sundry biases and subjectivities, must be compared with the flawed self-understandings and preferences of individuals attempting to determine their life plans for themselves" (Trebilcock & Keshvani, 1991, p. 590), ultimately favoring private contractual ordering of marriage and divorce despite its inevitable deficiencies. Private agreements allow some ongoing flexibility. Contractual agreements can be modified or terminated at any time with the consent of both parties (Mahoney, 1997). Most estate planning tools also may be modified or revoked at any time (using set procedures) by the grantor or creator.

Nonetheless, certain disadvantages and risks are associated with relying principally on contractual methods to establish legally enforceable rights and duties in stepfamilies. First, marital agreement and estate plan preparation can be a lengthy and expensive process when professional expertise (prudently) is employed. Thus, it is not a feasible option for many stepfamilies who otherwise would benefit if they were able to clarify relational expectations. Estate plans also should be reviewed regularly and updated in response to changed personal circumstances, requiring further time and money, not to mention methodical follow-through. Second, if disputes arise that fall outside of family and probate law provisions (e.g., stepparents contracting to support stepchildren), only contract remedies will be available and may require even more time and cost to establish and resolve a claim (Mahoney, 1997). In any case, if a stepfamily ends through divorce or death, step relationships clearly receive little legal protection.

Third, private agreements concerning minor children are subject to court approval (Gregory et al., 2001) and thus retain inherent uncertainty. Although legal parents' wishes for their children carry considerable weight in court, children's welfare always takes priority, and nonbinding support, visitation, and custody agreements must be judicially evaluated according to the child's best interests standard (Mahoney, 1997; Malia, 2005). In general, judicial interpretation and discretion are risk factors in any court proceeding.

Fourth and finally, contractual agreements customarily overemphasize economic and obligation issues rather than validating or enhancing noneconomic marriage benefits and legal family roles and rights. Public interests and the greater good may suffer because, although private approaches may clarify a stepparent's role in certain individual cases, they do not help legitimize or institute consistent expectations for residential and nonresidential stepfamily members (Malia, 2005).

Through stepchild adoption, however, stepparents formally and publicly can acquire full parental rights and duties from a terminated legal parent. This option is discussed at length in the next section.

STEPPARENT TRANSFORMATION INTO PARENT VIA STEPCHILD ADOPTION

Although private contractual arrangements are one path to solidify stepparents' rights and obligations, stepchild adoption to date is the most reliable way to resolve legal ambiguities regarding the stepparent's role and establish a permanent legal relationship between a stepparent and stepchild (Chambers, 1990; Mason, 1998). The number of adoptions in the United States has approximated 130,000 per year, and more than half involve children adopted by stepparents or other relatives (Mahoney, 1999). The majority stepchild adoption rule is consistent with the traditional stranger adoption "fresh start" paradigm, except that parent-child ties are completely severed with only one biological parent rather than both (Wendel, 2005). Prior to a stepchild adoption, under established adoption law principles, the legal status of the noncustodial parent (who again is usually the biological father) must be terminated by either voluntary consent or court order (by being declared unfit). The legal status of parent, with its corresponding rights and duties, then is transferred fully to the adoptive stepparent (Mahoney, 1999). Consequently, adoptive stepparents—now parents—are not likely to identify themselves as stepparents (Ganong et al., 1998).

Empirical research is scarce regarding the impact of variations in state adoption laws and the issues and concerns that stepfamilies consider before stepchild adoption (Ganong et al., 1998). Research that does exist focuses almost exclusively on stepfather-stepchild adoptions (Malia, 2005). Wolf and Mast (1987) and Ganong et al. (1998) explored factors that stepfamily members consider when contemplating adoption. Wolf and Mast interviewed 55 couples where the stepparent (only two were stepmothers) adopted a stepchild. Ganong et al. interviewed 32 residential parents and stepparents and 22 children (ages 10 to 19) from 16 stepfamilies; 14 were stepfather-mother households, and two were complex households in which both adults were stepparents to residential children. Common motives identified in the studies for stepchild adoptions included (a) creating family unity; (b) desiring to be a "regular" (nuclear) family; (c) sharing a surname; (d) legitimizing family roles, support relationships, or a good stepparent-stepchild relationship; and (e) severing ties from the noncustodial parent. Interestingly, Ganong et al. found that only one family they interviewed had adopted a stepchild. Relevant identified barriers to stepchild adoption included (a) an actively involved nonresidential parent, (b) anticipated hostile legal proceedings and angry interactions over requests to surrender parental rights, (c) financial concerns, and (d) not wanting continuing obligations and ties if the remarriage ended in divorce. And, although Wolf and Mast identified transferring legal rights to stepparents as an adoption motive for postadoption stepfamilies, the lack of legal ties between stepfamily members was not a key adoption motive identified by most pre- or nonadoptive stepfamilies interviewed by Ganong et al.

Edwards et al. (1999) interviewed British residential and nonresidential parents as well as stepparents (46 participants in total) and found complex and ambivalent tensions between two main themes, both of which can be seen as being in American as well as British children's best interests: (1) Children need biological parents, and (2) children need social families. Middle-class respondents were the most comfortable with and advocated for children needing coparenting biological parents. Working-class respondents, in contrast, were more concerned with children needing social families, contending that the two (biological and step) residential parental figures in a child's household should take precedence—akin to (re)creating a hybrid nuclear family home (Wendel, 2005). Most respondents concurred that stepparents need some form of legal status but preferably without disempowering the nonresidential parent (Edwards et al., 1999). Relationship quality and extensive time spent together were seen as legitimate justifications for formalizing the connection between a residential stepparent and stepchild. Respondents were split equally among recommending (a) traditional adoption (full rights and duties transferred), (b) establishing parental responsibility (shared rights and duties among multiple parents), and (c) recommending both approaches as options (Edwards et al., 1999; Malia, 2005).

Finally, Marsiglio (2004) explored through in-depth interviews 25 married and 11 informal stepfathers' experiences with claiming stepchildren as their own. Only five married participants had legally adopted their stepchildren, but a few others were considering doing so. Marsiglio's analyses revealed several salient properties and conditions that may influence stepfathers' perceptions of stepchildren and the claiming process as well as efforts to develop a sense of "we-ness" (group belonging) and a fatherlike identity (Malia, 2005). Most relevant here were (a) the properties of solo-versus shared-father identity as well as seeking public recognition and (b) the condition of whether the biological father was present and involved in the child's life. For most of these participants, the biological father was only peripherally, if at all, involved with the child. Yet, some stepfathers developed a shared-father identity. These stepfathers felt as if they had claimed a child even though the child's father was actively involved, and they sometimes served as ally to the biological father, facilitating access and a positive relationship between father and child. At the same time, the participants expressed the importance to them of being acknowledged as a legitimate father figure by community members and the law (Marsiglio, 2004).

OPEN AND THIRD-PARENT ADOPTIONS

Some states in the United States recognize *open, incomplete,* or *cooperative adoptions,* allowing certain legal ties, under extraordinary circumstances, to remain unsevered between adopted children and their former family of origin (Mahoney, 1999; Wriggins, 2000). Open adoptions are similar to France's *simple* (versus *plenary*) *adoptions* (see Mignot, this volume). In response to various legal commentators and courts advocating for more flexible options to encourage and facilitate stepchild adoptions (Mahoney, 1999), a growing minority of states have established special *stepparent adoption* exceptions (Wendel, 2005). These special rules create the possibility of enforceable postadoption visitation rights for the former noncustodial parent or extended family, such as grandparents and siblings (Mahoney, 1999). In addition, a child adopted by a stepparent effectively has three parents from whom she or he can inherit (Wendel, 2005). That is, the stepparent adoption exception inheritance provision provides that the biological parent-child relationship is only partially severed so that—unlike in the classic adoption scenario—the child can inherit from and through the "former" parent (although not the other way around). Full parental and inheritance rights between the child and stepparent still are established, and the parental and inheritance rights between the child and the biological parent married to the adoptive stepparent are not affected (Uniform Probate Code Art. 2 §114(b), Comment revised in 1993).

Wendel (2005) also discussed *de facto stepparent adoptions*, what he referred to as *step-partner adoptions*, a similar trend recognized in a minority of jurisdictions that has expanded the definition of stepparent to permit legal standing to petition for adoption for unmarried stepparents or *second parents*, that is, qualified partners who are not, or are no longer, married to a custodial parent (Comment to 1994 Uniform Adoption Act Art. 4 §102). However, the progressive three-parent inheritance provision for stepparent adoptions is not extended to de facto stepparents, leading to inequitable and, arguably, unconstitutionally discriminatory results. Wendel outlined parallel public policy justifications for both stepparent and de facto stepparent adoptions to not completely sever children's parental relationships with their biological parents. Arguments include, first, that extending enhanced three-parent inheritance rights is in the best interest of dependent children, whether in a stepfamily or cohabiting family. Second, although the former parent has waived his or her right to inherit from and through a child by consenting to an adoption, the child has no legal say in a stepparent or de facto stepparent adoption, and thus it would be inequitable to terminate the child's inheritance rights. Third, children in both scenarios likely have established, long-term connections with the parent to be legally displaced and his or her relatives.

With respect to inheritance laws, therefore, the stepparent adoption rule discriminates against children adopted by de facto stepparents (Wendel, 2005). The distinction made appears to be illogical and unjust, and, arguably, the states should extend the three-parent inheritance rights rule to children adopted by de facto stepparents. Similarly situated children should be treated equitably under the Equal Protection Clause of the 14th Amendment (Wendel, 2005). Further, the U.S. Supreme Court clearly has held that it is unconstitutional to discriminate against illegitimate children—to punish children for what are perceived to be the sins of unmarried (or gay or lesbian) parents—as a means of trying to influence the conduct of their parents. Wendel contended that stepparent and de facto stepparent adoptions constitute *third-parent adoptions* and that consistent third-parent adoption rule provisions should be defined and applied, effectively expanding the exclusive status of legal parenthood akin to open adoptions.

In sum, the stepfamily adoption-related studies outlined here support the value of having all U.S. state jurisdictions, not just the extant minority, permit open and third-parent adoptions (Wendel, 2005). The findings demonstrate (a) the diverse, complex range of existing stepfamily circumstances and (b) that important concerns for stepfamily members include legally legitimizing stepparent-stepchild bonds as well as allowing children to be able to maintain a meaningful relationship with both biological parents. However, just as with private contracting and estate planning, the legal adoption process generally requires a significant amount of time, effort, and money from families. Therefore, adoption may not always be feasible for stepfamilies.

THE IMPORTANCE OF FOSTERING MULTIPLE PARENTAL RELATIONSHIPS

It is well understood that children need to experience secure attachments for optimal development (Kelly & Lamb, 2000). The importance of continuity and stability in children's lives following the divorce of their biological parents or a parent and stepparent is well documented in the literature (Amato, 2000). Stability can be created in different ways: (a) regular contact with residential and nonresidential caregivers, (b) regular schedules or predictable routines and separations, (c) living in one geographic location (although children can and do adapt to more than one household), (d) consistent and appropriate care and discipline, and (e) affection and acceptance from caregivers (Kelly & Lamb, 2000). During custody disputes, children often are solicited about which parent they prefer to live with. Although this grants children some autonomy and power over their living situations, such responsibility commonly is neither appreciated nor age-appropriate (Malia, 2005). Children frequently experience loyalty conflicts between separated or divorced parents (Edwards et al., 1999) and do not need the burden of having to choose one over the other (Trinder, 1997). However, they do benefit measurably from being consulted about living arrangements. Substantial research supports the notion that, ultimately, maintaining meaningful relationships with both parents is a critical factor in children's adjustment to divorce (Amato, 2000; Opie, 1993) and in maximizing children's psychological well-being (Kelly & Lamb, 2000; Malia, 2005).

Children's long-term interests may be hindered if a biological parent's rights have been terminated voluntarily, for example, to end an unwed father's potential duty of support or to permit stepchild adoption (Mahoney, 1997; Ramsey & Abrams, 2001). This may be true even in the rare cases when the parent was found legally unfit (Eagle, 1994). It can be important to allow for the possibility that children eventually may establish an attachment with a noncustodial parent later in life, even if at first they may be uninterested in a relationship with a parent with whom they have had little contact or scarcely know. For instance, Edwards et al. (1999) found that some noncustodial fathers' perceptions over time shifted to recognize the importance of their relationships with their children in ways that they had not considered while still married to the children's mother and sharing a household. So, for various reasons, even though it may be in a stepchild's best interests to remain in the custody of or be adopted by a stepparent, it may not be in the child's best interests to sever all ties to the biological parent (Trinder, 1997; Woodhouse, 1994). Even in cases where relationships with all biological and nonbiological parents are inappropriate or unimportant at an early stage of a child's life, fostering relationships with multiple parents may be meaningful and important for the child at a later stage of life (Eagle, 1994; Woodhouse, 1994).

Residential stepfathers often make substantial contributions to family household income, helping to cover basic living costs and improving their stepchildren's material well-being (Edwards et al., 1999; Fine, 1997; Mason, 1998). For instance, incomes of stepfamilies tend to be 3 to 4 times greater than incomes of single mothers (Mason). Anderson, Kaplan, and Lancaster (2001) found that differences were smaller among blended families than across families when comparing paternal financial expenditures for step- and biological children. However, stepparents usually are characterized as providing custodial biological parents with discretionary, secondary financial assistance, and, although such support is expected (Ganong, Coleman, & Mistina, 1995), typically it is not an enforceable legal duty. Many noncustodial biological fathers have residential (step)children whom they support (Hofferth & Anderson, 2003), and they may feel financially stretched by the burden of contributing to two households, especially if the custodial mother of their biological children has remarried (Mason, 1998). These findings seem consistent with the argument that obligations "embedded in social parenthood may be more extensive and durable than those of natural parenthood" (Edwards et al., 1999, p. 87). Overall, existing research indicates that stepfathers do share economic resources with their stepchildren and contribute to the stepfamily's economic viability. Policy reforms legitimizing these discretionary functions would further enhance support possibilities by reinforcing the value of stepfathers' contributions (Malia, 2005).

Although not all stepparents develop close relationships with their stepchildren, many provide needed care and stability for them (Hofferth & Anderson, 2003; White & Gilbreth, 2001). With the goal of fostering stepchildren's well-being, even weak emotional attachments cannot be discounted when stepparents provide economic and other forms of adult support (Mason, 1998). Nonbiological caregivers can form close emotional relationships with children in their care that are similar to those of biological parent-child family ties (Coleman & Ganong, 1990; Rossi & Rossi, 1990). Some research findings suggest that noncustodial fathers also might not feel able to justify continued relationships with their children merely on the basis of biological links, instead seeing time together, affinity efforts, and relationship quality as justifying ongoing ties (Edwards et al., 1999; Malia, 2005).

White and Gilbreth (2001) studied stepchildren's relationships with both biological fathers and stepfathers. They found support for the *accumulation model* that maintains that both fathers often play an active and important role in (step)children's lives. They also found a significant positive association between quality of relationship with stepfathers and child outcomes (see also Pryor, this volume). Grotevant, Ross, Marchel, and McRoy (1999) found that multiple parents cooperating in open adoption family networks can enhance children's socioemotional well-being. Stepparents may act as key mediators in stepfamilies (Walker, 1992), and biological and nonbiological parents can, and sometimes do, work collaboratively for the children's best interests (Grotevant et al., 1999; Marsiglio, 2004). Additional evidence that children can accumulate fathers was found by Hofferth and Anderson (2003) when they examined the engagement, availability, participation, and warmth of (step)fathers with their residential (step)children in unmarried, cohabiting, and married families. The authors reported that marriage, rather than biological ties, differentiated and increased levels of paternal involvement and investment, as did younger age of a child and lack of additional financial obligation to any nonresidential children.

This body of research supports the contention that stepfamily members generally will benefit from policy reforms facilitating multiple, secure parental relationships for (step)children. Such progressive reforms could help foster children's emotional and psychological well-being, as well as their financial security, reducing reliance on state welfare (all legitimate governmental interests) by codifying present discretionary stepparent contributions and endorsing further stepparent-stepchild involvement. At the same time, reforms need to avoid discouraging nonresidential parental investment (Malia, 2005; Romesberg, 1999). Evidence from stepparents and both residential and nonresidential parents suggests that stepfamilies recognize the legal and family tensions involved in trying to establish constructive stepparenting and coparenting roles within the present limited legal family framework. However, further research is needed to clarify (a) stepfamily members' perspectives on existing and prospective federal and state policies affecting stepfamilies and (b) the ramifications of legal reforms that would more consistently acknowledge or invasively regulate step relationships (Malia, 2005).

In sum, maintaining multiple parental relationships in stepfamilies has been associated with better child outcomes (White & Gilbreth, 2001; Pryor, this volume). Stepparents can play an important role in parenting and financially supporting their stepchildren (Fine, 1997; Rossi & Rossi, 1990), particularly in the context of the tendency for contact between children and their noncustodial parents (typically fathers) to diminish over time (Amato, 2000; Mason, 1998; Thompson & Amato, 1999). On the other hand, many noncustodial parents do maintain contact with their children, at least to some degree, through the years (Thompson & Amato, 1999), and children usually experience a substantial loss when they are cut off from a parent (Woodhouse, 1994). Step relationships vary greatly in complex, dynamic ways. However, Fine (1997) has argued that empirical evidence supports the importance of clarifying the stepparent role to facilitate resource sharing, relationship investment, and family adjustment for stepfamily members. Stepparent-stepchild role ambiguity and lack of agreed understanding of stepparenting roles and responsibilities often exacerbate problems between stepparents and stepchildren (De'Ath, 1997; Ganong & Coleman, 1997). Recognizing a legitimate role for each parental figure in a child's life could help minimize loyalty conflicts and normalize stepfamily experiences for children as well as validate the unique, key parental contributions made by step- and biological parents (Malia, 2005).

DIVERSE LEGAL AND SOCIAL SCIENCE STEPFAMILY POLICY PROPOSALS

Laws and public policies help define and shape the concepts of social normalcy and deviancy (De'Ath, 1997). Thus, it is particularly significant that stepparents' interests and roles historically have been virtually ignored in U.S. family and probate law, despite the prevalence of stepparents (Malia, 2005). Stepfamily formation creates dynamic, complex familial structures, often encompassing more than two parents, a phenomenon that conventional policy makers are not well versed in addressing (Mason, 1998). The lack of consistent, accepted societal parenting expectations for stepfamilies and the obstacles confronting stepparents have prompted legal and social science scholars to advocate for policy reforms clarifying stepparent rights and responsibilities (Malia, 2005; Skinner & Kohler, 2002).

LEGAL VERSUS SOCIAL SCIENCE REFORMS

Malia (2005) has summarized selected stepparent family policy proposals made by legal commentators and family scholars, categorized according to (a) advocacy goals and assumptions, (b) legal status and parenting authority, (c) financial support obligations, (d) shared parenting and stepchild adoption, (e) visitation and access, and (f) custody. As a general trend, relevant public policy reforms that have been proposed by *legal scholars* remain within established legal precedent but try to strike a better balance between strict guidelines (too limiting or invasive) and broad judicial discretion (too unpredictable). Although such a conservative approach may result in more realistically enforceable policy changes that are less likely to be constitutionally challenged, it also limits creative innovations that can reflect complex, real-world family experiences and needs (Malia, 2005). Most legal reform proposals (e.g., Bartlett, 1999; Chambers, 1990; Goldstein, 1995; Mahoney, 1997, 2005) focus on establishing consistent criteria for limiting or extending stepparent financial support obligations as well as strengthening de facto parent standing, with the intent that courts will more seriously consider stepparent visitation or custody requests as being in stepchildren's best interests.

Overall, proposals by *social science researchers* are more likely to advocate for using a normative-adaptive perspective on stepfamily functioning (Ganong & Coleman, 1997) to push the law well beyond its existing limits (Malia, 2005). Even though Popenoe (1994), a proponent of the sociobiological family perspective, has argued to the contrary and contends that stepfamilies should be actively discouraged, most social science reform proposals (e.g., Ganong et al., 1998; Kavanagh, 2004; Mason, 1998; Skinner & Kohler, 2002) are consistent with the approach taken in this chapter and assume that validating stepfamilies as an authentic institutionalized family form is a worthy policy goal. Thus, recommendations emerging from this perspective emphasize that stepparent rights should match obligations and that the exclusive parenthood doctrine should be expanded to legally recognize multiple parents in order to minimize unwarranted loss for children (Malia, 2005). In addition to policy proposals and issues incorporated elsewhere in this chapter, two divergent examples are highlighted here.

First, Mason et al. (2002) have argued for (a) expanding the legal definition of family to encompass step relationships and (b) restricting judicial discretion to encourage more predictable results. The authors contended that the common law *de facto parent* doctrine should be fully established in the United States as a new parental category for (married) stepparents and other similar caregivers. De facto parents would be empowered as an additional parent with clearly delineated rights and responsibilities, while not invalidating any existing rights and duties of biological parents. For federal and state policy purposes, a stepparent would be treated essentially the same as the biological parent while married, with the same rights, duties, and presumptions in relation to his or her stepchildren, including a support obligation. In the case of divorce or death of either the biological or de facto parent, these rights and duties would continue in some form, depending on length of the marriage (Mason et al., 2002). In the event of divorce, the step-parent could be obligated for child support (including medical and other benefits) for a limited duration, perhaps half the length of the marriage. A de facto parent would have standing to seek not only visitation but also custody when a marriage ends due to divorce or the biological parent's death. On the death of a stepparent, minor dependent stepchildren—but, the authors argued, not necessarily independent adult stepchildren—would be treated identically to biological children for purposes of inheritance and benefits. Finally, because the de facto parent category could extend beyond married stepparents to other classes of parental figures (such as cohabiting partners), and a lack of legal ties may represent varying levels of long-term commitment, consent by a biological parent and an application process may be appropriate to establish de facto parent status (Mason et al., 2002).

In contrast, Brashier (2005) has provided a cautionary perspective, arguing for probate law to (a) restrict the unduly optimistic and broad default definition of a deceased person's family for inheritance purposes and (b) increase authorized judicial discretion for case-by-case analyses of available evidence regarding the appropriate degree of membership inclusiveness for a particular individual's biological and social family. The author aptly pointed out that policy debates have concentrated on spouse-like and parent-child relationships and neglected the changing relationships among other family members in blended stepfamilies, such as those among step- and half-siblings. Brashier focused on a default rule in most states that entitles surviving half-blood relatives to share equally with whole-blood relatives in an intestate estate. He contended that an increasing number of individuals who have only one common parent or ancestor between them may have no social or emotional ties and may not even be aware of each other's existence. "Consanguinity alone does not truly make them a family" (p. 140) and is inadequate as the sole criterion for determining inheritance shares. Brashier asserted that criticisms of the default rule are not based on antiquated notions of half-blood relatives being somehow inferior to whole-blood relatives. Rather, such bright-line rules or all-or-nothing approaches lead to unjustifiable results and ignore a central truth: that modern family ties and relationships along half-blood lines run the gamut. Although admittedly not a perfect solution, Brashier recommended that states instead should invest probate courts with generous discretion in determining the intestate shares of half-blood survivors. Evaluations for limited inclusion would be based primarily on objective factors (because a deceased person's intentions and definition of family clearly cannot be directly verified) evidencing a "shared upbringing" of half-blood siblings during significant portions of childhood or, perhaps alternatively, "significant family interaction" over time with the deceased person (p. 193).

Brashier (2005) illustrated the position that, due to the complexity and variability of step- and biological family ties, some degree of fluidity in family and probate law must be maintained. Bright-line rules run the risk of being overly broad and unfairly penalizing certain individuals and relationships (Knaplund, 2006). Thus, multiple, interested perspectives should be sought and considered to develop credible policy reform proposals and minimize unjustifiable results. However, the extensive fact-finding costs of case-by-case probate inquiries advocated by Brashier as the solution likely would outweigh potential benefits produced for particular deceased persons and their heirs. In contrast, the de facto parent category plan proposed by Mason et al. (2002) includes comparatively objective family and probate rules that are likely to promote impartial, evenhanded treatment of (step)families and predictable consistency in implementation. Mason et al.'s framework does not hold that stepfamilies and intact nuclear families are indistinguishable. Rather, it is designed to avoid undermining biological family ties while legally expanding and legitimizing prevalent stepfamily roles. The proposal in total is not unreasonable or overly broad, but, as with any policy change, unforeseen complications or individual case injustices may result. Additionally, an expansion of parental rights could result in increased demands for access to the courts (Romesberg, 1999). On the other hand, Mason et al. implied that no special legal paperwork or court involvement would necessarily be required to establish de facto parent status or its attached rights and duties, unless a stepfamily was severed by death or divorce or an unmarried parental figure sought to apply for the status.

Another key issue to clarify is whether, and by what objective criteria, nonresidential stepparents or those who nominally, if ever, interact with their stepchildren should and would be considered de facto parents. Perhaps application procedures similar to Great Britain's Children Act of 1989 (Edwards et al., 1999; Walker, 1992) for establishing residence orders (for stepparents to assume and share parental rights and duties with biological parents) may be adapted and used in the United States (Edwards et al., 1999; Fine, 1997; Walker, 1992).

In essence, the de facto parent category policy reforms would establish as the default standard a more inclusive notion of family and shared responsibility. Stepfamilies for which these default provisions are improper or undesirable then may choose "opt-out" legal options to modify obligations or otherwise delineate a person's intentions, interests, and wishes. Prenuptial agreements, wills, and other estate planning documents could be utilized to partially exclude or completely disinherit certain stepfamily members, just as individuals may do now with legal biological relatives. The tangible and intangible costs associated with traditionally clarifying stepfamily roles, which often are prohibitive for middle- and working-class Americans, thus would be minimized. The impetus instead would be on individuals to modify or limit their obligations. Often such persons should employ estate planning in any case because of disparate financial accountability or substantial joint family or separate property interests.

CLOSING THOUGHTS

As diverse, conflicting stepfamily policy proposals continue to be articulated across the United States, family scholars and practitioners advisably might take an active role in stepfamily legislative policy making to ensure that judicial guidelines and legislative measures are grounded in empirical evidence (Fine, 1997; Skinner & Kohler, 2002). Family policy reform is faced with the challenge of maintaining a delicate balance among divergent private and public interests and intentions related to complex step relationships. Nonetheless, focusing on the overarching goals of advancing children's welfare and strengthening diverse family roles and forms can help guide policy makers through the quagmire (Malia, 2005).

Existing probate and family laws insufficiently define stepparents' rights and obligations to their stepchildren. Current laws are shaped by prevailing negative cultural perspectives regarding stepfamilies, essentially " 'channeling' people into nuclear families through a web of incentives and disincentives" (Young, 1998, p. 511, citing Schneider, 1992). Lack of legal recognition undermines stepparents' authority in their dealings with the outside world and also may impair internal stepfamily functioning and effective parenting (Mason et al., 2002). Courts have been hesitant to grant de facto rights or to attach obligations to unwilling stepparents (Skinner & Kohler, 2002), probably reasonably concluding that attempts to force continued relationships and support would be ineffective, counterproductive, and even detrimental for the stepchildren. What little progress that has occurred in state and federal family law seems geared toward increasing stepparent financial support obligations without concurrently increasing stepparental rights or recognition of the important roles that many stepparents play in their stepchildren's lives (Malia, 2005). Probate law generally now recognizes half-blood relationships but not stepfamily ties. Private contractual options and permanent adoption are available to clarify stepfamily rights and duties. However, they require extensive cost and effort and inadequately address underlying issues of validating diverse stepfamily relationships while not usurping biological ties.

The deeply rooted legal limitation most consistently challenged in policy reform proposals is that children are prohibited from having more than two legal parents. Common sense indicates that this legal limitation conflicts with many stepchildren's daily lived experiences of multiple parental figures. Available research findings have shown that children are capable of and can benefit from multiple concurrent attachments (Kelly & Lamb, 2000; White & Gilbreth, 2001; Woodhouse, 1994). Step relationships increasingly have come to be viewed as including potentially long-lasting bonds that exist independently of the marriage that created the connection (Fine, 1997; Hans, 2002). A more inclusive legal definition of family could help institute normative-adaptive stepfamily role expectations and duties as well as provide a safety net to better protect dependents' well-being and minimize unnecessary loss for children (Mason et al., 2002). At a time in the United States when proportionally fewer children reside with two biological parents, more children live in economically strained conditions, and the government seems less likely to provide support, "the 'channeling function' of law . . . should be contemplating ways of encouraging more people to feel greater levels of [connection and] responsibility for more children" (Young, 1998, p. 555).

Consistently flexible and inclusive stepfamily policy reforms, such as the formalized *de facto parent* category proposed by Mason et al. (2002), should be uniformly adopted across U.S. jurisdictions in order to expand the legal definition of family to allow for the potential for more than two legal parental figures rearing children. With such a policy shift, legal impetus would be transferred to a default standard of shared responsibility and care-based family inclusiveness (Kavanagh, 2004). For situations where the new default rules would not suffice, opt-out options, via estate planning and marital agreements, should be available to modify family obligations. "Opt-in" legal options, such as open or third-parent adoptions (Wendel, 2005) and de facto parent applications for unmarried parental figures (Mason et al., 2002), also are recommended.

REFERENCES

Amato, P. R. (2000). The consequences of divorce for adults and children. *Journal of Marriage and the Family, 62,* 1269–1287.

Andersen, R. W. (2003). *Understanding trusts and estates* (3rd ed.). Newark, NJ: Matthew Bender.

Anderson, K. G., Kaplan, H., & Lancaster, J. B. (2001). *Men's financial expenditures on genetic children and stepchildren from current and former relationships* (Population Studies Center Research Report No. 01–484). Ann Arbor: University of Michigan.

Bartlett, K. T. (1999). Improving the law relating to postdivorce arrangements for children. In R. A. Thompson & P. R. Amato (Eds.), *The postdivorce family: Children, parenting, and society* (pp. 71–102). Thousand Oaks, CA: Sage.

Bartlett, K. T. (2001). Principles of the law of family dissolution: Analysis and recommendations. *Duke Journal of Gender Law and Policy, 8,* 1–85.

Brashier, R. C. (2005). Consanguinity, sibling relationships, and the default rules of inheritance law: Reshaping half-blood statutes to reflect the evolving family. *SMU Law Review, 58*, 137–194.

Cahn, N. R. (2004). Adoptees, families, step-families and inheritance. *Adoption Quarterly, 8*, 57–66.

Chambers, D. L. (1990). Stepparents, biologic parents, and the law's perception of "family" after divorce. In S. D. Sugarman & H. H. Kay (Eds.), *Divorce reform at the crossroads* (pp. 108–127). New Haven, CT: Yale University Press.

Cherlin, A. (1978). Remarriage as an incomplete institution. *American Journal of Sociology, 84*, 634–650.

Coleman, M., & Ganong, L. (1990). Remarriage and stepfamily research in the 1980s: Increased interest in an old family form. *Journal of Marriage and the Family, 52*, 925–940.

De'Ath, E. (1997). Stepfamily policy from the perspective of a stepfamily organisation. *Marriage and Family Review, 26*, 265–279.

Duran-Aydintug, C., & Ihinger-Tallman, M. (1995). Law and stepfamilies. *Marriage and Family Review, 21*, 169–192.

Eagle, R. (1994). The separation experience of children in long-term care: Theory, research, and implications for practice. *American Journal of Orthopsychiatry, 64*, 421–434.

Edwards, R., Gillies, V., & McCarthy, J. R. (1999). Biological parents and social families: Legal discourses and everyday understandings of the position of stepparents. *International Journal of Law, Policy, and the Family, 13*, 78–105.

Fine, M. A. (1997). Stepfamilies from a policy perspective: Guidance from the empirical literature. *Marriage and Family Review, 26*, 249–264.

Fox, G. L., & Blanton, P. W. (1995). Noncustodial fathers following divorce. *Marriage and Family Review, 20*, 257–282.

Ganong, L. H., & Coleman, M. (1997). How society views stepfamilies. In I. Levin & M. B. Sussman (Eds.), *Stepfamilies: History, research, and policy* (pp. 85–106). New York: Haworth Press.

Ganong, L. H., Coleman, M., Fine, M. A., & McDaniel, A. K. (1998). Issues considered in contemplating stepchild adoption. *Family Relations, 47*, 63–71.

Ganong, L. H., Coleman, M., & Mistina, D. (1995). Normative beliefs about parents' and stepparents' financial obligations to children following divorce and remarriage. *Family Relations, 44*, 306–315.

Gary, S. N. (2000). Adapting intestacy laws to changing families. *Law and Inequality: A Journal of Theory and Practice, 18*, 1–82.

Giarmarco, J. H. (2006). The five levels of estate planning for unmarried couples. *Prudential Financial Brochure*, 1–12. Available from www.disinheritirs.com/brochures/The_Five_Levels_of_Estate_Planning_for_Unmarried_Couples.pdf.

Goldstein, M. (1995). The rights and obligations of stepparents desiring visitation with stepchildren: A proposal for change. *Probate Law Journal, 12*, 145–171.

Gregory, J. D., Swisher, P. N., & Wolf, S. L. (2001). *Understanding family law* (2nd ed.). Newark, NJ: Matthew Bender.

Grotevant, H. D., Ross, N. M., Marchel, M. A., & McRoy, R. G. (1999). Adaptive behavior in adopted children: Predictors from early risk, collaboration in relationships within the adoptive kinship network, and openness arrangements. *Journal of Adolescent Research, 14,* 231–247.

Hans, J. D. (2002). Stepparenting after divorce: Stepparents' legal position regarding custody, access, and support. *Family Relations, 51,* 301–307.

Hofferth, S. L., & Anderson, K. G. (2003). Are all dads equal? Biology versus marriage as a basis for paternal investment. *Journal of Marriage and the Family, 65,* 213–232.

Kavanagh, M. M. (2004). Rewriting the legal family: Beyond exclusivity to a care-based standard. *Yale Journal of Law and Feminism, 16,* 83–143.

Kelly, J. B., & Lamb, M. E. (2000). Using child development research to make appropriate custody and access decisions for young children. *Family and Conciliation Courts Review, 38,* 297–311.

Knaplund, K. S. (2006). Grandparents raising grandchildren and the implications for inheritance. *Arizona Law Review, 48,* 1–22.

Levine, B. (1996, Fall). Divorce and the modern family: Providing in loco parentis stepparents standing to sue for custody of their stepchildren in a dissolution proceeding. *Hofstra Law Review, 25,* 315–352.

Mahoney, M. M. (1997). Stepfamilies from a legal perspective. *Marriage and Family Review, 26,* 231–247.

Mahoney, M. M. (1999). Open adoption in context: The wisdom and enforceability of visitation orders for former parents under Uniform Adoption Act. *Florida Law Review, 51,* 89–142.

Mahoney, M. M. (2005). Forces shaping the law of cohabitation for opposite sex couples. *Journal of Law and Family Studies, 7,* 135–204.

Malia, S. (2005). Balancing family members' interests regarding stepparent rights and obligations: A social policy challenge. *Family Relations, 54,* 298–319.

Malia, S. (2007a). *Estate planning recommendations for stepfamilies and individuals.* Available from the author.

Malia, S. (2007b). *Marital agreements: Issues for couples and stepfamilies.* Available from the author.

Marsiglio, W. (2004). When stepfathers claim stepchildren: A conceptual analysis. *Journal of Marriage and the Family, 66,* 22–39.

Mason, M. A. (1998). The modern American stepfamily: Problems and possibilities. In M. A. Mason, A. Skolnick, & S. D. Sugerman (Eds.), *All our families* (pp. 95–116). New York: Oxford University Press.

Mason, M. A., Fine, M. A., & Carnochan, S. (2001). Family law in the new millennium: For whose families? *Journal of Family Issues, 22,* 857–881.

Mason, M. A., Harrison-Jay, S., Svare, G. M., & Wolfinger, N. H. (2002). Stepparents: De facto parents or legal strangers? *Journal of Family Issues, 23,* 507–522.

Meyer v. Nebraska, 262 U.S. 360 (1923).

Mnookin, R. H., & Maccoby, E. (2002). Facing the dilemmas of child custody. *Virginia Journal of Social Policy and the Law, 10,* 54–88.

Opie, A. (1993). Ideologies of joint custody. *Family and Conciliation Courts Review, 31,* 313–326.

Popenoe, D. (1994). Evolution of marriage and stepfamily problems. In A. Booth & J. Dunn (Eds.), *Stepfamilies* (pp. 3–28). Hillsdale, NJ: Erlbaum.

Quinn, J. B. (2007, February 12). Wills and other ways. *Newsweek*, 61–62.

Ramsey, S. H., & Abrams, D. E. (2001). *Children and the law in a nutshell*. St. Paul, MN: West Group.

Romesberg, L. A. (1999). Common law adoption: An argument for statutory recognition of non-parent caregiver visitation. *Suffolk University Law Review, 33*, 163–184.

Rossi, A. S., & Rossi, P. H. (1990). *Of human bonding: Parent-child relations across the life course*. New York: Aldine de Gruyter.

Santosky v. Kramer, 445 U.S. 745 (1982).

Schneider, C. E. (1992). The channeling function in family law. *Hofstra Law Review, 20*, 495–532.

Seltzer, J. (1994). Intergenerational ties in adulthood and childhood experience. In A. Booth & J. Dunn (Eds.), *Stepfamilies* (pp. 89–96). Hillsdale, NJ: Erlbaum.

Skinner, D. A., & Kohler, J. K. (2002). Parental rights in diverse family contexts: Current legal developments. *Family Relations, 51*, 293–300.

Thompson, R. A., & Amato, P. R. (1999). Introduction. *The postdivorce family: Children, parenting, and society* (pp. xi–xxiii). Thousand Oaks, CA: Sage.

Trebilcock, M., & Keshvani, R. (1991). The role of private ordering in family law: A law and economics perspective. *University of Toronto Law Journal, 41*, 533–590.

Trinder, L. (1997). Competing constructions of childhood: Children's rights and children's wishes in divorce. *Journal of Social Welfare and Family Law, 19*, 291–305.

Troxel v. Granville, 530 U.S. 57 (2000).

Walker, J. (1992). Stepfamilies and parental responsibility: Who makes the decisions? In B. Dimmock (Ed.), *A step in both directions: The impact of the Children Act 1989 on stepfamilies*. London: STEPFAMILY Publications.

Wendel, P. (2005). Inheritance rights and the step-partner adoption paradigm: Shades of the discrimination against illegitimate children. *Hofstra Law Review, 34*, 351–403.

White, L., & Gilbreth, J. G. (2001). When children have two fathers: Effects of relationships with stepfathers and noncustodial fathers on adolescent outcomes. *Journal of Marriage and the Family, 63*, 155–167.

Wolf, P. A., & Mast, E. (1987). Counseling issues in adoptions by stepparents. *Social Work, 32*, 69–74.

Woodhouse, B. B. (1994). "Out of children's needs, children's rights": The child's voice in defining the family. *Brigham Young University Journal of Public Law, 8*, 321–341.

Wriggins, J. (2000). Parental rights termination jurisprudence: Questioning the framework. *South Carolina Law Review, 52*, 241–267.

Young, A. H. (1998). Reconceiving the family: Challenging the paradigm of the exclusive family. *American University Journal of Gender and the Law, 6*, 505–555.

Younger, J. T. (1996). Responsible parents and good children. *Law and Inequality: A Journal of Theory and Practice, 14*, 489–520.

CHAPTER 23

Where to from Here? Stepfamilies and the Future

JAN PRYOR

UBIQUITY, DIVERSITY, AND CHANGE

THE NUMBERS are compelling. In the United States, Teachman and Tedrow (Chapter 1) tell us, 40% of mothers and nearly 33% of children will spend some time in a stepfamily. Stepfamilies are the most rapidly growing household structure in the United States, with the numbers of *cohabiting* stepfamily households doubling in the 10 years between 1990 and 2000. If nothing else, these statistics justify a committed and ongoing focus on the well-being of adults and children living in stepfamilies. One in three children is a proportion of our young that deserves our efforts to understand and support their families.

The task of paying attention to stepfamilies becomes particularly challenging when we acknowledge the impressive diversity and complexity of stepfamilies. For example, Teachman and Tedrow emphasize the fact that stepfamilies form not just as a result of the death of a parent or the divorce of parents, but through several other pathways. Thirty-three percent of children and 25% of mothers enter stepfamilies that form after a nonmarital birth; parental separation, divorce, or death is not a feature of children's lives in this mode of entry. Children's experiences in this situation are rather different from those who have experienced the loss of a resident parent from their household. Diversity is evident, too, in the numerous household structures that come into the category of stepfamilies. Stepfamilies, then, are potent exemplars of the diversity seen more generally in families, encompassing biological and social relationships, cohabitation and marriage, and same-sex relationships. They range from simple structures in which a man becomes the social father of his stepchild from early infancy or even before, to the complicated and usually challenging composition that includes biological children from both families of origin, plus half-siblings born after the stepfamily is formed.

Accompanying ubiquity and diversity in stepfamilies is the phenomenon of change that renders them a moving target for those who attempt to understand their dynamics. All families, of course, undergo change as the individuals in them grow and develop and face challenges; for stepfamilies, though, the rate and complexity of change seems especially complicated. So, for example, as well as changes we might expect to see as children move through childhood and adolescence, in stepfamilies we must also consider changes accompanying the passing of time since formation and membership changes as boundaries are negotiated and renegotiated. Unfortunately too, statistics also tell us that stepfamilies are comparatively unstable family forms, being more likely on average to deconstruct than are first families.

The first wave of scholarly interest in stepfamilies was led largely by clinicians, who based their insights and conclusions on their work with troubled stepfamilies. It was not until the 1980s that nonclinical researchers entered the field in any number and began to examine the functioning of nonclinical samples of stepfamilies. In many ways the conclusions of the two groups overlap. However, clinicians tended to emphasize the primacy and salience of the parental relationship, seeing this as the conductor of the family orchestra and the linchpin that stood the best chance of holding the family together. In contrast, early researchers focused on the stepparent-stepchild relationship, seeing that as pivotal to the well-being of the family as a whole. More recently other aspects of stepfamilies have received attention: the parent-child relationship (see Cartwright, Chapter 9), experiences of individual stepfamily members (e.g., mothers, Smith, Chapter 7; fathers, Robertson, Chapter 6; stepmothers, Coleman, Troilo, & Jamison, Chapter 16), and sibling relationships (Baham, Weimer, Braver, & Fabricius, Chapter 8). Lawrence Ganong's chapter in this book (Chapter 17) also addresses the emerging realization that, as with other families, intergenerational relationships in stepfamilies both exist and need to be understood. And, pervading the attention to dyads and to individuals is a persistent acknowledgment of the family system, the interrelating of relationships and individuals: the constellation of people and relationships in stepfamilies.

CHALLENGES FOR THE LAW

Calls to legitimize relationships in stepfamilies, especially the stepparent-stepchild relationship, come from many quarters (e.g., Edwards, Gillies, &

Ribbens McCarthy, 1999; Malia, 2005). However, the diversity and complexity of stepfamilies render legitimation problematic, and, as Malia (Chapter 22) and Atkin (Chapter 21) attest, countries approach the task in varying and usually inadequate ways. The variable nature of stepfamilies—for example, a man raising a stepchild from infancy in a long-term stepfamily situation, a stepparent who may be one of several partners who enter and leave the mother's household—means that legal solutions are not straightforward. Yet for reasons of inheritance, day-to-day authority to make decisions on behalf of children, and stepchild-stepparent relationships after stepfamily dissolution, it is apparent that some frameworks for legitimizing this relationship need to be pursued.

CONTEXTS OF STEPFAMILIES

An important dimension of stepfamily functioning that has been somewhat neglected is the context in which families are established and function. The importance of culture, for example, is evident in the chapters by Nozawa (Chapter 4) and Coltrane, Gutierrez, and Parke (Chapter 5). The overlapping of two historic family systems (the stem family and salaryman husbands and their wives) place strains on Japanese stepfamilies that are specific to Japanese history and culture. Coltrane et al. note both similarities and differences in stepfathers in Mexican American and European American families. Another aspect of context is noted by Ganong (Chapter 17). Countries and cultures vary in their acceptance of cohabitation by adults, and because many stepfamilies are cohabiting households, attitudes to cohabitation have an impact on their functioning in the communities in which they live. An interesting exception to this, however, is described by Snoeckx and her colleagues in Chapter 12 where they find that national and cultural variables are not as important for the distribution of household tasks as economic resources specific to the family. In general, however, as stepfamilies become more ubiquitous it may be that their dynamics change as they become increasingly normative as a household and family structure. In this regard, Claxton-Oldfield (Chapter 2) notes a slight reduction in stereotyping in his later work, at least in the acknowledgment by participants of stereotyping and their reluctance to use it.

CHALLENGES AND DIFFICULTIES
FOR STEPFAMILIES

A persistent theme permeating perceptions of stepfamilies by researchers, clinicians, lawyers, and stepfamilies themselves is the high level of difficulty and challenge faced by those who form and live in stepfamilies.

Comparisons of outcomes for children raised in stepfamilies with those raised in stable first families indicate that as a group they are at increased risk for adverse outcomes (Amato, 1994; Pryor & Rodgers, 2001). As with other areas of research, however, analyses that make careful distinctions between the different kinds of stepfamilies show that it is children in blended or complex stepfamilies who tend to do poorly (Dunn, Deater-Deckard, Pickering, & O'Connor, 1998; Hetherington & Jodl, 1994). As one stepmother put it, stepfamilies curdle, they don't blend.

Several chapters in this book attest to the difficulties faced by stepfamilies. Coleman et al. (Chapter 16) vividly depict the challenges and tensions for stepmothers; stigmatized as "wicked," stepmothers face the contradictory demands of being a good mother (the "mother myth") at the same time that they have scant authority to do so from their stepchildren, the children's biological mother, and sometimes the stepmother's own partner. Coleman et al. note the particular ambiguity of the role of the nonresident stepmother who does not have the authority in her own home to mother, yet is put in the position of having to do so when her partner's children are staying. As shared care and joint custody arrangements become more commonplace, we might expect this situation to be faced by many more women.

Similarly, Robertson (Chapter 6) chronicles the tasks facing stepfathers as they negotiate their roles in face of the tight alliance often in place between biological parents and children. At the same time, as Cartwright (Chapter 9) points out, that relationship faces its own problems when a stepfamily forms and mother and children adjust to another adult in their lives. Mothers, as Smith (Chapter 7) attests, are the pivot points for all the relationships in a stepfamily as they juggle partnership and parenting. All these rearrangements, as stepfamilies are formed, call for herculean levels of adaptability, flexibility, tolerance, and steadfastness—levels for which some families have neither the will nor the resources. Chapters 19 and 20 document efforts to date to support stepfamilies through the use of interventions. Nicholson et al. (Chapter 20) note, however, the difficulties in recruiting stepfamilies to take part in programs because of their desire not to be seen as different and in need of support.

Perhaps the most pessimistic perspective is the evolutionary psychology framework adopted by Mignot (Chapter 3) in regard to French stepfamilies as an explanation for stepfamily dynamics. If one accepts this framework, then the prognosis for stepfamilies is indeed grim: Stepparents of both sexes are biologically programmed to neglect, abuse, and even kill their stepchildren. The arguments for and against this position are well known, and, as Mignot acknowledges, it is difficult to find empirical evidence that entirely supports or refutes the evolutionary psychology position. This perspective fails, however, to acknowledge the frequency with which nonrelated adults form close and enduring bonds with children in a variety of situations, including stepfamilies. Its danger lies particularly in its deterministic aspects and its power to stigmatize stepfamilies, who, it is clear, have always existed and are an increasingly important feature of families in the twenty-first century. Rather than accept a negative, pessimistic, and possibly flawed framework for understanding stepfamily dynamics, it is more constructive to identify and reinforce those factors that confer resilience for stepfamilies.

LOOKING FORWARD

Several chapters in this volume take an optimistic stance toward stepfamilies by focusing, in the main, on the wide network of family members rather than individuals or dyads. Baham et al.'s (Chapter 8) chapter demonstrates, for example, the complex interrelationships surrounding sibling relationships and offers a framework for future research that takes into account the web of networks in stepfamilies. Similarly, I show in Chapter 15 that not only can a nonresident parent make a positive contribution to children's well-being in stepfamilies, but relationships with stepparents, nonresident parents, and resident parents can all benefit children. Robertson (Chapter 6) found that most stepfathers regarded contact between their stepchildren and nonresident parents as neutral or beneficial for their relationships with their stepchildren, and over 60% thought that contact had no adverse effects or benefited the children. Marsiglio and Hinojosa (2007) suggest a somewhat similar scenario, in which stepfathers might foster father alliances between the nonresident father and themselves. These findings are suggestive of an increasingly collaborative milieu in which several parents (and grandparents as well) can work together to foster children's well-being in stepfamilies.

A particularly promising perspective is one that considers the stepfamily as a social unit rather than a collection of dyads and individuals. Figure 23.1 depicts one way of considering possible links among whole-family constructs and well-being at both individual and group levels for stepfamilies. In the following sections I address communication and routines and rituals as part of family dynamics, and boundaries and identity as whole-family constructs.

Communication in Stepfamilies

Afifi (Chapter 13) provides a cogent summary of recent and promising areas of research that examine communication strategies in stepfamilies. In an earlier work (under her former name; Golish, 2003), Afifi identified "strong" and "struggling" stepfamilies. This delineation was made by

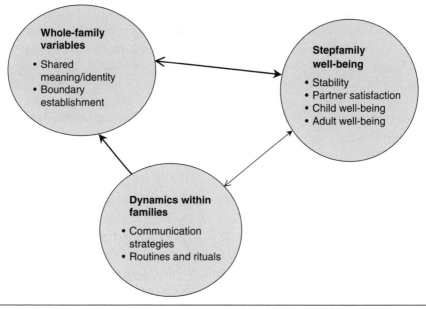

Figure 23.1 Suggested Associations among Whole-Family Variables, Dynamics within Families, and Well-being.

combining the judgments of three members of each family of their stepfamily as being strong or struggling. If all three members agreed that the family was strong, that family was in the strong category; all others were in the "having more difficulty" category. The communication factors that typified the strong families included supportive communication, active listening, communicating a sense of inclusion, everyday talk, openness, direct confrontation of problems, humor, and redefining conflict as positive.

ROUTINES AND RITUALS

Family rituals are symbolically imbued patterns of behavior that embody meaning and have the ability to foster communication, reflection, and affirmation of shared understandings. They have three partially overlapping functional aspects: to develop, convey, and modify meaning; to link individual family members to a shared intersubjectivity or understanding about their identity as a family group; and to provide opportunities for families to reflect, to bring together past, present, and future, and to convey reassurance about stability and continuity. Routines can become rituals if and when they carry meaning for the people involved in them (see Pryor, 2006). For all families, and in particular for stepfamilies in the early stages of formation, routines and rituals can provide a valuable resource for developing and sustaining a coherent sense of family.

Rituals, perhaps especially rituals arising from routines, have the capacity to foster meaning making at both the dyadic level and the whole-family level. A stepparent may, for example, make a habit of taking his or her stepchild to sports practice or music lessons every week. Over time this routine may take on meaning for them both and have the effect of strengthening the developing relationship between them. Similarly, parents in a stepfamily may set aside an evening to do something together without the children; the pattern of this behavior may take on significance for them as well as providing an opportunity to strengthen their relationship. For stepfamilies, rituals may be especially salient in the negotiation and understanding of roles and meanings for the complex group that constitutes the family.

ESTABLISHING FAMILY BOUNDARIES

Family boundaries comprise rules that define membership and functions of the various subsystems in a family system. They also help to regulate the emotional distance among family members and between the family and outsiders. The task for stepfamilies—to establish who is in and who is out, and when—is comparatively complex. Figures 23.2 and 23.3 contrast the situation for first families and stepfamilies.

Boundaries in first families are comparatively straightforward. Although in many cases grandparents and extended family members live in the household, the genetic relationships are usually apparent, and the rules of membership are developed over time in a sequence that sees the parental relationship established first, followed by membership expanding with the births or adoption of children.

The comparative complexity of the stepfamily situation is evident. There is often confusion between genetic and household boundaries, and, given the constantly changing membership of the household, flexibility is needed to accommodate the coming and going of individual members. The stepparents' children, for example, may spend time in the stepfamily household, and the children in the household may spend time with their nonresident parent and his or her new partner and their children.

Not surprisingly, then, boundary ambiguity is a recognized characteristic of stepfamilies. It occurs when family members are unsure who is in or out of the family, or who is performing what roles or tasks in the family system (Stewart, 2005). Membership can be both physical (living in the household) and psychological (seen as family members by at least some of the household; e.g., nonresident parents of stepchildren). Kay Pasley (1987) and Susan Stewart (2005) have examined boundary ambiguity in stepfamilies. Pasley found that 40% of remarried couples reported physical and/or psychological boundary ambiguity. Physical ambiguity is

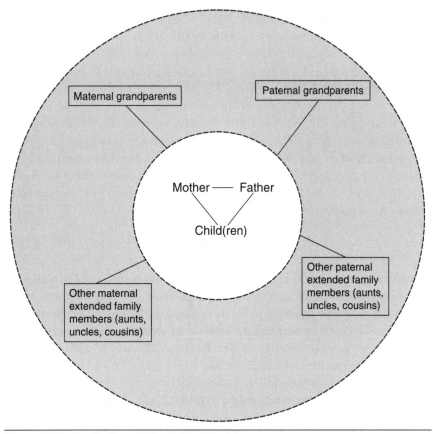

Figure 23.2   Family Boundaries in First Families.

defined as a discrepancy in reports between partners about who, physically, are members of the family (children and stepchildren both in and outside of the household); psychological ambiguity refers to who partners consider to be members of the family. Stewart measured only physical ambiguity in families who were part of the National Study of Families and Households; she found that a quarter of stepfamilies showed ambiguity in their reporting of children and stepchildren in the family. She found, too, that ambiguity was more likely in the case of children being older, in stepfamilies who had been together for a shorter time, in more complex families, and when children lived outside the household.

There is speculation that boundary ambiguity might be related negatively to well-being in stepfamilies. It is argued that where family members have differing cognitions about family factors, including who belongs and who does not, there is potential for conflict and the undermining of the parents' relationship. However, Pasley (1987) found no links between boundary ambiguity and marital integration and adjustment. Stewart's (2005)

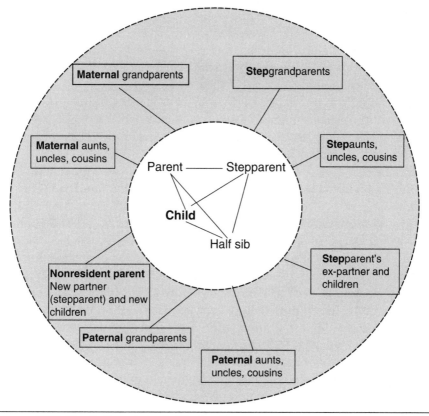

Figure 23.3 Family Boundaries in Stepfamilies.

findings were similar for men, but not for women; women in her sample were more likely to report high levels of disagreement and chances of separation where there was boundary ambiguity.

Given the need for flexibility in stepfamilies regarding membership, it may be that under some conditions boundary ambiguity (and in particular psychological ambiguity) is beneficial. Family members may agree to disagree about membership, at least in the early stages of the family's life cycle. Patterson and Garwick (1994) describe higher order family characteristics of being "consensus-sensitive" or "distance-sensitive" in relation to agreement among family members; in the phases of negotiation and renegotiation it might be adaptive for stepfamilies to be distance-sensitive.

SHARED FAMILY MEANING

The concept of family meaning is a central part of family stress models, in particular the Family Adjustment and Adaptation Response model (Patterson,). Two levels of meaning have been identified: situational meaning, in which the individual's and family's subjective definitions of capabilities and demands on the family were considered in relation to each other; and family identity or global meaning, referring to stable cognitive beliefs about the relationships of family members with each other and of the family unit to the larger community.

This model was developed in the context of families facing a stressor. If we regard the establishment of a stepfamily as a potential major stress for individuals and families as a whole, then it is possible to relate this model to stepfamily formation and stability over time.

Situational meanings occur when stepfamilies are first forming and when members begin to construct some meanings about the family in terms of membership and roles. It is at this phase that agreement may not be either necessary or important; although a shared *working* definition of the family may be in place, members may agree to disagree about its details.

Family meaning or identity is collectively constructed over time; it is not just agreement or consensus, but is a new construct that reflects stable aspects of what it means to be part of this family. In her framework Patterson (2002) suggests that family identity includes rules and norms for behavior, role assignments, and definitions of internal and external boundaries. In practice, stepfamilies may need to retain flexibility in these specific aspects of their family identity as roles and membership change from week to week. Indeed, it may not be possible to have agreement about membership, for instance when some individuals, such as stepchildren outside the household, do not regard themselves as family members. Schneider (1968) describes kinship as a "diffuse, enduring solidarity," a state that may be difficult or impossible for some stepfamilies to reach. Allan, Hawker, and Crow (Chapter 14) suggest that rituals serve to signify differences and boundaries in stepfamilies by excluding stepkin from family celebrations such as birthdays. Stepfamilies may have to accept that family membership and identity differ among individuals. However, to the extent that a stable family identity is established over time, stepfamily well-being may be enhanced.

A commonly used measure of family togetherness is family cohesion, which encompasses feelings of closeness and belongingness to the family group. In the Resilience in Stepfamilies study (Pryor, 2004) we were able to look at whether cohesion predicted well-being in children (adult well-being was not measured). On children's reports, both family cohesion and family expressiveness were associated with prosocial behavior, externalizing behavior, and peer problems, with higher cohesion being beneficial. Children's perceptions of cohesion and expressiveness also predicted *parents'* assessments of externalizing and peer problems.

Furthermore, given the possibility that family members may well have discrepant perceptions of family dynamics, we were also interested to investigate in a preliminary way the possible associations between discrepancies and children's outcomes. Analyses showed that discrepancies between children's and parents' assessments of family cohesion were associated with hyperactivity, externalizing, and self-concept in children. Discrepancies between parents' and stepparents' views of cohesion predicted anxiety and externalizing behavior in children. Externalizing was most strongly predicted by the discrepancy between parents' and stepparents' views of family cohesion. We have some preliminary evidence, then, that family cohesion is a correlate of well-being in children, although we were not able to determine the direction of effects. There remains a large gap in our empirical examination and understanding of the links between whole-family variables such as cohesion and identity, and well-being.

THE SALIENCE OF TIME

Through much of the writing on stepfamilies run threads of time and of uncertainty. This is especially true in regard to the early phases of establishment. when flexibility, adaptability, and compromise appear to characterize successful stepfamily living (see Afifi, Chapter 13). The parallel paths of deciding who is kin and who is not and of establishing roles and a sense of family identity both call for tolerance of uncertainty and ambiguity. Levin (1997) describes mothers who adopt a "wait and see" model of behavior, allowing roles to evolve and change over time. Writing as a clinician, Papernow (Chapter 18) advocates compartmentalization of relationships in the early phases, rather than attempting to establish the instant love and cohesion so yearned for by new stepfamilies. Rather, she suggests that consolidation of dyadic relationships should be a priority. In her study of strong and struggling stepfamilies, Golish (2003) noted that strong families created a common ground for members over time and undertook a slow and flexible process of developing family membership and identity. Allowing for different rates of psychological traveling time for individual family members appears to be beneficial. Children, and especially adolescents, will take far longer than the adults who formed the stepfamily to accept that this is, indeed, *their* family, and some may never do so.

WHERE TO FROM HERE?

Establishing a robust and stable stepfamily is not easy, and neither is the task of gathering and integrating knowledge about them. It is by now a cliché that stepfamilies are incomplete institutions with few scripts or guidelines for their roles. It is increasingly the case, however, that many other families and households fall outside the traditional structure for which there are clear scripts for behavior. It might be time to drop this implicitly negative phrase in regard to stepfamilies, in the interests of reducing stigmatization from within the scholarly community. Ganong and Coleman (2004) have called for a strengths and resilience approach to stepfamilies rather than the deficit view that is so often adopted.

It is comparatively easy to continue to document the difficulties faced by stepfamilies. More difficult and far more productive is a focus on what strengthens stepfamilies and renders them resilient. As well as the need for sophisticated statistical tools to match their complexity, we need to continue the search for conceptual frameworks that capture the wider scenario of stepfamilies, beyond their households. At the same time, qualitative studies that are sensitive to the lived reality of stepfamily living are invaluable for informing both theory and larger survey studies. Although change is the signature tune of stepfamilies that renders them difficult to study, it may be that some kinds of changes are beneficial. Higher profiles as numbers increase, for example, may be lowering the stigmatization experienced by many. Finally, tolerance of ambiguity and making haste slowly seem to be fruitful paths toward the stability that is beneficial for all family groups.

We have, I believe, reason to be cautiously optimistic. In the very best scenarios children in stepfamilies have four parents who love and nurture them. The paths to stability and successful functioning in stepfamilies are demanding and sometimes torturous; it is to be hoped that this book points to ways in which they can both be helped and help themselves toward being happy families.

REFERENCES

Amato, P. (1994). The implications of research findings on children in stepfamilies. In A. Booth & J. Dunn (Eds.), *Stepfamilies: Who benefits? Who does not?* Hillsdale, NJ: Erlbaum.

Dunn, J. K., Deater-Deckard, K., Pickering, K., & O'Connor, T. G. (1998). Children's adjustment and prosocial behaviour in step-, single-parent, and non-stepfamily settings: Findings from a community study. *Journal of Child Psychology and Psychiatry, 39*(8), 1083–1095.

Edwards, R. V., Gillies, V., & Ribbens McCarthy, J. (1999). Biological parents and social families: Legal discourses and everyday understandings of the position of stepparents. *International Journal of Law, Policy and the Family, 13*(1), 78–105.

Ganong, L., & Coleman, M. (2004). *Stepfamily relationships: Development, dynamics, and interventions.* New York: Kluwer Academic/Plenum Press.

Golish, T. D. (2003). Stepfamily communication strengths: Understanding the ties that bind. *Human Communication Research, 29*(1), 41.

Hetherington, E. M., & Jodl, K. M. (1994). Stepfamilies as settings for child development. In A. Booth & J. Dunn (Eds.), *Stepfamilies: Who benefits? Who does not?* (pp. 55–79). Hillsdale, NJ: Erlbaum.

Levin, I. (1997). Stepfamily as project. *Marriage and Family Review, 26*, 123–133.

Malia, S. (2005). Balancing family members' interests regarding stepparent rights and obligations: A social policy challenge. *Family Relations, 54*(2), 298–319.

Marsiglio, W., & Hinojosa, R. (2007, August). Managing the multifather family: Stepfathers as father allies. *Journal of Marriage and the Family, 69*, 845–862.

Pasley, K. (1987). Family boundary ambiguity: Perceptions of adult stepfamily members. In K. Pasley & M. Ihinger-Tallman (Eds.), *Remarriage and stepparenting: Current research and theory* (pp. 206–224). New York: Guilford Press.

Patterson, J. (2002, May). Integrating family resilience and family stress theory. *Journal of Marriage and the Family, 64*, 349–360.

Patterson, J., & Garwick, A. (1994). Levels of family meaning in family stress theory. *Family Process, 33*, 287–304.

Pryor, J. (2004). *Resilience in stepfamilies*. Wellington, New Zealand: Ministry of Social Development.

Pryor, J. (2006). *Beyond demography: History, rituals and families in the twenty first century* (Blue Skies Reports). Wellington, New Zealand: Families Commission.

Pryor, J., & Rodgers, B. (2001). *Children in changing families: Life after parental separation*. Oxford: Blackwell.

Schneider, D. (1968). *American kinship: A cultural account*. Englewood Cliffs, NJ: Prentice-Hall.

Stewart, S. D. (2005). Boundary ambiguity in stepfamilies. *Journal of Family Issues, 26*(7), 1002–1029.

Author Index

133, 134, 142, 152, 154, 158, 162, 169, 186,
187, 188, 193, 194, 195, 209, 210, 211, 214,
219, 220, 221, 231, 232, 233, 236, 240, 241,
244, 277, 279, 299, 300, 301, 306, 307, 308,
310, 311, 336, 374, 376, 394, 397, 399, 400,
404, 407, 410, 411, 412, 443, 456, 457, 460,
461, 472, 474, 476, 477, 485, 486, 545, 546,
558, 562, 563, 564, 565, 583
Garasky, S., 347
Garber, T., 48
Garcia Coll, C., 106
Gardner, C. O., 157
Garstka, T. A., 41
Garwick, A., 581
Gary, S. N., 545, 546, 553, 554
Gately, N. J., 245
Gates, G., 40
Gauthier, A., 335
Ge, X., 251
Geist, C., 279, 280, 281
Gelles, R. J., 166, 177
Genovese, T., 382
Georgiades, K., 179
Gerard, J. M., 269
Germano, L. M., 237
Gerson, R., 327
Giarmarco, J. H., 546, 550, 551
Giarrusso, R., 307, 336
Gibbard, S. D., 468, 472, 474, 475
Gibbins, R., 151
Gibson, D., 46
Gignac, M. A. M., 313
Gilbreth, J. G., 102, 103, 104, 131, 299, 346, 354,
355, 356, 357, 363, 365, 460, 563, 564, 569
Giles-Sims, J., 125, 166, 460
Gillcrist, K., 48
Gillies, V., 323, 364, 540, 549, 559, 561, 562, 563,
567, 574, 575
Gillman, S., 313
Gingrich, R., 33
Gladstone, J., 335, 409
Glick, P., 5, 8, 175
Goeke-Morey, M., 251, 253, 254, 257, 267, 269,
271
Goldberg, W. A., 254
Golding, J., 127, 128, 156, 158
Goldscheider, C., 411, 412
Goldscheider, F., 17, 278, 411, 412
Goldstein, M., 565
Golish, T., 243, 300, 301, 302, 303, 304, 306, 307,
310, 312, 578, 583
Gonzales, N. A., 106
Goode, W. J., 371
Goodman, R., 359
Goodyear, C., 42, 46
Gooley, S., 493, 501
Gottainer, G., 102, 300, 309
Gottlieb, B. H., 313
Gottman, J., 104, 232, 241, 448, 449
Grace, M., 354
Graham, P., 135
Granovetter, M., 340

Gravetter, F. J., 45, 46
Green, R., 218, 305, 494
Gregory, J. D., 547, 556, 557
Griswold del Castillo, R., 101
Grizzle, G. L., 226
Gross, P. H., 42
Grotevant, H. D., 563
Grych, J. H., 251, 253, 255, 256, 257, 258, 261,
265, 271, 272, 444
Guisinger, S., 384, 460
Gupta, S., 282
Gutierrez, D. G., 108
Guttman, J., 44, 45, 46

Hahlweg, K., 493, 510
Hajal, F., 197
Halford, K., 455, 457, 474, 477, 478, 502, 510,
511, 512, 514, 516
Hamilton, H. A., 311, 355, 356
Handal, P. J., 258
Hanna, S. L., 304
Hans, J., 410, 411, 545, 550, 554, 555, 556, 569
Hanson, T. L., 151, 158, 159, 163, 164, 167, 168,
170
Hardesty, C., 128
Harknett, K., 461
Harlow, L., 237
Harold, G., 251, 252, 253, 254, 255, 256, 257,
258, 265, 267, 269, 271, 272
Harper, A. M., 300
Harris, K. M., 105
Harris, R., 510
Harrison, M., 218, 349
Harrison-Jay, S., 245, 545, 546, 547, 565, 566,
567, 568, 569
Harrop, J. W., 166
Harter, K., 254
Haruna, H., 93
Harvey, D. M., 300
Hashima, P. Y., 166
Haskey, J., 125, 135
Hawker, S., 396
Hawkins, A. J., 132
Hawkins, N., 156, 158
Hayano, T., 80
Hays, S., 374
Heard, H. E., 105
Heaton, T. B., 461, 475
Heen, S., 449
Heinrichs, N., 493, 510
Helms-Erikson, H., 177, 179
Henderson, H. J., 469, 473, 474
Henderson, S. H., 170, 186, 212, 214, 216, 252,
457, 459, 460, 478, 486
Henley, K., xix
Hennigen, L., 310
Henry, C. S., 299, 311, 402, 405
Henry, R. G., 459
Hetherington, E. M., 102, 104, 125, 127, 128,
129, 130, 131, 132, 134, 144, 153, 158, 162,
163, 164, 166, 168, 170, 171, 175, 176, 178,
186, 210, 211, 212, 213, 214, 215, 216, 217,

Subject Index